SIXTH EDITION

SALES MANAGEMENT
Concepts and Cases

Douglas J. Dalrymple
Indiana University

William L. Cron
Southern Methodist University

JOHN WILEY & SONS, INC.

New York • Chichester • Weinheim • Brisbane • Toronto • Singapore

Acquisitions Editor	Ellen Ford
Marketing Manager	Karen Allman
Senior Production Editor	Jeanine Furino
Designer	Laura Boucher
Illustration Coordinator	Anna Melhorn
Cover Image	Todd Davidson/*Image Bank*

This book was set in Novarese Medium by University Graphics, Inc. and printed and bound by Donnelley/Crawfordsville. The cover was printed by Lehigh Press.

This book was printed on acid-free paper

Library of Congress Cataloging-in-Publication Data:

Dalrymple, Douglas J.
    Sales management : concepts and cases / Douglas J. Dalrymple,
William L. Cron.—6th ed.
      p. cm.
    Includes bibliographical references and index.
    ISBN 0-471-19197-3 (cloth : alk. paper)
    1. Sales management.   2. Sales Management—Case studies.
I. Cron, William L., 1949– . II. Title
HF5438.4.D34 1998
658.8'1—dc21
                                     97-30041
                                        CIP

Printed in the United States of America

10 9 8 7 6 5 4 3 2 1

ABOUT THE AUTHORS

Douglas J. Dalrymple is Professor of Marketing in the School of Business at Indiana University. He received his DBA degree in marketing from Michigan State University and his MS and BS degrees from Cornell University. Professor Dalrymple has taught at the University of California, Los Angeles, the Georgia Institute of Technology, the University of San Diego, and the University of North Carolina, Greensboro. His research emphasizes forecasting and sales force issues, and he regularly teaches sales management, marketing management, and services marketing courses. Publications in which his articles have appeared include *Journal of Personal Selling & Sales Management, Decision Sciences, Industrial Marketing Management, International Journal of Forecasting, Journal of Business Research, Business Horizons, California Management Review,* and *Applied Economics*. Professor Dalrymple is the author or coauthor of 22 marketing books including Marketing Management: Text and Cases (6th ed.), Basic Marketing Management, Cases in Marketing Management, a computerized Sales Management Simulation (4th ed.), and two retailing texts. His books and articles have been translated into Spanish, Chinese, Japanese and Hebrew.

William L. Cron is Professor of Marketing in the Edwin L. Cox School of Business at Southern Methodist University. He received his DBA from Indiana University. He has been an active teacher, trainer, researcher, and consultant in sales and sales management. His research on a variety of sales and management topics has been published in the *Journal of Marketing Research, Journal of Marketing, Journal of Personal Selling & Sales Management, Academy of Management Journal, Journal of Vocational Behavior,* and *Industrial Marketing Management,* among other journals and proceedings. Professor Cron is a member of the Editorial Review Board for the *Journal of Marketing, Journal of Personal Selling & Sales Management,* and *Journal of the Academy of Marketing Sciences*.

PREFACE

This book is designed to help students learn sales management concepts and how to apply them to solve business problems. Most marketing students start their careers as salespeople and they need to understand the role of the sales manager to function effectively in their jobs and prepare themselves for promotion. Effective management of salespeople is critical to business success because many goods and services demand personal contacts to close the sale. However, selling costs are growing rapidly and managers must know how to handle this resource effectively. Customer contact is a key weapon in the marketing game, and managers need experience in this area if they expect to move up the executive career ladder.

▶ APPROACH AND OBJECTIVES

Sales Management focuses on the activities of first-line field sales managers. To function effectively as managers, students must know how salespeople perform their jobs. With this in mind, we have positioned chapters on personal selling, account relationships, territory management, and sales ethics near the front of the book to emphasize how salespeople interact with customers and prospects. This information is particularly useful for students who have not taken—and for schools (such as SMU) that do not offer—courses in personal selling.

Our approach to sales management is comprehensive, up-to-date, and practical. We use many real-world examples and present them in an easy-to-read style. Stories in boxes highlight recent developments, topical issues, and unique sales strategies. Special emphasis is placed on current issues of managing strategic account relationships, team development, diversity in the work force, sales force automation, and ethical issues. We conclude each chapter with several detailed cases so that students can apply what they have learned by resolving realistic business dilemmas.

▶ CHANGES IN THIS EDITION

The first edition of Sales Management had 12 chapters, 31 cases and came packaged in 485 pages of text. Over the years adopters, reviewers and editors have asked us to add topics, new learning aids, and more cases. As a result the fifth edition ended up with 16 chapters, 49 cases and over 800 pages. With the new sixth edition we have chosen to reduce the length of the book to make it easier for students to use. Our goal was to shorten the book by eliminating extraneous material without hurting coverage of important topics. For example, we combined the two evaluation chapters so the book now has 15 chapters to match the number of weeks in most semester courses. Also we added seven new cases to the sixth edition and the total number of cases was reduced to 33. We would note that although all the chapters have been shortened they have been thoroughly revised with new material, updated tables, figures, and references. Chapter consultants, practicing sales managers and consultants, have reviewed each chapter for currency and inclusiveness of topics critical to cutting-edge sales management.

▶ LEARNING AIDS

- **Chapter Objectives.**   Each chapter begins with a set of objectives to show students what they will learn.
- **Boxed Inserts.**   Each chapter has one or more boxed examples that highlight recent sales management trends, issues, or strategies, including technology issues.
- **Summaries.**   All chapters end with a summary that wraps up the concepts and discussion.
- **Review Questions.**   Each chapter has a set of review questions that emphasize the most important topics.
- **Problems.**   Each chapter ends with a group of problems that encourage students to apply the concepts they have learned.
- **Key Terms.**   Key terms are highlighted in the text and listed at the end of each chapter.
- **In Class Exercises.**   Eight chapters have in class exercises to encourage students to evaluate the roles of salespeople and managers in realistic job situations.
- **Case Studies.**   Thirty-three cases for class discussion and written assignments are grouped at the end of each chapter. These meaty cases challenge students to apply sales management principles to real situations.
- **Appendixes.**   Discussions on "In Class Exercises" and "Getting a Job in Sales" at the end of the book help students learn how to use in-class exercises effectively, as well as how to write application letters and creative résumés.
- **Indexes.**   Case, Author, Company, and Subject indexes help students find information and examples.

▶ SUPPLEMENTS

Successful sales management courses require a well-written text and an effective set of supplementary teaching materials. We have assembled an outstanding package of these aids to support *Sales Management*.

- **Instructor's Resource Guide.**   Includes suggested course syllabi, chapter outlines, lecture notes, lecture enhancement examples, case notes, answers to end-of-chapter problems, and role play instructor notes. It also includes a test bank with a wide assortment of multiple-choice and true/false questions for each chapter. The test bank is available on computer disks; it allows you to compose exams on a personal computer.

- **Personal Selling Videotapes.** A set of 17 short (three- to five-minute) selling tapes prepared by Wilson Learning Corporation. These tapes provide models of good sales skills, mistakes to avoid, and coaching suggestions for sales managers. Integrated with text discussion.

- **Sales Management Simulation.** Encourages students to practice their sales management skills in a game environment by making decisions on hiring, deployment, retraining, termination, compensation, forecasting, and the design of sales contests for a field sales force. The new fourth edition updates game parameters, allows decisions to be input on work disks, and features the sales of computer network servers. Student manual sold separately or as a set packaged with this text. Instructors manual available.

- **TTG Territory Mapping Program.** Helps students design new sales territories for Case 11-2 on a personal computer.

- **Sales Manager Software.** Assists students in performing a computer evaluation of individual salespeople in Cases 15-2 to 15-3.

- **Sales Call Planning Software.** Helps students use a computer to allocate sales calls to customers in Case 5-2.

- **Forecasting Diskette.** The FORECAST program allows students to make projections to solve problems and case studies. Includes naive, moving average, exponential smoothing, projective, simple regression, and multiple regression techniques. Allows optimization of smoothing constants and the length of moving averages.

- Powerpoint Transparencies for lecture planning and note taking are available to both professors and students any may be downloaded from the book's Website at *www.wiley.com/college*.

▶ ACKNOWLEDGMENTS

This book could not have been published without the spirited comments and suggestions from a host of colleagues and reviewers. Although we don't have room to mention everyone, we would like to express our appreciation to the following managers and professors, who provided valuable tips for the sixth edition,

Ramon A. Avila, Ball State University
Keven M. Elliot, Mankato State University
Rolf Hackman, Western Illinois University
Rita Larkin, Temple University
Melissa S. Loder, West Virginia Wesleyan College
Chip E. Miller, Pacific Lutheran University

as well as numerous reviewers on previous editions, whose comments and suggestions live on:

Zafar Ahmed

Ramon A. Avila

Joseph P. Clayton
*Executive Vice President,
Marketing & Sales*
Thomson Consumer Electronics

Robert Collins

Jill W. Croft
National Sales Manager
Disc Manufacturing, Inc.

J. Kevin Cummings
National Sales Manager
ABTco, Inc.

Robert P. Eschino
Executive Vice President
Gold

William I. Evans
Principal
The Evans Group

Daniel Gardiner

James Gray

Bill Greenwood

John Hawes

Karen E. James

Madhav Kacker

Thomas Leigh

Richard Leventhal

Elaine Notorantino

Keith Paulson

B. J. Polk
Associate Director—Marketing
Procter & Gamble Distributing Co.

J. Tim Prevost
Director—Sales & Marketing
Stuart C. Irby Co.

Robert Roe

Jose Rosa

Bob Smiley

Fred Smith

Winston Stahlecker

William Strahle

Harish Sujan and his
class of 25
MBA students
Pennsylvania State University

Shelley Tapp

A special acknowledgment is due to the sales and marketing executives and consultants who served as chapter consultants to this book. They both reviewed the chapters and offered important insights into the chapter's subject matter. The result of their efforts is a text that is both practical and cutting-edge with respect to current sales and sales management practices. We are deeply indebted to the contributions of the following people:

Robert Conti
Vice President
The Alexander Group, Inc.

Neil Cronin
*Director of Taining and
Specialist Manager*

David Henry
General Sales Manager
CBS Radio: KVIL

Don James
Principal
Human Dimensions, Inc.

Christopher Jander
National Account Manager
GTE

Michael Mahan
Account Manager
IBM

George Michaud
*Director of Environment/Health
Safety & Ethics Northern Telecom*

David Pinals
President
TTG, Incorporated

John Schreitmueller
Senior Cice President and Partner
Reedie & Company, L.C.

Jerry Willet
National Sales Manager
Software Spectrum

We also want to thank all the people at John Wiley & Sons who helped develop this book. Ellen Ford our editor, worked tirelessly to upgrade and improve the sixth edition. Our production editor, Jeanine Furino, has been a great help in guiding the book through the many steps of the production process.

The book could not have been completed without the work of our secretaries Linda Sharp, Brenda Crohn, and Julie Hutcheson, who cheerfully typed endless drafts and revisions. In addition, we want to acknowledge the computer programming assistance of Chris Vesper of Marquise Micro Applications of Indianapolis, Indiana and the help of Chris and Jessica Bryant and Jennifer Cron in developing the test bank and teacher's manual that accompanies this text.

Finally, we want to thank our wives, Nancy and Deborah, for their help and encouragement.

BRIEF CONTENTS

▶ **PART I / SALES MANAGEMENT FUNCTIONS AND STRATEGIES**

CHAPTER 1 / Introduction to Selling and Sales Management   1

CHAPTER 2 / Strategic Planning and Budgeting   30

▶ **PART II / DEVELOPING THE SELLING FUNCTION**

CHAPTER 3 / Personal Selling   72

CHAPTER 4 / Account Relationship Management   123

CHAPTER 5 / Territory Management   169

CHAPTER 6 / Sales Ethics   218

▶ **PART III / SALES GOALS AND STRUCTURE**

CHAPTER 7 / Estimating Potentials and Forecasting Sales   251

CHAPTER 8 / Organization   282

▶ **PART IV / BUILDING A SALES PROGRAM**

CHAPTER 9 / Recruiting and Selecting Personnel   328

CHAPTER 10 / Sales Training   376

CHAPTER 11 / Territory Design   418

▶ **PART V / LEADING AND MOTIVATING THE SALES FORCE**

CHAPTER 12 / Leadership   444

CHAPTER 13 / Motivating Salespeople   481

CHAPTER 14 / Compensating Salespeople   529

CHAPTER 15 / Evaluating Performance   562

APPENDIX A / Role Play Guidelines   A-1

APPENDIX B / Getting a Job in Sales   A-2

Key Term & Subject Index   I-1

Author Index   I-3

Company Index   I-6

Case Index   I-8

CONTENTS

► PART I / SALES MANAGEMENT FUNCTIONS AND STRATEGIES

CHAPTER 1 / Introduction to Selling and Sales Management   1

Selling and Sales Management 2
The Sales Management Process 3
Sales Management in Action 1-1: **Selling in Other Countries** 4
Total Quality Management 7
The Field Sales Manager's Job 8
Sales Management in Action 1-2: **Turning It Around in Cleveland** 9
Career Paths 13

CASES

1-1   The Case Method 18
1-2   Arapahoe Pharmaceutical Company 21
1-3   Salco Chemicals SA 26

CHAPTER 2 / Strategic Planning and Budgeting   30

"When You Buy the Iron, You Get the Company" 31
Strategic Management Planning 32
Sales Management in Action 2-1: **"Sales as an Internal Position"** 33
Strategic Marketing Planning 37
Sales Management in Action 2-2: **"Some Threats Require A Response"** 38
Strategic Sales Force Decisions 39
Sales Technology 2-1: **"The Net Effect"** 41
The Sales Budget 47
Quality Sales Management 51
Ethical Situations 53

CASES

2-1   BSI 58
2-2   Shanandoah Industries (A) 63
2-3   Sales Management Simulation 69

► PART II / DEVELOPING THE SELLING FUNCTION

CHAPTER 3 / Personal Selling   72

An Electronic SOS 73
Basic Types of Selling Approaches 74
Pre-Interaction Phase: Pre-Call Planning Skills 76
The Interaction Phase 79
Sales Management in Action: 3-1: **Are You a Sales Person?** 80
Sales Management in Action: 3-2: **You're Not Prepared! You Don't Listen! . . .** 81
Needs Discovery Skills 82
Sales Management in Action 3-3: **The Stuff Is No Good** 86
Post-Interaction Phase 92
Selling Technology 3-1: **A Virtual Reality Demonstration . . .** 87
Sales Management in Action 3-4: **What Would You Say if You Were Called an "Okyakusama"?** 94
Selling Technology 3-2: **How to Save 5 Hours a Week . . .** 96
Ethical Situations 94
Sales Force Automation 95
Sales Techology 3-3: **A Mobile Office** 98
Total Quality Management 99

CASES

3-1   Royal Corporation 104
3-2   Mediquip SA 117

CHAPTER 4 / Account Relationship Management   123

Partners 124
Organizational Purchasing Process 125
Sales Management in Action 4-1: **Marketing or Restructuring** 128
Buying Center 130
Sales Management in Action 4-2: **Safety Shoes for the Benefits Office** 132
Sales Management in Action 4-3: **How Many People Does it Take to Buy a Window?** 134
Building Relationships 134
Relationship Binders 139

Sales Management in Action 4-4: National Culture and
Selling in France   141
Ethical Situations   142
Quality Sales Management: Cross-Functional Teams
143
Appendix: Buying A Test Stand   147

CASES

4-1   Centrust Corporation   149
4-2   Pepe Jeans   159
4-3   Negotiating A Channel Relationship   166

CHAPTER 5 / Territory
Management   169

Allocating Time at IBM   170
Sales Force Productivity   171
Sales Management Technology 5-1:
Road Warriors   172
Locating and Qualifying Prospects   173
Sales Management In Action 5-1:
A Perfect "10"   174
Sales Management Technology 5-2:
Researching Prospect Profiles On-Line   175
Sales Management In Action 5-2:
Would You Sell to Crooks?   176
Minimum Account Size   179
Sales Management In Action 5-3:
Are They "Hot," "Warm" or "Cold"?   179
Account Analysis and Time Allocation   183
Sales Management In Action 5-4:
Intel: Salespeople Who Don't Call on Customers
187
Managing Territory Profitability   189
Territory Coverage   190
Personal Time Management   191
Management's Role   192
Sales Management in Action 5-5: One of the Most
Important Things a Sales Manager Does   193
Sales Management Technology 5-3: Management by
Planning   195

CASES

5-1   Hanover Bates Chemical Corporation   200
5-2   Zygar Pharmaceuticals   204

CHAPTER 6 / Sales Ethics   218

Why Ethics Are Important   219
Modeling Ethical Behavior   219
Whose Ethics are Relevant?   220

Sales Management in Action 6-1: **Over Selling at Sears**
221
Making Decisions on Ethical Problems   224
Common Sales Ethics Issues   227
Sales Management in Action 6-2: **The Ethics of Selling
Infant Formula**   232
Whistleblowing   232
Government Regulation   233
Building a Sales Ethics Program   235

CASES

6-1   Texxon Oil Company   241
6-2   Dave MacDonald's Ethical Dilemmas   247

▶ **PART III / SALES GOALS AND
STRUCTURE**

CHAPTER 7 / Estimating Potentials and
Forecasting Sales   251

What Is Market Potential   252
Subjective Sales Forecasting   255
Objective Sales Forecasting   257
Selecting Forecasting Programs   263
Sales Management Tools 7-1: **Commercial Forecasting
Programs**   265

CASES

7-1   Parker Computer   269
7-2   Mead Products   271
7-3   Bates Industrial Supply   280

CHAPTER 8 / Organization   282

Hewlett-Packard Reorganizes   283
Organizational Principles   283
Specialization   288
Sales Management in Action 8-1:
What, Another One?   287
Major Accounts Program   292
Sales Management in Action 8-2:
What More Can We Do for You?   293
Telemarketing   295
Independent Sales Agents   298
Sales Management in Action 8-3: **From Employee to
Partner**   299
Number of Salespeople   301
Sales Management in Action 8-4:
How Many Salespeople are Enough?   302
Evolving Sales Force Organizations   304
Sales Management in Action 8-5:
"What? Only a 20 Percent Raise?"   304

Sales Management in Action 8-6:
   Help Wanted Now—A Temporary Sales Force
   306
Ethical Situations 307
CASES

   8-1   Jefferson-Pilot Corporation   313
   8-2   Shanandoah Industries (B)   326

► PART IV / BUILDING A SALES PROGRAM

CHAPTER 9 / Recruiting and Selecting Personnel   328

Recruiting at Procter & Gamble 329
Planning Cycle 330
Sales Management in Action 9-1: **"Which Seller Belongs Where"** 336
Sales Management in Action 9-2: **"Everything Will Be All Right"** 338
Recruiting 339
Selecting Prospects 343
Sales Management in Action 9-3: **Why Did You Do That?** 349
Sales Management in Action 9-4: **From Socialist to Sales Rep** 352
Validating the Hiring Process 355
Sales Management in Action 9-5:
   "Who Should We Hire in Belgium?" 355
Ethical Situations 356
Experiential Exercise 361
CASES

   9-1   Fortress Electrical Tape Company   363
   9-2   Adams Brands   370

CHAPTER 10 / Sales Training   376

Sales Training at IBM 377
Why Train Salespeople? 378
Planning for Sales Training 380
Sales Management in Action 10-1: **Getting Customers into the Act** 381
Developing the Training Program 384
Sales Management in Action 10-2: **Getting a Quick Start** 388
Sales Management in Action 10-3: **The Sales Training Book Club** 390
Sales Management Technology 10-1: **Training Without Travel** 391
Sales Management in Action 10-4:
   "They Really Paid Attention" 392

Evaluating Sales Training 393
Follow-Up 394
Additional Sales Trainging Issues 395
Experiential Exercise 400
CASES

   10-1   Westinghouse Electric Corporation   402
   10-2   Sandwell Paper Company   410

CHAPTER 11 / Territory Design   418

Why Use Territories? 419
Sales Management in Action 11-1: **Territories by Design** 419
Territory Design Procedures 420
Designing Territories by Computer 429
Sales Management in Action 11-2: **Interactive Mapping Programs** 430
Territory Assignments 432
Ethical Issues 432
CASES

   11-1   D. F. Hardware Company   436
   11-2   Kent Plastics   440

► PART V / LEADING AND MOTIVATING THE SALES FORCE

CHAPTER 12 / Leadership   444

Where Is Richard Waxler? 445
Leadership 445
Leadership Styles 448
Team Building 449
Sales Management in Action 12-1: **The Case for Effective Team Building** 450
Coaching 452
Sales Meetings 454
Sales Management in Action 12-2: **It's Always Something** 456
Sales Force Personnel Issues 457
Ethical Situations 462
CASES

   12-1   First National Bank   468
   12-2   Romano Pitesti   476

CHAPTER 13 / Motivating Salespeople   481

The President's Club 482
What Is Motivation? 483
Individual Needs 484

Sales Management in Action 13-1: **The Chinese Need Hierarchy** 486
A Model of Motivation 489
Self-Management 492
Quotas 493
Incentive Programs 498
Sales Management in Action 13-2: **Why Incentive Plans Cannot Work** 501
Recognition Programs 502
Ethical Situations 504
CASES

13-1   Hong Kong Bank of Canada 510
13-2   General Electric Appliances 519

CHAPTER 14 / Compensating Salespeople
529

Compensation Objectives 530
Compensation Methods 534
Sales Management in Action 14-1:
Designing Compensation Plans to Cut Turnover 534
Sales Management in Action 14-2: **Dell's Drive for Profits** 539
Setting Pay Levels 540
Expense Accounts and Benefits 541
Assembling the Plan 543
Ethical Issues 545

CASES

14-1   Madison Fiber Corporation 550
14-2   Power & Motion Industrial Supply, Inc. 557

CHAPTER 15 / Evaluating Performance
562

Sales Performance Review 563
The Big Picture 565
Expense Analysis 566
Evaluating Salespeople 568
Behavior-Based Evaluation 569
Results-Based Evaluations 572
Using Models for Evaluation 574
TQM and Sales Force Efficiency 579
Ethical Issues 580
CASES

15-1   Practical Parties 586
15-2   York Electronics 592
15-3   Abbott, Inc. 597

APPENDIX A / In-Class Exercises   A-1

APPENDIX B / Getting a Job in Sales   A-2

Key Term & Subject Index   I-1
Author Index   I-3
Company Index   I-6
Case Index   I-8

▶ 1 ◀

Introduction to Selling and Sales Management

By working faithfully eight hours a day, you may
eventually get to be a boss and work twelve hours a day.
ROBERT FROST

LEARNING OBJECTIVES

After studying this chapter, you should be able to:

▶ Show how personal selling is used to encourage customer purchases.

▶ Define sales management and its relation to other marketing activities.

▶ Identify the activities performed by field salespeople and sales managers.

▶ Understand typical career paths in sales.

▶ SELLING AND SALES MANAGEMENT

This book introduces you to the worlds of personal selling and sales management. In today's environment, managers must learn to improve sales force productivity, reduce selling expenses, boost revenue, introduce new selling technology, and contend with a wave of corporate mergers. These challenges affect the size of the sales force, the way salespeople are organized, and the procedures used to manage them. Your objective in the future will be to find new ways to recruit, train, compensate, and motivate salespeople to respond to a constantly changing business environment.

Selling at Compaq and BriskHeat

Ten years ago, Compaq Computer followed IBM's strategy of using large branch sales offices. However, customers were unhappy because they did not get the help they needed. Compaq responded by closing three of eight regional sales offices and salespeople were told to operate out of their homes. Telemarketers were added to answer routine customer inquiries about products, prices, and availability. Each morning, field reps log onto Compaq's server network and download the information needed for the day's calls onto their notebook computers. On the road, Compaq salespeople can get into the database from any phone jack. The net result of these changes was a one-third reduction in the size of Compaq's salesforce, a cut in sales and administration expenses from 22 percent to 12 percent of sales, and a doubling of sales revenues.[1]

At Briskheat, a maker of industrial blankets, the problem was flat sales. A new sales manager fired the existing sales reps and replaced them with more aggressive, experienced salespeople. He also scrapped the complex salary, plus commission, plus bonus compensation program with a simpler, more focused plan. Under the new plan salespeople were paid a salary plus a 5 percent commission on first year's sales from a customer and 2 percent on sales in following years. This plan encouraged representatives to sign up new distributors. In two years, sales at Briskheat doubled and the company had 50 new distributors.[2] The Briskheat manager succeeded because he hired talented reps and created a climate that encouraged them to satisfy customers.

The Changing Marketplace

In today's expanding global marketplace, managers have to respond to changing customer needs. The emphasis today is on problem solving and this requires salespeople to interact with more people at each customer site. Also customers expect vendors to get involved earlier in product development and field sales teams to interface with buyers.

These innovations in the way suppliers and customers interact have brought changes in the way sales forces are organized, compensated, directed, and evaluated. Our goal with this textbook is to explain how salespeople operate in this new environment and how they should be supervised for maximum efficiency. We begin with a discussion on the selling process that provides an overview of the sales function.

Next, we discuss the activities performed by field sales managers. The final section of this chapter profiles the types of career paths that you can expect to find in your first sales job.

▶ THE SALES MANAGEMENT PROCESS

The sequence of activities that guides managers in the creation and administration of sales programs for a firm is known as the sales management process. First, the firm must come up with a selling strategy and a plan of action. Then sales management has to locate target customers and recruit, train, motivate, compensate, and organize a field sales force. The next phase of the process is concerned with the interactions between customers and salespeople. The results of successful salesperson/customer interactions are orders, profits, repeat customers, and after-sale service. The last phase of the process focuses on evaluation of the field sales force and the feedback of suggestions to senior managers so that they can modify plans for the future.

When managers do not follow a defined sales management process, chaos reigns and field reps merely react to customer requests rather than help them solve problems. When Filemon Lopez looked at the selling process at Comcast Cable, he found there were no systems to tell a salesperson how to convert leads into a sale.[3] There were no territories, salespeople sold advertising space on price rather than value, and lead generation was haphazard. Lopez instituted training classes that showed reps how to prospect, analyze needs, solve problems, and make value-driven sales. He also established sales territories so reps were not competing with each other and hired telemarketers to get leads for field reps. Now that Comcast Cable has a defined sales process, reps know what steps to follow and sales revenue is up 20 percent.

International Dimensions

The principles of sales management are universal and can be used in North and South America, Europe, and Asia. We believe that the fundamentals of personal selling and sales management are basically the same the world over. For example, research has shown that the decision to use company salespeople or independent reps does not vary significantly across international markets.[4] However, sometimes cultural and language differences call for adjustments in selling approaches. For example, Wyeth-Ayerst International sells pharmaceuticals in 100 countries and employs 50 international sales trainers. The skills component of their training programs emphasizing listening, asking the right questions, and probing for needs is the same throughout the world. Nevertheless, the company adapts training to local conditions in response to cultural differences.[5] Salespeople are taught when to drink tea (always in China), when to schedule appointments (after 10 in France), and when to close (more often in Australia). This book includes a number of international cases and overseas examples to better acquaint you with the special problems of global selling. Sales Management in Action 1-1 describes how several firms have expanded their sales efforts in Mexico with the passage of the North American Free Trade Agreement (NAFTA).

Sales Management in Action 1-1
Selling in Other Countries

With the passage of NAFTA, the Mexican market is opening and Joe Martorelli is going back to school. The 56-year-old executive has completed an intensive 10-week Spanish course and he listens to language tapes on the drive to work. If he could speak Spanish fluently, he would be in Mexico for 1 or 2 weeks a month selling spare parts for plastics and injection molding machines. His company plans to have 10 percent of its total revenue coming out of Mexico in five years. Joe has already signed up two independent reps to sell his spare parts in Mexico.

Microsoft has been in Mexico for several years and has a staff of 50 salespeople. Half sell software to wholesalers who service retail dealers and half act as liaison for major accounts. Xerox has hired 110 independent reps who sell copying equipment to small retailers. They also have 70 salespeople who handle the top corporate and government accounts. Xerox also sells direct to larger dealers and is now selling $300 million of copiers a year in Mexico. Microsoft and Xerox's success suggests it is important to work with Mexican distributors or independent reps or hire local salespeople.

Source: Geoffrey Brewer, "New World Orders," *Sales & Marketing Management*, January 1994, pp. 59–63.

Strategic Sales Planning

Sales management focuses on the administration of the personal selling function in the marketing mix. This role includes the planning, management, and control of sales programs, as well as the recruiting, training, compensating, motivating, and evaluating of field sales personnel. *Sales management* can thus be defined as:

The planning, implementing, and control of personal contact programs designed to achieve the sales and profit objectives of the firm.

This definition suggests that sales management is concerned with strategic decision making, as well as with carrying out marketing plans. For example, sales executives often become involved in the design and development of marketing programs, and contribute to changes in the product line, the pricing of products and services, and the selection of advertising campaigns. Sales managers are involved in developing strategies for accessing different markets and building account relationships. *Sales managers* and the salespeople they supervise are in an excellent position to obtain information about customer needs, product applications, and market conditions. This knowledge of the market allows sales managers to contribute to corporate decision making. Our discussion of the strategic planning issues in sales management appears in Chapter 2.

Developing the Selling Function

Personal selling is critical to the sale of many goods and services and can be defined as:

Direct communications between paid representatives and prospects that lead to purchase orders, customer satisfaction, and postsale service.

The relationships between selling and other elements of the marketing mix are highlighted in Figure 1-1.

Marketing programs are designed around four elements of the marketing mix: products to be sold, pricing, promotion, and distribution channels. The promotion component includes *advertising, public relations, personal selling,* and *sales promotion* (point-of-purchase displays, coupons, and sweepstakes). Note that advertising and sales promotion are nonpersonal communications, whereas salespeople talk directly to customers. Thus, where advertising and sales promotion "pull" merchandise through the channel, personal selling provides the "push" needed to get orders signed. With public relations, the message is perceived as coming from the media rather than directly from the organization. Personal selling involves two-way communication with prospects that allows the sales message to be adapted to the special needs of the customer.

When objections are raised, the salesperson is there to provide appropriate explanations. Advertising can only respond to objections that the copywriter *thinks* are important to customers. Furthermore, personal selling can be directed to qualified prospects, whereas a great deal of advertising and sales promotion is wasted because many people in the audience have no use for the product. Perhaps the most important advantage of personal selling is that it is considerably more effective than advertising, public relations, and sales promotion in closing sales.

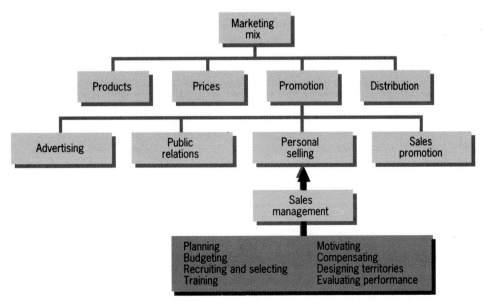

Figure 1-1: Positions of Personal Selling and Sales Management in the Marketing Mix

The steps salespeople go through to convert prospects into repeat buyers are described in Chapter 3. Next, it is important that you understand how salespeople manage individual accounts and conduct negotiations (Chapter 4). Chapter 5 explains how salespeople manage a territory and route themselves between customers. Salespeople are continually confronted with ethical dilemmas; some background on these problems is needed so that informed decisions can be made (Chapter 6).

Sales Goals and Structure

Sales planning is easier when managers have good data on where potential customers are located and how much they can be expected to buy. Sales managers need to be able to project sales for existing accounts and territories. A variety of techniques that can be used to estimate potentials and forecast sales are presented in Chapter 7.

A third dimension of sales planning is concerned with designing organizational structures. An example of a typical line *sales organization* in a medium-sized firm is shown in Figure 1-2. The diagram shows 96 field reps reporting to 8 district sales managers. This wide *span of control* (1/12) means that there are few opportunities for promotion within the line structure. Thus, sales managers have to be creative to find ways to motivate people and keep turnover under control. A detailed analysis of sales organization decisions on reporting relationships, specialization, telemarketing, and sales agents is provided in Chapter 8.

Building a Sales Program

Sales managers are responsible for hiring enough salespeople with the appropriate skills and backgrounds to implement the sales strategy. Research has revealed that failure is more likely among candidates who lack initiative, organization, enthusiasm, customer orientation, and personal goals.[6] This means that good sources must be found for new hires, and those who are weak in these areas must be carefully screened out. Recruiting issues are covered in Chapter 9.

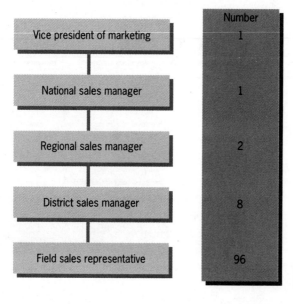

Figure 1-2: Sales Organization in a Medium-Size Firm

After salespeople have been hired, they must be trained before they are sent into the field. Sales managers are responsible for making sure that training is completed, and they often conduct some of the classes. Most training is to familiarize salespeople with the company's products, services, and operating procedures, with more limited time devoted to development of selling skills. Sales training is expensive, and it is the sales manager's job to select the most cost-effective methods, location, and materials. A detailed discussion of training is given in Chapter 10.

The next step in the sales management process is to assign salespeople to individual territories to minimize travel and contact costs (Chapter 11). The proper design of sales territories helps the sales department provide optimum customer service and satisfaction at an acceptable cost.

Managing the Sales Force

Effective sales managers know how to supervise and keep track of what their reps are doing. Sales managers also provide *leadership* to inspire their people to grow and develop professionally to achieve the revenue goals of the firm (Chapter 12). Good leaders provide models of behavior for employees to emulate, often developing strong mutual trust and rapport with subordinates. Leadership styles vary, but effective leaders are adept at initiating structure, that is, organizing and motivating employees, setting goals, enforcing rules, and defining expectations.

Sales managers use a variety of tools in their efforts to motivate salespeople to work more efficiently and effectively. One popular approach, called *expectancy theory*, is explained in Chapter 13. Other techniques that have proved to be effective motivators include sales meetings, quotas, sales contests, and recognition awards. It is amazing how well nonfinancial awards such as pins and plaques work with field sales reps.

The most powerful motivator for salespeople is a well-designed compensation package. There is nothing like money to attract and motivate salespeople to work hard (Chapter 14). A key task for sales managers is to come up with an effective mix of salary, bonuses, commissions, expenses, and benefits without putting the firm's profitability in jeopardy.

The last step in the sales management process is to evaluate the performance of the sales force. This involves analyzing sales data by territory and product breakdowns (Chapter 15). It also means reviewing selling costs and measuring the impact of sales force activities on profits. Now that the sales management process has been presented, we turn to a discussion of TQM.

► TOTAL QUALITY MANAGEMENT

Companies have begun focusing on improving the quality of products for an increasingly global market no longer protected by national economic policies. One approach is the collection of activities and perspectives known as *total quality management* (TQM).[7] By the 1990s, the ideas of being "customer driven," "delighting the customer," and "exceeding customer expectations," had reached almost a religious intensity in some organizations. Yet marketing and sales remained largely a new frontier for the quality movement. TQM originated in manufacturing and only now is being applied in sales by American companies, such as Ford, Xerox, Harley-Davidson, and Allen Bradley.

Increasingly, the areas closest to the customer, marketing and sales, provide a vital link in any organization's efforts to respond rapidly to changing market conditions.

TQM is built on the ideas of W. Edwards Deming, Joseph Juran, and Kaoru Ishikawa. In its simplest form, TQM is a comprehensive master plan for continuously improving quality in an organization. Built into the notion of TQM are some fundamental ideas:

- Making continuous improvements
- Having zero defects
- Doing it right the first time
- Understanding that employees closest to the situation know best how to improve it

Throughout this book, sales applications of TQM will be emphasized. The Alexander Group recently conducted a survey of how TQM principles were being applied in sales organizations.[8] Among other things, the study found that of the companies surveyed:

- Almost all measured customer satisfaction.
- Sixty-three percent were able to show improvement in their selling processes, particularly in the way salespeople were spending their time.
- Almost two-thirds were able to correct problems that ate up sales force time.
- Over three-fourths felt that they still lacked adequate data from their marketing information system (MIS) departments.
- Marketing and sales were focusing on shared goals, especially with respect to profitability. Less than half of the companies, however, felt that sales and marketing had an effective relationship.
- Very few companies had torn down functional barriers among departments.

These results suggest that progress is being made but that much remains to be accomplished.

▶ THE FIELD SALES MANAGER'S JOB

The basic responsibilities of sales managers are to direct the salespeople who report to them. Specifically, sales managers must set objectives, develop plans, execute programs, and evaluate performance. First-line sales managers are usually promoted to their jobs from the ranks of the sales force after a year or more of selling experience. The median age of newly appointed field sales managers is about 35 with about 6½ years of prior sales experience. Research has shown that there is a significant positive correlation between the appointment of new sales managers and subsequent performance.[9] New managers are younger than those they replace, and their enthusiasm and fresh ideas boost the sales of the salespeople they supervise. The bottom line is that you can make a difference with a career in sales management. An example showing how a new manager turned Xerox's Cleveland sales office around is described in Sales Management in Action 1-2.

Sales Management in Action 1-2
Turning It Around in Cleveland

When Frank Pacetta took over the Cleveland district sales office for Xerox, morale was low, turnover was high, and revenue was the lowest of the 11 districts in the region. Only one Xerox rep was making cold calls in downtown Cleveland, the district's biggest market, and customers were complaining about erratic service and slipshod billing. Pacetta knew he had to rebuild relations with customers so he hired seven more sales reps. This reduced the number of large customers per rep so important customers got more attention. Pacetta spent lavishly on promotional campaigns and customer parties, like a $17,000 golf outing. In the office he created a fraternity atmosphere with parties and pep rallies and recognition for birthdays and anniversaries. He also showered reps with plaques and praise for jobs well done. He creates elaborate sales contests with some winners getting $2,500 to $3,000 extra per year. Others win videocassette recorders, microwave ovens, or vacation trips.

Pacetta believes reps should do everything they can to get an order. Not long ago Pacetta made a bid to Packard Electric to replace 82 Toshiba copiers. When two Packard officials came to the office for a demonstration of a printing system they were asked what prices and conditions Xerox had to meet to get the copier bid that day. Once he obtained this information, Pacetta frantically called headquarters for approval to make a new lower bid. He got the "go ahead" and the $600,000 order. Pacetta has also weeded out employees who fail to meet his pumped up sales targets.

Pacetta believes sales reps should be well groomed. He hands out shoe polish, asks overweight reps to slim down, and requires that shirt collars be heavily starched. He even demands clean-shaven faces. His dress code and management style have not appealed to everyone, but in his first year the Cleveland district soared to No. 1 in the region and No. 4 among Xerox's 65 districts.

Source: James Hirsch, "To One Xerox Man, Selling Photocopiers Is a Gambler's Game," *Wall Street Journal*, September 24, 1991, p. 1.

Pacetta's Selling Tips

- Prepare customer proposals at night and on weekends.
- Never say no to a customer—everything is negotiable.
- Make customers feel good by sending cards for birthdays, etc., take them to lunch and ball games.
- Meet customers' requirements even if you must fight your own bureaucracy.
- Do things for customers you don't get paid for, like solving billing problems.
- Know competitive products better than they do.
- Be early for meetings.

Job Skills

Although sales managers reach their positions in an organization because of their sales ability, their continued success depends on administrative talents. Two skills essential in sales management are organizational ability and leadership. Research has shown that the traits needed for effective leadership include intelligence, motivation, energy, human relations skills, persuasiveness, ambition, perception of social cues, and personal impact.[10] Sales managers must be able to organize their own time, and they must also be able to set up procedures to ensure an efficient sales office. Clerks need to be trained to process orders, handle inquiries, and expedite shipments so that the office runs smoothly even when sales managers are away. Perhaps the most difficult tasks for sales managers are organizing personnel into territories, scheduling appropriate training and sales meetings, making sure sales reports are submitted on time, and being available to talk with reps when needed. Since salespeople are continually on the road, these tasks are made easier when the reps are equipped with pagers, car phones, fax machines, and personal computers.

Sales managers have a difficult job, but they operate in line positions with direct responsibility to achieve the sales and profit objectives of the firm. Thus, sales revenue is generally used to measure a manager's organizational and leadership ability and to reward those who exceed their quotas. These rewards not only include higher salaries, but sometimes a quick route to upper-level executive positions as well.

Time Allocations

An excellent way to learn about sales management is to ask a representative group of sales managers how they spend their time (Table 1-1). Most people are surprised to find that the largest proportion of a sales manager's time (29 percent) is spent selling. Sales managers typically spend 17 percent of their time in face-to-face conferences with customers and another 12 percent talking with them on the phone.

Table 1-1   Sales Managers' and Salespersons' Time Allocations

Job Responsibility	Managers' Time Allocation (in Percent)	Salespersons' Time Allocation (in Percent)
Selling	29%	56%
Face-to-face	(17)	(31)
Via telephone	(12)	(25)
Administration	24	15
Account service/coordination	17	11
Travel/waiting	15	18
Internal meetings	14	—

Source: Adapted from data presented in William A. O'Connell and William Keenan, Jr., "The Shape of Things to Come," *Sales & Marketing Management* (January 1990), p. 39; and *Sales Force Compensation Survey* (Chicago: Dartnell Corp., 1996), p. 20

These findings dispel the common misconception that sales managers sit behind desks issuing orders. For example, when Dan LeFever took over as sales manager for Bard Access's Northeast district he began to travel three days a week with his reps to meet with customers and help tailor presentations to buyers' needs. He found that the buying center for his vascular instruments had shifted from doctors to administrators who based decisions on cost. LeFever counseled his eight salespeople to broaden their prospect list to include chief financial officers, materials directors, and others involved in equipment decisions.[11] Two salespeople were not able to make this change and had to be replaced. By working closely in the field to train and motivate his salespeople, LeFever was able to move his district from last to first and earned a promotion to director of sales of the Davol Division of Bard, Inc.

Research shows that sales managers spend a significant amount of time selling to their own accounts. This activity can take time away from important administrative responsibilities. However, in some cases this activity can be justified. Occasionally the sales manager will handle one or more large accounts because they merit and need his or her attention. In smaller firms, there may not be a need for a full-time sales manager, in which case the sales manager is likely to handle personal accounts along with administrative responsibilities. Other reasons for selling personal accounts are more difficult to justify. A customer may request that the sales manager handle an account, often because of an existing relationship between the manager and the customer developed earlier in the manager's sales career. Personal accounts may also be used to supplement the sales manager's salary through commissions earned from these sales. Since commissioned salespeople sometimes earn more than salaried managers, a few choice accounts may be reserved for the sales manager in order to attract qualified people to this position. Few of these reasons, however, present a defensible argument for selling personal accounts. In fact, most large, successful firms do not allow their managers to use their valuable time in this activity.

Administration   Administrative duties take about one-quarter of the available time of sales managers and 17 percent of the time of field salespeople. For managers, these activities include management of field sales offices, training, preparation of budgets, expense control, and administration of compensation programs. Sales managers must continually deal with people both to help new hires get adjusted and to improve the selling skills of more experienced members of the sales team. For example, Jan Howard of MONY insurance boosted the revenue of her top producer group $2.3 million a year and won a Best Sales Force award from *Sales & Marketing Management* magazine by helping them become more efficient.[12] Jan had the reps keep track of their activities and pointed out where they were wasting time on meetings and paperwork. By delegating some of this work and making better use of technology, face-to-face time with customers increased from 8 hours a week to 13 hours and sales boomed.

Managers also spend time consulting with salespeople who are performing below standard. The performance of many of these people can be improved by encouragement, personal counseling, retraining, or assignment to a new territory. Poor sales records are occasionally the result of serious personal problems. Sales managers must know how to recognize and deal with such difficult situations and when to refer people to professional help. Poor performance may also be a function of factors beyond the control of the salesperson such as unusual competitive activity, loss of a key customer, or weak company support. In other cases, problem salespeople are the result of poor hiring decisions.

Sales managers typically spend only a small amount of time reviewing salespersons' compensation programs. This does not imply that compensation planning is unimportant, but rather that wage administration is usually concentrated on and achieved in fairly short periods of time every 6 or 12 months. Indeed, compensation is one of the key factors in attracting, motivating, and retaining field salespeople. Because sales is such a particularly demanding profession, wages tend to be higher than those paid to employees at equivalent levels in other functional areas within the firm. Table 1-2 presents the typical compensation paid for sales positions in 1996.

Account Service/Coordination   Students sometimes wonder why sales managers spend 17 percent of their time servicing accounts compared to only 11 percent for salespeople (Table 1-1). The reason is that customers need an advocate within the firm to make sure their interests are protected. Sales managers share responsibility with salespeople for seeing that customers' orders are processed and delivered on time. This means that sales managers help coordinate customers' needs with the production department to make sure that quality and service standards are maintained. They also work to gain credit approval, and they check with customers to make sure that postsales adjustments and service are satisfactory.

Travel   Typical sales managers spend about 15 percent of their time traveling (Table 1-1). This is less than the 18 percent spent by field salespeople who are on the road four or five days a week. Sales managers have larger territories than salespeople but travel less often. The most common reasons for sales manager travel are to keep in touch with conditions in the field, to help close important sales, and to observe and train field sales reps.

Table 1-2   Total Compensation for Field Sales Personnel, 1992

Job Title	Average
Top sales executive	$99,000
Regional sales manager	78,700
District sales manager	69,600
Senior salesperson	55,600
Intermediate sales rep	43,300
Entry-level rep	33,700

Source: Adapted from data in *Sales Force Compensation Survey* (Chicago: Dartnell Corp., 1996), pp. 68–73.

Meetings   Sales meetings are important training and motivational tools for field reps, and it is not surprising that sales managers spend 14 percent of their time on this activity. When Steve Bannigan, the new sales manager of McBride Electric, had his first meeting with his sales team he found that only two thought of themselves as salespeople.[13] The rest saw themselves as "estimators" who just priced electrical work and took orders. To give his team more of a sales focus, Bannigan held a series of meetings to develop basic selling skills so they could solicit business and close orders. As a result McBride Electric has been growing between 10 and 25 percent per year and salespeople now compete for sales awards. Meetings are also used to explain company-designed sales programs to field reps. Sales managers spend most of their time executing marketing plans created by other executives, and meetings are a useful way to get this work done. Now let us move on to career planning.

▶ CAREER PATHS

We believe it is important for students to understand how someone moves into the position of sales manager and what the opportunities are for further advancement. Sales managers almost always begin their *career paths* as salespeople.

Rob Prazmark

When Rob Prazmark graduated from college, his first job was selling Xerox copy machines in Buffalo, New York. After learning the basics, he moved on to sell ad space at an independent television station. Then he got a job selling ABC network news time. He was so creative at squeezing extra cash from each sale that he was offered a sales vice president's position at ISL Marketing at the young age of 31. In this job he had to find 11 sponsors for the Olympic Games and raise $300 million. The key sale was a $20 million pitch to Visa; from then on, Prazmark made each successive campaign even more successful. Prazmark's skyrocketing career shows that a basic foundation in selling often leads to a progression of increasingly rewarding sales positions.[14]

Sales trainees with undergraduate degrees are promoted into sales management positions after a few years of field selling experience. The amount of time required to make this step depends on the ability of the individual, the size of the firm, and the types of products sold. In some organizations that sell directly to consumers, it is possible to become a sales manager after six months. A person may spend 5 to 10 years in several positions before being promoted to sales manager in a firm marketing industrial products. An example of sales career paths for Hallmark Cards is now presented.

Hallmark Cards

Sales careers with consumer product firms begin in the field, where trainees gain valuable experience that becomes the springboard for promotions into other mar-

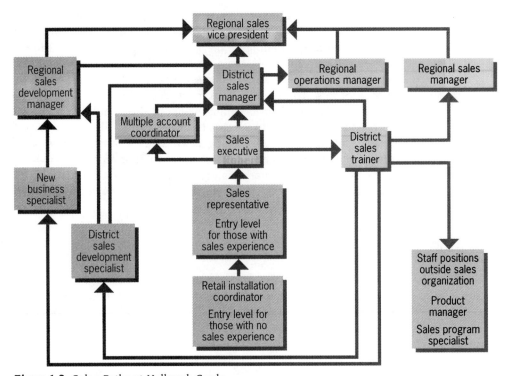

Figure 1-3: Sales Paths at Hallmark Cards

keting areas. At Hallmark Cards, salespeople start as retail installation coordinators (Figure 1-3) if they lack field sales experience. This allows new hires to familiarize themselves with customers and their needs before they move up to a position as a sales representative. Each sales representative is assigned a geographic territory that consists of several counties and about 30 retail accounts. Sales representatives work with their retail accounts to improve space productivity, visual appeal, personal selling skills, inventory control, and local advertising programs.

Successful reps move up to the position of sales executive with more responsibility and larger accounts. From this position, some people move to jobs as multiple account coordinators, district sales trainers, or district sales managers. The position of multiple account coordinator is designed for career salespeople who are not interested in staff or sales management positions. Hallmark thus offers three promotion opportunities for people who want to stay in sales rather than management.

District sales trainer is an important job at Hallmark Cards, as it can lead to a job as a regional sales trainer, district sales development specialist, new-business specialist, or staff positions outside the sales organization. Promotion to district sales manager at Hallmark usually takes 7 to 10 years and can lead to a position as one of four regional sales vice presidents. A key advantage of a sales career at Hallmark is the wide variety of positions available that provide experience needed to climb the ladder of success.

► SUMMARY

This chapter has introduced you to the topics of personal selling and sales management. Where personal selling focuses on direct contacts with prospects, sales management is concerned with the planning, implementation, and control of personal contact programs to satisfy customers and achieve the objectives of the firm. First we explained the role of personal selling in the marketing program of the firm. You cannot do a good job as sales manager until you thoroughly understand the job of a field sales representative. We then looked at the typical sales manager's job, which embraces such activities as selling, personnel management, training, preparation of budgets, administration, and financial analysis. Since sales managers continually deal with people, they must be able to organize and lead others if they expect to be successful. The chapter concludes with a discussion of career paths open to people in sales.

► KEY TERMS

Advertising	Public relations
Advertising pull	Sales management
Business products	Sales manager
Career paths	Sales organization
Consumer products	Sales promotion
Expectancy theory	Sales representative
Leadership	Span of control
Personal selling	Total quality management (TQM)
Personal selling push	

► REVIEW QUESTIONS

1. Where does personal selling fit within the marketing program of the firm?
2. What types of activities are included in the job of the sales manager?
3. How does the job of the person selling consumer products differ from that of the person selling business products?
4. Which activity of a sales manager takes up the most time?
5. If advertising is a *pull* strategy, what strategy does personal selling represent?
6. What advantages does personal selling have that advertising does not have?
7. Name two job skills that are essential to the success of sales managers.
8. Explain how a field salesperson becomes a sales manager.
9. Describe how career paths move between line and staff positions in a sales organization.

10. How do sales managers spend the 14 percent of their time that is devoted to meetings?

11. How much did a typical district sales manager earn in 1995?

▶ PROBLEMS

1. Research has shown that women reps pay more attention to detail, are better listeners, and do more consultative selling and relationship building than male salespeople. Does this mean that sales managers should hire more women than men?

2. Many salespeople spend several nights a week on the road away from their families. Should you as sales manager allow your reps to make daily phone calls home and charge them to their expense accounts?

3. Phil Tumminia, director of the Glassboro State College Development Fund in southern New Jersey, made a cold call on a local industrialist in 1990, and asked for and received a gift of $1,500. On succeeding calls, he got $3 million for the library, $20 million for the business school, and finally $100 million for a new engineering school. Why did personal sales calls work better than direct mail, phone calls, or media advertising for this tiny college's development program?

4. BeautiControl Cosmetics sells skin care products direct to consumers with a sales force of 47,000 consultants. Their sales of $75 million are small compared to Mary Kay, which has $950 million in volume. BeautiControl recruits reps by offering a 4 percent override commission to salespeople who bring in new consultants. The new reps have to pay $250 for orientation and education videos. BeautiControl has 12 sales meetings around the country in January to inspire their consultants. Field reps receive a constant stream of recognition and financial awards. Can a small direct sales firm like BeautiControl compete with giants like Mary Kay and Avon? What would you recommend to increase the size of their sales force?

5. Ascom Timeplex equipped 300 salespeople with laptop computers to allow electronic order processing. As a result, order cycle time was reduced 50 percent, accuracy increased 25 percent, and order processing costs delined 20 percent. Explain how improved sales force efficiency could pay the estimated $2.1 million cost of automating the Ascom Timeplex salespeople.

6. Firms that sell complex analytical software are relying more on sales teams to work with customers. One salesperson can never know everything about the product. As sales manager, how would you improve communications among member of sales teams and increase their incentive to work together?

7. Sales consultants are advising that women sales representatives should move away from dresses and slacks and adopt a more professional look. Is it part of your job as sales manager to tell your reps what to wear? If so, how should this be done?

8. Many small firms cannot afford a full-time sales manager to train and direct a sales team of four to six reps. A Utah company offers the services of a part-time sales manager for a fee of $750 per month. Under what conditions would it pay to hire a part-time sales manager?

9. A sales manager for a large industrial firm said, "We make a great effort to hire salespeople who recognize that their role is being both a salesperson and a part of their distributor's business." What did the sales manager mean by this?

10. Precision Cutting Tools manufactures industrial products for a national market. Until recently, they employed 12 salespeople to call on accounts. Dissatisfied with the results, the sales manager discharged all 12 in favor of 9 independent manufacturer's representatives. (Manufacturer's reps are not employed by the company; usually they sell for a number of companies.) The rep in this case sold other industrial products along with the Precision line to the same customers. Immediately, sales began to increase, old business was retrieved, and new accounts were acquired. What possible reasons might explain this? What are the advantages and disadvantages of manufacturer's reps compared to an in-house sales force?

11. To combat a decline in industry sales of lawnmowers and garden tractors, Simplicity Manufacturing increased its field sales force from 21 to 28. These salespeople called on 750 retail outlets and provided them with display and promotional services. Simplicity offered dealers unlimited matching co-op advertising allowances, and its salespeople helped dealers cut and paste together improved ads. The salespeople also planned promotional schedules and made media contacts for the dealers. As a result of these activities, Simplicity sales increased 20 percent. Which was more important in increasing sales, the larger sales force or the advertising program?

► EXPERIENTIAL EXERCISE

A good way to learn about sales management is to spend a day with a real sales manager. Your assignment is to contact a sales manager and arrange to observe his or her activities during a typical day. Keep a log of how the sales manager's time is spent and compare it with the data in Table 1-1. Write a report describing your experience and the manager's activities. Use the Yellow Pages to identify prospects and then phone to arrange an appointment. Remember that direct sales organizations like Avon, Mary Kay, and Tupperware have local sales managers who are good prospects for observation. Also, most towns have car dealers with sales managers who can be approached. If you have difficulty finding a cooperative sales manager, contact the local chapter of the Sales and Marketing Executives Club or the American Marketing Association, or ask your instructor for help.

► REFERENCES

1. ROLPH E. ANDERSON, "Personal Selling and Sales Management in the New Millennium," *Journal of Personal Selling & Sales Management*, Vol. 16 (Fall 1996), p. 24.

2. GEOFFREY BREWER, "To the Max," *Sales & Marketing Management*, March 1996, pp. 48–55.

3. ANDY COHEN, "Designing the Process, Starting Over," *Sales & Marketing Management*, September 1995, pp. 40–44.

4. JOHN S. HILL and RICHARD R. STILL, "Organizing the Overseas Sales Force: How Multinationals Do It," *Journal of Personal Selling and Sales Management*, Vol. 10 (Spring 1990), p. 61.

5. ANDY COHEN, "Small World, Big Challenge," *Sales & Marketing Management* (June 1996), pp. 69–73.

6. MARK W. JOHNSTON, JOSEPH F. HAIR, JR., and JAMES BOLES, "Why Do Salespeople Fail?" *Journal of Personal Selling and Sales Management*, Vol. 9, No. 3 (Fall 1989), p. 61.

7. The following discussion is based on James Cortada, TQM *for Sales and Marketing*

Management (New York: McGraw-Hill, 1993).

8. Information based on a presentation by Jerome A. Colletti, "Total Quality Management and Sales Organizations" (September 28, 1993).

9. ROBERT W. ARMSTRONG, ANTHONY PECOTICH, and BRAD MILLS, "Does the Sales Manager Make a Difference? The Impact of Sales Management Succession Upon Departmental Performance," *Journal of Personal Selling & Sales Management* (Fall 1993), p. 22.

10. DONALD B. GUEST and HAVVA J. MERIC, "The Fortune 500 Companies' Selection Criteria for Promotion to First Level Sales Management: An Empirical Study," *Journal of Personal Selling & Sales Management*, Vol. 9, No. 3 (Fall 1989), p. 51.

11. WILLIAM KEENAN, "Bravo: 10 Managers Show What It Takes to Lead and Succeed," *Sales & Marketing Management* (August 1995), p. 39.

12. GEOFFREY BREWER, "Celebrate Good Times," *Sales & Marketing Management* (October 1995), pp. 53–54.

13. CHARLES BUTLER, "Why the Bad Rap?" *Sales & Marketing Management* (June 1996), pp. 62–63.

14. "Rob Prazmark Goes for the Gold," *Sales & Marketing Management* (December 1990), pp. 24–25.

► SELECTED READINGS

CHURCHILL, GILBERT A., NEIL FORD, and ORVILLE C. WALKER, *Sales Force Management* (Homewood, Ill.: Richard D. Irwin, 1996).

INGRAM, THOMAS N., and RAYMOND W. LAFORGE, *Sales Management: Analysis and Decision Making* (Chicago: Dryden Press, 1992).

STANTON, WILLIAM J., RICHARD H. BUSKIRK, and ROSANN L. SPIRO, *Management of a Sales Force* (Homewood, Ill.: Richard D. Irwin, 1995).

CASE

1-1 THE CASE METHOD

The objective of the case method is to introduce a measure of realism to business education. The case method forces you to deal with problems as they actually occur in a business environment. Each case is a written description of the facts surrounding a particular business situation.

Benefits and Limitations

The case method becomes an effective learning device when you are encouraged to analyze the data presented and to formulate your own set of recommendations. Since each case is different, the solution you develop for one case cannot be randomly applied to other problems. This raises a question of what you actually learn by working with business cases. One obvious benefit is that the preparation and discussion of case studies helps you improve your skills in oral and written expression. In addition, the case method provides an easy way for you to learn about current business practices and methods. Perhaps the most important advantage of the case method is the experience it provides in thinking logically about different sets of data. The development of your analytical ability and judgment is the most valuable and lasting benefit derived from the case method.

Most cases, including those in this book, are drawn from the experience of real firms. Typically, the names and locations are disguised to protect the interests of the companies involved. In addition, final decisions are usually omitted to enhance the problem-solving orientation of the cases, thus permitting you to reach your own conclusions without being forced to criticize the actions taken by others. The case approach departs from the typical business situation in that the business executive normally does not have the facts presented as clearly and neatly as they are in casebooks. Problem solving in business usually involves extensive data collection, something that has been essentially completed for you when you work with the cases in this book.

A Framework for Analysis

There are many ways for you to approach the analysis of business cases. Each instructor has his or her own ideas on the number and nature of the steps that are involved. We believe that the following four-step procedure is a logical and practical way to begin.

1. Define the problem.
2. Formulate the alternatives.
3. Analyze the alternatives.
4. Recommend a solution.

The Problem

Once you are familiar with the facts of the case, it is important to isolate the central problem. Until this is done, it is usually impossible to proceed with an effective analysis. Normally you can get an idea of the central problem in a case by looking at where the case falls on the course outline. Instructors usually discuss a topic first and then assign a case to see if you understand the concepts that have been presented. Your instructor might provide questions to help you start your analysis. You should look at the questions as guides for action rather than as specific issues to be resolved. In no way are the questions designed to limit the scope or breadth of the discussion.

The Alternatives

The second step is the definition of possible alternatives to resolve the problem around which the case is organized. Some of these are obvious from the materials supplied in the case and from the statement of the main issue. Others you may have to supply.

Three or four alternatives are usually enough for most case problems. Only a foolish student would try to analyze 10 different alternatives in a six-page report. One alternative that you should always consider is the maintenance of the status quo. Sometimes doing nothing is the best course of action to follow.

The Analysis

The most crucial aspect of the case method is the analysis of alternatives. This section is usually where the student's grade is determined. To analyze is to separate into parts to find out the nature, proportion, function, and underlying relationships in a set of variables. Thus, to analyze is to dig into and work with the facts to uncover associations that may be used to evaluate possible courses of action. Your analysis should begin with a careful evaluation of the facts presented in the case. Be sensitive to the problem of sorting relevant material from that which is peripheral or irrelevant. Some cases include information designed to distract and confuse the careless reader. In reviewing a case, you must be very careful to distinguish between fact and opinion. Also you have a responsibility to make sure that the facts are consistent and reliable. Sometimes cases contain errors (either by accident or by design), and your instructor may prefer to remain silent.

Sometimes the most important facts in a case are obscurely buried in some chance remark or seemingly minor statistical exhibit. You must be careful to sift through the data to uncover all the relationships that apply to the alternatives being considered. This usually means that the quantitative information must be examined using a variety of ratios, graphs, tables, or other forms of analysis. Rarely are the data presented in the form most appropriate to finding a solution, and your instructor will expect you to work out the numbers.

Frequently, you will find gaps in the data provided in the cases. This means you must make assumptions if the analysis is to continue. You should be aware of and able to defend the assumptions you make. Also, a complete analysis is not one-sided. A review of a business situation is not sound unless both sides of important issues are examined. This does not mean that you must mention every point, but you should refute major opposing arguments where possible.

If after reviewing the facts you decide that you do not have enough information to reach a decision, you might wish to recommend that the decision be postponed pending the results of further research. Normally, however, "get more information" is not an acceptable solution in a business case. Decisions often cannot wait the length of time necessary to conduct good research. In addition, it is unlikely that we can ever expect to have all the information that we think we need. Because of the cost of research and the penalties of delay, business decisions are almost always made under conditions of uncertainty. If you say you need more information, your instructor may be tempted to conclude that you do not know how to analyze the facts available or are too lazy to collect more information.

You are expected to base your analysis on the evidence presented in the case, but this does not mean that other information cannot be used. You should utilize facts that are available to the trade, and information that is general or public knowledge. You can also use relevant concepts from other disciplines, such as accounting, statistics, economics, psychology, and sociology. The criterion in using "outside" material is that it must be appropriate to the particular situation. For example, you should not use data published in 1996 to make decisions in a case dated 1992. For this book we have attempted to select cases that provide you with enough information to complete the analysis. In some situations, however, you may wish to collect additional materials from the library.

Recommendations

After you have carefully analyzed the data and alternatives, you are in a position to make recommendations. Sometimes more than one course of action will look attractive. This is not an unusual situation, since most cases do not have a single "right" solution. Still, you must come up with a set of specific recommendations. To arrive at a solution, you must judge the relative risks and opportunities offered by the various alternatives. The optimum choice is the one that provides the best balance between profit opportunities and the risks and costs of failure. You should make a clear-cut decision and avoid qualifications and other obvious hedges. Instructors are much more concerned with the way a particular decision was reached than they are with the individual alternative selected.

If you feel that the collection of additional information is the only feasible solution to a case, you must provide support for this decision. First, you should state exactly what the research will show and how this information will be used. In addition, you

should indicate the research methodology to be followed and the anticipated cost of the study. After you have completed these tasks, you will be in a position to decide whether additional research is needed.

Writing the Report

We believe that students who prepare written reports do a better job of analyzing business problems. Writing a good report takes a certain skill, however, and we would like to suggest a few ideas that may be of help.

When instructors read reports, they look to see whether students fully understand the situation and whether their interpretation of the facts is reasonable. They also like to see papers that are objective, balanced, consistent, and decisive. Perhaps the most common error made by students writing case reports is to repeat the facts that have been provided. Instead of analyzing the data in light of the alternatives, students frequently repeat statements that appear in the case, with no clear object in mind. Nothing upsets an instructor more than reading a paper that devotes several pages to telling what he or she already knows about the case.

Another deficiency often observed in written reports is a lack of adequate organization. Students who have this fault will begin with the first thought that comes into their heads and continue, in almost random fashion, until they run out of ideas. The end result is a paper that has no beginning and no end and often consists of one long paragraph. To avoid this problem, some instructors require reports to be presented in outline form. The condensed nature of such reports sometimes makes them hard to follow, and we prefer the more readable narrative approach.

One system of organization that has proved effective divides the report into four sections. The sections are designated by Roman numerals and are arranged in the following order:

I. Problem statement

II. Alternatives

III. Analysis: List subheadings

IV. Recommendations

The problem statement is brief—rarely running more than one or two sentences. Students should take the time to construct a good lead sentence because first impressions are important. Lead sentences that combine several disjointed phrases connected by commas are not likely to impress your instructor or help you get an A. The alternatives section should be limited to three or four workable approaches to the problem. Students who consider all possible solutions will just confuse the grader. The analysis section makes up the bulk of the report and should include a number of subheadings. These might include evaluations of the data or discussions of the influence of the data on the alternatives. A good analysis is more than just a list of advantages and disadvantages of each alternative. Some of the topics that could be considered in the analysis section include:

1. Span of control
2. Training
3. Sources of salespeople
4. Alternative compensation plans
5. Impact on contests or quotas
6. Redesigning sales territories
7. Effects on company sales, costs, and profits

The recommendations section should be relatively short and concise. A list is quite appropriate. This is not the place to evaluate the facts or to hedge your position. Recommendations should be quite specific and they can be given priorities such as first do this and then do that. A common error of students is to let their report die at the end. They do a good job of stating the problem and analyzing the facts, but they fail to come up with a hard-hitting set of recommendations. Reports that end with a vague group of suggestions about reorganizing the sales force or revising the compensation plan are likely to receive B − or C grades.

There is no optimum length for a written case analysis. The report should be long enough to cover the subject adequately but no so long that it bores the instructor and the class. Obviously, written reports must be neat, legible, and free of errors in grammar and spelling. Remember to run Spell-Check before you print your report. Business professors are not hired to teach English composition, but they do expect certain minimum standards of performance in written expression. Their standards for written work are reflections of what the business community expects from college graduates.

Summary

Case analysis is designed to give students an opportunity to develop a productive and meaningful way of thinking and expressing themselves about business problems. Remember, however, that solutions to problems are worthless unless they can be sold to those in a position to act on the recommendations. The case approach provides students with practical experience in convincing others of the soundness of their reasoning.

CASE

1-2 ARAPAHOE PHARMACEUTICAL COMPANY*

As he reread the annual report that he had prepared for Phil Jackson, his regional sales manager, John Ziegler, shook his head and kept repeating to himself, "What a year!"

He could not forget the surge of pride he felt when his district sales manager asked him to call Phil

*This case was prepared by Professor Richard C. Leventhal of Metropolitan State College in Denver, Colorado. Reproduced by permission.

Jackson to let him know whether or not he wanted to accept a promotion to district sales manager for the Dallas area. As he remembered, he couldn't get to the telephone quickly enough, and it was only after Phil had asked him how his wife had taken the news, that he realized that he had forgotten to ask her. He immediately telephoned Lynn and found that she was thrilled both with his promotion and the move to Dallas even though neither one of them had been there before. Lynn was particularly pleased that her company had a sales opening in Dallas and she felt that she could obtain a transfer to that city. John once again expressed his appreciation to his sales manager for all of the help that she had given him so that he could qualify for the promotion.

John had joined Arapahoe Pharmaceutical as a sales rep immediately after graduating from San Francisco State University. While he had been interested in science in high school, and he had taken one course in chemistry and another course in biology at San Francisco State, he was more interested in marketing communications. When Arapahoe Pharmaceuticals recruited at the college in his junior year and again in the spring of his senior year, John decided that he might combine the interests in science and marketing communications as a sales representative. He was interviewed, hired, and assigned to a territory near Omaha in Betsy Warner's district. John's willingness, personality, and communications skills, plus Betsy's encouragement and guidance, helped him in quickly achieving above average productivity and allowed him to win a transfer to a territory in the greater metropolitan Denver area. The new territory offered him additional experience in working with food and drug chain headquarters, large hospitals, and drug wholesalers. John reviewed these experiences with considerable pleasure as he recalled the events of the past year. Betsy worked regularly with him, and delegated to him some of the training of new sales reps, which he found both challenging and rewarding, especially when the new sales trainee did well. His selling skills flourished as did his income and the recognition of his achievements by Betsy and the regional sales manager. A year later he was selected to attend his company's leadership training program, which was a milestone in his career.

Even before his first trip to Dallas, John was asked by Tom Boyle, the general sales manager, to spend a couple of days at the corporate headquarters in Philadelphia with him and various department heads in marketing, legal and human resources. They were all very complimentary about his past performance and how much he deserved his promotion. However, each of them in a different way seemed to repeat the same message: "Managing people is different from selling products." How well the events of the past year were to bear that out. The thrust of Boyle's message was a bit different. He wanted John to realize that he had full confidence in his ability, that John had earned his promotion, and that although John was a sales rep one day, and a district sales man-

ager the next, the company recognized the change wouldn't take place overnight and it would provide him with further training. In the meantime, Boyle advised John that the Dallas district was productive, operating efficiently, and staffed with well-trained sales reps, and that he was not expecting John to "Sweep the district clean" and make radical changes. He also emphasized that (1) John should give the sales reps in Dallas time to get to know him and he them; (2) he would be surprised and disappointed to discover that all the reps didn't operate with the same level of efficiency that he did nor use the same methods he used when he was a rep; (3) he shouldn't try to correct too many deficiencies at one time; (4) telling someone to do something doesn't necessarily get it done; (5) everyone doesn't remember hearing something the same way; and (6) it's better to have three sales reps working with you than ten working for you.

One year later, John realized that at the time he and Boyle talked, he didn't understand or appreciate the full meaning of that advice. The legal department wanted him to be aware of his increased responsibilities as a manager in speaking or acting for the company. The various departments in sales, marketing and human resources emphasized the importance of his new role and his support in administering the company's promotional programs and gaining the compliance of his sales reps. Increasingly, he realized the duality of his role as a member of management and of the field sales force. The sales management training programs he attended during the succeeding months reinforced these points and helped prepare him for the types of problems he was to encounter.

His introduction to the ten sales reps in the Dallas district went quite well. His predecessor, Chuck Morgan, who was retiring after 30 years with Arapahoe, fully reviewed all of the sales statistics for the district and the human resource records of the sales reps. He also gave him the benefit of his thoughts for the future and what John's immediate concerns should be. John had inherited a district that was operating on target both for sales and expenses, and appeared to have no major personnel problems other than one territory that had been open for four weeks. Chuck even had two resumes on promising candidates who needed processing.

John telephoned both applicants and scheduled interviews for the following week, along with trips of two days each with two of his sales reps. The interviews seemed to go well, but they took almost a full day. On his first day at his office the following week, John called the references and previous employers of both applicants, scheduled a second interview several days later with Larry Palmer, the most promising applicant, and, in accordance with the company's interviewing procedure, set up an information session with Larry and his wife for the following evening. Since this was John's first session of this type, he was pleased that it went well. Jean Palmer, Larry's wife, had numerous questions about transferring, the amount of travel, and how much extra time that her husband would have to spend responding to e-mail and other computer-type reports. John was glad that he was able to address her concerns. The telephone conversations with the other applicant's references and previous employers had been an interesting experience and tended to confirm what the applicant had said, except in two instances. A previous employer and one reference were guardedly enthusiastic about the applicant. When John pressed the issue, the reference refused to say more, while the previous employer provided specifics which confirmed an earlier impression John had noted at the initial interview. Comments about Larry Palmer all emphasized the great personality he had and what a terrific job they thought he would do in sales. Following the second interview with Larry Palmer and the spouse information session, John completed the company's applicant appraisal reports on both applicants and decided that Larry was the better of the two. He telephoned his regional sales manager, Phil Jackson, to set up a final interview for Larry. Then he faxed Phil his applicant appraisal reports, and wrote the other applicant a polite turndown letter.

The day following Larry's interview, Phil Jackson called to say that while he had some misgivings, he had hired Larry to begin training in a class at the regional office the first of the month. John's reaction was a sigh of relief because of all of the time he had put into the screening, and the hope that he wouldn't have to do that too often. The reports that he completed on his first field trips with his reps took longer to prepare than he anticipated. Coupled with the correspondence and appraisal reports on the applicants, John realized that communications were going to be a bigger part of the job than he had realized. He would have to learn how to use the computerized information system in a more effective and efficient manner if he were to have the necessary time for his other responsibilities.

John's relationship with his sales reps seemed to go well during the first few months on the job, with the exception of Dick McClure, an above average producer, aged 50, with 12 years experience, and the senior man in the district. Dick had been described by Chuck Morgan as a friendly, outgoing individual with a good sense of humor and a highly individualistic style of selling. As John worked with Dick, he was able to confirm in Dick's interaction with his customers, the general description Chuck had given him. However, Dick was curt with John, relatively subdued, and at other times almost hostile. For the next several working trips, John tried to ignore Dick's conduct and concentrated on the calls that they were making and the objectives that they were trying to achieve. At a recent sales meeting, Dick seemed to take delight in being argumentative and disruptive until John jokingly asked him if he would like to take over the sales meeting. After that, Dick settled down but made almost no contribution to the discussions for the rest of the meeting.

The situation came to a head immediately following a physician call, during which Dick introduced John without indicating who he was or his purpose for being there. The physician's reaction was: "Oh a new rep, eh?" and to Dick, "Are you being promoted?" This forced Dick, somewhat embarrassed, to indicate that John was his new district sales manager. As they left the office, it was clear that Dick was furious, as he muttered in a sarcastic manner, "Are you being promoted?" John decided that it was time to take action, whereupon he said emphatically, "Dick, I don't know what is eating you, but I think that it's time that we get it out in the open. You've been complaining from the day that I arrived. You're sarcastic, uncooperative, and just as cool as ice. If you and I are going to continue to work together, things had better change. I don't know what I have done that has upset you, but whatever it is or whatever I've said, it certainly wasn't intentional and I'm sorry. You're too good a person to go around perpetually angry. What the heck is bothering you?"

Dick's reaction was an angry, somewhat subdued and embarrassed, "I just guess it's not really your fault or anything that you did. I've been here 12 years and I'm the best rep in this district. Chuck even told me so. And bam—you get promoted and I'm left hung out to dry. Man, that's gratitude for you!"

Now that the problem was out in the open, John realized how long Dick had been carrying his anger locked up inside himself, and felt sorry for him. With that, he said, "Dick, I've sure been blind. Let's knock it off and sit down somewhere to talk this thing out." Three hours later they shook hands and parted on a much better understanding. Their relationship improved steadily, and now as John reflected on the district's productivity for the past year, he realized that Dick's support had been of paramount importance in terms of the district's overall success.

Thinking about the successful year reminded him of Peggy Doyle, the sales trainee who was doing such a terrific job. She was the one who had taken Larry Palmer's place. When he thought of Larry Palmer he winced thinking about the mistake that he had made. Larry was the first sales rep that he had recruited. He had completed the basic sales training class, but just barely. The report from the sales training manager was anything but encouraging. Larry had difficulty acquiring the necessary product knowledge and his scientific communication skills were marginal at best. The qualities that saved him from being dropped from the sales training class were his desire, his willingness to work, and the fact that he was such a great guy—everybody loved him! Notwithstanding Larry's shortcomings, John was convinced he could turn Larry around. He worked with him every opportunity he had, quizzed him, coached him, and drilled him in an effort to improve his knowledge and skills so that Larry could be able to capitalize on his sincerity and personality.

As the months wore on, John became increasingly aware that while Larry's customers liked him, he couldn't sell and his sales showed it. It was a tough decision John had to make to let Larry go, and an even tougher decision to implement, but John realized it really was in everyone's best interests. As he looked back on all the time and effort he had put into Larry's ultimate failure, John realized that it was at the expense of the time and effort he should have spent with his more productive sales reps. He also realized that in spite of the overwhelming evidence, he had carried Larry much longer than he probably should have, and was thankful that Phil Jackson did not remind him of it. Sometimes, however, events have a bright side. As much as John regretted the amount of time that it took to recruit Larry's replacement, he felt that he had lucked out with Peggy Doyle. She seemed to do everything right. In the four months since she'd been in the territory, sales had taken a noticeable increase and her enthusiasm was infecting the other sales reps in the district. John hoped her progress and productivity would continue on in this manner for a long time to come. Some performance data for Peggy and the other reps are shown in Exhibits 1 and 2.

Peggy's performance, however, did not eliminate the logjam that recruiting her had created in John's other activities. Her interviews, reference checking, early sales orientation and training, plus the extra time he had spent over the last few months helping Larry try to succeed, extended the intervals since he

Exhibit 1: Performance Data for Sales Reps in the Dallas/Ft. Worth District

Sales Rep	Last Year's Sales	This Year's Sales	Sales Quota Current Year
Larry Palmer[a]	$180,000	$181,000	$275,000
Dick McClure	450,000	583,000	535,000
Peggy Doyle[b]	—	120,000	150,000
Tom Jones	445,000	555,000	550,000
Bill Morrison	465,000	560,000	550,000
Sam Hanna	435,000	535,000	525,000
Jared Murphy	365,000	370,000	420,000
Marty Nakai	475,000	625,000	575,000
TOTALS	$2,815,000	$3,529,000	$3,580,000

[a]Sales and quota figures are for eight months.

[b]Peggy Doyle has been in her territory for only four months, there is no sales figure for the previous year. This year's sales and quota are for four months.

Exhibit 2: Input Factors Affecting Territory Coverage in the Dallas/Ft. Worth District

Sales Rep	Number of Sales Calls	Annual Expenses ($)	Physicians in Territory
Larry Palmer[a]	800	$6,300	1,600
Dick McClure	1,500	9,300	2,100
Peggy Boyle[b]	400	2,500	1,650
Tom Jones	1,300	8,000	1,850
Bill Morrison	1,350	8,300	1,800
Sam Hanna	1,350	8,500	1,900
Jared Murphy	1,050	7,800	2,000
Marty Nakai	1,550	9,800	2,200
TOTALS	9,300	$60,500	15,100

[a]Number of sales calls and expenses are for an eight-month period.

[b]Number of sales calls and expenses are for a four-month period.

last worked in the field with his above average sales reps, to the extent that several were beginning to make humorously sarcastic comments about being "orphans." John tried to explain that they were practically self-sufficient, while others needed his help more urgently. While they were willing to listen, John could see that they weren't buying into his excuse.

To further compound the problem, he received an e-mail that his semiannual appraisal interviews were to begin within 30 days. This would be the second time he would be holding these performance reviews, but it would be the first time alone since Phil Jackson had helped him. As John began to review the trip reports and correspondence in each sales rep's file, along with sales performance data generated from the company's computerized database (Exhibits 1 and 2), he realized the files of the above average producers were relatively thin. If it hadn't been for performance data, John would have been at a serious loss to justify his appraisal of their productivity.

Preparing for and conducting the performance reviews took a lot of time and this was when he really earned his salary. When the reps and John had different evaluations, the differences were resolved and then it became a matter of jointly agreeing on a plan of action to close the gap between actual and desired performance. As difficult as it was to achieve the agreement at times, and harder still to implement the agreed upon plan, John felt that it was at this point that he was making a significant contribution to the success of the company and the growth and development of the individual sales rep in the district.

The second appraisal and counseling session of the year had its peaks and valleys. It had been a pleasure to provide several with the recognition their performances merited, and to help them to further define the goals they would achieve for the forthcoming year. The case of Jared Murphy was another matter. Jared had been in the training class at the time John was hired. He had done reasonably well, but hadn't really lived up to his potential. Lately, Jared seemed to have lost interest. When John challenged Jared's own evaluation of his performance Jared sheepishly commented that he "wondered whether you'd let it pass." When John pressed him for an explanation of his performance in view of the potential in his territory, Jared quickly replied: "I didn't know you cared that much."

John also stated he felt that Jared had sufficient experience and intelligence to exert the necessary self-discipline to do what was required without a lot of personal attention from him. At this point, John said: "Jared, I think that it's time to decide whether or not you really have a future with Arapahoe. You definitely have the capabilities to be an above average performer. If you really want to do a better job, "I'll make every effort to help you to do a better job, but you will have to help me and really want to work at it. So what I want you to do is to go home, think about what I said, talk it over with your wife, and we will get together next Wednesday and make a plan for your future."

The problem John faced with Marty Nakai was almost the opposite. Marty was a young, single sales rep who had three years' experience in a territory that required quite a bit of travel in the Texas panhandle. He had about every good quality anyone could want in a salesperson, except maturity and self-control. He was smart, eager, highly motivated, and extremely ambitious. His favorite question of John was: "What else do I have to do to get promoted?" and he posed that question on every field trip and frequently at sales meetings. In addition, John could count on Marty calling him home on weekends. In a way, John wished he had more sales reps who were as productive and as eagerly cooperative, but he also wished that Marty would develop more patience and self-discipline. While John certainly didn't want to do anything to dampen Marty's enthusiasm, he was running out of ways to help Marty grow up.

As he thought about the challenges he had with his reps and the logjam he had created as a result of his recruiting activities, he realized that he had to formalize a set of objectives and specific plans for the coming year to discuss with Phil Jackson during his own coming appraisal session. Although the year had been a successful one, their performance on a couple of major products could have been at a higher level and he would have to figure out some kind of action plan to correct that situation. And then there were the territory revisions to be done to take advantage of the growth potential in the Ft. Worth area. Not the least important or urgent matter he needed to address was to evaluate his own performance during the past year and to set some personal objectives.

In addition, John had to prepare some written comments on the performance of each of his reps for the past year to put in their personal files. He thought he should calculate some ratios from the data in Exhibits 1 and 2 such as sales growth, sales to quota, sales per call, sales per physician, expenses per call, and selling expenses as a percent of sales to include in his report on each rep. Also he had to decide what to do about Jared and Marty. Overall, John saw his problems were really people problems and people opportunities, and their interaction and interdependence were what made his job both challenging and fun.

CASE

1-3 SALCO CHEMICALS S.A.*

Paul Dumont was promoted to the position of National Sales Director in Salco Chemicals, one of Belgium's smaller chemical companies. He was 31 years old, educated in business administration, and had a degree in engineering. Before being promoted, Dumont had spent four years as a salesperson with Salco. Later he worked for two years as assistant to the company's Export Sales Director. Now he was reassigned back to the domestic sales force where he

*This case was prepared by Professor Kamran Kashani as the basis for class discussion rather than to illustrate either effective or ineffective handling of a sales force management situation. Copyright © by IMEDE, Lausanne, Switzerland. Reproduced by permission.

had started, this time as its administrative head. The assignment was to some degree motivated by a desire on the part of the management, in the words of one executive, "to shape things up a bit in our own backyard."

One of the first tasks undertaken by Dumont was an assessment of the salespeople covering Belgium. Three problem salespeople emerged from his analysis. The first tended to cover, almost exclusively, the industrial accounts in his territory, thus ignoring the potential in the consumer accounts. The second was an older salesperson who seemed to have exhausted his energy and whose territory sales reflected it. The last was a young and newly recruited person whose performance in the field showed a significant deterioration, thought to be the result of family problems.

Dumont believed the three cases were serious enough to require a quick decision. He was considering a number of alternative courses of action with regard to each of the three salespeople.

Background

Salco was the manufacturer and marketer of a wide line of chemicals with industrial and consumer applications. The products were sold directly to the industrial accounts but were distributed through consumer product distributors to retail stores.

The company's Belgian sales force was organized into six territories, with each territory covering one or more of the country's provinces. A salesperson was assigned to each of the geographic territories where he or she sold to both the industrial and the distributor accounts. As explained by the National Sales Director, "The responsibilities for the industrial and distributor sales are combined because neither is large enough to support one additional salesperson in each territory."

The market in which Salco competed was highly competitive, with more than 20 small and medium-sized local and other European manufacturers selling similar products to industry and consumers. Said one marketing executive with Salco:

> The product formulations among the different producers are more or less the same. We know it and so do our customers. As a result, the only leverage one could have in this market is through sales coverage. The better we cover each territory and the more sales push is exerted at the account level, the better our chances for improving our market share. It's that simple.

In the last two years, Salco's Belgian domestic sales had stagnated in spite of an estimated growth of about 15 percent in market potential. In this period, volumes had fallen below the planned levels, causing concern among management. Dumont had been assigned to the national sales force soon after the former director had left the company for personal reasons.

Michel Cornet

Michel Cornet had been with Salco for the last three years. Before joining the company, he had worked in a local manufacturing firm as assistant to the procurement manager. He was 43 years old, married, and had two children.

In his analysis of individual salespeople, Dumont had noticed that Cornet's sales had come almost exclusively from industrial accounts. The surprising fact was that the total territory volume had shown growth over the three years Cornet had been with the company. More industrial accounts and greater sales per account were responsible for the growth in sales (see Exhibit 1).

Although Dumont had seen Cornet before, he did not know him well. In a recent meeting he had held with all the salespeople together, Dumont had found Cornet somewhat aloof and uninvolved. In the meeting, Cornet had responded rather aggressively to a question posed by another salesperson. It was Dumont's impression that Cornet could be very inflexible and even stubborn on issues where he disagreed with other parties.

The impression was later reinforced in an interview that Dumont had held with Cornet. After Dumont had explained the need for a balanced coverage of distributor and industrial accounts, Cornet responded.

> You have to look at it this way: Either I come up with the sales volume you need or I don't. If my total sales meet or exceed the territory targets, what difference does it make where they come from? For the last three years, I have put my best into developing new industrial accounts which have more than compensated for the drop in distributor sales. I have met the territory targets every year.

Cornet continued, "Besides, I like dealing with the factory people. I speak their language."

Toni Vestmar

Toni Vestmar was the most senior salesperson at Salco. He had been with the company for almost 15 years. He was 56 years old and had recently become a grandfather.

Vestmar's territory was geographically the second largest one in Belgium. It had been undeveloped when he joined the company. But over the years, the volume of sales had grown as more accounts were added. Vestmar's long coverage of the territory seemed to have paid off handsomely in terms of good

Exhibit 1: Territory Sales by Type of Account

	Sales by Year in Thousand Belgian Frans				
	Year 1	Year 2	Year 3	Year 4	Year 5
MICHEL CORNET					
Industrial sales	29,280[a]	29,760[a]	38,976	45,504	48,960
(Number of accounts)	(60)	(59)	(65)	(73)	(78)
Average sales per account	488	504	600	623	628
Distributor sales	9,120	9,888	8,832	5,280	1,920
(Number of accounts)	(12)	(12)	(11)	(5)	(2)
Average sales per account	760	824	803	1,056	960
Total territory potential[b]					265,920
TONI VESTMAR					
Industrial sales	45,120	46,560	47,328	48,000	48,480
(Number of accounts)	(87)	(89)	(90)	(91)	(91)
Average sales per account	519	523	526	527	533
Distributor sales	10,752	11,520	12,192	11,808	11,904
(Number of accounts)	(14)	(15)	(17)	(15)	(15)
Average sales per account	768	768	717	787	794
Total territory potential					288,960
WILLIAM HOUTTE					
Industrial sales	—[a]	—[a]	—[a]	44,160[a]	44,544
(Number of accounts)				(53)	(55)
Average sales per account				833[a]	810
Distributor sales	—[a]	—[a]	—[a]	3,744[a]	3,936
(Number of accounts)				(5)	(7)
Average sales per account				849	562
Total territory potential[b]					240,000

[a]Territory covered by a different salesperson.

[a]Territory potential, estimated by Dumont using experience with other territories, reflects the market size for each territory.

relations with the distributors and buyers. While looking into the salesman's file, Dumont had come across several letters from customers complimentary to Vestmar. One distributor called him "the best partner I have in this business." Another recent letter from an industrial buyer had praised Vestmar as the "most reliable salesperson we deal with." Still another buyer had praised his "nonaggressive" selling approach.

The problem, as perceived by Dumont, however, was that Vestmar's territory sales had shown little growth in the last five years. No new accounts had been added for several years, and sales per account had remained more or less constant (see Exhibit 1). From the sales call reports Dumont had seen in the file, it appeared as though Vestmar was concentrating his sales effort on the accounts in or around his home-

town. The frequency of sales calls for the nearby accounts was far more than that for the distant accounts, which required half a day's travel by car. In Dumont's words, "The territory has lost its dynamism; it needs new blood."

Dumont had known Vestmar when he himself was a salesman with Salco. He remembered him as a congenial, easygoing fellow who seemed to cherish his independence and autonomy. He recalled vividly a statement of Vestmar's in that meeting with the salespeople: "Nobody knows my area better than I do. Somebody has to spend 15 years in that territory before telling me what is the right thing to do."

In a subsequent interview Dumont had held with him, Vestmar was surprisingly irritated when the question of growth in territory volume was raised: "I have developed that territory and I know its potential.

No 'wonder kid' can tell me that my territory can produce more sales than what I am delivering. My customers buy from me because they know and trust me. Hard sell just doesn't work with these people." On the subject of territory coverage, Vestmar had responded: "I call those accounts where I feel there is potential. I don't just call because they are there." Vestmar had concluded the meeting by saying, "Maybe if I were an inexperienced salesman and 20 years younger I could be pushed around and told what to do. But I have been a salesman all my life, and at 56 I deserve recognition, not direction."

William Houtte

William Houtte was in his second year with Salco when Dumont returned to the national sales force. He had a technical degree from a local school and had worked for an electrical appliance manufacturer as a salesperson before joining Salco. At 27, Houtte was the youngest person on the sales force. He had recently been married.

Houtte's territory was geographically small but highly concentrated in terms of industrial accounts. His sales performance in the first year on the job was considered acceptable. A number of new accounts had been opened, but sales to several of the older accounts had declined. Overall, however, the volume of sales was maintained (see Exhibit 1). For the second year, Houtte was slated for a sizable increase in sales volume. But actual sales in recent months had fallen far below the targets and even below last year's volume for the same period.

The problem, Dumont believed, was the result of a deterioration in the territory coverage. Houtte's sales call reports showed a serious decline in the number of accounts he visited daily. Some customers even had taken the initiative of calling the Salco sales office to find out why Houtte had not visited them lately. Dumont believed that if the current pattern continued, the territory's sales could suffer seriously in the long run.

Although Dumont had not had a chance to get to know the new salesman, he had heard from the office staff that Houtte was "not a sociable type," "lacked self-confidence," and seemed to "show a disregard for the selling profession." The few times Dumont had seen Houtte around the office, he had noticed his longer-than-average hair, bushy sideburns, and colorful ties. His appearance was a definite contrast to that of the older salespeople.

Dumont had also heard that Houtte was experiencing marriage problems. His wife apparently had left him and was living with her family. Some suggested that Houtte's recent performance in the field was at least in part due to this personal problem.

In an interview to which Houtte had come an hour late, Dumont had raised the performance issue. The salesman, who seemed clearly apologetic, had said only "I know I am not doing as well as you expect me to. I need more time."

Dumont wondered what courses of action were appropriate for his three problem salespeople.

▶ 2 ◀

Strategic Planning and Budgeting*

"SHARING A VISION"

Two men were struggling to get a large crate through the door. They struggled and struggled, but the crate would not budge. Finally, one man said to the other, "We'll never get this crate in." Replied his partner, "I thought we were trying to get it out."

*Chapter Consultant: Joseph P. Clayton, President & COO, Frontier Telecommunication.

LEARNING OBJECTIVES

After studying this chapter, you should be able to:

▶ Know what is meant by strategic management planning.

▶ Distinguish the major steps involved in strategic marketing planning.

▶ Describe the impact of strategic planning on selling and sales management.

▶ Identify the two strategic sales force decisions and their implications for selling and sales management.

▶ Discuss the purpose and scope of a sales force budget.

▶ Describe the key concepts involved in Sales Force Quality.

"When You Buy the Iron, You Get the Company"

This is the philosophy of Caterpillar Inc. (Peoria, Ill.), which sells machinery and engines worldwide. Despite sales of $10.2 billion, the company faces the twin challenges of global competition and a sputtering global economy. Part of Caterpillar's strategy for winning in such a tough environment is to strengthen its network of 2,400 independent dealers. Says Pat Dalton, business operations manager for Caterpillar's North American commercial division, "We want the entire distribution network to focus on the customer first." Dealer owners, for example, attend classes taught by top Caterpillar managers.

Caterpillar's 2400 salespeople are instrumental in implementing its strategy. In 1992, Caterpillar introduced "customer sensitivity training" for all of its salespeople. Among other things, the sales force learns how to train customers to operate the machinery. "Our salespeople must demonstrate the benefits of our products," says Dalton, "to show why buying our products will help the customer make more money. We want our salespeople to roll up their sleeves and work closely with customers to be business partners with them."

Sales force compensation has also been adjusted to reward the sales force for being good dealer partners. Salespeople don't receive bonuses just for meeting quotas; they can accumulate bonus points for scoring high on product knowledge tests, customer-satisfaction surveys, and evaluations from their managers.[1]

This example shows how one company is attempting to meet its objectives in a highly competitive environment. They are trying to be successful based on the competitive advantage of their strong dealer network. As the primary company contact with the dealers, the sales force is critical to the success of the strategy. As this case illustrates, strategic decisions will usually have implications for the sales force in terms of how the market is accessed and the type of relationship desired with the customer. These decisions make up the sales force strategy, which, in turn, has implications for the budget plan and how the sales force is managed. In this case, training, compensation, and individual salesperson evaluation were adjusted to reflect the "partnering" focus of Caterpillar's strategy.

The purpose of this chapter is to show the implications of business and marketing strategy for sales management. We do not attempt to explain organization or marketing strategy. This is better accomplished elsewhere (see Selected Readings at the end of this chapter). Instead, we focus most of our attention on sales force strategy and budgeting.

The sequence of topics to be covered is depicted in the diagram on the next page. Key sales force decisions are made within the limits set by the organization. *Strategic management planning* consists of the steps taken by the organization to ensure the long-term survival and growth of the business. In contrast, *strategic marketing planning* involves the allocation of resources to programs designed to achieve specific marketing objectives derived from the organization's overall objectives.[2] The *sales force strategy* is derived from the marketing strategy and includes decisions about how to access the target market and the type of relationship the company will have with its customers. Finally, the strategic plan must be converted into an operating budget.

Budgets are working documents that help sales managers keep track of expenses. Actual results can be compared to budgeted figures, and any changes in the objectives and strategies planned for the subsequent period can be recommended.

▶ STRATEGIC MANAGEMENT PLANNING

Strategic planning is employed to make better use of company resources and to create and sustain an advantage over the competition. At a basic level, competitive

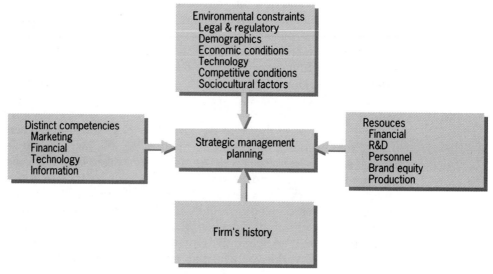

Figure 2-1: Factors Influencing Strategic Management

advantage arises from a firm's choice of markets to serve, its distinct competencies, and the deployment of resources that gives it an edge over its competition in chosen markets. The factors influencing the strategic management planning process are depicted in Figure 2-1. Marketing and the sales force should both be intimately involved in an organization's strategic planning process because they understand the customers' wants and how they value the fulfillment of needs.

Business Mission

A well-defined business mission provides a sense of direction to employees and helps guide them toward the fulfillment of the firm's potential. The basic character of an organization's business is defined by the *three* Cs—customers, competitors, and the company itself. Top managers should ask "What is our business?" and "What should it be?" The idea is to determine an overarching mission from a consideration of the firm's history, resources, distinct competencies, and environmental constraints. The *business mission* is a statement about (1) the types of customers it wishes to serve, (2) the specific needs to be fulfilled, and (3) the means or technologies by which it will fulfill these needs. Thus organizations will not only know the focus of their business, they will also be able to identify strategic opportunities.

As the competitive environment changes, companies may need to alter their mission. Sales Management in Action 2-1 describes how marketplace changes affect field sales activities. Merck and Company, the $4 billion pharmaceutical firm, has adjusted to meet the needs of the evolving customer base in the health care industry. In the past, Merck's 3000 salespeople called primarily on individual physicians. Now reps must also call on business administrators of hospitals, health maintenance organizations (HMOs), and preferred provider organizations (PPOs), which have vastly different information needs. One change has been to reorganize the sales force so that more people are calling on the managed-care customers. Merck has also had to

---

Sales Management in Action 2-1
"Sales as an Internal Position"

Pharmaceutical companies are finding that their customer base is changing from individual physicians to hospital administrators and head pharmacists at HMOs as a result of efforts to reduce costs in the health care industry. Direct selling and electronic channels are radically changing what the sales force does in this industry. Its activities must be integrated back into marketing and distribution. As a result, salespeople and sales managers are likely to be more internally focused. As "case managers," they may be responsible for everything from order processing to distribution, sales, and after-sales servicing. This will result in the customer having a single point of contact with the pharmaceutical firm.

Source: William Keenan, Jr., "Reengineering Salespeople Out of a Job," *Sales & Marketing Management* (December 1993), p. 61.

adjust their training by adding team building and negotiating and by developing more expertise on the managed-care environment in general.[3]

Establishing Goals

Once the mission for an organization has been decided on, the next step is to translate the mission into the *organization's goals*—specific objectives by which performance can be measured. These objectives are usually stated in terms of profits, sales revenue, unit sales, market share, survival, and social responsibility. Firms will typically pursue multiple objectives. Procter & Gamble, for example, seeks a 10 percent after-tax profit and a doubling of sales revenue every five years.

When priorities change, the sales force is often affected. Faced with heavy competitors such as Procter & Gamble, demanding retailers, and mature markets, Scott Paper Company switched its mission from gaining volume at any cost to profitability. This called for massive changes in how Scott's 500 salespeople related to the retail

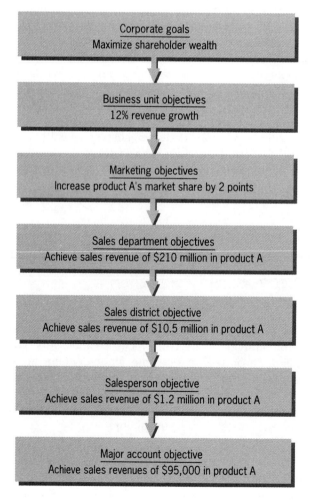

Figure 2-2: Hierarchy of Sales Objectives

trade. "It's no longer a volume or promotional approach to customers," states one Scott marketer, "it's a lot more than that. It's understanding brands and how the consumer's response to various actions on our part is timed so that we can eliminate waste and improve profit." To support this changed relationship, sales training has been altered to include market knowledge and understanding marketing data in order to arrive at the most profitable product mix for both the company and the customer. Not all salespeople were able to adapt to the discipline required in this new business approach. To reinforce this new approach, Scott shifted its compensation plan from volume to profitability.

The Scott Paper example illustrates another important characteristic of organizational goals: the hierarchical nature of the goals. Measurable organizational goals must be communicated down the organizational structure. Figure 2-2 illustrates this point by showing how an organizational sales goal is translated into a key account goal.

Strategies

Once business objectives have been decided on, the next step is to translate them into strategies. *Strategy* is the means an organization uses to achieve its objectives. Several classification schemes have been developed to delineate better the overall thrust of a strategy. One of the most popular is Porter's *generic business strategies*.[4] According to Porter, all successful businesses focus on one of three generic strategies—*low cost, differentiation,* or *niche*. Each of these strategies is described in Figure 2-3. Each strategy is based on offering a distinct market value based on corporate strengths. In

---

Low Cost Strategy:
Vigorous pursuit of cost reductions from experience and tight cost control.

Sales Force Role:
Service large current customers, pursue large prospects, minimize costs, sell on the basis of price, often with significant order-taking responsibilities.

Differentiation strategy:
Creating an offering perceived as being unique leading to high brand loyalty and low price sensitivity.

Sales Force Role:
Sell non-price benefits, order-generating, servicing and responsive to needs of customers. High quality sales force usually required.

Niche Strategy:
Servicing a target market very well, focusing all decisions with the target market needs in mind, dominating sales with the segment.

Sales Force Role:
Experts in the operations and opportunities associated with a target market. High margins needed, focus on non-price benefits, and allocate selling time to the target market.

Source: Adapted from William Cron and Michael Levy, "Sales Management Performance Evaluation: A Residual Income Perspective," *Journal of Personal Selling and Sales Management* (August 1987), p. 58.

Figure 2-3: Generic Business Strategies and the Role of the Sales Force

the computer business, NCR follows a differentiated strategy. They offer standard chip designs and software used by competitors and are price competitive with high-end rivals such as IBM and Compaq. They hope to differentiate their offering through the support and services provided by the NCR sales organization.[5] NCR is pursuing a broad differentiation strategy since they are deemphasizing price, promoting service and support, and attempting to meet the needs of a broad base of customers.

One of the most widely recognized analytical tools for developing strategies is *business portfolio analysis*, developed by the Boston Consulting Group (BCG). This approach helps large firms allocate resources by breaking their organization into individual profit centers called *strategic business units* (SBUs). Ideally, an SBU is a product line or group of products (1) for which plans can be developed independently, (2) that has its own competitors and unique set of customer needs that it fulfills, and (3) that has one manager with profit responsibility. Depending on relative market share and market growth rate, one of four growth strategies are recommended—*build, hold, harvest,* or *divest*. These strategies are described in Figure 2-4, along with the primary sales tasks associated with each strategy.

The role of the sales force will also vary according to the types of markets in which the firm competes and the firm's reliance on existing versus new products. Miles and Snow have developed a typology of business strategies in which firms are labeled as *prospectors, analyzers,* or *defenders*. See Figure 2-5 for a description of each strategy and the role of the sales force. One study in the financial services industry found that the

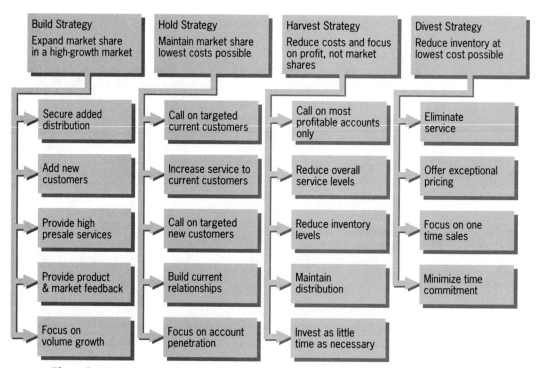

Figure 2-4: Business Portfolio Analysis and Sales Force Strategy

Prospector Strategy:
Attempt to pioneer in market/product development. Offer many new products. Willing to sacrifice short-term profits to gain a long-term stronghold in a market.

Sales Force Role:
Focus on sales volume with an emphasis on prospecting and account penetration.

Defender Strategy:
Offer a limited, mature product line in predictable markets in the late growth or mature stage of the product life cycle. Emphasize low cost and high volume.

Sales Force Role:
Primary emphasis is on maintaining current customer base. Very little prospecting is needed. Customer service is emphasized along with full distribution and profitability.

Analyzer Strategy:
Selectively choose high growth markets while holding onto mature markets. Make fewer new product offerings than prospectors and are less committed to stability and efficiency than defenders.

Sales Force Role:
Must balance multiple roles: servicing existing customers, prospecting for new customers, uncovering new applications, holding onto distribution of mature products and supporting campaigns for new products.

Source: Adapted from William Cron and Michael Levy, "Sales Management Performance Evaluation: A Residual Income Perspective," *Journal of Personal Selling and Sales Management* (August 1987), p. 58.

Figure 2-5: Miles and Snow's Business Strategies and the Role of the Sales Force

sales function was most important for defenders. One reason for this is that new product ideas often come from customers whom salespeople are servicing. The "Gladiator" bar-coded scanning device, for example, was developed by Symbol Technologies, Inc., based on suggestions made by a customer and brought to the attention of the company by the sales force.[6] This information often emanates from asking "What is the customer trying to accomplish in his or her business?"

▶ STRATEGIC MARKETING PLANNING

Strategic marketing planning is a process whereby an organization allocates marketing mix resources to reach its target markets. This planning process is similar to the overall strategic management planning process in that it begins with a situation analysis. This information is then used to segment the market and choose target markets on which to concentrate the firm's marketing resources. The third step is to develop the complete marketing mix. Each of these steps has important selling and sales management implications.

Situation Analysis

Suppose that you are the head of marketing for Glaxo Holdings PLC, a large pharmaceutical company. You have been very successful to date spending 20 percent of your revenues on marketing and sales. Most of the money goes to the army of sample toting representatives who call on individual doctors to get your drugs prescribed. More and more doctors, however, are joining managed-care organizations. One of the largest managed health care networks is Kaiser, which plans to buy more than $700 million worth of pharmaceuticals this year. In order to reduce costs, however, Kaiser has cracked down on having representatives in their facilities. All representatives, called detailers in the industry, must abide by 32 rules, including not being able to visit a facility without an appointment.[7] Why are the growth of managed care and Kaiser's actions significant factors for Glaxo to consider when developing its marketing strategy? Will Glaxo come to rely less on its sales force to promote its products? At what point in time should Glaxo change its marketing strategy? These are but a few of the questions raised by Glaxo's situation analysis.

This is the essence of *situation analysis*—taking stock of where the firm or product line has been, where it is now, and where it is likely to end up in the future. This analysis must often take into account legal, economic, competitive, customer, and technological factors. Sales Management in Action 2-2 describes how technological changes caused severe financial problems for Encyclopedia Britannica Corporation. As the primary contact with customers, the sales force is often critically involved in gathering information for a situation analysis. In the Glaxo situation, a special 45-person sales team was formed to help determine how to deal with managed-care networks.

Segmentation and Target Marketing

Marketing programs require a customer focus to be effective. This requires that marketing segment the market and select target markets. *Market segmentation* involves aggregating customers into groups that (1) have common needs and (2) will respond similarly to a marketing program. *Target marketing* refers to the selection and prioritizing of segments to which the company will market.

Sales Management in Action 2-2
"Some Threats Require a Response"

First published in Edinburgh, Scotland 225 years ago, Encyclopaedia Britannica sales peaked at $650 million in 1990. In the early 1990s, personal computers continued to penetrate the consumer household market and CD-ROM technology gained acceptance. Competitors entered the encylcopedia market with CD-ROM packages at prices ranging from $99–$395. Britannica's management decided to continue to market through a direct sales force of 2,300 people. The typical Encyclopaedia Britannica sells for $1,500 and pays the salesperson a commission of $300. Despite the high commission, it is tough to sell against a high-tech version priced far lower. Sales have drastically declined and the company is in severe financial trouble.

Source: David Cravens, "The Changing Role of the Sales Force," *Marketing Management*, 4 (Fall 1995), No. 2, p. 51.

These marketing decisions have obvious implications for how salespeople set priorities and allocate their time among different customers. Sometimes the sales force must be reorganized to implement a targeted marketing program. Hewlett-Packard Company decided to target companies with three characteristics: significant worldwide presence, large size, and high growth potential. In all, 1000 accounts were selected for the Global Accounts Program, which includes locating technical and selling teams at the headquarters of the account. Revenue growth in these accounts is more than 10 times the growth rate in the $350 billion information technology industry. As a further effort to target specific customers, H-P has developed separate sales organizations for discrete manufacturing, process industries, financial services, and telecommunications customers.[8] In this reorganization, H-P is attempting to ensure that markets targeted in its marketing plan receive the intended attention and sales support.

Marketing Mix Program

Having settled on specific marketing goals and identified the target market, the third step in the planning process is to design the proper *marketing mix*—price, product, promotion, and channels. Once again, an important change in any of these elements usually necessitates changes in the sales force plan. It was found, in a recent study of 219 organizations who had introduced a new product, that nearly every element of the sales management program was modified by a significant proportion of responding firms. The most likely change was in quotas with compensation and sales support elements also likely to be changed.[9]

Sales is only one element of the promotion mix. Coordination between the various promotion mix elements is especially important. When recently introducing a new printer, Hewlett-Packard sent sales kits to customers and dealers, followed by a mailing program and telemarketing. Next, they sent sales reps to the dealerships to make follow-up calls and give management briefings. Afterward, a committee of dealers met to evaluate the success of the program. This marketing program included a coordinated effort among advertising, sales promotion, channels of distribution, and the sales force.[10]

▶ STRATEGIC SALES FORCE DECISIONS

Throughout the remainder of this text, many important issues are discussed with respect to organizing, building, leading, and controlling an organization's selling effort. As is argued throughout this text, marketing and sales squarely focus on the customer. Two management decisions in particular have an important and pervasive impact on the sales force and an organization's sales management program—(1) how the company will access its customers and (2) the type of relationships the company wishes to have with its various customers.

Market Access

The typical customer base of many organizations consists of a few very important customers in terms of sales and profits. Figure 2-6 shows a triangle with the horizontal dimension representing the number of customers and the vertical dimension the size

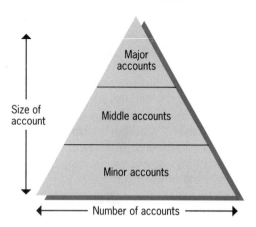

Figure 2-6: Customer Base Triangle

of the accounts. There are typically a few major accounts at the top and many "minor" accounts at the bottom. All too often, the traditional sales force found it difficult to meet the needs of the top accounts and it was too expensive to call on the large number of small accounts. At IBM, for instance, 20,000 distributors and resellers, referred to as "business partners," have become the primary sales force for small and medium-sized accounts.[11] Technology has also created alternatives to face-to-face selling for accessing and servicing customers. See Sales Technology 2-1, "The Net Effect."

Most large companies do not access their markets in only one way—through a direct sales force, for instance, or through distributors. To defend their customer base, expand market coverage, and control costs, companies today are adopting multiple methods for reaching different target markets. IBM, for example, once sold computers through the company's 5,000-person sales force. When low-cost computers hit the market, IBM reacted by expanding into new channels. Now they sell through dealers, value-added resellers, catalog operations, direct mail, and telemarketing. In total, IBM added 18 new channels in addition to their own sales force to communicate with customers.[12]

To provide better local service in the face of intense price competition from foreign firms, many firms are turning to distributors or wholesalers. The Gates Rubber Company establishes strong partner relationships with its distributors in order to compete with price competition from offshore manufacturers. The sales force's role in Gates' marketing strategy is critical. Among other responsibilities, they must determine the distributor's objectives and needs, provide product knowledge, share information regarding industry trends, and communicate Gates' expectations of the distributor.[13] As this example illustrates, commitment to distributors will impact sales force activities.

In some cases, sales force involvement has been restricted to certain steps within the selling cycle. The system developed by Wright Line, Inc., a leading supplier of accessories used to store, protect, and provide access to computer tapes, diskettes, and other media, focuses the sales force where it can be most effective. For years, it sold only through a direct sales force responsible for all steps in the selling cycle— lead generation, qualifying, preselling, closing, postsales service, and account man-

---

Sales Technology 2-1
"The 'Net Effect"

More and more marketers are turning to the Internet in search of new, improved ways to link with customers and suppliers. One company, Industry.Net, is going one step further in bringing together companies that have something to sell with companies that have something to buy. Through Industry.Net, more than 200,000 companies are reaching the more than 150,000 buyers that are attracted to the site each day. Large companies like FedEx, Holiday Inn, and Air Products & Chemicals, Inc. are finding success on the Internet:

- FedEx has set up their Web site so that instead of calling a customer service center, Web surfers just type their package ID number to get an update on the location of their package.
- Holiday Inn allows guests to check availability and price, and book rooms at any of its 2,100 hotels.
- Air Products & Chemicals Inc. has its complete product catalogue online in an interactive format that will allow customers to conduct searches for Air Products offerings by typing in what they're looking for.

Source: Tom Dellecave, "The 'Net Effect," *Sales and Marketing Management* (March 1996), pp. 17–21.

---

agement. Now direct mail and telemarketing perform the complete selling cycle for small and medium-sized customers. Telemarketing is also responsible for generating and qualifying leads among big customers, and a special technical support group handles postsales servicing for large customers. These changes have resulted in adjustments to sales force deployment, training, and compensation.[14]

An increasingly popular alternative for accessing markets is to establish an *alliance* with another organization in a joint venture to sell products to specific markets. This strategy has often been used to expand globally. AT&T, for example, has negotiated a variety of computer sales partnerships with companies in France, Germany, Italy, Belgium, and the Netherlands.[15] The Chrysler Corporation has contracted with Hyundai Motor Company to sell certain Chrysler products in South Korea.[16] General Mills and Nestle SA have set up a joint venture to form a separate company for marketing breakfast cereal throughout Europe.[17]

The net effect of these developments has been, first, that many large firms have reduced the size of their field sales forces by focusing them on medium and large size accounts. Second, firms have come to rely more on direct selling alternatives to generate sales volume. Third, firms have had to struggle with the problems of coordinating the means of accessing the market. IBM, for instance, attempts to limit the direct competition between its value-added resellers and its direct sales force by crediting 85 percent of the volume generated by resellers in the salesperson's territory against the salesperson's annual sales quota.[18]

Account Relationship Strategy

A firm's *account relationship strategy* refers to the type of relationship a firm intends to develop with its customers. Some firms, for instance, take a transactional approach to customers because customers can quite easily switch their business from one supplier to another, depending on which offers the lowest price. Other firms may establish contractual relationships with their key customers. Still other suppliers rely on the personal relationships between customers and their salespeople.

The management of account relationships has grown more varied and strategic in today's business-to-business environment, defining how a company competes in the marketplace.[19] Impetus for this development includes industry mergers and acquisitions, global competition, information technology, maturing markets, and more sophisticated customers. Figure 2-7 contrasts traditional marketing views with those of relationship marketing.

Relationship marketing may take a variety of forms, each having major implications for the sales force. While there is no strong consensus regarding the description of all the new relationship marketing forms, Figure 2-8 illustrates several alternatives.

Account relationships differ in both their purchasing and selling approaches.[20] A customer's purchasing practices may vary from transactional to programmatic purchasing practices. *Transactional purchasing* provides solutions to specific operational problems and is negotiated largely with lower-level management. *Programmatic purchasing*, on the other hand, usually involves multiple business solutions addressing strategic customer issues for the entire enterprise. A high degree of interorganizational intimacy is required, and corporate-level management plays a significant role in these relationships.

Customer relationships may also differ in the selling approaches taken by a supplier. A *reactive selling approach* identifies and responds to demand opportunities with a product-oriented solution focusing on features, functions, and price performance.

Traditional View	vs.	Relationship View
The ultimate purpose of marketing is to make a sale	vs.	The ultimate purpose of marketing is to create a customer
The objective is to make the sale and find the next customer	vs.	The objective is to satisfy the customer you have by delivering superior value
Growth comes primarily from finding customers	vs.	Growth comes primarily from enhanced product offerings for existing customers
Supplier is valued for its products and services	vs.	Supplier is valued for its present and future problem solving capabilities

Source: Presentation by Frederick Webster, "Relationships in Marketing" at Summer Marketing Educator's Conference, August 8, 1993.

Figure 2-7: Traditional versus Relationship Marketing

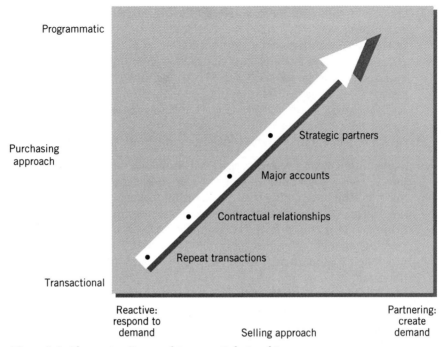

Figure **2-8:** Alternative Types of Account Relationships

The selling process is fairly routine and often focused on lower levels in the buying organization. At the other end of the spectrum is a *partnering selling approach* which focuses on creating demand. A partnering selling approach includes such elements as visible executive commitment, joint planning, open information technology, cross-training and consulting, and joint resource leveraging. Notice that the four relationships in Figure 2-8 are depicted on the diagonal. This suggests that an appropriate convergence of selling and purchasing approaches is needed for a particular relationship to be successful.

The role of the sales force differs for each type of relationship. These relationships and accompanying sales force roles are discussed in the remainder of this section.

Repeat Transactions   Most business-to-business transactions take place as part of an ongoing relationship between supplier and customer. This relationship is based on the nurturing elements discussed in Chapter 4, including a history of trust, bargaining, value, and meeting or exceeding customers' expectations. The efforts of Jim Roberts, a salesperson with Holston Building Supply, to sell oak balusters and other parts for staircases to a small chain of lumberyards in east Tennessee illustrates the advantages and limitations of this type of account relationship. While the customers had long purchased other Holston products, they informed Jim that they were quite satisfied with their present supplier of staircase parts and had excellent profit margins on these items. Jim persisted, however, asking, "Just give me a chance to prove that you could sell even more and make better margins with our products." When the buyer did give them a trial run, they sold so well that he soon switched completely to Holston's stair parts. "I would not have had the slightest chance of getting him to try our line," says Roberts, "no matter how good my arguments might have been, if I had not already established a solid, trusting relationship with him."[21] Notice that the personal relationship between Jim and the account was critical to obtaining the sale and that trust was a key element in the relationship. On the other hand, another supplier of staircases offering a higher profit margin and able to generate equal demand is likely to take the business from Jim in the future.

Contractual Relationship   *Contractual relationships*, wherein a supplier and buyer enter into a legal agreement for a specific period of time, are quite common in industrial markets. The information needs and upper management involvement of both parties are typically greater than in the *repeat transaction* relationship because of the greater economic importance of the relationship to both buyer and seller. In these longer-term buyer-seller relationships, prices are an outcome of a negotiation process based on mutual dependence. Quality, delivery, and technical support become more important.

Despite the long-term focus of contractual relationships, they are often arm's length and adversarial in nature, pitting the customer against the vendor in a battle focused on low price. The automobile industry prior to the 1980s provides a good example of the pitfalls in contractual relationships.[22] Automobile manufacturers for decades had purchased from thousands of vendors, with many vendors for each item. The relationships were fundamentally and intentionally adversarial. Vendors were seen as competing for an "unfair" share of the profits created by the final product. Competitive bidding around extremely tight product specifications was used to control vendor share of the business, though several other vendors were given smaller shares to keep pressure on the low-priced supplier. While producing lowest list prices, this adversarial system of contractual relationships led to higher total system costs and was often detrimental to the quality of the final product.

Major Account Relationships   In recent years, customers have been downsizing their supplier base, and replacing their myriad vendors with a very small number of hopefully long-term relationships offered only to a select few suppliers. Ford Motor Company is reducing its supplier base from 52,000 to 5,000. A widely quoted figure is that customers are working today with one-third fewer suppliers than they did 10 years ago. The seller's response to the emergence of very large and powerful customers was to develop a system for managing *major account relationships*. A major account management system, sometimes known as "national account management," may take many forms but generally means that a supplier attempts to develop a system of superior customer responsiveness based on an outstanding support system. SmithKline Beecham, for example, was able to develop a new product to meet K-Mart's specifications in only 4 months instead of the usual 12 months. This was attributed to the major account team's work with K-Mart and the support they received from SmithKline.[23]

Companies with major account programs include such well-known organizations as AT&T, IBM, Procter & Gamble, Pitney Bowes, Federal Express, and Dow Chemical.

When successful, major account management systems represent a change in the philosophy of customer commitment. Sales and profits are increased by growing with the customer, as opposed to expanding the customer base itself. To be successful, however, there must be a mutual commitment to the relationship that eschews short-term opportunities to take advantage of the partner. Armed with the powerful weapon of very large volumes, for instance, General Motors bullied their suppliers into setting drastically lower costs. By aggressively pursuing grab-a-bigger-share-of-the-pie strategies, GM was able to reduce purchasing costs by $4 billion, but at a cost of lost supplier loyalty and trust. During periods of short supply, when the shoe was on the other foot, scarce capacity went to support GM competitors, who had earned supplier loyalty.[24]

Strategic Partners   Under the continuing need to remain competitive by reducing costs and dissatisfied with traditional purchasing relationships, some buyers and suppliers have come together to form strategic partnerships. *Strategic partnerships* are buyer-seller relationships in which both partners are highly dependent on each other and establish a pattern of cooperation virtually unknown in traditionally adversarial relationships.[25] Successful strategic partnerships are characterized by (1) a shared vision of the partnering possibilities, (2) an intimacy between two organizations based on mutual trust and sharing, and (3) a strategic impact on both organizations producing real added productivity and value.[26] Joint product, service, and infrastructure, for example, are often found in strategic partnerships. Many of America's premier industrial firms such as GE, IBM, DuPont, Monsanto, and Honeywell have established strategic partner relationships with customers such as American Airlines, Ford, Milliken, Procter & Gamble, and the federal government.

This radically different type of relationship is often initiated by the customer. In 1989, Chrysler was on the ropes. One of its responses was to change the way it did business with its suppliers. Instead of forcing suppliers to win its business anew every two years and focusing on lowest list price, it decided to give suppliers business for the life of a model and beyond. Excruciatingly detailed contracts gave way to oral agreements. Instead of relying solely on its own engineers to create the concept for a new car and design all the car's components, Chrysler now involves suppliers. Instead of Chrysler dictating price, the two sides now strive together to lower the costs of making cars and to share the savings. Today Chrysler has improved its market share and profitability significantly by speeding up product development, lowering development costs, and reducing procurement costs.[27]

The Chrysler example illustrates some ways in which strategic partnering relationships are different from traditional supplier relationships. Following are some of the ways in which other companies have made strategic partner relationships work:

- Suppliers are involved in the early stages of need identification, specification, and new-product development. Texas Instruments targets key emerging accounts in which they participate in these firms' product design process as early as possible and, in doing so, suggest improvements that enable these firms to design products that fully capitalize on the strengths and capabilities of TI system products.

- In conventional relationships, the primary players were the salesperson, the customer service representative, and perhaps a design engineer. With strategic partnering the supplier fields a team that interfaces with the customer on a regular basis, and includes a variety of functional areas and management levels. John Deere workers, for instance, solve production problems with their counterparts at suppliers such as McLoughlin Body Co.[28]

- In strategic partnering relationships there is an unusually high degree of intimacy resulting in immediate responsiveness from suppliers, sharing of information, and radical empowerment of suppliers. For instance, a small group of nine suppliers, called "in-plants," work on-site, full time at Bose. This insider status gives them unparalleled opportunities to grow with the customer and to influence requirements for their products. Based on their access and knowledge, the suppliers decide what, when, and how much of a particular product or service is needed, and write orders to themselves to make it happen.[29]

The sales force's role, the structure of the sales program, and even the sales philosophy differ for each type of relationship. For instance, as the buyer-seller relationship becomes more sophisticated and complex, the sales force's role as the primary point of contact between customer and supplier often diminishes. The focus also shifts from volume to management and maintenance of the relationship. A comparison of the old and new relationship is summarized in Figure 2-9. The skills needed, compensation, incentive programs, and evaluation criteria all need to be adjusted from those of a general field sales force to be appropriate for these relationships.

Summary   One of the key ideas expressed up to this point is that a sales force strategy should be derived from the business and marketing plans of the organization. Numerous company examples have been presented to illustrate this idea. The other

Traditional	Partnership
Little recognition or credit for past performance.	Recognition of past performance and track record.
No responsibility for supplier's profit margins	Recognition of suppliers' need to make a fair profit.
Little support for feedback from suppliers	Feedback from suppliers encouraged.
No guarantee of business relationship beyond the contract.	Expectations of business relationship beyond the contract.
No performance expectations beyond the contract.	Considerable performance expectations beyond the contract.
Adversarial, zero-sum game.	Cooperative and trusting, positive-sum game.

Source: Jeffrey Dyer, "How Chrysler Created an American Keiretsu," *Harvard Business Review*, (July–August 1996) p. 50.

Figure **2-9**: Strategic Partnership Relationship Comparison

Sales Managers' and Marketing Executives' Product Classifications by Strategy

		Sales Manager Classification				
		Build Strategy	**Hold Strategy**	**Harvest Strategy**	**Divest Strategy**	**Total**
Marketing	Build strategy	71[a]	22	2	0	95
executive	Hold strategy	29	57	3	1	88
classification	Harvest strategy	10	49	23	6	88
	Divest strategy	21	21	27	25	94
	Total	129	149	55	32	365

[a]A total of 71 sales managers classified their products as build strategies out of 95 or so classified by marketing executives.

important idea is that a sales force strategy should include two key decisions: (1) the organization's strategy for accessing the target markets defined within the marketing plan and (2) the type of account relationships that will be pursued—repeat transactions, contractual, major account, and strategic partners.

One of the difficulties that may arise in executing a marketing strategy is that the sales force may not understand and execute the product strategy. The ability of sales managers to understand marketing strategies and apply them in the field has been examined in some recent research.[30] Table 2-1 shows how marketing executives and sales managers classified products into four basic strategies. If the views of the two groups matched perfectly, then all the numbers would be on the diagonal. Instead, sales managers tended to be more aggressive in pushing products that marketing wanted to either divest or harvest. Not only does there appear to be widespread misallocation of selling time and effort, but continued emphasis on building product sales volume when inappropriate may also cause the company's relationship with its customers to suffer. What is the firm's strategy, by the way, when marketing says they are doing one thing but sales says another?

Strategic planning implies that choices will have to be made. One of these choices is the allocation of resources. Indeed the marketing and sales force strategy is often motivated by cost and revenue considerations. One of the outcomes of the strategic planning process should be to set an operating budget for controlling the implementation of the strategy. The next section concentrates on how sales force budgets can be set and administered.

▶ THE SALES BUDGET

Budgets are a key element used by sales managers in planning programs to reach their objectives. A *sales budget* is essentially a set of planned expenses that is prepared on an annual basis. The sales budgeting process is described in Figure 2-10. Sales budgeting begins when senior management designs a marketing plan and sets spending levels for advertising and sales promotion. Once these demand creation factors

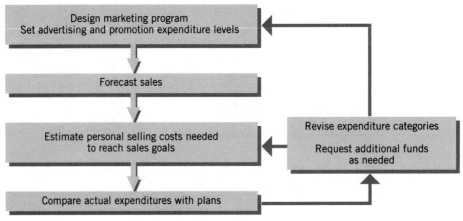

Figure 2-10: The Sales Budgeting Process

are determined, sales forecasts can be made (forecasting is discussed in Chapter 7). The sales forecast, in turn, provides a guide for estimating how many salespeople will be needed. Sales managers must also project travel and other expenses for the sales force. Next, the actual expenditures for a period are compared with the budget. When expenditures exceed planned levels, the sales manager has to revise the categories or ask for more funds. The main concerns in preparing budgets are to decide how much to spend on personal selling and how to allocate the money across various selling activities.

Sales Budget Planning

For budgeting purposes, it is usually necessary to further refine and identify the strategic avenues for achieving an overall sales volume target. For instance, the overall sales target may be broken down by geographic area, region or district. Many companies have found that the *Customer-Product Matrix* shown in Figure 2-11 is a very useful tool for analyzing the basic revenue generating avenues of the firm. This matrix identifies four strategic sources of sales revenue based on a combination of new and/or current customers and products. The reason companies have found this to be a useful analysis tool is that the sales job and resulting expenses are quite different for each quadrant in the matrix. New Business Development revenues (new customers and new products) will require much higher training and promotion expenses, for instance, than Account Management revenues (current customers and products). Even the sales force compensation plan can be quite different depending on the quadrant representing the source of company revenues. This is discussed further in Chapter 14 on compensation. The point being made here is that a sales figure for each of these four sources of revenue illustrated in the customer-product matrix should be budgeted so that the total of the four quadrants equals the company's total sales volume target. This analysis will help considerably in the determination of expense budgets and in designing an overall sales program.

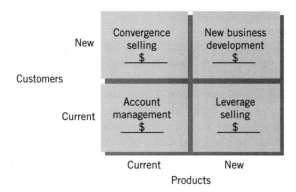

Figure 2-11: The Customer-Product Matrix

How Much to Spend?

Perhaps the most popular method for determining a sales budget is the *percentage of sales method*. This technique bases a sales budget on what managers think is a reasonable percentage of planned revenues. The percentage is usually derived from historical spending patterns and industry standards for a particular line of trade. Table 2-2, for example, provides the average sales force expenses for 19 major industries. A typical firm selling industrial services spent 6.9% of sales on sales force expenses.

Table 2-2   Sales Force Selling Expenses as a Percentage of Sales

	Sales Force Total Cost as a Percentage of Sales		Sales Force Total Cost as a Percentage of Sales
COMPANY SIZE		**INDUSTRY**	
Under $5 Million (MM)	14.7%	Business services	1.7
$5–$25 MM	10.5	Chemicals	2.9
$25–$100 MM	7.9	Communications	9.8
$100–$250 MM	3.5	Educational services	47.9
Over $250 MM	6.8	Electronics	4.2
		Fabricated metals	10.8
PRODUCT OR		Health services	19.9
SERVICE		Hotels & other lodgings	21.4
Industrial products	4.1	Instruments	2.3
Industrial services	6.4	Machinery	10.1
Office products	9.4	Manufacturing	13.6
Office services	8.1	Office equipment	9.0
Consumer products	5.4	Paper and allied products	6.8
Consumer services	7.9	Printing and publishing	12.0
		Retail	6.1
		Trucking and warehousing	12.2
		Wholesale (consumer goods)	3.7
		Wholesale (industrial goods)	9.5
		Average	**6.9%**

Source: Sales Force Compensation Survey (Chicago: Dartnell Corp., 1992), p. 109.

There are several notable drawbacks to the percentage of sales approach. There is no guarantee, for instance, that the use of industry percentages in setting sales budgets will lead to optimal results for individual firms. Note in Table 2-2 that smaller firms tend to spend a bigger percent of sales on the sales force than do larger firms. Another drawback is that with this approach budget allocations for selling expenses change in the same direction as sales. The percentage base, however, may not provide the appropriate amounts of funds when market conditions change. If a firm is losing market share, for instance, an intensified selling effort may require greater funding than would be appropriated under the percentage of sales method.

Despite its drawbacks, the percentage of sales method is practical and provides useful standards for comparison. A company might adjust the industry average according to its own needs and plans, trying sales budgets that are higher or lower than average to see if they lead to greater effectiveness. This latter approach is similar to the objective-and-task budgeting method described in many marketing textbooks.

Where to Spend It?

Sales managers set target figures for the various selling expense categories for each planning period. The goal is to keep actual expenditures at, or under, the budgeted figures to ensure that overall financial objectives are achieved. Some of the more common *expense classifications* are:

- Sales force salaries, commissions, and bonuses
- Sales manager salaries, bonuses, and commissions
- Social Security
- Retirement plans
- Hospitalization and life insurance
- Automobile
- Travel, meals, lodging, and entertainment
- Samples and other sales aids
- Recruiting and training
- Clerical and secretarial services
- Office rent and utilities
- Office supplies and postage

The amounts budgeted for the different expense categories tend to vary widely by product and type of customer. Often managers make their initial allocations using the previous year's budget, and adjust for inflation and program changes.

Budget Administration

One of the prime benefits of sales budgets is that they force managers to think about how marketing funds should be spent. Decisions must be made about whether sales representatives should receive more training, whether more money should be spent to purchase complementary hockey tickets, whether to provide more sample books, or to increase bonuses, and so on. Budgets, therefore, aid sales managers in designing the optimal combination of the marketing variables under their control.

Another advantage of a budget is that it facilitates the control of sales operations. If sales objectives are not being reached, for instance, the manager can see from the budget how much money has been spent in each expense category and where adjustments are needed. In this case the sales manager might be able to use funds from the training budget to buy prizes for a sales contest.

Budget administration has been greatly simplified in the past few years with the development of the *electronic spreadsheet*. Computer programs like Lotus 1-2-3 and Excel and the widespread availability of personal computers have made it easier to keep track of sales force expenditures.

QUALITY SALES MANAGEMENT

Regardless of the particular strategy chosen by an organization for marketing its products and services, TQM recommends certain approaches in executing a strategy. The following concepts from the quality movement apply directly to sales and sales management.[31]

Information

A basic tenet of quality programs is that decisions should be based on facts. Knowing what your competition actually does and not what you think it does, for instance, has long been a recommended part of strategic and marketing planning. Comparing your processes with the best process in other companies, known as *benchmarking*, is relatively new.

Quality-driven organizations build customer databases that provide salespeople information on all kinds of transactions with customers (e.g., billing, what is on order, contacts, previous revenues, average order quantities, and so forth) so as to improve service. At both IBM and Westinghouse, salespeople are responsible for gathering increasing amounts of such information, while their firms work to integrate existing files to build a composite view of customers.

Not only is more information gathered, but the information collected is different. For one thing, more information is collected on how well things are being done, not just on what gets done. For example, the speed with which orders are processed is measured daily, not just how many orders were placed this month. Providing information more frequently, in trend format, is also a characteristic of TQM.

Tasks and Processes

Important to improving quality is the notion that tasks should be looked at as processes, as families of activities. Documenting all the steps required, for instance, from taking an order from a customer to delivering it means that you have to understand how orders are taken, communicated back to the office, entered into an order processing system, communicated to the warehouse, scheduled for delivery, and ultimately shipped and, if need be, installed. A similar sequence of actions should be specified for handling customer service complaints. Thinking of a business as pro-

Prospect Identification	Competitive Analysis
Customer Feedback	Compensation
Skills Development	Order Processing
Service and Repair	Distribution/Delivery
Revenue and Profit Accounting	Pricing
Telephones	Sales and Planning
Supplier Relations	Market Segmentation
Quotas and Measurements	Product Liability
Organization	Service Quality
Complaints	

Figure 2-12: Possible Sales Force Quality-Related Processes

cesses instead of functions can have dramatic impacts on the organization. Consider the following:

- AT&T: The Network Systems Division reorganized its entire business around processes so that budgets are set by process and bonuses are awarded to employees based on customer evaluations.
- *General Electric*: The Lighting business scrapped its vertical structure and adopted a horizontal design based on more than 100 processes and programs.
- *Eastman Chemical Company*: Identified five major processes in the sales function: customer satisfaction, employee satisfaction, training, market intelligence, and productivity measurement and budgeting.[32]

Figure 2-12 lists a number of important sales processes.

When they first examine processes, companies find that they can be improved. At some point, however, they cannot improve the existing process any further. To improve beyond that point requires a radically *new* process. A radically new order entry process may be required—for instance, customers ordering directly from the warehouse instead of placing orders with salespeople. Setting radically higher performance objectives, time to deliver an order for example, and developing new processes is referred to as *reengineering*.[33]

Cycle Time Reduction

Cycle time is the time needed to complete a particular process. In the quality world, part of the definition of improvement is the reduction in the amount of time required to perform a process—reducing the time needed to place an order, for instance. Cycle time reduction in sales would include ways to reduce the selling cycle from three months to one. Faxing orders to the office instead of mailing them is an example of cycle time reduction in the order entry process.

The biggest benefit of quality improvement efforts to reduce cycle time is that it contributes directly to elimination of errors, delays, and bottlenecks while improving the ability to do things right the first time. This often requires using technology such as computers and fax machines. AT&T's recently unveiled INTUITY system provides multimedia delivery of territory reports, sales prospects, and up-to-date pricing. A fully integrated sales presentation can be delivered with voice, text, and full-motion video to a prospect's desktop computer. This will speed sales flow through communnications.[34]

These quality principles are just starting to be incorporated into the selling and sales management thought and practice, but they have wide-ranging implications for the sales program. In recognition of their significance, quality issues are raised in each of the following chapters.

► ETHICAL SITUATIONS

In sales, as in other professions, you will face a variety of day-to-day situations requiring you to make decisions that trade off one alternative course of action for another. In some cases, decisions may have legal ramifications. More often, decisions reflect personal values and ethics. Most chapters in this text have a section called "Ethical Situations," which presents situations requiring trade-off type decisions.

When a manufacturer's salespeople sell through distributors, their time and knowledge are valuable resources to the distributors. The time they spend with the distributor's sales force is especially valuable to the distributor. Distributors look to the manufacturer's sales force to provide their salespeople with product and market information. This involves leading sales meetings and spending one-on-one time with the customers of individual salespeople in their territory. Distributors frequently call on manufacturers' salespeople to accompany their own salespeople to help close an important deal.

Conflicts sometimes occur because customers and prospects are covered by more than one distributor carrying the manufacturer's line of products. This can give rise to friction and even ethical questions. What would you do, for instance, if you were called by two distributors to help close a deal with the same prospect? Should there be a company policy or guideline for such situations? What if one does not exist? An even more common problem is deciding how much time to spend with the sales force of each distributor in your territory. Remember, you are a valuable sales resource to these distributors. How should you allocate your time? What factors should you consider?

A whole different set of tensions is likely to arise in a strategic partner relationship with a customer, as opposed to a repeat-transaction relationship. It would not be unusual for you, as a member of the Procter & Gamble sales team located at WalMart, to be aware of valuable competitive information since you have access to WalMart's computer information system. Should you provide information about upcoming competitors' promotion programs to your headquarters? Should you check with WalMart's management first? What would you do if a Wal-Mart executive told you about a plan to change their merchandising program in a way that would be detrimental to P&G

but asked you not discuss this with your people at headquarters? What additional factors would affect your decision? As you can see, intimacy has its hazards.

▶ SUMMARY

The sales force strategy and management structure should be planned and designed within the context of an organization's overall business strategy and its marketing strategy. The strategic management process includes defining a business mission, setting specific measurable goals for the organization, and deciding on a strategy for meeting these objectives. A well-defined business mission should provide a sense of direction for the organization, defined in terms of customers, competitors, and the company itself. Goals should be measurable and should guide goal setting throughout the organization. Strategies should be based on developing a sustainable competitive advantage.

Strategic marketing planning is a process whereby an organization allocates marketing mix resources to reach its target markets. This process starts with a situation analysis that consists of taking stock of where you have been, where you are now, and where you are likely to go in the future. The next step is to define market segments and to choose target markets. Once you have made these decisions, an appropriate marketing mix program should be designed, including integration of the various promotion tools.

The sales force strategy should follow from and be consistent with the earlier business and marketing strategy decisions. Two decisions will have an overall influence on the sales force program—how the firm will access the target markets and the types of relationships it wishes to establish with its customers.

Sales budgets follow from the long-term strategic plans of the organization. Sales budgets are essentially a set of planned revenues and expenses that are prepared on an annual basis. How much is spent on personal selling and sales force expenses will vary from industry to industry and among competitors within an industry.

Total quality management (TQM) is a broad set of processes designed to enhance a firm's competitive advantage. Its key concepts include continuous improvements, zero defects, doing it right the first time, and recognizing that the employees closest to the situation know best how to improve it. TQM represents a different way of thinking about business. The amount and type of information, the emphasis on tasks as part of a process, and the emphasis on cycle time reduction directly affect the sales force.

▶ KEY TERMS

Account relationship strategy	Build strategy
Alliances	Business mission
Analyzers	Business portfolio analysis
Benchmarking	Contractual relationship

Cycle time
Defenders
Differentiation
Divest strategy
Electronic spreadsheet
Expense classifications
Generic business strategies
Harvest strategy
Hold strategy
Low cost
Major account relationships
Market segmentation
Marketing mix
Niche
Organizational goals
Partnering selling approach

Percentage of sales method
Programmatic purchasing
Prospectors
Reactive selling approach
Reengineering
Repeat transactions
Sales budget
Sales force strategy
Situation analysis
Strategy
Strategic business units (SBUs)
Strategic management planning
Strategic marketing planning
Strategic partnership
Target marketing
Transactional purchasing

▶ REVIEW QUESTIONS

1. How do sales strategies evolve from corporate objectives?

2. What are the steps involved in strategic management planning?

3. What is included in a business mission? What is its purpose?

4. What are the characteristics of a good organizational goal?

5. What are the differences between business portfolio analysis, strategic business units, generic business strategies, and the Miles and Snow typology of business strategies?

6. What is the difference between strategic management planning and strategic marketing planning? How are they related?

7. Which comes first, target marketing or market segmentation? Why?

8. What do build, hold, harvest, and divest strategies imply for the sales force?

9. Do senior marketing executives agree with their sales managers on the classification of products into build, hold, harvest, and divest strategies?

10. What are the alternative means available for accessing a customer base and what are the implications for selling and sales management?

11. What are the different types of account relationships, how do they differ, and what are the implications for the sales force?

12. Why do sales organizations use budgets?

13. Why should sales targets be established for each quadrant in the customer-product matrix?

14. How does a firm decide how much to spend on field selling?

15. Why is TQM considered a strategic approach to business?

16. What are the basic quality issues in the sales force?

17. What ethical situations may arise for salespeople when selling to and through distributors?

▶ PROBLEMS

1. Synesis Corporation markets computer-based training programs to large corporations. How might they segment their market? What would be the implications for the sales force if they chose to use a focused, differentiated strategy?

2. Why do you think corporations have been slow to apply TQM principles to the sales force when the focus of TQM is on the customer? On what issues is the sales force likely to resist attempts to implement a TQM program?

3. "You should partner with each of your customers." Do you agree with this statement? Are there any dangers involved in following this advice?

4. How would a company know if they should establish a strategic customer partnering relationship? What are the signals? What would be some of the major issues involved in establishing such a program? How long do you think it would take to establish the program?

5. What would be involved in the basic sales job, that is, the activities salespeople are expected to perform, for each quadrant of the customer-product matrix? What differences in the sales program (e.g., organization, compensation, training, recruiting, evaluation) would be needed to support these activities? How would the sales manager's job differ between the four quadrants?

6. The sales forces of most health care product manufacturers placed a premium on product expertise. Sales personnel were literally product-solution specialists who were relied upon by physicians, nurses, pharmacists and others for their product and service expertise. In a dramatic shift in emphasis, hospitals are applying managed care principles to control costs. They have established rules regarding treatment for particular diagnoses (formularies) carry fewer product lines, provide their own product analysis and expertise, and have restricted salesperson access to key department personnel such as physicians and nurses. How are these changes likely to affect the customer relationship strategies of health care product suppliers?

▶ REFERENCES

1. GEOFFREY BREWER, "The Tough Get Going," *Sales & Marketing Management* (September 1993), p. 61.

2. This organization is based on ERIC BERKOWITZ, ROGER KERIN, STEPHEN HARTLEY, and BILL RUDELIUS, *Marketing* (Burr Ridge, Ill: R. D. Irwin, 1994), pp. 33–56.

3. WILLIAM KEENAN, JR., "The Tough Get Going," *Sales and Marketing Management* (September 1993), p. 62.

4. MICHAEL PORTER, *Competitive Strategy* (New York: Free Press, 1980).

5. JOHN WILKE, "NCR Is Revamping Its Computer Lines in Wrenching Change," *Wall Street Journal*, (June 20, 1990), A1–A6.

6. "Tapping Your Customer Resources," *Sales Management Bulletin*, No. 1311 (August 30, 1993), pp. 4–5.

7. GEORGE ANDERS, "Managed Health Care Jeopardizes Outlook for Drug 'Detailers,'" *Wall Street Journal* (September 1, 1993), p. A1.

8. Presentation by MANUAL DIAZ, "Sales Force Conversion: From Volume to Value" (September 28, 1993).

9. THOMAS WOTRUBA and LINDA ROCHFORD, "The Impact of New Product Introductions on Sales Management Strategy," *Journal of Personal Selling and Sales Management* (Winter 1995), pp. 35–51.

10. "Kotler Foresees Integrated Future," *Business Marketing* (September 1993), p. 85.

11. TIM CLARK, "Marketing Alliances Starting to Pay Off," *Business Marketing* (May 1993), p. 46.

12. ROWLAND MORIARTY and URSULA MORAN, "Managing Hybrid Marketing Systems," *Harvard Business Review* 68 (November––December 1990), p. 146.

13. "Distributor Networks," *Sales Manager's Bulletin*, 1307 (June 30, 1993), pp. 1–2.

14. MORIARTY and MORAN, "Managing Hybrid Marketing Systems," p. 153.

15. RICHARD HUDSON, "AT&Ts Computer Business Is Planning to Build Sales Partnerships in Europe," *Wall Street Journal* (May 11, 1990), p. B5.

16. BRADLEY STERTZ, "Chrysler's Search for Broader Alliances Intensifies Amid Strong Internal Debate," *Wall Street Journal* (June 19, 1990), p. A4.

17. JOHN STERLICCHI and CHARLOTTE KLOPP, "Europe Faces Invasion by U.S. Cereal Makers," *Marketing News* (June 11, 1990), p. 2.

18. "IBM to Shift More Business to Resellers," *Sales & Marketing Management* (March 1995), p. 36.

19. This section is based on the discussion in FREDERICK WEBSTER, "The Changing Role of Marketing in the Corporation," *Journal of Marketing*, 56 (October 1992), pp. 1–17, and Roger Brooksbank, "The New Model of Personal Selling: Micromarketing," *Journal of Personal Selling and Sales Management*, 15 (Spring 1995), pp. 61–66.

20. For more on how partnering relationships differ, see DAN DUNN and CLAUDE THOMAS, "Partnering with Customers," *Journal of Business & Industrial Marketing*, 9 (1994), pp. 34–40.

21. EDWARD DOHERTY, "How to Steal a Satisfied Customer," *Sales and Marketing Management* (March 1990), p. 45.

22. This discussion based on JAMES WOMACK, DANIEL JONES, and DANIEL ROOS, *The Machine That Changed the World* (New York: HarperCollins, 1991).

23. Based on a presentation by GREGORY BRADLEY, National Accounts Director, SmithKline Beecham Consumer Brands, September 28, 1993.

24. NEIL RACKHAM, LAWRENCE FRIEDMAN, and RICHARD RUFF, *Getting Partnering Right* (New York: McGraw-Hill, 1996), p. 5.

25. This definition is based on that provided by FREDERICK WEBSTER, "The Changing Role of Marketing in the Corporation," *Journal of Marketing*, 56 (October 1992), p. 7.

26. RACKHAM et al., *Getting Partnering Right*.

27. JEFFREY DYER, "How Chrysler Created an American Keiretsu," *Harvard Business Review* (July–August 1996), pp. 42–56.

28. JOHN MAGGS, "U.S. Paper, Car Parts Makers Decry Japan Business Tactic," *Journal of Commerce and Commercial* (October 17, 1991), p. 3.

29. URBAN LEHNER and ALAN MURRAY, "Selling of America," *Wall Street Journal* (June 19,1990), pp. A1, A12.

30. WILLIAM STRAHLE, ROSANN SPIRO, and FRANK ACITO, "Marketing and Sales: Strategic Alignment and Functional Implementation," *Journal of Personal Selling and Sales Management* (Winter 1996), pp. 1–20.

31. The discussion in this section is based on JAMES CORTADA, *TQM for Sales and Marketing Management* (New York: McGraw-Hill, 1993).

32. JOHN BYRNE, "The Horizontal Corporation," *BusinessWeek* (December 20, 1993), pp. 78–79.

33. For more on reengineering, see MICHAEL HAMMER, "Reengineering Work: Don't Automate, Obliterate," *Harvard Business Review*, 68 (July–August 1990), pp. 104–113.

34. JAMES KIMBALL, "Salespeople Likely Market for INTUITY," *Business Marketing* (February 1994), p. 19.

▶ SELECTED READINGS

KEARNS, DAVID, and DAVID NADLER, *Prophets in the Dark: How Xerox Reinvented Itself and Beat Back the Japanese* (New York: Harper Business, 1992).

KERIN, ROGER, VIJAY MAHAJAN, and RAJAN VARADARAJAN, *Contemporary Perspectives on Strategic Market Planning* (Boston: Allyn & Bacon, 1990).

McKENNA, REGIS, *Relationship Marketing* (Reading, MA: Addison-Wesley Publishing Co., 1991).

NANUS, BURT, *Visionary Leadership* (San Francisco: Jossey-Bass, 1992).

RACKHAM, NEIL, LAWRENCE FRIEDMAN and RICHARD RUFF, *Getting Partnering Right* (New York: McGraw-Hill, 1996).

SCHONBERGER, RICHARD, *Building a Chain of Customers: Linking Business Functions to Create the World Class Company* (New York: Free Press, 1990).

CASE

2-1 BSI*

With four people and sales of $5.5 million, Barro Stickney, Inc. (BSI), had become a successful and profitable manufacturers' representative firm. It enjoyed a reputation for outstanding sales results and friendly, thorough service to both its customers and principals. In addition, BSI was considered a great place to work. The office was comfortable and the atmosphere relaxed but professional. All members of the group had come to value the close, friendly working relationships that had grown with the organization.

Success had brought with it increased profits, as well as the inevitable decision regarding further growth. Recent requests from two principals, Franklin Key Electronics and R. D. Ocean, had forced BSI to focus its attention on the question of expansion. It was not an easy decision, for expansion offered both risk and opportunity.

Company Background

John Barro and Bill Stickney established their small manufacturers' representative agency, Barro Stickney, Inc., ten years ago. Both men were close friends who left different manufacturers' representative firms to join as partners in their own "rep" agency. The two

*This case was prepared by Professor Erin M. Anderson of INSEAD, Fontainebleau, France. Reproduced by permission.

worked very well together, and their talents complemented each other.

John Barro was energetic and gregarious. He enjoyed meeting new people and taking on new challenges. It was mainly through John's efforts that many of BSI's eight principals had signed on with BSI. Even after producing $1.75 million in sales this past year, John still made an effort to contribute much of his free time to community organizations in addition to perfecting his golf score.

Bill Stickney liked to think of himself as someone a person could count on. He was thoughtful and thorough. He liked to figure how things could get done and how they could be better. Much of the administrative work of the agency, such as resource allocation and territory assignments, was handled by Bill. In addition to his contribution of $1.5 million to total company sales, Bill had a Boy Scout troop and was interested in gourmet cooking. In fact, he often prepared specialties to share with his fellow workers.

A few years later, as the business grew, J. Todd Smith (J.T.) joined as an additional salesperson. J.T. had worked for a nationally known corporation, and he brought his experience in dealing with large customers with him. He and his family loved the Harrisburg area, and J.T. was very happy when he was asked to join BSI just as his firm was ready to transfer him to Chicago. John and Bill had worked with J.T. in connection with a hospital fund-raising project, and they were impressed with his tenacity and enthusiasm. Because he had produced sales of over $2 million this past year, J.T. was now considered eligible to buy a partnership share of BSI.

Soon after J.T. joined BSI, Elizabeth Lee, a school friend of John's older sister, was hired as office manager. She was cheerful and put as much effort into her work as she did coaching the local swim team. The three salespeople knew they could rely on her to keep track of orders and schedules, and she was very helpful when customers and principals called in with requests or problems.

Most principals in the industry assigned their reps exclusive territories, and BSI's ranged over the Pennsylvania, New Jersey, and Delaware area. The partners purchased a small house and converted it into their present office, located in Camp Hill, a suburb of Harrisburg, the state capital of Pennsylvania. The converted home contributed to the family-like atmosphere and attitude that was promoted and prevalent throughout the agency.

Over the years, in addition to local interests, BSI and its people had made an effort to participate in and support the efforts of the Electronics Representative Association (ERA). A wall of the company library was covered with awards and letters of appreciation. BSI had made many friends and important contacts through the organization. Just last year, BSI received a recommendation from Chuck Goodman, a Chicago manufacturers' rep, who knew a principal in need of representation in the Philadelphia area. The principal's line worked well with BSI's existing portfolio, and customer response had been quite favorable. BSI planned to continue active participation in the ERA.

Each week BSI held a five o'clock meeting in the office library, where all members of the company shared their experiences of the week. It was a time when new ideas were encouraged and everyone was kept up-to-date. For example, many customer problems were solved here, and principals' and members' suggestions were discussed. An established agenda enabled members to prepare properly. Most meetings took about one to one and one-half hours, with emphasis placed on consensus of the group. It was during this group meeting that BSI would discuss the future of the company.

Opportunities for Expansion

R. D. Ocean was BSI's largest principal, and it accounted for 32% of BSI's revenues. Ocean had just pro-

moted James Innve as new sales manager, and he felt an additional salesperson was needed in order for BSI to achieve the new sales projections. Innve expressed the opinion that BSI's large commission checks justified the additional effort, and he further commented that J.T.'s expensive new car was proof that BSI could afford it.

BSI was not sure that an additional salesperson was necessary, but it did not want to lose the goodwill of R. D. Ocean or its business. Also, while it was customary for all principals to meet and tacitly approve new representatives, BSI wanted to be very sure that any new salesperson would fit into the close-knit BSI organization.

Franklin Key Electronics was BSI's initial principal and had remained a consistent contributor of approximately 15% of BSI's revenues. BSI felt its customer base was well suited to the Franklin line, and it had worked hard to establish the Franklin Key name with these customers. As a consequence, BSI now considered Franklin Key relatively easy to sell.

A few days previously, Mark Heil, Franklin's representative from Virginia, perished when his private plane crashed, leaving Franklin Key without representation in its D.C./Virginia territory. Franklin did not want to jeopardize its sales of over $800,000 and was desperate to replace Heil before its customers found other sources. Franklin offered the territory to BSI and was anxious to hear the decision within one week.

BSI was not familiar with the territory, but it did understand that there was a great number of military accounts. This meant there was a potential for sizable orders, although a different and specialized sales approach would be required. Military customers are known to have their own unique approach to purchase decisions.

Because of the distance and the size of the territory, serious consideration was needed as to whether a branch office would be necessary. A branch office would mean less interaction with and greater independence from the main BSI office. None of the current BSI members seemed anxious to move there, but it might be possible to hire someone who was familiar with the territory. There was, of course, always the risk that any successful salesperson might leave and start his or her own rep firm.

In addition to the possibilities of expanding its territory and its sales force, BSI wanted to consider whether it should increase or maintain its number of principals. BSI's established customer base and its valued reputation put it in a strong position to ap-

Exhibit 1: BSI Client Portfolio

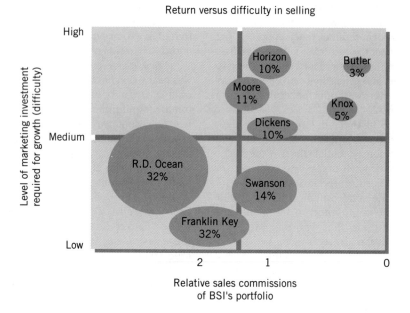

Notes and Explanation

This chart evaluates the amount of sales effort (difficulty in selling) necessary in order to achieve a certain percentage of sales in BSI's portfolio (return). Difficulty in selling is measured by the level of marketing investment required for growth. Stickney's estimate is shown on the vertical axis. Return for this investment is measured by the relative sales commissions as a percentage of BSI's portfolio, shown on the horizontal axis. If BSI's time were evenly divided among its eight principals, each would receive 12.5% of the agency's time. The x-axis shows each principal's time allocation as a proportion of 12.5%, the "par" time allocation. The area of each ellipse reflects each principal's share of BSI's commission revenue.

Additional Comments

- Swanson's products are being replaced by the competition's computerized electronic equipment, a product category the firm has ignored. As a result, the company is losing its once prominent market position.
- Although only small amounts of effort are required to promote Ocean's product line to customers in the current sales territory, Ocean is extremely demanding of both BSI and other manufacturers' representative firms.
- According to a seminar at the last ERA meeting, the maximum safe proportion of a rep firm's commissions from a single principal should be 25–30%. Also, at the meeting, one speaker indicated that if a firm commands 80% of a market, it should focus on another product or expand its territory rather than attempt to obtain the remainder of the market.
- The revenue for investment for the manufacturers' representative firm comes from one or more of several sources. These sources include reduced forthcoming commission income, retained previous income, and borrowed money from a financial institution. Most successful firms expand their sales force or sales territory when they experience income growth and use the investment as a tax write-off.

proach potential principals. If, however, BSI had too many principals, it might not be able to offer them all the attention and service they might require.

Preparation for the Meeting

Each member received an agenda and supporting data for the upcoming meeting, asking them to consider the issue of expansion. They would be asked whether BSI should or should not expand its territory, its sales force, and/or the number of its principals. In preparation, they were each asked to take a good, hard look at the current BSI portfolio and to consider all possibilities for growth, as well as the effect any changes would have on the company's profits, its reputation, and its work environment.

It was an ambitious agenda, one that would de-

termine the future of the company. It would take even more time than usual to discuss everything and reach a consensus. Consequently, this week's meeting was set to take place over the weekend at Bill Stickney's vacation lodge in the Poconos, starting with a gourmet dinner served at 7:00 P.M.

Before the meeting, Bill Stickney examined the sources of BSI's revenue and the firm's income for the previous year, in addition to estimating the future prospects for each of BSI's lines, considering each line's market potential and BSI's level of saturation in each market. Finally, he estimated the costs of hiring a new employee, both in the current sales territory and in the Washington/Virginia area. Immediately before the meeting, Elizabeth finished compiling Bill's data into four charts (Exhibits 1–4).

Exhibit 2: Estimation of Cost of an Additional Sales Representative

Compensation Costs for New Sales Representative
Depending upon the new sales representative's level of experience, BSI would pay a base salary of $15,000–$25,000, with the following bonus schedule:

0% firm's commission revenue up to $500,000 in sales
20% firm's commission revenue 1st half million dollars in sales over $500,000
25% firm's commission revenue for the next half million dollars in sales
30% firm's commission for the next half million dollars in sales
40% firm's commission sales above two million dollars in sales

Estimate of Support Costs[a] for New Representative[b]	
Search applicant pool, psychological testing, hiring, training[c], flying final choice to principals for approval[d]	$28,000
Automobile expenses, telephone costs, business cards, entertainment/ promotion	$22,000
Insurance, payroll taxes (Social Security, unemployment compensation)	$16,000
Total expenses	$66,000
Incremental expenses for new territory	
Transportation (additional mileage from Camp Hill to Virginia)	$ 2,000
Office equipment and rent (same regardless of headquarters location)	$ 4,000
Cost of hiring office manager[e]	$18,000
Total incremental expenses	$24,000

[a]Rounded to the nearest $1,000.

[b]In the current territory.

[c]Excludes the lost revenue from selling instead of engaging in this activity (opportunity cost).

[d]Although legally rep agencies are not required to show prospective employees to principals, it is generally held to be good business practice.

[e]Discretionary.

Exhibit 3: Statement of Revenue (Total Sales Revenue, 1985: $5.5 Million)

Principal	Estimated Market Saturation	Product Type	Sales/ Commission Rate	Share of BSI's Portfolio	Commission Revenue
R. D. Ocean	High	Components	5%	32%	$96,756
Franklin Key	High	Components	5%	15%	$45,354
Butler	Low	Technical/computer	12%	3%	$9,070
Dickins	Low	Components	5%	10%	$30,236
Horizon	Medium	Components	5.5%	10%	$30,237
Swanson	High	Components	5.25%	14%	$42,331
Moore	Medium	Consumer/electronics	5.25%	11%	$33,260
Knox	Low	Technical/communications	8.5%	5%	$15,118

Exhibit 4: Statement of Income for the Year Ending December 31, 1985

Revenue	
Commission income	$302,362
Expenses	
Salaries for sales and bonuses (includes Barro and Stickney)	$130,250
Office manager's salary	$20,000
Total nonpersonnel expenses[a]	$128,279
Total expenses	$278,529
Net Income[b]	$ 23,833 (7.9% of revenue)

[a]Includes travel, advertising, taxes, office supplies, retirement pension, automobile expenses, communications, office equipment, and miscellaneous expenses.

[b]Currently held in negotiable certificates of deposit in a Harrisburg bank.

CASE

2-2 SHANANDOAH INDUSTRIES (A)*

Late in the evening of August 8, 1986, Charlton Bates, president of Shanandoah Industries, called Dr. Thomas Berry, a marketing professor at a private university in the Northeast and a consultant to the company. The conversation went as follows:

BATES: Hello, Tom. This is Chuck Bates. I'm sorry for calling you this late, but I wanted to get your thoughts on the tentative 1987 advertising program proposed by Mike Hervey of Hervey and Berham, our ad agency.

BERRY: No problem, Chuck. What did they propose?

BATES: The crux of their proposal is that we should increase our advertising expenditures by $400,000. They indicated that we put the entire amount into our consumer advertising program for ads in several shelter magazines.

BERRY: That increase appears to be slightly above your policy of budgeting 5 percent of expected sales for total promotion expenditures, doesn't it? Hasn't John Bott [vice president of sales] emphasized the need for more sales representatives?

BATES: Yes. John has requested additional funds. You're right about the 5 percent figure too, and I'm not sure if our sales forecast isn't too optimistic. Your research has shown that our sales historically follow the industry almost perfectly, and trade economists are predicting about a 13 percent increase. Yet, I'm not too sure.

BERRY: Well, Chuck, you can't expect forecasts to always be on the button. The money is one thing, but what else can you tell me about Hervey's rationale for putting more dollars into consumer advertising?

BATES: He contends that we can increase our exposure and tell our story to the buying public—increase brand awareness, enhance our image, that sort of thing. He also cited data from *Home Furnishings* magazine which showed that the newly affluent baby boomers [consumers between the ages of 25 and 40] are almost three times more likely to buy dining room furniture and twice as likely to buy living room furniture than their elders in the next year. All I know is that my contribution margin will fall to 25 percent next year due to increased labor and material cost.

BERRY: I appreciate your concern. Give me a few days to think about the proposal. I'll get back to you soon.

After the parting remarks, Dr. Berry began to think through Charlton Bates's summary of the proposal, Shanandoah's present position, and the furniture industry in general. He knew that Bates expected a well-thought-out recommendation on such issues and a step-by-step description of the logic he used to arrive at his recommendation.

The Company

Shanandoah Industries is a manufacturer of medium- to high-priced living room and dining room wood furniture. The company was formed at the turn of the century by Bates's grandfather. Charlton Bates assumed the presidency of the company upon his father's retirement in 1982. Forecasted year-end gross sales in 1986 were $50 million; before-tax profit was $2.5 million.

Shanandoah sells its furniture through 1000 high-quality department stores and furniture specialty stores nationwide, but not all stores carry the company's entire line. The company is very selective in choosing retail outlets. According to Bates, "Our distribution policy, hence our retailers, should mirror the high quality of our products."

The company employs 10 full-time salespeople

*This case was prepared by Professor Roger A. Kerin of Southern Methodist University. Reproduced by permission.

and 2 regional sales managers. Sales personnel receive a base salary and a small commission on sales. A company sales force is atypical in the furniture industry since most furniture manufacturers use sales agents or representatives who carry a wide assortment of noncompeting furniture lines and receive a commission on sales. "Having our own sales group is a policy my father established 25 years ago," noted Bates, "and we've been quite successful having people who are committed to our company. Our people don't just take furniture orders; they are expected to motivate retail salespeople to sell our line, assist in setting up displays in stores, and give advice on a variety of matters to our retailers and their salespeople."

In 1985 Shanandoah allocated $2.45 million for total promotional expenditures for the 1986 operating year, excluding the salary of the vice president of sales. Promotion expenditures were categorized into four groups: (1) sales expense and administration; (2) cooperative advertising programs with retailers; (3) trade promotion; and (4) consumer advertising. The cooperative advertising budget is usually spent on newspaper advertising in a retailer's city. Cooperative advertising allowances are matched by funds provided by retailers on a dollar-for-dollar basis. Trade promotion is directed toward retailers and takes the form of catalogs, trade magazine advertisements, booklets for consumers, and point-of-view materials, such as displays, for use in retail stores. Also included in this category is the expense of trade showings. Shanandoah is represented at two showings per year. Consumer advertising is directed at potential consumers through shelter magazines. The typical format used in consumer advertising is to highlight new furniture and different living room and dining room arrangements. The dollar allocation for each of these programs in 1986 is shown in Exhibit 1.

Exhibit 1: Allocation of Promotion Dollars, 1986

Sales expense and administration	$ 612,500
Cooperative advertising allowance	1,102,500
Trade advertising	306,250
Consumer advertising	428,750
Total	$2,450,000

Source: Company records.

The Industry

The household wood furniture industry is composed of over 1400 firms. Industry sales at manufacturers' prices were $6.3 billion in 1985 and were forecasted to reach $7.1 billion in 1986. California, North Carolina, Virginia, New York, Tennessee, Pennsylvania, Illinois, and Indiana are the major furniture-producing areas in the United States. Major furniture manufacturers include Ethan Allen, Bassett, Henredon, and Kroehler. No one firm captured over 3 percent of the total household wood furniture market.

The buying and selling of furniture to retail outlets centers on manufacturers' expositions at selected times and places around the country. At these *marts*, as they are called in the furniture industry, retail buyers view manufacturers' lines and often make buying commitments for their stores. However, Shanandoah's experience has shown that sales efforts in the retail store by company representatives account for as much as one-half of the company's sales in any given year. The major manufacturer expositions occur in High Point, North Carolina, in October and April. Regional expositions are also scheduled during the June–August period in locations such as Dallas, Los Angeles, New York, and Boston.

Furniture-Buying Behavior

Results of a consumer survey conducted by the company provide information on furniture-buying behavior. Selected findings from the consumers survey are reproduced in Exhibit 2. Other findings from this research are as follows:

- Ninety-four percent of the respondents enjoy buying furniture somewhat or very much.

- Eighty-four percent of respondents believe that "the higher the price, the higher the quality" when buying home furnishings.

- Seventy-two percent of respondents browse or window-shop furniture stores even if they don't need furniture.

- Eight-five percent read furniture ads before they actually need furniture.

- Retail outlets used by respondents:
  Furniture specialty stores (32 percent)
  Furniture gallery stores (28 percent)
  Department stores (14 percent)

Exhibit 2: Selected Findings from the Consumer Survey[a]

Question: If you were going to buy furniture in the near future, how important would the following factors be in selecting the store to buy furniture? (Base 449)

Factor	Very Important	Somewhat Important	Not Too Important	Not at All Important	No Answer
Sells high-quality furnishings	62.6%	31.0%	3.8%	1.1%	1.5%
Has a wide range of different furniture styles	58.8	29.2	8.2	2.9	.9
Gives you personal service	60.1	29.9	7.8	.9	1.3
Is a highly dependable store	85.1	12.7	1.1	—	1.1
Offers decorating help from experienced home planners	26.5	35.9	25.4	10.9	1.3
Lets you "browse" all you want	77.1	17.8	3.3	.7	1.1
Sells merchandise that's a good value for the money	82.0	15.6	.9	.2	1.3
Displays furniture in individual room settings	36.3	41.2	18.7	2.4	1.3
Has a relaxed, no-pressure atmosphere	80.0	17.1	1.6	—	1.3
Has well-informed salespeople	77.5	19.8	1.6	—	1.1
Has a very friendly atmosphere	68.2	28.1	2.4	—	1.3
Carries the style of furniture you like	88.0	10.0	.9	—	1.1

Question: Please rank the following factors as to their importance to you when you purchase or shop for case-goods furniture, such as a dining room or living room suite, 1 being the most important factor, 2 being second most important, and so on, until all factors have been ranked. (Base 449)

	1	2	3	4	5	6	7	8	9	10	NA
Construction of item	24.1%	16.0%	18.5%	13.1%	10.5%	6.9%	4.9%	1.6%	.2%	1.1%	3.1%
Comfort	13.6	14.7	12.9	12.3	12.7	10.9	8.2	4.5	4.0	2.4	3.8
Styling and design	33.6	19.8	11.1	9.6	4.7	7.3	4.5	1.6	2.9	1.6	3.3
Durability of fabric	2.2	7.6	9.8	14.5	15.1	14.7	12.9	5.6	5.8	7.8	4.0
Type and quality of wood	10.9	17.8	16.3	15.8	14.7	5.8	5.3	3.1	4.9	2.0	3.4
Guarantee or warranty	1.6	3.8	1.6	5.3	8.7	10.0	13.8	25.2	14.5	11.1	4.4
Price	9.4	6.2	8.7	8.5	10.0	12.5	14.2	11.8	6.9	8.0	3.8
Reputation of the manufacturer or brand name	6.2	3.6	4.7	5.6	6.2	6.2	12.7	17.1	22.7	11.6	3.4
Reputation of retailer	1.6	1.8	1.6	2.4	4.0	7.3	7.4	13.6	22.0	34.5	3.8
Finish, color of wood	4.7	7.6	10.2	8.0	8.9	13.4	10.7	10.0	10.2	12.7	3.6

Question: Below is a list of 15 criteria that may influence what furniture you buy. They are ranked from 1 as most important to 5 as least important. (Base 449)

	1	2	3	4	5	No Answer
Guarantee or warranty	11.4%	11.1%	26.3%	16.9%	5.3%	29.0%
Brand name	9.1	6.5	14.3	25.6	11.6	32.9

Exhibit 2: (*continued*)

	1	2	3	4	5	No Answer
Comfort	34.7	27.8	14.5	8.5	4.7	9.8
Decorator suggestion	4.0	2.4	2.7	8.2	44.8	37.9
Material used	14.9	24.1	14.9	13.4	6.2	26.5
Delivery time	.7	.5	1.3	2.9	55.2	39.4
Size	7.6	10.7	13.6	30.9	4.0	33.2
Styling and design	33.4	17.8	21.8	13.6	2.2	11.2
Construction	34.3	23.6	13.1	11.4	2.9	14.7
Fabric	4.0	25.6	24.9	14.0	4.5	27.0
Durability	37.0	19.4	13.6	6.9	4.9	18.2
Finish on wooden parts	5.8	14.7	16.7	10.7	16.7	35.4
Price	19.4	21.8	16.0	10.9	15.4	16.5
Manufacturer's reputation	4.2	9.1	15.4	22.9	14.3	34.1
Retailer's reputation	2.2	4.7	10.5	21.2	26.5	34.9

Question: Listed below are some statements others have made about their homes and the furniture pieces they particularly like. Please indicate, for each statement, how much you agree or disagree with each one. (Base 449)

Statement	Agree Completely	Agree Somewhat	Neither Agree nor Disagree	Disagree Somewhat	Disagree Completely	NA
I wish there was some way to be really sure of getting good-quality in furniture	61.9%	24.7%	4.7%	4.2%	3.6%	.9%
I really enjoy shopping for furniture	49.2	28.3	7.6	9.8	4.2	.9
I would never buy any furniture without my husband's/wife's approval	47.0	23.0	10.9	9.8	7.1	2.2
I like all the pieces in the master bedroom to be exactly the same style	35.9	30.7	12.7	11.1	7.6	2.0
Once I find something I like in furniture, I wish it would last forever so I'd never have to buy again	36.8	24.3	10.0	18.9	9.1	.9
I wish I had more confidence in my ability to decorate my home attractively	23.1	32.3	12.5	11.6	18.7	1.8
I wish I knew more about furniture styles and what looks good	20.0	31.0	17.1	13.4	16.7	1.8

Exhibit 2: (*continued*)

Statement	Agree Completely	Agree Somewhat	Neither Agree nor Disagree	Disagree Somewhat	Disagree Completely	NA
My husband/wife doesn't take much interest in the furniture we buy	6.5	18.0	12.3	17.8	41.4	4.0
I like to collect a number of different styles in the dining room	3.3	10.5	15.2	29.8	38.3	2.9
Shopping for furniture is very distressing to me	2.4	11.6	14.3	18.0	51.9	1.8

Question: Listed below are some factors that may influence your choice of furnishings, 1 being most important, 2 being second most important, and so on until all factors have been ranked. (Base 449)

	1	2	3	4	5	No Answer
Friends and/or neighbors	1.3%	16.9%	15.8%	22.1%	41.7%	2.2%
Family or spouse	62.8	9.4	14.3	9.8	2.0	1.7
Magazine advertising	16.3	30.3	29.6	17.6	4.2	2.0
Television advertising	1.1	6.7	14.7	32.5	42.3	2.7
Store displays	18.9	37.2	22.1	14.0	5.6	2.2

Question: When you go shopping for a *major* piece of furniture or other smaller pieces of furniture, who, if anyone, do you usually go with? (Base 449—multiple response)

	Major Pieces	Other Pieces
Husband	82.4%	59.5%
Mother or mother-in-law	6.2	9.1
Friend	12.0	18.9
Decorator	4.2	1.6
Other relative	15.6	15.4
Other person	2.9	3.3
No one else	5.1	22.3
No answer	.9	3.1

Question: When the time comes to purchase a *major* item of furniture or other smaller pieces of furniture, who, if anyone, helps you make the final decision about which piece to buy? (Base 449—multiple response)

	Major Pieces	Other Pieces
Husband	86.0%	63.5%
Mother or mother-in-law	2.4	4.5
Friend	3.6	8.0
Decorator	3.1	2.7
Other relative	10.1	12.9
Other person	.1.6	1.8
No one else	7.1	24.3
No answer	.9	2.2

*Survey interviews were conducted using shopping center intercepts at five cities throughout the United States. A total of 449 responses were obtained in the survey.

Sears, Ward's, and Penney's (8 percent)
Discount furniture outlets (7 percent)

- Ninety-nine percent of respondents agree with the statement "When shopping for furniture and home furnishings, I like the salesperson to show me what alternatives are available, answer my questions, and let me alone so I can think about it and maybe browse around."

- Ninety-five percent of respondents say that they get redecorating ideas or guidance from magazines.

- Forty-one percent of respondents have written for a manufacturer's booklet.

- Sixty-three percent of respondents say that they need decorating advice for "putting it all together."

The Budget Meeting

At the August 8 meeting attended by Hervey and Bernham executives and Shanandoah executives, Michael Hervey proposed that Shanandoah's 1987 expenditure for consumer advertising be increased by $400,000. Cooperative advertising and trade advertising allowances would remain at 1986 levels. Hervey further indicated that shelter magazines would account for the bulk of the incremental expenditure for consumer advertising.

John Bott, Shanandoah's sales vice president, disagreed with the budget allocation and noted that sales expenses and administration costs were expected to rise $50,000 in 1987. Bott believed an additional sales representative was needed to service Shanandoah's accounts since 50 new accounts were being added. He estimated that the cost of the additional representative, including salary and expenses, would be at least $50,000 in 1987. "That's

about $100,000 for sales expenses that have to be added into our promotional budget for 1987," Bott noted. He continued:

> We expect sales of about $50 million in 1986 if our sales experience continues throughout the remainder of the year. Assuming a 13 percent increase in sales in 1987, that means that our total budget would be about $2,825,000, if my figures are right, or a $375,000 increase over our previous budget. And I need $100,000 of that. In other words, $275,000 is available for other kinds of promotion.

Hervey's reply to Bott noted that the company planned to introduce several new styles of living room and dining room furniture in 1987 and that these new items would require advertising to be launched successfully. He agreed with Bott that increased funding of the sales effort might be necessary and thought that Shanandoah might draw funds from the cooperative advertising allowance and trade promotion.

Bates interrupted the dialogue between Bott and Harvey to mention that the $400,000 increase in promotion exceeded the 5 percent percentage-of-sales policy by $25,000. He pointed out that materials cost plus a recent wage increase were forecast to squeeze Shanandoah's gross profit margin and threaten the company's objective of achieving a 5 percent net profit margin before taxes. "Perhaps some juggling of the figures is necessary," he concluded. "Both of you have good points. Let me think about what's been said and then let's schedule a meeting for a week from today."

As Bates reviewed his notes from the meeting, he realized that the funds allocated to promotion were only part of the question. How the funds would be allocated within the budget was also crucial. Perhaps a call to Tom Berry would be helpful in this regard, he thought.

C A S E

2-3 SALES MANAGEMENT SIMULATION*

The Sales Management Simulation (4th ed.) is a computer game in which you operate a sales force in competition with other firms in a search for fame and fortune. SMS allows you to select salespeople, set prices, and make other decisions during each round of game play. Your decisions are processed on a computer, and you will receive regular printouts showing the impact of your choices on sales, profits, and customer satisfaction.

The Selling Environment

The sales force is the primary focus in this simulation game. Thus, performance in the simulated environment depends on your skill in selecting high-quality salespersons and deploying them effectively over the various regions of the country. Although the product and advertising are the same for all teams, you may adjust your prices, sales force compensation levels, sales contests, and market research requests each period of play.

The Industry

Your team will act as the managers of the sales force of one of three to five companies making up the industry. All companies are independent divisions of large firms in the mushrooming office machine industry. The firms manufacture and sell two models of computer servers that are designed for a variety of industrial and consumer markets.

The Product

Many offices are buying network servers to improve communications efficiency. These machines are spe-

*This simulation was developed by Professor Emeritus Ralph Day and Professor Douglas J. Dalrymple of Indiana University and Professor Harish Sujan of Penn State University.

cial computers that allow networks of personal computers to communicate with each other. The basic model will handle networks with 20 machines and the advanced model will work with up to 50 machines.

Each of the companies in this simulation has announced an initial price of $3500 for its basic machine and $5500 for its advanced model. There will be no quantity or cash discounts. The purchase price from manufacturing divisions is initially $3150 for the basic unit and $4,500 for the premium model. This transfer price is based on full overhead and administrative expenses and a contribution by manufacturing to the corporate overhead and profit. The gross margins retained by the Sales Department must cover all compensation and expenses of the sales force, transportation costs, and inventory or expediting costs and generate a contribution from sales operations to corporate overhead and profit.

The Market

The market for your product is divided into 10 clearly defined geographic regions. Your plant and national headquarters are located in the Midwest. All shipments are made directly to the customer from the factory by motor freight to eliminate the need for regional warehouses. Industry practice calls for the seller to pay the freight, and in your company the Sales Department pays for shipping.

The servers you will sell are potentially useful in a variety of offices that are widely, but far from uniformly, dispersed throughout the country. You can expect that many firms will first experiment with one or two units before considering wider uses of the machines for their offices. Also, customers can choose from among a half-dozen server suppliers with similar products and prices. Therefore, server salespersons must have a good grasp of their product's features, have an understanding of office problems, be skilled in selling, and have the drive and persistence to handle the "tough-close" situations they are likely to encounter.

The Sales Force

As the simulation begins, a single field sales manager (FSM) is responsible for the supervision of all the company's active salespeople and conducts the on-the-job portion of the sales training program. When the sales force organization was approved by top management, the general sales manager (GSM) was allowed to hire a second FSM as soon as the number of field salespeople reached 10 and was required to hire the second FSM if the size of the sales force reached or exceeded 12 salespersons. GSMs' salaries are $64,000 per year ($16,000 per quarter), and travel expenses will be $10,000 per year ($2500 per quarter). The salary for FSMs is $48,000 per year ($12,000 per quarter), and expenses are $14,000 per year ($3,500 per quarter). The costs of maintaining the sales office, including the cost of the administrative assistant, a customer service coordinator, secretarial support, rent, telephone expense, postage, and office supplies, will be $200,000 per year ($50,000 per quarter).

To get into the market quickly, an initial sales force of ten salespersons will be hired and trained on an emergency basis. Highly qualified salespersons will be sought and given a brief but intensive training program prior to the beginning of the first quarter of sales operations. They will be provided unusually close support from the FSMs and technical people from the factory during the first quarter. All salespeople beyond the initial ten will be required to complete a three-month training program consisting of two months of training in the headquarters and factory and one month in the field. Training programs will start at the beginning of a quarter so that graduates can be assigned to a territory at the beginning of the following quarter.

Up to five salespersons can be either hired for training or retrained in each quarter. This means up to five trainees may be hired at the same time as the initial ten salespersons. The student manual for the game contains 55 application forms from those applicants who passed an initial screening by the corporate personnel manager. A number of applicants who lacked the basic communications skills required for selling and/or lacked the background education needed to acquire the skills used in selling servers were rejected by the personnel manager. The personnel manager's evaluation after each interview is provided for each application. Applicants in the first group of 20 who are passed over are generally *not* available for the following quarter. Instead, a new group of five applicants (for up to five positions) will be made available each quarter.

All salespersons are paid an initial base salary of $28,000 per year ($7000 per quarter). While in the training program, this is the total compensation. Once in the field, the salesperson receives an additional commission of 2 percent of the sale price. Therefore, a salesperson who averaged 45 basic units per quarter would earn $12,600 in commissions (45 × 4 × $3500 × .02 = $12,600) plus base salary for a total of $40,600 per year. The earnings of salespersons and their contributions to the firm's overhead and profit are influenced by factors other than the individual salesperson's ability and effort.

The average travel expense for field salespersons is $12,000 per year ($3000 per quarter). New salespeople in the training program have travel expenses only in the third month of the quarter, and this averages $1000. If any of the ten original salespersons appear to be performing poorly and you think it might be the result of inadequate training, you can bring them to headquarters for retraining. Established salespersons receive their customary expense allowance while in the training program. If an analysis of sales results and other information suggests that a salesperson might be more effective in a different region, a salesperson may be transferred at the end of any quarter. Company policy recommends paying a moving allowance of $5000 whenever a salesperson is transferred. There is some risk that a salesperson might quit instead of accepting a transfer. Salespersons may quit for other reasons, especially if a sharp drop in commissions should occur. Salespersons can be fired at the end of any quarter. Your company pays a $3000 severance allowance in lieu of notice of termination.

Summary

The setting for this simulation is an office equipment industry consisting of three to five firms that make similar products and are on an equal footing at the beginning of the game. Although advertising is the same for all firms, each company can change selling prices, sales force compensation levels, and the amount spent on sales contests during each period of play. The main basis of competition will be the field-selling activities of the firms. Each team may hire an initial sales force of up to ten persons and will assign them among 10 geographical regions according to estimates of potential and assumptions about the strategy of competitors. Additional salespersons can be hired as the game proceeds, and established salespersons can be reassigned or retrained. Performance as reflected by share of the market will depend on the team's skill in selecting and assigning its salespersons. Performance as reflected by cumulative net profit will depend on the team's ability to control costs, as well as its ability to obtain sales. Additional information on the operation of the game is available in the student manual.

Copies of the Sales Management Simulation Participant's Manual (4th ed.) and the SMS Instructor's Manual with the game diskette (version 8.3) can be obtained from

John Wiley & Sons
605 Third Avenue
New York, NY 10158

Telephone inquiries concerning the SMS should be made to

Ellen Ford, Editor
John Wiley & Sons
605 Third Avenue
New York, NY 10158
(212) 850-6054

▶ 3 ◀

Personal Selling*

People are more apt to buy when they're talking than when you're talking!
RON WILLINGHAM

*Chapter Consultants: Neil Cronin, Regional Sales Manager, John Wiley & Sons, Inc., and William Evans, President, Evans & Associates.

LEARNING OBJECTIVES

After studying this chapter, you should be able to:

▶ Describe the basic types of selling approaches.

▶ Describe the skills utilized in the selling process.

▶ Understand the opportunities for total quality management in selling.

▶ Discuss the reasons for sales force automation.

▶ **AN ELECTRONIC SOS**

Exxon Chemical Co. wanted a software-development tool that would help it blend off-the-shelf software packages with the oil giant's custom business applications. Project manager Ed Baugh, head of the sales team for CAP Gemini Sogeti, a French computer-services giant, was aware that his customer had for five months combed the market without finding a solution to their problem. Baugh's sales team had also determined that building the tool from scratch would take at least 18 months, too long for Exxon's needs.

Hoping CAP Gemini's 17,000 software engineers and technicians might have a lead, Baugh sent out an electronic SOS across the company intranet. Forty-eight hours later, an engineer with CAP Gemini's British unit responded that he knew of a software tool that might be tailored to meet Exxon's needs. Within three weeks, Baugh presented a solution to Exxon and clinched a hefty development contract.[1]

The CAP Gemini sale described above is indicative of how sales is changing today. A sales team is frequently involved rather than a single salesperson. Sales force automation is often critical to successfully compete. Addressing a critical customer solution often requires marshaling diverse resources within the selling company. Sales managers are taking on a greater selling role than in the past as companies downsize and industry consolidation results in larger individual customers.

Before we talk further about sales management, it is vital that you have a general understanding of personal selling. Sales managers are usually promoted from field sales, and they are expected to be well versed in the art of personal selling. In addition, sales managers need selling skills in order to train, coach, and evaluate field sales personnel, and earn their respect.

This chapter is designed to provide you with a basic understanding of the selling process. To facilitate discussion and help you organize the skills involved, the selling process is divided into three phases:

- **Preinteraction.** Actions that are initiated prior to interaction with key decision makers requiring skills in precall planning.
- **Interaction.** Actions initiated while interacting with decision makers, calling on skills in relating, discovery, advocating, handling objections, and closing.
- **Postinteraction.** Activities following a transaction involving supporting skills.

These three phases and the skills associated with each phase are specified in Figure 3-1.

It is important to note that these steps are ordered in a logical sequence for discussion purposes. The actual process may backtrack to earlier phases many times before concluding in a sale. These phases are highly interrelated, and it may be difficult to specify the exact step at a specific point in a sale. Finally, it should be recognized that the process is not necessarily completed in a single sales call.

As we discuss each skill, we will point out its purpose or objective, as well as strategies for achieving these objectives. In many cases, common mistakes to be avoided are also highlighted. Throughout the discussion, company practices and viewpoints of sales executives have been included to facilitate your learning. After

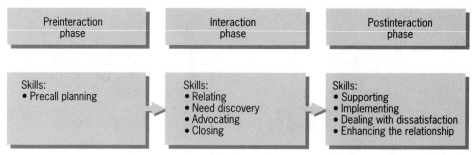

Figure 3-1: Phases and Steps of the Selling Process

you have achieved a basic understanding of the selling process, sales force automation is discussed. First, different basic types of selling approaches are discussed.

▶ BASIC TYPES OF SELLING APPROACHES

Sales consultants have devised numerous titles or labels for the selling approaches they teach, but most are based on one of the following basic selling process models—stimulus-response, need-satisfaction, and problem-solution. Each approach is appropriate in certain situations. Accompanying a description of these sales approaches is an analysis of situations in which each is most efficient and effective.

Stimulus-Response

With a *stimulus-response presentation*, a series of statements are constructed about an offering, so as to stimulate a positive response by the customer. This is often referred to as *benefitizing* an offering. Benefitizing means translating features of a product into benefits believed to be of value to the customer. A benefit of a new software package, for example, may be the ease with which it can be learned by employees. At an extreme, specific statements are developed using phrases that tend to elicit a positive response. These may include words such as *user-friendly, satisfaction guaranteed, productivity improvement*, and *no money down*. The ease-of-learning benefit may be stated as "Clear, easy-to-follow, step-by-step instructions containing no confusing buzzwords." This is referred to as a *canned presentation* because the same basic presentation is given to each customer.

The stimulus-response approach is most appropriate in situations where a product is standardized or when the benefits are generally the same for all customers. In such a situation, the sales pitch can be studied and refined to such a degree that even voice tone can be studied for its impact on sales.[2] Since standardized sales presentations are easiest to learn, they are also used where the sales force is relatively inexperienced and employee turnover is high. Such is the case with many direct marketing organizations such as Mary Kay Cosmetics, Cutco, and Avon Products. This also helps to ensure uniform, high-quality presentations. This selling approach is particularly dangerous, however, when listening to customers is necessary to enhance the relationship.

Need-Satisfaction

A *need-satisfaction presentation* is oriented to discovering and meeting customers' needs. Needs discovery is achieved by skillfully asking questions that will elicit a customer's buying needs. This type of selling requires more selling skill because unless it is tactfully handled, customers may become irritated by the questions or find them intrusive. Needs discovery takes place early in the selling cycle, often during the first call, and replaces the presentation as the most important step in the selling process.

A needs-satisfaction selling model is most appropriate when two conditions exist: when the *dollar value of the sale is significant enough* to cover the added time required by the selling process and when *different benefits need to be emphasized* for different customers. An office manager of a law firm, for example, is likely to look for different reproduction qualities in a laser-jet printer than would an administrator of a school district. In both cases, a salesperson would need to investigate the nature of the documents to be produced, along with the capabilities of their present printers. The sales force must be trained to ask the right questions to uncover customer needs that will lead to a purchase decision. The general line sales forces of most consumer goods and office products companies are trained to use this selling model. The key is to develop good listening skills, as opposed to concentrating on how to respond to what the customer is saying.

Problem-Solution

A *problem-solution presentation* is similar to the need-satisfaction method in that both involve an analysis of each customer's circumstances. The primary difference is that a problem-solution selling process is based on more formal studies of the customer's operations. Instead of identifying the customer's needs on the first sales call, the early selling objective is to get the customer's permission to conduct a formal study. The sales rep or sales team will conduct the study and submit a written proposal based on the study. A formal presentation, perhaps by a team including a salesperson, management, and technical personnel, often accompanies the proposal.

This selling model usually involves a very significant dollar expenditure, and the selling cycle may be quite long. The types of products being sold by this selling approach include computer systems, advertising campaigns, telecommunications systems, and information systems. The problem analysis study may be so involved that the customer may be asked to pay to have it performed. EDS's customers for instance, may be asked to pay several hundred thousand dollars for a study of their computer systems to determine if EDS can help them. It is not unusual for clients to pay several advertising agencies to research and prepare a proposed ad campaign before deciding which agency will be awarded the account.

Which is the best selling approach? There is no unequivocal answer to this question. The most appropriate approach will depend, among other factors, on the offering, the professionalism of the sales force, the dollar value of the transaction, and the type of customer involved. With small chains or individual grocery stores, for example,

Procter & Gamble may use a needs-satisfaction selling style, but with major accounts such as Wal-Mart, a problem-solution approach may be most appropriate.

In the next part of this chapter, the skills associated with each phase of the selling process are presented. Most of the discussion is based on the *Counselor* selling method developed by Wilson Learning.

▶ PREINTERACTION PHASE: PRECALL PLANNING SKILLS

As the term *precall planning* implies, this stage occurs when you collect your thoughts and organize your sales strategy prior to meeting the buyer face to face. A recommended approach to precall planning is to ask yourself a series of questions.

What Do I Want to Accomplish?

Many selling experts have stated simply that salespeople should not make a call unless they can specify an *action* that they want the client or prospect to take. Don't set an objective like "to collect information" or "to build a good relationship." Here are some examples of good objectives:

- The client agrees to supply information on historical inventory levels.
- The client tells you who will be involved in the purchase decision.
- The client arranges for a meeting with the chief design engineer.
- The client agrees to a trial run on the system.

Note that each of these examples calls for the customer to take a specific action. The reason objectives should be stated in terms of actions is that the salesperson will know whether the objectives have been met. Also, note that the first two objectives involve gathering information.

In more complex selling situations involving multiple calls over a period of time, an action may be more subtle. For example, it may take several calls to fully educate a buyer on the benefits of the product. Alternatively, you may be calling to ensure that the customer is satisfied after the sale or to handle a specific customer complaint.

What Do I Know About the Prospect?

Precall planning is also a good opportunity to review relevant information about buyers and their company. Information that may be useful to know about an individual includes exact spelling and pronunciation of the name, title, age, residence, education, buying authority, clubs and memberships, hobbies, and idiosyncracies. A medical equipment salesperson, for example, was finding it very difficult to get doctors at the hospital to give him time to make a presentation. The doctors were usually under extreme time pressure while at the hospital and were concerned about their immediate patients. He found out that many of the doctors belonged to a health club near the hospital and that in this environment the doctors were more relaxed and

What is the size of their business?

Who are the prominant executives and other key personnel?

Who are their competitors and on what basis do they compete?

What product lines do they sell and what markets do they serve?

Do they have any previous experience with our company?

Where, how, when, why, and by whom will the products be used?

What are the prospects for future sales volume and what is the upside potential?

Figure 3-2: Some Important Pretransactional Information

willing to listen to his sales pitch. He eventually became the top salesperson in his district—and an accomplished racquetball player.

You should also review what you know or do not know about the buyer's organization. Figure 3-2 gives a list of some of the questions that a salesperson should be able to answer about a customer. This information is often critical when planning a presentation and when demonstrating competency, trust, and commitment to the buyer.

Where Can I Find the Information?

When you know what information you need to make a successful sales call, you can usually identify a number of sources for obtaining the data. These sources include company records, salespeople, customer employees, published information, and observation. Observation of the prospect's business operations provides a wealth of information to the experienced salesperson. By observing a prospect's retail operations, for instance, a veteran consumer goods salesperson can tell a lot about a buyer's pricing strategy, merchandising strategy, vendor preferences, and deal proneness.

The World Wide Web is an emerging and powerful source of information ranging from customer information to competitive information to industry information. For instance, you can find out information about industry trade associations and a list of companies in different industries at www.mfginfo.com. Several other locations on the Web are excellent for identifying and locating prospects (e.g., www.switchboard.com). More on sales force automation is presented at the end of this chapter.

What Am I Going to Say?

All salespeople should have at least a general idea of how they will initially start the sales presentation, what questions they will ask, and what benefits they plan to present. Salespeople should anticipate concerns a customer is likely to raise and prepare strategies for addressing these concerns. This is where prior experience in making cold calls is particularly helpful.

A useful process when preparing to call on clients is to put yourself in their position. What would you want to know about your company and its products if you were the buyer? If you are prepared to address these questions, then you are probably ready for the call and have a much better chance of success. Figure 3-3 shows some of the questions about you and your company that a client is likely to have when there is no prior experience on which to rely. Note that while these questions may be in the client's mind, they are often not asked. However, these questions may prevent a sale if left unanswered.

One other suggestion that has proven to be useful in a variety of situations is to visualize a successful sales encounter. This technique simply means creating a mental picture of the sequence of events that will lead to accomplishing your call objective. With practice, this exercise should help you to reduce your anxieties and increase your confidence.

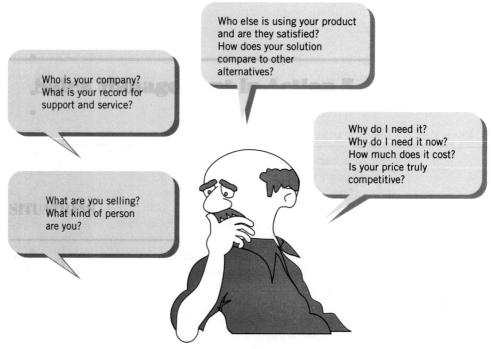

Figure 3-3: A Buyer's Questions

▶ THE INTERACTION PHASE

The *interaction phase* generally refers to what takes place when face-to-face with a customer. Our discussion of this phase of the selling process focuses on three skills that are important in all business and social interactions: relating, discovering, and advocating. In addition, there are two skills that are critical to successful selling: gaining access to key personnel and closing the sale. We start with gaining access.

Gaining Access

Usually, appointments are fairly easy to get with established customers, but this can be more difficult when prospecting, especially with the senior officers of a company. Following are three commonly used alternatives for gaining access to decision makers.

Direct Personal Contact   The most difficult approach occurs when the call is the first meeting and there have been no prior attempts to communicate with the prospect. In making a personal visit, the salesperson has the opportunity to look over the facilities of the prospect and to become better prepared to talk with the buyer.

However, problems are likely to occur. The person may be busy, and the salesperson must wait. The key is not to waste the time. Use this time to learn more about the prospect from other people in the organization, prepare for other scheduled calls, or complete necessary reports. A more difficult problem is the negative reaction of buyers to people calling on them without an appointment. Many purchasing agents do not like meeting with a salesperson who simply "walks in without an appointment."

Phoning Ahead   Using the telephone to approach prospects has a number of advantages. Appointments make better use of the salesperson's time and reduce the hours spent in waiting rooms. Even prospects who are too busy to see anyone often will answer the phone and give salespeople a chance to introduce themselves and set up a future meeting.

The major problem with a phone approach is that it is too easy for prospects or their secretaries to turn someone down over the telephone. Salespeople, therefore, must develop tactics to secure the cooperation of switchboard operators and receptionists. Referring to buyers by their first name, for example, implies familiarity with the buyer.

Personal Letters   The first approach to a prospect may be made by means of a personal letter. Letters are more difficult than phone calls for the secretary to screen. In addition, letters allow the person to include brochures that describe the product assortment and benefits, enabling prospects to learn more about a potential supplier than they can over the phone. Letters can also invite the prospect to special showings of the product or describe gifts offered to those who make appointments. Approach letters should close by suggesting dates for a meeting. This may also be accomplished by a follow-up phone call. In doing so, the salesperson focuses the prospect's attention on the issue of *when* to meet rather than *whether* to meet. The use of a hand-delivered personal letter is described in Sales Management in Action 3-1.

Sales Management in Action 3-1
Are You a Salesperson?

Early in his career, W. Patrick Hughes sold tax shelters for the Boston firm of Cheverie and Co. Since the product required a minimum investment of $50,000, he decided that CEOs would be good prospects. "I was so new I didn't know how things should be done," Hughes says, "so I didn't get caught up in the write-a-letter-make-a-call routine." Instead, he made cold calls on corporate headquarters in his Connecticut territory. "I have a letter of introduction for Mr. Smith," he'd tell the receptionist, handing her an envelope containing a handwritten letter on linen stationery. Hughes did his best not to look like a salesperson. He never carried a sample case or a sales kit. Recalling the psychology of the technique, Hughes believes that it depended on his ability to differentiate himself in the mind of the secretary. Therefore he made it a point not to sit with other vendors while awaiting her arrival in the reception area. When the secretary arrived, he would hand her the letter saying that he'd be happy to call or phone at Mr. Smith's convenience. "She found out I was a real person," he says, "and that neutralized the primary line of defense." He nearly always got in to see the CEO, even though the letter said nothing more than the usual sales letter. "I think I succeeded because the CEOs were curious," says Hughes. "They'd never seen anyone use this approach before."

Source: Martin Everett, "Selling to the CEO," *Sales & Marketing Magazine* (November 1988), p. 61.

Relating Skills

In most social situations, there is a level of tension or defensiveness on the part of people meeting for the first time. This defensiveness, refered to as *relationship anxiety*, is especially likely to occur when meeting a salesperson.[3] This anxiety arises because people don't like to be sold, they like to buy. In one sense, the role of the salesperson is help the customer buy wisely. This calls for well-developed *relating skills*, which refers to the ability to put the other person at ease in a potentially tense situation. The first few moments of the selling encounter are important because people formulate initial impressions at this time. One study found that buyers formulate impressions about salespeople's competence, trustworthiness, and likability based on nonverbal visual cues.[4] To help establish rapport, salespeople should first hand a business card to the prospect and introduce themselves. The prospect then can both see and hear the salesperson's name. A sample introduction might go as follows:

"Hello, Mr. Smith, I am Mary Johnson of the Hamilton Company, and I am here today to see if we can help you save money on your duplicating budget."

Ms. Johnson tells who she is, the purpose of the visit, and that she plans to focus on a possible customer benefit (lower costs). Many salespeople prefer using this type of opening. It is simple, direct, and informative.

Usually the prospect responds by asking the salesperson to sit down and continue the discussion. It is important to realize that in these first few seconds of an interview the prospect is making a number of crucial judgments about the salesperson and the company he or she represents. Salespeople's habits and appearance are often used to evaluate a company. Dress must be appropriate for the occasion. Common mistakes committed by many salespeople are described in Sales Management in Action 3-2.

Although nonbusiness topics are often discussed initially in the selling process, one field study comparing effective and ineffective sales presentations observed that very little nonbusiness discussion occurred during successful sales calls with established customers. Buyers were interested in what the salesperson had to say because they felt that the salesperson could help them in their business. They also respected the salesperson's time demands. Ineffective salespeople spent more time discussing nonbusiness issues and relating as friends rather than providing solutions to business problems.[5] The message is clear: Don't overdo the nonbusiness pleasantries before getting down to business. If the customer gives signals that he or she is pressed for

Sales Management in Action 3-2
You're Not Prepared! You Don't Listen! You Promised!

An Executive Advisory Panel was asked to describe the most typical gaffes they have seen salespeople commit. Following are some excerpts from their responses: "The first rule of selling is to know how your product or service impacts or adds value to your client," stated Jeri Sessler of A.T. Kearney in Illinois. "If you don't know anything about your client and have no conception of how your offering can be employed by him or her, you have no right to be there." "There are times when salespeople just won't let their clients talk," noted Gary Slavin, president of Multimedia Marketing, Inc. "The salesperson thinks it's more important for him or her to be heard. They don't realize how important listening is in determining the needs of their customer. Consequently, they wind up talking themselves out of a sale." "I've seen many salespeople who overpromise the delivery of their product and simply don't follow up enough," said Maria DiNuzzo of John H. Harland Company in New York. "To avoid this, I suggest they develop a contact sheet of all their accounts in order to make sure they call each one periodically and see them as often as possible."

Source: Kerry Rottenberger-Murtha, "What Common Mistakes Do Your Salespeople Make?" *Sales and Marketing Management* (May 1993), pp. 28–29.

Propriety	Acting and dressing appropriately for the situation and showing the buyer due respect. *Example*: Waiting to be asked to be seated or handing the buyer a business card.
Competence	Demonstrating competence at your job. *Example*: Give references from third parties who are pleased with you and your company.
Commonality	Showing the buyer that you hold similar interests and views in at least some areas. *Example*: Common acquaintances or outside interests.
Intent	Revealing to the buyer the purpose of the call, as well as the process to be used and the payoff to the buyer. *Example*: "I'm not just here to sell you a package. I would like to examine your current package. You may be able to save money."

Figure 3-4: Means of Reducing Relationship Anxiety

time, then get on with the call. The key is being flexible and focusing on the other person.

Much more is involved in demonstrating relating skills than simply getting a dialogue started between you and the buyer. Figure 3-4 discusses four strategies by which salespeople can reduce relationship tension. It is critical that a salesperson utilize each of these means to reduce tension quickly when meeting with a prospect. With established customers a relationship already exists; thus many of the rules of the relationship are already set. However, salespeople should constantly make an effort to reinforce these impressions.

▶ NEEDS DISCOVERY SKILLS

After establishing initial rapport with the prospect, the salesperson should begin a customer *needs discovery*. Remember, customers do not buy products or services; they buy a set of benefits that solve problems or enhance opportunities. Contractors do not want a bulldozer; they want dirt moved quickly and at low cost. Plant managers do not buy computer-controlled milling machines; they are interested in reduced setup time, closer tolerances, and fewer defects. Thus the job of the salesperson is to discover the true needs and then inform the prospect about the characteristics, capabilities, and availability of goods and services that can address these needs.

Research has shown that there is a direct relationship between the number of needs a salesperson uncovers and selling success. A study by Xerox of over 500 sales calls revealed that successful sales calls contained three times more identified needs than failed calls.[6]

What you perceive as being a good relationship and a distinct set of customer needs is not enough to make the sale. The buyer must also perceive the same needs.[7] To recommend a solution to a need that the buyer does not perceive or does not rank high in importance will fall on deaf ears. In fact, this recommendation will probably hinder further progress toward a sale because buyers may conclude that you do not really understand their situation. Therefore, needs discovery is much more than just matching your products or services to needs you perceive the buyer has. Needs discovery is about understanding the buyer's perceptions of his or her needs. In the new model of personal selling in today's business environment, 80 *percent of the selling process focuses on discovering and matching customer needs.*[8]

Identifying Motives

In selling to other businesses, the situation is complicated because both task and personal motives influence the purchasing decision. *Task motives* can be defined as the logical, practical, or functional reasons for buying. They usually involve either money or productivity. Typical money motives may include cost savings or profit increases. Productivity motives may involve increasing output, increasing quality, or reducing effort. Organizations tend to emphasize different task issues in their culture, so it is important for salespeople to understand these tendencies.[9]

At the same time, people will have personal motives for purchasng a product or service. Personal motives are the individual preferences that spur a person to buy. They are generally psychological in nature and involve relationships with other people. *Personal motives* include the need for respect, approval, power, and recognition. The *respect*-oriented buyer wants to demonstrate and prove his or her expertise. These buyers are interested in research that not only supports your product or service, but also reinforces the work they have already done. Buyers focusing on *approval* want to be sure that others affected by the decision to buy will be pleased. They are responsive to products or services that reduce conflict and provide minimum risk. Buyers interested in *power* are looking for ways to gain greater control over some real, practical aspect of their situation. Products or services that will give them the ability to make quicker decisions, choose from among more options, or get desired results in a better way will be most appealing. For some buyers, the desire for *recognition* is the dominant personal motive. They are interested in products or services that give them greater visibility and provide opportunities to demonstrate their leadership ability. These people are often unique or innovative in their approach to problem solving. While respect and approval motives are somewhat timid and defensive, power and recognition are fairly aggressive in nature.

Personal motives for buying are very powerful, especially for the purchase of small-dollar items. It is important for a salesperson to identify these motives for each person involved in the buying process. Discovery of personal motives is challenging because they are rarely stated by the buyer. In many cases, buyers may be reluctant to share their personal agendas because of their political sensitivity in the organization. More likely, they have not engaged in the self-analysis required to be aware of these underlying personal motives. Nevertheless, you must infer these motives from the actions and statements of the buyer.

Questioning

Discovering a customer's perceived needs naturally involves asking *questions* and actively *listening* to the customer's responses. Asking questions is not as easy as it may first appear. Not only do you want to know perceived needs, but you want to gain the information in a way that does not irritate or alienate buyers and helps them to better understand their own needs.

Questions may be classified as closed-ended or open-ended. *Closed-ended questions* can be answered with a simple "yes" or "no" or by selecting from a list of responses. "Would you like delivery Friday, or is Monday of next week all right?" These questions are easy to answer, and are used to gain buyer feedback and commitment. *Open-ended questions* cannot be answered with a simple "yes" or "no" and are used to identify a topic. "How are the new tax laws affecting your decision regarding the purchase of fleet cars for your salespeople?"

Sales experts have identified several types of questions that may be used in the discovery process.

- **Permission.**   This closed-ended questioning technique involves asking the buyer for permission to ask questions or to probe further into a subject. It is designed to put the buyer at ease and observe social courtesies. "May I ask you a few questions about your current shipping process?"

- **Fact finding.**   These are questions that focus on factual information about the business, the person, and the current situation. Factual information might include a question such as: "Who is your current supplier of sutures?" A follow-on question about the buyer's current situation might be: "Do you have a JIT arrangement with Ethicon in supplying sutures?"

- **Feeling finding.**   These are open-ended questions that try to uncover the feelings of the buyer toward a situation and the potential consequences of the situation. These inquiries help to determine the buyer's perceptions and the importance of the need. "How do you feel about your current inventory levels in sutures?" "What affect does this level of inventory have on your operating costs?"

- **Checking.**   At this point, the seller is checking to see if he or she understands exactly what the buyer has said and to get agreement from the buyer concerning the statement. "If I understand you correctly, you have said that you are happy with the quality of your current supplier but feel that you may be able to get the same quality of service at a lower price from another supplier. Is that accurate?" This type of question may result in an open or closed type of answer.

Discovering a customer's needs usually requires a series of questions. This process usually begins with a *permission question* and *open-ended questions*, followed by *fact-finding* and *feeling-finding questions* and *checking questions*. Effective salespeople are also good listeners. This means that they are actively involved in listening to the buyer (e.g., by nodding the head in agreement, smiling, taking notes). However, before arriving at a response, salespeople should not focus on their own response to the buyer's statement, but rather on hearing all that the buyer has to say.

Companies that uncover customers' real needs are in a better position to fill them. Consider again the Exxon sale discussed at the beginning of the chapter. The CAP Gemini Sogeti sales team not only needed to know that Exxon was actively seeking a software integration solution, but that the solution was needed immediately.

Team Selling

With today's more complex problems and solutions, the execution of the discovery process is also changing. Now a team of people may be involved in the process of discovering and providing solutions to customer needs. At Allegiance, Inc. (formerly the Baxter Healthcare Division of Baxter, Inc.) a person called a sales generalist may be responsible for discovering customer problems and needs. Due to the breadth and technical complexity of product lines Allegiance sells the sales generalist can call on a person called a surgical generalist, an I.V. systems generalist, a distribution generalist, and a variety of product specialists to uncover and address customer needs. In other words, Allegiance is organized to discover and meet different levels of customer needs.

Advocating

Following the discovery of customer needs, the skill that takes on critical significance is advocating. A*dvocating skills* refer to the ability to clearly and fully present a solution that customers can see helps to address their needs. In this section, two aspects of advocating are considered: (1) presenting a specific solution to a problem and (2) addressing customer concerns regarding the solution being proposed.

Solution Presentation   The objective of the presentation is to convince the customer that the goods and services that are offered match the customer's requirements and satisfy his or her needs. It is very important to understand, however, that the purpose of the sales presentation isn't just for your prospects to understand what you are selling. The purpose is for them to visualize the end-result benefits—how your product or service will satisfy their task and personal needs.[10]

A sales presentation is primarily a discussion of a series of product features connected with benefits that the buyer has indicated are important during the previous needs discovery stage and is followed by evidence that the benefits will in fact be delivered. *Features* are tangible or intangible characteristics of the product or service. For example, a feature of a long-distance telephone service may be that billings are based on one-tenth of a minute rather than the usual full-minute increments. This feature may be emphasized because the task motive of this buyer is judged to be cost savings. A benefit is a statement about how a product or service can be or can help a customer. Therefore, the salesperson may state the benefit of the previous billing feature in the following terms:

> "What this means is that on a call of 2 minutes and 6 seconds, you will be billed for only 2.1 minutes. Other companies would bill you for 3 minutes. This will provide you with a significant cost savings on your monthly telephone bill."

Sales Management in Action 3-3
"The Stuff Is No Good"

Salespeople must always be careful not to exaggerate the benefits of their products because the courts may find that these claims constitute warranties for their products. But is it legal to make disparaging remarks, such as the above statement, to a client or prospect? In *Testing Systems v. Magnaflux* (1966) the salesperson selling Spotcheck, a chemical used to test commercial and industrial materials, made this statement about a competitor's product, named Flaw Finder. The court found that general statements of product superior-

ity, even when made in the form of exaggerated, unfavorable statements about a competitor's product, are permissible. In this same case, however, the salesperson also claimed that Flaw Finder was only about 40 percent as effective as Spotcheck. The court found this to be an "assertion of fact" and therefore actionable.

Source: Karl Boedecker, Fred Morgan, and Jeffrey Stoltman, "Legal Dimensions of Salespersons' Statements: A Review and Managerial Suggestions," *Journal of Marketing*, 55 (January 1991), pp. 70–80.

Notice that the feature (one-tenth-of-a-minute billings) is connected directly with a specific *benefit* (billed for 2.1 versus 3 minutes). Also, notice that while the feature is product or service centered, the benefit focuses on the buyer and is related to a motive (cost savings). The benefit is being sold, not the feature. There is also research to suggest that benefit statements are most powerful when connected to an explicit need expressed by the customer.

Finally, some *evidence* should be offered to support the idea that one-tenth-of-a-minute billing is a significant savings. Evidence may include presenting the product or a model of the product, showing test results, testimonials from satisfied customers, or trial periods. In the long-distance telephone service example, the salesperson may use testimonials from satisfied customers, as well as actual savings from other installations or test results to show savings. With any presentation, salespeople have to be careful in what they say about competitive products; see Sales Management in Action 3-3.

Perhaps the most widely used means of providing evidence to prove problem-solving claims is the use of *demonstrations*. Demonstrations encourage participation and often allow the buyer to experience the product benefits firsthand. Communication is improved by involving more of the buyer's senses than just hearing. A good demonstration should impress, even startle, a buyer so that interaction is stimulated. T*he objective is to get the prospect to ask questions and to become more involved in the selling process.* Demonstrations shift the focus from selling to showing how the buyer's needs will be fulfilled.

Demonstrations become more of a problem when selling heavy equipment. Heavy machinery salespeople, for instance, may encourage prospects to observe the

---

Selling Technology 3-1
A Virtual Reality Demonstration

Technology is making better and more effective office demonstrations possible. AMSCO International, Inc. has equipped its two dozen salespeople in the company's decontamination and surgical equipment with virtual reality software for their laptop computers. This software allows reps to instantly tailor presentations to customers' needs. If a customer doesn't quite grasp something about a machine, then the rep can have the customer see the aspect of a machine they have questions about. The customer sees the product in three dimensions, just as if it were truly in front of them. At a recent trade show, AMSCO took this idea one step further by including a virtual reality demo with head gear that allowed attendees to actually walk though the machines. It was a big hit at the show.

Source: Andy Cohen, "Introducing the Virtual Sales Call," *Sales & Marketing Management* (May 1996), p. 44.

---

equipment in action at a construction site, factory, or office. As a less expensive alternative, demonstrations are often made in the prospect's office through the use of visual aids. Audiovisual equipment is used primarily because it improves retention and recall of sales messages. Since people receive over 80 percent of their knowledge from their sense of sight, salespeople who use visual reinforcement as they talk are in a better position to communicate products' benefits to prospects. Selling Technology 3-1 discusses how one firm is taking office demonstrations a step further.

Written Sales Proposals In today's competitive world, most prospects want to "see it in writing." There is simply too much at stake to make a poor decision. This is especially true of *complex sales*. Complex sales meet one or more of the following criteria:

- The offering provides a sophisticated or innovative business solution.
- The offering's benefits are not readily apparent.
- Buying approval involves more than one person.
- The offering addresses a complicated business problem.
- Team selling is involved.

Although proposals may be organized in various ways, a proposal should convey the following five quality dimensions:

- **Reliability:** identifies solutions and strategies to achieve the prospect's needs and wants.
- **Assurance:** builds trust and confidence in your ability to deliver, implement, and produce benefits.

- **Tangibles:** enhances and supports your message and invites readership.
- **Empathy:** confirms your understanding of the prospect's business and needs.
- **Responsiveness:** develops proposal in a timely manner.[11]

Formal sales proposals have the advantage that everything is in writing and there is less chance of misunderstanding. Written proposals also improve communication when purchase decisions are made at buying or executive committee meetings that are off-limits to salespeople. Sales proposals have a durability that allows them to be read and evaluated over a period of time. However, written sales proposals take a lot of time and money to prepare, and for many selling situations they may not be cost effective.

Addressing Customer Concerns Customer concerns about a proposed solution to a problem are likely to arise in any sales presentation. In traditional sales training, these concerns were often refered to as "objections." David Mercer, in his book *High Level Selling*, expresses well our reasons for preferring the term "concern" rather than "objections" when he says:

> Even using the term "objections," I believe, puts a sales professional in the wrong frame of mind. It immediately relegates the whole sales call to an adversarial game of verbal tennis, instead of concentrating on helping the prospect. I believe that he should be on the same side of the net as the prospect; this automatically makes verbal tennis impossible.[12]

Ideally, a customer's most fundamental concerns should have been uncovered in the discovery phase before recommending a solution. Since customers are not likely to be aware of all their concerns until faced with making a decision, customer concerns are probably best thought of as a natural part of any sales presentation and should be viewed by the salesperson as an opportunity rather than a hurdle. Research on presentations by Xerox salespeople found that successful calls have 50 percent more objections than failed calls.[13] When prospects raise concerns, they are actually showing interest and are asking for more information. They may be trying to make a clearer connection between their needs and your offering. Instead of being passive buyers, they are actively involved in the buying process. The most difficult prospect is one who does not say anything during the presentation, refuses to buy, and gives no reason for the decision. Xerox has also found that failed calls contain significantly more customer statements of indifference than successful calls. Concerns should be welcomed as a chance to get the prospect involved and to expand the discussion into areas of concern to the buyer. Most concerns are nothing more than innocent questions and should be viewed as an opportunity for deeper insight into customer needs.

Once *rapport is established*, most buyers have no reason to want to score points at the salesperson's expense. It is important that salespeople distinguish between real and pseudoconcerns. Each type is described below, along with ideas about how to approach these concerns.

Real concerns arise in most sales presentations. Concerns are likely to be about your company, product, timing, or price. In a well-developed selling situation, a need concern should not arise, since it should have been established earlier, when qualifying the prospect and during the needs discovery phase of the selling cycle. Many sales professionals view these concerns as pleas for more information, which is an effective point of view to maintain.

The question remains as to how to handle real concerns raised by buyers. Wilson Learning Corporation suggests a method for handling objections that it refers to by the acronym LSCPA. The process involves the following steps:

- *Listen* to the buyer's feelings.
- *Share* the concerns without judgment.
- *Clarify* the real issue with questions.
- *Problem-solve* by presenting options and solutions.
- *Ask for action* to determine the commitment.

These steps are recommended because buyers are in no frame of mind to listen to a logical clarification or solution when they are feeling tense. A customer concern is a signal that the buyer is feeling discomfort with the buying process. It is a natural part of the process. The listening and sharing steps help to reduce tension by helping the buyer get objections out in the open and showing that you care enough to acknowledge and try to understand them. Listen actively and encourage the buyer to talk. Don't think about how you will respond while listening to the buyer. In the sharing stage, you are trying to demonstrate understanding of the buyer's feelings. Listening and sharing take maturity, energy, and patience. Remember that the buyer is not attacking you personally, so concentrate on not being defensive.

The clarifying step often takes the form of a question, such as "It seems to me you are saying . . . " This step will often uncover misinterpretations. When this happens, you need to go back to the beginning of the process in order to listen to and share new understandings with the buyer to demonstrate your acceptance and to help the buyer relieve tension.

How the problem-solving stage is handled will depend on the concern and the situation. One strategy is to present a list of the pros and cons for the action requested. Another approach is to admit that the concern is valid but to point out advantages that compensate for the concern. Alternatively, a case history could be presented describing how another prospect purchased the offering and benefited.

Salespeople must learn to distinguish between real concerns and *pseudoconcerns*, or excuses. Pseudoconcerns are designed to hide the fact that the prospect just doesn't want to show his or her hand or make the decision yet. People often fear change and may not trust their own decisions. For example, the following concerns may be valid in some situations, but they usually are employed to get rid of salespeople:

- "I'll get back to you."
- "I'm too busy right now."
- "Our budget is tight this year."

The astute salesperson recognizes such excuses, sometimes choosing to ignore them and continue with the presentation. If the concern is legitimate, the customer will bring it up again and the salesperson can handle it then. As with real concerns, one of the best ways to uncover the real reason for the excuse is to ask questions that call for action by the buyer. Some suggestions for responding to the above excuses include the following:

- "If you are too busy now, may I see you for half an hour this afternoon at three, or would tomorrow morning at nine be better?"

Closing Skills

Closing occurs when a salesperson asks for a commitment from the customer. In a simple selling situation, such as in inventory replenishment, the commitment is for an order. Only 10% of sales calls in most major business-to-business relationships result in an order. In the other sales calls the customer is asked to commit to advancing the buying process.

Many salespeople find this the most difficult step of the selling process and are very reluctant to close. As one sales manager said when asked about the common mistakes salespeople make, "I think one of the big mistakes salespeople tend to make is not asking for the order."[14] The major reason salespeople are so hesitant to close seems to be fear of rejection. If salespeople do not ask for the order, they cannot be turned down and thereby they avoid embarrassment or disappointment. All professional purchasing agents, however, expect a sales representative to attempt to close. It is the job of the salesperson to make the first move. Research shows that it is important to keep a positive attitude for a sales presentation to be effective.[15] If you have successfully performed the earlier steps in the selling process, the close will follow naturally. In this case, closing is simply asking for a decision when you're pretty sure a person is going to say "Yes."

When to Close   An often-heard suggestion is to "close early and close often." This advice is not consistent with efforts to build trusting relationships with customers and is inherently adversarial in nature. The buyer is likely to see asking for the order before being ready to buy as pushy. "You can be too pushy because if you want the sale too badly and become overly aggressive, your client is going to close up and start pushing to end the meeting," notes Tim McCarthy, director of sales and marketing for The Gregory Group.[16]

Does this mean that successful salespeople expect to close only once? No. Often there are undisclosed needs that still need to be addressed. One of your customer's needs may be the need to have other people listen to them. Salespeople must be prepared to use multiple closes. It is often said that most acceptances are made on the fifth closing attempt.

If undiscovered needs are likely to exist and multiple closes are often required, how does a salesperson avoid being pushy while uncovering hidden needs and getting the sale? We suggest the use of *trial closes*. While closes call for decisions, trial closes are questions that ask for opinions that will serve as indicators of how close the buyer is to making a purchase decision. You may, for example, ask:

- How does this look to you?
- How important is this to you?
- Is this what you had in mind?
- Will this equipment be consistent with what you have now?

If a prospect makes a positive response to one of these questions, the salesperson can assume that the customer is leaning toward buying and can move directly to the final close. The salesperson should be prepared to continue the sales presentation, however, if the prospect does not appear ready to make a decision. He or she may then proceed, boldly but discreetly, to ask the simple question "Why?" This question will help the salesperson uncover the real needs of the buyer.

Successful salespeople learn to time their closing remarks on the basis of *buying signals* given by the buyer. These cues can take the form of gestures (the customer nods in agreement, picks up the product and examines it closely, or leans back in his or her chair) or they can be verbal comments. When prospects make comments like these:

- "Shipments must be completed in five months?"
- "We like the speed-control feature."
- "Would we be able to install the custom model within three weeks?"

the salesperson should recognize them as signs of interest and shift to a specific closing routine. Notice that each of these signals suggests an action by the buyer, not just a problem.

Closing Techniques   There are many different closing techniques and salespeople have personal preferences, depending on the circumstances. This suggests that salespeople need to be familiar with a number of closing techniques so that they can choose methods that are appropriate for each selling situation. Two popular closing techniques are the alternative choice close and the summary close:

Alternative Choice   When the prospect is faced with a variety of colors and models, the *alternative choice* close may be effective. With this technique, the salesperson poses a series of questions designed to narrow the choice and help the prospect make a final selection. For example:

"These couplings can be packed in units of 24 or cases of 72. Which is more convenient for you?"

Summary Close   One of the best closes provides a summary of the benefits accepted during the call, combined with an action plan requiring the customer's commitment.

SALESPERSON: George, you have said that our word processor has more memory, better graphics, and is easier to use than other machines you have seen. Is that correct?

PROSPECT: Yes.

SALESPERSON: Well, I recommend that you lease one of our machines for three months, and the lease payments will apply to the purchase price if you decide to keep it.

In a Xerox-sponsored study of 500 sales calls, the *summary close* gave a 75 percent success rate, and in only 7 percent of the calls was the summary method a failure.[17]

There are myriad other closing techniques that have been suggested and can be found in any selling textbook. There are popular business books entirely devoted to presenting different closing techniques.[18] While some of the techniques are very creative, in practice, most veteran salespeople prefer one of the more straightforward closes discussed in this section. It is our belief that if the previous steps have been performed correctly, the close may be kept simple. "If the salesperson has a clear vision of what benefits his or her product or service has to offer and he or she has made those benefits tangible for the prospect," says Arnold Wechsler, president of Wechsler Partners, Inc., "there's no reason for the salesperson not to be blunt in asking for the sale."[19] Perhaps part of the problem is terminology. "I've never been a believer in *closing*," a sales consultant once said, "because my objective is to *open* a relationship."

▶ POSTINTERACTION PHASE

A sale only begins the relationship between buyer and supplier. Once a salesperson has helped a buyer make a purchase, attention shifts to the follow-up activities. *Follow-up* refers to all the efforts involved in servicing the sale and building a lasting and growing relationship. Customers expect after-sale service, and it is frequently the job of sales representatives to make sure that these activities are carried out.

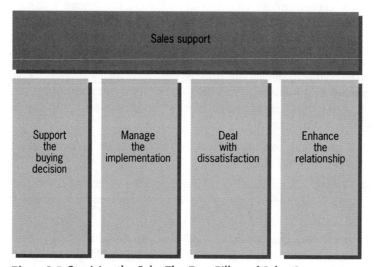

Figure 3-5: Servicing the Sale: The Four Pillars of Sales Support

The Wilson Learning Corporation has identified four pillars of sales support involved in after-sales follow-up. These are shown in Figure 3-5. *Supporting the buying decision* means reducing any anxiety that may arise with the purchasing decision. This may be accomplished through a follow-up sales call or by sending a card or letter thanking the buyer for the order. *Managing the implementation* includes offering support services, assisting with any personnel training, and reporting implementation and utilization progress. *Dealing with dissatisfaction* may include responding in an empathetic manner to any problems that arise. Salespeople should always be on the alert to *enhance the relationship* by being available, ensuring that the quality of the offering is maintained, and being a source of information, help, and ideas. It is very important to perform these activities successfully because the bulk of most salespeople's volume is in repeat business.

Delivering after-sale service is more difficult than it sounds because salespeople have to depend on the actions of others. Other people run the trucks to get the product to the customer. Other people service the product to keep it operating. Someone else sends out the manuals and bills to the customer. However, if something goes wrong, the salesperson is the one the customer turns to for relief. Therefore, salespeople must learn to follow up on *everything* that they request others to do for the customer.

An example of the power of follow-up occurred at a paper products company. The company handled many complex orders and prided itself on not missing one delivery date in four years. To highlight its achievements, the firm attached a new sheet to the monthly invoice that showed requested delivery dates and actual delivery times. A final column gave the number of days behind or ahead of schedule that the firm delivered the orders. This helped emphasize the company's excellent record, and it has led to considerable new business.

Follow-up also refers to callbacks to check the status of prospects who don't buy on the initial call. Some salespeople who get put off on a first call fail to go back when the prospect may just need a little extra time or help to make a purchase decision. As a general rule, when an order is not obtained on the initial call, the salesperson should express appreciation for the time made available and suggest a later visit. In this way, the salesperson shows continued interest in helping the prospect and in getting the order. When leaving, the salesperson should inquire if there are any brochures, samples, or other information that the prospect needs before they meet again.

Whenever salespeople leave without an order, they should immediately write down what they have learned about the prospect—for example, the prospect's chief concerns, who makes the final decision, and the prospect's primary needs. If the salesperson made any critical mistakes during the presentation, they should be noted so that they will not be repeated on the next visit.

Salespeople who do not follow up on sales are unlikely to establish long-term relationships with customers or secure repeat business. Purchasing agents expect postsale service, and it is the salesperson's responsibility to see that they remain satisfied. The importance of salesperson follow-up in Japan is described in Sales Management in Action 3-4.

Sales Management in Action 3-4
What Would You Say If You Were Called An "Okyaku-Sama"?

Are Japanese salespeople different from American salespeople? According to George Leslie, president of Meitec Inc., the answer is yes. "Today's Japanese sales reps, if they're good," says Leslie, "still behave as if they're at the bottom of the social ladder, respecting and trying to satisfy their customers. In fact, customers are often referred to as okyaku-sama, sama used in reference to God, the emperor, and others deserving honor." Japanese salespeople are trained to assume immediate responsibility for any difficulties that are associated with their product. Japa-

nese salespeople are team players, who are fanatically proud of their company. U.S. salespeople, on the other hand, are often taught the merits of independent action and are rewarded with commissions that reinforce the image of independence and responsibility. As industries mature and selling becomes much more complex, traditional salesperson orientations are changing in the United States.

Source: George Leslie, "U.S. Reps Should Learn to sell 'Japanese Style,'" *Marketing News*, 24 (October 29, 1990), p. 6.

▶ ETHICAL SITUATIONS

Attempts to influence people's decisions may lead to ethically questionable situations. Working independently of direct supervision, salespeople must often make a decision on their own about the ethics of a certain behavior. Personal judgments about ethical issues may not be easy. It is common to find disagreement as to whether a behavior is unethical. Consider the following situations:

- Making statements to an established customer exaggerating the seriousness of the customer's problem in order to obtain a bigger order or other concessions

- Having higher prices or other, less generous payment terms for buyers for which you are the sole supplier than for firms for which you are one of two or more suppliers

- Because it increases the likelihood of a sale, attempting to reach and influence other departments (such as engineering) directly when the customer has a corporate rule that only the purchasing department may be contacted

- Making claims about your offering that are exaggerated or not based on fact.

These and other situations are likely to arise sometime during your career in sales and sales management. Do you feel these represent unethical behaviors? This question was put to over 200 salespeople in the electronics industry in the United States.[20] Fifty-six percent felt that exaggerating problems was unethical, but 26 percent felt that such behavior was ethical. The rest were not sure. The less competitive price situations elicited almost an even split between salespeople who felt the behavior to be ethical versus those who felt it was unethical. Only 19 percent felt that going around the purchasing department was unethical.

It is clear that people differ in their judgments about the ethics of specific behaviors. Likewise, many behaviors of questionable ethical quality may appear to be insignificant or minor. Be careful. After all, tapes of White House conversations in 1972 indicate that the participants did not feel that there would be much of an uproar over bugging Democratic party headquarters. A good starting point is to clarify and understand the company's position on these issues.

▶ SALES FORCE AUTOMATION

Computers are becoming an integral part of selling and sales management as salespeople and sales managers find new ways to employ computers in field sales. In a recent survey, 80 percent of the pharmaceutical and health care companies responding indicated that they were spending money on *sales force automation* (SFA). See Figure 3-6 to find out which other industries are spending money on SFA.

A number of factors account for this intense interest in SFA. These include high selling costs, emphasis on customer satisfaction, closer and longer customer relations, and the need for coordination between sales, customer service, and marketing. Technical developments also have fostered this growing interest. Computer costs have dramatically declined, the power of portable computers has increased, and standards have developed for computer processors as well as electronic mail, communications, and electronic data interchange (EDI).

In this section, we will focus on computers and applications for salespeople. In later chapters, we will discuss management's computer applications in designing sales territories, compensation plans, and evaluating performance. We first look at what companies hoped to achieve by creating computerized sales support systems. Next,

Industry	Percentage of firms spending money on SFA
Pharmaceuticals/health	80%
Autos/heavy equipment	67%
Computer/software	65%
Consumer products	64%
Telecommunications	59%
Insurance	58%
Media/entermainment	56%

Figure **3-6:** Who's Spending Money on SFA

we examine some current developments in the use of automation in sales and marketing management.

Reasons for Computerization

Companies have plunged into SFA for a variety of reasons. As the opening vignette to this chapter indicates, advances in communications technology are fostered by and encourage development of team selling. Some companies were seeking to enhance the professionalism of the sales force, generate higher sales, and increase selling time. An example showing how computers can help salespeople save five hours per week is described in Selling Technology 3-2. Although some companies have achieved outstanding results in these areas, achieving SFA objectives has been elusive for others.

A recent report on computerization in sales published by the Conference Board, a business research organization, sheds some light on the benefits companies have derived from computerized sales support systems. By far the single most important benefit of computerization is management of the sales force. This is also supported by studies showing that sales management software, primarily hiring and training related, represents $6 out of every $10 spent on sales and marketing software.[21] Companies also list better sales performance and productivity, access to data, and faster response to customers as important benefits they have derived from instituting computer support systems. Figure 3-7 lists additional benefits salespeople derive from computer technology. An example of how Monsanto Corporation has attempted to realize these benefits in a mobile office is described in Selling Technology 3-3. Companies indicated, however, that on average, computerization did not lead to a sustainable competitive advantage.

Though the benefits of computerization may be difficult to quantify, companies seem to be convinced that computerization is necessary to stay competitive. Accord-

---

Selling Technology 3-2
How to Save 5 Hours a Week or Do 10 Days of Work in 15 Minutes

Saving five hours a week is what has been accomplished by a new computer data network used by salespeople with the Frito-Lay division of PepsiCo. The network is designed to help salespeople get a handle on many of the more time-consuming aspects of selling. In addition, a "trade development system" has been introduced that helps account executives pinpoint situations where supermarket managers can build profits by promoting more Frito-Lay products. With this system, presentations to store managers can be created in just 15 minutes by having a computer analyze sales data on any of the company's 200 different products. These presentations used to take 10 days or more to put together.

Source: Arthur Bragg, "Getting Face-to-Face with Customers," *Sales & Marketing Management* (February 1991), p. 46.

Use	Benefits
Order entry	Orders are entered/received as soon as they are placed, resulting in faster delivery and better customer service.
Price changes/product announcements	Predictable delivery; entire sales staff empowered with the same information at the same time.
Meeting setup and confirmation	Speeds response time. Eliminates phone tag.
Account planning and management	Decisions and updates easily and immediately announced to everyone dealing with an account.
Proposal writing	Salespeople can quickly get input from peers, managers, and/or financial people, shortening the turnaround time necessary to get a proposal to a client.
Internal communications	Removes time and geographic constraints. Managers can send immediate information on special situations with instructions on what action to take. Managers can make pricing/special favor decisions more quickly and efficiently because salespeople can get the necessary information into their managers' hands faster.

Figure **3-7:** Sales Force Automation Benefits

ing to the Software Publishing Association, unit sales of sales and marketing application software increased by 36 percent in 1992 to $5.75 billion.[22] To get a better idea of what companies are doing with all this software, we will discuss some specific applications of sales force automation.

SFA Technology Developments

If it is not here today, it will probably be here tomorrow. It is a mistake to think of computerization only in terms of what can be done today. We will take a look at some of the current developments in technology for sales force automation, including open systems, pen and tablet computers, wireless technology, artificial intelligence, and multimedia.[23]

Open Systems   *Open systems* refers to the ability of disparate technologies to communicate due to the standardization of systems. Some current marketplace standards include Microsoft's MS-DOS and Windows; Novell Netware, which has over 70 percent of the microcomputing networking market; and the Unix operating system, which is marketed by every major computer supplier in the world. Whether these products will still be dominant in the years ahead isn't the important issue. What is important is that standards developed for electronic mail, communications, and EDI allow information to be passed between different vendor products. As a result, salespeople are able to transmit sales call data by attaching their palmtop computer to a notebook computer for high-speed data transfer to the home office computer. Information from the home office will be downloaded with equal ease.

Selling Technology 3-3
A Mobile Office

St. Louis-based Monsanto Corporation has equipped salespeople in two of their divisions with seven-pound laptops plus software. According to Information Systems Manager Thomas Tucker, "The idea behind the mobile office and sales system is that the salesperson will spend less time in a walled office and, therefore, more time with customers." The laptops are equipped with four major software systems: A mail module with a corporatewide electronic mail system, including a report distribution function that permits downloading of sales reports. An account management system that includes, among other things, account profiles, key contacts, sales plans, pricing, complaints, and "things to do." Generic office systems for word processing, presentation graphics, and other applications. Special-purpose software for sales forecasting and product selection for specific accounts.

Source: Arthur Bragg, "Getting Face-to-Face with Customers," *Sales & Marketing Management* (February 1991), p. 48.

Pen and Notebook Computers   *Pen* and *tablet* computers, initially developed in the late 1980s, play a significant role in many sales forces. These devices include those that recognize handwriting using a stylus and those that use touch technology. Ultimately expected to be the size of a pad of paper, these computers are expected to replace paper-based forms including telephone directories, calendar appointment schedules, notepads, and calculator functions. These devices are empowering the sales force by allowing them to tap into company databases instead of working through sales managers or other headquarter personnel for marketing research, credit, production, and shipping information.

Wireless Technology   *Wireless communication technologies* have advanced to the point of being a viable alternative to traditional land-line communication technology. The first commercially available network, ARDIS, was jointly developed by IBM and Motorola for use by IBM's service organization. It was made available to the public in 1991. With wireless technology, salespeople are able to send or receive data anytime or anywhere. It also offers real-time links to corporate host computer systems, providing clients and customers higher levels of service. Most important, the cost of this technology is expected to continue to decrease by 50 percent to 75 percent.

Artificial Intelligence   Expert systems or *artificial intelligence* (AI) software technology made significant advances during the 1980s and early 1990s. *Expert systems* refer to highly specialized applications in which the system makes decisions similar to those of a person who has expert knowledge of the subject. Based on the architecture of the human brain, AI software systems may be used in complex sales environments to help determine the most qualified prospects, the most effective sales methods to use with those prospects, and the most effective way to solve customers' problems. The possibilities for this technology are exciting.

Multimedia   *Multimedia* is the blending of several technologies, including voice, sound, video, still pictures, monochrome and color graphics, and traditional computer applications. Federal Express equipped its 1,200 account executives with a multimedia information system which allows reps to download photos, drawings, and video/audio clips for customer sales presentations. In addition to their use In sales presentations, other multimedia applications include interactive sales training and order entry systems complete with pictures and video-captured product demonstrations. When combined with voice-response capabilities, these media may eventually replace other methods of ordering products and services.

SFA Issues

As noted earlier, SFA is generally quite expensive and some companies have found it difficult to quantify its benefits. In addition a number of time related issues may arise with respect to realizing the potential benefits of SFA. In particular, salespeople may conclude that there will be too great an amount of time needed to become proficient in using available software, and avoid using the technology. Non-selling time may increase as salespeople take on more tasks, proposal preparation for instance, that used to be performed by support personnel. Time spent on data entry may also be prohibitive. Advances in software technology are helping to address these time related issues, but management should be aware of the need to address these issues to avoid resistance from the sales force to adopting the new technology that is available.

▶ TOTAL QUALITY MANAGEMENT

At the core of a quality-driven sales organization's activities is its collection of processes by which the business is run. Performance of each process needs to be measured and an effort made to continuously improve performance. Sales force automation can help improve performance, sometimes dramatically. Consider Ascom Timeplex, which recently equipped its 300 account executives with Apple Computer's PowerBooks in an effort to improve its business-order cycle time.[24]

One of the important processes in Timeplex's selling cycle is developing customer proposals for the sale of large communication networks. Karter Smith, an account executive with Timeplex, describes the process prior to the introduction of automation: "After huddling with my sales engineer, I'd prepare a quote or proposal and hand it over to an administrator, who had it typed. When I got it back, I reviewed it to make sure it was correct; then I'd worry about having someone fax or mail it to the client. The customer invariably made changes, and I'd have to insert them by hand, calculate the new costs, and double-check, again, the quote and the drawings that always accompanied it."

With Timeplex's new computers, account executives are able to prepare quotes and proposals at the customer's site, as well as handle client-induced changes and calculate the resulting costs during the sales call. An account executive describes how he won a major telecommunications carrier account from two competitors: "A customer using an RFP (request for proposal) called me in with the two other vendors. During our meeting, he made twelve changes to the proposed network that affected my preliminary quote, drawings, and paperwork. I took out my PowerBook, edited the quote, and, using the customer's printer, gave him a revised quote, cover letter, terms and conditions, and network drawings, all within a few minutes. One competitor took four weeks to provide the same documentation; the second competitor, over five weeks."

As a result of the proposal-generating ability and other capacities of their automation system, Timeplex has realized significant benefits, including the following:

- Order cycle time slashed by 50 percent
- Order accuracy improved by 25 percent
- Order administration costs cut by 20 percent

▶ SUMMARY

Sales managers are first-line supervisors of field salespeople and need to understand the personal selling process. This process requires that salespeople develop many skills. For example, they must know how to prospect, arrange meetings, and establish rapport with strangers. They also must develop skills in needs analysis, oral presentations, handling customer concerns, and demonstrating product benefits. Many times, salespeople will need coaching in overcoming their reluctance to ask for an order. In most selling situations a key goal is to cultivate long-term relationships with customers; as a result, good follow-up service is critical.

Many salespeople now routinely use computers to help improve selling efficiency. Computers can eliminate paperwork and delays of order processing, help find prospects, solve customer problems on the spot, cut ordering errors, and save time. Personal selling is the backbone of most marketing programs, and effective selling procedures help ensure the success of marketing efforts.

▶ KEY TERMS

Alternative choice close	Expert systems
Artificial intelligence (AI)	Fact-finding questions
Benefits	Features
Benefitizing	Feeling-finding questions
Buying signals	Follow-up
Checking questions	Multimedia
Closed-ended questions	Needs discovery
Closing	Need-satisfaction presentation
Complex sales	Open-ended questions
Demonstrations	Open systems
Establishing rapport	Pen computers

Permission questions
Personal motives
Precall planning
Problem-solution presentation
Pseudoconcerns
Real customer concerns
Relationship anxiety
Relating skills

Sales force automation (SFA)
Stimulus-response presentation
Summary close
Tablet computers
Task motives
Trial close
Wireless technology

► REVIEW QUESTIONS

1. What questions should be asked when preparing to call on a prospect or customer? What is the purpose of each question?

2. What is a salesperson trying to accomplish during the approach step of the selling process?

3. How is building rapport with a prospect different from needs discovery, and how are they related?

4. Why is needs discovery such a critical part of the sales presentation?

5. What kinds of questions may a salesperson ask to determine the needs of the buyer?

6. Explain the different presentation methods. Which is most popular? When should a salesperson use each method?

7. What is a salesperson trying to accomplish during a sales presentation?

8. How should a salesperson distinguish between a valid objection and a pseudo-objection?

9. How should a salesperson handle a real objection raised by a buyer?

10. When should the salesperson attempt to close the sale?

11. What is the difference between a trial close and a final close?

12. Describe three different types of closes.

13. Why is follow-up so important in most sales jobs?

14. What are companies trying to achieve through sales force automation, and what are they likely to achieve?

15. What developments in computer technology are likely to have a significant impact on sales forces?

► PROBLEMS

1. A young insurance salesperson had an appointment with an executive (a former top-notch industrial salesperson) to sell life insurance. The older person, empathetic to the young man, sat patiently as the young man rambled on for 20 minutes, jumping from one point to the next, without any sense of continuity. Finally, the executive couldn't stand it any longer and roared for the salesperson to stop. "Son, this is the worst sales talk I've ever heard in my 30 years in sales. I'll tell you what; I'm going to buy your life insurance policy if you'll just listen to my advice. Get yourself a memorized sales talk. Doesn't your company supply you with a sales talk you can use so that you can present the material in a logical

way?" The young man responded, "Yes sir, I do have a memorized sales talk. This is the talk I use on executives who are former salespeople. It seems to work quite well, don't you agree?" Can any lessons be extracted from this story? Why do some industries use the memorized sales talk, while others use a less structured presentation?

2. "Selling yachts is a little different than selling brushes door to door," says the owner of a marine center in Connecticut. "Don't call them boats," he goes on to say. "Boats float. Yachts create. Also, never try to close a sale. Lay back and let the customers decide what they want to buy and how it should be equipped." Is this approach suitable to all high-priced products? Is it suitable to any low- or medium-priced goods? Which ones?

3. Talking to the person with responsibility and authority for purchasing is considered critical for success. Dave Douglas of Western Electronics is an exception to that rule. "If a purchasing agent shows any reluctance to my product, I go right to engineering and ask the department to specify my line." Are there any problems with this approach? Do you think Douglas's sales approach is the same for engineering and purchasing?

► EXPERIENTIAL EXERCISE

A better understanding of the role of personal selling can be obtained by traveling for a day with a field salesperson. Your assignment is to contact a salesperson and arrange to observe his or her activities for a day. Keep a log of how much of the salesperson's time is spent on meetings, travel, and waiting, and how much is spent talking to customers. Write a report describing your experience and the salesperson's activities. The Yellow Pages and your college placement office can be used to identify firms with salespeople in your area. Local chapters of Sales and Marketing Executives clubs and the American Marketing Association are also good sources of salespeople for this assignment.

► REFERENCES

1. GAIL EDMONDSON, "One Electronic SOS Clinched the Deal," *Business Week* (February 26, 1996), p. 83.

2. ROBERT PETERSON, MICHAEL CANNITO, and STEVEN BROWN, "An Exploratory Investigation of Voice Characteristics and Selling Effectiveness," *Journal of Personal Selling & Sales Management* (Winter 1995), pp. 1–15.

3. THOMAS STAFFORD, "Conscious and Unconscious Processing of Priming Cues in Selling Encounters," *Journal of Personal Selling & Sales Management* (Spring 1996), pp. 37–44.

4. TONY HENTHORNE, MICHAEL LATOUR, and ALVIN WILLIAMS, "Initial Impressions in the Organizational Buyer-Seller Dyad: Sales Management Implications," *Journal*

of *Personal Selling & Sales Management* 3 (Summer 1992), pp. 57–66.

5. SAUL GELLERMAN, "The Tests of a Good Salesperson," *Harvard Business Review* (May–June 1990), pp. 64–72.

6. *Exchange*, 17 (Stamford, Conn.: Xerox Learning Systems, 1990), p. 3.

7. This discussion is based on material from the Wilson Learning Corporation, *The Counselor Salesperson* (1996).

8. ROGER BROOKSBANK, "The New Model of Personal Selling: Micromarketing," *Journal of Personal Selling & Sales Management* (Spring 1995), 15, 61–66.

9. ARUN SHARMA and UAJNADINI PILLAI, "Customers' Decision-Making Styles and their Preferences for Sales Strategies:

Conceptual Examination and an Empirical Study," *Journal of Personal Selling & Sales Management*, 16 (Winter 1996), pp. 21–34.

10. We don't mean to leave the impression that logical deduction is all that is involved. For more on presentation influencing techniques see: TOMMY WHITTLER, "Eliciting Consumer Choice Heuristics: Sales Representatives," *Journal of Personal Selling & Sales Management*, 14 (Fall 1994), pp. 41–54.

11. Based on ROBERT KANTIN and MARK HARDWICK, *Quality Selling Through Quality Proposals* (Dallas, Tex.: Minehan Quality Press, 1991).

12. DAVID MERCER, *High-Level Selling* (Houston, Tex.: Golf Publishing, 1990), p. 130.

13. *Exchange*, p. 3.

14. KERRY ROTTENBERGER-MURTHA, "What Common Mistakes Do Your Salespeople Make?" *Sales and Marketing Management* (May 1993), p. 28.

15. DAVID STRUTTON and JAMES LUMPKIN, "Problem- and Emotion-Focused Coping Dimensions and Sales Presentation Effectiveness," *Journal of the Academy of Marketing Science*, 22 (Winter 1994), pp. 28–37.

16. ROTTENBERGER-MURTHA, "Common Mistakes," p. 28.

17. *Exchange*, p. 3.

18. See, for example, JOHN FENTO, *Close! Close! Close!* (Amsterdam: Pfeiffer and Company, 1993).

19. ROTTENBERGER-MURTHA, "Common Mistakes," p. 28.

20. ALAN DUBINSKY, MARVIN JOLSON, RONALD MICHAELS, MASAAKI KOTABE, and CHAE UN LIM, "Ethical Perceptions of Field Sales Personnel: An Empirical Assessment," *Journal of Personal Selling & Sales Management*, 4 (Fall 1992), pp. 9–21.

21. *Computer-Based Sales Support* (Report No. 9: The Conference Board, 1990).

22. THAYER TAYLOR, "SMA Software: Something New, Something Old," *Sales and Marketing Management* (May 1993), p. 22.

23. This section is based on the following sources: ROLPH ANDERSON, "Personal Selling and Sales Management in the New Millennium," *Journal of Personal Selling & Sales Management*, 4 (Fall 1996), pp. 17–32; WENDY CLOSE, "A Software Diet to Fatten Sales," *Sales and Marketing Management* (October 1992), pp. 76–82; MICHAEL HUCKS, "The Technology Connection," *Sales and Marketing Management* (February 1992), pp. 42–48; THAYER TAYLOR, "Getting in Step with the Computer Age," *Sales and Marketing Management* (March 1993), pp. 52–59.

24. THAYER TAYLOR, "The Automated Wake-Up Call," *Sales Marketing Management* (August 1993), pp. 64–67.

▶ SELECTED READINGS

ANTHONY, RAY and MALCOM KUSHNER, *High Octane Selling: Boost Your Creative Power to Close More Sales* (New York: Amacom, 1995).

HANAN, MACK, *Consultative Selling* (New York: Amacom, 1990).

KISHEL, GREGORY, and PATRICIA KISHEL, *Build Your Own Network Sales Business* (New York: Wiley, 1992).

MATHEWS, JACK, *Sales Driven* (Chicago: Probus, 1993).

MINNINGER, JOAN, and BARBARA GOALTER, *The Perfect Presentation* (New York: Bantam Doubleday Dell Publishing Group, 1991).

PEOPLES, DAVID, *Presentation Plus*, 2nd ed. (New York: Wiley, 1992).

RACKHAM, NEIL, SPIN *Selling* (New York: McGraw-Hill, 1987).

C A S E

3-1 ROYAL CORPORATION*

As Mary Jones, a third-year sales representative for the Royal Corporation, reviewed her call plans for tomorrow, she thought about her sales strategy. It was only July but Jones was already well on her way toward completing her best year, financially, with the company. Last year, she had sold the largest dollar volume of copiers of any sales representative in the Northeast and was the tenth most successful rep in the country.

But Jones was not looking forward to her scheduled activities for the next day. In spite of her excellent sales ability, she had not been able to sell the Royal Corporate Copy Center (CCC). This innovative program was highly touted by Royal's upper management. Jones was one of the few sales reps in her office who had not sold a CCC. Although Jones had an excellent working relationship with her sales manager, Tom Stein, she was experiencing a lot of pressure from him of late because he could not understand her inability to sell CCCs. Jones had therefore promised herself to concentrate her efforts on selling CCC even if it meant sacrificing sales of other products.

Jones had five appointments for the day—9:00 A.M., Acme Computers; 9:45 A.M., Bickford Publishing; 11:45 A.M., ABC Electronics; 12:30 P.M., CG Advertising; and 2:00 P.M., General Hospital. At Acme, Bickford, and ABC, Jones would develop CCC prospects. She was in various states of information gathering and proposal preparation for each of the accounts. At CG, Jones planned to present examples of work performed by a model 750 color copier. At General Hospital, she would present her final proposal for CCC adoption. Although the focus of her day would be on CCCs, she still needed to call and visit other accounts that she was developing.

*This case was prepared by Hubert Hennessey and Barbara Kalunian of Babson College. Copyright © by Hubert Hennessey and Barbara Kalunian. Names and locations have been disguised. Reproduced by permission.

Royal Introduces CCC Concept

Two years ago, Royal had introduced its Corporate Copy Center facilities management program (CCC). Under this concept, Royal offered to equip, staff, operate, and manage a reproduction operation for its clients on the clients' premises (see Exhibit 1). After analyzing the needs of the client, Royal selected and installed the appropriate equipment and provided fully trained, Royal-employed operators. The CCC equipment also permits microfilming, sorting, collating, binding, covering, and color copying, in addition to high-volume copying.

The major benefits of the program include reproduction contracted for at a specified price, guaranteed output, tailor-made capabilities, and qualified operators.

As she pulled into the Acme Computers parking lot, Jones noticed that an unexpected traffic jam had made her 10 minutes late for the 9:00 A.M. appointment. This made her uncomfortable, as she valued her time and assumed that her clients appreciated promptness. Jones had acquired the Acme Computers account the prior summer and had dealt personally with Betty White, Director of Printing Services, ever since. She had approached White six months earlier with the idea of purchasing a CCC, but had not pursued the matter further until now because Betty had seemed very unreceptive. For today's call, Jones had worked several hours preparing a detailed study of Acme's present reproduction costs. She was determined to make her efforts pay off.

Jones gave her card to the new receptionist, who buzzed White's office and told her that Jones was waiting. A few minutes later, Betty appeared and led Jones to a corner of the lobby. They always met in the lobby, a situation that Jones found frustrating but apparently was company policy.

"Good morning, Betty, it's good to see you again. Since I saw you last, I've put together the complete analysis on the CCC that I promised. I know you'll be excited by what you see. As you are aware, the con-

Exhibit 1: CCC: It Makes So Much Sense

	To see what Royal Corporate Copy Center can do for you—and for your operating budget—take a minute to explore the true cost of your present system, outlined in the chart below. As you can see, it includes those "hidden" reprographic expenses that many organizations fail to consider.	The CCC concept is a familiar one, of course. Many progressive organizations are now utilizing similar arrangements for their food service and data processing programs.
Labor	Operator (hr × 4.3 wks) Secretary (hr × 4.3 wks) Executive (hr × 4.3 wks) Supervisor (hr × 4.3 wks)	CCC provides expert operators and experienced reprographic management; all labor costs are included in one convenient monthly invoice.
Paid Benefits	Social Security Vacations Sick leave Pensions Medical plans	CC eliminates all "people problems"; your repro staff is on our payroll, and we pay for their benefits.
Recruiting and Training	Advertising costs Personnel time Interviewer time Operator time Supervisor time	No more recruiting and training—we handle that job, and we cover all related expenses!
Administrative Time	Purchase orders Filing work Calling service people Talking to salespeople	We handle all repro management; you receive a single monthly invoice for your entire repro system (and supplies).
Waste	Operator negligence Unauthorized copies Equipment malfunction	You pay only for the copies you use.
Downtime	Resulting in vendor charges, overtime costs, missed deadlines	Comprehensive backup capabilities at your local Royal Reproduction Center; job turnaround times are guaranteed at no extra cost to you!
Price Increases	Labor Materials Overhead Interest	The price includes everything, and it's guaranteed for the length of our agreement!
Space Requirements	Inventory File cabinets Additional equipment	Equipment and supplies are our responsibility, eliminating the need for anything extra on your part.
Chargeback Control	Clients Departments Individuals	At no charge, we maintain a log of all copies made for clients, departments, and individuals.

cept of a CCC is not that unusual anymore. You may recall from the first presentation that I prepared for you that the CCC can be a tremendous time and money saver. Could you take a few moments to review the calculations that I have prepared exclusively for Acme Computers?"

Betty flipped through the various pages of exhibits that Jones had prepared, but it was obvious that she had little interest in the proposal.

"As you can see," Jones continued, "the savings are really significant after the first two years."

"Yes, but the program is more expensive the first two years. But what's worse is that there will be an outsider here doing our printing. I can't say that's an idea I could ever be comfortable with."

Jones realized that she had completely lost the possibility of White's support, but she continued.

"Betty, let me highlight some of the other features and benefits that might interest Acme."

"I'm sorry, Mary, but I have a 10:00 meeting that I really must prepare for. I can't discuss this matter further today."

"Betty, will you be able to go over these figures in more depth a little later?"

"Why don't you leave them with me? I'll look at them when I get the chance." White replied.

Jones left the proposal with White, hoping that she would give it serious consideration, but as she pulled out of the driveway to Acme Computers, she could not help but feel that the day had gotten off to a poor start.

The Royal Corporation established the Royal Reproduction Center (RRC) Division in 1956. With 51 offices located in 24 states in the United States, the RRC specializes in high-quality, quick turnaround copying, duplicating, and printing on a service basis. In addition to routine reproduction jobs, the RRC is capable of filling various specialized requests including duplicating engineering documents and computer reports, microfilming, color copying, and producing overhead transparencies. In addition, the RRC sales representatives sell the Royal 750 color copier (the only piece of hardware sold through RRCs) and the Royal Corporate Copy Center program (CCC). Although the RRC accepts orders from "walk-ins," the majority of the orders are generated by the field representatives, who handle certain named accounts which are broken down by geographic territory.

At 9:45 A.M., Jones stopped at Bickford Publishing for her second sales call of the day. She waited in the lobby while Joe Smith, director of Corporate Services, was paged. Bickford Publishing was one of Jones's best accounts. Last year her commission from sales to Bickford totaled 10 percent of her pay. But her relationship with Joe Smith always seemed to be on unstable ground. She was not sure why, but she had always felt that Smith harbored resentment toward her. However, she decided not to dwell on the matter as long as a steady stream of large orders kept coming in. Jones had been calling on Bickford ever since Tim McCarthy, the sales representative before her, had been transferred. Competition among the RRC sales reps for the Bickford account has been keen. But Stein had decided that Jones's performance warranted a crack at the account, and she had proven that she deserved it by increasing sales 40 percent within six months.

"Good morning, Miss Jones, how are you today?" Smith greeted her. He always referred to her formally as Miss Jones.

"I'm fine, Mr. Smith," Jones replied. "Thank you for seeing me today. I needed to drop by and give you some additional information on the CCC idea that I reviewed with you earlier."

"Miss Jones, to be perfectly honest with you, I reviewed the information that you left with me, and although I think that your CCC is a very nice idea, I really don't believe it is something that Bickford would be interested in at this particular point in time."

"But Mr. Smith, I didn't even give you any of the particulars. I have a whole set of calculations here indicating that the CCC could save Bickford a considerable amount of time, effort, and money over the next few years."

"I don't mean to be rude, Miss Jones, but I am in a hurry. I really don't care to continue this conversation."

"Before you go, do you think that it might be possible to arrange to present this proposal to Mr. Perry (Tony Perry, V.P. Corporate Facilities, Joe Smith's immediate supervisor) in the near future? I'm sure that he would be interested in seeing it. We had discussed this idea in passing earlier, and he seemed to feel that it warranted serious consideration."

"Maybe we can talk about that the next time you are here. I'll call you if I need to have something printed. Now I really must go."

As Jones returned to her car, she decided that, in spite of what Smith had told her about waiting until next time, she should move ahead to contact Mr. Perry directly. He had seemed genuinely interested in hearing more about the CCC when she had spoken to him earlier, even though she had mentioned it only briefly. She decided that she would return to the office and send Perry a letter requesting an appointment to speak with him.

Although Jones was not yet aware of it, Joe Smith had returned to his desk and immediately began drafting the following memo to be sent to Tony Perry:

To: Tony Perry, V.P. Corporate Facilities
From: Joe Smith, Corporate Services
Re: Royal CCC

Tony:

I spoke at length with Mary Jones of Royal this morning. She presented me with her proposal for the adoption of the CCC program at Bickford Publishing. After reviewing the proposal in detail, I have determined that the program (a) is not cost effective, (b) has many problem areas that need ironing out, (c) is inappropriate for our company at this time.

Therefore, in light of the above, my opinion is that this matter does not warrant any serious consideration or further discussion at this point in time.

Royal 750 Color Copier

The Royal 750 color copier made its debut in 1973 and was originally sold by color copier specialists in the equipment division of Royal. But sales representatives did not want to sell the color copier exclusively and sales managers did not want to manage the color copier specialists. Therefore, the 750 was not a particularly successful product. In 1979, the sales responsibility for the color copier was transferred to the RRC division. Since the RRC sales representatives were already taking orders from customers needing the services of a color copier, it was felt that the reps would be in an advantageous position to determine when current customer requirements would justify the purchase of a 750.

Jones arrived back at her office at 10:45. She checked her mailbox for messages, grabbed a cup of coffee, and returned to her desk to draft the letter to Tony Perry. After making several phone calls setting up appointments for the next week and checking on client satisfaction with some jobs that were delivered today, she gathered up the materials that she needed for her afternoon sales calls. Finishing her coffee, she noticed the poster announcing a trip for members of the "President's Club." To become a member, a sales representative had to meet 100 percent of his or her sales budget, sell a 750 color copier, sell a CCC program, and sell a short-term rental. Jones believed that making budget would be difficult but attainable, even though her superior performance in 1982 led to a budget increase of 20 percent for 1983. She had already sold a color copier and a short-term rental. Therefore, the main thing standing in her way of making the President's Club was the sale of a CCC. Not selling a CCC this year would have even more serious ramifications, she thought. Until recently, Jones had considered herself the prime candidate for the expected opening for a senior sales representative in her office. But Michael Gould, a sales rep who also had three years' experience, was enjoying an excellent year. He had sold two color copiers and had just closed a deal on a CCC to a large semiconductor manufacturing firm. Normally everyone in the office celebrated the sale of a CCC. As a fellow sales rep was often heard saying, "It takes the heat off all of us for a while." Jones, however, found it difficult to celebrate Michael's sale. For not only was he the office "Golden Boy" but now, in her opinion, he was also the prime candidate for the senior sales rep position as well. Michael's sale also left Jones as one of the few reps in the office without the sale of a CCC to his or her credit. "It is pretty difficult to get a viable CCC lead," Jones thought, "but I've had one or two this year that should have been closed." Neither the long discussions with her sales manager nor the numerous in-service training sessions and discussions on how to sell the CCC had helped. "I've just got to sell one of these soon," Jones resolved.

On her way out, she glanced at the clock. It was 11:33. She had just enough time to make her 11:45 appointment with Sam Lawless, operations manager, at ABC Electronics. This was Jones's first appointment at ABC and she was excited about getting a foot in the door there. A friend of hers was an assistant accountant at ABC. She had informed Jones that the company spent more than $15,000 a month on printing services and that they might consider a CCC proposal. Jones knew who the competition was, and although their prices were lower on low-volume orders, Royal could meet or beat their prices for the volume of work for which ABC was contracting. But Jones wasn't enthusiastic about garnering the account for reproduction work. She believed she could sell ABC a CCC.

Jones's friend had mentioned management dissatisfaction with the subcontracting of so much printing. Also, there had been complaints regarding the quality of work. Investment in an in-house print shop had been discussed. Jones had assessed ABC's situation and had noticed a strong parallel with the situation at Star Electronics, a multidivision electronics manufacturing firm that had been sold CCCs for each of their four locations in the area. That sale, which occurred over a year ago, was vital in legitimatizing the potential customers in the Northeast. Jones hoped to sell ABC on the same premise that Fred Myers had sold Star Electronics. Myers had been extremely helpful in reviewing his sales plan with Jones and had given her ideas on points he felt had been instrumental in closing the Star deal. She felt well prepared for this call.

Jones had waited four months to get an appointment with Lawless. He had a reputation for disliking to speak with salespeople, but Jones's friend had passed along to him some CCC literature and he had seemed interested. Finally, after months of being unable to reach him by telephone or get a response by mail, she had phoned two weeks ago and he had consented to see her. Today she planned to concentrate on how adoption of the CCC program might solve ABC's current reproduction problems. She also planned to ask Lawless to provide her with the necessary information to produce a convincing proposal in favor of CCC. Jones pulled into a visitor parking space and grabbed her briefcase. "This could end up being the one," she thought as she headed for the reception area.

Jones removed a business card from her wallet and handed it to the receptionist. "Mary Jones to see Sam Lawless. I have an appointment," Jones announced.

"I'm sorry," the receptionist replied, "Mr. Lawless is no longer with the company."

Jones tried not to lose her composure, "But I had an appointment to see him today. When did he leave?"

"Last Friday was Mr. Lawless's last day. Mr. Bates is now operations manager."

"May I see Mr. Bates, please?" Jones inquired, already knowing the response.

"Mr. Bates does not see salespeople. He sees no one without an appointment."

"Could you tell him that I had an appointment to see Mr. Lawless? Perhaps he would consider seeing me."

"I can't call him. But I'll leave him a note with your card. Perhaps you can contact him later."

"Thank you, I will." Jones turned and left ABC, obviously shaken. "Back to square one," she thought as she headed back to her car. It was 12:05 P.M..

Jones headed for her next stop, CG Advertising, still upset from the episode at ABC. But she had long since discovered that no successful salesperson can dwell on disappointments. "It interferes with your whole attitude," she reminded herself. Jones arrived at the office park where CG was located. She was on time for her 12:30 appointment.

CG was a large, full-service agency. Jones's color copy orders from CG had been increasing at a rapid rate for the past six months, and she had no reason to believe that their needs would decrease in the near future. Therefore she believed the time was ripe to present a case for the purchase of a 750 color copier. Jones had been dealing primarily with Jim Stevens, head of Creative Services. They had a good working relationship, even though on certain occasions Jones had found him to be unusually demanding about quality. But she figured that characteristic seemed to be common in many creative people. She had decided to use his obsession with perfection to work to her advantage.

Jones also knew that money was only a secondary consideration as far as Stevens was concerned. He had seemingly gotten his way on purchases in several other instances, so she planned her approach to him. Jones had outlined a proposal which she was now ready to present to Jim.

"Good morning, Jim, how's the advertising business?"

"It's going pretty well for us here. How's things with you?"

"Great, Jim," Jones lied, "I have an interesting idea to discuss with you. I've been thinking that CG has been ordering large quantities of color copies. I know that you utilize them in the presentations of advertising and marketing plans to clients. I also know that you like to experiment with several different concepts before actually deciding on a final idea. Even though we have exceptionally short turnaround time, it occurred to me that nothing would suit your needs more efficiently and effectively than the presence of one of our Royal 750 color copiers right here in your production room. That way, each time that you consider a revision, one of your artists will be able to compose a rough, and you can run a quick copy and decide virtually immediately if that is the direction in which you want to go, with no need to slow down the creative process at all."

"Well, I don't know; our current situation seems to be working out rather well. I really don't see any reason to change it."

"I'm not sure that you're fully aware of all the things that the 750 color copier is capable of doing," Jones pressed on. "One of the technicians and I have been experimenting with the 750. Even I have discovered some new and interesting capabilities to be applied in your field, Jim. Let me show you some of them."

She reached into her art portfolio and produced a wide variety of samples to show Stevens. "You know that the color copier is great for enlarging and reducing as well as straight duplicating. But look at the different effects we got by experimenting with various sizes and colors. Don't you think that this is an interesting effect?"

"Yes, it really is," Stevens said loosening up slightly.

"But wait," Jones added, "I really have the ultimate to show you." Jones produced a sheet upon which she had constructed a collage from various slides that Stevens had given her for enlarging.

"Those are my slides! Hey, that's great."

"Do you think that a potential client might be impressed by something like this? And the best part is, you can whip something like this up in a matter of minutes if the copier is at your disposal."

"Hey, that's a great idea, Mary. I'd love to be able to fool around with one of those machines. I bet I'd be able to do some really inventive proposals with it."

"I'm sure you would, Jim."

"Do you have a few minutes right now? I'd like to bounce this idea off of Bill Jackson, head of Purchasing, and see how quickly we can get one in here."

Jones and Stevens went down to Jackson's office. Before they ever spoke, Jones felt that this deal was closed. Jim Stevens always got his own way. Besides, she believed she knew what approach to use with Bill Jackson. She had dealt with him on several other occasions. Jackson had failed to approve a purchase for her the prior fall on the basis that the purchase could

not be justified. He was right on that account. Their present 600 model was handling their reproduction needs sufficiently, but you can't blame a person for trying, she thought. Besides, she hadn't had Stevens in her corner for that one. This was going to be different.

"How's it going, Bill? You've met Mary Jones before, haven't you?"

"Yes, I remember Miss Jones. She's been to see me several times, always trying to sell me something we don't need," he said cynically.

"Well, this time I do have something you need, and not only will this purchase save time, but it will save money, too. Let me show you some figures I've worked out regarding how much you can save by purchasing the 750 color copier." Jones showed Jackson that at their current rate of increased orders of color copies, the 750 would pay for itself in three years. She also stressed the efficiency and ease of operation. But she knew that Jackson was really only interested in the bottom line.

"Well, I must admit, Miss Jones, it does appear to be a cost-effective purchase."

Stevens volunteered, "Not only that, but we can now get our artwork immediately, too. This purchase will make everyone happy."

Jones believed she had the order. "I'll begin the paperwork as soon as I return to the office. May I come by next week to complete the deal?"

"Well, let me see what needs to be done on this end, but I don't foresee a problem," Jackson replied.

"There won't be any problem," Stevens assured Jones.

"Fine, then. I'll call Jim the first of next week to set up an appointment for delivery."

Jones returned to her car at 1:00. She felt much better having closed the sale on the 750. She had planned enough time to stop for lunch.

During lunch, Jones thought about her time at Royal. She enjoyed her job as a whole. If it weren't for the pressure she was feeling to sell the Corporate Copy Center program, everything would be just about perfect. Jones had been a straight "A" student in college, where she majored in Marketing. As far back as she could remember, she had always wanted to work in sales. Her father had started out in sales, and enjoyed a very successful and profitable career. He had advanced to Sales Manager and Sales Director for a highly successful Fortune 500 company and was proud that his daughter had chosen to pursue a career in sales. Often they would get together, and he would offer suggestions that had proven effective for him when he had worked in the field. When Jones's college placement office had announced that a Royal college recruiter was visiting the campus, Jones had immediately signed up for an interview. She had known several recent graduates who had obtained positions with Royal and were very happy there. They were also doing well financially. She was excited at the idea of working for an industry giant. When she was invited for a second interview, she was ecstatic. Several days later, she received a phone call offering her a position at the regional office. She accepted immediately. Jones attended various pretraining workshops for six weeks at her regional office in preparation for her two-week intensive training period at the Royal Training Headquarters. This training consisted of product training and sales training.

She had excelled there and graduated from that course at the head of her class. From that point on, everything continued smoothly—until this problem with selling the CCC.

After a quick sandwich and coffee, Jones left the restaurant at 1:30. She allowed extra time before her 2:00 appointment at General Hospital, located just four blocks from the office, to stop into the office first, check for messages, and check in with her sales manager. She informed Tom Stein that she considered the sale of a 750 to CG almost certain.

"That's great, Mary. I never doubted your ability to sell the color copiers, or repro for that matter. But what are we going to do about our other problem?"

"Tom, I've been following CCC leads all morning. To tell you the truth, I don't feel as though I've made any progress at all. As a matter of fact, I've lost some ground." Jones went on to explain the situation that had developed at ABC Electronics, and how she felt when she learned that Sam Lawless was no longer with the company. "I was pretty excited about that prospect, Tom. The news was a little tough to take."

"That's okay. We'll just concentrate on his replacement now. It might be a setback. But the company's still there, and they still have the same printing needs and problems. Besides, you're going to make your final presentation to General Hospital this afternoon, and you really did your homework for that one." Stein had worked extensively with Jones on the proposal from start to finish. They both knew that it was her best opportunity of the year to sell a CCC.

"I'm leaving right now. Wish me luck."

He did. She filled her briefcase with her personals and CCC demonstration kit that she planned to use for the actual presentation and headed toward the parking lot.

Jones's appointment was with Harry Jameson of General Hospital. As she approached his office, his receptionist announced her. Jameson appeared and led her to the board room for their meeting. Jones was surprised to find three other individuals seated around the table. She was introduced to Bob Goldstein, V.P. of Operations, Martha Chambers, Director of Accounting, and Dr. J. P. Dunwitty, Chairman of the Board. Jameson explained that whenever an expenditure of this magnitude was being considered, the hospital's Executive Committee had to make a joint recommendation.

Jones set up her demonstration at the head of the table so that it was easily viewed by everyone and began her proposal. She presented charts verifying the merits of the CCC (Exhibits 2 and 3), and also the financial calculations that she had generated based upon the information supplied to her by Jameson.

Forty minutes later, Jones finished her presen-

Exhibit 2: Why Royal Corporate Copy Center?

No hidden costs	Allows you to devote full time to your business
No downtime	Departmental budget control
No capital investment	RRC full center support
No recruiting or training	Tailor-made system
No people problems	Full write-off
No inventory problems	Guaranteed cost per copy
Increased quality	Short-term agreement
Expert operators-plus	Trial basis
Guaranteed turnaround time	

Exhibit 3: What Is Royal Corporate Copy Center?

Royal Corporate Copy Center is the means whereby Royal will equip, staff, operate, and manage a reproduction operation for you on your own premises. First, we analyze your needs, then we select and install the appropriate equipment. Second, we provide two fully trained, Royal-employed operators and professional reproduction management. Finally, we schedule all work and protect you with comprehensive backup capabilities at our Reproduction Center . . . and you receive just one monthly bill for the entire package.

General Hospital Copying Objectives

1. To lower on-hand inventory of forms.
2. To be able to upgrade or relocate equipment if needed.
3. To have a competent full-time operator as well as backup operators.
4. To increase productivity.
5. To be more cost efficient.
6. To try 89-day trial option period.
7. To eliminate downtime.
8. To eliminate waste.
9. To assure fast turnaround.
10. To establish an inventory control system for paper and copier supplies.
11. To install an accurate departmental charge-back system.
12. To improve copy quality.
13. To eliminate queuing time.
14. To allow administrative support personnel to devote their full time to General Hospital's daily business.
15. To eliminate having to worry about service on machines.

General Hospital Offset vs. Printing

1. You won't eliminate all your related printing problems, such as:
    A. You still have to keep Savin copiers for short run lengths.
    B. You will still have waste problems.
    C. You still need plates and printing supplies.
    D. Messy and complicated.
    E. Must have dependable operator every day and someone for vacations.
    F. Still have to vend some printing.
    G. Won't be able to cut down inventory of forms on hand; have to have long run lengths to be profitable and long turnaround for two-sided copying.
    H. You will be running a copying print shop, yet it is not state of the art.
    I. Very noisy; wouldn't be able to be put in this building. Might have to find other location or keep in old building.
    J. Hospital—only 3 out of about 15 on the North Shore area have printing presses—those that do have large duplicators do 100,000 to 200,000 in volume per month besides long-run lengths on presses.
2. You would lose all of the extra benefits the Royal Corporate Copy Center would give you. (See attached)
3. For the first full year because of expense for press, your cost would be $14,890 higher than Royal Copy Center, and your estimated price increases over the next two years would not be fixed, thus still costing you more for a less efficient operation.

Royal Corporate Copy Center Will Satisfy These Objectives in the Following Manner:

1. By having a high-speed duplicator and professional operator, you will be able to order forms on an as-needed basis. This will lower your present inventory by at least 80 percent, thus freeing up valuable space for other use.

2. Because of the flexibility that Royal Corporate Copy Center gives you, you have the opportunity to change or upgrade equipment at any time. If relocation of equipment is necessary because of changes in the Hospital's structure, this can be done also.

3. Royal Corporate Copy Center will provide a trained, professional operator whose hours will conform to General Hospital's. Regardless of vacation schedules, sickness, or personal absences, a competent operator will report to General Hospital every day. If these operators do not meet with General Hospital's satisfaction, they can be changed within 24 hours. Because Royal will supply the operators, you will be relieved of this person as a staff member. Benefits, sick time, and vacation will be taken care of by Royal. You will receive operators for your facility 52 weeks a year.

4. Our people will report directly to your supervisor for their assignment the same as any other employee under your supervision. These people will be able to sort incoming jobs as we have discussed or may be used for other work in the copy center at nonpeak times. These people would also be available to pick up copying work from various central locations throughout General Hospital at specified times, thus eliminating the need for people to come to the copy center. These people may also be used to operate other types of equipment that General Hospital has.

5. By having a Royal Corporate Copy Center program at General Hospital and letting Royal take care of all your duplicating needs in a professional manner, your copying costs will become much more cost efficient. We believe that the cost savings alone in the first year could be upward of 10–15 percent and would increase as your copy volume grows with you. Your present system does not offer several of the important benefits that Royal Corporate Copy Center offers; these benefits will now be included in one fixed cost—in dollars and cents by not having to pay for these services; this is where the additional 10–15 percent cost savings per year could come in. We also will give you a fixed reproduction cost so that you can budget more accurately. We will also fix all of your costs for the next three years (that includes supplies, machine, support, and operators) if you sign a three-year agreement at the end of the trial period. This will enable you to save upward of another 10 percent per year.

6. We at Royal feel very confident about this program and its success. We therefore wish to minimize our customers' risk for installing a new program. We feel we are able to do this by offering a trial option period of up to 89 days. This program works in the following way: General Hospital must sign a trial option pricing addendum and a three-year agreement. This will put into action the following:

    A. $1,050.00 per month credit off the original pricing for the first partial month, the first full month, and the second full month (total of $3,150.00).

    B. At the end of the trial option period, General Hospital can elect to
        1) Remain on the 3-year agreement.
        2) Execute a 90-day, 1-year, or 2-year agreement with applicable pricing.
        3) Cancel the agreement, without liquidation damages.

7. With Royal Facilities Management, you will never experience downtime. Your work will always be done timely. We will back up the machines with a backup copier running the work there or send it to our closest center to be completed and returned. By being a Royal Corporate Copy Center customer, General Hospital will always receive priority on service. Also, our operators will be able to handle more extensive types of service to the equipment.

8. General Hospital will be charged only for the copies ordered. This will eliminate all of your present waste that is involved with offset.

Exhibit 3: (*continued*)

9. By having trained Royal operators, turnaround on work should decrease. These operators will know how to run jobs on the equipment properly and in the fastest way so that productivity and turnaround time will improve.

10. Royal will order all toner and developer, thus eliminating the need for General Hospital to make large commitments and maintain large inventories. We will also order paper for you on a weekly basis if you so choose.

11. Royal will install an accurate departmental charge-back system, allowing General Hospital to accurately account for all copies. You will receive a copy of this breakdown each month.

12. Royal will provide trained operators guaranteeing high-quality copies. By using a Xerographic process, you will always have consistently high-quality copies.

13. By providing General Hospital with skilled operators, copying and duplicating requirements will be met in a timely fashion, eliminating the need for General Hospital employees to stand and wait to use other equipment. In essence, General Hospital employees will be free to do General Hospital business; Royal will fulfill the copying and duplicating requirements.

14. Administrative personnel will no longer have to worry about salespeople, service problems, obtaining purchase orders, or buying supplies.

15. All machines used will be the responsibility of Royal for service and maintenance.

General Hospital Cash Flow (One-Year Period), Royal Corporate Copy Center vs. Present System

Corporate Copy Center				Hospital
Royal 900	Equipment			Obsolete presses & mimeo
$ 6,500.00	Supplies and paper			$ 42,189.00
Included	Toner and developer			0
Included	Labor			$ 22,496.00
Included	Benefits			$ 2,681.00
Included	Administrative time			?
Included	Management time			?
Included	CCC benefits			None
Eliminated	Savin 680 rental			$ 4,534.00
Eliminated	Small Savin I rental			$ 1,080.00
Eliminated	Smaller Savin II rental			$ 1,320.00
Eliminated	Savin copying cost			$ 2,400.00
Eliminated	Vending (forms that could be kept in-house)			$ 7,000.00
Eliminated	Issuing of P.O.s			$ 500.00
Eliminated	Expense for present building			$ 2,500.00
$ 80,310.00 ($.029 per copy)	Royal Corporate Copy Center (200,000 copies)			—
$ 86,810.00	Total cash flow			$ 86,700.00
	Fixed	Price Increases	Est.	
$ 86,810.00	0	15 months	5%	$ 91,035.00
$ 89,414.00	3%	2nd year	9%	$ 99,228.00
$ 91,202.00	2%	3rd year	9%	$108,158.00
$267,426.00	Projected 3 year cost			$298,421.00
$ 30,995.00	Projected 3 year savings			None

Exhibit 3: (*continued*)

Recommendation

Royal feels at this time that it would be very beneficial for General Hospital to change from their present reproduction system of two offset presses, mimeograph equipment, several smaller copiers, and a collator to a Royal 900 and a professional operator under the Royal Corporate Copy Center program. Royal feels it would be beneficial for General Hospital to effect this change presently for the following reasons:

1. Professional people would replace a part-time operator (20 hours) and an operator that is on leave (20 hours).

2. State-of-the-art equipment would replace the present presses, which are very old and outdated.

3. The large amount of waste presently experienced would be eliminated.

4. The high maintenance cost for the presses would be eliminated.

5. Hand collating and off-line collating would be eliminated.

6. Poor and inconsistent quality in the copies would be eliminated.

7. The backup problem would be eliminated.

8. You would have better turnaround and accountability.

9. Some of the smaller copiers and lower copy volumes on the smaller copiers would be eliminated.

10. You would receive all other Royal Corporate Copy Center benefits unattainable with your present program.

---

tation and began fielding questions. The usual concerns were voiced regarding hiring an "outsider" to work within the hospital. But the major concern seemed to revolve around the loss of employment on the part of two present printing press operators. One, John Brown, had been a faithful employee for more than five years. He was married and had a child. There had never been a complaint about John personally, or with regard to the quality or quantity of his work. The second operator was Peter Dunwitty, a recent graduate of a nearby vocational school and nephew of Dr. Dunwitty. Although he had been employed by the hospital for only three months, there was no question about his ability and performance.

In response to this concern, Jones emphasized that the new equipment was more efficient, but different, and did not require the skills of experienced printers like Brown and Dunwitty. She knew, however, that this was always the one point about the adoption of a CCC program that even she had the most difficulty in justifying. She suddenly felt rather ill.

"Well, Miss Jones, if you'll excuse us for a few minutes, we'd like to reach a decision on this matter," said Jameson.

"There's no need to decide right at this point. You all have copies of my proposal. If you'd like to take a few days to review the figures, I'd be happy to come by then," said Jones, in a last-ditch attempt to gain some additional time.

"I think that we'd like to meet in private for a few minutes right now, if you don't mind," interjected Dunwitty.

"No, that's fine," Jones said as she left the room for the lobby. She sat in a waiting room and drank a cup of coffee. She lit a cigarette, a habit that she seldom engaged in. Five minutes later, the board members called her back in.

"This CCC idea is really sound, Miss Jones," Jameson began. "However, here at General Hospital, we have a very strong commitment to our employees. There really seems to be no good reason to put two fine young men out of work. Yes, I realize that from the figures that you've presented to us, you've indicated a savings of approximately $30,000 over three years. But I would have to question some of the calculations. Under the circumstances, we feel that maintaining sound employee relations has more merit than switching to an unproven program right now. Therefore, we've decided against purchasing a CCC."

Jones was disappointed. But she had been in this situation often enough not to show it. "I'm sorry to hear that, Mr. Jameson, I thought that I had presented a very good argument for participation in the CCC program. Do you think that if your current operators decided to leave, before you filled their positions, you might consider CCC again?"

"I can't make a commitment to that right now. But feel free to stay in touch," Jameson countered.

"I'll still be coming in on a regular basis to meet all your needs for other work not capable of being performed in your print shop," Jones replied.

"Then you'll be the first to know if that situation arises," said Jameson.

"Thank you all for your time. I hope that I was of assistance even though you decided against the purchase. If I may be of help at any point in time, don't hesitate to call," Jones remarked as she headed for the door.

Now, totally disappointed, Jones regretted having scheduled another appointment for that afternoon. She would have liked to call it a day. But she knew she had an opportunity to pick up some repro work and develop a new account. So she knew she couldn't cancel.

Jones stopped by to see Paul Blake, head of staff training at Pierson's, a large department store with locations throughout the state. Jones had made a cold call one afternoon the prior week and had obtained a sizable printing order. Now she wanted to see whether Blake was satisfied with the job, which had been delivered earlier in the day. She also wanted to speak to him about some of the other services available at the RRC. Jones was about to reach into her briefcase for her card to offer to the receptionist when she was startled by a "Hello, Mary!" coming from behind her.

"Hello, Paul," Jones responded, surprised and pleased that he had remembered her name. "How are you today?"

"Great! I have to tell you, that report that you printed for us is far superior to the work that we have been receiving from some of our other suppliers. I've got another piece that will be ready to go out in about an hour. Can you have someone come by and pick it up then?"

"I'll do better than that. I'll pick it up myself," Jones replied.

"See you then," he responded as he turned and headed back toward his office.

"I'm glad I decided to stop by after all," Jones thought as she pressed the elevator button. She wondered how she could best use the next hour to help salvage the day. When the elevator door opened, out stepped Kevin Fitzgerald, operations manager for Pierson's. Jones had met him several weeks earlier when she had spoken with Ann Leibman, a sales rep for Royal Equipment Division. Leibman had been very close to closing a deal that would involve selling Pierson's several "casual" copying machines that they were planning to locate in various offices to use for quick copying. Leibman informed Jones that Tom Stein had presented a CCC proposal to Pierson's six months earlier but the plan was flatly refused. Fitzgerald, she explained, had been sincerely interested in the idea. But the plan involved a larger initial expenditure than Pierson's was willing to make. Now, Leibman explained, there would be a much larger savings involved, since the "casual" machines would not be needed if a CCC were involved. Jones had suggested to Fitzgerald that the CCC proposal be reworked to include the new machines so that a current assessment could be made. He had once again appeared genuinely interested and suggested that Jones retrieve the necessary figures from Jerry Query, Head of Purchasing. Jones had not yet done so. She had phoned Query several times, but he had never responded to her messages.

"Nice to see you again, Mr. Fitzgerald. Ann Leibman introduced us, I'm Mary Jones from Royal."

"Yes, I remember. Have you spoken with Mr. Query yet?"

"I'm on my way to see him right now," Jones said, as she thought that this would be the perfect way to use the hour.

"Fine. Get in touch with me when you have the new calculations."

Jones entered the elevator that Fitzgerald had been holding for her as they spoke. She returned to the first floor and consulted the directory. Purchasing was on the third floor. As she walked off the elevator on the third floor, the first thing that she saw was a sign that said, "Salespeople seen by appointment only, Tuesdays and Thursdays, 10 A.M.–12 noon."

"I'm really out of luck," Jones thought. "Not only do I not have an appointment, but today's Wednesday. But I'll give it my best shot as long as I'm here."

Jones walked over to the receptionist, who was talking to herself as she searched through a large pile of papers on her desk. Although Jones knew she was aware of her presence, the receptionist continued to avoid her.

"This could be a hopeless case," Jones thought. Just then the receptionist looked up and acknowledged her.

"Good afternoon. I'm Mary Jones from Royal. I was just speaking to Mr. Fitzgerald who suggested that I see Mr. Query. I'm not selling anything. I just need to get some figures from him."

"Just a minute," the receptionist replied as she walked toward an office with Query's name on the door.

"Maybe this is not going to be so bad after all," Jones thought.

"Mr. Query will see you for a minute," the receptionist announced as she returned to her desk.

Jones walked into Mr. Query's plushly furnished office. Query was an imposing figure at 6'4", nearly 300 pounds, and bald. Jones extended her hand, which Query grasped firmly. "What brings you here to see me?" Query inquired.

Jones explained her conversations with Ann Leibman and Kevin Fitzgerald. As she was about to ask her initial series of questions, Query interrupted. "Miss Jones, I frankly don't know what the hell you are doing here!" Query exclaimed. "We settled this issue over six months ago, and now you're bringing it up again. I really don't understand. You people came in with a proposal that was going to cost us more money than we were spending. We know what we're doing. No one is going to come in here and tell us our business."

"Mr. Query," Jones began, trying to remain composed, "the calculations that you were presented with were based upon the equipment that Pierson's was utilizing six months ago. Now that you are contemplating additional purchases, I mentioned to Mr. Fitzgerald that a new comparison should be made. He instructed me to speak with you in order to obtain the information needed to prepare a thorough proposal," Jones tried to explain.

"Fitzgerald! What on earth does Fitzgerald have to do with this? This is none of his damn business. He sat at the same table as I six months ago when we arrived at a decision. Why doesn't he keep his nose out of affairs that don't concern him. We didn't want this program six months ago, we don't want it now!" Query shouted.

"I'm only trying to do my job, Mr. Query, I was not part of the team that presented the proposal six months ago. But from all the information that is available now, I still feel that a CCC would save you money here at Pierson's."

"Don't you understand, Miss Jones? We don't want any outsiders here. You have no control over people that don't work for you. Nothing gets approved around here unless it has my signature on it. That's control. Now I really see no need to waste any more of my time or yours."

"I appreciate your frankness," Jones responded, struggling to find something positive to say.

"Well, that's the kind of man I am, direct and to the point."

"You can say that again," Jones thought. "One other thing before I go, Mr. Query. I was noticing the color copies on your desk."

"Yes, I like to send color copies of jobs when getting production estimates. For example, these are of the bags that we will be using during our fall promotion. I have received several compliments from suppliers who think that by viewing color copies they get a real feel for what I need."

"Well, it just so happens that my division of Royal sells color copiers. At some time it may be more efficient for you to consider purchase. Let me leave you some literature on the 750 copier which you can review at your leisure." Jones removed a brochure from her briefcase. She attached one of her business cards to it and handed it to Query. As she shook his hand and left the office, Jones noted that she had half an hour before the project of Blake's would be ready for pick-up. She entered the donut shop across the street and as she waited for her coffee, she reviewed her day's activities. She was enthusiastic about the impending color copier sale at CG Advertising, and about the new repro business that she had acquired at Pierson's. But the rest of the day had been discouraging. Not only had she been "shot down" repeatedly, but she'd now have to work extra hard for several days to ensure that she would make 100 percent of budget for the month. "Trying to sell the CCC is even harder than I thought it was," Jones thought.

CASE

3-2 MEDIQUIP S.A.*

On December 18, Kurt Thaldorf, a sales engineer for the German sales subsidiary of Mediquip, S.A., was informed by Lohmann University Hospital in Stuttgart that it had decided to place an order with Sigma, a Dutch competitor, for a CT scanner. The hospital's decision came as disappointing news to Thaldorf, who had worked for nearly eight months on the account. The order, if obtained, would have meant a sale of DM 2,370,000 for the sales engineer.[1] He was convinced that Mediquip's CT scanner was technologically superior to Sigma's and, overall, a better product.

Thaldorf began a review of his call reports in order to better understand the factors that had led to Lohmann University Hospital's decision. He wanted to apply the lessons from this experience to future sales situations.

Background

At the time, the computer tomography (CT) scanner was a relatively recent product in the field of diagnostic imaging. This medical device, used for diagnostic purposes, allowed examination of cross sections of the human body through display of images. CT scanners combined sophisticated X-ray equipment with a computer to collect the necessary data and translate them into visual images.

When computer tomography was first introduced in the late 1960s, radiologists had hailed it as a major technological breakthrough. Commenting on the ad-

vantages of CT scanners, a product specialist with Mediquip said, "The end product looks very much like an X-ray image. The only difference is that with scanners you can see sections of the body that were never seen before on a screen—like the pancreas. A radiologist, for example, can diagnose cancer of the pancreas in less than two weeks after it develops. This was not possible before CT scanners."

Mediquip was a subsidiary of Technologie Universelle, a French conglomerate. The company's product line included, in addition to CT scanners, X-ray, ultrasonic, and nuclear diagnostic equipment. Mediquip enjoyed a worldwide reputation for advanced technology and competent after-sales service.

"Our competitors are mostly from other European countries," commented Mediquip's Sales Director for Europe. "In some markets they have been there longer than we have, and they know the decision makers better than we do. But we are learning fast." Sigma, the subsidiary of a diversified Dutch company under the same name, was the company's most serious competitor. Other major contenders in the CT scanner market were FNC, Eldora, Magna, and Piper.

Mediquip executives estimated the European market for CT scanners to be around 200 units per year. They pointed out that prices ranged from DM 1.5 to DM 3.0 million per unit. The company's CT scanner sold at the upper end of the price range. "Our equipment is at least two years ahead of our most advanced competition," explained a sales executive. "And our price reflects this technological superiority."

Mediquip's sales organization in Europe included eight country sales subsidiaries each headed by a managing director. Within each country, sales engineers reported to regional sales managers, who, in turn, reported to the managing director. Product specialists provided technical support to the sales force in each country.

---

*This case was prepared by Kamran Kashani of IMD, Lausanne, Switzerland. Copyright © 1991 by the International Institute for Management Development (IMD), Lausanne, Switzerland. Reproduced by permission.

[1] For the purposes of this case, use the following exchange rates for the Deutschmark (DM): DM 1.00 = SF 0.85, $0.60, Ecu 0.50, £0.35.

Buyers of CT Scanners

A sales executive at Mediquip described the buyers of CT scanners as follows:

> Most of our sales are to what we call the public sector, health agencies that are either government-owned or belong to nonprofit support organizations such as universities and philanthropic institutions. They are the sort of buyers that buy through formal tenders and have to budget their purchases at least one year in advance. Once the budget is allocated, it must then be spent before the end of the year. Only a minor share of our CT scanner sales goes to the private sector, profit-oriented organizations such as private hospitals or private radiologists.
>
> Of the two markets, the public sector is much more complex. Typically, there are at least four groups that get involved in the purchase decision: radiologists, physicists, administrators, and people from the supporting agency—usually the ones who approve the budget for purchasing a CT scanner.
>
> Radiologists are the ones who use the equipment. They are doctors whose diagnostic services are sought by other doctors in the hospital or clinic. Patients remember their doctors, but not the radiologists. They never receive flowers from the patients! A CT scanner could really enhance their professional image among their colleagues.
>
> Physicists are the scientists in residence. They write the technical specifications which competing CT scanners must meet; they should know the state of the art in X-ray technology. Their primary concern is the patient's safety.
>
> The administrators are, well, administrators. They have the financial responsibility for their organizations. They are concerned with the cost of CT scanners, but also with what revenues they can generate. The administrators are extremely wary of purchasing an expensive technological toy that will become obsolete in a few years.
>
> The people from the supporting agency are usually not directly involved with decisions as to which product to purchase. But since they must approve the expenditures, they do play an indirect role. Their influence is mostly felt by the administrators.

> The interplay among the four groups, as you can imagine, is rather complex. The power of each group in relationship to the others varies from organization to organization. The administrator, for example, is the top decision maker in certain hospitals. In others, he is only a buyer. One of the key tasks of our sales engineers is to define for each potential account the relative power of the players. Only then can they set priorities and formulate selling strategies.

The European sales organization at Mediquip had recently started using a series of forms designed to help sales engineers in their account analysis and strategy formulation. (A sample of the forms, called Account Management Analysis, is reproduced in Exhibit 1.)

Lohmann University Hospital

Lohmann University Hospital (LUH) was a large general hospital serving Stuttgart, a city of one million residents. The hospital was part of the university's medical school. The university was a leading teaching center and enjoyed an excellent reputation. LUH's radiology department had a wide range of X-ray equipment from a number of European manufacturers, including Sigma and FNC. The radiology department had five staff members, headed by a senior and nationally known radiologist, Professor Steinborn.

Thaldorf's Sales Activities

From the records he had kept of his sales calls, Thaldorf reviewed the events for the period between May 5, when he learned of LUH's interest in purchasing a CT scanner, and December 18, when he was informed that Mediquip had lost the order.

May 5:

Office received a call from a Professor Steinborn from Lohmann University Hospital regarding a CT scanner. I was assigned to make the call on the professor. I looked through our files to find out if we had sold anything to the hospital before. We had not. I made an appointment to see the professor on May 9.

May 9:

Called on Professor Steinborn, who informed me of a recent decision by university directors to set aside

Exhibit 1: MEDIQUIP S.A: Account Management Analysis Forms (condensed version)

Key Account: _____

ACCOUNT MANAGEMENT ANALYSIS

The enclosed forms are designed to facilitate your management of:

1. A key sales account
2. The *Mediquip* resources that can be applied to this key account

Completing the enclosed forms, you will:

- Identify installed equipment, and planned or potential new equipment
- Analyze purchase decision process and influence patterns, including:
  —Identify and prioritize all major sources of influence
  —Project probable sequence of events and timing of decision process
  —Assess position/interest of each major influence source
  —Identify major competition and probable strategies
  —Identify needed information/support
- Establish an account development strategy, including:
  —Select key contacts
  —Establish strategy and tactics for each key contact, identify appropriate *Mediquip* personnel
  —Assess plans for the most effective use of local team and headquarters resources

KEY ACCOUNT DATA

☐ Original (Date: _____)   Account No.: _____   Type of Institute: _____
☐ Revision (Date: _____)   Sales Specialist: _____   Bed Size: _____
                             Country/Region/District: _____   Telephone: _____

1. CUSTOMER (HOSPITAL, CLINIC, PRIVATE INSTITUTE)
   Name: _____
   Street Address: _____
   City, State: _____

2. DECISION MAKERS—IMPORTANT CONTACTS

INDIVIDUALS	NAME	SPECIALTY	REMARKS
Medical Staff Administration Local Government State Government			

3. INSTALLED EQUIPMENT

TYPE	DESCRIPTION	SUPPLIED BY	INSTALLATION DATE	YEAR TO REPLACE	VALUE OF POTENTIAL ORDER
X-ray Nuclear Ultrasound RTP CT					

Exhibit 1: (*continued*)

4. PLANNED NEW EQUIPMENT

TYPE	QUOTE		% CHANCE	EST. ORDER DATE		EST. DELIVERY		QUOTED PRICE
	NO.	DATE		1980	1981	1980	1981	

5. COMPETITION

COMPANY/ PRODUCT	STRATEGY/ TACTICS	% CHANCE	STRENGTH	WEAKNESS

6. SALES PLAN   Product: _____ Quote No.: _____ Quoted Price: _____

KEY ISSUES	Mediquip's PLAN	SUPPORT NEEDED FROM:	DATE OF FOLLOW-UP/REMARKS

7. ACTIONS—IN SUPPORT OF PLAN

SPECIFIC ACTION	RESPONSIBILITY	DUE DATES			RESULTS/REMARKS
		ORIGINAL	REVISED	COMPLETED	

8. ORDER STATUS REPORT

REVISION DATE	ACCOUNT NAME AND LOCATION	ISSUES/ COMPETITIVE STRATEGY	ACTIONS/ STRATEGY	RESPON-SIBILITY	% CHANCE	EXPECTED ORDER TIMING	WIN/LOSE

funds next year for the purchase of the hospital's first CT scanner. The professor wanted to know what we had to offer. Described the general features of our CT system. Gave him some brochures. Asked a few questions, which led me to believe other companies had come to see him before I did. Told me to check with Dr. Rufer, the hospital's physicist, regarding the specs.

Made an appointment to see him again ten days later. Called on Dr. Rufer, who was not there. His secretary gave me a lengthy document on the scanner specs.

May 10:

Read the specs last night. Looked like they had been copied straight from somebody's technical manual.

Showed them to our Product Specialist, who confirmed my own hunch that our system met and exceeded the specs. Made an appointment to see Dr. Rufer next week.

May 15:

Called on Dr. Rufer. Told him about our system's features and the fact that we met all the specs set down on the document. He did not seem particularly impressed. Left him with technical documents about our system.

May 19:

Called on Professor Steinborn. He had read the material I had left with him. Seemed rather pleased with the features. Asked about our upgrading scheme. Told him we would undertake to upgrade the system as new features became available. Explained that Mediquip, unlike other systems, can be made to accommodate the latest technology, with no risk of obsolescence for a long time. This impressed him. Also answered his questions regarding image manipulation, image processing speed, and our service capability. Just before I left, he inquired about our price. Told him I would have an informative quote for him at our next meeting. Made an appointment to see him on June 23 after he returned from his vacation. Told me to get in touch with Carl Hartmann, the hospital's general director, in the interim.

June 1:

Called on Hartmann. It was difficult to get an appointment with him. Told him about our interest in supplying his hospital with our CT scanner, which met all the specs as defined by Dr. Rufer. Also informed him of our excellent service capability. He wanted to know which other hospitals in the country had purchased our system. Told him I would provide him with a list of buyers within a few days. He asked about the price. Gave him an informative quote of DM 2,850,000—a price my boss and I had determined after my visit to Professor Steinborn. He shook his head, saying, "Other scanners are cheaper by a wide margin." I explained that our price reflected the fact that the latest technology was already built into our scanner. Also mentioned that the price differential was an investment that could pay for itself several times over through faster speed of operation. He was noncommittal. Before leaving his office, he instructed me not to talk to anybody else about the price. Asked him specifically if that included Professor Steinborn. He said it did. Left him with a lot of material about our system.

June 3:

Went to Hartmann's office with a list of three hospitals similar in size to LUH that had installed our system. He was out. Left it with his secretary, who recognized me. Learned from her that at least two other firms, Sigma and FNC, were competing for the order. She also volunteered the information that "prices are so different that Mr. Hartmann is confused." She added that the final decision will be made by a committee made up of Hartmann, Professor Steinborn, and one other person, whom she could not recall.

June 20:

Called on Dr. Rufer. Asked him if he had read the material about our system. He had but did not have much to say. I repeated some of the key operational advantages our product enjoyed over those produced by others, including Sigma and FNC. Left him some more technical documents.

On the way out, stopped by Hartmann's office. His secretary told me that we had received favorable comments from the hospitals using our system.

June 23:

Professor Steinborn was flabbergasted to hear that I could not discuss our price with him. Told him about the hospital administration's instructions to that effect. He could not believe this, especially when Sigma had already given him their quote of DM 2,100,000. When he calmed down, he wanted to know if we were going to be at least competitive with the others. Told him our system was more advanced than Sigma's. Promised him we would do our best to come up with an attractive offer. Then we talked about his vacation and sailing experience in the Aegean Sea. He said he loved the Greek food.

July 15:

Called to see if Hartmann had returned from his vacation. He had. While checking his calendar, his secretary told me that our system seemed to be the "radiologists' choice," but that Hartmann had not yet made up his mind.

July 30:

Visited Hartmann accompanied by the regional manager. Hartmann seemed to have a fixation about the price. He said, "All the companies claim they have the latest technology." So he could not understand why our offer was "so much above the rest." He concluded that only a "very attractive price" could tip the balance in our favor. After repeating the operational advantages our system enjoyed over others, including those produced by Sigma and FNC, my boss indicated that we were willing to lower our price to DM 2,610,000 if the equipment were ordered before the end of the current year. Hartmann said he would consider the offer and seek "objective" expert opinion. He also said a decision would be made before Christmas.

August 14:

Called on Professor Steinborn, who was too busy to see me for more than ten minutes. He wanted to know if we had lowered our price since the last meeting with him. I said we had. He shook his head and said with a laugh, "Maybe that was not your best offer." He then wanted to know how fast we could make deliveries. Told him within six months. He did not say anything.

September 2:

The regional manager and I discussed the desirability of inviting one or more people from the LUH to visit the Mediquip headquarter operations near Paris. The three-day trip would give the participants a chance to see the scope of the facilities and become better acquainted with CT scanner applications. This idea was finally rejected as inappropriate.

September 3:

Dropped in to see Hartmann. He was busy but had time to ask for a formal "final offer" from us by October 1. On the way out, his secretary told me there had been "a lot of heated discussions" about which scanner seemed best suited for the hospital. She would not say more.

September 25:

The question of price was raised in a meeting with the regional manager and the managing director. I had recommended a sizable cut in our price to win the order. The regional manager seemed to agree with me, but the managing director was reluctant. His concern was that too big a drop in price looked "unhealthy." They finally agreed to a final offer of DM 2,370,000.

Made an appointment to see Hartmann later that week.

September 29:

Took our offer of DM 2,370,000 in a sealed envelope to Hartmann. He did not open it, but he said he hoped the scanner question would soon be resolved to the "satisfaction of all concerned." Asked him how the decision was going to be made. He evaded the question but said he would notify us as soon as a decision was reached. Left his office feeling that our price had a good chance of being accepted.

October 20:

Called on Professor Steinborn. He had nothing to tell me except that "the CT scanner is the last thing I want to talk about." Felt he was unhappy with the way things were going.

Tried to make an appointment with Hartmann in October, but he was too busy.

November 5:

Called on Hartmann, who told me that a decision would probably not be reached before next month. He indicated that our price was "within the range," but that all the competing systems were being evaluated to see which seemed most appropriate for the hospital. He repeated that he would call us when a decision was reached.

December 18:

Received a brief letter from Hartmann thanking Mediquip for participating in the bid for the CT scanner, along with the announcement that LUH had decided to place the order with Sigma.

▶ **4** ◀

Account Relationship Management*

The sale, then, merely consummates the courtship, at which point the marriage begins. How good the marriage is depends on how well the seller manages the relationship.
THEODORE LEVITT

*Chapter Consultant: Chris Jander National Accounts Manager RELTEC.

LEARNING OBJECTIVES

After studying this chapter, you should be able to:

▶ Explain the steps in the professional purchasing process.

▶ Identify the different buying influences of people in the buying center.

▶ Explain how relationships evolve and what constitutes critical nurturing relationships with customers.

▶ Describe critical factors in the evolution of relationships.

▶ PARTNERS

Owens-Brockway's partnership with a major beverage producer began with a business lunch in the client's executive dining room. Owens, the Glass Container Division of Owens-Illinois (Toledo, Ohio), had been selling glass containers to the beverage producer for a number of years. "As I recall, the company's worldwide sourcing director and I were talking about cost-reduction opportunities," notes account executive Henry A. Casazza, Jr. "The director had attended the Owens-Brockway Glass School and was familiar with the blow-mold concept. That was the gestation of a partnership agreement that was termed the Multi-Serve Juice Rationalization Program," he reports.

The beverage company was expanding its product line by offering its product in many new sizes and shapes. This offered the marketing advantage of differentiation but was also very costly. Teams from each side were reviewing crucial issues, such as how to standardize the bottling line and how much time it would take to change over to new molds. Owens-Brockway's program was chosen over that of another supplier and resulted in a multiyear agreement.

In commenting on the partnership, Casazza stresses, "Partnering has emotional costs. You must develop a very trusting relationship. And you and the customer need mutual reasons to lock into each other for a period of time." Casazza emphasizes that partnerships "require relationships with all departments. You'll work with plant, marketing, logistics, operations, and traffic personnel—and in virtually every aspect of the business."

"The account manager usually makes the initial contact and steers the agreement through," he notes. "However, that individual requires the support of all the others—on both sides—all of whom become part of the partnering team."[1]

This chapter focuses on building lasting and profitable relationships with customers, referred to as *accounts*. Chapter 3's discussion of the selling process focused primarily on an individual sales call. In professional selling to other businesses, multiple calls are typically required to close a sale, and transactions usually take place within the context of an ongoing relationship. The Owens-Brockway example illustrates some of the most important developments in business-to-business marketing—selling teams, buying centers, close cooperation between buyers and sellers, strategic project involvement, long-term relationships, and a high level of trust. This chapter examines each of these issues and provides practical examples of their significance.

One additional point that should not go unnoticed in the Owens example is that companies are increasingly looking for significant growth opportunities within current accounts. In a recent Gallup survey, over 60 percent of responding salespeople indicated that it took one or two calls to consummate a sale with existing customers, but only 18 percent indicated a sale could be made to new customers with only this number of calls.[2] Results of a recent study by Weeks and Kahle further underscores the importance of existing customers in meeting sales objectives. This study investigated whether the amount of time spent calling on established accounts versus potential new accounts affected sales force performance. The results show that neither the total amount of time spent face-to-face with customers nor the amount of time prospecting is related to performance; only the time spent with established accounts has a positive impact on performance.[3]

Our discussion of relationship management begins by presenting the typical stages in the business-to-business purchasing process. Examples of different types of account relationships will be discussed within the context of each stage. The concept of a buying center is introduced, along with the development of selling teams. Following this, our focus changes to understanding how relationships evolve and when certain factors are likely to influence this evolution. We conclude the chapter with a discussion of ethical situations that may arise in account relationships and quality selling.

▶ ORGANIZATIONAL PURCHASING PROCESS

To help salespeople in their account and territory planning, purchasing of new products can be viewed as a process consisting of six stages (Figure 4–1).[4] It is important for salespeople to know an account's purchasing stage because it will help determine what actions they may wish to take to influence the purchase decision. The nature of each stage is changing rapidly in today's business environment, where many buyers and suppliers are working with greater cooperation to establish a competitive advantage. These developments are very significant in selling today and are reflected in the following discussion.

Need Recognition

The first stage occurs when the account *recognizes that a need exists*. This recognition may come from inside the firm, such as when a manager observes a bottleneck in a production process or when existing machinery breaks down. External sources of *need recognition* include advertisements, trade shows, and calls by salespeople.

One of the first things a salesperson needs to know about business-to-business buying behavior is the concept of *derived demand*. Professional buyers do not purchase for themselves, but rather to help produce goods and services for resale. This suggests that suppliers can gain a competitive advantage by knowing and understanding the needs of the customers' customers.[5] This also means that the demand for industrial goods is derived from demand for the client's final product.

Derived demand is an important idea because it determines who the sales force calls on, what customer benefits are emphasized, and how much of a product or service is ultimately sold. To convince GTE to carry its line of ethernet connections,

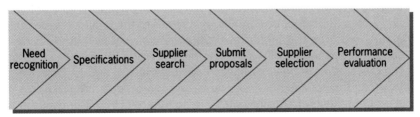

Figure 4-1: Flow Diagram of the Account Purchasing Process

for example, RELTEC demonstrated to apartment owners the advantages of ethernet connections for the computer needs of their customers. Since the apartment's client turnover could be reduced by this feature, the apartment owners convinced GTE to include RELTEC's ethernet connection with its product lines.

Specifications

During this stage, the characteristics or specifications of the product are established, as well as the quantity of items to be purchased. This is usually dictated by the anticipated demand for the organization's products and by the technological requirements of its operations. Consequently, a precise statement of the requirements and tolerances is often developed and referred to as a product's *specifications*. This stage is often critical for potential suppliers because final specifications can favor one product over another. Therefore, selling the benefits of a technology is often critical at this point in the purchasing process. Each supplier may emphasize different product features, so getting specifications established that are best met by your offering may be critical to landing the sale.

In some of the more advanced and successful partnering relationships, customers work with suppliers to meet product specifications. Take the case of Johnson Controls, Inc., chosen to supply seats for Chrysler's new small car, Neon. Johnson was able to meet Chrysler's cost target but fell far short on safety, weight, and comfort. Ten Chrysler engineers met with 10 Johnson counterparts, led by the sales director. After five 11-hour days, they agreed on weight, cost, and performance targets and subsequently helped Johnson meet these targets.[6] This example also illustrates that in more advanced buyer-seller relationships, the supplier is actually chosen prior to completion of detailed technical specification which are jointly developed by the supplier and customer.

Search for Suppliers

Because of strong competition in many industries, manufacturers are under pressure to reduce the costs of parts and raw materials. Purchased materials represent from 30 to 80 percent and average 50 percent of an original manufacturer's (OEM) total product cost.[7] This means that buyers are likely to spend considerable time searching for new, low-cost suppliers during the third step of the selling process. Some firms and government organizations even publish solicitations to help find bidders. The length of the search is likely to depend on the significance of the purchase to the buying organization.[8]

Supplier search is not without costs. Costs associated with identifying viable alternative suppliers include time, travel, educating vendors, cost of misunderstandings, and postsale problems. Partially as a result of these and other costs, customers are greatly reducing the number of suppliers with whom they do business. Figure 4–2 shows the magnitude of supplier reductions made by some large customers. Consider the Owens-Brockway and Johnson Controls examples of cooperative problem solving between buyers and sellers. A buyer would not have the resources to establish this type of working relationship with a large number of suppliers of the same product or service.

| | Number of Suppliers | | Percent |
	Previous	Current	Change
Xerox	5,000	500	−90%
Motorola	10,000	3,00	−70%
Digital Equipment	9,000	3,000	−67%
General Motors	1,800	1,000	−45%
Ford Motor	1,800	1,000	−44%
Texas Instruments	22,000	14,000	−36%
Rainbird	520	380	−27%
Allied Signal Aerospace	7,500	6,000	−20%

Source: John Emshwiller, "Suppliers Struggle to Improve Quality as Big Firms Slash Their Vendor Roles," *Wall Street Journal*, August 16, 1991, p. B1.

Figure 4-2: Supplier Reduction Trends

Proposals

The fourth stage in the purchasing process is the acquisition and evaluation of *proposals*. It is important to know the seller's criteria for evaluating alternative offerings. In purchasing materials and equipment, for example, building contractors may consider service, quality of product, supplier support, low price, and/or reputation for fair dealing among their most important purchasing criteria when choosing suppliers. The relative importance of these criteria, however, may vary from one contractor to the next. One contractor may place more importance on low price, while another may be more concerned about the willingness of the supplier to stand behind the product. To win a contract, it is important that a supplier's proposal is written toward meeting the customer's priorities. See Sales Management in Action 4–1 for an example of how one consulting company's proposal missed the mark. Then again, if suppliers are judged by the customer as being about equal on these criteria, friendship with the supplier, the salesperson's personality, or that of the supplier may be determining factors in the sale.

Increasingly, the proposal follows an in-depth audit of the buyer's operating processes. This is likely to be the case when the seller employs a *systems selling* approach. Systems selling is used when a firm is selling a system of products, services, and assistance necessary to carry out a complex process or function in the buyer's organization. Bottomley and Associates, Inc. (Atlanta, Ga.), for example, will do an operational assessment of the medical records department in a hospital evaluating how the department processes its work, its procedures, adherence to performance standards, and interface with the rest of the hospital. Bottomley will submit a proposal to the hospital to take over total management of the hospital's record department, including having the hospital's employees become Bottomley's employees, if the audit indicates that cost savings are feasible within predetermined performance standards. In addition, they may suggest purchasing encoders, imaging software, and other computer software. Bottomley's CEO, Larry Gerdes, indicated that the audit takes two

Sales Management in Action 4-1
Marketing or Restructuring?

The consulting manager had a whole team spend a month on a proposal for a point-of-sale system for a major retail client's marketing department. Because he had worked with the retailer on systems in finance, operations, and distribution, the manager felt he had an inside track on this system. His company did not get the project. He tells why:

"We had some great contacts within MIS, but they weren't willing to talk much about the new point-of-sale system until they'd put out a bid and received proposals from all interested vendors. We got some points of view on technology that other bidders probably didn't have, but nothing you could really take to the bank."

"A few months after we lost the proposal, the client granted us a post-mortem. It turned out the issue was not really point-of-sale data

for the marketing department, although that's what was stated in the specifications. The real issue was that the client anticipated consolidation of its retail stores and consolidation is a good time to build a marketing system and tighten the link between customers and product marketing. But in terms of what they were really looking for, they wanted someone who specifically had experience developing systems in the middle of a radical restructuring. We actually had that experience, but we never knew this was an issue to them, so it never went into our proposal. The winning vendor was all over this point; we saw their proposal, and the entire document reeked of restructuring."

Source: Neil Rackham, Lawrence Friedman, and Richard Ruff, *Getting Partnering Right*, (New York: McGraw-Hill, 1996), pp. 83–84.

to three days to perform, the report takes one week to complete, and it may take the hospital three to four months to make a decision on whether to give Bottomley a five-year contract. The whole selling cycle takes less than six months.

Supplier Selection

In many cases, the final *supplier selection* decision is made by a *buying committee*. The buying committee may be made up of personnel from a variety of functional areas affected by the decision, often including management from finance, operations, purchasing, manufacturing, and marketing. As the earlier discussion suggests, however, some companies are moving away from a long and thorough analysis of multiple suppliers to a long-term focus on a limited number of suppliers.

Price is usually a crucial factor in business-to-business marketing, especially for commodity-type items, for which there are many comparable alternatives from which to choose. With consumer goods, the emphasis on price is often inversely related to derived demand for the product. As the perceived value of the product falls in the eyes of the ultimate consumer, dollars previously spent on product improvement and advertising are temporarily shifted to price reductions. Agreement with this change in marketing strategy and passing along consumer price incentives to the retailer's shelves is one of the key dynamics within a partnering relationship between manufacturer and retailer.

As is true in the other stages of the purchasing process, the role of price in many buyer-seller relationships is changing in today's competitive environment. One change is that instead of looking just for a low price, some buyers are realizing that by working together with sellers, they can operate more efficiently and effectively in satisfying the needs of the ultimate consumer. As a result, Hewlett-Packard has instituted a Global Accounts Program with a dedicated sales team for each of its top 1,000 accounts. The sales team consists of technical and marketing consultants who are located at the headquarters of the customer, not in a Hewlett-Packard sales office.[9]

Performance Evaluation

Once the goods are delivered, evaluation begins. The *performance evaluation* focuses on both the product and the supplier, and may include a formal value analysis and/or a vendor analysis.

Value analysis, developed during the 1940s by General Electric as a basis for cost reduction, is a detailed analysis of vendor offerings focusing on the relative cost of providing a necessary function or service at the desired time and place with the necessary quality. Value analysis focuses on total cost, not just invoice cost. For repetitively purchased items, *possession costs* (i.e., costs related to holding inventory) and *acquisition costs* (e.g., costs associated with originating requisitions, interviewing salespeople, expediting deliveries, receiving and editing invoices, follow-up on inaccurate and late deliveries) usually far exceed the price on the invoice that the customer pays for the product.[10]

Vendor analysis is similar to value analysis but focuses on the vendor by looking at such things as delivery reliability, product quality, price, service, and technical competence. Vendor analysis focuses on eliminating marginal suppliers in order to reduce contact costs and improve efficiency. General Motors, for example, used vendor analysis to help concentrate its steel purchases among a smaller number of suppliers. GM felt it could get better service and prices by favoring a few vendors with most of its steel business.

In some high-tech industries there is a movement away from extensive vendor analysis. Instead, suppliers are offering a warranty that says in effect the supplier will share the cost of any changes in specifications that are needed during a period of time. The supplier is essentially sharing in the customer's risk while reducing the selling and purchasing cycle.

Repeat Purchases

The steps shown in Figure 4–1 apply mostly to purchases of products and supplies new to the organization, especially those involving significant risk. The purchasing of significantly modified products will also tend to follow this six-step process. Repeat purchases, also known as *straight rebuys*, involve a less complicated process, since a customer is reordering a product that has been purchased many times before without any modification requirements. These purchases are usually made from among a single or limited number of approved suppliers. Further, the decision is usually limited to one of quantity and delivery, rather than a complete respecification of the product's requirements. A far more limited number of people, usually in the purchasing and operations departments, are given responsibility for ordering products in straight rebuy situations.

Summary

This section discussed the distinct phases of organizational purchasing to illustrate the typical process and to demonstrate how suppliers can win or lose the sale at any point in this process. Selling in such situations requires a high degree of customer intimacy—knowing what problems the customers have, their priorities, expectations, needs, and culture.[11] Likewise, it is important that salespeople know who within the customer's organization is involved in the purchasing decision and understand their role in the process. The next section provides a framework for understanding the roles people play in the process and how their perspectives and needs may differ.

► BUYING CENTER

Because organizational purchasing decisions usually involve multiple people, the term *buying center* is used to refer to all of the people formally or informally involved in the purchasing decision. The buying center changes over time and is not a formal department in the organization. The number of people included in the buying center may vary from 1 to 15 or more, depending on a number of factors, including how many departments use the item, the dollar value of the purchase, and the product's degree of technical sophistication. Four people, for instance, are typically involved in the purchasing of new office equipment: a purchasing agent, an office manager, a controller, and a supervisor of the department using the equipment. Each of these people is likely to have a unique perspective and purchasing concern when selecting an office equipment supplier.

A *purchasing concern* refers to the issue or criterion that a member of the buying center will consider when deciding whether to approve or recommend either a purchase or a specific supplier. Each member of the buying center will have certain purchasing concerns. Purchasing concerns may be grouped into one of three types: economic buyers, user buyers, and technical buyers. An individual buying center member may have multiple concerns, but these concerns are expected to be held by at least one individual in any major purchasing situation.[12] A fourth person must also be present for the sale to be successfully concluded. This person is referred to as an advocate. Each of these four roles is described in this section.

Economic Buyer

An *economic buyer* is the person or committee who has the power to give final approval to buy your product or service. These people have the money to make a purchase and are able to release the cash to buy should they choose to do so. The focus of the economic buyer is not exclusively on price or technology, but also on performance; that is, what will the organization get in return for spending this money?

Obviously this buyer must be identified in each sale. Although these people are rarely very far down in the organization, their exact organizational position will depend on a number of factors. The economic buyer is likely to be further up the organizational ladder in the following situations:

- The more expensive the product
- The more depressed the organization's business condition
- The less experience the customer has with you, your firm, and the product
- The greater the potential impact a wrong purchase decision will have on the organization

The person who assumes the role of economic buyer may change if the role the product or service performs for the customer changes. The regional Bell operating companies (RBOCs) of a downsized AT&T, for example, are experiencing this in the telecommunications industry. The role played by telecommunications has changed as a result of the movement toward distributed data processing and networked computer systems.[13] Many companies now view telecommunications as a strategic asset rather than just "utilities." This has far-reaching implications for sales and marketing in the industry. "In the last three years," says a vice president of operations at AT&T, "we have changed from selling to purchasing agents and dealing with only the communications managers. We have expanded our horizons to where we must gain acceptance with people in the customer organization who are policy makers." This change in focus has necessitated many changes in AT&T's sales practices; for instance, the RBOCs' sales force training has been beefed up to place more emphasis on strategic business decision making in addition to the usual technical training of salespeople.

User Buyer

The role of *user buyers* is to determine the impact of the purchase on the job that they or their people perform. Their focus is much narrower than that of the economic buyer because they are primarily concerned with their own operating areas or departments. As users, they represent a very powerful buying influence and one that is important for the seller to identify. This point is made quite well in the now-famous story of 3M's Post-It notes. Initial efforts to sell the stick-on notes to office managers met with little success. It wasn't until 3M gave secretaries and office workers free samples that the notes took off.

Identifying user buying influences may be more complex than often anticipated. In selling axles for trucks, for example, there are at least three sets of users involved.

First, there are the manufacturing engineers who design manufacturing processes. Second, there are the people on the manufacturing line at the assembly plant who fit the axle onto the truck. Third, the ultimate end-user is the customer who buys the truck. In recognition of this, some leading-edge axle supply companies are questioning their customer's customers directly about the performance of their axles.[14]

Technical Buying Influence

The role of *technical buyers* is to act as gatekeepers by screening out products and suppliers that do not meet the needs of the buying organization. Their function is to narrow down the choices to those alternatives that are most likely to fulfill particular organizational objectives. In other words, these people can't say "Yes," only "No."

These buyers are called technical buyers because they focus on the quantifiable aspects of the product or service as they relate to the product's specifications. A number of people may perform this function, including engineers, legal counsel, and purchasing agents. In our earlier truck axle example, product engineers and designers would probably assume this role. See Sales Management in Action 4-2 for an unusual example of a technical buyer for nonslipping shoes. Often, however, purchasing agents take a leading role as technical buying influences.

One problem salespeople have experienced with some technical buyers is that they take on the appearance of the economic buyer, that is, the person who makes the final decision. This may occur because of the person's screening function and also out of self-deception or an attempt to elevate their perceived importance within the organization. At any rate, salespeople may be misled, and as a result, a purchase

---

Sales Management in Action 4-2
Safety Shoes for the Benefits Office

The High Test Safety Shoes Company manufactures and sells a variety of shoes designed to protect workers from job-related injuries. They sell a nonslipping shoe to the airlines that workers wear when performing repairs and maintenance on airplanes. One key user buying influence High Test must sell is the personnel and benefits department of the airlines because once every six days an airline worker will fall off the wing of a plane. These accidents may result in higher insurance rates, workman's compensation, and other medical-related expenses, not to mention the cost of possibly replacing the injured employee. If High Test can show that their shoes can reduce accidents and lower the costs associated with accidents, it is addressing the concerns of the personnel and benefits office of the airline, an important buying influence in this case.

Source: John Caslione, "Strategic Sales Planning," presented in "Leading the High-Performance Sales Organization," October 7, 1993.

decision may be a surprise to them because the competition has dealt with the real economic buyer.

Advocate

In a complex selling situation involving multiple buying influences, it has been suggested that salespeople need to develop a special relationship with a buying influence referred to as an *advocate*. The role of the advocate is to help guide you in the sale by providing critical information about the organization and the people involved in the purchase decision. These people may be internal or external to the buying organization. They do not necessarily make the sale or make referrals, but they are willing to provide key information about those who do influence the sale. They are often able to sell for you when you cannot be there, for example during purchasing committee meetings. Their motivation for providing this information is that they are convinced that your product is best for the organization, and therefore they have a personal interest in seeing that you get the sale. This person is obviously critical, and must be selected and developed with care. Others in the buying center must feel that the person is trustworthy and competent. Ideally, the advocate will be recognized by others in the buying center as a group leader and major influence. One way to identify a good advocate, in fact, is to listen for the person that other people in the buying center refer to a lot. A strong advocate may be important to the seller's long-term success, since people are less apt to change after having established a publicly stated position.[15]

Summary

The buying center concept has several important implications for salespeople in business-to-business selling. First, salespeople must be quite diverse in their knowledge and flexible in their behavior. Salespeople may find themselves, for example, selling to purchasing agents, engineers, production managers, and controllers in order to close a sale. People are likely to be much more involved in the sales message when it is tailored to their functional area.

Second, the people involved in each stage of the purchasing process and their role in the process may change. Purchasing agents, for example, have been found to have the greatest influence during the later stages of the purchasing process. They are experts at negotiation and tend to know a lot about the suppliers' and competitors' product offerings and terms of sale. Production, on the other hand, is usually most influential during the need identification stage, while engineering is most involved in establishing specifications. To further illustrate these points, the appendix at the end of this chapter reviews the purchase of an automotive test stand. Sales Management in Action 4-3 illustrates that the buying center concept may be very important even when selling relatively moderately priced, low-tech products.

Third, be sure that you know who the real decision-makers are. There is a tendency for people to exaggerate their role in any decision. In addition, most people enjoy the special treatment—golf or dinner—a supplier may extend to the decision-makers in a big potential sale.

Sales Management in Action 4-3
How Many People Does it Take to Buy a Window?

The answer is, probably more people than you thought it would take. Marvin Windows, a rapidly growing manufacturer of windows and patio doors, has achieved sales of $230 million by understanding that architects, building owners, remodelers, building supply dealers, and builders all influence the window purchase decision. Marvin tailors its messages to the requirements of each decision influencer. Architects are important in setting specifications, so Marvin stresses design flexibility that meets aesthetic and budget constraints. The emphasis is on the soft sell, technical support, visual excitement, and design options rather than price. Remodelers, on the other hand, want windows that fit existing spaces and minimize installation charges, so Marvin positions itself as a made-to-order window manufacturer. For these people, Marvin uses a more aggressive sales approach and exhibits a large number of traditional windows. Builders are looking for technical support, details such as frame size, and design options, rather than the lowest price. When addressing building supply dealers, the company focuses on how its Windows enhance profitability through high resale margins. The line of windows stays the same, but Marvin Windows has been very successful because they understand their customers' needs and tailor the sales pitch to meet the needs of each influencer in the buying decision process.

Source: Kate Bertrand, "Divide and Conquer," *Business Marketing* (October 1989), pp. 49–53.

▶ BUILDING RELATIONSHIPS

In 1976, a Digital Equipment Corporation regional sales manager commented, "Our products sell themselves. My only constraint is not enough sales reps to function as order takers."[16] In 1991, 15 years later, Digital was sending all its salespeople to account development workshops focusing on relationship selling. "Having a superior product is not good enough," commented a Digital senior executive. "Customers want and expect more, especially trust and responsiveness."[17]

Most marketers would agree that they would like to establish a long-term relationship with their customers to ensure a stream of purchases and an upgrading of the equipment each client purchases over time. Like Digital, many companies are emphasizing to their salespeople the importance of understanding how to build and enhance professional relationships at all levels in the organization.[18] It is up to the individuals in both buyer and seller organizations to cement a professional relationship by adding value, meeting expectations, developing trust, and having a willingness to bargain. These "relationship binders" are discussed further in the next section.

According to research in social psychology, growing relationships evolve through five general stages: (1) awareness, (2) exploration, (3) expansion, (4) commitment, and

Relationship Stage	Description	Key Selling Objectives
Awareness	Recognition that a supplier may be able to satisfy an important need.	1. Gain customer's attention. 2. Demonstrate how the product/service can satisfy a need.
Exploration	A tentative, initial trial with limited commitments by both parties. This trial period may go on for an extended period of time.	1. Gain initial acceptance. 2. Build a successful relationship.
Expansion	Expanding the interactions, commitments, and rewards for each party in the relationship.	1. Get to know customers and their business better. 2. Look for additional ways to help the customer.
Commitment	The commitment by both the buyer and seller to an exclusive relationship.	1. Interaction at levels between the buyer's and seller's organizations. 2. Early supplier involvement in development processes. 3. Long-term focus to the relationship.
Dissolution	Total disengagement from the relationship. This may occur at any point in the relationship.	1. Look for warning signals. 2. Attempt to reinitiate the relationship.

Figure 4-3: Stages in a Buyer–Seller Relationship

(5) dissolution.[19] Although it may be difficult to determine exactly when a relationship progresses to each stage, each represents a major shift in the nature of the relationship; consequently, salespeople should be aware of these changes and proceed accordingly. These five stages of *relationship evolution* and the objectives associated with each stage are summarized in Figure 4-3.

Awareness

This stage refers to a recognition by the client that a seller may be a viable source for a particular product or service. Commitments at this stage are nonexistent or very limited. Buyers' and sellers' actions are largely unilateral; that is, they are each looking out solely for their own objectives.

While this stage may seem obvious in beginning a relationship, it makes a subtle but important point. Relationships are based on a number of sales calls, and customers want to know who you and your company are before they are ready to spend much time with you and certainly before making any commitments. The Ball Corporation recognizes this explicitly in its selling strategy, which they refer to as the *planned selling approach*. Ball Corporation is a packaging company with a high-technology base. Its products consist of glass, metal cans, barrier plastic packaging, and industrial product lines and items used in space technology. The purpose of the first sales call is to explain further who the Ball Corporation is. On subsequent calls, salespeople tell buyers about each of the four product groups.

The importance of this stage and the validity of Ball Corporation's selling approach are backed by research comparing the sales approaches of average and higher-performing salespeople. This research found that higher-performing salespeople felt that assessing the prospect's knowledge of the seller's company and discussing the prospect's background were more important activities in the initial sales call than did lower-performing salespeople. Conversely, lower-performing salespeople felt that making a complete presentation and explaining each product benefit was more important than did higher-performing salespeople.[20]

Exploration

When both parties develop a heightened sense that the possibility for mutual benefit exists, this signals the beginning of the exploration stage of the relationship. The buyer is willing at this point to make a greater effort to explore the seller's offering and capabilities. The Ball Corporation, for example, invites prospects and their fellow decision-makers to visit its research labs, a manufacturing plant, and corporate headquarters in Muncie, Indiana. A certain level of interest must have been developed up to this point for a buyer to commit time to this type of visit.

From the seller's perspective, the selling process shifts to understanding the unique needs and viewpoints of the account in order to better understand whether and how a product can be of benefit. At this point, buyers are more willing to share their needs and feelings with a seller. This suggests that salespeople should be aware that usually buyers will be unwilling to share their true concerns with a salesperson on the first visit. The relationship has not yet progressed to this point of heightened trust and interest.

The exploration stage focuses on a *trial relationship*. If feasible, trial purchases (small quantities or tests) may take place in an effort to better understand the benefits, consequences, and costs or problems associated with a product. For example, it is common in the furniture industry for large furniture chains to purchase a sofa from a manufacturer for the purpose of examining its durability, workmanship, and general appearance. Recall from the opening vignette on Owens-Brockway that teams from Owens-Brockway and the beverage producer met to review crucial issues with respect to the cost of glass containers for its beverage line. There must be a certain level of trust and expectation of success to commit to this type of relationship. At this point, however, the relationship is very fragile, allowing for relatively easy termination.

Expansion

During this phase, the parties have experienced some of the benefits and problems associated with the relationship and attempt to expand the benefits. Returning again to the Owens-Brockway example, Owens was awarded a five-year contract as a result of its work with the beverage producer. At the end of this period, it will need to renegotiate. How strong Owens-Brockway's position will be at that time will depend on how well it has lived up to its agreement.

Expansion doesn't simply refer to increased sales, though this will usually occur in a good relationship. Expansion also occurs in the joint activities in which a seller and customer may engage. These activities include tool development and product design, value analysis and cost targeting, design of quality control and delivery systems, and long-term planning.[21] This also suggests that one of the distinguishing characteristics of this stage is increased dependency between supplier and buyer. Both parties will have made unique investments in the form of personnel, time, and information sharing.

In some cases, increased business will take place naturally because a customer's business grows over time. However, salespeople should not expect sales to increase as a natural phenomenon; they must be earned. As suggested earlier, calling on existing customers is often the most productive use of a salesperson's time. One practical suggestion for increasing business with an existing account is to survey, either formally or informally, as many parts of the customer's business as possible and examine in some detail all aspects of the operation. For each department visited, a comprehensive report of its requirements should be produced. In the context of what the salesperson is selling, the following elements should be established:

1. **Existing uses.**   What limits current operations? What makes current operations more difficult than they need be? Which of these difficulties are most important? What do managers see as their worst problems?

2. **Possible needs.**   What do managers need to make their operations better? What do they need to make their lives easier and more pleasant?

3. **Possible solutions.**   What does the client think might be the best solutions?

4. **Possible new uses.**   What new operations does the client believe might be possible? Which ones are favored?

5. **Decision criteria.**   In supporting any solution, what would the business and personal criteria be?

One of the important benefits of this type of survey is that it will provide the salesperson with the knowledge necessary to demonstrate expertise in the customer's business. The United Parcel Service (UPS), for example, will set up private branch exchange, and telecommunications services, as well as perform time-and-motion studies for its clients. What does this have to do with the delivery of packages? These value-added services make UPS more valuable to the customer, often resulting in access to decision-makers higher up in the organization.

Commitment

This stage consists of a high degree of commitment by the buyer and seller to their relationship. The commitment is more than just between individuals, it is also between organizations. In fact, a buyer may commit to purchase from only one supplier, while a supplier sells exclusively to one buyer within a specified trading area.

- Ford Motor Company is reducing its supplier base from 52,000 to 5,000—a reduction of over 90 percent.
- AlliedSignal's plants used to buy valves, pipes, and fittings from 400 suppliers. Now it has packed all that business into a $10 million-a-year contract with one supplier.[22]
- Scott Aviation has cut back its supplier base from 800 to less than 250.[23]

Customers are consolidating their supplier base for a very straightforward reason. Customers are under a lot of pressure. Cheap technology, easily available information, and the explosion of global markets have commoditized their businesses and driven down their prices. In response, customers are looking to suppliers as a resource where there is potential to find new productivity and competitiveness.

Customer evaluation is also more important, especially in a *strategic partnering* relationship, because a supplier is more dependent on the client's success for his or her own success. The supplier must select a winner with which to establish a committed relationship. Some important considerations when choosing a customer with which to partner include the following:

- **Potential for impact.**   Is there some real value for both parties that can come out of partnering that could not be achieved from a traditional supplier relationship?
- **Common Values.**   Is there sufficient commonality of values—what the parties consider to be important? In particular, it is important that both companies be ethical and look at quality and the quality process similarly.
- **Good environment for partnering.**   How does each party look upon the partnership—long-term relationship versus profit on the sale, future oriented or present? Are there frequent interaction and transactions between the two companies?[24]
- **Consistency with supplier's goals.**   Is a partnering relationship with this customer consistent with our own product and market strategy, and with our overall direction as a company?

Strategic partnering represents the extreme in interorganizational commitment. Even in more transactionally oriented buyer-seller relationships there may develop a deep level of personal and professional commitment between the parties. This is likely to be the time when the customer is most profitable for the supplier.

Dissolution

The possibility of disengaging from a relationship is not a direct consequence of commitment, but it is implicit at each stage. If the criteria discussed for each stage are not met in the relationship, then the parties may choose either to limit the relationship to one of the earlier developmental stages or to disengage from the relationship entirely.

The world of business is dynamic, and the forces of change require that the seller stay alert to the possibility of dissolution even when a relationship with a client is in a strong commitment stage. Specific issues that sellers should continually monitor include (1) increasing costs of transactions; (2) financial health of the client; (3) changing barriers to switching suppliers; (4) changes in key personnel; and (5) changing organizational needs, resulting in less relative value for the benefits of the seller's products and services.

Salespeople must be alert to signs that a relationship is changing. Following are five warning signals that a relationship may possibly change:[25]

1. **Missing information.** You are unable to specify the purchasing concern (e.g., economic, user, or technical buyer) of each person involved in the buying decision or there is a buying role for which you do not have the name of the person fulfilling this role.

2. **Uncertainty about information.** You are unsure about what a piece of information means to the sale. For example, you may not know how a change in the size of new retail stores affects your client's merchandising strategies.

3. **Uncontacted buying influence.** Each buying influence should be contacted, either by the salesperson or by someone else from the selling organization. For example, Saga, Coca-Cola, and Hewlett-Packard employ a strategy of like-rank selling to cover all the bases of a sale. This means that salespeople contact people at a comparable level in the client's organization.

4. **Customer personnel new to the job.** This occurs when a new person comes to the customer's organization or is transferred from another part of the organization. This person must be sold on the existing relationship.

5. **Reorganization.** Like the new buying influence, when people assume a new role, they must be sold. That is, the relationship changes when people change, even though the name of the account stays the same. Reorganizations can be particularly difficult because a person's role may change, even though the person occupies the same office and has the same title.

All of these examples point to the same conclusions: (1) relationships are based on people and (2) you should expect and anticipate changes in relationships over time in a selling environment. These warning signals also suggest that you should not put all your eggs in one basket. Don't put all your faith in one customer or one person within an organization. Cross-check information to find and fix any problems that may arise.

▶ RELATIONSHIP BINDERS

It should be obvious from the previous discussion that there are certain factors that drive parties, whether individuals or organizations, to progress to a fully committed relationship. Salespeople should be aware of these factors. This section reviews four important underlying factors necessary for a fully developed relationship that every salesperson and marketer should know and understand—value, expectations, bargaining, and trust.[26]

Value

Value refers to the perception that the rewards exceed the costs associated with expanding the relationship. For the seller, highly committed relationships provide the opportunity to leverage its skills and resources, develop long-term customers, and build strong competitive positions. Investment in building relationships may be considerable, so the financial returns must also be significant to justify their cost.

Value to a buyer is not always the lowest list price; it may also be time savings, labor savings, or greater sales of the customer's products. Value must ultimately reach the customer's customers in the form of cheaper products, wider choices, and quicker access to those choices.

Consider Motorola, Inc.'s approach to selling customized pagers. Motorola's pager sales force will use the customer's own specifications to design the pager system just right for the customer's needs. The specs, put together on a laptop computer by the Motorola sales rep, are sent via modem to the company's factory. This individualized product development, however, requires an investment of time and effort on the part of the buyer. Motorola executives feel that it is partially this initial investment by the customer that makes them so resistant to competition.[27]

Expectations

In any relationship, the involved parties develop *expectations*, sometimes referred to as *rules* or *norms*, with respect to acceptable conduct and performance. Acceptable behavior varies by individual preferences, company policies, and national cultures. See Sales Management in Action 4-4 for a discussion of the cultural tendencies of different countries.

In some strategic relationships, buyers and sellers derive a mutually agreed-upon set of team values. These are sometimes put in writing in order to remind all members that these are the accepted standards of conduct of the relationship to which every individual must subscribe. Each may agree, for instance, to be the advocate for the other partner within their own company. It is especially important to ensure that new members to the team are aware of and comply with these values.

Salespeople must be careful not to encourage unfavorable buyer expectations as a result of present behaviors. If a salesperson agrees to a special price discount at the request of a buyer, for example, then this may become standard practice as far as the buyer is concerned, and some sort of discounting will be expected in the future. Because of this behavior, many companies, such as IBM and Procter & Gamble, do not give their salespeople the flexibility to discount prices in order to avoid the development of a discounting rule.

Expectations also develop with respect to performance. Customer performance expectations include the performance of the product, as well as a number of service activities such as frequency of sales calls, notification of price changes, lead time in delivery, order fill rate, emergency orders, and installation. A recent study comparing the performance perceptions of salespeople and buyers in a wide variety of industries shows that there is considerable inaccuracy in salespeople's perceptions of buyers' performance expectations.[28] Furthermore, accuracy in identifying the buyer's performance rules is related to high sales performance. Interestingly, salespeople in this

---

Sales Management in Action 4-4
National Culture and Selling in France

Because people from the same country are conditioned by similar background, educational, and life experiences, they are likely to have similar cultures or dispositions to see things a certain way. Researchers have classified national cultures along four dimensions:

- Uncertainty avoidance: how people accept and handle uncertainty and tolerate opinions and behaviors different from their own

- Individualism: the extent to which people enjoy individual freedom and are expected to take care of their nuclear family alone

- Power distance: the extent to which inequalities in power and wealth are condoned and supported

- Masculinity: whether traditional masculine values such as assertiveness, respect for superachievers, and acquisition of money and material possessions are valued versus feminine values such as nurturing, concern for the environment, and championing the underdog

Relative to other countries, for example, France displays a strong tendency to avoid uncertainty and a willingness to condone and encourage inequalities in power and wealth. When selling in France, emphasis should be placed on such factors as established name brand, superior warranty, and money-back guarantees as uncertainty reducers. An appeal to the status value of the offering is also likely to be favorably received in France. Individuals will develop their own styles, but it is very helpful to be aware of national cultures in international sales.

Source: Sudhir Kale, "The Cultural Domain of Cross-National Buyer–Seller Interactions," presented at the American Marketing Association's Summer Educator Conference, August 1993.

---

study with more experience were less accurate in their buyer performance expectations.

To encourage accuracy in customer assessment, some companies require their salespeople to provide a written assessment of their key customers once a year. This assessment process involves answering a series of questions, however, writing the answers down helps to identify key assumptions, inconsistencies, and missing information. This assessment could be done every time a competitor wins a key piece of business.

Bargaining

Bargaining refers to the willingness to negotiate each party's obligations, benefits, and burdens. Two aspects of bargaining are of particular interest in the buyer-seller context. First, buyers must perceive a willingness on the part of the seller to negotiate on significant factors in the relationship. Thus, while a firm may be unwilling to negotiate the price, it should demonstrate considerable flexibility in other important areas such as delivery service, maintenance agreements, installation, and so on. Second, sellers should engage in bargaining early in the relationship in order to avoid misconceptions regarding future obligations and norms of conduct. There may be some reservations among salespeople, especially new ones, about engaging in such bargaining out of fear of losing the sale. Veteran salespeople are probably more aware of the hazards of not bargaining early in the relationship. They have probably learned that the costs of terminating a relationship are higher when a customer is alienated later in the relationship.

It is also important to keep in mind that customers want and expect to bargain. They will likely want to bargain even if you have offered your best price. You should be able to offer something other than price, like equipment documentation, training, support, and supplies. Remember, the "best deal" in your opinion may not be the customer's "best deal."

Trust

Trust refers to the belief that an individual's word or promise can be believed and that the long-term interests of the customer will be served. Trust in salespeople and their companies has been found to be essential to buyers' evaluation of the quality of a relationship and to establishing working partnerships.[29] How does a salesperson earn the trust of a buyer? Studies of buyers and sellers have shown that the five most important trust-earning attributes of salespeople are the following:

- **Dependability.**   Salespeople who follow through on their promises.
- **Competence.**   Salespeople who know what they are talking about.
- **Customer orientation.**   Salespeople who put buyers' interests ahead of their own.
- **Honesty.**   Salespeople who tell the truth.
- **Likability.**   Salespeople whom the buyer enjoys knowing.[30]

Other studies have found that salespeople tend to overestimate, relative to buyers, the importance of likability and product competence as trust-building elements.[31] Consequently, salespeople may rely too much on likability and product knowledge.[32]

► ETHICAL SITUATIONS

Building close relationships with individual customers may also give rise to ethical issues. Strategic partnering calls for disclosure of information, for example, future strategic plans that would not usually be disclosed in a more traditional arm's-length relationship. In this situation, salespeople must be careful not to reveal this information to direct or indirect competitors of the customer. This is probably most likely to happen when attempting to establish your expertise with a new prospect. As the primary contact with a partner, you may well be given information that the partner does not want you to share even with other people in your own company.

Another delicate situation that is likely to arise is associated with the need to contact all members of the buying center who may influence the purchase decision.

What if the customer's organization has a policy against salespeople talking directly with the end-user of a product or service? The end-user may be a production engineer in a factory, for example, or a doctor in a hospital. Should you try to get around these policies in an effort to influence the sale? What if there is no company policy against your talking with a user but the purchasing agent has asked you not to contact this person?

Based on the development expectations within a relationship, what if the customer or partner engages in unethical behavior or if salespeople from other companies do so? Is this sufficient justification for your taking retaliatory actions? In an interesting study of overselling of an expensive product that is not needed by the customer, results indicated that sales managers did not accept this excuse. In fact, they tended to be harsher in their recommended punishment when unethical behavior by either a customer or a competitor was mentioned as justification for unethical behavior by a salesperson.[33]

▶ QUALITY SALES MANAGEMENT: CROSS-FUNCTIONAL TEAMS

In focusing on improving processes and satisfying the customer, many companies are forming cross-functional teams of people to address specific problems and to interface with customers. Following are examples of teams that some companies have set up to satisfy customers' expectations:

- To meet their goal of creating "customer delight," the Morris Paper Company (Mars, Pa.) has created a sales team composed of representatives from sales, marketing, credit, logistics, and technical services involved in the selling cycle.

- G. D. Searle & Company (Skokie, Ill.) has implemented a feedback system involving customers as consultants. Departments most commonly involved in consulting with customers are marketing, corporate medical and scientific affairs, R&D, manufacturing, legal, regulatory, training, human resources, sales operations, corporate communications, and quality control.

- To reduce miscommunications between the sales department and other internal departments, BBN Software Products (Cambridge, Mass.) implemented a Total Quality Sales Management (TQSM) process in which the first step was to create a TQSM team comprised of representatives from sales, marketing, manufacturing, engineering, finance/accounting, and distribution.

As the above examples illustrate, teams are being formed in a variety of ways to perform a variety of functions. RELTEC for instance, helps the customer form a cross-functional team to meet with their sales teams. RELTEC has found that this helps to identify opportunities and handle problems. Selling teams are most often formed for one or a combination of the following reasons:

- *Rapidly changing technology.* New products are being added and old ones have improved at such a rapid pace that individual salespeople cannot stay current.

- **Customer consolidation.**   Individual customer operations are becoming so geographically diverse and important to the supplier that a team approach is needed and financially justified.
- **Demanding customers.**   Customers are demanding solutions to problems that individual salespeople are not equipped to handle.
- **Competitive advantage.**   Teams bring more of an organization's competencies to bear on the customer's problems so as to gain an advantage over competition.

Many of the current business developments discussed in this and previous chapters suggest that selling teams will become more prominent in the future, so companies are well advised to figure out how to form, manage, and direct selling teams.[34] These issues are addressed throughout the remaining chapters of this text.

▶ SUMMARY

In order to sell to organizations, a salesperson must know how organizations purchase. The selling process is intertwined with the buying process. The buying process in most organizations consists of a series of stages, which include need recognition, establishing specifications, searching for suppliers, gathering proposals, selecting suppliers, and evaluating performance. What occurs during each step will depend on the nature of the purchase and the type of relationship the buyer and seller enjoy.

Effective salespeople recognize that people in the buying center perform various roles and are involved in the purchasing process at different stages. It is important that salespeople identify all those involved in the process, as well as the nature of their involvement. Regardless of functional area or level in the organization, people in the buying center will assume one of three roles: economic buyer, technical buyer, or user buyer. In addition, salespeople should selectively choose and cultivate an advocate in the buying center.

Most transactions take place within the context of a buyer-seller relationship. The purchasing process and the purchase decision are likely to depend on the nature and quality of the relationship between the buyer and seller organizations. It is helpful, therefore, for salespeople to know the evolution of relationships and the factors that will drive the level of commitment and interdependence in a relationship. These factors include value, trust, expectations, and bargaining.

▶ KEY TERMS

Acquisition costs	Derived demand
Advocate	Economic buyer
Bargaining	Expectations
Buying center	Need recognition
Buying committee	Performance evaluation

Planned selling approach

Possession costs

Proposals

Purchasing concerns

Relationship evolution

Specifications

Straight rebuys

Strategic partnering

Supplier search

Supplier selection

Switching costs

Systems selling

Technical buyer

Trial relationship

Trust

User buyer

Value

Value analysis

Vendor analysis

▶ REVIEW QUESTIONS

1. What is the sequence of stages in an organizational purchasing process?

2. How does a straight rebuy differ from an initial purchase?

3. Explain the concept of derived demand and tell why it is so important to industrial salespeople.

4. Why are multiple buying influences so common in industrial selling?

5. What functional areas may be included in the buying center when an industrial organization is making an initial purchase of a highly technical product?

6. How is the economic buying influence different from the user and technical buying influences?

7. Purchasing agents often get involved in making value analyses of the products they buy. How does this affect the activities of field salespeople?

8. How does establishing a strategic partnering relationship with a buyer change the purchasing process?

9. What factors are most important in developing trust in an account relationship?

10. Why is it so important for salespeople to tell purchasing agents when they visit other buying influences within an organization?

11. What are the warning signals that an account relationship may possibly change?

12. What are the five stages through which a relationship may progress over time? How does the relationship change during each stage?

13. What are the most important ways in which salespeople can earn trust from buyers?

14. How can a salesperson increase sales to existing customers?

15. What type of person should a salesperson select as an advocate in the purchasing process?

▶ PROBLEMS

1. The General Services Administration (GSA) of the U.S. government has decided that it can save money by refurbishing government offices and putting people in smaller spaces. Westinghouse Furniture Systems believes it has just the right equipment for this job. How-

ever, Westinghouse's 150 furniture salespeople think of Uncle Sam as a buyer swathed in red tape. What can Westinghouse do to make it easier for its salespeople to sell to the government and for GSA to buy from Westinghouse?

2. Rockport makes several lines of special shoes for the rapidly growing aerobic walking market. Most of the shoes are styled as dress or casual models, but 20 percent are now styled as athletic shoes. These athletic walking shoes will be sold by a new channel called the "athletic specialty store." Rockport is trying to decide whether to expand its present sales force of 28 reps or to hire 8 agents with athletic shoe experience to concentrate on this new segment of the market. Based on your knowledge of professional buyer behavior, which approach should Rockport follow? Why?

3. The Micro Switch Division of Honeywell manufactures and markets sensors and related equipment. In the past, a sales call consisted of showing the sensors to purchasing agents and asking them what they thought of the product. Micro Switch is now trying to position itself as a factory automation expert. Instead of showing products, salespeople are selling a package of automation solutions. Will purchasing agents go for this new approach? Why or why not?

4. Edward A. Chapman, Exhibits Manager at AT&T, has found that women are more successful at trade show selling than men. What are the factors involved in industrial buying behavior and what are the qualities of purchasing agents that would help explain this difference?

5. The Lowell Corporation makes and sells a line of specialized hand tools for use by mechanics and assembly-line workers. When the president asked one of the company's sales reps about the effectiveness of advertising in attracting new business, the rep opened his desk and showed him a stack of inquiries generated by the company's ads. When asked what he was doing with the inquiries, the rep replied, "Nothing—they're all catalog collectors; they're a waste of my time." As a result of this conversation, the president thought about installing a computerized follow-up system to answer all inquiries and provide better lists of prospects. Should Lowell install the system and send letters and follow-up cards to purchasing agents? Why is it so difficult to get reps to go after new buyers?

6. Services Shipping, Inc., provided trucking services to large customers. It had an excellent reputation for reliable scheduling and careful handling. With decreasing regulation, Services' management decided that they needed more of a marketing orientation. They wanted to build and maintain long-lasting, profitable relationships with their customers. Services invested time and effort to study customers' shipping needs and were especially good at helping customers plan for their needs. After two years, Services' managers were very disappointed with the results. Customers were pleased with the new marketing approach and frequently complimented Services, but sales were down. Low-cost competitors were particularly bothersome. What went wrong? Why didn't customers want to commit to long-term relationships?

► EXPERIENTIAL EXERCISE

Make an appointment to interview an industrial purchasing agent. Ask the buyer to explain how parts, raw materials, or equipment are bought at his or her company. Prepare flow diagrams showing all the steps in the purchase process. Write a report comparing your diagrams with the model found in this chapter. Explain how a salesperson could make use of your charts.

▶ APPENDIX: BUYING A TEST STAND

An affiliated company had requested a test stand for automobile engines. The product research supervisor assigned the project to the section head of the mechanical division, who set the technical specifications for the test stand purchase. Next, the technical buyer took over and, based on his experience, requested credit checks for two potential suppliers. The buyer then made on-site visits to these suppliers and requested bids on the test stand. Proposals submitted by two firms were evaluated by the technical buyer, and a choice was made during a meeting with the group head of the mechanical division. A requisition for the test stand then had to be approved by the section head of the mechanical division and the business manager. The last step in the process required the technical buyer to issue a purchase order to buy the stand from supplier A.

Salespeople who wanted to influence the purchase of the test stand should have spent most of their time calling on the technical buyer and the group head of the mechanical division. These key influences set the specifications, searched for suppliers, and chose the winning bid. Secondary attention would have been allocated to the business manager and the section head of the mechanical division, who had to approve the order. One conclusion suggested by this example is that buying a test stand was complicated because it involved five executives and 13 different steps. In addition, the buyer was very thorough and actually visited two potential suppliers.

▶ REFERENCES

1. "Ultimate Edge," *Sales Manager's Bulletin* (September 15, 1993), pp. 1–2.

2. ALLISON LUCAS, "Leading Edge," *Sales & Sales Management* (June 1995), p. 13.

3. WILLIAM WEEKS and LYNN KAHLE, "Salespeople's Time Use and Performance," *Journal of Personal Selling & Sales Management* (Winter 1990), pp. 29–37.

4. For further development of the purchasing process, see MICHELE BUNN, "Taxonomy of Buying Decision Approaches," *Journal of Marketing* (January 1993), pp. 38–56.

5. DANIEL SMITH and JAN OWENS, "Knowledge of Customers' Customers as a Basis of Sales Force Differentiation," *Journal of Personal Selling & Sales Management*, 15 (Summer 1995), pp. 1–16.

6. "Chrysler's Neon," *Business Week* (May 3, 1993), p. 119.

7. CHARLES O'NEAL and KATE BERTRAND, *Developing a Winning JIT Marketing Strategy* (Englewood Cliffs, N.J.: Prentice-Hall, 1991).

8. JAN HEIDE and ALLEN WEISS, "Vendor Consideration and Switching Behavior for Buyers in High Technology Markets," *Journal of Marketing* (July 1995), pp. 30–43.

9. Presentation by MANUAL F. DIAZ, General Manager of Marketing and Sales for Hewlett-Packard at the seminar "Reinventing the Sales Organization," The Conference Board, September 28, 1993.

10. THOMAS NOOREWIER, GEORGE JOHN, and JOHN NEVIN, "Performance Outcomes of Purchasing Arrangements in Industrial Buyer-Vendor Relationships," *Journal of Marketing* (October 1990), pp. 80–93.

11. For more on understanding buyer decision making, see ARUN SHARMA and RAJNANDINI PILLAI, "Customers' Decision-Making Styles and The Preferences for Sales Strategies: Conceptual Examination and Empirical Study," *Journal of Per-*

sonal Selling & Sales Management. 16 (Winter 1996), pp. 21–34.

12. This discussion is based on concepts presented in ROBERT MILLER, STEPHEN HEIMAN, and TAD TULEJA, *Strategic Selling* (New York: William Morrow, 1985), pp. 83–87.

13. B. G. HOVOVICH, "Marketing After the Break-Up," *Business Marketing* (November 1991), pp. 14–16.

14. B. G. HOVOVICH, "Revolutionary Marketing," *Business Marketing* (March 1993), pp. 36–38.

15. ROBERT KRAPFEL, JR., "An Advocacy Behavior Model of Organizational Buyers' Vendor Choice," *Journal of Marketing,* 49 (Fall 1985), pp. 51–59.

16. STEPHEN DOYLE and KURT ENGEMANN, "How to Teach a Marketing Case About a Supplier Changing Its Selling Strategy from Transactional to Relationship," *Marketing Education Review,* 2 (Spring 1992), p. 41.

17. DOYLE and ENGEMANN, "How to Teach," p. 41.

18. ROBERT BLATTBERG and JOHN DEIGHTON, "Managing Marketing by the Customer Equity Test," *Harvard Business Review* (July–August 1996), pp. 136–144.

19. For more on relationship development see JAMES C. ANDERSON, "Relationships in Business Markets: Exchange Episodes, Value Creation, and Their Empirical Assessment," *Journal of the Academy of Marketing Science,* 23 (1996), pp. 346–350.

20. GERRARD MACINTOSH, KENNETH ANGLIN, DAVID SZYMANSKI, and JAMES GENTRY, "Relationship Development in Selling: A Cognitive Analysis," *Journal of Personal Selling & Sales Management,* 4 (Fall 1992), pp. 23–34.

21. JAN HEIDE and GEORGE JOHN, "Alliances in Industrial Purchasing: The Determinants of Joint Action in Buyer-Supplier Relationships," *Journal of Marketing Research,* 27 (February 1990), p. 25.

22. SHAWN TULLY, "Purchasing's New Muscle," *Fortune* (February 20, 1995), p. 79.

23. These examples and the discussion of which customers to partner with are from NEIL RACKHAM, LAWRENCE FRIEDMAN, and RICHARD RUFF, *Getting Partnering Right* (New York: McGraw-Hill, 1996), p. 4.

24. For more on the influencers of a customer's long-term orientation, see SHANKAR GANESAN, "Determinants of Long-Term Orientation in Buyer-Seller Relationships," *Journal of Marketing,* 58 (April 1994), pp.1–19.

25. MILLER et al., *Strategic Selling,* pp. 101–105.

26. For more on additional relationship binders, see DAVID T. WILSON, "An Integrated Model of Buyer-Seller Relationships," *Journal of the Academy of Marketing Science,* 23 (1996), pp. 225–245.

27. DON PEPPER and MARTHA ROGERS, "In One-to-One Marketing Customer Interaction Vital," *Business Marketing* (February 1994), p. 9.

28. DOUGLAS LAMBERT, HOWARD MARMORSTEIN, and ARUN SHARMA, "The Accuracy of Salespersons' Perceptions of Their Customers: Conceptual Examination and an Empirical Study," *Journal of Personal Selling & Sales Management* (Winter 1990), pp. 1–9.

29. For more information, see JAMES ANDERSON and JAMES NARUS, *Journal of Marketing,* 54 (January 1990), pp. 42–58, and LAWRENCE CROSBY, KENNETH EVANS, and DEBORAH COWLES, "Relationship Quality in Services Selling: An Interpersonal Influence Perspective," *Journal of Marketing,* 54 (July 1990), pp. 68–81.

30. JOHN SWAN, FRED TRAWICK, and DAVID RINK, "Measuring Dimensions of Purchaser Trust of Industrial Salespeople," *Journal of Personal Selling & Sales Management* (May 1988), pp. 1–9.

31. JON HAWES, KENNETH MAST, and JOHN SWAN, "Trust Earning Perceptions of Sellers and Buyers," *Journal of Personal Selling & Sales Management* (Spring 1989), pp. 1–8.

32. For more on building trust in business relationships, see ROBERT MORGAN and

Shelby Hunt, "The Commitment-Trust Theory of Relationship Marketing," *Journal of Marketing*, 58 (July 1994), pp. 20–38.

33. Joseph Bellizzi and D. Wayne Norwell, "Personal Characteristics and Salesperson's Justifications as Moderators of Supervisory Discipline in Cases Involving Unethical Salesforce Behavior," *Journal of the Academy of Marketing Science*, 19 (1991), pp. 11–16.

34. For more on how teams operate, see Dawn Deeter-Schmelz and Rosemary Ramsey, "A Conceptualization of the Functions and Roles of Formalized Selling and Buying Teams," *Journal of Personal Selling & Sales Management*, 15 (Spring 1995), pp. 47–60.

▶ SELECTED READINGS

Clancy, Kevin, and Robert Shulman, *The Marketing Revolution* (New York: HarperCollins, 1993).

Crosby, John, *Managing the Big Sale* (Chicago, Ill.: American Marketing Association, 1996).

Miller, Robert, Stephen Heiman, and Tad Tuleja, *Conceptual Selling* (New York: Warner Books, 1989).

Sherlock, Paul, *Rethinking Business-to-Business Marketing* (New York: Free Press, 1992).

Vavra, Terry, *After-Marketing: How to Keep Customers for Life Through Relationships Marketing* (Homewood, Ill.: Business One Irwin, 1992).

Wylie, Peter, and Mardy Grothe, *Can This Partnership Be Saved?* (Dover, N.H.: Upstart Publishing, 1993).

CASE

4-1 THE CENTRUST CORPORATION*

While at the Chicago airport, I was awaiting a flight to Los Angeles. I checked voice mail and there was another message from Bill Short, who is Vice President of Strategic Planning. He was concerned over the apparent loss of Joysco Technological Surgeries (JTS). The message was: "Please call me tomorrow at 7:00 A.M. to discuss the loss of JTS. I am extremely disturbed at losing this account. I have reviewed your records on this account through the last quarter. The records do not have third-quarter profiles." He continued, "Be prepared to discuss how you approached this strategic account and why we lost the business.

*This case was prepared by John Cheneler and Professor William Cron of Southern Methodist University. Neither names nor financial data are intended to reference anyone or a particular business. All cataract surgery information is accurate; however, competitive and product information has been modified for reasons of company security.

As the most senior sales representative for Centrust, I am discouraged that you have not called before now to discuss this matter."

Each quarter, the field sales force downloads all account profiles and sales activities from their laptops to home office computers. Current-quarter records are due next week, containing information that Bill Short has not yet examined. I decided it would be a good idea to look over all of the information on this account which had been logged on my laptop for the last eight months. If I could discover why this account was lost, obviously I could make some changes in my selling strategy.

It was only a week ago that I had caught a flight to Cincinnati on a sales call to JTS, only to be frustrated by this account. I was certain that prior to my arrival, everything was in order to close this sale. I was shocked that JTS had purchased what I believed to be a substantially inferior surgical system for performing cataract surgery from Bayson Laboratories. Bayson Labs is a relative newcomer in the medical supplies field, and JTS always had dealt with vendors who have an established reputation. I was given no indication that any other vendor was being seriously considered for this purchase.

As I reflected on the situation, I wondered how much the loss of the JTS sale would impact my division in the upcoming budget for the year. I also wondered how the loss would impact my own position.

The Cataract Surgery Market

The cataract surgery market has grown tremendously over the last decade. Much of this growth occurred as a result of Medicaid and Medicare reimbursement for the procedure. In 1993, there were 6,000,000 cataract surgeries performed in the United States, of which almost 65 percent were covered by government Medicare and Medicaid programs. Cataracts typically occur in patients after forty-five years of age. When patients develop cataracts, the lens of their eye forms an opaque mass and light rays are unable to pass to the back of the eye. With the diminishing ability of the lens to pass light, patients will eventually go totally blind. Estimates indicate that 35 percent of the population will develop cataracts. Approximately 40 percent of all Medicare and Medicaid patients can be certified as needing cataract surgery.[1]

There are 12,000 board-certified eye surgeons in the United States. The number of board-certified eye surgeons is the only specialty that has not grown in total members in the last 10 years. Only under the rarest conditions would any doctor other than an eye surgeon perform cataract surgery. The average reimbursement for an office visit by Medicare, Medicaid, and most private insurance payers in 1993 was $72.00. Most patients will see a surgeon five times, including pre- and postsurgery visits. The average gross income after three years of practice for eye surgeons in 1993 was $2,000,000 for either a sole practitioner or one in a group practice. Net income for an eye surgeon in the United States during this year was $494,543, (less costs for opening the practice and paying off student loans).

[1]Information on the profiles of cataract surgeons and the number of procedures supplied by the U.S. Office of Medical Statistics, Washington, D.C.

Cataract surgery is a procedure requiring superb skills, yet it is not time-consuming; the surgery can be performed in less than one hour. Patients feel little, if any, discomfort, and the surgery is usually performed on an outpatient basis. In 1993, the total cost for the procedure was $8,200, with the surgeon receiving $3,000. As recently as three years ago, the total cost for the procedure was $17,000, with a $5,000 surgeon's fee. Today, surgeons typically operate two days a week, averaging 10 surgeries weekly.

Most eye surgeons practice for 50 weeks each year. Surgeons also offer ancillary services such as offering eyeglasses and contact lenses, thus offering a complete package to their patients. Frequently, a surgeon will lease space to an optometrist, receiving a percentage of the profits, typically 10 percent.

Eighty percent of eye surgeons prefer to be sole practitioners. A sole practitioner will usually need two nurses and a receptionist to manage four examination rooms. The remaining eye surgeons belong to large group practices. The average group practice has four surgeons with 12 examination rooms. In 1993, the cost to open a practice with equipment for examinations and office supplies was $720,000.[2] On average, a first-year surgeon will owe $195,000 for schooling and resident training.

With increased competition and better equipment, many hospitals are fighting to maintain market share by having the latest equipment available. In the early stages of the cataract surgery market, all surgery was performed at hospitals. Soon off-site surgery centers began to compete actively with hospitals for the patients of large surgical group practices.[3] Now some large group practices are even soliciting other surgeons to use the group's facilities for performing cataract surgeries, rather than going to either hospitals or off-site surgery centers.

Suppliers and Equipment

The main competitors in this market are the established medical vendors that have broad lines of med-

[2]Financial data on the costs of maintaining an ophthalmological practice found yearly in *News in Ophthalmology*, a private trade publication.

[3]Off-site surgery centers are conveniently located centers for performing a variety of surgeries in which the patient needs to stay for less than a day. Surgeries that can be performed at these centers include removal of gallbladders, cosmetic surgery, liposuction, and cataract surgery.

ical products. Two of the major competitors are Alcon Laboratories and Storz Medical, Inc. Centrust's loss of patent protection on its new product line allowed competitors to obtain previously protected digital/laser technology by copying Centrust's new products. Competitors' R & D departments were able to alter their surgical product lines with Centrust's technology and market to Centrust's accounts. The competition was also very aggressive at targeting other surgical specialties with these modified products. The purchaser was often unaware that this technology originally belonged to Centrust.

Most of the full-line vendors in the cataract surgery market carried a complete line of products. Niche manufacturers were typically able to hold market share for only two or three years. Vendors have offered lines of diagnostic units, surgical units, and disposable instruments. Centrust, along with Storz and Alcon, offered office products, but margins on these products are very thin.

Diagnostic Units

Diagnostic units are used to determine the relative focal ability of an eye. Even though a physician can determine that a patient suffers from eye degeneration with a routine examination, there is still a need to quantify eyesight to justify the need for cataract surgery.

While a patient places his or her chin on a leather strap, a laser beam is projected into the eye. The patient reads a series of randomly generated letters or numbers. The diagnostic unit predicts how much eyesight will be regained by the patient after surgery. When cataract surgery is completed, patients will see as well as they did using the diagnostic unit. An examination can be performed in less than five minutes.

Centrust introduced the first diagnostic unit in 1990 and offers the highest-priced diagnostic unit on the market at $60,000. Competitors have attempted either to continue to sell the Snellen Chart method, using dilation, or to use a variation of the Centrust diagnostic unit, though with limited success.[4] Competitors' products range in price from $4,500 to $27,000. Surgeons considered Centrust's diagnostic

unit as the only one currently on the market in which they could have 100 percent confidence in diagnosis. The U.S. government had ruled only the Centrust unit as acceptable in confirming the need for cataract surgery for Medicaid and Medicare patients without a second medical opinion. No other competitor is currently able to offer a product that can duplicate this process with as much reliability. Centrust was quite successful in selling this unit by emphasizing that it lasts for the life of a medical practice and, further, that no dilatation drops are needed. Centrust was the only vendor offering lifetime warranties on diagnostic products for eye care.

Surgical Units

The price for a surgical unit used in cataract surgery varied between $200,000 and $600,000. This price differential was due solely to the name recognition of the vendor and the number of modifications needed to adapt the unit to other equipment in the operating room as opposed to distinguishable product difference. Modifications can be as simple as adapting electrical outlets or as complex as writing computer programs to link the unit to other surgical units.[5]

The surgical unit is a large console, usually four feet long by two feet wide by five feet tall. It consists of a computer that sends an electric impulse to handheld cutting tools, tubing for flowing fluid into the surgery area and suctioning the fluid back, and several exasperating tubes to remove the lens of the eye after incision. The minuscule pieces of material around the lens must be removed without damaging the surrounding area. The surgery site is smaller than the size of a period on a piece of paper. Most units offered by manufacturers appear to have similar capabilities; therefore, surgeons and hospitals often shopped vendors on price. Seldom would surgeons be aware of the difference in a vendor's products. In the past, surgeons always purchased the highest-priced unit, believing that quality and price were absolutely related. As their surgical techniques improved, surgeons were less willing to pay higher

---

[4]The Snellen Chart consists of rows of letters or numbers that decrease in size with each row. One major concern of a physician is that patients will often memorize the letters after repeated examinations.

[5]Centrust was not aggressive in requiring the purchaser to share the costs of modifying surgical units, in which extensive modifications could add up to 50 percent to the cost of the unit. In 1990 Centrust made major modifications to 11 percent of their units; in 1993 the percent of units requiring adjustments soared to 38 percent.

Exhibit 1:

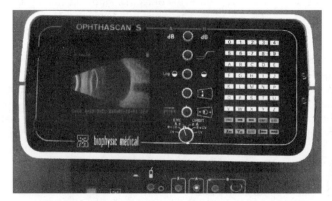

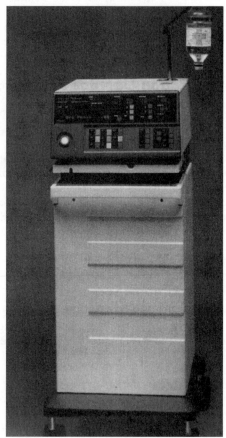

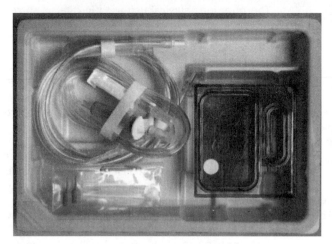

prices unless they observed a distinct difference in product quality. Hospital surgery management viewed a surgical unit, however, as much more critical for their success in attracting doctors and patients than a diagnostic unit.

Disposable Instruments

Disposable cutting instruments used in cataract surgery typically cost $170. Every surgical procedure requires a new set of disposable surgical hand pieces each time an incision is made. Disposable hand pieces are plugged into surgical units which supply electrical current, along with proper irrigation and aspiration.[6] After completion of the surgery, disposable cutting tools and gauze patches must be discarded. Little difference exists among the disposable products of various vendors; therefore, most disposable instruments were purchased primarily based on the lowest price available through distributors. Pictures of a diagnostic unit, a surgical unit, and a disposable instruments pak are shown in Exhibit 1.

[6]The hand-held piece makes a quite thin incision along the lens of the eye, and the surgeon removes the lens and extraneous materials with suction tubes supplied via the unit. The cleaner the incision, the quicker the recovery of the patient.

Centrust Corporation

Centrust has been a pioneer in the development of digital/laser technology in the medical field. They started almost exclusively as a fledgling medical manufacturer in New York City, with a limited product line. However, in the last few years with the introduction of new diagnostic products, Centrust had grown to a leadership position in medical diagnostics and surgical products for cataract eye surgery. See Exhibit 2 for financial information on Centrust. Few medical companies enjoy Centrust's reputation for quality.

Although the technology for the diagnostic unit is protected by patents, the cataract surgery units and disposable instruments are not. With its superior manufacturing processes, however, R & D was able to modify slightly its line of surgical units to fit the needs of off-site surgery centers and other medical specialties. The delicate aspirating capabilities of the surgical unit, for instance, have been modified for use by vascular surgeons in nerve and vascular reattachment. The success of product extensions depends on both the identification of viable extension opportunities and the manufacturer's reputation. Most successful vendors develop a strong association with a particular specialty and use this relationship for product line extensions. Due to Centrust's success in the cataract area and resulting selling time demands, the sales force has not been aggressive in promoting Centrust's products to other specialties.

Centrust's marketing strategy had been to establish their reputation through aggressive promotion of their high-quality products. The margins on cataract equipment had been high, but with increased competition and product maturity, they had declined. After 1992, numerous competitors for Centrust's digital/laser products appeared. This was not unusual, as typically a breakthrough product could hold market share for only three years or less.

With its reputation and high margins, Centrust was able to attract extraordinarily skilled and established sales representatives plus similarly qualified sales managers. The sales force consisted of six sales representatives, three sales managers, and one national sales director. There had been no turnover in the sales force in the last two years. The average sales representative had over 10 years' industry experience and covered a large territory.

Centrust had watched their market share dwindle from 70 percent in 1990 to 42 percent in 1993. The total U.S. sales for equipment in cataract surgery in 1992 was $1.075 billion, up from $579 million in 1990, not including disposable instruments. In reaction to this, the strategic planning unit developed a New Account Planning Program (NAPP), which Centrust hoped would return the company to its previous high level of performance. NAPP is described in Exhibit 3.

Although other companies relied on distributors when selling disposable instruments, Centrust sells all of its medical products directly to the health care

Exhibit 2: Centrust, Inc.: Income Statement and Statement of Retained Earnings for the year ending December 31, 1993 (in millions)

	1990	**1991**	**1992**	**1993**
Sales revenues	$436.6	$515.5	$558.5	$456.1
Cost of sales	330.6	372.7	385.4	345.8
Gross margin	106.0	142.8	173.1	110.3
Expenses				
Depreciation	$24.0	$24.1	$24.4	$24.6
Sales expenses	28.1	30.3	32.5	34.1
Other expenses	10.9	10.7	10.3	10.2
Income taxes	18.9	35.0	48.7	19.1
Total expenses	81.9	100.1	$115.9	88.0
Net income	$24.1	$42.7	$57.2	$22.4
Less: Cash dividends	7.2	12.8	17.2	6.7
Net retained earnings	$16.9	$29.9	$40.0	$15.7

Exhibit 3: National Account Planning Program (NAPP)

NAPP is an effort by Centrust to change the selling behavior of the sales force to a more consultative approach, emphasizing account relationship building, value-added selling, identification of product line extension opportunities, an account tracking system, and coordination with management. Following is a brief description of this program.

1. *Relationship Building:* With all important members of the buying center, build a relationship based on trust, rapport, and meeting each member's concerns and expectations. Backgrounds on people who may be involved in the purchase include the following:

Marketing Manager:	Promotes the hospital and is often involved in its strategic planning.
Hospital Administrator:	Acts as CEO of the hospital. Concerned with financial matters and the strategic direction of the hospital. Usually does not have a technical background in medicine.
Purchasing:	Establishes and maintains vendor relationships and ensures continuous supply at the lowest price. Usually a business or liberal arts education.
Reimbursement Officer:	Determines and tracks billing of patients and third parties (e.g., insurance and government) to meet government guidelines. Usually has some medical background.
Head of Nursing:	Primary user of many medical supplies; acts as a budget director for surgery and is highly influential in deciding which products will be used in surgery.
Safety Director:	Concerned with government safety regulations compliance and exposure to lawsuits. Frequently a highly technical individual; often an engineer.
Head of Surgery:	Usually a senior, well-respected surgeon who is highly influential in the hospital. Would have worked solely with one hospital in the past; this is not necessarily the case today.

2. *Value-Added Selling:* With hospitals' recent emphasis on low price, emphasis should focus on nonprice benefits, such as demonstrating technical superiority of equipment and instruments, fewer complications following surgery, lower cost per surgery due to greater speed, value in hospital's marketing to doctors, and exceeding government-mandated safety specifications.

3. *Product Line Extension Opportunities:* In an effort to expand sales opportunities for current cataract equipment, salespeople should be on constant alert for opportunities to apply cataract technology to other medical specialties.

4. *Opportunity Tracking System:* In order to better track the current selling situation, salespeople are to classify all sales opportunities into one of the following classifications:

"Unqualified"	When salesperson thinks there may be an opportunity but has not identified all buying influences.
"Qualified"	When a need has been verified, there is a confirmed intention to buy, and funding is available within a defined time frame.
"Best"	All influencers have been identified and concerns addressed, and there is a 90 percent probability of a sale.

5. *Management Coordination:* Salespeople are to update management quarterly on the status of all opportunities. In addition, management is to be personally involved in all "Best Opportunities" valued at more than $500,000, must approve all equipment discounts, and should be notified of all line extension opportunities by completing Form LEO-2000.

provider, relying on distributors to promote only office supplies. Centrust does not want to lose control of their medical products to distributors. The competition has been extremely active in using a distribution network over the last two years. Distributors provide a local inventory of products, logistical services, filling customers' reordering needs, and supplying manufacturers with market information. Armed with market information from their distributors, for instance, competitors have been quite successful in imitating Centrust's disposable cutting tools and promoting these to other specialties.

Market Purchasing Behavior

To complete the selling cycle for a surgical system, sales representatives need to work through several layers of approval. Sales representatives typically meet with several individuals to identify their needs and to demonstrate the product's advantages. This process becomes quite confusing if the sales representative tries to sidestep anyone influential in the decision-making process. The commitment to buy medical products is seldom impulsive; therefore, sales representatives who try to complete the sale without total buyer commitment to the product will become frustrated. A successful sales representative must be prepared to allot several months to gain the endorsement and commitment of everyone involved in the process.

To keep the selling process flowing, effective sales representatives must find a champion, either inside or outside the hospital, to help promote their products and to identify potential roadblocks hindering completion of the sale. The purchasing agent, for instance, may not be the most influential individual in the decision process. The head nurse, rather than the surgeon, most often purchases disposable surgical products and determines the budget. Hospital management may desire a particular surgical unit based on low price, but surgeons in many specialties may influence the decision in another direction by demonstrating that the slightly higher-priced unit has more applications. Each purchase decision is unique, though multiple people are always involved.

The medical community has come under greater scrutiny in the last few years concerning the purchase and costs of medical care. With the impending gov-

ernment legislation, purchasing agents have been instructed to acquire products at the lowest possible price. Often, the value of products and services is not readily apparent. Very seldom are vendors able to sell a purchasing agent on any point other than price without first establishing strong relationships with everyone influential in the decision process.

Laptop Records of Account Activities

The following notes appear in their original grammatical form as copied from laptop notes. The sales representative is required to input daily activities on all accounts.

Business Practices at JTS

JTS is a rather large surgical hospital that has a solid business reputation. They performed the most surgical procedures in a three county region that served seven million residents. In an effort to retain the most skilled surgeons, JTS had one of the highest compensation programs in the industry and their turnover rate was low throughout the hospital. JTS had published several brochures recently that indicated they were establishing Total Quality Management (TQM) programs this year. I thought it might be advantageous to link this to Centrust.

January 6

JTS had been targeted as being an account that had tremendous profit potential by our Strategic Analysis Department. During a scheduled appointment with B. J. Avery, JTS Director of Purchasing, we examined the new product lines that Centrust is offering. I assessed the potential purchases of this account as 4 diagnostic units, 16 surgical units, and around 4,000 disposable surgical instruments for the first year. The total potential is $10.5 million.

Spent the day doing informational interviews at the JTS facility. Developed a list of people who I think will be influential in the purchasing decision. The buyers assured me that Centrust had maintained a positive relationship in the past with delivery, service and quality. Spent two hours looking around to obtain information about their business. I noticed that there was a business services unit that actually marketed medical services and products.[7] Made an appointment to see Avery's boss, the Vice President of Purchasing, for the morning of January 22 and the Head of Surgery for the afternoon of January 22.

January 22

Met with Sandy Adams, who has been the Vice President of Purchasing for three years. In the past I had been able to sell at JTS without needing to meet Sandy Adams. I was informed that all bids must be at the lowest market price. I must find users of the products to champion the full price. Dropped off the proper brochures to show Sandy Adams the features of our products that fit perfectly into their existing surgical protocols. I have classified JTS as a "Qualified Opportunity."

I met with Dr. Stenz (a leading surgeon who works with JTS) to discuss the technical aspects of Centrust products. He appeared more comfortable with Centrust after understanding the surgical benefits of our products over our competitors' products. He seemed to be impressed by our products.

I asked if any other competitor had established solid relationships with JTS and I was guaranteed that we were in the "driver's seat." It was even suggested that I stop by the office of Dr. Stenz and speak with his four associates. We also discussed the delivery process and training. The order for $10.5 million from JTS should be coming soon and we are in a position to hold full price. Stenz does not feel that we will need to discount very much to JTS. He also indicated that he would be purchasing for his office seven diagnostic units; an unusually large order for an established practice. I wonder?

January 24

Stopped by to see the associates of Dr. Stenz. I was surprised that no one was aware that I was coming. Stenz had seemed so enthusiastic and promised that he would arrange my visit with his associates and pass along the brochures I

gave him. Even though I was disappointed that they were unprepared for my visit I used this as an opportunity to speak with the office manager, whom I found was influential in the office's buying process.

One interesting development is that I found out during the meeting with the office manager that there were two other competitors that had spoken with the hospital and other surgeons during the last month. Dr. Stenz had assured me that there was no real competition. I am not worried too much since I know from the December Vendors Trade Show in New Orleans that there is no threat for upcoming products from any other vendor.

February 3

Called on JTS to check on the Purchasing Department's progress concerning the order. Took the Purchasing Vice President's Assistant to lunch to find new information. The discussion centered around the politics of the organization. Learned that they felt we are being too aggressive and need to slow down. I took this as an opportunity to discuss our company and try to establish a rapport rather than focus on true selling product. After lunch I stopped by surgery to see if any competitors' products were being used. It seemed like a smorgasbord of products with no one vendor in dominance.

Made an appointment to see the Nursing Head of Surgery on the 14th. It's interesting. When I mentioned this to the Purchasing Assistant, he said, "Go ahead and do that, but remember we are the ones who sign all the purchasing orders."

February 14

It's Valentines Day so I stopped by with candy and flowers for the Surgical Nursing Department. This has always paid off well. The atmosphere was light and everyone was very receptive to listening to benefits of our products. They seemed to be pleased with what I told them. Looks as though the "ducks are being lined up." Look for the order soon!

March 16

Called Stenz to schedule an appointment since I will be in the area in April. He said that I

---

[7]Even though hospitals are traditionally thought of as nonprofit, they will often have marketing and promotion departments that are extremely aggressive.

needed to talk to H. M. Jones over at JTS. Found out that Jones was the Head of Safety at JTS. Made an appointment for April 23 and sent a follow-up letter and brochures on every product that we could possibly offer. I am not sure who this individual is but I am sure his role will be explained at our meeting.

April 23

I arrived at JTS and initiated a discussion with H. M. Jones concerning purchases on the original "bid." I was surprised to find that Jones was rather unsophisticated and appeared confused by both the literature and our conversation. Centrust had hired the finest ad agency in the city to prepare these brochures for a high school level education. Jones may actually understand the material and is simply testing me. I'm sure I passed the test. The last question I asked was, "If this is all clear, do you have any other questions?" The reply I got was "nope!"—another duck lined up!!!! I have moved JTS' classification up to a "Best New Opportunity."

May 15

Received a phone message from Stenz stating that our prices on the diagnostic units for his office are too high, and I need to come down on price immediately. I called and was unable to reach him, but I did speak with an associate who told me that they were actually looking for an order that might be twice as large as my original estimate but the problem is that we are too high on price. I asked him if they were basing this opinion on a price relative to someone else or if our price was too high in general. They assured me that their business could not support our prices. I set an appointment on May 18 to speak in person with everyone in their office.

May 18

I had prepared new proposals in accordance with the practices of Centrust. There had been an offer by our Vice President of Sales to attend the meeting, but I felt comfortable that I would finalize this sale in ninety days so I rejected the suggestion. I proposed to the Strategic Analysis Department that we offer a new pricing struc-

ture for Dr. Stenz and his associates if they are able to help us get the JTS contract. After some arm twisting I was given the authority to discount Stenz's order by 25% on the condition that they help us obtain the JTS order. All I need now is the JTS account. The shipment of diagnostic units to Stenz' office is scheduled for July 1, with some modification of mounting devices to fit on their examination equipment. Stenz wants this order rushed, but modifications always require a minimum of thirty days from R & D. I am sure he will negotiate on our behalf to JTS. Stenz said he would set an appointment with B. J. Avery at JTS for June 16.

June 16

I was shocked to find that Stenz was not present for the meeting at JTS. When I called Stenz' office, they said they were nervous about meetings with JTS. For the first time, I found out that they now compete with JTS over some surgical business.[8] Avery was very pleasant, but informed us that our prices appeared to be quite high. I explained that this was due to the "state of the art technology" and that the price is actually reasonable. He asked if I might supply him with technology specifications to verify this statement. While this may not be standard protocol, I agreed to share the information I had with him. I also stated that we would share anything else that they needed after the order was delivered. I again mentioned to Avery that in an earlier meeting everyone had agreed that pricing would not be an issue. He asked me to return on July 7 and meet with the purchasing board. I asked why it was necessary to meet with this board. He said that it was a formality that was rarely used; however, with the size of this order he wanted another opinion. I asked if there was anything else we needed to cover and he said, "No, I am comfortable for now. I am also looking forward to finalizing this transaction."

---

[8]It is becoming very competitive for the cataract business, with the ability of cataract surgeons to perform surgery in their offices. The U.S. Food and Drug Administration has been quite liberal on the restrictions of in-office surgery for this field.

July 7 morning

Tried to see Dr. Stenz before heading to JTS. The delivery of the 7 diagnostic units had occurred and training was complete. The staff was not using the system and I am concerned about this. I'll bring this up with Dr. Stenz at the meeting with JTS this afternoon. With the discount I had given them they must be happy. Normally this discount is reserved for long-term accounts. All in all everything appeared to be in control.

July 7 afternoon

My meeting with the purchasing board took only three minutes. They were totally unaware of what we were to discuss. Since Avery had been so concerned about my meeting them, I was frustrated that they were not prepared for the meeting. Once again, Avery assured me that everything was OK and that we will meet on August 1st to finalize the sale.

August 1

When I arrived for my scheduled meeting with Sandy Adams and B. J. Avery, there was a note left for me at the front desk from Sandy Adams. It read:

> Sorry to miss you this time around. We are busy with R & D helping with the installation of new diagnostic and surgical equipment. Again, sorry you lost this business. Better luck next time.
> Sandy Adams

I stopped by Adams' office and found a helpful secretary who informed me that Bayson Laboratories had won the business. They had apparently had a price similar to Centrust's.

Next, I proceeded to Avery's office and had the following conversation:

B. J. AVERY: Oh Hi! I was unaware that you were stopping by today. Did we have an appointment?

(I didn't let on that I had read the note and acted as though all was still in order. I wanted to see if I could gain some information as to what had happened)

ME: No, I was in the area and wanted to see if you were close to arriving at your decision. Is there anything more that I can supply you with?

B. J.: No, I received the new brochures that you sent and passed them along to everyone that you indicated in your letter. I believe that everyone was quite impressed with them. The videos that you sent were very professional too. All in all, I would say that you have done an excellent job of presenting your company and your products.

ME: I am happy that you feel that way, and I hope that we will soon be engaging in a long-term relationship. As I indicated to you in one of our last meetings, we will also be able to offer substantial discounts with multiple units installed.

B. J.: This was a hard decision, but we have decided to purchase all of our surgical products from Bayson Laboratories. There was no real reason other than that was the decision by all parties. We do want to thank you for your trouble. I have a meeting in five minutes, so I hope you will forgive me. Here is a note I was about to send you.

There was nothing different in this note from the one left by Sandy Adams. It appeared that they both wrote these together.

I left JTS more confused than ever as to how I lost the sale. This was not what I had expected. JTS had been started by two surgeons who had been associated with the developers of the digital/laser technology. When Centrust purchased the technology years ago, JTS had been an advocate of us. To me this loss was totally unexpected; we were completely in control of this process. I wonder what happened. What could possibly have gone wrong?

C A S E

4-2 PEPE JEANS*

John Miln, managing director of Pepe U.K. Ltd., knew that despite its great success in the United Kingdom denim jeans market, his company faced problems. After five years of large annual increases, sales growth had flattened and begun to decline. Miln had commissioned a survey of attitudes toward Pepe among its retail outlets, and this had shown that some of its independent retailers were unhappy at the changes that had come with Pepe's growth. They felt that their close personal ties with the company had been lost and replaced with "big company" systems. At the other extreme, many of the buyers for nationwide multiple chains felt that the company needed to become more professional and systematized. These differences led Miln to reconsider the critical success factors in dealing with retailers. Should he put more marketing effort into managing his distribution channels or into supporting the Pepe brand image in the market?

The Background to Pepe's Success

Pepe began to produce and sell denim jeans in 1974. From the late 1970s onward, the company achieved enormous growth. Despite losing some ground from a peak in 1990, it sold 3.3 million pairs of jeans in the United Kingdom during 1991. This amounted to more than 10 percent of the sales value in the U.K. jeans

market, making Pepe second only to Levi Strauss. From its head office in Willesden, Pepe was now marketing a full range of casual clothing, although most of its sales remained in jeans. Sales outside the United Kingdom had grown to account for nearly half the total turnover of £72 million. In 1991, a record profit of £4.3 million was achieved, as shown in Exhibit 1.

Pepe's success was the result of a unique approach in a product market that had been dominated by strong brands and limited variety. Pepe presented a range of jeans styles which offered a better fit than traditional "5-pocket western" jeans—particularly for women customers. The Pepe range of basic styles was modified each season, but each style kept its identity with a slightly whimsical name featured prominently on the jeans and on the point-of-sale material. Variations such as modified washes, leather trim, and even designer wear marks were applied to respond to changing fashion trends. Exhibit 2 shows the principal styles for men and women and their importance in terms of total Pepe sales in the United Kingdom.

Pepe was the first U.K. company to treat jeans as a fashion item and to present retailers with a new collection each season. A team of young, in-house designers were responsible for developing new styles and the accompanying point-of-sale material. Pepe became associated with an offbeat, designer image that was very different from the traditional jeans brands and appealed strongly to young people. Many of its product and point-of-sale innovations—such as clip-on key rings and bold 1950s-style labeling—were copied throughout the industry. However, none of the competitors was as successful as Pepe in maintaining a reputation for fresh design and product variety.

*This case was prepared by Professor Kenneth Simmonds, David Bramley, and Chris John of the London Business School. Copyright © 1990 Kenneth Simmonds.

Exhibit 1: Pepe Group Financial Performance
Profit and Loss Account

	1991 (£m)	1990 (£m)
Turnover	72.2	50.2
Cost of sales	43.1	34.2
Gross profit	29.1	16.0
Operating expenses and interest	20.7	10.1
Profit before tax	8.4	5.9
Taxation	2.9	2.0
Profit after tax	5.5	3.9
Distributions, etc.	1.2	1.0
Retain profit	4.3	2.9

Balance Sheet

	1991 (£m)	1990 (£m)
Current assets		
Stock	6.5	5.4
Debtors	19.6	13.5
Cash	3.9	2.2
	30.0	21.1
Fixed assets	4.8	3.0
	34.8	24.1
Current liabilities	18.0	11.9
Bank loans	4.2	—
Capital and reserves	12.6	12.2
	34.8	24.1

Exhibit 2: Principal Pepe Denim Jeans Styles

Styles	Percentage of Pepe U.K. Sales Value
Men's	
Comfort	19
Macho	15
Drifter	7
Cowboy	4
Eddie	3
Louie	3
Women's	
Betty	14
Jane	4
Ella	3
Ellis	2
Gladys	2

Pepe's sales were predominantly to customers in the 15 to 24 age range, and customer brand awareness was very high. Pepe's brand share was almost exactly the same for men and women, unlike most of the other major brands that sold a higher proportion to men. Pepe had a high repeat-buying rate, with some users rebuying a particular style because of its fit, and the more fashion-conscious owning a range of styles.

Pepe's brand strength was such that its retail price of around £25 for standard jeans was matched only by Levi's price. This brand strength had emerged without any significant use of advertising. In 1990 and 1991 a limited amount of television advertising had been undertaken, but it was hard to tell if it had made an impact on sales. Indeed, there was still uncertainty about how the Pepe brand, which depended on a wide variety of products constantly being redesigned, should be presented. Inevitably, the brand had become less "radical" since it was now present in all the nationwide multiples and had a substantial market share.

Pepe had built its distribution in the United Kingdom by concentrating on small, independent retailers to whom it had offered close cooperation and easy credit terms. Pepe's approach had brought it a distinct advantage, given the minimal retailer support offered by many of the leading brands. Many accounts had been with Pepe since the company's founding and had built their entire business around the Pepe range. Indeed, some of these retailers were family relations of the company's founders. By keeping its distribution with small independents in the initial stages, Pepe had avoided the price pressures of buyers for the multiple chains. Pepe also reached younger, more fashion-conscious consumers, who tended to shop at small independents rather than at nationwide multiple stores.

Manufacture of Pepe's denims was carried out on contract by around 30 independent factories in Hong Kong. These factories worked on a "cut/make/trim" basis. Pepe supplied them with exact patterns, material specifications, and instructions for the final washing process. The company had developed close working relationships with its manufacturers, and it consistently achieved high standards of product quality and delivery reliability. The variable cost of manufacturing and bringing a pair of jeans into the United Kingdom was £6.50. Orders for manufacture had to be placed six months in advance of delivery in the United Kingdom. The six month-lead time comprised

Exhibit 3: Brand Shares for Total Market (percentage)

Brand	1983	1988	1991
Levi	19	17	17
Pepe	< 1	6	10
Wrangler	17	10	8
Lee	< 1	5	5
Easy	—	2	4
Marks and Spencer	2	4	5
Other	61	56	51
Total	100	100	100

denim ordering, manufacturing, finishing and washing, transport by sea freight, customs clearance, and dispatch in the United Kingdom. Orders to Hong Kong were always based on firm forward orders from retailers in the United Kingdom. As a matter of policy, the company never carried stocks of finished goods. Pepe's management felt that holding stock in a fashion-based market was too risky, even for standard lines. In any event, until recently, growth in sales had outstripped the company's capacity to supply the product.

The U.K. Demand for Jeans

Throughout the 1980s, annual sales of denim jeans in the United Kingdom varied between 40 and 50 million pairs. Early in the period, fashion trends shifted to-

ward other kinds of casual and sports wear and sales declined, but the decline was offset by increased sales of designer jeans partly through Pepe's entry into the market. What had been a market for high volumes of standardized products shifted toward variety, design, and more flexible manufacture. Traditional brands were hit hard by this change. The response of the largest, Levi, was a large-scale advertising campaign and the revival of their original "Levi 501" jeans. These measures were highly successful for Levi and had the knock-on effect of strengthening sales of all kinds of denims. By 1991 the United Kingdom's annual volume had stabilized at around 50 million pairs. The average retail price of a pair of jeans in 1991 was £19.50, but there were wide variations. A pair of exclusive-label, high-fashion jeans could cost up to £50. Some own-label and unbranded products were sold by chain stores for £13. For the leading volume brands, prices varied from £20 to £35.

Fashion and demographic forces were expected to have a continuing impact on denim sales. Fashion trends could simply shift away from denim, although it was hard to imagine so serviceable and well-established a fabric being replaced completely. The 15 to 24 age group—which purchased over half of the current denim output—was declining 3 percent annually. This trend was expected to continue.

Competing Brands

Exhibit 3 shows trends in market share for the main brands. Exhibits 4 and 5 break down brand perfor-

Exhibit 4: Sales of Jeans by Outlet and by Brand, 1991 (percentage)

	Outlet Type				
	Independent	Multiple	Mail Order	Market Stall + Other	Total
Share of Total Market	34	31	11	24	100
Share of Outlet Sales					
Levi	22	16	13	12	17
Pepe	16	8	2	7	10
Wrangler	6	6	19	8	8
Lee	6	4	1	5	5
Easy	2	6	7	1	4
Marks and Spencer	—	16	—	—	5
Other	48	44	58	67	51
Total	100	100	100	100	100

Exhibit 5: U.K. Sales of Jeans by Age Group and by Brand, 1991 (percentage)

	Age Group				
	15–19	20–24	25–34	35–44	45+
Share of Total Market	29	25	26	14	7
Brand Share of Age Group Sales					
Levi	16	20	18	15	13
Pepe	13	13	8	4	1
Wrangler	5	6	12	11	9
Lee	5	7	4	3	2
Easy	5	4	4	1	1
Marks and Spencer	1	2	7	10	12
Other	55	48	47	56	62
Total	100	100	100	100	100

mance according to type of retail outlet and age group of customers. Each of the competing brands had a distinctive market profile.

- Levi was the leading brand in the market. Long-established and with almost universal brand awareness, Levi's name was almost synonymous with denim jeans. Two distinct product lines were presented: the ultratraditional 501s, and standard lines that had moved some way toward being designer jeans. Levi had spent heavily on television and cinema advertising, directed mainly at its 501 line. It was the price leader in the market, with 501s retailing at around £35 and standard lines at around £25. Levi manufactured in Europe.

- Wrangler was a traditional jeans brand that had declined from its heyday in the late 1970s. It had stuck with its original western, male-oriented image and undertook some television advertising to support it. It also manufactured in Europe.

- Lee was owned by the same company as Wrangler but was closer to Pepe in terms of being a designer jeans brand. Lee was a strong brand but lacked Pepe's well-established reputation for variety and design. The line was manufactured in Ireland.

- New brands such as Easy, Zeus, and 2nd Image were now appearing on the market.

These were higher-fashion, designer brands that sought to emulate Pepe's success. Easy was the largest. Like Pepe, it manufactured in the Far East, but it tended to target high-volume multiple outlets. Zeus and 2nd Image were much smaller European manufacturers. They aimed at independents, where retailers were more likely to accept newer, more radical styling.

- Retailers' "own brands" had increased their share throughout the 1980s, mainly by appealing to older consumers. Marks and Spencer was the major make. It offered competitively priced, high-quality products and had developed its expertise through imitating other brands' styles. It did not display Marks and Spencer's "St. Michael" labeling prominently. In addition, in a market with almost no barriers to entry, there was a proliferation of minor brands and cheap, unbranded jeans, making up nearly half the total market. An increasing number of these were low-cost imports from the Far East.

It had been estimated that 25 percent of jeans customers actually specified the brand they wished to buy when they entered a store. The remaining 75 percent tended to try on two to three pairs and choose the pair that fit and suited them best. Unlike Pepe, which now sold a wide range of fashion goods, the main competitors sold principally jeans and a limited range of accessories.

Distribution Channels

Manufacturers generally sold jeans directly to retailers at around 50 percent of the price that they felt the product's brand strength, quality, and design could sustain at the retail level. They looked to retailers to take a 100 percent markup on cost, although retailers had varying attitudes toward price cutting.

There were various channels of distribution to the consumer. Exhibit 4 gives the breakdown of sales among them.

- *Multiples* were nationwide chains that tended to stock all the best selling brands. Typically, purchasing was carried out by a central staff of professional buyers, supported by sophisticated forecasting systems. They ordered very large quantities but tended to be conservative in taking on new brands and styles. Because of their high-volume purchases, they generally achieved an 8 to 10 percent discount on the manufacturers' prices. They had their own merchandisers and in-store look, and they made only limited use of manufacturers' point-of-sale material. Multiples would almost always maintain prices at 100 percent markup on the manufacturers' price before their buying discount.

- *Mail-order outlets* purchased and maintained prices in a similar way.

- *Independents* varied from those that sold nothing but denim products through fashion "boutiques" that stocked only a very small range of designer products. They also varied from well-laid-out "High Street" stores that charged the recommended retail price to discount stores that cut prices and sold jeans along with a wide range of discounted goods. A typical High Street independent would hold around two-thirds of its stock in two or three main brands and the remainder in a number of smaller brands. It would tend to keep the same main brands but change and experiment with sales of smaller brands.

- *Wholesalers* also operated in the market. They did not generally obtain their products directly from manufacturers but from retailers who either had excess stock or had deliberately overordered. Large amounts of product were available for all the main brands, at be-

tween 50p and £1 above the manufacturers' listed supply prices. The wholesalers supplied discount stores and market traders who invariably sold at much less than the recommended retail price.

Pepe's U.K. Distribution System

Independents

Some 75 percent of Pepe sales went through 1,500 independent outlets throughout the United Kingdom. Of these sales, 80 percent were concentrated in just 25 percent of the 1,500 outlets. The company was present in most outlets that sold branded jeans, and increasing retail coverage was no longer an objective. However, while some outlets sold the whole range of Pepe products, many sold just a few lines. The company maintained contact with its independent retailers via a group of 10 agents who were self-employed, although working exclusively for Pepe. Each agent was responsible for retailers in a particular area of the country. The agents were paid a 5 percent commission on sales which was forfeited if any of the accounts to which they sold failed to settle their bills with Pepe.

This agency system had not been changed since Pepe was established. They were employed on a "handshake," with no formal written contracts, but for many years none of the agents had left. All the agents had come to know the retailers in their areas very well and maintained good relations with them. Pepe was convinced that good relations with independent retailers had been vital in building up distribution of the brand. The agents aimed to see retailers three to four times each year in order to present the new season or midseason collection and to take sales orders. Because the number of accounts had grown so dramatically, contact was now often achieved by holding a presentation—often in a hotel—to serve several retailers in a particular locale. The agents only rarely visited the actual shops of many of the retailers. The agents did no retail merchandising, and Pepe did not employ any specialists for this purpose. Point-of-sale material was supplied to retailers directly from the head office. Information about retail and market trends was passed back from the agents to Pepe's head office at a quarterly meeting in Willesden and via regular telephone calls.

Agents took orders from retailers for six-month

delivery on all items from basic jeans through to fashion accessories. Once Pepe received an order, the retailer had only one week in which to cancel because of the need to place immediate firm orders in Hong Kong in order to meet the delivery date, and because of the company's long-standing policy of not holding stocks in the United Kingdom.

Multiples

Once the Pepe brand had been established as a success, the multiples had become keen to stock it. Multiples' orders had grown to 25 percent of Pepe's total sales, and a Key Accounts manager had recently been employed to deal directly with the buyers of the 10 multiple customers. These 10 customers had between them over 1500 outlets nationwide. Planning and supply were relatively easy with the multiples because of the volumes of their purchases. However, the multiples argued repeatedly that they wanted access to large stocks of product and flexible supply, which, because of its operational constraints, Pepe was not prepared to provide. The multiples had to make firm orders for six-month delivery in exactly the same way as the independents. Pepe was aware that other firms had much more flexible arrangements with the multiples but considered this to be a reflection of their relatively weaker brands. Pepe had in fact experimented with holding certain amounts of stock for two of the smaller multiples. This arrangement had worked reasonably well, but Pepe was wary of extending the experiment to any of the larger chains, as it did not wish to be left with large stocks on hand because a multiple decided to push some other brand.

Head Office Systems

Once an order had been taken and confirmed, the rest of the process up to delivery was administered by the head office in Willesden. The retailer could check on the status of orders and deliveries on its account by telephone. Six telephone operators were backed up by the information available from sales, manufacturing, and dispatch in Hong Kong and from the agents in the field. Since its founding, Pepe had prided itself on being flexible and friendly in dealing with its retailers. However, this approach had become more difficult now that it was a much bigger company. Information flows were harder to manage, and it was no longer possible for all the telesales operators to be familiar with all the accounts. A system of account

classification was in operation, but it was intended mainly to identify accounts that were bad credit risks.

In order to deal with these problems, Miln had brought in more professional sales management and had partly computerized the sales control system to minimize paperwork. Yet he had to admit that this expansion of the fixed cost base of the company had so far not brought any tangible financial benefit.

Survey of Pepe Retailers' Attitudes

In order to identify more closely what seemed to be growing problems, Miln commissioned an interview survey of Pepe's retailers. A representative cross section of both multiples and independents was asked about all aspects of Pepe's performance and how the company compared with its competitors.

Independents

There was universal agreement among the independents that Pepe was second only to Levi in terms of brand pull. Although they were highly impressed by Levi's advertising, they were ambivalent about Pepe's recent campaigns. Independents praised the fit, quality, and variety of Pepe's jeans, although many thought that they had become much less of a "trend-setter" than in their early days. It was felt that Pepe's variety of styles and quality were their key advantages over their closest competitors, such as Levi and Lee. For the 75 percent of customers who came into a shop without specifying a particular brand, one of Pepe's styles would always provide a good fit.

All the independents were well aware that Pepe stock was freely available from wholesalers at only slightly higher prices than from the company itself. Many who bought their regular merchandise from Pepe and tried to charge the full retail price were upset by this. They felt that Pepe was failing to discriminate between themselves and outlets that sold by discounting prices.

Many independents were also unhappy with Pepe's requirements that firm orders be placed six months in advance, with no possibility of amendment, cancellation, or repeat ordering. Half of those questioned said that Pepe's business had already suffered because of its order-taking policies. They claimed that Pepe's order system meant that they ordered less and tended to stock out of particular sizes and styles. Some went as far as to say that Pepe's sales would increase by around 10 percent with a more flexible ordering system. Distortions in sales were most acute for the best-selling denim lines.

Different styles and sizes naturally sold at different speeds at different times, so retailers always expected to have some inventory that took quite a time to move and some gaps in their coverage. With six months' orders, however, gaps took a long time to fill, and overordering of a particular size or style could not be adjusted for a long time. What the retailers would have liked was some method of limited returns, exchange, or top-up in order to overcome the worst of these problems.

Orders could often be placed with Pepe's smaller competitors for delivery in a matter of weeks—or even days in some cases—although stock availability tended to be sporadic. Lee and Easy carried large stocks in the United Kingdom and could often deliver on order. Easy also took orders for two-month delivery on their basic product lines. Levi still required retailers to place orders six months in advance. However, an initial order carried options for large repeat-order quantities, and amendments to quantities and to the mix of sizes and styles were possible up to one month before delivery. In particular, the details of the wash for an order—one of the most volatile fashion features—could be specified at this later date.

Most of the other major brands employed in-house sales representatives rather than agents to deal with retailers. Levi's representatives called at the shops of their largest accounts at least once a month and had a network of retail merchandisers in support. As well as taking new orders, Levi's representatives had access via portable terminals to an on-line stock control system. They would use this system to try to adjust deliveries, depending on the retailer's sales performance and stock position. In a few cases, the representative would help the retailers in forecasting and stock requirements, not only for Levi goods but also for the whole of their range. Some retailers used Levi merchandisers to help them arrange the layout of their shop displays.

This level of service was a relatively recent innovation by Levi. Levi seemed to be making special efforts at some of the accounts where Pepe's sales were highest. Seventy-five percent of the retailers questioned thought that it had made dealing with Levi significantly easier than dealing with Pepe. However, some still preferred dealing with Pepe's "streetwise" agents rather than Levi's more systems-dependent representatives.

In terms of making deliveries correctly and on time, Pepe was at least as good as its competitors. However, some retailers found it hard to get information or to settle problems with the telephone sales staff. Several reported that they had had disputes about what seemed to be trivial matters such as returning a few pairs of erroneously delivered jeans. Some even stated that Pepe's attitude was arrogant, that it had the attitude of "take it or leave it." They felt that over the past couple of years they had lost the close contact that used to exist with the head office. The new systems at the head office seemed to have aggravated the problems rather than helped to remove them.

Multiples

The multiples' buyers were similarly convinced of Pepe's continuing brand strength. However, they were even more outspoken than the independents about Pepe's lack of flexibility in supply. One even claimed that she "only bought Pepe because she had to." They were all very quick to point out that other brands took a different approach.

All of Pepe's major competitors kept in weekly contact with the multiples in order to review nationwide sales data for the previous week. Pepe's contact had increased since the arrival of the Key Accounts manager, but Pepe still did not communicate as much excitement about sales levels as its competitors. For instance, Easy would often meet with the multiples' buyers three times a week. Lee apparently had three Key Accounts managers working with the multiples, despite having less than half of Pepe's sales to them.

The subject that produced the most annoyance with the multiples was Pepe's provision of information from the head office. They found it hard to get information on the status of orders and deliveries. Some became incensed when they were not forewarned of potential problems with delivery. The multiples were in general less interested than independents in point-of-sale material, and they were not interested at all in using manufacturers' retail merchandisers. However, Levi's merchandisers still made visits to multiples' stores apparently in order to gather data. Lee also visited multiples' stores and even gave out prizes to multiples' sales staff who sold the most Lee jeans. The multiple buyers were not in favor of these activities, but they were tolerated.

Miln's Dilemma

Naturally, Miln was disturbed by the results of the survey. He felt that some of the complaints—particularly those from multiple buyers—were an inevitable result of Pepe resisting dependence on retailers. Some of the problems seemed to be straightforward matters of operational efficiency; others had more to do with basic policies such as the agent system and the holding of stocks. It struck him that many of his competitors' activities seemed to be carried out for their own benefit as much as for the retailers'.

The general belief of Pepe's management was that brand strength was still high and that this was Pepe's most important weapon in dealing with retailers and consumers. They believed that companies that had failed in the jeans market had done so either because they tried to sell the wrong product or let their brand strength weaken. They thought that the main issue that faced Pepe was to manage its brand to continue to appeal to the existing customers as they got older, and to make renewed efforts toward the diminishing number of young people in their market. They were against holding stocks because they believed there was a danger that retailers would treat the company as a "cash and carry" supplier and that this would ultimately weaken the brand. The debate on these issues became even more intense when early 1992 figures seemed to show that the decline in U.K. sales was continuing unabated.

CASE

4-3 NATIONAL SAXONY CARPET COMPANY*

The carpet industry is extremely competitive at all levels, from manufacturing, to wholesaling, to retailing. Some experts say that the only people making any money in the industry are the fiber manufacturers, such as DuPont and Monsanto. Because of intense competition, carpet manufacturers make concessions to key wholesalers and large retailers when it is necessary to get their business.

Most carpet manufacturers will pay up to 50 percent of the cost of a cooperative advertising program for distributors or large retailers, and sometimes even more if the expected volume of sales is high. A co-op advertising program consists of a fund held by the carpet manufacturer for the distributor or retailing organization to be used for local advertising, usually in newspapers but occasionally on television or radio. Typically the manufacturer would pay 50 percent of the advertising expense and the distributor or retailers would pay the balance. The actual split is negotiable.

*This case was prepared by James T. Strong and Jon M. Hawes of the University of Akron. Reproduced by permission.

The amount that the manufacturer puts into the fund is usually a percentage of the distributor's (or retailer's) purchases and ranges from 1 to 10 percent, based on their negotiated agreement. Thus, if the fund was based on 10 percent of the distributor/retailer purchases for a given time period (typically six months or one year) and purchases totaled $100,000, the amount that the manufacturer would have contributed to the fund would be $10,000. Assuming in this example that the co-op program is a 50/50 split, the distributor or retailer has to match (dollar for dollar) all advertising appropriations spent from the fund established by the manufacturer. For a $1,000 ad, $500 would come from the fund set up by the manufacturer and $500 would be paid by the distributor or retailer. Appropriations to the fund can be based on actual sales to the distributor or retailer over some previous period of time, such as the past six months or one year. Alternatively, future sales can be estimated and funds can be provided "up-front" to support initial advertising efforts in the local market.

The manufacturer's contribution to a co-op fund comes out of their margin. Given the industry's highly competitive and dynamic nature, it is safe to say that *everything* regarding co-op advertising arrangements is negotiable.

Another area for negotiations is the cost of samples and displays. Samples and displays are used by retail and wholesale salespeople to sell the line. Samples and displays are very expensive and retailers, distributors, and manufacturers all hate to pay for them. Carpet manufacturers try to collect enough revenue for samples and displays to break even (so they say). Without adequate sampling of a carpet line in retail showrooms, sales will suffer.

Sampling is especially important in the "cut to order" business. Cut orders are pieces of carpet that are custom cut to the job size as requested by the retailer, based on the ultimate consumer's needs. When cut orders are purchased, the reseller does not have to stock a roll of that carpet style and color. A significant disadvantage for the manufacturer who sells by the cut order system is that eventually there is only a small amount of carpet left on the roll. The remaining amount becomes a "remnant" that cannot be sold at regular prices because it is too small. Due to the high cost of carrying inventory and cutting the rolls to a particular size as well as the necessary markdowns of remnants, manufacturers and distributors who offer this service must charge a premium price for cut orders. This higher price typically results in relatively high profits for firms selling carpet cut to order.

The Potential Seller

National Saxony Carpet Company (NSCC) is based in Dalton, Georgia. The firm specializes in manufacturing residential saxony carpet in wool, nylon, and wool blends. Saxony is a type of carpet that is classic in its styling. It has a cut pile and is usually offered in a solid color. National Saxony Carpet Company sells primarily to floor covering distributors and its products are widely distributed throughout most of North America. NSCC has been in business for over 25 years serving the needs of the mainstream and high-end residential saxony carpet niche and is a relatively large firm within its industry.

While selling primarily through distributors, National Saxony Carpet Company also sells directly to some large carpet retailers such as New York Carpet World, Einstein Moomjy, and Don's Carpet Barn. In addition, NSCC also sells a private label line of essentially the same products to wholesale distributors.

They sell the carpet to medium and small retailers, designers, and decorators at a 10 to 30 percent price premium over the large retailer's costs for similar goods. Selling direct to large retailers is a common practice in the carpet industry. Distributors are aware of this practice and usually seem resigned to accept it as a fact of life. This form of dual distribution does cause some channel conflict, especially when large retailers gain significant price advantages over what smaller competitors must pay for the same products that are distributed through the traditional distributor channel arrangement.

Presently, NSCC is trying to make a deal with a floor covering distributor to handle all of their product lines in Ohio. National Saxony Carpet Company has existing distribution arrangements in the surrounding areas of Michigan and Western Pennsylvania, but lacks access to the Ohio retail carpet market.

Some significant and well known advantages of the NSCC product lines include the following:

1. Comprehensive coverage across price and style points for the mid-to-high-end market.

2. Excellent assortment of colors—twice the number of colors (48) usually offered by manufacturers.

3. Excellent inventory services are provided by NCSS. This enables the distributor to offer a broad color assortment without an excessive investment in its own inventory.

4. Good delivery service.

5. Generally high quality products.

6. Superb wool products, both in styling and construction. In fact, no domestic producer can match the quality and price (value) that NCSS offers for its wool products. European manufacturers sell wool products of comparable quality, but their transportation costs result in a price at least 15 percent higher.

No manufacturer's competitive offering is absolutely perfect for each potential distributor. Some disadvantages of the product lines marketed by National Saxony Carpet Company include the following:

1. Some competitors offer lower prices.

2. The company is not flexible on complaints—NCSS will not issue a credit unless the carpet has a manufacturing defect.

3. A very strict credit department.

The Potential Buyer

The potential buyer is Mid-States Carpet Distributors (MSCD) located in Columbus, Ohio, with a branch in Pittsburgh, Pennsylvania. Mid-States Carpet Distributors sells carpet, vinyl, wood, and other flooring products to retailers, designers, and decorators in Ohio and in Western Pennsylvania. MSCD is independently owned and operated, has been in business for 35 years, and is well financed with a good credit rating. They have a good reputation with dealers for reliable service (i.e., adequate stock and inventory), good products, and fair customer policies. While the company is generally well respected, some of its products are considered "too high priced" by some of its current and potential accounts.

The Assignment

The third sales interaction between National Saxony Carpet Company and Mid-States Carpet Distributors is scheduled for next week. Both parties are interested in making a final decision on whether or not to enter into a sales agreement. If a productive exchange relationship is not likely, both parties would like to determine this as soon as possible so that they can find alternative business partners. Prior meetings have been cordial and informative, but neither side has made any commitments. During the last meeting NSCC offered MSCD the set prices shown in Exhibit 1.

To receive these prices, National Saxony Carpet Company has proposed that Mid-States Carpet Distributors buy 10 rolls of each style on the initial order. There are 100 yards per roll, and at roll price this amounts to an opening order of $91,500. Industry practices suggest that this is a fairly conservative request of a distributor. NSCC would be very happy, however, to take a larger initial order from MSCD (a loaded distributor is a loyal distributor).

Exhibit 1: NSCC's Pricing Proposal*

Product Line	Roll Price	Cut Order Price
Product line 1 (high end pure wool)	$30.00	$37.50
Product line 2 (80% wool, 20% nylon)	23.50	29.37
Product line 3 (100% Dupont Stainmaster nylon)	16.40	20.50
Product line 4 (100% Monsanto Wear-Dated nylon)	13.75	17.19
Product line 5 (generic nylon)	7.85	9.80

*All prices are quoted on a per-square-yard basis.

The cost of display samples for Mid-States Carpet Distributors to support the line will be $20,000. Mid-States could attempt to recover the costs of these samples by billing its customers. Traditionally, MSCD has been able to recover about 50 percent of its sample costs with this policy. National Saxony Carpet Company has offered a 2 percent co-op fund with a yearly accrual and a 50/50 split. Money would be available in the fund after the first year of sales for local advertising.

Additional information will be provided by your instructor. A confidential set of materials will be provided to the NSCC selling team. The MSCD buying team will also receive a set of confidential information. Under no circumstances should this material be shared across the buying and selling teams. Your instructor will assign students to NSCC selling teams and MSCD buying teams. Your assignment is to prepare a negotiation strategy and formal proposal and then negotiate an agreement with an opposing team during a class session. Good luck.

▶ 5 ◀

Territory Management*

It almost goes against the nature of salespeople to think about time; they just want to hit the road and sell.
MARTY WILEY
(Vice President of Marketing and Sales, Loctite Corporation)

*Chapter Consultant: Jerry Willett National Sales Manager Software Spectrum.

LEARNING OBJECTIVES

After studying this chapter, you should be able to:

▶ Tell how companies are attempting to increase sales force productivity.

▶ Calculate the cost per sales call.

▶ Determine the break-even sales volume.

▶ Describe four methods for allocating selling time to different customers and tell when each method should be used.

▶ Devise a travel plan for effectively and efficiently covering a territory.

▶ Understand how to develop your own time management program.

▶ Explain the role of the sales manager in territory management.

► ALLOCATING TIME AT IBM

After 20 years with IBM in a variety of sales, sales management, and sales training positions, David Mercer was recalling one of his earliest experiences:

I well remember when I was an IBM trainee and had been given my first territory to develop. I spent an inordinate amount of time on a small food wholesaler which had been foolish enough to admit that it wanted to improve its financial systems. Over seven or eight extended calls I eventually developed a 50-page proposal, which just about managed to justify the $50,000 or so I was asking them to invest in the smallest mainframe computer. I ultimately lost the order. They actually bought a new electric typewriter and a new desktop electronic calculator at a total cost of less than $1,000.

Identifying your opportunities and using your time wisely is important with current customers as well as new prospects. According to Mercer:

In IBM I rarely worked on more than 10 or so accounts that I knew would deliver better than 90 percent of my business in the next year. I didn't totally ignore the next 20 or 30 accounts, which would give me almost all the remaining 10 percent, but they received significantly less attention. I didn't totally ignore the 100+ accounts which might provide, at best, 1 or 2 percent; like many sales professionals, I am too greedy for my own good. But I covered these marginal accounts by mass marketing activities—only getting personally involved when they actually asked to place an order. Even then, the size of the order usually made the business unproductive.[1]

As David Mercer's experiences indicate, the difference between rookie salespeople and experienced sales professionals often starts with their attitude toward their territory. Salespeople must carefully analyze their resources, opportunities, and constraints. All accounts and sales opportunities are not equally important. Likewise, time available for face-to-face communications with customers is an important constraint on performance.

The purpose of this chapter is to show how salespeople can be more productive by working smarter, that is, by working more efficiently. Up to this point, we have concentrated on selling effectiveness: how to make a good sales presentation and how to cultivate a profitable long-term relationship. This chapter examines how salespeople should effectively use their available selling time.

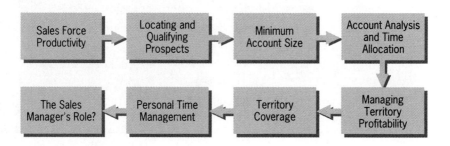

The first part of our discussion focuses on various tools for better planning the use of your selling time. We begin by discussing the importance of new customer prospecting and present various methods for generating qualified prospects. The remainder of the chapter focuses on allocating time among existing customers. First, we show how to determine the minimum size account a salesperson should try to sell, followed by a discussion of how to allocate time among selling opportunities. Several methods for allocating time are presented, including the single factor, the portfolio, decision models, and the sales funnel.

In addition to allocating time properly, productivity can be improved by increasing the amount of time available for selling. One way to increase selling time is to minimize the time spent traveling between accounts. Several methods for reducing travel time are presented. Another way to increase selling time is to exercise better management of your personal time. We conclude with a discussion of what role sales management should play with respect to territory management. First, we more closely examine the issue of sales force productivity.

► SALES FORCE PRODUCTIVITY

For many companies, selling costs have risen faster than sales volume, while sales force productivity has suffered. The conclusion of one widely quoted study on sales force productivity over a 10-year period through 1987 was that selling costs were rising almost twice as fast as average sales volume per salesperson. With the cost of an average sales call for industrial goods at $227.27, the crisis in sales force productivity has not escaped top management's attention.[2] Efforts to improve sales force productivity have focused on two areas: (1) increasing the amount of time salespeople spend selling and (2) focusing salespeople's time on high-productivity priorities.[3]

Selling Time

Over the past decade, the amount of time that the average salesperson spends not selling has increased. *Nonselling time* includes such tasks as completing expense reports, doing other paperwork, attending meetings, handling customers' complaints, expediting orders, training customers to use your product or service, traveling, and selling internally to your own company. Figure 5-1 shows how salespeople spend their time. On average, salespeople report spending only 30 percent of their time in face-to-face selling. Waiting, traveling, and performing administrative tasks, on the other hand, account for 37 percent of their time.

Improving the amount of time spent in face-to-face selling is an opportunity for producing significant productivity gains. A task force at one Fortune 100 company estimated that a 10 percent improvement in the time its sales force spent selling would generate more than a 5 percent increase in overall sales volume. Sales Management Technology 5-1 provides examples of how other companies are trying to increase selling time and decrease costs through new technology integration and by eliminating field sales offices.

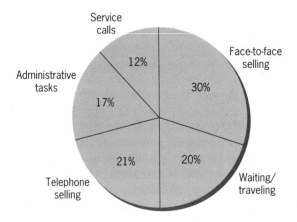

Figure 5-1: How Salespeople Spend Their Time

Sales Management Technology 5-1
Road Warriors

Unlike traveling salespeople of yore, who carried battered suitcases, today's salespeople carry the latest technology: laptop computers with modem and fax boards, cellular phones, pagers, and printers or graphics display devices. These "road warriors" are able to create "virtual offices" as a result of these portable technologies. As a result, companies such as Aetna Life & Casualty, Arthur Andersen & Company, AT&T, Ernst & Young, Dun & Bradstreet, IBM, and Pacific Bell are able to reduce the leasing costs of offices. AT&T estimates that it has saved more than $24 million in real estate expenses associated with its 6,000 member sales force. Following are some examples of how companies are making information more accessible and reducing administrative chores through technology:

- Apple Computer salespeople use computers to send customized information to prospects, schedule follow-up calls, and alert themselves 60 days before a contract expires.

- Armstrong World Industries' salespeople are able to develop customer cost estimates on site.

- Owens-Corning Fiberglass uses computers to reduce the 20 pounds of reports a salesperson receives per month.

- When confronted with a new competitive product, DuPont's salespeople can check their computers to see if another salesperson has seen the product and find out how it was countered.

- IBM says that laptop use by salespeople saves 4.4 hours per week that had been spent traveling to branch offices to get answers to customers' questions and has increased time with customers by 2.8 hours per week.

Sources: Patrick Flanagan, "Here Come the 'Road Warriors,'" Management Review (September 1993), pp. 36–40; and Thayer Taylor, "Going Mobile," *Sales & Marketing Management* (May 1994), pp. 94–106.

Account and Product Focus

A second strategy for increasing sales force productivity is to get salespeople to focus more of their effort on strategic accounts and products. In 1996 there were over $659 billion of mergers and acquisitions in the United States. The net result has been a concentration in sales to a few, very important customers. The top 10 percent of all customers represent, on average, 50 percent of total sales volume, while the top 20 percent of all customers represent, on average, 75 percent of total sales volume.

At first glance, it would appear obvious that salespeople should spend their time with the top 50 percent of their customers and especially with the top 20 percent. Unfortunately, many factors entice salespeople and management to provide sales coverage to a large number of customers. Once a customer has been added to the list, for instance, it is against human nature to reduce that coverage. The top 20 percent may be geographically dispersed throughout a territory, with customers in the bottom 50 percent often located next door. Further, in total the bottom 50 percent still represent significant volume and commissions. Some of the bottom 50 percent have the potential to become major customers, and some of the bottom 50 percent are the salesperson's best and oldest friends in the business. Consequently, it is quite easy to not spend enough time with the *right* accounts performing the *right* activities.[4]

One approach to increase sales force productivity is to focus sales force time on prospects that have a high probability of becoming important customers. The next section discusses the importance of prospecting for new customers and company efforts to increase sales force efficiency in this area.

▶ LOCATING AND QUALIFYING PROSPECTS

One of the most important tasks of many salespeople is to prospect for new customers. A sale cannot occur until you have a potential buyer, and a widely quoted rule of thumb is that it takes a business-to-business salesperson five or more calls before closing a new account. *Prospecting* is necessary for a number of reasons:

- Existing accounts are lost to competitors.
- Clients go out of business or merge with other businesses.
- An organization may have the goal of increasing its customer base.
- New products may be better suited to new customers, rather than to present customers.

For these and other reasons, many salespeople spend a good proportion of their time looking for new customers. The key to building sales in a territory through prospecting is not just spending time at it, but spending time with prospects that are likely to become good customers. Therefore it is important that salespeople build a good prospect profile.

Building a Prospect Profile

Not all businesses will want or need your product or services. Some will clearly be a waste of your time, while others will not buy enough to make it worth your time. You must first decide what factors determine who is a good prospect. This means building a *prospect profile*, which is simply a profile of what the best prospect looks like. How a prospect profile helped one company is described in Sales Management in Action 5-1.

A starting place for building this profile is a review of the target markets for your products, as specified in your marketing plan. Allnet Communications Services, a small long-distance phone company in Michigan, defines their target niche as small- to medium-sized business that bill between several hundred dollars and several tens of thousands of dollars per month. This target was identified to avoid head-to-head competition with AT&T, MCI, and Sprint. If a target market has not been clearly identified, then a new salesperson may need to rely on the past experience of other salespeople in the company by asking them what types of business provide their most valuable customers. Veteran salespeople are probably best advised to examine their own past successes.

If you are selling blood processing machines, for example, then your best prospects may be hematologists (hospital consultants specializing in analyzing and treating blood disorders). Upon closer examination, the hottest prospects may be young (under 30) and trained at a handful of teaching hospitals.

The blood processing example points out a few important aspects of building a profile. First, the profile is defined in terms of demographics, the physical character-

Sales Management in Action 5-1
A Perfect "10"

At Southwest Network Services in Austin, Texas, management has decided that better prospecting success can be achieved by working smarter instead of harder. So instead of focusing on generating more prospects, they have developed a tool to help salespeople be more organized and effective in working the prospects they already have. To do this they have created a prospect profile consisting of 12 characteristics, such as current vendor, percent savings, equipment specs, payback period, etc. Next to each characteristic is a rating scale ranging from 1 to 10 in value. After the first call, the salesperson answers all 12 characteristic questions. The total score is added and then divided by 12. If the prospect's score is above 8.5, Southwest knows that the prospect historically and objectively is likely to buy, and the salesperson keeps working on it. If the score is 7.5 or lower, the salespeople know they are bucking the odds and should stop working on that account.

Source: David S. Kemp, "Pray For Us All," *Sales & Marketing Management* (March, 1993), p. 8.

Sales Management Technology 5-2
Researching Prospect Profiles On-Line

"Knowledge is power," as the saying goes, and information on just about every company and industry is out there somewhere on-line. The benefit to salespeople is that on-line services can be a great source of information on prospects and client companies.

As selling focuses its attention on addressing customer problems, it takes more and more time to research and discover the needs of a client. This is where on-line services can help. Once on-line, you can access databases containing government statistics, journals, books, and up-to-date newswires. There are also about 7,000 newsgroups, and any number of bulletin boards, forums, and roundtables that cover almost every subject

imaginable. Web sites useful for target marketing and identifying new customers include www.census.gov:80/stat-abstract or www.city.net. A good site for identifying the top businesses in a geographic market area is www.toplist.com. If you are in the information technology business, for instance, you can receive by e-mail a report on any company within 15 minutes from reports.infowizard.com.

Perhaps the most important and most widely used source of information for salespeople is the customer's own homepage. These sites regularly provide sales, financial, product, location, press release, and stock information.

---

istics that define the individual buying environment. In the blood processing example, demographics included the customer's business, age, and educational background. Other examples of demographics frequently used to build a prospect profile include the following:

- Size of the business
- Age of the equipment to be replaced
- Geographic distance from shipping points
- Product line specialty

This information often can be obtained before meeting with the prospect. At Southwest Networks in Austin, Texas, salespeople keep a written profile of 12 characteristics on all leads. The purpose of the profile is to tell salespeople how good a prospect a lead is and when to walk away from the lead.[5] Sales Management Technology 5-2 discusses obtaining this information on-line.

Building a Prospect List

With an ideal profile clearly in mind, a list of prospects should be developed. Here's the question that many companies are asking: Does it make sense for salespeople to spend four days out of five prospecting for new business? Companies are increasingly answering No.[6] Some of the more widely used methods being used to identify good prospects include direct inquiries, trade shows, directories, referrals, and cold canvassing.

Direct Inquiry   All companies receive direct inquiries about products or services from potential customers. People making direct inquiries are often good prospects because they are, in effect, requesting that a salesperson call. While some inquiries are unsolicited, the most common ways to generate leads are with advertising, direct mail, and trade shows. Advertising is not always used to sell the product or service, but it is an excellent vehicle for locating prospective customers. The fact that the potential customer initiates the contact allows salespeople to concentrate their efforts on those prospects most likely to purchase.

The quality of leads generated by advertising may vary, depending on the promotional copy in the advertising. Someone responding to an ad stating that a sales-

---

Sales Management in Action 5-2
Would You Sell to Crooks?

There is perhaps no more dramatic change in a business environment than that occurring in Eastern Europe, which in the early 1990s is between communism and capitalism. No one has to tell Sepp Leimgruber, area director of Hungary and the Czech Republic for Rank Xerox, how difficult it can be to sell in this environment.

Rank Xerox, a joint venture between Xerox and the Rank Organization of Britain, has been selling photocopiers in Eastern Europe since 1964. The company believes the sales potential in Eastern Europe and the former Soviet Union is fantastic. The former Soviet Union, which has about 50,000 copiers, is estimated to need 2.5 million to 5 million. Eastern Europe has about 100,000 copiers and is estimated to need at least 1 million.

To realize this potential, significant obstacles must be overcome. To get around the shortage of convertible currencies in the area, a company must be adept at counter trade—arranging the sale of Eastern Euro-

pean and Soviet goods to earn the hard currency to pay for photocopiers. Perhaps Leimgruber's most important problem is deciding who are the best customers for Xerox photocopiers.

The problem is that the only people with the necessary capital to be independent copier dealers are those who were corrupt Communist officials or those involved in money changing or other black-market activities. "Nobody but the big crooks have the money," says Leimgruber, "and the question is whether you, as a respectable company, want to do business with the crooks." Leimgruber is continuing to look for the honest entrepreneurs who are slowly emerging in Eastern Europe. His primary prospect profile is people with expertise who might have worked for state-owned companies and are eager to go out on their own.

Source: Steven Prokesch, "Xerox Drives for Pole Position in Race for Eastern Europe Markets," *The Dallas Morning News* (December 31, 1990), p. 1D.

person will call on them is a more qualified lead than one offering a prize as a reward for completing the inquiry. The former indicates a greater commitment to further buying action.[7] In consumer markets, direct mail is usually sent to a large potential audience. Although the response rate is typically very small, frequently less than 1 percent, the expense is fairly low especially relative to sales force time.

In business-to-business marketing a hybrid of direct mail is called "indirect" mail. Trade publications carry advertisements directed at specific segments of the business community. The advertisement contains a *"bingo"* card that allows the reader to request more information about certain products. Some of the problems you may encounter in searching for prospects in foreign countries are described in Sales Management in Action 5-2.[8]

Trade Shows Trade shows are also an excellent vehicle for generating good prospects. It is estimated that more than 145,000 firms participate in over 8,000 trade shows at a cost of $10 billion annually. The National Restaurant Show held annually in Chicago draws more than 100,000 food buyers and business owners. One of the reasons for the growing popularity of trade shows is the relatively low cost per customer contact, around $89 per qualified contact. A qualified contact is a customer contact whose interest in purchasing has been verified. Another reason is that, at trade shows, organizations can project a coherent and consistent message to all prospects through exhibit structure, graphic and product displays, product demonstrations, and other support material. While some sales are consummated at trade shows, more likely the lead is passed on to the appropriate salesperson. In fact, some trade shows do not permit the writing of orders.[9]

Directories Special *direct inquiry directories* and open-to-bid announcements are important sources of leads for many firms. For example, the T*homas Register of American Manufacturers* provides names, addresses, and other information compiled by types of products and by state. Furthermore, the firms in the *Register* are scored according to their assets, which enables the salesperson to judge the size of each potential customer.

Referrals With *referrals*, a satisfied customer is asked to provide the names of others who might be interested in a product. In some cases, the person may also supply an introduction of the salesperson to the prospects. The advantage of referrals is that the person can say things about the salesperson and the product line that might not be as credible coming directly from the salesperson.[10]

One residential protection agency uses an interesting referral technique. The company holds a "walkthrough party" after completing an alarm system installation. The customer is encouraged to invite up to four neighbors or friends to observe the well-organized indoctrination in the use of the system. The conversion rate on subsequent presentations to people who were present at the walkthrough party is over 90 percent.[11]

Cold Canvassing *Cold canvassing* involves contacting prospective customers without appointments; that is, salespeople call on firms or knock on doors until they find good prospects. Direct sales organizations such as Avon Products have had success with this approach. It is also used with some regularity by salespeople selling office supplies, air conditioning, cash registers, paper supplies, and insurance. Cold canvassing is used in these situations because the target markets for these products are fairly broad. The use of cold calls allows salespeople to concentrate their efforts in the best geographic areas and to fill gaps in their schedules. For example, if a stationary salesperson has an appointment canceled in the middle of the day, the time until the next scheduled call can be spent making cold calls on other potential customers in the same building or immediate area. The drawback to this approach is that it does not encourage calling on high-quality prospects. A salesperson could spend time soliciting low-quality prospects. Canvassing may also be accomplished by telephone.

As the above discussion suggests, there are a variety of methods for identifying high-quality prospects. Salespeople are limited only by their own imagination and initiative.

Qualifying Prospects

Once salespeople have a list of leads, they must identify or *qualify a prospect*, that is, determine if the prospect is likely to be converted to a buying customer. Companies often initially qualify leads by telephone because of the lower cost of doing so. For example, Dow Corning, a specialty chemical affiliate of Dow Chemical and Corning Glass Works, uses an inside sales staff to qualify by telephone some of the 80,000 leads it generates annually.

To effectively qualify a prospect, the salesperson needs information about customer needs, buying authority, and ability to pay. Each of these are discussed below.

Needs   The most qualified leads are those that have a use for the seller's goods or services and are planning to buy in the near future. A prospect that is satisfied with the present supplier and has no desire to change is going to be very difficult to convert into a customer. You will sell such a prospect only if you can discover a desire or need that is not being fulfilled adequately with the present supplier and get the buyer to focus on these needs. This is not an easy task. Even if the prospect has an immediate need that you can meet and a desire to buy, you must still determine if the size and profitability of potential orders are sufficient to warrant further attention. A telephone qualifying approach is described in Sales Management in Action 5-3.

Buying Authority   Beyond the question of customer needs is the issue of buying authority. The plant manager may want a milling machine, but if he or she does not have the authority to buy, then a sales call may help give a favorable impression but will not necessarily produce a signed order. Business-to-business salespeople often have problems identifying who has the authority to buy within an organization because of the number of people who have a role in making a purchasing decision. Methods for identifying the buying authority were presented in the preceding Chapter 4.

Ability to Pay   Finding prospects who want a product and also have the authority to buy is not enough if they lack the financial resources to pay for it. Selling products that must be repossessed later for nonpayment of bills is not the way for salespeople to get ahead. Hence, salespeople should make an initial screening of prospects on their ability to buy. The objective is to eliminate prospects who represent too high a

---

Sales Management in Action 5-3
Are They "Hot," "Warm," or "Cold"?

Atlantic Software Corporation of Denver sells computer-based accounting and estimating systems priced from $6,000 to $150,000. Customers include construction companies, specialty subcontractors, developers, and real estate managers.

A few years ago, Atlantic was having a common problem. Salespeople were spending too much of their time chasing prospects that were either not qualified to buy or not planning to purchase for some time. To overcome the problem, Atlantic started telequalifying leads generated by advertising. Telequalifiers identify the prospect's indus-try, budget, buying time frame, software-purchasing decision makers, and the competitive products they are considering.

The telequalifiers label leads as "now," "hot," "warm," or "cold." "Now" leads are relayed immediately by telephone to Atlantic's salespeople; the rest are mailed. The program's revenues from first-time customers came to $500,000 the first year. Revenues on new business from leads increased to $1.5 million in the second year.

Source: Kate Bertrand, "Streamlining Field Sales Through Automation," *Business Marketing* (May 1988), p. 62.

---

credit risk. Credit ratings are readily available from banks and credit services such as Dunn and Bradstreet.

One study on how salespeople qualify prospects found that successful salespeople differed from less successful salespeople in how they thought about prospects. While both groups of salespeople generally used the same cues to qualify a prospect (e.g., income, need, etc.), successful salespeople utilized higher qualifying standards and were more likely to cut their losses early. For example, they required a higher credit rating or a greater need for the product or service to consider a lead to be a hot prospect.[12] This is another example of how wasted time can hurt productivity and that time management is critical to sales success.

▶ MINIMUM ACCOUNT SIZE

Prospecting for new accounts is only a part of the overall job in most sales positions. In all likelihood, you will be given a list of existing accounts which will account for most of your sales volume. An important starting point in managing your territory is to determine the minimum size customer on whom you should be calling. A salesperson's time is valuable and expensive and should not be wasted pursuing unprofitable sales opportunities.

The individual salesperson should be able to determine the long-term value of a customer. For example, salespeople should know customers' short-term growth potential, as well as their territory's competitive and demand situations. If supplied with proper direct selling expense information, salespeople are in an excellent position to determine the *minimum account size* on which to call.

Cost per Call

The first step in addressing the minimum customer size issue is to calculate what it costs to make a sales call. *Cost per call* will be a function of the number of calls you make per day, the number of days available to call on customers, and your direct selling expenses. Direct selling expenses include compensation, travel, lodging, entertainment, and communications. These expenses are referred to as *direct selling expenses* because they can be attributed to an individual salesperson. In other words, the company would not have incurred these costs if a salesperson had not been present in the territory.

The procedure for computing the average cost per call is illustrated in Table 5-1 for an industrial sales representative with an average-size territory. In this example, compensation includes salary, commissions, and bonuses, as well as fringe benefits such as insurance and social security. These total $69,000, which is about average for an industrial salesperson.[13] Other direct selling expenses equal $21,250, for a total direct selling expense of $90,250.

For this salesperson, 205 days a year are available for selling. If the average

Table 5-1 Computing the Cost per Call for an Industrial Products Salesperson

Compensation		
Salary, commissions, and bonus	$60,000	
Fringe benefits (hospital, life insurance, Social Security)	9000	$69,000
Direct Selling Expenses		
Automobile	7000	
Lodging and meals	5250	
Entertainment	2250	
Communications	3500	
Samples, promotional material	1750	
Miscellaneous	1500	21,250
Total Direct Expenses		$90,250
Calls Per Year		
Total Available Days		260 days
Less:		
Vacation	10 days	
Holidays	10 days	
Illness	5 days	
Meetings	18 days	
Training	12 days	55 days
Net Selling Days		205 days
Average Calls per Day		3 calls
Total Calls per Year (205 × 3)		615 calls
Average Cost per Call ($90,250/615)		**$146.75**

number of calls per day is 3, then under normal circumstances the total number of calls for the entire year is 615 (3 × 205). Using these estimates, the representative can now compute the cost of an average call as $146.75 ($90,250/615).

How does the cost per call of $146.75 compare to that of other salespeople? According to one survey, the median cost per call in 1993 for consumer goods salespeople was $210.87; it was $227.27 for industrial goods and $213.64 for services.[14]

Break-Even Sales Volume

Break-even sales volume, the sales volume necessary to cover direct selling expenses, will help determine the minimum size customer that should be pursued. In addition to the cost per call, calculating the break-even volume requires that we also know the number of calls necessary to close a sale and what direct selling expenses should be as a percentage of total sales. Calls to close may be based on your own experience or that of other salespeople in the company, while the target for direct selling expenses should be provided by management.

Both the number of sales calls needed to close a sale and direct selling costs as a percentage of sales will vary considerably among industries and even between companies in the same industry. Table 5-2 shows these numbers for 10 industries. The number of calls needed to close a sale varies from 2.8 in the construction industry to 5.3 in the instruments industry. Sales costs as a percentage of sales are 19.3 percent in business services but only 2.8 percent in rubber and plastics.

Armed with this information, break-even sales volume for an individual sale can be calculated as follows:

$$\text{Break-even sales volume} = \frac{\text{Cost per call} \times \text{number of calls to close}}{\text{Sales costs as a percentage of sales}}$$

If the sales representative is in the chemicals industry, where 2.8 calls are needed to close a sale and sales expenses are 3.0 percent of sales, then the break-even sales

Table 5-2   Selected Statistics on Cost per Call and Number of Calls Needed to Close a Sale

Industry	Cost per Call	Number of Calls Needed to Close a Sale	Sales Costs as a Percentage of Total Sales
Business services	$ 46.00	4.6	19.3%
Chemicals	165.80	2.8	3.0
Construction	111.20	2.8	3.2
Electronics	133.30	3.9	12.0
Food products	131.60	4.8	9.6
Instruments	226.00	5.3	10.3
Machinery	68.50	3.0	13.0
Office equipment	25.00	3.7	15.0
Printing/publishing	70.10	4.5	8.3
Rubber/plastic	248.20	4.7	2.8

volume would be $13,697 ([$146.75 × 2.8]/.03). As a point of comparison, break-even sales volume for an average salesperson in the instruments industry is $11,629 ([$226.00 × 5.3]/.103). Notice that the higher cost per call and greater number of calls, needed to close an order in the instrument industry, are more than offset by the fact that direct selling costs are normally 10.3 percent of sales in this industry, compared to 3 percent in the chemicals industry.

In many industries, salespeople's primary function is to facilitate straight rebuys. Remember, straight rebuys consist of sales to replenish inventories of products already used by a customer, with no significant modification in the specifications for the product. This is the primary responsibility of most consumer and industrial goods wholesale salespeople. Instead of examining the number of calls needed to close the sale, in this case the number of calls made each month on an account may be substituted in the break-even sales volume equation to arrive at a break-even volume per month. For example, if the cost per call is $146.75, the number of calls made on a customer is four times a month, and selling costs are 9 percent of sales, then a customer should place, on average, $6,522 worth of business with a salesperson each month ([$146.75 × 4]/.09).

Break-even sales volume can also be calculated when prospecting for new customers. The calculations are the same, though the sales volume and sales calls per month figures are estimates rather than historical facts. This suggests that estimates of future account sales and service requirements are important when prospecting.

Territory Management Implications

Having performed a break-even analysis, how can a salesperson use this information? Should a salesperson reduce the number of calls made on the account in our previous example if the account does not place at least $6,522 of business with the salesperson each month?

The real world of selling is rarely simple or straightforward. Other factors must be considered before dropping a customer or reducing the selling effort. For example, sales to a customer may be growing; a customer may be located next door to a major account, so a call takes little time and there is no real travel time involved. More important, a customer may purchase a mix of high-profit products, so that average gross margins are 25 percent higher than average.

Top management may choose to address the smaller, less profitable accounts in ways other than reducing the number of sales calls made on these accounts. The Gillette Company's Safety Razor Division decided to hire part-time merchandisers to assist salespeople in calling on individual small retailers. The Commercial Systems Division of Hewlett-Packard hired inside sales and technical reps to work the phones. Alternatively, a plumbing fixtures manufacturer chose to raise prices to discourage the "worthless" small customer orders that were disrupting its production scheduling. These small orders became the most profitable. The new higher prices more than compensated for the costs; customers weren't changing suppliers because of high switching costs; and competitors had shied away from these small accounts because of the conventional wisdom in the industry regarding their profitability.

As you can see from these examples, the minimum size customer on which a salesperson should call depends on the direct selling costs involved, the number of sales calls made over a period of time, and the cost structure of the company, as well as other considerations. There is rarely a hard-and-fast dollar volume below which a customer's business should not be pursued. However, when supplied with the right information, sales professionals will know each account well enough to judge if it is likely to become a profitable one.

► ACCOUNT ANALYSIS AND TIME ALLOCATION

Break-even account analysis provides a starting place from which to determine the minimum size account that should be called on. This analysis does not fully address the issue of how much time should be allocated to prospecting and how much to existing accounts in a territory. *Account analysis* refers to estimating the present and future importance of accounts to your business and allocating time in a way that maximizes sales productivity.

Single-Factor Model

The easiest and most widely used models for allocating salespeople's time are single-factor models. These models examine a single customer characteristic, such as current sales volume, to arrive at an initial allocation of sales calls.

An example of a *single-factor allocation model* based on total sales volume is presented in Table 5-3. This is referred to as ABC *account classification*. Customers are first arrayed according to their total sales volume. The top 15 percent of all accounts are classified as A accounts, the next 20 percent are classified as B's, and the remaining accounts are classified as C's. Column 4 is a calculation of each type of account's sales as a percentage of total territory sales. In this example, A's generate 65 percent of total territory sales, B's account for 20 percent, and C's represent only 15 percent. Based on surveys, these results are fairly typical for a variety of businesses.

If sales force performance is based on total revenue, then effort should be allocated according to sales volume. All too often customers are treated equally, so that each customer is called on with the same frequency. Columns 5 and 6 in Table 5-3 illustrate the problem with making equal numbers of calls on all customers. Notice that if you treat all accounts as equal, say by calling on each account weekly, then you would be spending 65 percent of your time on your C accounts. A call on an A customer, however, is on average 20 times as productive as a call on a C customer.

Table 5-3 ABC Account Classification

Account Classification	No. of Accts. (1)	Percent of Total Accts. (2)	Sales (000) (3)	Percent of Total Sales (4)	Total Calls per Classif. (5)	Sales ($) per Call (6)
A	21	15	$910	65	105	$8667
B	28	20	280	20	140	2000
C	91	65	210	15	455	462
Totals	140	100	$1400	100	700	$2000

Spending too much time with C customers may allow the competition to steal an A customer through better service.

The main limitation of single-factor models such as the ABC account classification procedure is that they do not include all the factors that should be considered when evaluating an account. They do not consider customer growth potential, for example, or the opportunity to obtain greater account penetration (a greater share of the account's total purchases) or account profitability. On the other hand, salespeople are likely to make better time allocation decisions with the ABC systematic approach than when relying totally on judgment and intuition.

Portfolio Models

Portfolio models attempt to overcome the limitations of single-factor models by taking into consideration multiple factors when determining the attractiveness of individual accounts within a territory. Selling effort is allocated so that the most attractive accounts receive the most selling effort.[15]

Portfolio models are a general class of models that attempt to prioritize the value or attractiveness of a salesperson's portfolio of accounts by measuring and classifying accounts on a number of criteria. For instance, one company classified its portfolio of accounts according to their average gross margin and the cost to service each account. The Pharmaseal Surgical Division of Baxter Healthcare Corporation instituted a customer classification system based on the type of hospital (e.g., teaching/research, regional medical center, government/federal, community), location (rural versus urban), and size. Sales effort and marketing programs were designed for each type of customer within the classification system. What criteria a company uses to classify its customers will depend on their competitive situation and what the sales force is asked to accomplish.

Figure 5-2 illustrates one well-known portfolio model. This model classifies

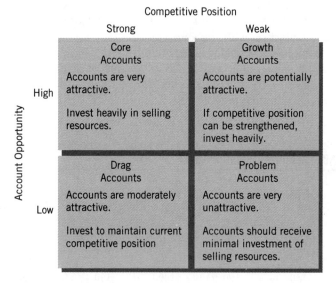

Figure 5-2: Portfolio Model of Effort Allocation
Source: Adapted from Raymond W. LaForge, David W. Cravens, and Clifford E. Young, "Improving Salesforce Productivity," *Business Horizons,* (September-October 1985), p. 54. Copyright 1985 by the Foundation for the School of Business at Indiana University. Reprinted by permission.

accounts into one of four categories by determining account attractiveness based on two criteria: account opportunity and competitive position. *Account opportunity* refers to the magnitude of an account's present and future need for the salesperson's offering. Ratings of account opportunity may be based on the account's present and projected growth rate, its financial health, and its present and future strength in the marketplace. *Competitive position*, the second dimension on which accounts are classified, refers to the strength of the salesperson's present relationship with an account. Competitive position may be on outcome measures such as an account's total gross profit dollars, account penetration, type of contract, and compliance with the contract. Additional indicators of competitive position may focus on the account relationship and may include the account's attitude toward the company and familiarity with the decision makers in the account. Once all accounts have been rated on both dimensions, we can proceed to prioritize our accounts by splitting them at the median of both dimensions and forming a four-quadrant grid, as shown in Figure 5-2.

As an extension of single-factor customer classification models, portfolio models offer several benefits that single-factor models do not:

- They help the sales team to identify the important customer and relationship issues.
- They facilitate communication and sharing of judgments and assumptions between salespeople and sales managers.
- They help isolate information gaps and set priorities for customer data collection and analysis.
- They force the sales team to think about the future and consider ways of achieving a more desirable portfolio configuration.

Decision Models

While portfolio models have the advantage of using multiple characteristics to classify accounts, several shortcomings remain. First, accounts must still be grouped into the four quadrants for the purpose of allocating sales calls. Differences between firms in the same quadrant are therefore not taken into consideration. Second, the process does not arrive at an optimal allocation of sales calls.

Decision models for allocating sales calls overcome these two shortcomings by focusing on the response of each account to the number of sales calls made over a period of time. Although mathematically elegant, these models consist of two parts. The first part consists of developing the relationship between the number of sales calls over a period of time and sales to a particular account. This is referred to as a *sales response function*. The response function may be derived either through regression analysis on historical data or judgmentally. With judgment-based decision models, salespeople are first given information about how many times they called on a particular account over a period of time and the resulting sales generated. Salespeople are then asked what they think sales will be in the coming quarter if the same number of calls are made on the account, if the number of sales calls is decreased by 50 percent, if they make no sales calls, and if they make the maximum number of sales calls possible.

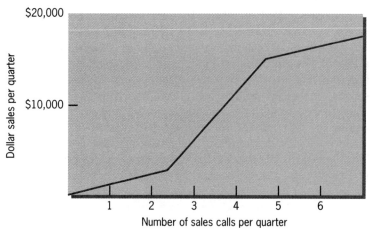

Figure 5-3: Number of Sales Calls Response Function

These estimates are used to construct a sales response function like the one shown in Figure 5-3.

Note that customers are assumed not to respond dramatically when only one or two calls are made per quarter, but sales are expected to increase dramatically when the number of calls increases from two to four. The response function flattens out after four calls, suggesting that there is little left for the salesperson to accomplish by calling on the account more than four times in a quarter.

The second part of these models uses the individual response functions to allocate calls so as to maximize sales. Essentially, these models continue to allocate sales calls to an account until more sales can be generated by calling on another account. For example, a third and fourth call may be allocated to the account in Figure 5-3, but greater sales are likely to be generated by calling on another account rather than by allocating a fifth call to this account.

The allocation task in decision models is complex and involves a large number of calculations as the number of accounts in a territory increases. Therefore, computer models such as CALLPLAN have been developed. CALLPLAN is an interactive computerized program based on decision model logic. CALLPLAN is self-instructing, and salespeople can work with the model at remote computer terminals using simple conversational language. Research results on the use of decision models have consistently supported the use of these models, with sales improvements ranging from 8 to 30 percent.[16]

Sales Funnel

Despite the advantages of sophisticated call allocation programs, they are not appropriate for all situations. For an example of when they would not be appropriate, see the example of Intel salespeople in Sales Management in Action 5-4. More commonly, a long selling cycle may limit their usefulness of these models.

Sales Management in Action 5-4
Intel: Salespeople Who Don't Call on Customers

A large number of Intel's salespeople don't call on customers. Instead they call on software vendors, information technology buyers, and retail outlets—companies that are traditional partners and customers of PC manufacturers. These salespeople don't sell the microprocessors made by Intel; instead they sell the idea of PCs on every desk and in every household. Salespeople are also responsible for knowing what is going on in those industries that impact Intel. For instance, Intel is represented on most software standards committees. That gives Intel a voice in what shape such things as the Internet will take. It's a voice Intel uses to foster consumer and corporate interest in PCs—rather than low-end devices that don't require Intel processors.

When the sale is not a straight rebuy to replenish existing inventories, the selling cycle can be quite long. This is especially true in industrial goods and high-tech markets, as well as in major account selling where more effort is required and many people may be involved in the purchase decision. An 18-month selling cycle is typical, for example, in the Traffic Control Division of 3M. Likewise, new product introductions are more time-consuming in most industries. In such situations, the single-factor, portfolio or decision models are not appropriate.

In complex selling situations or when significant time is spent prospecting for new accounts, the *sales funnel* approach is more appropriate. Initially developed for training salespeople at Hewlett-Packard, this system categorizes and prioritizes sales opportunities or objectives, not accounts.[17] This is necessary because a salesperson or sales team may have multiple selling objectives at one account at the same time. He or she may be attempting to get a pilot installation in one of the client's departments, for example, while wanting to upgrade to a more sophisticated piece of equipment in another department.

Each sales opportunity is categorized based on the level of uncertainty in meeting the opportunity:

1. **Unqualified opportunities.** In this case data suggest that a possible need exists, but this need has not been verified with key people in the account. For example, you have found out that a customer's existing contract with a competitor is about to expire. The selling job needed in this situation is to qualify the account by verifying that a need exists according to the criteria discussed earlier in this chapter.

2. **Qualified opportunities.** A qualified opportunity must meet four criteria:
   - The need has been verified with at least one of the buying influences (i.e., the technical, user, or economic buyers discussed in Chapter 3).

- There is a confirmed intention to buy a new product or service, replace an existing one, or switch suppliers.
- Funding for the purchase has been approved or already exists.
- There is an identified time frame within which the purchase will be made.

3. **Best few opportunities.**   All the buyers have been contacted and their needs identified, and in your judgment have been sufficiently met to make the sale. You have all but eliminated luck and uncertainty in the sale and are at least 50 percent along in the *selling cycle*. That is, it should take you half as long to close these sales as is normal in your territory.

The term *sales funnel* is derived from figuratively placing the sales opportunities in a funnel, with unqualified opportunities just outside the top of the funnel; qualified opportunities inside the funnel, depending on the probability of closure and the position in the selling cycle; and the few best opportunities at the bottom of the funnel.

In the sales funnel shown in Figure 5-4, each numbered bubble represents a unique selling opportunity. Notice that the qualified opportunities are divided into those with a 50 percent probability of closure and those with a 75 percent probability. This distinction is made to portray the current situation more clearly and to facilitate communication between salesperson and sales manager. The situation in Figure 5-4 appears to be healthy in that there are a number of opportunities likely to be closed in the current period but an even larger number of opportunities for future sales results. Some companies will alter the shape of the funnel to reflect the number of opportunities at each level, which quickly indicates the present and future health of the territory.

At first glance, it would seem best to work on your best few and qualified opportunities, while spending whatever time remains on unqualified opportunities. The problem with this approach is that when given low priority, prospecting rarely occurs.

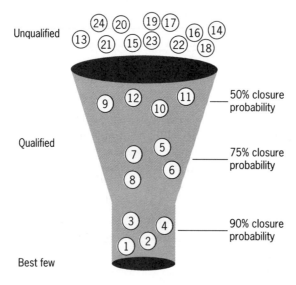

Figure 5-4: Sales Funnel

Having closed the best few and exhausted the qualified opportunities, there is nothing left to replace these opportunities. Therefore, experts suggest the sequence of (1) closing your best few sales opportunities first, (2) prospecting for unqualified opportunities next, and (3) working the qualified opportunities last to ensure a constant and predictable flow of sales over time.[18] It is always important to keep the funnel full through prospecting.

Because there are probably many sales opportunities during any review period, only the major deals and core or growth accounts should be included in the sales funnel. This will allow both the salesperson and manager to identify critical sales objectives accurately, monitor progress over time, and plan their time for meeting key sales objectives.

▶ MANAGING TERRITORY PROFITABILITY

Faced with tough buyers in mature markets, some companies are beginning to evaluate their salespeople on the profitability of their territory. Profit, of course, is the difference between net price and the actual cost to serve a customer. There can be dramatic differences between accounts both in price and in cost.[19] Why is this true?

Looking at service costs first, service costs may vary dramatically among accounts. Some accounts are located far from the salesperson's normal route. Some order by phone, while others require endless sales calls to close a deal or to place even a routine order. Some customers demand intensive presale services like applications engineering and custom design support, while others accept standard designs.

The size of the order will often influence both production and distribution costs. Costs may also vary according to preferred transportation mode, number of receiving locations for an order, and opportunities to back-haul. In postsale servicing, some customers will require services such as user training, installation requirements, technical support, and repair and maintenance agreements, while others will not.

Although legal constraints, such as the Robinson-Patman Act, encourage uniformity of pricing, customers generally pay quite different prices. Some customers are able to negotiate lower prices and higher discounts because of their size or ability to bargain. Others are able to negotiate lower prices because of their in-house technical and maintenance abilities. And some customers exploit deals and promotions more than others or buy a mix of products that have lower gross margins.

The dispersion of customer profitability should be managed by the sales force in at least three ways:

1. **Allocation of effort.** Salespeople can manage their time allocation according to the profit opportunity an account represents. Distributors of disposable medical supplies, for instance, look for small or single-doctor family practices because these practices use a lot of disposable supplies, such as exam table paper, and they tend to be less price sensitive since they do not usually have a dedicated purchasing manager.

2. **Mix of products.** Most salespeople sell a number of product lines with quite different gross margins. Salespeople should allocate their efforts based on both volume opportunity and profitability of the product line. Management at Loctite

Corporation, a manufacturer of industrial sealants and adhesives, compensates its sales force so as to emphasize the sales of its larger, more profitable console adhesive applicators rather than the pencil applicators.

3. **Price concessions.** Salespeople should be very reluctant to offer price concessions in order to close a sale. Not only do they encourage the buyer to negotiate discounts in the future, but even a small concession can have a dramatic impact on profits. Studies indicate that companies giving salespeople wide latitude to negotiate price discounts are not only less profitable, but also grow less rapidly than those with tight control over sales force price discounting.[20]

The shift to managing territory profits requires that companies first pinpoint their costs, measure account profitability, and provide this information to the sales force.

▶ TERRITORY COVERAGE

After salespeople have determined their time allocation, they still have the problem of selecting a sequence of calls, or *sales routes*, that will minimize travel time and expense. Recall from our discussion at the beginning of the chapter that, on average, 20 percent of salespeople's time is spent traveling and waiting. Careful scheduling can produce substantial benefits. The task of selecting sales routes is usually handled by the salesperson, but at some companies it is developed by the sales manager or staff specialists. The rapidly increasing costs of automobiles and automobile repairs, as well as the possible savings in time, have encouraged many firms to employ more sophisticated technologies to find the best travel routes.

Techniques used to schedule and route salespeople have received considerable attention from management scientists; the issue has become known as the *traveling salesperson problem*. The dilemma is usually stated as a search for a route through the territory that allows a salesperson to visit each customer and return to the starting point with a minimum expenditure of either time or money. A variety of techniques have been employed to search for the best routes, including linear, integer, nonlinear, and heuristic programming, and branch-and-bound methods. Discussion of these complex procedures is beyond the scope of this book.[21]

A simpler way to find the best sequence of calls, and one that is often just as effective in minimizing travel time and costs, is to plan a travel route based on four basic rules:

1. The route should be circular.
2. The route should never cross itself.
3. The same route should not be used to go to and from a customer.
4. Customers in neighboring areas should be visited in sequence.

Circular routes are reasonable because salespeople usually start at a home base and then return to it at the end of the sales trip. Likewise, if sales routes cross, a salesperson knows that a shorter route was overlooked. Sometimes a salesperson will be forced to use the same route to go to and from a customer because of local road conditions or scheduled appointments, but this should be avoided when possible.

Other Factors

In reality, other factors often interfere with plans that appear to be ideal on paper. In geographic routing problems, other factors such as availability of good roads, traffic flows at different times of the day, traffic lights, and congestion often lead to a different route than that originally planned. This does not mean that operations research approaches are not of value; they are an excellent starting point for your analysis.

One additional factor to consider is the work schedule of the account. The best approach is to travel when clients are not available, thereby not wasting valuable selling time. If customers are not available early in the morning, then this may be a good time to get in the most travel miles. As a result, you may make your first call on the customer farthest from your home, rather than making a circular route. Better routing usually comes with experience and greater familiarity with the territory.

▶ PERSONAL TIME MANAGEMENT

Time management was recently rated the third most popular subject in business training programs. Seventy-one percent of firms provide salespeople with training in time management.[22] There is no reason to wait until you are out of school, however, to begin learning good time management skills. The time pressures on students today are quite severe.

A key aspect of managing time effectively is to recognize and control things that tend to waste time. Following is a list of what salespeople consider to be some of the most common time wasters:[23]

1. Telephone interruptions
2. Drop-in visitors
3. Lack of self-discipline
4. Crises
5. Meetings
6. Lack of objectives, priorities, and deadlines
7. Indecision and procrastination
8. Attempting too much at once
9. Leaving tasks unfinished
10. Unclear communication

Note that the top two time wasters are telephone interruptions and drop-in visitors. The rest of the time wasters, such as lack of discipline, lack of objectives, and procrastination, indicate poor self-management by the salesperson. How different is this list from the one you would make for yourself?

A key step in time management is preparing a list of personal and professional goals and then pursuing them one step at a time. Planning does not have to be elaborate to be useful. Simply writing down a list of things you want to do tomorrow is a good place to start. The next step is to rank the tasks on the basis of their

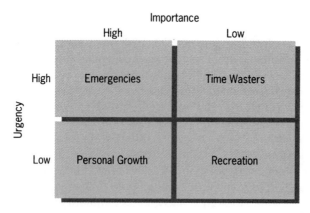

Figure 5-5: Personal Time Management

importance. Then when you start the day, begin task 1 and stay with it until it is completed. Recheck your priorities and begin task 2. Continue with tasks as long as they remain most important.

Once people get into the habit of daily planning, the next step is to plan a week or more ahead. Many salespeople, for example, are required to prepare weekly call plans. The idea is to encourage salespeople to plan a series of calls for each day, to call ahead for appointments, and to make better use of their time. A useful device that helps with planning is a small diary for the pocket or purse. Carrying a diary allows you to keep track of appointments and to reschedule them as needed.

Stephen Covey, a well-known consultant in personal and professional development, advises people to analyze their time management using a framework like the one shown in Figure 5-5.[24] *Importance* refers to activities that are of importance to you in meeting your objectives. *Urgency*, on the other hand, is the time pressure we feel to perform certain activities. Notice that we may feel this pressure for both important and relatively unimportant activities. According to Covey, activities in the Emergencies and Recreation quadrants will generally take care of themselves. Where people can really gain control over their lives is to spend less time on Time Wasters and more on Personal Growth activities. Time Wasters (high urgency but low importance) include phone calls, some meetings, and unnecessary administrative work—in other words, things that demand our immediate attention. Personal Growth activities (low urgency but high importance) are easily put off but are very important to our future growth and development. Activities in this category may include reading professional journals or books, enrolling in professional development or executive courses, getting to know how other functional areas operate, or prospecting for new customers. Notice that for many people these activities can be postponed indefinitely. Considering both urgency and importance may provide us with a useful perspective on how we can spend our time more productively.

▶ MANAGEMENT'S ROLE

Up to this point, territory management has been addressed from the salesperson's viewpoint. What, if any, is the role of sales management in helping salespeople successfully manage their sales territories? There is, of course, no simple answer. While managers agree that territory management is very important, what works for one company may not work for another. In general, management practice in this area runs along a continuum from very close supervision to hands-off management. Each approach has its merits.

Close Supervision

In some companies, salespeople are given very little freedom to schedule their time. In an extreme case, daily itineraries and routes are developed by the staff at headquarters. This usually occurs only in sales situations in which a salesperson has a set list of customers that need to be seen on a frequent and consistent basis in order to replenish inventory. Less extreme are managers who require daily call reports or weekly itineraries from each salesperson. At Ziegler Tools, an Atlanta industrial distributor, salespeople are required each week to fill out detailed itineraries and call reports, which are compared to quarterly itineraries.

Why do some companies believe in such close supervision? One reason is their belief about the behavior of salespeople. Turner Warmack, vice president of sales and marketing at Ziegler Tools, states, "Generally speaking, salespeople are poor managers and can be thrown off course pretty easily. What we feel our system does is help them focus their efforts." The key here is the word *help*. At Ziegler Tools, the salesperson has the last word on any territory management issues. The sales manager is there to help. The Ziegler plan is explained in more detail in Sales Management in Action 5-5.

Sales Management in Action 5-5
"One of the Most Important Things a Sales Manager Does"

This is a quote from a sales manager with an industrial adhesives manufacturer. He was referring to territory planning and monitoring. At Ziegler the sales manager holds an annual meeting with each salesperson to discuss the previous year's sales, key accounts, account growth, and areas for new business. Then the sales manager and the salesperson categorize accounts and decide how often to call on them in the upcoming year. Once they decide on the frequency of calls, the salespeople write their quarterly itineraries. Each account must be visited at least once a quarter or the salesperson does not receive a commission on orders placed during that period. The itineraries are either approved by the sales manager or sent back to be rewritten. These quarterly reports are then saved and checked later against the weekly itineraries and call reports. The objective of this routine is to help people become better organized so that they can be free to do more selling. As one manager said, "You can't just say, 'Here's your territory, go get 'em.' "

Source: Bill Kelley, "How Much Help Does a Salesperson Need?" *Sales & Marketing Management* (May 1989), p. 32.

Hands-Off Management

At the other end of the spectrum are sales managers who do not require their salespeople to submit call reports and detailed reviews of customer status. Typical of this approach is Rick Horn, president of Stahl Company, a specialty truck body manufacturer, who states: "I didn't feel I had to tell them what to do. They were big boys and knew their territory. All I wanted to know is where they were in case I had to reach them." No call reports are required, except from rookie salespeople, and then only for the first six months. Weekly itineraries are required. Larry Eisenhauer, president of Datacom, an electronics representative firm, is also a hands-off manager. He does not even require an itinerary from his 13 salespeople; he lets quarterly commission reports keep him up-to-date on how his salespeople are managing their territories. "Every time they're doing paperwork or attending a meeting they don't have to," he says, "they're not out getting orders."

Recommendations

You may run into many different management opinions on how much and when sales managers should get involved in territory management. Research seems to suggest that close supervision may be appropriate for even veteran salespeople, and may be effective in lowering salespeople's role conflicts and the ambiguity associated with the job.[25] While you should generally consider a system that is right for you, your salespeople, and your company, a few general rules are important for new sales managers to keep in mind:

1. You should be aware of the management style with which you and your salespeople are most comfortable and productive. There are successes associated with the use of each style. Which is most consistent with the culture of your company?

2. You should consider the experience and maturity of your sales force in deciding on the appropriate style of management. The younger and less experienced the salespeople, the closer the supervision should be in order to provide the kind and amount of feedback required and frequently desired by rookies. Older, more experienced people will probably understand your need to know what is going on in their territory but are likely to resent a requirement of daily call reports. You should ask yourself: Is it really necessary for me to know what my people are doing each day, or is a monthly or quarterly status review sufficient? Even sales managers who believe in giving salespeople considerable freedom still must stay on top of what is happening in the territory. What if a salesperson leaves suddenly and goes to a competitor? The sales manager cannot afford to have the territory be a complete mystery.

3. Cold calling and prospecting are a special case, regardless of management style. There is general agreement that extra attention should be given to these activities when they are part of the sales job.

Management involvement in territory planning is likely to be impacted by other business developments, such as the radical downsizing of local sales branch offices and company downsizing resulting in sales managers being assigned larger sales

---

Sales Management Technology 5-3
Management by Planning

Management by Planning (MBP) is a system introduced by Intel Corporation to help sales managers monitor the performance of sales reps who aren't seen as often because Intel has chosen to close most of its sales offices. MBP rolls the corporate strategic objectives down to the sales district level and the individual salesperson level. To help the district achieve its strategic goals, the district manager and individual salesperson mutually agree on specific tactics and goals for individual accounts. Salespeople are responsible for keeping up to date in their portable computers their tactical goals and success in achieving them. They are also responsible for uploading to a central database. Periodically, a manager will call up each salesperson's record to check the status of his or her goals. If the manager sees that results are not meeting expected levels, the manager visits the territory to determine whether this failure is due to a specific situation in the marketplace or whether there is a problem with that particular salesperson. This helps the district sales manager stay close to territory developments even though he or she is managing more salespeople.

Source: Thayer Taylor, "Going Mobile," *Sales & Marketing Management* (May 1994), pp. 94–106.

---

units. Sales Management Technology 5-3 talks about how Intel Corporation is addressing these developments with a new system called Management by Planning.

▶ SUMMARY

Over the past decade, sales force productivity has lagged behind the double-digit increase in selling costs. As a result, top executives are giving increased emphasis to improving sales force productivity by increasing the amount of time salespeople spend face-to-face with customers. New technology such as laptop computers and cellular phones is being incorporated into sales forces to fight this battle.

A second method of improving sales force productivity is to increase the focus of salespeople on the most important accounts and strategic products. Due to a number of developments in business over the past decade, sales are becoming increasingly consolidated among a few very important accounts. Salespeople must respond to these changes by adjusting the amount of effort that they allocate to these accounts.

Cost per call and break-even analysis were demonstrated to show there is a minimum size necessary to justify a salesperson's efforts. A number of tools for making time allocations decisions were also reviewed. The simple ABC account classification model is most appropriate for sales situations in which servicing a limited number of current customers is the primary responsibility of the salesperson. In more complex selling situations, portfolio or decision models are more appropriate. The sales funnel approach is useful when prospecting is a significant aspect of the job and when the selling cycle is very long.

Salespeople spend a considerable part of their time traveling and waiting, so time savings from optimal routing among customers can be significant. While a number of complex mathematical solutions to the traveling salesperson problem are possible, a nearly optimum solution based on a few simple decision rules is often sufficient.

This chapter concludes with a discussion of different approaches to help salespeople manage their territories. Management styles vary from very close day-to-day management to a hands-off approach. Regardless of the approach, it is important for sales managers to be familiar with each territory, especially the key accounts, and to be prepared to help salespeople when they need it.

► KEY TERMS

ABC account classification
Account analysis
Account opportunity
Best few opportunities
Break-even sales volume
CALLPLAN
Cold canvassing
Competitive position
Cost per call
Decision models
Direct inquiry directories
Direct selling expenses
Minimum account size
Nonselling time
Portfolio analysis

Portfolio models
Prospecting
Prospect profile
Qualified opportunities
Qualify a prospect
Referrals
Sales funnel
Sales response function
Sales routes
Selling cycle
Single-factor allocation model
Time management
Traveling salesperson problem
Unqualified opportunity

► REVIEW QUESTIONS

1. Explain how salespeople typically spend their time.

2. What are sales executives doing to increase sales force productivity?

3. What has caused sales to become concentrated among a few customers in today's business environment?

4. Why should salespeople periodically review the minimum size account they should be calling on?

5. How can salespeople determine the minimum size customer that they should call on?

6. Why does the break-even sales volume differ for different salespeople?

7. Distinguish between the following types of time allocation models: single-factor, portfolio, decision models, and sales funnel.

8. Should salespeople give priority to prospecting overqualified sales opportunities?

9. What are the four basic rules for designing routes to cover a sales territory?

10. What do you think management's role should be in helping salespeople manage their territory?

11. What steps can you take today to better manage your time as a student?

12. Why are accounts likely to be quite different in profitability?

13. What can salespeople do to increase territory profitability?

14. Explain why sales volume may vary dramatically from one period to the next using the sales funnel format.

▶ PROBLEMS

1. You are a rookie salesperson with Associated Medical Supplies, Inc., a wholesaler of disposable medical supplies. As a new salesperson, you are finding it difficult to convince accounts to change from their current suppliers. The doctors with whom you are having the most success tend to be small, single practices located in rural areas. Competition for these accounts is not as intense, perhaps because their purchases are fairly small. They usually place about $900 worth of business with you a month. Nevertheless, they seem to be most appreciative of your coming each week to take inventory of their supplies and write an order. Furthermore, it is better than no sales at all. Lately your boss has been getting after you because productivity has not increased as much as he had hoped when he placed you in the territory. In particular, direct selling costs, including compensation, are currently 15 percent of net sales, whereas the total company target is for direct sales costs to be 10 percent of net sales. In light of this, you are wondering if spending time on small rural physicians is the best way to manage your territory. You have calculated that your cost per call is currently $34.50. Should you be calling on these small physician practices? What is the smallest size customer you should pursue in order to meet your company's selling cost objectives? What actions might you wish to consider in managing your territory better?

2. As a salesperson for Strength Footwear, Inc., you have been very successful. Your commissions are well over $70,000 per year. Demand for your product line is strong, but so is the demand on your time. You work your territory 220 days a year and can make four calls a day. The maximum number of times you need to see any account is every other week, but you need to call on each account at least once a quarter. To help you allocate your time according to sales results, you have gathered the following information on customer sales:

Accounts	Sales Last Year
Top 10 accounts	$150,000
Next 10 best accounts	37,500
Next 10 best accounts	37,000
Next 20 best accounts	56,250
Next 20 best accounts	55,500
Next 20 best accounts	18,750
Last 20 accounts	15,000
	$370,000

Develop and justify a call schedule for allocating time across the 110 customers in your territory.

3. You are concerned about your productivity and have decided to analyze your account allocation strategy. You sell outdoor sportswear to women's retail clothing stores. The sportswear segment of women's clothing has been growing rapidly, though some retailers have been quicker than others to recognize and take advantage of the opportunity. You have compiled the following account information from this past year:

Account	Account Opportunity	Competitive Position	Sales Calls	Sales
Designer Depot	High	Strong	24	$60,000
Fashion Conspiracy	High	Strong	22	57,000
Clothes Time	High	Weak	15	29,500
Moda Fashion	Low	Weak	15	20,000
Peachtree	Low	Weak	17	21,000
Tomorrow Fashion	High	Weak	18	36,000
Reprise	Low	Strong	24	34,250
Plus Fashions	Low	Strong	22	35,000
Casual Girls	High	Weak	10	14,000
Another Season	Low	Strong	21	37,000
Bandiera's	Low	Weak	15	20,500
Sports Locker	High	Strong	20	53,000

Assume that these accounts are representative of all of your accounts. Construct a portfolio model and assess your effort allocation. Where do time allocation problems seem to occur? Why might this happen? Develop a more productive effort allocation strategy, given the information available.

▶ REFERENCES

1. DAVID MERCER, *High-Level Selling* (Houston, Tex.: Gulf Publishing, 1990), pp. 21–22.

2. "1993 Sales Manager's Budget Planner," *Sales & Marketing Management* (1993), p. 65.

3. WILLIAM O'CONNELL and WILLIAM KEENAN, "The Shape of Things to Come," *Sales & Marketing Management* (January 1990), pp. 36–41.

4. O'CONNELL and KEENAN, "Things to Come," p. 40.

5. DAVID S. KEMP, "Pray for Us All," *Sales & Marketing Management* (March 1993), p. 8.

6. For more discussion of how companies are efficiently identifying qualified prospects, see NANCY ARNOTT, "Selling Is Dying," *Sales & Marketing Management* (August 1994), pp. 82–86.

7. MARVIN JOLSON and THOMAS WOTRUBA, "Prospecting: A New Look at This Old Challenge," *Journal of Personal Selling & Sales Management*, 4 (Fall 1992), p. 65.

8. For more information on generating leads, see DORIS VAN DORAN and THOMAS Stickney, "How to Develop a Database for Sales Leads," *Industrial Marketing Management*, 19 (August 1990), pp. 201–208.

9. For more information on trade shows, call or write to Trade Show Bureau, 1660 Lincoln Street, Suite 2080, Denver, Colorado 80264-2001 or call 303-860-7626.

10. JOLSON and WOTRUBA, "Prospecting," p. 61.

11. JOLSON and WOTRUBA, "Prospecting," p. 61.

12. DAVID SZYMANSKI and GILBERT CHURCHILL, "Client Evaluation Cues: A Comparison of Successful and Unsuccessful Salespeople," *Journal of Marketing Research*, 27 (May 1990), pp. 163–174.

13. "1993 Sales Manager's Budget Planner," p. 62.

14. "1993 Sales Manager's Budget Planner," p. 63.

15. RAYMOND LAFORGE, DAVID CRAVENS, and CLIFFORD YOUNG, "Improving Salesforce Productivity," *Business Horizons* (September–October 1982), pp. 50–59.

16. RAYMOND LAFORGE, DAVID CRAVENS, and CLIFFORD YOUNG, "Using Contingency Analysis to Select Selling Effort Allocation Methods," *Journal of Personal Selling & Sales Management* (August 1986), p. 23.

17. This discussion is based on ROBERT MILLER and STEPHEN HEIMAN, *Strategic Selling* (New York: William Morrow, 1985), pp. 234–269.

18. MILLER and HEIMAN, *Strategic Selling*, p. 249.

19. SHAPIRO et al., "Manage Customers for Profits," pp. 101–108.

20. JOSEPH VACCARO and DEREK COWARD, "Managerial and Legal Implications of Price Haggling: A Sales Manager's Dilemma," *Journal of Personal Selling & Sales Management*, 13 (Summer 1993), pp. 79–85.

21. For further information on the traveling salesperson problem see WAYNE WINSTON, *Operations Research: Applications and Algorithms* (Belmont, Calif.: Duxbury Press, 1994) and G. D. Eppon, F. J. Gould, C.P. Schmidt, and Rick Hesse, *Introductory Management Science* (Englewood Cliffs, N.J.: Prentice-Hall, 1993).

22. "1993 Sales Manager's Budget Planner," p. 75.

23. MICHAEL LEBOENT, "Managing Your Time, Managing Yourself," *Business Horizons* (February 1980), p. 42.

24. STEPHEN COVEY, *The 7 Habits of Highly Effective People* (New York: Simon & Schuster, 1989).

25. For more information see BERNARD JAWORSKI, VLASIS STATHAKOPOULOS, and SHANKER KRISHNAN, "Control Combinations in Marketing: Conceptual Framework and Empirical Evidence," *Journal of Marketing*, 57 (January 1993), pp. 57–69.

▶ SELECTED READINGS

BROOKS, WILLIAM, *Niche Selling* (Homewood, Ill.: Richard D. Irwin 1992).

DOUGLASS, MERRILL, and DONNA DOUGLAS, *Time Management for Teams* (New York: Amacom, 1992).

HUNAN, MACK, and PETER KARP, *Competing on Value* (New York: Amacom, 1991).

MOSKOWITZ, ROBERT, *How to Organize Your Work and Your Life* (New York: Doubleday, 1993).

CASE

5-1 HANOVER-BATES CHEMICAL CORPORATION*

James Sprague, newly appointed northeast district sales manager for Hanover-Bates Chemical Corporation, leaned back in his chair as the door to his office slammed shut. "Great beginning," he thought. "Three days in my new job and the district's most experienced sales representative is threatening to quit."

On the previous night, James Sprague, Hank Carver (the district's most experienced sales representative), and John Follett, another senior member of the district sales staff, had met for dinner at Jim's suggestion. During dinner, Jim had mentioned that one of his top priorities would be to conduct a sales and profit analysis of the district's business in order to identify opportunities to improve the district's performance. Jim had stated that he was confident that the analysis would indicate opportunities to reallocate district sales efforts in a manner that would increase profits. As Jim had indicated during the conversation, "My experience in analyzing district sales performance data for the national sales manager has convinced me that any district's allocation of sales effort to products and customer categories can be improved." Both Carver and Follett had nodded as Jim discussed his plans.

Hank Carver was waiting when Jim arrived at the district sales office the next morning. It soon became apparent that Carver was very upset by what he perceived as Jim's criticism of how he and the other district sales representatives were doing their jobs—and more particularly, how they were allocating their time in terms of customers and products. As he concluded his heated comments, Carver had said:

This company has made it darned clear that 34 years of experience don't count for anything . . . and now someone with not much more than two years of selling experience and two years of pushing paper for the national sales manager at

corporate headquarters tells me I'm not doing my job. . . . Maybe it's time for me to look for a new job . . . and since Trumbull Chemical (Hanover-Bates's major competitor) is hiring, maybe that's where I should start looking . . . and I'm not the only one who feels this way.

As Jim reflected on the scene that had just occurred, he wondered what he should do. It had been made clear to him when he had been promoted to manager of the northeast sales district that one of his top priorities should be improvement of the district's performance. As the national sales manager had said, "The northeast sales district may rank third in dollar sales but it's our worst district in terms of profit performance."

Prior to assuming his new position, Jim had assembled the data presented in Exhibits 1 through 7 to assist him in his work. The data had been compiled from records maintained in the national sales manager's office. Although he believed that the data would provide a sound basis for a preliminary analysis of district performance, Jim had recognized that additional data would probably have to be collected when he arrived in the northeast district (District 3). To provide himself with a frame of reference, Jim had also requested data on the north-central sales district (District 7). This district was generally considered to be one of the best, if not the best, in the company. Furthermore, the north-central district sales manager, who was only three years older than Jim, was highly regarded by the national sales manager.

The Company and Industry

The Hanover-Bates Chemical Corporation was a leading producer of processing chemicals for the chemical plating industry. The company's production process was, in essence, a mixing operation. Chemicals purchased from a broad range of suppliers were mixed according to a variety of user-based formulas. Company sales in 1996 had reached a new high of

---

*This case was prepared by Professor Robert W. Witt of The University of Texas, Austin. Reproduced by permission.

Exhibit 1: Summary Income Statements (thousands), 1992 to 1996

	1992	1993	1994	1995	1996
Sales	$39,780	$43,420	$38,120	$43,960	$47,780
Production expenses	23,868	26,994	24,396	27,224	29,126
Gross profit	15,912	16,426	13,724	16,736	18,654
Administrative expenses	5,212	5,774	5,584	5,850	6,212
Selling expenses	4,048	4,482	4,268	4,548	4,798
Pretax profit	6,652	6,170	3,872	6,338	7,644
Taxes	3,024	2,776	1,580	2,852	3,436
Net profit	$ 3,628	$ 3,394	$ 2,292	$ 3,486	$ 4,208

Exhibit 2: District Sales and Gross Profit Quota Performance (thousands), 1996

District	Number of Sales Reps	Sales Quota	Sales Actual	Gross Profit Quota[a]	Gross Profit Actual
1	7	$7,661	$7,812	$3,104	$3,178
2	6	7,500	7,480	3,000	3,058
3	6	7,300	6,812	2,920	2,478
4	6	6,740	6,636	2,696	2,590
5	5	6,600	6,420	2,620	2,372
6	5	6,240	6,410	2,504	2,358
7	5	5,440	6,210	2,176	2,260
		$47,600	$47,780	$19,040	$18,654

[a]District gross profit quotas were developed by the National Sales Manager in consultation with the district managers and took into account price competition in the respective districts.

Exhibit 3: District Selling Expenses, 1996

District	Sales Rep Salaries[a]	Sales Rep Commissions	Sales Rep Expenses	District Office	District Manager's Salary	District Manager's Expenses	Sales Support	Total Selling Expenses
1	$354,200	$38,852	$112,560	$42,300	$67,000	$22,920	$139,000	$776,832
2	286,440	37,400	101,520	42,624	68,000	24,068	142,640	702,692
3	314,760	34,060	108,872	44,246	70,000[b]	24,764	140,000	736,722
4	300,960	33,180	98,208	44,008	65,000	22,010	132,940	696,306
5	251,900	32,100	85,440	42,230	66,000	22,246	153,200	653,116
6	249,700	32,530	83,040	41,984	67,000	22,856	134,200	631,310
7	229,700	35,060	89,400	44,970	63,000	23,286	117,500	602,916
								$4,797,830

[a]Includes cost of fringe benefit program, which was 10 percent of base salary.

[b]Salary of Jim Sprague's predecessor.

Exhibit 4: District Contribution to Corporate Administrative Expense and Profit, 1996

District	Sales (thousands)	Gross Profit (thousands)	Selling Expenses	Contribution
1	$ 7,812	3,178	$ 776,832	$2,401,168
2	7,480	3,058	702,692	2,355,308
3	6,812	2,478	737,058	1,740,942
4	6,636	2,590	696,306	1,893,694
5	6,420	2,372	653,116	1,718,884
6	6,410	2,358	630,752	1,727,248
7	6,210	2,620	600,516	2,019,484
	$47,780	$18,654	4,797,272	$13,856,648

$47,780,000, up from $43,780,000 in 1995. Net pretax profit in 1996 had been $7,644,000, up from $6,338,000 in 1995. Hanover-Bates had a strong balance sheet and the company enjoyed a favorable price-earnings ratio on its stock, which was traded on the over-the-counter market.

Although Hanover-Bates did not produce commodity-type chemicals (e.g., sulfuric acid and others), industry customers tended to perceive minimal quality differences among the products produced by Hanover-Bates and its competitors. Given the lack of a variation in product quality and the industrywide practice of limited advertising expenditures, field sales efforts were of major importance in the marketing programs of all firms in the industry.

Hanover-Bates's market consisted of several thousand job-shop and captive (i.e., in-house) plating operations. Chemical platers process a wide variety of materials including industrial fasteners (e.g.,

screws, rivets, bolts, washers), industrial components (e.g., clamps, casings, couplings), and miscellaneous items (e.g., umbrella frames, eyelets, decorative items). The chemical plating process involves the electrolytic application of metallic coatings such as zinc, cadmium, nickel, and brass.

Regardless of the degree of plating precision involved, quality control is of critical concern to all chemical platers. Extensive variation in the condition of materials received for plating requires a high level of service from the firms supplying chemicals to platers. This service is normally provided by the sales representatives of the firm(s) which supply the plater with processing chemicals.

Hanover-Bates and the majority of the firms in its industry produced the same line of basic processing chemicals for the chemical plating industry. The line consisted of a trisodium phosphate cleaner (SPX), anesic aldehyde brightening agents for zinc plating

Exhibit 5: District Sales and Gross Profit Performance by Account Category, 1996

District	Sales by Account Category (thousands)			
	(A)	(B)	©	Total
Northeast	$1,830	$3,362	$1,620	$6,812
North-Central	1,502	3,404	1,304	6,210

District	Gross Profit by Account Category (thousands)			
	(A)	(B)	©	Total
Northeast	$712	$1,246	$520	$2,478
North-Central	660	1,450	510	2,620

Exhibit 6: Potential Accounts, Active Accounts, and Account Call Coverage, 1996

District	Potential Accounts			Active Accounts			Account Coverage (total calls)		
	(A)	**(B)**	**(C)**	**(A)**	**(B)**	**(C)**	**(A)**	**(B)**	**(C)**
Northeast	90	381	635	53	210	313	1297	3051	2118
North-Central	60	286	499	42	182	216	1030	2618	1299

(ZBX), cadmium plating (CBX), and nickel plating (NBX), a protective postplating chromate dip (CHX), and a protective burnishing compound (BUX). The company's product line is detailed in Exhibit 7.

Company Sales Organization

The sales organization consisted of 40 sales representatives operating in seven sales districts. Sales representatives' salaries ranged from $28,000 to $48,000 with fringe-benefit costs amounting to an additional 10 percent of salary. In addition to their salaries, Hanover-Bates's representatives received commissions of 0.5 percent of their dollar sales volume on all sales up to their sales quotas. The commission on sales in excess of quota was 1 percent.

In 1994, the national sales manager of Hanover-Bates had developed a sales program based on selling the full line of Hanover-Bates products. Anticipated benefits included the following: (1) sales volume per account would be greater and selling costs as a percentage of sales would decrease; (2) a Hanover-Bates sales representative could justify spending more time with such an account, thus becoming more knowledgeable about the account's business and better able to provide technical assis-

tance and identify selling opportunities; (3) full-line sales would strengthen Hanover-Bates's competitive position by reducing the likelihood of account loss to other plating chemical suppliers (a problem that existed in multiple-supplier situations).

The national sales manager's 1994 sales program had also included the following account call frequency guidelines: A accounts (major accounts generating $24,000 or more in yearly sales)—two calls per month; B accounts (medium-size accounts generating $12,000 to $23,999 in yearly sales)—one call per month; C accounts (small accounts generating less than $12,000 yearly in sales)—one call every two months. The account call frequency guidelines were developed by the national sales manager after discussions with the district managers. The national sales manager had been concerned about the optimum allocation of sales efforts to accounts and felt that the guidelines would increase the efficiency of the company's sales force, although not all of the district sales managers agreed with this conclusion.

It was common knowledge in Hanover-Bates' corporate sales office that Jim Sprague's predecessor as northeast district sales manager had not been one of the company's better district sales managers. His attitude toward the sales plans and programs of the national sales manager had been one of reluctant

Exhibit 7: Product-Line Data

Container Product	Size	List Price	Gross Margin	Sales (000)
SPX	400 lb drum	$160	$56	$7,128
ZBX	50 lb drum	152	68	8,244
CBX	50 lb drum	152	68	7,576
NBX	50 lb drum	160	70	9,060
CHX	100 lb drum	440	180	8,820
BUX	400 lb drum	240	88	6,952

compliance rather than acceptance and support. When the national sales manager succeeded in persuading Jim Sprague's predecessor to take early retirement, he had been faced with the lack of an available qualified replacement.

Hank Carver, who most of the sales representatives had assumed would get the district manager's job, had been passed over in part because he would be 65 in three years. The national sales manager had not wanted to face the same replacement problem again in three years and had wanted someone in the position who would be more likely to be responsive to the company's sales plans and policies. The appointment of Jim Sprague as district manager had caused considerable talk, not only in the district but also at corporate headquarters. In fact, the national sales manager had warned Jim that "a lot of people are expecting you to fall on your face. They don't think you have the experience to handle the job, in particular, and to manage and motivate a group of sales representatives most of whom are considerably older and more experienced than you." The national sales manager had concluded by saying, "I think you can handle the job, Jim. I think you can manage those sales reps and improve the district's profit performance, and I'm depending on you to do both."

CASE

5-2 ZYGAR PHARMACEUTICALS*

Zygar Pharmaceuticals was formed in 1970. Two consulting research cardiologists from the Parke-Davis division of Warner Lambert, Dr. Dale R. Fox and Dr. Caren Conners, began the company in Yardley, Pennsylvania. Initially, Zygar was little more than an independent sales office, with 10 people handling part of the Parke-Davis product line in the northeastern and mid-Atlantic states.

All that changed in 1982 with Food and Drug Administration (FDA) approval of Zilene, a drug developed and patented by Fox and Conners for patients suffering from coronary artery spasms (angina). The drug interferes with slow inward (depolarizing) electrical currents in myocardial tissues, relaxing the coronary vascular muscles and dilating the coronary arteries. Such a drug was of interest to both cardiologists and general practitioners. Normally, a patient with symptoms of angina would be referred to a cardiologist. If a drug regimen was indicated, the cardiologist would prescribe an antianginal drug and return the patient to the care of her or his primary physician. While the general practitioner usually continued to prescribe the selected drug, he or she could change the prescription if changes in the patient's condition over time warranted it.

Because Zilene would compete with several antianginal and antiarrhythmic drugs already produced by Parke-Davis, Drs. Fox and Conners resigned their consulting positions and took Zygar Pharmaceuticals private. Warner Lambert, however, was initially licensed to manufacture Zilene for the start-up company.

While only 3 salespeople stayed with the new company, by 1990 Zygar's sales organization had grown to 85 sales reps, 8 sales managers, and 1 vice president of sales. The vice president, Alan Machin, was one of the three who stayed with the company after the changeover. In addition to Zilene, by the spring of 1990 Zygar's product line included one cerebral vasodilator (Gaspar), which was of particular interest to physicians specializing in oncology and internal medicine, one bronchial dilator (Bendine), and two antidepressants.

Zygar's corporate headquarters remained in Yardley, Pennsylvania. However, by early 1990, the company had built one manufacturing facility in the Mercer County, New Jersey, free trade zone and another manufacturing facility in Bloomington, Indiana. A regional sales office (leased) had been located in Orange County, California, in early 1993. A second re-

*This case was prepared by William Strahle and Dale R. Fox of Rider College. Reproduced by permission.

gional sales office in Savannah, Georgia, is currently under consideration.

Zygar's salespeople are expected to make between six and eight calls a day, including calls on pharmacies. Physicians to be called on are separated by their sales potential (the 1's have the highest potential and the 3's have the lowest) and by how difficult they are to see (X's are the hardest to see and E's are the easiest). Machin has always liked to see his detailers try to build their schedules around the times the X-1's and M-1's are available, though new doctors are given priority because their potential is unknown. While each salesperson is expected to call on pharmacists to update their doctors' "script-writing" habits, most of them are too busy filling prescriptions to be seen until late afternoon. Alan has always insisted, however, that sales reps visit pharmacists *before* calling on a new doctor to get a handle on the physician's prescription-writing tendencies so that they can tailor their presentation better in the initial getting-acquainted visit.

In June 1993, Fox and Conners received FDA approval for Rodine, a new vasodilator. Like Zilene, Rodine acts to depress myocardial irritability and conduction. Like Gaspar, Zygar's cerebral vasodilator, Rodine acts to increase cerebral blood flow as well. However, its primary benefit to patients is that it also safely reduces ventricular arrhythmias. This combination of attributes makes Rodine a drug that can be used not only by cardiologists and general practitioners, but also by surgeons and those specializing in internal medicine. In anticipation of its release, the number of inquiries received by the company about the new drug was phenomenal. Zygar's switchboard was swamped. At Machin's urging, Fox and Conners agreed with his plan to expand the sales force and to hire between 10 and 15 new trainees.

A problem quickly arose. How could Machin efficiently train both new hires and the sales reps in the field to describe (detail) the new drug without a sales meeting of some kind? Zygar's national sales meeting had already been held in New Orleans in February (as it is every year), and Alan knew that Fox and Conners would never authorize a second meeting for the introduction of just one drug. Both Fox and Conners wanted their salespeople to concentrate on "what they got paid for"—selling. The election of a president who was hostile to the medical community also made many routine expenditures problematic.

In addition, Conners had been pressuring Machin to lower his organization's selling costs. Conners had estimated the cost of putting a Zygar detailer in front of one physician at $280. While the industry average was $300 per visit, Conners had expressed her concern that Machin's salespeople were spending too much time in the wrong physician's office waiting to see a doctor at the wrong time and reading four-year-old copies of *Gourmet Magazine*. Since 1991, the company had provided each salesperson with a laptop personal computer for record keeping at a cost of $2,200 per unit. Although the software had a basic call-planning program, few of the detailers had mastered it and were using it regularly. Alan knew that he also had to find a way to teach his sales reps to make better use of their time and to use their computers to better advantage.

Finally, one particular sore point was Zygar's focus on meetings and the use of meetings quotas. In order to get in front of more physicians, Machin had encouraged his reps to try to schedule at least two presentations a month with groups of doctors who shared an interest in or tended to prescribe similar types of drugs. Because Zygar was a fairly small company, Machin didn't want his salespeople calling on the same doctor more than twice a year. From his perspective, this would force his detailers to see more doctors with different specializations and result in more complete coverage in each of their rather large territories. Scheduling a breakfast or luncheon meeting at a hospital for six or eight physicians would allow the salesperson to see a doctor more than twice a year. Whether a guest speaker was scheduled or the detailer just gave a quick stand-up presentation, the networking opportunities involved would, at the very least, help build goodwill between the rep and the physicians. Unfortunately, most of Machin's salespeople did not look for the opportunity of arranging meetings when doing their call planning.

Machin decided to call Dr. William Strahle, managing partner of Time & Territory Management. TTM is a subsidiary of Implementation Research Associates that specializes in handling tour routing and call planning issues. Strahle suggested developing a training diskette for all Zygar salespeople that could be used by reps as they waited in a doctor's office for their appointment. Interested, Machin agreed to hear Strahle out. From this point on, reader, you are Alan.

The Meeting

Okay, Alan, let's turn on your computer. I see it's an IBM compatible. Good; now let the system boot up. Insert the diskette in the appropriately sized disk drive. Now, type **a:**[1] or the letter associated with the disk drive. Good; now type the word **zygint** and hit the enter key. This will give you the initial screen in the Tag Along Trainer.

Zygar Pharmaceuticals Sales Planner Exercises

D - ONE DAY PLANNER EXERCISES
W - WEEK PLANNER EXERCISES

E - EXIT PROGRAM

OPTION

TTM Time & Territory Management, Inc.
Copyright 1991

As you can see, Alan, the Tag Along Trainer consists of two major portions, the Day Scheduler and the Week Scheduler.

The Week Scheduler should be used to learn and reinforce priorities for matching locations with the day of the week on which they should be visited. The program reads in a database of physicians and pharmacies and information about these physicians, such as their type of practice, the date they were last visited, the drugs they prescribe, and the days and times when they are most accessible. The physicians are already grouped into locations. The program allows the salesperson to decide which locations should be visited on which days and to evaluate their decisions.

The detailer will be given feedback about the decisions and suggestions about how to query the database for helpful information.

The Day Scheduler assumes that the decisions about which location to visit on each day have been made. Zygar's detailers must schedule the actual appointments, using the physicians' accessibility, po-

---

[1] Words and phrases typed by the computer that require a response from you will be underlined. Commands that you should give by typing words, letters, and numbers will be typed in **bold** characters. The computer will know that you have finished typing the command when you hit the enter key.

tential, date of the last visit, and other information. After scheduling the physicians, either through one-on-one contact or meetings, and scheduling their meals, they can evaluate their decisions for each day of the week against the schedules selected by yourself and senior Zygar sales managers. Next, your salespeople will be led through a practice walk-through of the Week and Day Schedulers. Then we will give a description of the screens that may be accessed for information to help them make their decisions.

After choosing the letter **W** to enter the week program, your salespeople will see a screen like the following:

```
OPTION
--------------------------------------------------------SCREENS --------------------------------------------------------
C - Counts for Location       L - List by Location         E - Exit Week Program
D - Counts for Day            A - Appointment Notes        V - Evaluate Assignment
                              P - Physician Codes
```

Remember that the purpose of the Week Scheduler is to determine which location your detailers will visit each day of the week. There are seven locations, and they want to assign exactly one for each day of the week, Monday through Friday. Two of the locations aren't assigned. Below is a brief description of the meaning of each of the options:

C—Counts for Location   Use this if you want a count of the number of physicians who can meet on each day at a given location.

D—Counts for Day   Use this if you want a count of the number of physicians at each location who can meet on a given day.

L—List by Location   This will give a brief list, on one screen, of the physicians, the code of their type of practice, and the days of the week and times they are most likely to be available.

A—Appointment Notes

These are three pages of detailed information about the physicians at a particular location.

P—Physician Codes

This is a list of the meanings of the four-letter codes associated with the type of practice.

E—Exit Week Program

Use this to exit the week program.

V—Evaluate Assignment

This will give you a discussion of the optimal location assignments so that you can compare your assignments.

Okay, Machin, now try it on your own. Read the following text and simultaneously work through the week program. You are going to determine the location that should be visited on Tuesday. The first thing you should do is obtain counts for Tuesday.

Type **D** to get counts for the day.

Type **T** to let the program know you are interested in counts for Tuesday. Now you should see a screen that looks like the one below.

From this screen, it is clear that location 1 is the most likely choice to visit on Tuesday, since there are eight physicians who are usually available on Tuesdays. But it is also important for the detailer to consider whether assigning location 1 to Tuesday eliminates visiting location 1 on a more appropriate day. Thus the detailer should examine physician availability at location 1 on other days by using the C—Counts for Location option.

Type **C** to get counts for the location.

The number of physicians at location 1 that can meet on T is 8

The number of physicians at location 2 that can meet on T is 5

The number of physicians at location 3 that can meet on T is 1

The number of physicians at location 4 that can meet on T is 2

The number of physicians at location 5 that can meet on T is 2

The number of physicians at location 6 that can meet on T is 1

The number of physicians at location 7 that can meet on T is 2

OPTION

---SCREENS ---

C - Counts for Location	L - List by Location	E - Exit Week Program
D - Counts for Day	A - Appointment Notes	V - Evaluate Assignment
	P - Physician Codes	

Type **1** to let the program know you want counts for location 1. You should get the following screen:

The number of physicians at location 1 that can meet on Monday   is 5

The number of physicians at location 1 that can meet on Tuesday   is 8

The number of physicians at location 1 that can meet on Wednesday   is 2

The number of physicians at location 1 that can meet on Thursday   is 3

The number of physicians at location 1 that can meet on Friday   is 4

OPTION
--SCREENS --
C - Counts for Location   L - List by Location   E - Exit Week Program
D - Counts for Day   A - Appointment Notes   V - Evaluate Assignment
                            P - Physician Codes

By examining this screen, you can see that assigning location 1 to Tuesday will not eliminate any better assignments.

Finally, you should browse through the physicians and see whether they are more likely to be seeing physicians one-on-one or using meetings, and how long it has been since most of the physicians have been visited. This can be done by choosing the

L—List by Location

and the

A—Appointment Notes

options on the screen. The three screens contained in the appointment notes are listed on the next page. After referring to the appointment notes, it is clear that the physicians have not been visited for quite some time and that there are a variety of times when they may be visited. The actual scheduling of the day is left for the Day Scheduler. This hierarchical planning is typical in complicated operations. You are now ready to assign the other locations. Why don't you give it a try?

```
                    Notes on Location 1                          Page 1

ONCO         Dr. Bruce Anshutz              Oncologist          Hospital
10/19/90     Appointment    Tu, F              4:00 - 5:00 PM
             Canistan-md Bendine-hi Mycostatin-lo Cardizem-lo

INTM         Dr. Jerrold Baker              Internal Medicine   Office
12/02/90     Appointment    M, Tu             11:00 - 1:00 PM
             Zilene-hi Cardizem-hi Bendine-lo Canistan-lo

CARD         Dr. Thomas Cloyd               Cardiologist        Hospital
12/27/90     Appointment    Tu                3:00 - 5:00 PM
             Zilene-md Cardizem-hi Vasotec-lo

SURG         Dr. Merle Drew                 General Surgeon     Hospital
02/01/91     Appointment    M, Tu, Th         1:00 - 3:00 PM
             Amphotericin B-hi Naprosyn-hi Bendine-md Canistan-lo


OPTION
-------------------------------------------------SCREENS-------------------------------------------------
                             1 - Page One of Notes
R - Return to Selections     2 - Page Two of Notes
                             3 - Page Three of Notes
```

```
                    Notes on Location 1                          Page 2

CARD         Dr. David Giltner              Cardiologist        Office
10/19/90     Appointment    M, Tu             8:00 - 10:00 AM
             Zilene-md Cardizem-md

GENP         Dr. Mark Haring                General Practice    Office
Not seen     New            M, Tu, W, Th, F   Anytime
             UNKNOWN

GENP         Dr. Frederick Isaacs           General Practice    Office
12/28/90     Appointment    M, W, F           8:00 - 10:00 AM
             Zilene-hi Cardizem-hi Naprosyn-hi Ansaid gel-md Canistan-md

SURG         Dr. George Justus              General Surgeon     Hospital
02/01/91     Drop in        Tu, Th            2:00 - 5:00 PM
             Amphotericin B-hi Naprosyn-hi Bendine-md Ansaid gel-md


OPTION
-------------------------------------------------SCREENS-------------------------------------------------
                             1 - Page One of Notes
R - Return to Selections     2 - Page Two of Notes
                             3 - Page Three of Notes
```

```
                    Notes on Location 1                          Page 3

    GENP        Dr. John Pollock              General Practice      Office
    02/01/91    Drop in        Tu, F          Anytime

                Bendine-hi Zilene-hi Naprosyn-md Cardizem-lo Canistan-lo

    PHAR        Richard Leyda                 Pharmacist           Store
    12/28/90    Drop in        Any day        Anytime
                ALL DRUGS











    OPTION
    -----------------------------------------------SCREENS-----------------------------------------------
                                    1 - Page One of Notes
    R - Return to Selections        2 - Page Two of Notes
                                    3 - Page Three of Notes
```

Finished? Good. Now let's look at the walk-through for the Day Scheduler. From the initial screen, you should choose the **D** option to enter the Day Scheduler. Now you will get a screen that asks you which day you want to schedule.

Type **P** for Practice Walkthrough. The practice walkthrough will lead you and your sales reps through scheduling a Monday. The Day Scheduler uses different schedules than the Week Scheduler, but the location assignments have already been done. You should get the screen shown on page 212.

The list you and your salespeople see in the center of the screen is a shorthand form of physician information and sales and accessibility potential at location 7 for the walkthrough to be scheduled on Monday. Although the codes are necessary due to the limited space on a screen, they will become more familiar as you work with the program. Here is a brief description of the options you can choose from the bottom of the menu:

P—Physician Codes	This lists the different physician practices and their associated four-letter codes.
S—Accessibility and Sales Potential	This list shows what the accessibility and sales potential codes mean. The letters have to do with access, the numbers relate to the sales potential.
E—Exit This Day	This will allow you to exit the program for the current day.
R—Return to Current Day	This will allow you to refresh the screen with the basic information on the current day.
A—Appointment Notes	This is a detailed list of all the information about the physicians, such as the drugs they prescribe and when they are most likely to be available.
C—Change the Day	This allows the detailer to change the day they are scheduling.

```
                    This is a listing of the physicians at location 7 for
                                      Walkthrough

                                        85 MIN
                                     driving time

                         GENP                    M-1
                         PHAR                    E-1
                         CARD                    X-2
                         CSUR                    X-2
                         GENP                    E-1
                         GENP                    E-3
                         CARD                    M-2
                         ORTH                    M-2
                         INTM                    E-2
                         PHAR                    E-1


    OPTION
    ---------------------------------------------SCREENS ---------------------------------------------

    P - Physician Codes   S - Accessibility & Sales Potential   E - Exit This Day
               R - Return to Current Day   A - Appointment Notes
               C - Change the Day          D - Schedule the Day
```

D—Schedule the Day

This puts the detailer into a deeper part of the program where the actual scheduling occurs. There will be a new set of options at this level.

To gain some experience with the options and the meaning of the codes:

Type **P** to see a list of the abbreviations of the practice types.

Type **S** to see a list of the accessibility and sales potential codes.

Type **A** to see a detailed list about the physicians. Be sure to examine all three pages. A printout of these screens is given on the next page. You will want to refer to it later.

Now type **R** to return to the current day.

You and your detailers can refer to these screens at almost any time. Now enter the D—Schedule the Day portion of the program.

Type **D** and you should see a different screen with a few different options.

Number	at Location 7	Appointments	
I		7 AM ---- CARD	X-2 --------
2		8 AM ---- GENP	E-1 --------
3		9 AM ---- CARD	M-2 --------
4		10 AM ---- GENP	E-3 --------
5		11 AM ---- INTM	E-2 --------
6		12 PM ---- CSUR	X-2 --------
7		1 PM ---- ORTH	M-2 --------
8		2 PM ---- GENP	M-1 -------
9		3 PM ---- PHAR	E-1 --------
10		4 PM ---- PHAR	E-1 --------
		5 PM ----	--------
11	MEETING	6 PM ----	
12	MEAL		
13	MEET--MEAL		

OPTION
--SCREENS---
P - Physician Codes   S - Accessibility & Sales Potential   E - Exit Scheduler
I - Insert Appointment   U - Undo Appointment   A - Appointment Notes
V - Evaluate Schedule   R - Return to Schedule

Notes on Location 7		Page 1
GENP M-1 12/17/90	Dr. William Chestnut General Practice Appointment M, W, F 1:00 - 3:00 PM Vasotec-hi Mycostatin-hi Naprosyn-md Zilene-hi Bendine-md	Office
PHAR E-1 01/18/91	William W. Yu Pharmacist Drop in Any day Anytime ALL DRUGS	Store
CARD X-2 12/10/90	Dr. James Touloukian Cardiologist Appointment M 6:30 - 8:00 AM Cardizem-hi zilene-md Vasotec-lo	Office
CSUR X-2 11/21/90	Dr. Richard Fry Cardiovascular Surg Appointment M, Tu, F 12:00 - 1:00 PM Bendine-md Mycostatin-hi Naprosyn-hi	Office

OPTION
--SCREENS---
                                I - Page One of Notes
R - Return to Selections   2 - Page Two of Notes
                                3 - Page Three of Notes

```
                        Notes on Location 7                         Page 2

  GENP   E-1     Dr. Robert Boomer           General Practice        Office
    12/14/90     Drop in        M, F           7:00 - 9:00 AM
                 Zilene-hi Naprosyn-hi Bendine-hi Feldene gel-lo


  GENP   E-3     Dr. Allan Dunn              General Practice        Office
    12/10/90     Walk in        M, F          10:00 - 11:00 AM
                 Zilene-lo Ansaid gel-lo Naprosyn-lo Feldene gel-lo


  CARD   M-2     Dr. Kermit Hibner           Cardiologist           Office
    12/14/90     Appointment    M, F           9:00 - 11:00 AM
                 Zilene-md Cardizem-md Vasotec-md


  ORTH   M-2     Dr. David Holtzclaw         Orthopedic Surgeon     Office
    12/15/90     Appointment    M, W, F       12:00 - 2:00 PM
                 Voltaringel-md Canistan-hi Naprosyn-md



  OPTION
  ----------------------------------------------SCREENS--------------------------------------------------
                                  1 - Page One of Notes
  R - Return to Selections        2 - Page Two of Notes
                                  3 - Page Three of Notes
```

```
                        Notes on Location 7                         Page 3

  INTM   E-2     Dr. Glen Ley                Internal Medicine      Office
    12/13/90     Drop in        M, Th, F      10:00 - 12:00 PM
                 Zilene-md Cardizem-md Canistan-md Mycostatin-lo


  PHAR   E-1     Diane Wells                 Pharmacist             Store
    01/18/91     Drop in        Any day       Anytime
                 ALL DRUGS











  OPTION
  ----------------------------------------------SCREENS--------------------------------------------------
                                  1 - Page One of Notes
  R - Return to Selections        2 - Page Two of Notes
                                  3 - Page Three of Notes
```

Although most of the options are the same as before, there are three new ones, and they will be discussed below.

I—Insert Appointment	This allows you to schedule a physician, pharmacy, meeting, or meal from a row on the left at some time slot on the right.
U—Undo Appointment	This allows you to remove a physician, pharmacy, meeting, or meal from a time slot on the right and place it back in a row on the left.
V—Evaluate Schedule	This will compare your schedule to the optimal schedule and allow you to move through a discussion of the optimal solution.

Now we will lead you through the scheduling of the walkthrough. You want to start by scheduling the physicians who are harder to see and who have higher sales potential. There are two such physicians at location 7:

CARD X-2 and CSUR X-2

From looking at the appointment notes, it is clear that you will be able to schedule CSUR at 12 P.M. and that you will schedule CARD for 7 A.M. You also will need to type the letter **R** after leaving the appointment notes to refresh the screen. Thus you need to insert CARD into a time slot. To do this:

Type **I** and then respond to the question by typing the
row **3** to identify CARD X-2. Then you must enter the time
7 AM to insert the appointment into the time slot.
Type **I** and then respond to the question by typing the
row **4** to identify CARD X-2. Then you must enter the time
12 PM to insert the appointment into the time slot.

You don't actually have to type the A.M. or P.M. part of the time. If you put a physician in an inappropriate time slot, you can use the undo option to move the physician back to the left side.

Of the remaining physicians, the one who is most difficult to see, yet who has high sales potential, is the

GENP M-1

From the appointment notes, it is clear that you can schedule the physician at either 2 P.M. or 3 P.M. At present, it is unclear which is better, so we will schedule him earlier, in the hope that the workday will be over sooner.

Type **I** and then respond to the question by typing the
row **1** to identify GENP M-1. Then you must enter the time
2 PM to insert the appointment into the time slot.

You don't actually need to type the P.M.

The remaining physicians who are more difficult to see and of relatively high sales potential are

CARD M-2   and   ORTH M-2

From the appointment notes, you can tell that you have a couple of different times when these can be scheduled. You should start by scheduling the ORTH at 1 P.M. since you've scheduled the CSUR X-2 at noon. You should schedule the CARD at 10 A.M., though you may have to undo it later.

Type **I** and then respond to the question by typing the
row **7** to identify CARD M-2. Then you must enter the time
10 AM to insert the appointment into the time slot.
Type **I** and then respond to the question by typing the
row **8** to identify ORTH M-2. Then you must enter the time
1 PM to insert the appointment into the time slot.

Again, the A.M. and P.M. are unnecessary.

Of the remaining physicians, the

GENP E-1

can be seen at 8 A.M. without conflicts.

Type **I** and then respond to the question by typing the
row **5** to identify GENP E-1. Then you must enter the time

8 AM to insert the appointment into the time slot.

The

INTM E-2

can be seen at 11 A.M. without interfering with other appointments.

Type **I** and then respond to the question by typing the

row **9** to identify INTM E-2. Then you must enter the time

11 AM to insert the appointment into the time slot.

The

GENP E-3

can only be seen at 10 A.M., so the CARD M-2 must be moved to 9 A.M. This involves undoing the CARD M-2, then inserting the CARD M-2 at 9 A.M., and then inserting the GENP E-3 at 10 A.M.

Type **U** and then respond to the question by typing the

time **10** to identify CARD M-2. Then you must enter the

row **1** to give him a temporary place to stay.

Type **I** and then respond to the question by typing the

row **1** to identify CARD M-2. Then you must enter the time

9 AM to insert the appointment into the time slot.

Now

Type **I** and then respond to the question by typing the

row **6** to identify GENP E-3. Then you must enter the time

10 AM to insert the appointment into the time slot.

Similarly, you can schedule the pharmacies at 3 P.M. and 4 P.M.

The final schedule you obtain should look like the following screen:

Number	at Location 7	Appointments	
1	GENP M-1	7 AM ----	--------
2	PHAR E-1	8 AM ----	--------
3	CARD X-2	9 AM ----	--------
4	CSUR X-2	10 AM ----	--------
5	GENP E-1	11 AM ----	--------
6	GENP E-3	12 PM ----	--------
7	CARD M-2	1 PM ----	--------
8	ORTH M-2	2 PM ----	--------
9	INTM E-2	3 PM ----	--------
10	PHAR E-1	4 PM ----	--------
		5 PM ----	--------
11	MEETING	6 PM ----	--------
12	MEAL		
13	MEET--MEAL		

OPTION

---SCREENS ---

P - Physician Codes   S - Accessibility & Sales Potential   E - Exit Scheduler

I - Insert Appointment   U - Undo Appointment   A - Appointment Notes

V - Evaluate Schedule   R - Return to Schedule

Now you want to evaluate the schedule and compare it to the optimal. To do this

Type **V**

and you should see a screen that looks like the following:

```
    The Optimal Schedule                    The Schedule You Developed

    7 AM ---- CARD      X-2 --------        7 AM ---- CARD      X-2 --------
    8 AM ---- GENP      E-1 --------        8 AM ---- GENP      E-1 --------
    9 AM ---- CARD      M-2 --------        9 AM ---- CARD      M-2 --------
   10 AM ---- GENP      E-3 --------       10 AM ---- GENP      E-3 --------
   11 AM ---- INTM      E-2 -------        11 AM ---- INTM      E-2 --------
   12 PM ---- CSUR      X-2 --------       12 PM ---- CSUR      X-2 --------
    1 PM ---- ORTH      M-2 --------        1 PM ---- ORTH      M-2 --------
    2 PM ---- GENP      M-1 --------        2 PM ---- GENP      M-1 --------
    3 PM ---- PHAR      E-1 --------        3 PM ---- PHAR      E-1 --------
    4 PM ---- PHAR      E-1 --------        4 PM ---- PHAR      E-1 --------
    5 PM ----           --------           5 PM ----
    6 PM ----           --------           6 PM ----


    You are correct on 12 out of 12 appointments



    OPTION
    ----------------------------------------------------SCREENS ----------------------------------------------------
                            R - Return to Selections
                D - Discussion of Solution      S - Scoring and Comparison
```

In order to see a written discussion of the schedule, you can choose **D**, choose **S** to see the scoring again, or choose **R** to return to the scheduling menu.

You are now ready to schedule the other days contained in the Day Scheduler. Try it.

▶ 6 ◀

Sales Ethics

*Make yourself a seller when you are buying
and a buyer when you are selling, and then
you will buy and sell justly.*
ST. FRANCIS DE SALES

LEARNING OBJECTIVES

After studying this chapter, you should be able to:

▶ Draw the line between good and bad sales tactics.

▶ Explain the moral bases for business ethics.

▶ Understand how to make decisions that involve ethical problems.

▶ Recognize the issues of common sales ethics.

▶ Distinguish when public awareness and government regulations are needed

▶ Discuss how to build a sales ethics program.

▶ WHY ETHICS ARE IMPORTANT

Sales ethics provides a moral framework to guide salespeople in their daily contacts with customers. Ethical dilemmas are common in selling because salespeople often have to make decisions in the field in response to customers' demands and competitive offers. For example, insurance sales agents receive little in-house ethics education and many work for firms that implicitly reward employees for engaging in questionable behavior.[1] Ethical problems also occur in the sale of property. A Chicago real estate broker has been charged with paying $84,000 to a Kmart real estate executive for the approval of the sale of three stores and for consideration in future Kmart transactions. Both the broker and the Kmart executive have been indicted on federal mail and wire fraud charges and are expected to plead guilty.[2]

Other ethical problems occur with the issue of harassment. We know of one sales manager who asks his salespeople to credit his personal frequent flyer account whenever they take trips on company business. Salespeople who refuse fear they may be penalized on their next performance review. This occurs despite surveys that show 94 percent of firms have rules allowing their reps to keep frequent-flyer miles for personal use.[3]

These examples suggest that the world of personal selling is full of ethical dilemmas. Sales managers must train reps on how to recognize these situations and what responses to make when they occur. Remember that *business ethics* is a code of moral behavior that governs the conduct of a business community. This chapter focuses on the ethical problems faced by salespeople and sales managers and provides you with a set of guidelines to make better decisions.

▶ MODELING ETHICAL BEHAVIOR[4]

Procedures for making ethical decisions in business organizations are described in Figure 6-1. The process begins with the characteristics of individuals who are confronted with ethical choices. If people start out with high moral standards, then the chances that ethical decisions will be made are enhanced. This suggests that hiring honest, principled salespeople is the first step in establishing high moral behavior in sales activities.

Part B of Figure 6-1 describes the sequence of activities a person goes through in making ethical decisions. First, you have to recognize the various alternatives, identify the affected parties, and consider the possible outcomes of your choices. Then you have to assign priorities to moral values and convert these intentions into actions. This decision process is moderated by the ethical standards of society, the organization, your peers, superiors, competitors, customers, and the law.

Part C of Figure 6-1 focuses on the outcomes of the ethical decision process. This can be measured in terms of job performance, customer satisfaction, and the achievement of organizational goals. For example, if salespeople who refuse to pay bribes to get business are supported by their managers, then the climate for ethical decision making is strengthened. On the other hand, if salespeople or sales managers who make ethical decisions are reprimanded and punished for their actions, then the

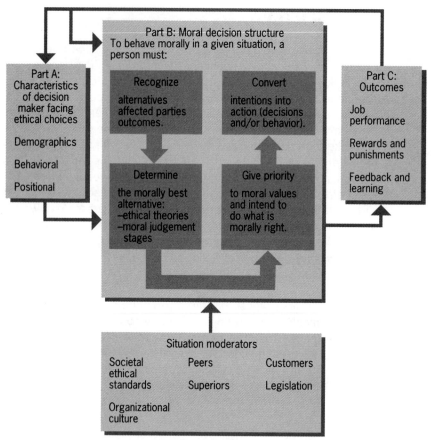

Source: Adapted from Figure 1 in Thomas R. Wotruba, "A Comprehensive Framework for the Analysis of Ethical Behavior, with a Focus on Sales Organizations," *Journal of Personal Selling & Sales Management*, Vol. 10 (Spring 1990), p. 31.

Figure 6-1: A Model of Ethical Decision Making

organization is apt to get into trouble. For example, a former sales manager at Dean Witter who was fired for refusing to condone improper activities by the firm's brokers received a $2.4 million arbitration award for false statements that appeared on his termination notice.[5]

Our discussion of sales ethics is built around the ethical decision-making process described in Figure 6-1. We begin by focusing on the ethical rules and moderating factors that influence ethical choices in part B of the diagram.

▶ WHOSE ETHICS ARE RELEVANT?

Ethical problems are usually the result of poor decisions by individual salespeople or company policies that encourage wrongdoing. For example, New York State inves-

Sales Management in Action 6-1
Overselling at Sears

In 1990 Sears converted its service advisors in its automotive centers from hourly wages to a commission program that paid employees solely on the amount of repairs customers authorize. They also instituted a program of requiring service advisors to meet sales quotas on specific auto parts during their workshifts. Sears instituted the new policies to trim costs and boost revenue.

After a year-long undercover investigation, California officials in 1992 sought to suspend Sears' license to perform auto repair work because of persuasive efforts by Sears service advisors to recommend unnecessary repairs to consumers. California officials found that unnecessary repairs were recommended 90 percent of the time at 38 Sears Service Centers that were investigated. Customers would come in to take advantage of an advertised discount on a brake job and would end up with new shocks and other parts that they didn't need. Soon New Jersey and 41 other states announced similar claims against Sears. As a result Sears discontinued the commission plan and dropped the fixed parts quotas for its service advisors.

Sears' experiment with unrealistic parts quotas proved to be a disaster for the company. The direct costs of settling claims that it sold unneeded parts amounted to $15 million. Sears has offered $50 rebates on 933,000 transactions for a potential liability of $46.7 million. Since the controversy erupted, business nationwide at the company's auto centers has fallen 15 percent or about $256 million a year. Much of the customer goodwill that Sears built up over the years at its auto centers has been lost by their misguided effort to boost short-term profits. Sears no longer does mechanical work at its auto centers and now specializes in the installation of tires, batteries, and shocks.

Unrealistic sales quotas encourage unethical overselling.

Sources: Craig Cox, "The Sins of Commissions," *Business Ethics*, September/October, 1992, p. 33; Gregory Patterson, "Sears' Brennan Accepts Blame for Auto Flap," *Wall Street Journal* (June 23, 1992), p. B1; Gregory Patterson, "Sears Will Pay $15 Million Settling Cases," *Wall Street Journal* (September 3, 1992), p. A4.

tigators found that an information services director solicited bribes from computer suppliers for a $1.2 million computer installation. Salespeople were asked to contribute $8,000 to a scholarship fund for the buyer's late son. Salespeople from Data General contributed the largest $1,000 gift to the fund and got the order for the computer. When the scam was uncovered, Data General was asked to remove the computer, the salespeople were fired, and the buyer was demoted. Data General was also barred from making any sales to the state for six months.[6]

This example suggests that hiring the right people—people with principles—can save money in the long run. However, even the right salesperson can go wrong if he or she is forced to operate under policies that promote misdeeds. For instance, Sears lost millions of dollars in fines and sales as the result of a sales quota system that encouraged overselling of unneeded parts at its auto service centers. A description of the Sears quota debacle is given in Sales Management in Action 6-1. Remember, there are often no laws or court decisions to guide salespeople in specific situations, and actions must be taken in the "twilight zone" between the clearly right and the clearly wrong. This means you must understand the different moral rules that are available to guide business managers (Figure 6-1, part B).

Role Morality

Perhaps the first place to look for guidelines on ethical behavior in the workplace is the job description. A *job description* is a set of rules or practices that define the role an employee is expected to play at work. It resembles a legal contract because it specifies the number of hours of work, starting and stopping times, and the goals that are to be accomplished. If an employee fails to live up to the legal rules of a job description, there are grounds for dismissal.

When an accurate and complete job description is available, employees are in a better position to resolve ethical problems when they occur. If Data General had a written policy stating that salespeople were not to donate to scholarship funds, hospital building funds, or special charities associated with customers, then it is unlikely that they would have gotten in such trouble with New York State officials. When job descriptions include questionable activities to be avoided, salespeople can respond that their job description does not allow them to make such payments.

The Ungolden Rule

A second argument for business ethics rests on the view that without some rules most business activities would be impossible. The *Golden Rule* helps you decide how you want to be treated in business and then to treat others the same way. This implies a logical consistency, so that like situations must be treated alike. For example, common morality says that cheating on exams is wrong. However, when students cheat, they are always trying to make exceptions for themselves. They are saying that they are exempt from the rules without being willing to grant the same privilege to others, for if everyone had the right to cheat on the exam, the professor would likely throw out the exam and no one would gain an advantage by cheating. Businesspeople follow the same routine when they use bribes to get orders and assume that others will follow the rules and not use bribes. A good part of the time, businesspeople are trying to "do unto others as they hope others will *not* do unto them." This is the U*ngolden Rule*, and it can cause serious moral confrontations.

The distinction between acceptable behavior and deception often occurs when businesspeople say they are operating by one set of rules when in fact they are playing by another. Take the example of department stores and the counting of guaranteed sale merchandise. To get new lines into department stores, it is common for salespeople to guarantee that the merchandise will sell within a certain period. However, counts on actual sales are made by store personnel without an inventory check by the salesperson. A store could take delivery of 500 sportswear items and then claim that only 350 were sold by the end of the time period. In this case, the store would be allowed to pay for only 350 pieces even though it may have sold the entire lot of 500. Thus the buyer was allowed to keep 150 items it did not have to pay for, in probable violation of the *Robinson-Patman Act*, which says that all buyers must be offered the same terms for the same merchandise.

Our argument suggests that when business activities are full of lies, broken promises, bribes, exaggeration, and concealment of pertinent facts, business practice is unstable and may be impossible. Minimum standards of morality are needed to allow business to function efficiently in our society.

Social Darwinism

The concept of *Social Darwinism*, based on the ideas of Charles Darwin and his theory of evolution, emerged in the latter half of the nineteenth century. Just as natural selection leads to stronger plant and animal species, free competition among business firms presumably leads to the survival of the fittest. That is to say, "natural laws" select the best and the most able firms to enhance the good of society.

With Social Darwinism, there are no ethical standards. The law is the law of the jungle. Government does not interfere, cutthroat competition eliminates the weak, and only the strong survive. Social Darwinism was quickly embraced by the robber barons of the nineteenth century because it perfectly reflected the climate of their everyday business activities. However, this philosophy is generally considered too ruthless for the 1990s—an era in which the U.S. government protects the interests of small businesses and consumers. As a personal ethic, Social Darwinism is not publicly endorsed because of its inherent inhumanity.

Machiavellianism

No discussion of ethics would be complete without some mention of Niccolò Machiavelli. Machiavelli was Secretary of State in the Florentine Republic in the sixteenth century and is widely known for his observations on human behavior and the workings of power. Many consider him to have been basically a realist—a person who focused on what is rather than on what ought to be. Machiavelli's political doctrine denied the relevancy of morality in public life and regarded expediency as the guiding principle. He was prepared to manipulate people and bend the laws of business to achieve his own goals. The opportunism that characterized Machiavelli's philosophy is reflected in the following quotation:

> Any person who decides in every situation to act as a good man is bound to be destroyed in the company of so many men who are not good. Wherefore, if a Prince desires to stay in power, he must learn how to be not good as the occasion requires.[7]

Dictionaries define *Machiavellianism* as the principles and methods of craftiness, duplicity, and deceit. Such practices are still employed by some sales executives to achieve personal or corporate goals. A survey of 98 salespeople revealed that salespeople with Machiavellian tendencies were less ethical than other salespeople.[8] Sales managers should avoid hiring people with Machiavellian traits and should retrain their existing people to avoid this type of bad ethics.

"When in Rome"

Another ethical standard that can guide the actions of executives is known as *conventional morality* or *situation ethics*. This philosophy is reflected in the familiar phrase "When in Rome, do as the Romans do." The emphasis shifts from the *individual* to what *society* thinks about the ethical issue; that is, the standard of morality becomes what is acceptable to others at a particular time and place. Thus, social approval is the ultimate test of right and wrong. With conventional morality, relationships to others are more important than end results.

With the *When in Rome* approach to morality, there are no absolute ethical standards to guide the actions of executives. Morality is based on social convention and group consensus. But the problem is that the majority can be wrong. Salespeople and sales managers sometimes justify cheating on expense accounts with the argument that "everybody does it" or "it's a way to reward salespeople with tax-free dollars." However, these are not acceptable reasons for violating organizational policy.

Another problem with conventional morality is that it is difficult for managers to adapt to changing contexts. Ten dollars given to a headwriter is a tip, but $10 given to a customs official to get a perishable product moving is a bribe. While both transactions represent payment for extra services rendered, one is socially acceptable and the other is not—in the United States. Often, in fact, what is moral, ethical, or common in one country is improprietous—or even illegal—in another. For example, hiring of relatives is called nepotism in the United States; in South America, it is viewed as an honorable family duty. Indeed, ethical dilemmas have become a serious, ongoing concern among the growing number of firms in multinational markets.

▶ MAKING DECISIONS ON ETHICAL PROBLEMS

Ethics is concerned with the effect of actions on the individual, the firm, the business community, and society as a whole. The relationships among the values and moral codes of conduct of these various entities was first described in Figure 6-1. A hierarchical diagram showing the order in which values evolve is given in Figure 6-2. Notice that the ethical values and standards of the business firm are derived from the general values and norms of society, and that business decisions represent a synthesis of the moral and ethical principles embraced by the various entities. Conflict is common because the values of the firm, as interpreted by its executives, may disagree with the values held by the individual. The difficult choice for managers is whether they should adhere to their own moral standards to solve problems or do what is expedient to maximize the short-run profits of the firm.

All too often when faced with ethical problems executives choose what is expedient rather than what is morally correct. When 400 executives were asked to play an "in-basket" game, 47 percent of top executives directed underlings to avoid write-offs that would hurt profits and 14 percent inflated sales figures to meet expectations.[9] The presence of a company ethics policy did not change the results. This tendency to sell out personal ethical standards for a chance at corporate glory means organi-

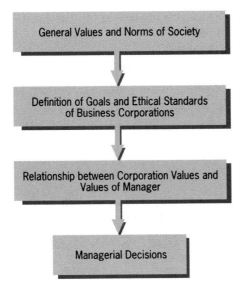

Figure 6-2: Making Decisions on Ethical Problems

zations need to foster a business climate that reinforces ethical behavior, and establish ombudsmen who train and provide guidance to salespeople on ethical dilemmas.

Ethical Checklist

To help managers make difficult moral decisions, General Dynamics suggests the following checklist:

1. Recognize the dilemma.
2. Get the facts.
3. List your options.
   Are they legal?
   Are they right?
   Are they beneficial?
4. Make your decision.

Applying this checklist to an employee who is operating below expectations helps explain how it works.

The Case of the Drug-Using Salesperson

Recognizing the Dilemma   Suppose sales manager Smith is concerned about Jones, who used to be the star member of the sales force. Jones's sales volume is slipping. At first, Smith ignores the problem. However, when customers start calling to complain about service, she can no longer put off deciding how to deal with the problem.

Assembling the Facts.   The next step in the decision process is to assemble all the relevant facts. Smith could start by asking questions of the other members of the sales force and of customers who can be trusted to tell the truth. Suppose these inquiries reveal that Jones's family life is stable but that a possible drug problem is interfering with normal sales-call patterns.

The sales manager could summarize the problem in the following manner:

1. Jones had an excellent sales record in the past, and the firm is having trouble finding good replacements for salespeople who leave.

2. Jones's apparent drug use is preventing him, a potentially good salesperson, from performing up to standard.

3. Jones's apparent drug use is hurting company sales and profits, and the situation must be corrected.

Any solution adopted should deal with all the facts. If some of the pertinent information is ignored, the sales manager is unlikely to find the best way to resolve the problem.

Making an Ethical Decision.   Alternative plans that deal with all aspects of the problem include the following:

1. Smith could have a talk with Jones and indicate her distress with sales in Jones's territory. The two could agree on a mutually acceptable quota, and Jones could prepare a plan to achieve the new goals. Smith could explain that she does not believe in telling people what to do with their personal lives, but she does expect that personal problems will not detract from performance on the job.

2. Smith could call Jones in and state that she is unhappy with Jones's poor sales and has heard rumors that Jones has a drug problem. Smith could give Jones an ultimatum that unless he submits to a drug test and takes care of the problem if the test is positive, his employment will be terminated. Smith would agree to set a reasonable sales quota and express confidence in Jones's ability to meet the goal.

3. Smith could tell Jones that she is concerned with the two problems of poor sales and possible drug use. Jones could be offered a three-month furlough at half pay to find a way to overcome his problem and could be told that a decision on reinstatement or termination would be made at the end of the furlough. Smith could suggest that Jones start seeing the company psychologist, explaining that the firm would like to keep Jones because of his impressive record of past successes. Temporary salespeople would be hired to cover Jones's territory during the furlough.

4. Smith could call Jones in and express her displeasure with Jones's poor sales and his possible drug problem. Jones could then be offered a choice of taking a drug test and going to a drug rehabilitation center for a month at company expense or of being let go. Temporary salespeople would be hired to cover Jones's territory during his absence.

The first of these solutions is a step in the right direction, but it may not be sufficient. Smith alludes to the drug problem but stops short of offering any help. The second plan faces the sales and drug problems squarely. However, it is not clear that Jones would be able to handle the pressure of the "reform or get fired" threat made by the sales manager. The third plan takes some of the pressure off Jones and offers help for the drug problem. But Jones may not be able or willing to stop using drugs and this plan may simply postpone the inevitable decision to dismiss him.

The last solution to the possible drug problem is attractive because it offers advantages for all participants. The sales manager is helped because Jones is removed from the territory and customers are handled by experienced reps. In addition, company sales volume in the territory should recover with the added attention. Furthermore, Jones is forced to confront his possible drug problem in a professional environment where chances for a recovery are enhanced. The main risk with this approach is that Jones may refuse the treatment and his potential contributions to the firm will be lost forever.

► COMMON SALES ETHICS ISSUES

Sales managers must make decisions in a wide variety of situations that have ethical dimensions. These include relations with superiors, salespeople, customers, competition, and dealers, and issues such as *sexual harassment*. There are no well-defined guidelines for moral conduct in each of the situations because what is right so often depends on the particular circumstances. Our objective is to raise some questions about business ethics and to point out potential problem areas.

Withholding Information

An important part of the salesperson's job is providing information on goods and services to customers. However, there are situations where the salesperson may be tempted to withhold information from the buyer. For example, suppose that an office equipment manufacturer has developed a new line of personal computers that will be available in 12 months. In the meantime, the firm plans to sell the old model until the new machines are available for sale. What does the salesperson say when a customer asks, "Will this machine be obsolete next year?" If the salesperson tells the truth, the customer is apt to wait and the sale may be lost. On the other hand, if the salesperson withholds the information, the customer will be unhappy when the new equipment makes his purchase obsolete. Withholding information can help the salesperson get immediate orders and raise commissions, but the firm may lose out on repeat orders from firms that feel they have been deceived.

Sabotaging Competitive Plans

Salespeople also face difficult decisions on what tactics are fair when battling competitive sales programs. For example, retail shelf space is vital to the success of many sales plans, and salespeople are continually trying to expand their share of this limited commodity. Should salespeople attempt to steal shelf space from their competitors when they get the chance to reorganize the shelf space? Would your decision be influenced by knowing that this practice is common in your industry? This is not an idle question; cookie salespeople have been known to get into fist fights over shelf space allocations in grocery stores.

Trade Secrets

Most people think of *trade secrets* as something to do with production processes, secret formulas, or patents. However, sales managers must realize that new-product information and marketing plans can also qualify as trade secrets. A few years ago, a case was filed over the theft of a rental car company's marketing strategy. Thus, when sales managers hire salespeople from other firms, they have to be careful about how much information they try to extract about the former employer. Clearly, it is unethical and perhaps illegal to hire someone from a competitor for the sole purpose of finding out what the other firm is planning to do.

Hiring and Firing

Various federal and state laws prohibit discrimination in hiring practices. Thus, firms that hire only white male Christians between the ages of 25 and 30 are breaking the law rather than operating unethically. An ethical problem, in contrast, usually requires considerable judgment as to the proper course of action—for example, in hiring candidates who are relatives of officers of the firm. Suppose a sales manager must choose between a man and a woman for a position as a field representative. Both candidates are well trained, but the man has somewhat more experience. Assume further that the woman is the daughter of a vice president of the company. If the decision is based strictly on qualifications, the man would get the position. However, the firm is under pressure from the federal government to hire women, so maybe she should get the position despite having somewhat lower qualifications. Although nothing has been said, the sales manager knows there could be personal advantages to finding a way to hire the vice president's daughter. Some would contend that hiring the woman instead of the man would be reverse discrimination and unethical. In this example, the sales manager must make a moral choice between what is best for the firm and what might enhance his or her own position in the firm.

Another sticky ethical question relates to hiring salespeople from competitors. The main advantages are that these people are trained and are likely to bring along some customers from their former employer. However, securing salespeople from competitors can increase selling costs and may lead to lawsuits if *trade secrets* are involved. Despite these risks, raiding competitors is common in the insurance, real estate, and stock brokerage fields. These firms operate on the premise that it is easier to hire successful agents than it is to train them. To prevent such practices, some firms have unwritten agreements that local competitors will not hire salespeople from each other. While this arrangement helps control selling costs, it often precludes salespeople from improving their positions by moving to another firm in the local area.

With so many firms concerned about reducing selling costs to boost profits, some companies are tempted to fire older salespeople who are paid high wages and to replace them with younger people who cost less. This approach is clearly illegal if it is part of a general plan to discriminate against older employees. However, the courts have ruled that it is legal to fire older employees if the decision is based solely on the need to reduce costs.[10]

An interesting finding in a cross-gender study indicates that women business students exhibit higher overall standards of ethical behavior than men. This suggests that hiring more women might reduce ethical problems in sales organizations and improve compliance with government guidelines on hiring minorities.

House Accounts

A touchy problem for sales managers is how to handle large and important customers. These older accounts often require special attention that exceeds the time and skills available from the salesperson assigned to the territory. Should these accounts be left with the district salesperson or shifted to headquarters as *house accounts*? This is not an easy decision because the accounts often generate high-commission income. The designation of a customer as a house account is usually defended on the grounds that it results in better service. However, the district salesperson who developed the account is apt to feel a proprietary interest because of the historical relationship with the client. Thus, a transfer to house account status is sure to be viewed as unfair by the salesperson losing the account. House accounts are clearly one area where firms need a specific and well-publicized policy so that misunderstandings and resentment can be avoided.

Expense Accounts

Most ethical abuse in a sales organization takes place with expense accounts. Salespeople are expected to spend money contacting customers and are then reimbursed for their expenses. The trouble is that they often claim higher expenditures than the amounts spent, keep the difference, and then do not report it to the Internal Revenue Service. A recent survey revealed that 25 percent of sales managers have caught a rep falsifying expenses within the past year.[11]

Sales managers must decide how tight controls on expense accounts should be. For example, if all salespeople who pad their expense accounts were fired, there would be few people left in the sales organization. Tight control on expense accounts could result in salespeople not traveling to contact out-of-the-way customers. However, liberal repayment for expenses invites investigations by the Internal Revenue Service and results in selling expense ratios that are higher than they should be.

A good solution to this problem is to monitor the actual expenses of some reliable salespeople for a month each year and then use these figures to set reimbursement amounts for all field reps. This approach greatly reduces the costs of processing expense accounts and keeps expense payments in line with actual experiences.

Gifts for Buyers

American business has a tradition of giving small *gifts for buyers* to express appreciation for past and future business. These gifts include novelties and samples given out by salespeople and gift-wrapped bottles of liquor at Christmas. The problem is that the gift giving may start out with a pair of hockey tickets and end up as a portable television set for the customer's den. How can a gift be distinguished from a bribe?

A survey of doctors by the Department of Health and Human Services revealed that 82 percent have received gift offers from drug salespeople to encourage them to prescribe their wares. Most physicians were offered small gifts such as pens and prescription pads, but each was offered at least one more substantial gift or payment. The average gift offers for each doctor amounted to $727 per year, but three offers for research funding amounted to $20,000 or more.[12] Abbott Laboratories and other infant formula makers have cultivated doctors' endorsements of their products by extending school loans, grants, payments for medical articles, and trips to conferences to pediatricians and medical students.[13]

Another survey of purchasing agents revealed that only 3 percent would not accept any favors, down from 17 percent in an earlier study. There seems to be more willingness today to accept gifts of clothing, pens, and calendars. The average annual value of favors accepted by purchasing agents was $132. To help control gift giving, 72 percent of firms have a written ethics policy. However, management guidance on gifts has slipped, and it is becoming difficult for salespeople to know what is right or wrong in a changing business environment.

Some firms have set rules that prohibit buyers from accepting any gifts, meals, or favors that might compromise their integrity. Although rules appear to solve the problem, they are hard to enforce. Another guideline is the Internal Revenue Service ruling that only $25 can be deducted each year for business gifts from a company to any one person. In the absence of explicit policies, sales managers and salespeople must judge what is a reasonable gift and what could be interpreted by others to be a bribe.

Bribes

The use of *bribes* to obtain business is widespread, and you must know what to do when you encounter or feel the need to engage in this practice. Bribery is fairly easy to spot in its most blatant forms. If a customer says that an order will be placed if a $20,000 commission is paid to a third party, then the salesperson can be sure that someone is being paid off. Bribes of this size are not only unethical, they can be illegal.

For example, the chief executive officer of Mid-American Waste System Inc. has been indicted on charges that he approved payment of bribes to members of the Gary, Indiana, city council to influence voting on a lucrative landfill contract. The indictment says that certain council members expected financial "help" for their upcoming elections and "all would prefer cash." Mid-American attempted to limit the funding to the $2,000 allowed for political contributions, but it eventually agreed to pay one council member $10,000 disguised as the purchase of two vehicles. Other council members received $5,000 in cash and $2,000 checks from Mid-American's political action committee.[14]

Foreign payoffs are so common that the U.S. Congress passed the *Foreign Corrupt Practices Act* to make it a criminal offense to offer a payment to a foreign government official to obtain or retain foreign business. However, no other industrialized nation has imposed such restrictions on its business managers. As a result, German and

Japanese firms are outbidding American firms and securing substantial business in Africa, the Far East, the Middle East, and Latin America. During a 13-month period ending in May 1995, U.S. firms lost contracts valued at $45 billion to foreign companies that pay bribes. Germany even allows firms to take a tax deduction for foreign bribes.[15] When the United States proposed discussing a rule outlawing bribery on government projects at a World Trade Organization meeting, the agenda item was opposed by some Southeast Asian Nations. This suggests that U.S. views on bribery are not shared by everyone.

The Foreign Corrupt Practices Act has been amended so now companies break the law only if they knowingly make an illegal payment.[16] Also, "grease payments" are now permitted to facilitate a routine matter such as getting a visa or a permit. In addition, it is proper to make payments allowed under the written laws of a foreign country. Although these changes have helped, American firms still find that they can't engage in activities their local competitors carry out every day.

Unfortunately, much of the bribery and extortion in business dealings is disguised to make it even more difficult for the businessperson to choose right from wrong. For example, a hospital asks for bids on some equipment and three suppliers all bid the same amount, higher than an out-of-town bid. In talking with one of the potential suppliers, the purchasing agent for the hospital gets a hint that the firm plans to continue its large annual gift to the hospital if it receives the contract. Is the gift in this case a bribe, or is it just good business? To whom should the contract be awarded? An example of the fine line between what is ethical and what is unethical in the marketing of infant formula is described in Sales Management in Action 6-2.

Entertainment

Providing entertainment for potential customers is standard practice in American business, but it can lead to ethical problems. The issue is often "How much is too much?" Most would agree that taking a customer to lunch is fair, reasonable, and expected. Few would argue against occasionally taking a client and spouse to dinner and a floor show. But what about the use of a company car or a weekend on the company yacht? On big orders, it is not unusual to fly personnel from the customer's plant to the supplier's headquarters in order to include plant tours and introductions to corporate executives as part of the sales presentation. Should the expenses of spouses taken on such trips be covered? Is it ethical to offer customers free use of the company hunting lodge in Canada? Sometimes out-of-town buyers are provided with call girls in addition to other forms of entertainment. What legitimately and ethically constitutes business "entertainment"?

An example of a difficult entertainment issue occurs when customers ask to be taken to topless bars. A recent survey revealed that 49 percent of male reps and 5 percent of female reps had taken customers to topless bars.[17] The survey also revealed that 72 percent of the visits were suggested by customers. Women reps generally do not like topless bars and feel that entertaining customers at these places gives men an unfair advantage over female salespeople. While 40 percent of firms do not allow reps to entertain at topless bars, many firms just look the other way. This example suggests that it is hard to solicit business on the basis of product

Sales Management in Action 6-2
The Ethics of Selling Infant Formula

The three leading suppliers of infant formula in the United States are Abbot Laboratories with 51 percent of the market, followed by Bristol-Myers' 27 percent and American Home Products' 11 percent. These companies have built this dominant market position by having networks of sales representatives work closely with hospitals and doctors. The companies provide doctors with cash grants for research, school loans, payments for medical articles, and pay for trips to conventions. They also make major contributions to hospitals for the privilege of giving away "discharge packs" of formula to mothers leaving hospitals. The market leaders have also agreed on an industry code to abstain from consumer advertising. This ban on advertising has been endorsed by the American Academy of Pediatrics. The academy says its opposition is based on the fear that consumer advertising would reduce breast feeding of babies. However, the objectivity of the academy is suspect when you realize that the formula industry contributes $1 million a year toward its budget and paid $3 million of the $10 million cost of its headquarters in Illinois in 1983. Also the formula companies regularly pick up the tab for cocktail receptions at the American Academy of Pediatrics biannual meetings. The academy's opposition to advertising has made it very difficult for new entrants such as Nestle and Gerber to break into the infant formula market.

The close cooperation among the three market leaders allowed them to increase the price of infant formula 207 percent since 1980 or six times the increase in the price of milk, its basic ingredient. Antitrust changes and bid-rigging allegations have recently caused the three market leaders to settle with the government for $230 million. The government fines appear to be primarily due to price-fixing charges rather than the payments to doctors and the American Academy of Pediatrics.

Are the actions of Abbot and the other market leaders just aggressive marketing or are they being unethical?

Source: Thomas M. Burton, "Methods of Marketing Infant Formula Land Abbot in Hot Water," *Wall Street Journal* (May 25, 1993), p. A1.

quality and service features when your competition is "buying" customers with exotic entertainment.

▶ WHISTLEBLOWING

A whistleblower is an employee who informs the public about immoral or illegal behavior of an employer or supervisor. Whistleblowing is a last-resort action that is justified when the employee has the appropriate moral motive. Before whistleblowing takes place, the person who has observed the unethical behavior should have exhausted all the internal channels for dissent. This means talking to your supervisor or the company ombudsman if one is available. Another test of whistleblowing is that the evidence should be strong enough to convince the average person that a violation is taking place. Furthermore, the observed moral violation should be serious enough to require immediate attention. Finally, the act of telling the public must have some chance for success. From a practical standpoint, it does not make sense to complain to the public unless something is going to be done about the problem. Why expose yourself to hardship if there is no moral gain?

Whistleblowing is not something employees take lightly because they know they may suffer if they "go public" with a moral problem. A typical example of what happens to a whistleblower occurred with a West Virginia bank manager who was fired for complaining about illegal overcharges for certain classes of his customers. The manager sued the bank and won an unfair firing judgment, but he received only $18,000 after paying his lawyer. Even worse, he was unable to find another bank job after applying to all the other banks in the state. The former banker was eventually forced to take a lesser job as a state bank examiner.

Why are whistleblowers treated so badly for simply following high personal moral standards? The problem seems to be that by speaking up, they violate the *role morality* that demands that employees should be loyal and keep their mouths shut. Management can be embarrassed by whistleblowers, and they often try to get rid of people they feel can't be trusted. To help encourage whistleblowers to come forward, federal laws have been modified to pay rewards of 15 to 30 percent of any recovery plus attorneys' fees. About 516 suits have been brought, with total recoveries of $358 million, and whistleblowers pocketed about $42 million. In one case, a whistleblower got $15 million in a Medicare fraud case. In another case, Chester L. Walsh received several million dollars for reporting a scam in which an Israeli air force general diverted money intended for jet fighter engines with the help of General Electric officials.[18]

Whistleblowing displays the classic conflict between the high ethical standards of individuals and the often lower morality found in the business world. The ultimate answer may occur when more firms set up formal internal mechanisms so that employees with moral problems to report are not ignored or punished.

▶ GOVERNMENT REGULATION

When business fails to operate in an ethical manner, there is usually a cry from the public and the media for more *government regulation*. Thus one of the basic roles of government is to set minimum standards of business morality and then to help enforce the rules. The judicial branch of government settles disputes over the interpretation of the regulations, and Congress writes new rules as they are needed. Some of the first government regulations in the United States affecting business were designed to protect the public from noncompetitive activities. The kinds of activities the laws are designed to prevent include a scheme by Mitsubishi Electric to force its dealers to charge premium prices for certain televisions. In this case, Mitsubishi agreed to refund $8 million to consumers. In another case, Manischewitz pleaded no contest to charges that it had agreed with other firms to fix the price of Passover matzo crackers. The company faced fines of up to $1 million for the violations. Federal agents are investigating whether Baxter International paid *kickbacks* to doctors to increase its Medicare revenues for home health care.[19]

Consumer Protection

A number of federal consumer protection laws have also been passed to set ethical standards for transactions between manufacturers and the consumer. For example, the common practice by dealers of inflating the prices of new cars was stopped by the Automobile Information Disclosure Act. This law requires manufacturers to attach labels to car windows that show the suggested price for the car, accessories, and transportation. Deceptive packaging has been attacked with the Fair Packaging and Labeling Act, which calls for standard package sizes and disclosure of the manufacturer's name or the distributor. Attempts by loan companies and retailers to mislead consumers on interest rates have led to the enactment of the Consumer Credit Protection Act. *Truth in lending* laws require full disclosure of annual interest rates and other charges on loans and credit sales. More recently, the Magnuson-Moss Warranty Act has increased the power of the FTC to regulate product warranties. New FTC rules require full disclosure of warranty terms and reduce the use of warranties as promotional gimmicks.

Why Are Regulations Needed?

Government often gets involved in business ethics when the problem is too big for individual firms to handle. For example, automobile exhaust is a major cause of air pollution, but it is difficult for an individual firm to solve the problem. If one company feels it is morally correct to install air pollution equipment on their cars, their costs will be higher than those of the competition. Thus the cars of the ethically lazy firm will be cheaper and more powerful, and they will literally run off with the market. In this situation, government regulation allows the well-intentioned business to be the good citizen it wants to be.

Although there are many arguments for a minimum of government regulation of business, there are also other problems with regulation. Businesspeople generally dislike government controls because they rob them of the flexibility needed to respond to changing conditions. Government rules established to solve problems in one decade are often obsolete by the next decade. For instance, the federal government got into the regulation of natural gas prices because gas is often shipped through interstate pipelines. As might be expected, the government tended to set gas prices low for maximum political gain. However, the drillers were more rational, and they slowed their search for new gas. As a result, the supply of natural gas declined until the price controls were removed.

Government attempts to legislate morality have not always worked. A case in point is the recent savings and loan scandal. Although a system of controls and inspectors was established, unscrupulous managers were able to bypass the rules and make political contributions to U.S. senators to gain special treatment. Obviously, just having rules is not enough; they have to be enforced if they are going to be effective.

We believe there should be a balance between too little government (savings and loan industry) and too much regulation (as occurred in the natural gas industry, where business was strangled by endless rules and red tape).

▶ BUILDING A SALES ETHICS PROGRAM

The moral climate of a business reflects the words and actions of its top executives. If management tolerates unethical behavior in the sales force, then there is little a member of the organization can do about it. Superiors set the moral climate and provide the constraints within which business decisions are made. Thus, the best way for a manager to build a strong sales ethics program is to get the backing of the board chairperson and the president of the company (Table 6-1). When this support is not available, there are sure to be ethical violations.

Codes of Ethics

Once a sales manager gains the support of top management, the next step is to prepare a written sales *ethics policy statement* that indicates to the sales force that the company believes in playing fair with customers and competitors. Research has shown that senior executives believe the adoption of a corporate code of ethics is the most effective way to encourage ethical behavior. A recent survey of 218 salespeople indicated that field reps want written policies that help them perform their jobs ethically.[20] Also, the policies need to be monitored on a regular basis to make sure that they are germane to the current selling arena. The advantage of a written ethics policy is that it allows the firm to be explicit about what activities are permissible and what actions violate company standards. This can be useful when customers, suppliers, or your boss ask you to participate in some unethical activities. If your company has a code of ethics, you can reply, "I'm sorry, but company policy forbids that," and graciously end a conversation about a shady deal. The vast majority of firms that got into trouble in the foreign payoff scandals had no written policies on commercial bribery. Today nearly all firms claim to have formal ethics codes, but only half ask employees

Table 6-1   Eight Ways to Keep Your Sales Force Honest

1. Get support from top management showing that they expect you to follow the spirit and letter of the law.
2. Develop and distribute a sales ethics policy.
3. Establish the proper moral climate. If the bosses follow the rules, then the troops are apt to do likewise.
4. Assign realistic sales goals. People who try to meet an unfair quota are more likely to rationalize their way to a kickback scheme.
5. Set up controls when needed. Watch people who live above their income.
6. Suggest that salespeople call for help when they face unethical demands.
7. Get together with your competition if payoffs are an industry problem.
8. Blow the whistle if necessary.

to acknowledge or sign them.[21] This suggests some firms need to make reps more aware of company ethical standards.

An example of what a written code of ethics should look like is provided by General Motors. GM's new policy is a 12-page document complete with instructional scenarios with fictional characters.[22] One scenario has a purchasing employee visiting the home office of a possible supplier where he was offered a chance to go to a Rams football game and mingle with top executives. This opportunity should be turned down. In another scenario an investment banking firm that helped with an acquisition for GM invites several GM employees to New York for a dinner and the gift of a mantel clock. In this case the dinner and the clock should be refused. GM's policy provides some wiggle room for employees outside the United States. Workers in certain countries may accept meals, gifts, or outings to comply with local business practices and to avoid being put at a competitive disadvantage. Also GM employees can continue providing gifts and meals to their customers, but only within limits. The most expensive restaurant in town is no longer appropriate. GM's policy requires GM employees to avoid violating the customer's gift policy.

Sales managers should also be ready to enforce company policies on bribery. A survey of industrial salespeople found highly supervised employees at bureaucratic firms more likely to act ethically than those at laissez-faire ones.[23] The results suggest that salespeople think about the risk of being caught. This means it pays to keep tabs on salespeople who appear to live beyond their income. It also means setting reasonable sales goals so that salespeople will not be tempted to cheat to reach an unfair quota. Salespeople should be encouraged to ask for assistance when they encounter unethical situations. If payoffs become too widespread, the sales manager should meet with the competition to work out a set of standards for the industry.

Ethics Training

Managers should remember that publishing a sales ethics code does not guarantee that it will be followed by field sales representatives. More and more companies are offering classes to make sure employees know what to do in morally ambiguous situations. In the case of pharmaceutical salespeople, research has shown that reps should stress the importance of long-term relationships with doctors and develop classes that enhance product and customer knowledge. Reps with the greatest expertise tend to act more ethically in their relationships with doctors.[24]

Honeywell revamped employees' training and replaced a vague policy manual with a detailed handbook. Some of the unacceptable practices spelled out in the handbook include catcalls, sexual jokes, and staring. Nearly three-quarters of DuPont's 90,000 U.S. staffers have taken harassment-prevention training dubbed "A Matter of Respect" and sexual harassment suits involving the company have fallen off. Corning is testing its first workshops on ethics because people who feel harassed on the job aren't productive workers.[25]

These programs bring groups of employees together with an instructor to find solutions to simulated moral dilemmas. By working through a number of scenarios, employees learn how to recognize problems, assemble facts, consider alternatives, and make decisions. They can also pick up some tips on how the company expects them to operate. At one session a salesperson asked, "When I check in at a motel, I get a coupon for a free drink; can I use it?" The correct answer was that it would be acceptable to use the coupon, but it would be wrong to accept $50 to stay there in the first place. At DuPont the course offers advice on what women should do when a male customer makes a pass and puts his hand on the saleswoman's knee. In this case she should firmly remove his hand and say, "Let's pretend this didn't happen." Some firms also include training sessions for men on how to avoid crude jokes and other forms of intimidation when dealing with women buyers. The idea behind ethics training is to make sure employees are equipped to handle real-world issues they are apt to encounter when calling on customers.

▶ SUMMARY

Sales ethics forms a code of moral conduct that guides sales managers and salespeople in their everyday business activities. Ethical decisions can be based on different rules including the self-interest of Social Darwinism, the unscrupulous expediency of Machiavellianism, or the more acceptable conventional morality of consensus. Perhaps the best way to solve ethical problems is the pragmatic approach, which involves an objective analysis of relevant facts and leads to more rational decisions. Areas in which the sales manager is likely to confront difficult ethical situations involve hiring, trade secrets, house accounts, whistleblowing, expense accounts, requests for payoffs, and customer gifts and entertainment. Sales managers are better equipped to deal with ethical dilemmas when they have the backing of top management and the firm has an explicit policy detailing ethical standards of behavior for its employees.

▶ KEY TERMS

Bribes	Kickbacks
Business ethics	Machiavellianism
Consumer protection	Robinson-Patman Act
Conventional morality	Role morality
Ethics policy statement	Sexual harassment
Foreign Corrupt Practices Act	Situation ethics
Gifts for buyers	Social Darwinism
Golden Rule	Trade secrets
Government regulation	Ungolden Rule
House accounts	When in Rome
Job description	Whistleblowing

▶ REVIEW QUESTIONS

1. Why is role morality a common guide in ethical dilemmas?
2. Why do businesspeople use the Ungolden Rule instead of the Golden Rule?

3. What are the ethics of Social Darwinism?

4. Why is sexual harassment so difficult to control?

5. Why have Machiavelli's ethics lasted for hundreds of years?

6. How do people who use When in Rome ethics get themselves in trouble?

7. When should the ethical values of the individual take precedence over the values of the firm?

8. What is the problem-solving approach to the solution of moral dilemmas?

9. How do you treat an alcoholic salesperson who has won sales contests in the past?

10. Should you hire less qualified salespeople who are relatives of officers of the firm?

11. What should you do about salespeople who cheat on their expense accounts?

12. When does a gift become a bribe?

13. How does a sales manager know when entertainment expenses are unethical?

14. Should sales managers run training classes on sales ethics?

▶ PROBLEMS

1. Recently a stockbroker pleaded guilty to conspiracy charges in San Diego for accepting $500,000 in bribes to promote the sale of certain stocks. Bribes amounting to 15 percent of the value of the stock sold to clients were paid in cash. What should stock brokerage firms do to reduce the chances that brokers would accept money to push certain stocks?

2. Boehringer Mannheim recently accused Johnson & Johnson's LifeScan division of encouraging their employes to spy on Boehringer Mannheim, steal a prototype glucose monitoring device, and acquire secret new product documents. What types of information can you ask your salespeople to collect about competitors and when does this information gathering become illegal?

3. A U.S. export licensing officer who earned $40,000 a year was convicted of receiving over $100,000 in gratuities in exchange for issuing licenses to ship sophisticated electronic equipment to China. The defendant, who is 35 years old, faces a maximum sentence of 25 years in jail and a fine of $350,000. What are the best ways to prevent middle-level managers from taking bribes and kickbacks?

4. A federal jury awarded $69.5 million to two former vice presidents of Ashland Oil who were fired for refusing to cover up bribes to an Omani official to obtain crude oil. Defendants in the case included the former chairman and current top officers of the company. Ashland settled the case by paying the two former executives $25 million. Do whistleblowers usually fare as well as these two executives when they report wrongdoing? What can be done to prevent top officials in a firm from participating in illegal activities?

5. A United Technologies employee has charged that the company's Sikorsky Division offered two Saudi princes a "bonus" of 3 to 5 percent of a $130 million portion of a $6 billion potential Blackhawk helicopter order. The employee is seeking $100 million in damages from United Technologies. What seems to be the motive of the employee in this case, and why are such "commissions" so common in foreign sales agreements? How should the company handle these demands for special favors?

6. For a year and a half, Del Monte Corporation tried to buy a 55,000-acre banana plantation in Guatemala, but the government said no. Then the company hired an influential business consultant and agreed to pay him nearly $500,000 if the deal went through. Suddenly, the

Guatemalan government reversed itself. Now Del Monte owns the profitable banana-growing properties, for which it paid $20.5 million. The consultant assured Del Monte that none of the cash went to any government officials. Did Del Monte do anything wrong? Would you have approved the payment to the consultant?

7. IBM attempted to get a sales engineer to accept early retirement by moving him from job to job. Although he had spent all of his career selling small computers to first-time buyers, IBM put him in charge of selling the most complex systems without any retraining. After failing this assignment, he was transferred several times, ending up in an abandoned sales office in Tinton Falls, New Jersey. When he refused early retirement again, employees entered his office in the middle of the night and removed all the furniture. The 59-year-old engineer sued IBM, claiming age discrimination, and was awarded $315,000 in a jury trial. What would have been a more ethical solution to this situation?

8. You have just been hired as a sales manager by the Beta Corporation, with a 35 percent increase in salary over your previous job. Beta paid all relocation expenses and has provided you with a new Buick Turbo for use in your work. At a cocktail party welcoming new employees, the national sales manager begins asking you detailed questions about the marketing plans and products of your former employer. How would you respond?

9. Due to changing conditions in China, businesspeople are encountering increased requests for special favors from government officials. These usually take the form of cash but may include U.S. college tuition for a son or daughter or sponsorship for immigration of the official to a Latin American country. One Hong Kong trading company that sells precision equipment routinely offers a Shanghai official rebates of 1 to 3 percent of a transaction. In return, the official provides exclusive "market research" on the procurement plans of local plants. Because orders depend on the availability of foreign currency, such research information is vital. Are these fees paid for sales leads morally acceptable? How do you decide whether to pay to help move a deal along?

▶ IN-CLASS EXERCISE

Assume you have taken over the territory of Henry Perkins, who has retired after 30 years with your firm. Henry was well liked by everyone and earned $60,000 in commissions on printing sales in his last year. You are having dinner with one of the best customers in the territory, Mary Stevens. Mary bought $100,000 in printing services from your company in the past year, and this business earned Henry $6,000 in commissions. You have been emphasizing to Mary how you plan to continue to give the same high-quality service that Henry was providing. Mary responds that she has recently talked to several other quality printers who also provide good service, and she wonders if you intend to continue Henry's special support activities. You say that you are not sure what special support Henry has been providing. Mary indicates that Henry paid $2,000 for a trip to Jamaica each winter to help relieve her arthritis. Discuss how you would respond in this situation in small groups in your class for seven minutes. Be prepared to continue the conversation when your instructor calls on your group.

▶ REFERENCES

1. K. DOUGLAS HOFFMAN, VINCE HOWE, and DONALD W. HARDIGREE, "Ethical Dilemmas Faced in the Selling of Complex Services: Significant Others and Competitive Pressures," *Journal of Personal Selling & Sales Management* (Fall 1991), p. 22;

"Doing the 'Right' Thing Has Its Repercussions," *Wall Street Journal* (January 25, 1990), p. B1.

2. ROBERT BERNER, "Two Men Charged in Plot to Bribe Ex-Kmart Official," *Wall Street Journal* (April 23, 1996), p. B8.

3. GEOFFREY BREWER, "On the Road Again," *Sales & Marketing Management* (January 1996), p. 50.

4. See THOMAS R. WOTRUBA, "A Comprehensive Framework for the Analysis of Ethical Behavior, with a Focus on Sales Organizations," *Journal of Personal Selling & Sales Management*, 10 (Spring 1990), pp. 29–42.

5. MICHAEL SICONOLFI, "Brokers May Sue Former Employers Over Firing Notices," *Wall Street Journal* (May 8, 1996), p. B7.

6. JOHN R. WILKE, "New York Will Bar Data General Sales to State Agencies Amid Bribery Inquiry," *Wall Street Journal* (October 8, 1992), p. A5.

7. NICCOLÒ MACHIAVELLI, *The Prince* (New York: Mentor Classics, 1952).

8. ANUSORN SINGHAPAKDI and SCOTT J. VITELL, "Analyzing the Ethical Decision Making of Sales Professionals," *Journal of Personal Selling & Sales Management* (Fall 1991), p. 9.

9. DAWN BLALOCK, "For Many Executives, Ethics Appear to Be a Write-Off," *Wall Street Journal* (March 26, 1996), p. C1.

10. MILO GEYELIN and STEPHANIE SIMON, "Court Rules Employers Can Fire Older Executives to Trim Costs," *Wall Street Journal* (July 16, 1991), p. B5.

11. GEOFFREY BREWER, "On the Road Again," *Sales & Marketing Management* (January 1996), p. 50.

12. "Most Doctors Get Gift Offers from Drug Firms, Survey Says," *Herald Times* (April 3, 1992), p. A5.

13. THOMAS M. BURTON, "Methods of Marketing Infant Formula Land Abbott in Hot Water," *Wall Street Journal* (May 23, 1993), p. A1.

14. JAMES P. MILLER, "Mid-American Waste System CEO Quits After Indictment on Bribery Charges," *Wall Street Journal* (April 17, 1996), p. B5a.

15. Review & Outlook, "Is Corruption an Asian Value?" *Wall Street Journal* (May 6, 1996), p. A14.

16. *Wall Street Journal* (June 20, 1989), p. B1.

17. ROB ZEIGER, "Sex, Sales & Stereotypes," *Sales & Marketing Management* (July 1995), pp. 46–56.

18. RICHARD B. SCHMITT, "It Can Pay to Be Whistle-Blower in Health Fraud," *Wall Street Journal* (September 2, 1993), p. B1; Amal Kumar Naj, "U.S. Joins Suit Against General Electric Officials," *Wall Street Journal* (August 15, 1991), p. A3.

19. PAUL M. BARRETT, "Mitsubishi Electric to Pay Consumers in Price-Fixing Suit," *Wall Street Journal* (March 28, 1991), p. A13; "U.S. Judge to Accept Plea of No Contest from Manischewitz," *Wall Street Journal* (April 26, 1991), p. C17; THOMAS M. BURTON, "Baxter Faces Probe of Fees Paid to Doctors," *Wall Street Journal* (September 9, 1991), p. A3.

20. ALAN J. DUBINSKY, MARVIN A. JOLSON, RONALD E. MICHAELS, MASAAKI KOTABE, and CHAE UN LIM, "Ethical Perceptions of Field Sales Personnel: An Empirical Assessment," *Journal of Personal Selling & Sales Management* (Fall 1992), p. 18.

21. *Wall Street Journal*, May 14, 1996, p. A1.

22. GABRIELLA STERN and JOANN S. LUBLIN, "New GM Rules Curb Wining and Dining," *Wall Street Journal* (May 5, 1996), p. B1.

23. *Wall Street Journal* (March 1, 1990), p. 1.

24. ROSEMARY R. LAGACE, ROBERT DAHLSTROM, and JULE B. GASSENHEIMER, "The Relevance of Ethical Salesperson Behavior on Relationship Quality: The Pharmaceutical Industry," *Journal of Personal Selling & Sales Management* (Fall 1991), p. 44.

25. JOANN S. LUBLIN, "Companies Try a Variety of Approaches to Halt Sexual Harassment on the Job," *Wall Street Journal* (October 11, 1991), p. B1.

► **SELECTED READINGS**

BEAUCHAMP, TOM L. *Case Studies in Business, Society and Ethics*, 3rd ed. (Englewood Cliffs, NJ: Prentice-Hall, 1993).

BEAUCHAMP, TOM L., and NORMAN E. BOWIE, *Ethical Theory and Business*, 4th ed. (Englewood Cliffs, NJ: Prentice-Hall, 1993).

DONALDSON, THOMAS, and PATRICIA H. WERHANE, *Ethical Issues in Business*, 4th ed. (Englewood Cliffs, NJ: Prentice-Hall, 1993).

VELASQUEZ, MANUEL G., *Business Ethics: Concepts and Cases*, 3rd ed. (Englewood Cliffs, NJ: Prentice-Hall, 1992).

CASE

6-1 TEXXON OIL COMPANY*

The retail gasoline marketing strategy of the major oil companies first began to develop in the early 1930s. Before 1910 gasoline was sold by livery stables, garages, and hardware, grocery, and general stores. However, by the mid-1920s, with the dramatic growth of automobile registrations, a clear need emerged for a new type of outlet. The result was the development of the gasoline service station, which quickly dominated the sale of gasoline.

History of Gasoline Marketing

Gasoline Service Stations

The initial demand for service stations was met by independent businesspeople who were eager to capitalize on the profit opportunity in this important venture. The result was intense competition among the major oil companies for exclusive representation by the higher-quality, independently owned retail outlets. This competition had two consequences for quality representation. First, the price of quality representation became quite high. Second, frequent brand switching by the independently owned outlets often disrupted major oil company coverage in an area.

For these and other reasons, the major oil companies began to integrate forward to control their key marketing facilities, either by outright ownership or by long-term leases. Forward integration also ensured

*This case was prepared by James M. Patterson of Indiana University.

that the outlets would sell only the brand of the owning company. It also permitted greater control over station appearance and operation. Such control is very important in the development of a favorable brand image for an unpackaged product like gasoline.

While the ownership and control of stations permit employee operation, most major companies have chosen to use independent dealers to run their service stations. Under this arrangement, the major oil company is both landlord and supplier.

This was not always so. Initially, it was quite common for the major oil companies to operate their stations with company employees. For a number of reasons, including the avoidance of chain store taxes, most majors moved away from direct station operation by the mid-1930s. The threat of unionization, as well as the desire to shift the burden of the often low returns from retailing to others, also entered into this decision.

Franchised Station Operation

The franchise relationship in the petroleum industry is unique in that the franchiser not only grants the franchisee the use of his trademark but often controls, and leases to the franchisees, the retail facility used by the franchisee. In addition, the franchiser is almost always the primary supplier of the franchisee's principal sale item: motor fuel. This relationship is often complex and is sometimes characterized by competing interests. There is also a substantial disparity of bargaining power between the supplier and the dealer. This disparity results in standard franchise agreements that translate into the dealer's continuing vulnerability to the demands and actions of the supplier.

The natural tensions that are created by this relationship have led to numerous complaints by dealers of unfair terminations or nonrenewals of their franchises by their supplier/landlords. Allegations have been made in court and before congressional committees that the refiner/landlord uses terminations and nonrenewals to compel franchised dealers to comply with the marketing policies of the franchiser, even though they are often at odds with the dealers' own economic interests.

While the relationship of the parties in a motor fuel franchise agreement is basically contractual, the franchiser often avoids the normal remedies for violations of the provisions. Moreover, the disparity of bargaining power that disadvantages the franchisee in negotiations leading to the execution of the agreement often manifests itself in one-sided remedies for contract violations. In addition, the franchiser is able to capitalize on this disparity in bargaining power to obtain greater flexibility with respect to his or her right to terminate the contractual relationship. As a result, termination of franchise agreements for contract violations has been repeatedly utilized, often for what to many seem to be minor infractions.

Franchiser/Franchisee Conflict

As in other franchise relationships, the parties to a motor fuel franchise believe the relationship will be a continuing one. This expectation is often fostered by the nature of the actions and sometimes by the statements of the franchiser. It is clearly in the dealer's best interest to build customer goodwill for the location and for the franchiser's brand and to develop customer loyalty for the services and products he or she offers. Consequently, the nonrenewal of a motor fuel franchise relationship can be almost as punitive as a termination during its term. In the case of nonrenewal, the reasonable expectations of the franchisee are destroyed. This loss is made even more severe in the case of the lessee/dealer since the dealer loses not only the goodwill generated for the franchiser's brand, but also the goodwill generated for service at a specific location. By contrast, landlord/suppliers are able to convert most of the goodwill generated by dealers to their own use. The losses from nonrenewal, therefore, fall more heavily on the lessee/dealer.

Disparity of bargaining power at the start of a franchise relationship may manifest itself in the use of termination as a remedy for contract violations. In addition, the prospect of nonrenewal of a franchise relationship may be used to coerce the dealer into accepting the franchiser's marketing policies against his or her better judgment. Threats are not even essential to the leverage that nonrenewal provides a franchiser over the activities of the dealer. The prospect is ever present, and the lessee/dealer can readily imagine and comprehend the implications of departing from the marketing policies of the franchiser, even if they are contrary to the dealer's own economic interests. This problem is made even more severe when the franchiser uses shorter franchise periods.

Congress enacted the Petroleum Marketing Practices Act in 1978.[1] The purpose of the law was to ensure that the grounds for termination and nonrenewal were not so broad as to deny dealers meaningful protection from arbitrary or discriminatory terminations and nonrenewals. The law also sought to establish uniform guidelines regarding the franchise relationship.

The drafters of the law also sought to accommodate the legitimate needs of a franchiser to terminate or not renew a franchise relationship by reason of certain serious specified actions of the franchisee.[2] The intention was to provide adequate flexibility so that franchisers might respond to changing economic conditions and consumer preferences.

Divorcement/Anticonversion Legislation

During this same period, Maryland enacted legislation to prevent refiner/marketers from taking back their dealer stations and operating them as company stores with their own employees. This reintegration was a natural outgrowth of the changes that were taking place in the marketing of gasoline during the

---

[1] Petroleum Marketing Practices Act, 15 U.S.C. 2801.

[2] The following are grounds for termination or nonrenewal of a franchise relationship: (1) failure to comply with reasonable and material provisions of the contract; (2) failure of the dealer to exert good faith efforts to carry out the provisions of the franchise; (3) the occurrence of an event that is relevant to the franchise relationship; (4) agreement between the parties; and (5) a determination made by the franchiser in good faith and in the normal course of business to withdraw from the retail marketing of motor fuel in the relevant geographic area.

1970s. High-volume, self-service, gasoline-only stations were the wave of the future. Unlike the traditional low-volume, full-service station, these new express stations could be operated with employees or contract labor as opposed to dealers. Moreover, the traditional dealer margins, which were based on low-volume full-service stations, were out of line with what was required for the new retail operations. Many dealers were getting rich at oil company expense. In fact, some dealers were making more money than the oil company managers supervising them.

Initially, this dealer-inspired divorcement legislation merely prohibited refiner/marketers from operating stations with their own employees. But since the refiners immediately challenged these laws on constitutional grounds, the dealers got their friends in the state legislature to enact legislation that would make it illegal for any service station that had been offering automotive repair service to continue to operate as a service station without also continuing to provide this service. No longer could a traditional station be razed and converted to an express, gas-only operation. Ultimately, both laws withstood constitutional challenge and were upheld as valid exercises of the state's police power.

These anticonversion laws served the dealers' goal of self-preservation because very few stations offering automotive service had ever been successfully operated by the refiners. Automotive service operations were too hard to control from headquarters. They required continuous, detailed supervision and local initiative for them to be profitable. As a result, the dealers knew that if automotive service at a location had to be continued by law, lessee/dealers would continue to be used to operate the station at that location.

Richie Highway Texxon Station

Governor Richie Highway is a true "gasoline alley." This highway is a major north–south four-lane road that runs from Baltimore to Annapolis. There is hardly a stretch along its 25 miles where a gasoline service station is not in sight. The road is a classic strip-retailing commuting corridor interspersed with several large shopping centers. The highway is heavily traveled, almost to the point of congestion. Most major brands, from Amoco to Sun, are represented on this highway. There is no significant private brand

presence, but Crown, a strong regional marketer that prices with the majors, has a strong presence. Prices are very competitive, since commuters driving to work notice the range of posted prices and fill up at the lowest-priced station on the way home.

Compared with the new, attractive stations, Texxon (MD–73) is an old-timer, having been built in 1959. The retail configuration is traditional. The building is a red brick colonial with two service bays and an automotive rollover car wash. The station has three pump islands with mechanical pumps and no canopy. The lighting and signage are old-fashioned. Nevertheless, the station has experienced good volume since the Texxon brand and credit card are well received. Texxon is one of the top gasoline marketers in Maryland and has nearly 200 stations statewide. Operating data for MD–73 appear in Exhibits 1 and 2.

Ron Kile, the most recent lessee/dealer to operate MD–73, took over the station in November 1982 and operated it under a succession of standard Texxon dealer agreements until the last one expired in November 1986. Kile paid $123,000 to the former dealer to acquire the business and goodwill of MD–73. Kile, as well as his father and brother, are personally obligated on the loans obtained to finance this business at MD–73.

At the time Kile acquired MD–73 in 1982, Texxon approved Kile as the Texxon franchisee. Texxon was also aware that Kile, who had previously managed MD–73 for the former dealer, had paid a substantial sum to acquire the business at MD–73.

Prior to the time that Kile acquired the business of MD–73, the dealer rep advised him informally that Texxon intended to renovate the station and convert it to an advanced marketing facility with an overhead canopy, computerized gasoline pumps, sales kiosk, and upgraded service bays. This understanding, however, was never put in writing and was not part of the franchise agreement.

Upon acquiring the business, Kile spent a great deal of effort and money to improve the premises, promote the sale of Texxon gasoline and products, and otherwise comply with the written franchise agreements.

The New Texxon Express Station

Shortly before Kile became the Texxon franchisee at MD–73, Texxon's real estate department acquired an older Hess-brand, gas-only station located approximately 1500 feet south of MD–73 on the same side of

Exhibit 1: Texxon Oil Company, Monthly Volume

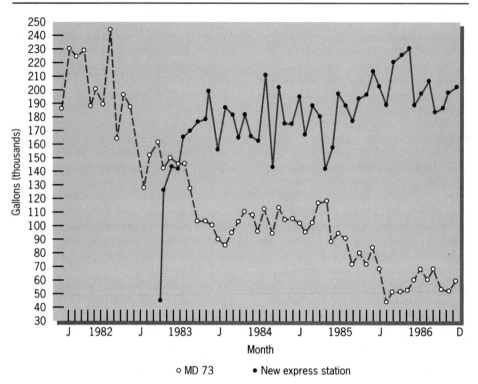

○ MD 73   ● New express station

the highway. The Hess station (which did not offer automobile repair service) was in plain sight of MD–73. Kile knew of this acquisition but was unclear about Texxon's plans for the Hess property.

In the spring of 1983, Texxon razed the Hess property and constructed a new state-of-the-art gasoline express station. The new outlet is operated by another Texxon franchisee, in compliance with the Maryland divorcement law, and is in direct competition with MD–73.

Shortly after the new express facility opened, Kile's business at MD–73 began to deteriorate rapidly. Gasoline sales at MD–73 dropped from 2,405,890 gallons in 1982 to 1,564,330 gallons in 1983. Moreover, despite repeated requests from Kile, Texxon refused to upgrade MD–73 or to give Kile any additional retail marketing tools or subsidies to compete with the new express station. Rather, the opposite was the case. Between 1983 and 1986, Texxon raised the rent on MD–73 from $1,992 to $3,371 per month.

The new express station, which opened in April

1983, prospered during this same period. From 1,371,000 gallons in 1983, its gallonage grew to 2,415,000 in 1986 (Exhibit 1). Initially, Kile sought to meet the competition of the new express station by cutting his price, but when this measure failed to slow down the loss of gallonage, he raised his price and sought to offset the loss of volume with a higher margin. But this strategy also failed, and operating profits continued their nosedive.

As a result of his concern over the deteriorating business and Texxon's failure to provide him with assistance, Kile began to experience considerable emotional distress. Increasingly, he withdrew from day-to-day operations and left the management of the facility to his employees. Since this withdrawal led to a deterioration in the appearance and quality of service at the station, it soon became a bone of contention between Kile and the Texxon station rep. Kile was cited several times by the rep for sloppy operations.

Obviously, Texxon knew that the new facility

Exhibit 2: Kile Texxon

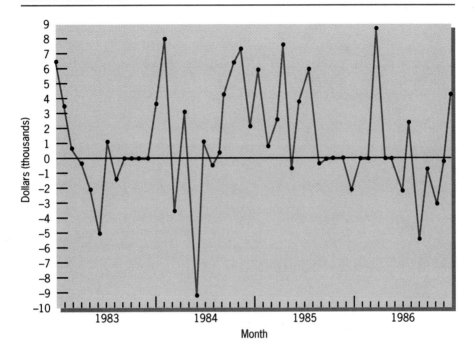

would be in direct competition with MD–73. However, it was Texxon's stated position that it would be "up to the market" to determine which location would survive. Kile was to be on his own in this struggle.

Consulting Report

In the summer of 1985, Texxon commissioned a study of MPSI Americas, Inc., a well-regarded Tulsa retail consulting firm, to examine the implication of an upgrade of MD–73. The proposed tactic would be to add a canopy and a 600-square-foot mini convenience store and to upgrade the pumps and other equipment. The MPSI computer model showed that this tactic would increase MD–73's gallonage by 29,000 gallons per month but would cut into the gallonage at the new Texxon express station by 2,500 gallons per month. The improvements would cost on the order of $160,000 to $175,000. Earlier, in November 1984, an MPSI study examining the consequences of closing MD–73 had estimated that Texxon would keep only 22,500 gallons of MD–73's then 137,664 monthly gallonage and would lose the rest to competitors up and down the street (Exhibit 3).

After three years of competition between the two

stations, and after Kile's volume had fallen to an all-time low of 35,000 gallons in February 1986, Texxon made the decision to abandon MD–73 and not to renew the franchise relationship with Kile at the expiration of the current agreement ending in November 1986. Kile, however, was not advised of this abandonment decision at that time.

With full knowledge that the franchise relationship would not be renewed, and possibly with an intent to circumvent Kile's potential purchase rights under the Petroleum Marketing Practices Act (PMPA),[3] Texxon began to document a case that would justify

---

[3]The act states that if a determination is made by the franchiser "in good faith and in the normal course of business . . . to convert the leased premises to a use other than the sale or distribution of motor fuel . . . or to sell the premises . . . or to materially alter or replace the premises . . . or if the renewal is likely to be uneconomical, the franchiser must first make a bona fide offer to sell, transfer or assign to the franchisee such franchiser's interests in such premises, or offer the franchisee the right of first refusal" 15 U.S.C. 2801, Section 102 D.

Exhibit 3: MPSI Study of the Impact of Closing MD–73

| Outlet Number | Brand Name | Tactic Results | | | Total |
		Tactic Increase	Tactic Decrease	Base Volume	
1	Amoco	3401		220,958	224,359
2	Merit	2472		133,368	135,840
3	Texxon	3411		171,898	175,309
4	Mobil	7438		138,247	145,685
5	BP	6177		187,552	193,729
6	Gulf	3542		124,004	127,546
7	Exxon	3081		105,760	108,841
8	Texxon	3407		118,468	121,875
9	Texaco	2177		70,071	72,248
10	Shell	2721		48,604	51,325
11	Mobil	3210		49,171	52,381
12	Gulf	5279		63,459	68,738
13	MD–73		137,664	137,664	0
14	New Express Station	12209		158,596	170,805
15	Exxon	3997		48,146	52,143
16	Sunoco	4492		53,931	58,423
17	Crown	17415		226,585	244,000
18	Texxon	3502		42,223	45,725
19	Amoco	5598		94,949	100,547
20	Shell	2584		210,661	213,245
21	BP	2422		152,217	154,639

the termination of Kile's franchise prior to abandonment. Whether or not it was Texxon's intention to circumvent Kile's purchase rights under PMPA, the fact remains that it was clearly not in Texxon's interest to have the MD–73 site remain a gas station after taking down the Texxon sign. Accordingly, on July 30, 1986, Texxon advised Kile that his franchise relationship was terminated and would not be renewed at the expiration of his lease on November 11, 1986. The grounds for termination involved such alleged infractions as failure to remain open for the full number of hours specified in the agreement; failure by Kile to operate the premises in a clean, safe, and healthful manner; and finally, failure by Kile to exert good faith efforts to carry out the provisions of the franchise by virtue of his high-price, low-volume policy.

In October 1986 Kile contracted for the sale of the business at MD–73. As part of this proposed sale, Kile was to assign the lease agreement for MD–73 to the prospective purchaser. However, Texxon refused to consent to the proposed sale, transfer, and assignment on the ground that Kile had already been notified of Texxon's proposed termination. On January 15, 1987, Kile relinquished possession of MD–73, and the station has been boarded up ever since.

CASE

6-2 DAVE MACDONALD'S ETHICAL DILEMMAS*

The following situations are real events experienced by the case writer. Only the names have been changed.

Halco Manufacturing

Dave MacDonald was excited when he got the unexpected phone call from Nicki Steele, a senior buyer from Halco Manufacturing.

"I know it's a year since we bought that prototype reel from you, but we just got a contract from the government to build 10 more 'bear traps' and we desperately need to hold our price on these units. Could you possibly sell us 10 new reels at the same price you charged last year?" Nicki inquired.

"I'll see what I can do and call you back today," Dave replied.

Dave immediately retrieved the file from the previous year and saw that they had supplied the reel for $6,990.00 F.O.B. the customer's warehouse. There was a breakdown of the pricing on the file:

Manufacturer's list price	$4,000.00
Special engineering charge (25%)	1,000.00
Total list price	5,000.00
Distributor discount (20%)	1,000.00
Distributor net cost	4,000.00
Estimated currency exchange (8%)	320.00
Estimated duty (22½%)	972.00

*This case was prepared by H. F. MacKenzie of Memorial University of Newfoundland, St. John's, Canada. The case was prepared as a basis for class discussion and is not intended to illustrate effective or ineffective handling of a management situation. All names in the case have been disguised. Copyright © 1994 by H. F. MacKenzie, Memorial University of Newfoundland, Faculty of Business Administration, St. John's, Newfoundland A1B 3X5. Reproduced by permission.

Estimated freight	245.00
Estimated brokerage	55.00
Estimated distributor cost, F.O.B. destination	5,592.00
Markup (25%)	1,398.00
Selling price, F.O.B. destination	$6,990.00

There were some notes on the file that Dave reviewed. The reel was designed as part of a "bear trap" on Canadian navy ships. These bear traps would hook onto helicopters in rough weather and haul them safely onto landing pads on the ship decks. The reel was really a model SM heavy-duty steel mill reel, except that some of the exposed parts were to be made of stainless steel to provide longer life in the saltwater atmosphere. There was a special engineering charge on the reel, as it was a nonstandard item that had to be specially engineered. The manufacturer had suggested at the time they quoted that Dave could keep the full 20 percent discount, as they thought there was only one other manufacturer capable of building this unit, and their price would likely be much higher.

When Dave got a price from the manufacturer on the 10 new units, he was surprised that they quoted a price of only $3,200.00 each, less 40/10 percent. When he asked that the price be verified, the order desk clarified the pricing. First, there had been a 20 percent reduction in all SM series reels. That made the manufacturer's list price only $3,200.00. Then, because there was a large quantity, the distributor discount was increased to less 40/10 percent instead of the 20 percent that was given on the original reel.

As Dave estimated his cost, things got better. The original reel was imported from the United States at 22½ percent duty as "not otherwise provided for manufacturers of iron or steel, tariff item 44603-1." In the interim, the company Dave worked for had gotten a duty remission on series SM steel mill reels as "machinery of a class or kind not manufactured in Canada, tariff item 42700-1," and the duty was remitted (and the savings supposedly passed on to the end customer). The currency exchange rate also improved in Dave's favor, and the estimated freight and brokerage charges per unit dropped considerably because of the increased shipment size. Dave estimated his new cost as follows:

Manufacturer's list price	$3,200.00
Distributor discount (40/10%)	1,472.00
Distributor net cost	1,728.00
Estimated currency exchange (2%)	35.00
Estimated duty (remitted)	0.00
Estimated freight	85.00
Estimated brokerage	14.50
Estimated distributor cost, F.O.B. destination	1,862.50

Now that he had all the figures, Dave had to decide what the selling price should be to his customer.

Crown Pulp and Paper Ltd.

Bill Siddall had been promoted to the position of salesperson, and he was pleased when he received an order for nearly $10,000 for stainless steel fittings from the new pulp mill being built in his territory. Unfortunately, he quoted a price that was 40 percent below his cost.

"We have to honor the price quoted," Bill insisted.

"I know if you let me talk to Rory, he'll let us raise the price," replied Dave MacDonald, the Sales Manager. "Rory used to be the purchasing agent at one of my best accounts before he came to the mill."

"No. You gave me responsibility for this account, and I want to build a good relationship with Rory myself. He gave us the order over two weeks ago. He can't change suppliers now because he needs the material next week, and I don't want to put him on the spot now because it would be unfair. Since this is our first order, I would like to supply it without any problems. We'll get back the money we lost on this order many times if we can get their future business. This material is needed for a small construction job, and they haven't even started to consider their stores inventory yet."

After much discussion, it was agreed that the order would stand, but Dave would call the fitting manufacturer's Sales Manager, Chuck Knowles, as the two men were good friends.

"We need some help on that last order we placed with you. Bill sold it at 40 percent below our cost," said Dave.

"How could that happen?" Chuck seemed amazed.

"Well," replied Dave, "you give us a 25 percent distributor discount, and we gave 10 percent to the customer due to the size of the order. What we forgot was to double the list price because the customer wanted schedule 80 wall thickness on the fittings instead of standard schedule 40. This was Bill's first large inquiry, and he made an honest mistake. He doesn't want me to get involved with the customer, and I don't want to force the issue with him, so I'm hoping you can help us on this one order. We expect to get a lot of business from this account over the next few years."

"I'll split the difference with you. What you're selling now for $0.90, you're paying $1.50 for, and if I give you an additional 20 percent discount, your cost will come down to $1.20. Can you live with that?" Chuck asked.

"It's a help. We appreciate it. We'll see you on your next trip to our territory, and I'll buy lunch."

"A deal. See you next month." The conversation ended.

When it was over, Dave was feeling reasonably satisfied with himself, but he still felt somewhat uneasy. He promised not to call Rory, and he promised not to interfere with the account, but he still thought something could be done.

On Saturday morning, Dave went to the Brae Shore Golf Club. He was confident that Rory would be there. Sure enough, at 8:00 A.M., Rory was scheduled to tee off. Dave sat on the bench at the first tee and waited for Rory to appear. Promptly, Rory arrived with Bob Arnold, one of his senior buyers. The three men greeted each other pleasantly, and Rory asked who Dave was waiting for.

"Just one of my neighbors. He was supposed to be here an hour ago, but I guess he won't show."

"Join us. We don't mind. Besides, we might need a donation this fall when we have our company golf tournament. We'll invite you, of course, and we'll invite Bill if he plays golf."

"He doesn't play often, but he's pretty good. Beat

me the last time we played. How is he doing at your mill? Is everything okay?" Dave asked.

"Checking up on him? Sure. He's fine. He made a mistake the other day when he went to see our mill-wright foreman without clearing it through my office first, but he'll learn. He'll do a lot of business with us because we want to buy locally where possible, and you have a lot of good product lines. I think he'll get along well with all of us as well. He seems a bit serious, but we'll break him in before long. We just gave him a big order for stainless fittings a few weeks ago, but we told him to visit at ten o'clock next time and to bring the doughnuts."

"I know," replied Dave. "Unfortunately, we lost a lot of money on that order."

"Your price was very low. I couldn't understand it because I knew your material wasn't manufactured off-shore. Did you quote the cheaper T304 grade of stainless instead of the T316 we use?"

"No. We quoted schedule 40 prices instead of schedule 80. The wall thickness for schedule 80 is twice as thick, and the price should have been double as well."

"Heck. Double the price. We'll pay it. I'll make a note on the file Monday. I know you're not trying to take us, and I can appreciate an honest mistake. At double the price, you might be a bit high, but you know we want to place the order with you anyway because you're local. Eventually we'll want you to carry some inventory for us, so we might just as well make sure we're both happy with this business."

Strait Structural Steel Ltd.

Dave MacDonald was sitting in the outer office waiting to see Stan Hope, the purchasing agent for Strait Structural Steel, a new account that had just begun operations in a remote coastal location about 40 miles from the nearest city. Stan had telephoned Dave the previous week and had an urgent request for four large exhaust fans that were required to exhaust welding fumes from enclosed spaces where welders were at work. The union had threatened to stop the project unless working conditions were improved quickly, and although Dave didn't sell fans at the time, he found a line of fans and negotiated a discount from the manufacturer, along with an agreement to discuss the further possibility of representing the fan manufacturer on a national basis.

When Stan gave the order to Dave for the fans, the two men discussed other products that Dave sold. Dave sold products for a company that was both a general-line and specialty-line industrial distributor. Included in the general-line products were such items as hand and power tools, cutting tools (drills, taps, dies), safety equipment, wire rope and slings, fasteners (nuts, bolts), and fittings (stainless steel, bronze, and carbon steel flanges, elbows, tees). Included in the specialty-line products were such items as electric motors and generators, motor controls, hydraulic and pneumatic valves and cylinders, rubber dock fenders, and overhead cranes. When the men finally met, they were almost instantly friends, and it was obvious that the opportunities for them to do further business were great. "One item that really interests me," said Stan, "is PTFE tape. We need some, and we will be using a lot of it."

"We have the largest stock of PTFE tape in the country," replied Dave. "We import it directly from Italy, but it's high quality and is the same standard size as all others on the market; ½ inch wide, .003 inch thick, and 480 inches long. How much are you interested in?"

"Let's start with 400 rolls," Stan suggested.

PTFE tape was a white, nonadhesive tape that was used as a pipe thread sealant. It was wrapped around the threads of pipe or fittings before they were screwed together to make a leakproof seal. The tape first came on the market in the late 1960s at prices as high as $3.60 per roll, but since then prices had dropped considerably. North American manufacturers were still selling the tape for list prices near $1.80 and were offering dealer discounts of between 25 and 50 percent, depending on the quantities that dealers bought. Dave was importing the tape from Italy at a landed cost of $0.17 per roll.

"We have a standard price of $1.00 per roll as long as you buy 200 rolls," Dave offered.

"No question. You have an excellent price. How much would you charge M H Sales?"

"I don't know. Who is M H Sales?" asked Dave.

"A small industrial supply company located in my basement. The 'H' is for Hope. I share the company with Bruce Malcolm, the 'M,' and he's in purchasing at Central Power Corporation. M H Sales is a small company, and we are looking for additional products to sell. Between Strait Structural and Central Power, we could sell several thousand rolls of PTFE tape each year."

McCormick Gleason Limited

Dave MacDonald telephoned Clarey Stanley, a Senior Buyer at McCormick Gleason Limited. "Clarey, I'm calling about that quote we made on Lufkin tapes. Can we have your order?"

"Sorry. Your price was high. I gave the order to Ken Stafford. You need a sharper pencil."

"How much sharper?" Dave asked.

"I can't tell you that. But you were close," Clarey replied. "By the way, Kenny called me from the stores department this morning, and he has a large shipment of electric relays that was delivered yesterday. They weren't properly marked, and he can't identify the ones with normally open contacts from the ones with normally closed contacts. Do you want them returned, or can someone see him and straighten it out here?"

"Tell him I'll see him immediately after lunch. I can tell them apart, and I'll see they get properly identified."

When the conversation ended, Dave made a note to see Clarey about the tapes. There was a problem somewhere. Dave knew his cost on Lufkin tapes was the lowest available, and he quoted 12 percent on cost because he really wanted the order. The order was less than $1,500, but it meant that Dave could place a multiple-case order on the manufacturer and get the lowest possible cost for all replacement inventory. That would increase the margin on sales to other customers who bought smaller quantities. There was no possibility that Stafford Industrial, a local, one-person, "out-of-the-basement" operation that bought Lufkin tapes as a jobber, not as a distributor, could match his price.

That afternoon, while waiting to see Ken MacKay, the Stores Manager, Dave noticed a carton from Stafford Industrial Sales being unloaded from a local delivery van. Although he knew that Stafford supplied quite a few maintenance, repair, and operating (MRO) supplies to this customer, Dave decided to play ignorant.

"What do you buy from Stafford Industrial?" he asked the young stores clerk who was handling the package.

Opening the carton, the clerk read the packing slip. "It says here we ordered 144 measuring tapes, ¾ inches wide by 25 feet long."

"Are those things expensive?" Dave asked.

"Don't know. There's no price on the packing slip. Clarey Stanley in purchasing ordered them. You could talk to him." The clerk continued to unpack the shipment. As he did, Dave noticed that the tapes were manufactured offshore and were poor in quality compared to the Lufkin tapes that he sold and that he quoted to Clarey Stanley the previous day.

"Aren't those supposed to be Lufkin tapes?" Dave asked.

"Not that I know. The packing slip just says tapes. Wait, and I'll haul our copy of the purchase order." The clerk went to a filing cabinet next to his desk and returned with a carbon copy of the purchase order. "No, it just says tapes. It doesn't specify any brand."

There was something wrong, and Dave was determined to get an answer.

7

Estimating Potentials and Forecasting Sales

*The pace of events is moving so fast that unless
we can find some way to keep our sights on tomorrow,
we cannot expect to be in touch with today.*
DEAN RUSK

LEARNING OBJECTIVES

After studying this chapter, you should be able to:

▶ Estimate market potentials.

▶ Seasonally adjust sales data.

▶ Understand judgmental forecasting.

▶ Calculate naive, moving average, and exponential smoothing forecasts.

► WHAT IS MARKET POTENTIAL?

One of the keys to sales management success is knowing where customers are located and being able to predict how much they will buy. Data on potentials are vital for designing sales programs, preparing budgets, and serving as benchmarks for the evaluation of sales force performance.

Market potential is an estimate of maximum demand in a time period based on the number of potential users and the purchase rate. Actual industry sales are usually less than market potential, as shown in Figure 7-1. For instance, the U.S. market potential for compact disc players could be defined as the total number of households based on typical purchases of one unit per family. Actual sales are less than potential because it takes time to convince people to buy expensive items like disc players and because some can't afford them. The industry purchase rate is a function of price levels, promotional expenditures, and the number of stores stocking the machines.

Company *sales potential* is a portion of total industry demand. It is the maximum amount a firm can sell in a time period under optimum conditions. As Figure 7-1 suggests, company sales will generally be lower than industry sales. The ratio of company sales to industry sales is a measure of the market share of the organization.

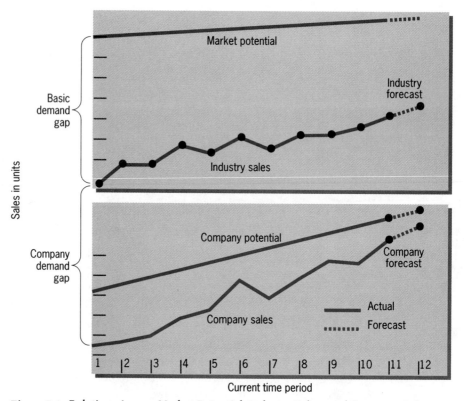

Figure 7-1: Relations Among Market Potential, Industry Sales, and Company Sales

In your position as sales manager, you will be asked to estimate current values for market and company potential for products assigned to your care. This can be tricky because the number of users and the purchase rate change over time. Also, price declines, industry promotions, and changing economic conditions can influence the size of the market. Besides measuring current levels of demand, you will be required to forecast into the future. These predictions are shown as the dashed lines for period 12 in Figure 7-1. Our discussion begins with demand measurement and shifts later in the chapter to the issue of forecasting.

Estimating Potentials

All estimates of potential are based on two key components; namely, the number of possible users of the product and the maximum expected purchase rate. Sometimes you can get estimates of these numbers from trade associations or commercial research associations. However, you have to come up with your own potential figures broken down by geographical area, industry, and customer type.

The easiest way of estimating the number of buyers is to use secondary sources. There are a wide variety of commercial data available that provide the potential number of buyers, size of firms, age of consumers, income levels, and locations. Dun's Marketing Services and *Sales & Marketing Management* magazine sell these data on diskettes for use with personal computers. You can also access potential data banks through computer networks on a fee basis. Large firms often have their own data banks that can be mined for potential information.

Purchase rates are usually derived from trade organizations or government publications. For existing products, you can use the ratio of current sales to the number of households or sales per person. These ratios can be obtained from trade publications like those from the Conference Board or calculated from published data. For example, average demand per household could be derived by dividing total industry sales for an area by the number of households. In the case of new products, managers may estimate conversion rates from experience with other items. If a similar product was sold to 4 percent of U.S. households the first year, then this rate could be applied to obtain demand estimates for new merchandise.

Buying Power Index Method

Market potentials for consumer goods are usually estimated by constructing indexes from basic economic data. Perhaps the most popular multifactor index of area demand is the *Buying Power Index* (BPI) published in August of each year by *Sales & Marketing Management* magazine. This index combines estimates of population, income, and retail sales to give a composite indicator of consumer demand in specific states, metropolitan areas, counties, and cities in the United States.

Data used to calculate the Buying Power Index for the Sacramento, California, area are summarized in Table 7-1. The figures show that Sacramento Metro area has 0.576 percent of the U.S. income, 0.554 percent of retail sales, and 0.565 percent of the U.S. population. These three numbers are weighted to give a Buying Power Index for Sacramento Metro of 0.567.

Thus, an area with only 0.565 percent of the U.S. population has 0.576 percent of

Table 7-1   Data Used to Calculate Buying Power Index

	1995 *Effective Buying Income*		1994 *Total Retail Sales*		1995 *Estimated Total Population*		Buying Power Index
	Amount ($000,000)	**Percentage of United States**	**Amount ($000,000)**	**Percentage of United States**	**Amount (000,000)**	**Percentage of United States**	
Total United States	$4,436,178	100.0%	$2,241,319	100.0%	262,313	100.0%	100.0
Sacramento Metro	25,572	.5764%	12,414	.5538%	1,482	.5653%	.5674

Source: "1995 Survey of Buying Power," *Sales & Marketing Management* (August 24, 1995), pp. B-2, B-3, B-4, C-13, C-19. Copyright © 1995 by *Sales & Marketing Management.* Reproduced by permission.

the national income. When retail sales for an area are less than the income and population bases, as in this example, there is strong evidence that people are spending money in surrounding counties. This suggests that managers must spread their promotional dollars over a fairly wide area if they expect to reach all the customers who live in the Sacramento Metro area.

Buying Power Index values are used to help managers allocate selling efforts across geographic regions. That is, the Buying Power Index suggests that Sacramento Metro, with 0.567 percent of the U.S. sales potential, should receive about 0.567 percent of the personal selling and advertising budgets for products in national distribution.

SIC Method for Business Markets

Business market potential can be built up from data made available through the U.S. *Census of Manufacturers.* The Census of Manufacturers is available every five years, so you may want to use updated figures from *Sales & Marketing Management's* annual *Survey of Industrial and Commercial Buying Power.* Both sources combine businesses into *Standard Industrial Classifications* (SICs) according to products produced or operations performed.

The first step in estimating potentials from census data is to identify all the SIC codes that make use of the product or service. This is usually accomplished by looking

Table 7-2   Estimating the Market Potential for Food Machinery in North Carolina

SIC Code	Industry	(1) Production Employees[a] (1000)	(2) Number of Machines Used per 1000 Workers[b]	Market Potential (1 × 2)
204	Grain milling	2.3	8	18.4
205	Bakery products	11.9	10	119.0
208	Beverages	1.9	2	3.8
				141.2

[a]From 1992 *Census of Manufacturers,* Geographical Area Series, North Carolina, p. NC 11.
[b]Estimated by the manufacturer from past sales data.

for industries that are likely customers, using judgment to pick likely codes from the SIC manual and running surveys of different types of firms to see where products are employed. Next, the firm must select an appropriate database for estimating the amount of the product that will be used by each SIC code. A food machinery manufacturer, for example, could review past sales data to determine the relationship between the number of its machines in use and the number of production workers in a particular industry. If the manufacturer found that 8 machines were used for every 1,000 grain milling employees, 10 for every 1,000 bakery workers, and 2 for every 1,000 beverage workers, then the market potential for North Carolina could be determined as shown in Table 7-2. Because grain milling (SIC No. 204) has 2,300 workers and 8 machines are used per 1,000 workers, the market potential would be 2.3 × 8, or 18.4 machines. Similar calculations for other codes yield a total market potential of about 141 machines for the state of North Carolina. The potential built up for North Carolina would then be added to estimates derived for other states to give national figures. These figures can be converted into annual measures of market potential by adjusting for the average life of the machines. If the machines last an average of 10 years, then 10 percent of the North Carolina potential of 141 units, or 14 machines, would be replaced each year. Estimates of company potential would be derived by multiplying annual demand potential by the firm's current market share.

▶ SUBJECTIVE SALES FORECASTING

Sales forecasting is concerned with predicting future levels of demand. These projections are vital for budgeting and planning purposes. For new products, there are a few simple routines that can be employed. The absence of past sales means that you have to be more creative in coming up with predictions of the future. Sales forecasts for new products are often based on executive judgments, sales force projections, surveys, and market tests. We will begin our discussion of forecasting techniques by focusing on subjective methods that are based on interpretations of business conditions by executives and salespeople.

Sales Force Composite

A favorite forecasting technique for new and existing products is the *sales force composite* method. With this procedure, salespeople project volume for customers in their own territory, and the estimates are aggregated and reviewed at higher management levels. Sales force composite forecasting was the most popular method used by 45 percent of the firms in a U.S. survey (Table 7-3). This technique is a favorite with industrial concerns because they have a limited number of customers and salespeople are in a good position to assess customers' needs. This technique was recently adopted by a medical products subsidiary of American Home Products.[1] Previously the sales forecast came down from headquarters and now the forecast is built up from estimates prepared by 120 field reps. When salespeople provide input they buy into the forecast and are more likely to achieve their sales quotas. The net result at the medical products firm has been improved sales forecast accuracy.

Table 7-3   Utilization of Sales Forecasting Methods by 134 Firms

Type	Method	Percentage of Firms That Used Regularly	Percentage of Firms That No Longer Used
SUBJECTIVE	Sales force composite	44.8	13.4
	Jury of executive opinion	37.3	8.2
	Intention to buy survey	16.4	18.7
	Industry survey	14.9	17.9
EXTRAPOLATION	Naive	30.6	9.0
	Moving average	20.9	15.7
	Percent rate of change	19.4	14.2
	Leading indicators	18.7	11.2
	Unit rate of change	15.7	18.7
	Exponential smoothing	11.2	19.4
	Line extension	6.0	20.9
QUANTITATIVE	Multiple regression	12.7	20.9
	Econometric models	11.9	19.4
	Simple regression	6.0	20.1
	Box-Jenkins	3.7	26.9

Source: Douglas J. Dalrymple, "Sales Forecasting Practices: Results from a United States Survey," *International Journal of Forecasting,* 3 (1987), p. 382.

Jury of Executive Opinion

This technique involves soliciting the judgment of a group of experienced managers to give sales estimates for proposed and current products. The *jury of executive opinion* was used by 37 percent of the firms described in Table 7-3. The main advantages of this method are that it is fast and it allows the inclusion of many subjective factors such as competition, economic climate, weather, and union activity. United Parcel Service forecasts are prepared by a group of senior executives using economic indicators such as the Consumer Price Index, historical sales data, and other trends.[2] These forecasts are then compared with predictions developed by salespeople and the differences are reconciled.

The continued popularity of jury of executive opinion shows that most managers prefer their own judgment to other less well-known mechanical forecasting procedures. However, available evidence does not suggest that the jury of executive opinion method leads to more accurate forecasting. Perhaps the main problem with the method is that it is based on experience, and it is difficult to teach someone how to forecast using this method.

Leading Indicators

Where sales are influenced by basic changes in the economy, *leading indicators* can be a useful guide in the preparation of sales forecasts. For example, 19 percent of the firms in Table 7-3 regularly use leading indicators in sales forecasting. The idea is to find a general time series that is closely related to company sales, yet is available several months in advance. Changes in the series can then be used to predict sales directly, or the series can be combined with other variables in a forecasting model. For example, General Electric has found that sales of dishwashers are closely related to the number of housing starts that occurred several months earlier. Obviously, the key issue is finding indicators that have forecasting value for particular products. Some of the more useful leading indicators include prices of 500 common stocks, new orders for durable goods, new building permits, contracts and orders for plant and equipment, and changes in consumer installment debt.

Because leading indicators do not give direct sales forecasts, they are often used to provide background material for subjective forecasting methods such as jury of executive opinion and sales force composite. Perhaps the greatest contribution of leading indicators is their ability to predict turns in a series. Most of the mechanical forecasting techniques that we will discuss do a very poor job of telling managers when a series is going to change direction. Leading indicators are sensitive to changes in the business environment, and they often signal turns in the economy months before they actually occur.

▶ OBJECTIVE SALES FORECASTING

We now shift our focus from opinion-based methods to objective techniques. These procedures are based on manipulations of historical data. Objective methods are more number oriented than those using the subjective approach.

Seasonal Adjustments

Before we talk about data-based forecasting techniques, you need to understand how seasonal factors influence predictions of the future. Sales forecasts are often prepared monthly or quarterly, and seasonal factors are frequently responsible for many of the short-run changes in volume. Thus, what may appear to be a good forecast may turn out to be a poor one because of a failure to consider seasonal factors. When historical sales figures are used in forecasting, the accuracy of predictions can often be improved by making adjustments to eliminate seasonal effects.

The first step in making *seasonal forecast adjustments* to a time series is to collect past sales figures for several years. Next, sales for months or quarters are averaged across years to build a seasonal index. In Table 7-4, four years of quarterly sales are averaged to give a rough indication of seasonal effects.[3] The quarterly averages are then divided by mean sales for all quarters to give seasonal index numbers. For example, when average sales of 58.0 for quarter 1 are divided by the mean for all quarters of 79.25, a seasonal index of 0.73 is obtained. This number says that seasonal factors typically lower first-quarter sales by 27 percent. Computers used in sales forecasting take these indexes and make forecasts for future periods.

Some students assume that because seasonal adjustments complicate the fore-

Table 7-4 Calculating a Seasonal Index from Historical Sales Data

Quarter	Year 1	Year 2	Year 3	Year 4	Four-Year Quarterly Average	Seasonal Index
1	49	57	53	73	58.0	0.73[a]
2	77	98	85	100	90.0	1.13
3	90	89	92	98	92.3	1.16
4	79	62	88	78	76.8	0.97

Four-year sales of 1268/16 = 79.25 average quarterly sales

[a]Seasonal index is 58.0/79.25 = 0.73.

casting process, they are not worth the time and effort required. However, there are two truths about seasonal adjustments that you should remember:

1. Seasonal adjustments are widely used in business.
2. Seasonal adjustments reduce forecasting errors.

Naive Forecasts

Time series forecasts rely on past data to provide a base for making projections about the future. The *naive forecast* is the simplest forecasting technique and is often used as a standard for comparison with other procedures. Thirty percent of the firms in Table 7-3 regularly use naive forecasts. This method assumes that nothing is going to change and that the best estimate for the future is the current level of sales. For example, actual sales of 49 units observed in quarter 1 in Table 7-4 can be used to predict sales in quarter 2. Naive forecasts for the last three quarters of year 1 would be

	Quarter 1	Quarter 2	Quarter 3	Quarter 4
Actual sales	49	77	90	79
Naive forecast		49	77	90

The error in the naive forecast for quarter 2 is the difference between 49 and 77. A formula for the *percentage forecasting error* is

$$\text{Percentage forecasting error} = \frac{\text{forecast} - \text{actual}}{\text{actual}}$$

This means the percentage error for the naive forecast in quarter 2 is

$$\text{Percentage error} = \frac{49 - 77}{77}$$

$$\text{Percentage error} = 36\%$$

If the data were seasonally adjusted, the forecasting error for quarter 2 would be only 1.3 percent. This example shows seasonal adjustments can lower forecasting errors.

MAPE

When you want to compare forecasting accuracy across several time periods, the *mean absolute percentage error* (MAPE) can be used. MAPE is the average percentage forecast error and is a popular way to measure accuracy. This technique looks at the average error without regard to whether the errors are positive or negative.

Trend Projections

The use of *trends* to project sales is a popular technique among business firms. With this method, the analyst estimates trends from past data and adds this figure to current sales to obtain a forecast. For example, in Figure 7-2 sales increased from 10 units in period 2 to 20 units in period 3, suggesting a trend of 10 units per period. A *unit rate of change* forecast for period 4 would combine current sales of 20 plus 10 units of trend for a total of 30. Trends can also be expressed as a *percentage rate of change*. With this method the 10 units of trend would be divided by the base of 10 units of sales to give a 100 percent growth rate. A 100 percent growth rate applied to current sales of 20 units would give a forecast of 40 units for period 4. Note that the percentage rate of change method and the unit rate of change procedure give different sales forecasts. When sales are increasing, forecasts prepared with the percentage rate of change approach will normally be higher than those obtained by other projective techniques. Research reported in Table 7-3 shows that the percentage rate of change

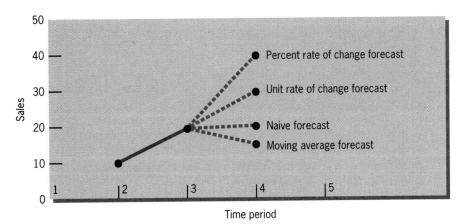

Figure 7-2: Comparing Trend Forecasting Methods

method is the most popular projective forecasting technique, followed by the unit rate of change.

Moving Averages

With the *moving average* method, the average revenue achieved in several recent periods is used as a prediction of sales in the next period. The formula takes the form

$$F_{t+1} = \frac{S_t + S_{t-1} + \cdots + S_{t-n+1}}{n}$$

where

F_{t+1} = *forecast for the next period*
S_t = *sales in the current period*
n = *number of periods in the moving average*

This approach assumes that the future will be an average of past achievements. For example, if sales in the last two periods went from 10 to 20, then a two-period moving average forecast would be 15 (Figure 7-2). Thus, when there is a strong trend in a time series, a moving average forecast always lags behind. However, this lag can be an advantage when sales change direction (suddenly increase or decrease). If actual sales decline to 17 units in period 4, as shown in Figure 7-2, then the moving average forecast will be more accurate than the trend projection methods.

Students must remember that a moving average really does move. For example, sales data from Table 7-4 can be used to make two-period moving average forecasts as follows:

	Quarter			
	---	---	---	---
	1	2	3	4
Actual sales	49	77	90	79
Two-period moving average			63	83.5

Thus periods 1 and 2 are averaged to give a forecast of 63 for period 3. Then period 1 is dropped and periods 2 and 3 are averaged to produce a forecast of 83.5 for period 4.

A crucial issue in using moving averages is determining the ideal number of periods (*n*) to include in the average. With a large number of periods, forecasts tend to react slowly, whereas a low value of *n* leads to predictions that respond more quickly to changes in a series. The optimum number of periods can be estimated by trial and error or with computer programs.

A characteristic of moving averages that distracts from their ability to follow trends is that all time periods are weighted equally. This means that information from the oldest and newest periods is treated the same way in making up a forecast. A popular technique that overcomes this problem is exponential smoothing.

Exponential Smoothing

An important feature of *exponential smoothing* is its ability to emphasize recent information and systematically discount old information. A simple exponentially smoothed forecast can be derived using the formula

$$\overline{S}_t = \alpha S_t + (1 - \alpha)\overline{S}_{t-1}$$

where

$\overline{S}_t$ = *smoothed sales for period t and the forecast for period t + 1*
α = *the smoothing constant*
S_t = *actual sales in period t*
$\overline{S}_{t-1}$ = *smoothed forecast for period t − 1*

The formula combines a portion (α) of current sales with a discounted value of the smoothed average calculated for the previous period to give a forecast for the next period.

An example using data from Table 7-4 is shown below with a smoothing constant of .4.

	Quarter			
	1	**2**	**3**	**4**
Actual sales	49	77	90	79
Smoothed forecast			60.2	72.1

The forecast for period 3 is obtained by taking .4 times the current sales in period 2 of 77 plus .6 times 49 which is the estimate of smoothed sales for the prior period [(.4 × 77) + (.6 × 49) = 60.2]. A forecast for period 4 would be obtained by multiplying .4 times the period 3 sales of 90 plus .6 times the smoothed forecast for period 3 [(.4 × 90) + (.6 × 60.2) = 72.1].

The major decision with exponential forecasting is selecting an appropriate value for the *smoothing constant* (α). Smoothing factors can range in value from 0 to 1, with low values providing stability and high values allowing a more rapid response to sales changes. Using a smoothing constant of 1.0 gives the same forecasts that are obtained with the naive method. Forecasts produced with a low smoothing constant, such as 0.2, lag behind, and forecasts generated with high values, such as 0.8, will likely overestimate sales at turning points. When historical data are available, the analyst can select a smoothing constant by trying out different α values to see which one forecasts best. When managers want to incorporate other variables in their forecasting, regression techniques have advantages.

Linear Regression

In *simple linear regression*, the relationship between sales (Y) and some independent variable (X) can be represented by a straight line. The equation of this line is Y = a

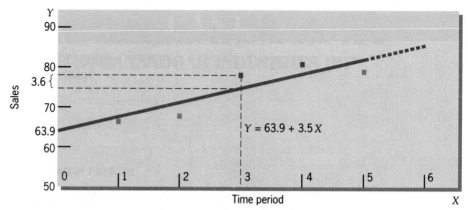

Figure 7-3: Fitting a Trend Regression to Seasonally Adjusted Sales Data

+ bX, where a is the intercept and b shows the impact of the independent variable. The key step in deriving linear regression equations is finding values for the coefficients (a, b) that give the line that best fits the data. The best fit can be obtained by employing a *least-squares procedure*, as illustrated in Figure 7-3, where sales (Y) have been plotted against time (X). The equation, Y = 63.9 + 3.5X, indicates that sales are 63.9 plus a trend of 3.5 for every unit of time. Two variable regression equations can be easily calculated using some pocket calculators or desk and laptop computers using Excel or other programs. A sample of some commercial programs available for sales forecasting are shown in Sales Management Tools 7-1.

A limitation of simple regression forecasting is the assumption that sales follow a linear pattern. Although this may hold for some series, others have cyclical patterns that are hard to track with linear equations. In this case, the analyst can base the forecasting equation on the logarithms of the time series data to produce improved forecasting equations.

Another problem is knowing how much past data to include in the calculation of the forecast. Usually all past data points are used to provide greater stability. Sometimes shorter regressions will do a better job of tracking changes.

The simple regression equations that have been described use time as the independent variable, which is common in sales forecasting. Other variables, such as income or the rate at which products are sold for junk, could be used if they are found to be closely related to sales. When sales seem to be associated with several independent variables, multiple regression procedures can be used to build a forecasting model.

Multiple Regression

With *multiple regression*, a computer is used to build forecasting models based on historical relationships between sales and several independent variables. Sales managers first have to find an appropriate set of independent factors that are related to the series being predicted. Some of the best variables for multiple regression equations are leading indicators such as housing starts, new orders for durable goods, and contracts for plant and capital equipment. These variables have the advantage that current values can be plugged into multiple regression equations to predict the future. A problem with multiple regression is that you need a lot of historical data to ensure that your model will forecast accurately. Generally, five observations are needed for every independent variable in the equation. Thus an equation with 3 predictor variables would need 15 observations. Frequently, 15 observations are not available for sales series and other methods must be selected. Despite the complexities of multiple regression forecasting, this technique was the most popular of the quantitative methods reported in Table 7-3 and was used regularly by 13 percent of the firms. A real data set that you can use to build a multiple regression forecasting equation is included with problem 6 (Table 7-5) near the end of this chapter.

Turning Points

The numerical forecasting methods we have discussed make projections from historical data, and almost all of them do a poor job of predicting turning points in a time series. Percentage rate of change, unit rate of change, and two-variable regression are all notoriously poor predictors of series that change direction. Naive, moving average, and exponential smoothing are somewhat better, as they tend to lag and then adapt to new information. If the identification of turning points is important to you, then the use of subjective procedures is often the best approach. These methods can pick up environmental cues that signal turning points frequently missed by numerical methods. Sometimes leading indicators can be included in multiple regression equations to help predict turning points.

▶ SELECTING FORECASTING PROGRAMS

Although some firms prefer judgmental methods, most sales forecasting today is done with computers. Thus a key task is finding a program that works for the time series you need to predict. Features you should look for include an ability to plot data, seasonally adjust data, and measure percentage forecasting errors. Also look for a program that includes naive, moving average, exponential smoothing, simple regression, and multiple regression procedures. An ideal program would also find optimal lengths for moving averages and optimal exponential smoothing constants based on an analysis of past data. The four forecasting programs described in Sales Management Tools 7-1 are only a small sample of the many commercial programs available.

Accuracy is one of the most important criteria in your selection of forecasting programs. Management expects you to find methods that perform for the types of products under your control. Research has shown that simple procedures such as naive, moving average, and exponential smoothing often have lower forecasting errors than other, more complex methods.[4] This suggests you should start with the basic procedures and move to more sophisticated models only when they are needed.

Sales Management Tools 7-1
Commercial Forecasting Programs

Vendor	Package	Description	Price
Applied Decision Systems	SIBYL	Eighteen distinct time series forecasting techniques.	$495
Delphus, Inc.	The Spreadsheet Forecaster	Curve fitting, seasonal decomposition, exponential smoothing, regression for monthly and quarterly data.	$79
Delphus, Inc.	Autocast II	Built-in expert forecasting system tests seasonality, outliers, trends, patterns, and automatically selects best forecasting model from nine alternatives.	$349
SmartSoftware, Inc.	SmartForecasts II	Expert system graphics and data analysis; projects sales, demand, costs, revenues; time series analysis, multivariate regression.	$495

Source: *Sales & Marketing Management* (December 1994), p. 66.

Since no one forecasting technique is best for all situations, some analysts employ several methods and then take the average of these projections as their final forecasts. Research shows that predictions based on averages of several procedures have lower errors than single-technique forecasts. However, this approach forces you to balance possible improvements in accuracy against the greater costs and complexity associated with preparing multiple forecasts.

Remember you must select techniques that can be sold to management. If managers cannot understand how forecasts are prepared, they are apt to reject the techniques in favor of their own judgmental forecasting methods.

▶ SUMMARY

An important part of your job as sales manager is to prepare estimates of current market potential and to make forecasts for the future. Estimates of potential are based on projections of the number of users and the expected purchase rate. Geographical measures of potential can be obtained by using the Buying Power Index and SIC code procedures. Sales forecasts are key inputs for business planning, and you must know how they are prepared. Forecasts of the future may be extensions of historical data or, in the case of new products, based on judgment. Examples of subjective forecasting methods include sales forecast composite, jury of executive opinion, customer surveys, and leading indicators. When you are working with historical data, you can often improve the accuracy of your forecasts by seasonally adjusting your data.

A variety of numerical sales forecasting techniques are available, and you need to understand how they work and where they should be employed. Detailed explanations have been presented for naive, moving average, exponential smoothing, and regression procedures. Your choice among these and other methods is a function of the length of the forecast, pattern of the data, cost, accuracy, and ease of understanding. Possibly the ideal forecasting procedure combines a numerical analysis of past data with your own interpretation of current developments.

► KEY TERMS

Buying Power Index (BPI)	Percentage rate of change
Exponential smoothing	Sales force composite
Jury of executive opinion	Sales forecasting
Leading indicator	Sales potential
Least-squares procedure	Seasonal forecast adjustments
Market potential	Simple linear regression
Mean absolute percentage error (MAPE)	Smoothing constant
Moving average	Standard Industrial Classification (SIC)
Multiple regression	Trend
Naive forecast	Unit rate of change
Percentage forecasting error	

► REVIEW QUESTIONS

1. What is the difference between sales potential and a sales forecast?

2. How do sales managers use the Buying Power Index?

3. Why is the jury of executive opinion method of forecasting so popular?

4. Where is the sales force composite method of forecasting used most often?

5. Why do managers often make seasonal adjustments when they prepare sales forecasts?

6. Explain why simple forecasting techniques such as the naive method often outperform more sophisticated techniques.

7. Why do the percentage rate of change and unit rate of change methods give different forecasts?

8. What causes the moving average method to be so accurate when a series changes direction?

9. What does the manager have to decide when using the exponential smoothing technique?

10. Describe the primary advantages of forecasting with trend regressions.

► **PROBLEMS**

1. Why do marketing managers need projections of market potential? How are they obtained?

2. Secure a copy of the computer FORECAST program from your instructor. Using the FORE-CAST program and the following data, forecast sales for periods 4 through 7, using naive, trend projections, moving average, and simple exponential smoothing. Compare MAPEs across methods for time periods 4 to 7. What length of moving average and smoothing constant works best? What are your forecasts for periods 8 and 9?

Period	1	2	3	4	5	6	7	8	9
Sales	15	18	16	20	22	19	25	?	?

3. Quarterly sales (thousands of dollars) for the Chester Furniture Company for the past four years have been as follows:

Quarter	Year				
	1	2	3	4	5
1	230	240	264	328	?
2	245	266	290	344	?
3	193	259	221	275	?
4	174	218	202	281	?

Using the FORECAST program, calculate seasonal indexes and adjust the data. Run seasonally adjusted naive, moving average, exponential smoothing, and linear regression forecasts through the data to see which method has the lowest MAPE. Select the best method and forecast sales for quarters 1 through 4 in year 5.

4. Sales (in thousands of dollars) for the Busy Bee Bakery for the past 15 time periods have been:

Period	Sales	Period	Sales	Period	Sales
1	2005	6	2360	11	3442
2	2150	7	2354	12	2948
3	1940	8	2682	13	3020
4	1770	9	2504	14	3079
5	2285	10	2329	15	3275

Using the FORECAST program, prepare sales forecasts for periods 6 through 15 using the naive, projection, moving average, exponential smoothing, and regression techniques. What length of moving average and smoothing constant work best? What method does the best job of tracking the data over periods 6 through 15? What is your forecast for periods 16 through 24?

5. The first optical scanner was installed in a supermarket in the United States in the second quarter of 1974. The number of optical scanners installed in each quarter through the

third quarter of 1979 is given. Estimate the number of scanners that were installed in the fourth quarter of 1979.

Year	Quarter			
	1	2	3	4
1974	0	1	3	1
1975	3	4	7	12
1976	10	15	17	19
1977	27	25	31	23
1978	47	67	95	137
1979	173	196	235	?

6. You are the sales manager for a manufacturer, and you have been asked to forecast company sales for the next six months. You have collected data on company sales and other variables for the last 38 semiannual time periods (Table 7-5). In addition, you have estimates for period 39 for most of your variables. You also have access to a FORECAST program that has multiple regression. Enter the data in Table 7-5. Calculate a correlation matrix and explain what it tells you about your variables. Create an equation to predict sales using all or a subset of your variables. Explain why you have included each variable and discuss the power of your equation. Forecast sales for period 39 using your multiple regression model.

► REFERENCES

1. WILLIAM KEENAN, "Numbers Racket," *Sales & Marketing Management* (May 1995), p. 66.

2. WILLIAM KEENAN, "Numbers Racket," *Sales & Marketing Management* (May 1995), p. 70.

3. The seasonal indexes derived in Table 7-4 are easy to explain, but most computer programs use a more sophisticated procedure known as the ratio to moving average method. See SPYROS MAKRIDAKIS, STEVEN C. WHEELWRIGHT, and VICTOR E. McGEE, *Forecasting: Methods and Applications*, 2nd ed. (New York: Wiley, 1983), pp. 137–141.

4. SPYROS MAKRIDAKIS, A. ANDERSEN, R. CARBONE, R. FILDES, M. HIBON, R. LEWANDOWSKI, J. NEWTON, E. PARZEN, and R. WINKLER, "The Accuracy of Extrapolation (Time Series) Methods: Results of a Forecasting Competition," *Journal of Forecasting*, 1 (April–June 1982), pp. 111–153, and Steven P. Schnaars, "Situational Factors Affecting Forecasting Accuracy," *Journal of Marketing Research*, 21 (August 1984), pp. 290–297.

► SELECTED READINGS

ARMSTRONG, J. SCOTT, *Long Range Forecasting*, 2nd ed. (New York: Wiley, 1985).

MAKRIDAKIS, SPYROS G., *Forecasting, Planning, and Strategy for the 21st Century*, (New York: Free Press, 1990).

OWEN, DUANE B., *Business Fluctuations and Forecasting* (Homewood, Ill.: Irwin, 1991).

WHEELWRIGHT, STEVEN C., and SPYROS MAKRIDAKIS, *Forecasting Methods for Management*, 5th ed. (New York: Wiley, 1989).

Table 7-5 Company Sales and Other Variables (Semiannual)

Period	Company Sales (thousands of dollars)	Personal Disposable Income (millions of dollars)	Dealer's Allowances (thousands of dollars)	Price (dollars)	Product Development Budget (thousands of dollars)	Capital Investments (thousands of dollars)	Advertising (thousands of dollars)	Sales Expenses (thousands of dollars)	Total Industry Advertising Budget (thousands of dollars)
1	5540.39	398	138	56.2058	12.1124	49.895	76.8621	228.80	98.205
2	5439.04	369	118	59.0443	9.3304	16.595	88.8056	177.45	224.953
3	4290.00	268	129	56.7236	28.7481	89.182	51.2972	166.40	263.032
4	5502.34	484	111	57.8627	12.8916	106.738	39.6473	258.05	320.928
5	4871.77	394	146	59.1178	13.3815	142.552	51.6517	209.30	406.989
6	4708.08	332	140	60.1113	11.0859	61.287	20.5476	180.05	246.996
7	4627.81	336	136	59.8398	24.9579	−30.385	40.1534	213.20	328.436
8	4110.24	383	104	60.0523	20.8096	−44.586	31.6456	200.85	298.456
9	4122.69	285	105	63.1415	8.4853	−28.373	12.4570	176.15	218.110
10	4842.25	277	135	62.3026	10.7301	75.723	68.3076	174.85	410.467
11	5740.65	456	128	64.9220	21.8473	144.030	52.4536	252.85	93.006
12	5094.10	355	131	64.8577	23.5062	112.904	76.6778	208.00	307.226
13	5383.20	364	120	63.5919	13.8940	128.347	96.0677	195.00	106.792
14	4888.17	320	147	65.6145	14.8659	10.097	47.9795	154.05	304.921
15	4033.13	311	143	67.0228	22.4940	−24.760	27.2319	180.70	59.612
16	4941.96	362	145	66.9049	23.3698	116.748	72.6681	219.70	238.986
17	5312.80	408	131	66.1843	13.0354	120.406	62.3129	234.65	141.074
18	5139.87	433	124	67.8651	8.0330	121.823	24.7122	258.05	290.832
19	4397.36	359	106	68.8892	27.0486	71.055	73.9126	196.30	413.636
20	5149.47	476	138	71.4177	18.2208	4.186	63.2737	278.85	206.454
21	5150.83	415	148	69.2775	7.7422	46.935	28.6762	207.35	79.566
22	4989.02	420	136	69.7334	10.1361	7.621	91.3635	213.20	428.982
23	5926.86	536	111	73.1628	27.3709	127.509	74.0169	296.40	273.072
24	4703.88	432	152	73.3650	15.5281	−49.574	16.1628	245.05	309.422
25	5365.59	436	123	73.0500	32.4918	100.098	42.9984	275.60	280.139
26	4630.09	415	119	74.9102	19.7127	−40.185	41.1346	211.25	314.548
27	5711.86	462	112	73.2007	14.8358	68.153	92.5180	282.75	212.058
28	5095.48	429	125	74.1615	11.3694	87.963	83.2870	217.75	118.065
29	6124.37	517	142	74.2838	26.7510	27.088	74.8921	306.80	344.553
30	4787.34	328	123	77.1409	19.6038	59.343	87.5103	210.60	140.872
31	5035.62	418	135	78.5910	34.6881	141.969	74.4712	269.75	82.855
32	5288.01	515	120	77.0938	23.2020	126.420	21.2711	328.25	398.425
33	4647.01	412	149	78.2313	35.7396	29.558	26.4941	258.05	124.027
34	5315.63	455	126	77.9296	21.5891	18.007	94.6311	232.70	117.911
35	6180.06	554	138	81.0394	19.5692	42.352	92.5448	323.70	161.250
36	4800.97	441	120	79.8485	15.5037	−21.558	50.0480	267.15	405.088
37	5512.13	417	120	80.6394	34.9238	148.450	83.1803	257.40	110.740
38	5272.21	461	132	82.2843	26.5496	−17.584	91.2214	266.50	170.392
39	?	485	125	81.6257	20.0000	40.000	85.0000	275.00	180.000

Source: Steven C. Wheelwright and Spyros Makridakis, *Forecasting Methods for Management*, 4th ed. (New York: Wiley, 1985), pp. 181–182.

CASE

7-1 PARKER COMPUTER*

Two engineers, Bill Parks and Anne Smith, founded Parker Computer in 1980. The company specialized in the manufacture of high-end personal computers and low-priced workstations for product design and other business applications. Bill was chairman of the board, and Anne was director of research and development. For the first 10 years of its life, Parker enjoyed steady growth in sales and profits. Parker's success was based on providing customers with superior computer performance at prices slightly above average. However, in 1993, aggressive price cutting by large competitors began to erode sales growth. Parker's revenue peaked in 1994 at $75 million.

Solving Parker's Problems

Although customers were willing to pay for high-quality computers in the 1980s, this strategy did not attract many buyers in the cost-conscious 1990s. Bill Parks realized that the company had to do a better job of both marketing and cost reduction. The company currently employed a small sales force but relied primarily on a network of local dealers to sell its computers to the business market. Bill knew that the company needed a stronger customer focus, so he hired a CEO with a marketing background. As a result, the company started to pay more attention to marketing activities and began to prepare detailed marketing plans for each product line. Jane Austin, a recent business graduate, was hired as a marketing assistant to help with the planning.

Part of Jane's responsibility was to estimate sales for the PC220 and PC440 computers for the next year. In the past, these forecasts had been developed using judgmental procedures. Jane knew that the CEO expected a more thorough analysis of sales trends for the 1996 marketing plan. When she was in school, Jane had acquired a copy of a computerized forecasting package from one of her professors. This seemed to be a good time to make use of the FORECAST program.

*This case was prepared by Douglas J. Dalrymple of Indiana University.

Computerized Forecasting

First, Jane copied the large FORECAST program onto the hard drive of her desktop computer. This made it easier for the computer to access the program and to store data files. Then she typed in FORECAST and hit the *enter* key. The title page of the program came up first, followed by a screen showing a basic spreadsheet. Down the left side of the screen were numbers from 1 to 200 designating individual observations. The spreadsheet was set up to hold 20 columns of data across the screen. The cursor appeared on the heading space above the first data column. Jane typed in "PC220" to identify sales of the high-end personal computer she planned to forecast. After she hit the *enter* key, the cursor moved down to the first data entry space. She then entered the quarterly sales figures for PC220 (Exhibit 1) in the first 12 spaces. Sales for 1993 were entered as observations 1 through 4, sales for 1994 were entered as observations 5 through 8, and sales for 1995 were entered as observations 9 through 12. After checking the numbers to be sure that they were correct, Jane hit the F10 key to access the options menu at the top of the screen. She moved the cursor to "file" and touched *enter* to get a small data access menu. Then she moved the cursor to "Save As" and hit the *enter* key to save the PC220 file on the hard drive for later use. Next, Jane used the F10 key to access the top menu and moved the cursor to the "Graphing" option to see the sales of PC220. She then printed out a plot of the sales data for inclusion in her marketing plan.

Forecasting Options

Jane was now ready to forecast, and she moved the cursor to the "Techniques" option in the top menu and hit the *enter* key. This brought up a window menu of nine separate forecasting methods to choose from. The first was the naive technique based on sales achieved in the previous period. If this procedure was chosen, Jane would have to decide whether to adjust the quarterly data seasonally or try any of three trend

Exhibit 1: Quarterly Sales for the PC220 and PC440

	1993		1994		1995	
Quarter	PC220	PC440	PC220	PC440	PC220	PC440
1	1950	770	3150	545	2924	350
2	2920	620	2600	450	3380	420
3	2560	623	3002	400	2554	310
4	3330	830	4250	639	2800	775

adjustments. The second method used a unit rate of change procedure and could also be seasonally and trend adjusted. Jane would have to specify whether these forecasts were based on the most recent change in sales or on an average of unit changes in recent time periods. A third procedure focused on percentage rates of change and offered similar options. A fourth method employed a simple linear regression against time. This procedure developed a forecasting equation and could be seasonally adjusted. A fifth moving regression approach developed a series of forecasting equations of a specified length. For example, a five-period regression equation based on data from periods 1–5 could be used to forecast period 6; then another equation based on periods 2–6 could be used to forecast period 7; and so on. With this technique, Jane would have to specify the length of the moving regression that she planned to use for forecasting.

Method 6 was a moving average procedure. This technique allowed both seasonal and trend adjustments. In addition, the program asked Jane to select the length of each moving average or to have the optimum value calculated automatically. A variation of the moving average known as *exponential smoothing* was the seventh technique in the package. Exponential smoothing is a weighted moving average that requires Jane to select a smoothing constant ranging from 0 to 1 for each time series. These smoothing constants (or α values) could also be calculated by the program to minimize forecasting errors. Method 8, called *Holts exponential smoothing*, used an α value to smooth the basic data and a second β value to smooth trend. To use this method, Jane would have to estimate α and β values from 0 to 1 for both of her time series. The FORECAST program also had a multiple regression procedure, but this was not appropriate for Jane's current forecasting problem.

Projecting Sales for the PC220

Jane decided to start her analysis with the naive technique. She moved the cursor to this procedure and touched the *enter* key. The program then asked her to indicate the range of data points to be used in making the forecasts. After hitting the *enter* key, Jane moved the cursor to the first data observation in row 1. Then she pushed *enter* and moved the cursor to the last data point in row 12 and hit *enter* again. The program then asked for the range of points to be forecasted. Since Jane planned to use simple regression as one of her techniques, she knew she had to allow five data points for the calculation of the regression equations. This meant that the first data point to be forecasted would be period 6 and the last would be period 16. Forecasts for periods 13 through 16 would be her projections for 1996. To accomplish this, she pressed *enter*, moved the cursor to observation 6, and pressed *enter* again. Then she moved the cursor to observation 16 and hit *enter*.

Next, the program asked Jane if she wanted to adjust her data and forecasts seasonally. This seemed to be a good idea, and she moved the cursor to the number two option for quarterly data and pressed the *enter* key. The program then asked if she wanted to trend-adjust the naive forecasts using three different methods. Jane decided to skip this step for now. When she hit the *enter* key again, a table of quarterly index numbers appeared on the screen. A print option came up next, and Jane moved the cursor to the "Yes" box to make a copy of the index numbers for inclusion in her marketing plan. Next, the program brought up seasonally adjusted sales forecasts for periods 6 through 16. Forecast errors were shown for periods 6 through 12 and averaged as a single MAPE value at the bottom of the screen. Next, Jane printed out the PC220 forecasts by moving the cursor to the "Yes" box on the print option menu.

After the results had been printed, the program returned to a new "Change Parameter" menu. This allowed Jane to change forecasting techniques, seasonal adjustments, trend adjustments, length of regressions, length of moving averages, or the size of smoothing constants. Once Jane had adjusted the parameters for a new forecast, she moved the cursor to option seven, "Run Forecast," and hit the *enter* key. Jane decided to try all the methods and options available in the FORECAST program to find the best procedures to forecast sales for the PC220 and PC440 for 1996. Just by looking at a plot of the data, it was not obvious whether seasonal and trend adjustments would improve the quality of her projections. Jane's goal was to find the procedures that gave the lowest

forecasting errors when predicting old sales data. Once she had finished with the PC220, she planned to enter data for the PC440 in the second column of her FORECAST spreadsheet.

One issue that Jane was concerned about was whether to report one set of quarterly forecasts for 1996 for each computer line or to average the forecasts of the best two or three methods. Although FORECAST allowed Jane to try many different techniques, it did not tell her which forecasts to include in her report. Also, the wide variety of options available in the program meant that she would have to spend several hours grinding out the numbers. On the other hand, Jane realized that if she attempted to make the forecasts using a pocket calculator, she would be spending several days on the project.

CASE

7-2 MEAD PRODUCTS*

"You know, this just might be the most fantastic product we've ever launched. I think it's really going to shake up the school supplies market!" The man who spoke was Bryant Crutchfield, Mead Products' New Ventures manager.

Crutchfield had just concluded a meeting in Wichita, Kansas, with Bob Crandall, the regional sales manager, where the two men had reviewed the results of a market test. The purpose of the test was to measure market acceptance of Trapper Portfolio and the Trapper Keeper Notebook.

As he prepared to depart Wichita Airport for Dayton, Ohio, Crutchfield felt good about the success of the test. A new unique product unlike anything else on the market—and a total sell-through in test market.

But Crutchfield also thought about plans for 1981 and the big question yet to be resolved. "How many can we sell nationally?"

*This case was prepared by Peter S. Carusone of Wright State University. Copyrighted by Peter S. Carusone.

Mead Corporation

Mead's traditional base is in forest products. From a strong base in pulp, paper, and paperboard, Mead has developed a family of related businesses. Lumber operations complement those in pulp. Other divisions convert paper and paperboard into packaging, containers, school supplies, and many more industrial and consumer products; some specialize in their distribution.

Still other Mead businesses provide additional growth opportunities and balance—engineered castings, molded rubber parts, distribution of piping and electrical supplies, and advanced digital systems for managing and reproducing vast amounts of information. See Exhibit 1 for a list of the Mead divisions and affiliates.

Innovation at Mead in the 1970s focused on areas beyond but closely related to its traditional businesses. Advanced and sophisticated product developments emerged from expertise and knowledge in printing technology, pollutant management, information handling, and digital technology.

Exhibit 1: Mead Divisions and Affiliates

Divisions
    Mead Paper—Chillicothe (OH)
    Mead Fine Paper
    Mead Publishing Paper
    Gilbert Paper
    Specialty Paper
    Mead Paperboard
    Mead Paperboard Products
    Mead Containers
    Mead Packaging
    Mead Pulp Sales, Inc.

Affiliates (50 percent owned)
    Georgia Kraft Company
    Brunswick Pulp & Paper Company
    Northwood Forest Industries Limited
    Schoeller Technical Papers, Inc.
    Mead Products
    Mead Merchants
    Gulf Consolidated Services
    Lynchburg Foundry
    Mulga Coal Company
    Murray Rubber
    Mead Data Central
    Mead Digital Systems
    Mead CompuChem
    Mead Office Services
    Mead Reinsurance

Mead Data Central's LEXIS and NEXIS are the world's most sophisticated services for text research of case law and news materials. Information is channeled into the system from the courts, Congress, news media, and other sources, and flows on demand to thousands of subscriber terminals in the professions, business, government, and education.

Ink-jet printing, which involved the parallel development of hardware and software by Mead Digital Systems, is a new technology that promises to revolutionize the printing industry in many fields. The process results from generating and directing millions of minute drops of ink—precisely and at high speed—to form words, numerals, and images. Ink-jet printing makes it possible to simultaneously compose and imprint personalized materials three times faster than any conventional method.

Mead's CompuChem special chemical analysis service has opened the nation's largest automated laboratory devoted exclusively to the analysis of priority pollutants. Client companies in the petroleum, coal, pulp, paper, rubber, and other industries ship samples to the SuperLab where materials that the Environmental Protection Agency has ruled as potentially hazardous are identified and measured (in parts per trillion).

The Mead Corporation's development philosophy was summarized in the company's 1980 Annual Report:

> Mead's underlying strategic principle is to devote its investment resources to market segments that are growing, that need products and services we are prepared to deliver, and that offer us the opportunity to build or retain a position of cost-effective leadership.

In 1980 Mead sales hit a record $2.7 billion, a 69 percent increase from 1976. The firm employs 25,000 men and women. Its world headquarters is located in Dayton, Ohio.

Mead Products

A division of Mead Corporation, Mead Products (formerly Westab) is the largest U.S. manufacturer and marketer of school and college supplies, stationery, photo albums, and home/office supplies. Westab was founded in 1927 (as the Western Tablet and Stationery Corporation) and merged with Mead Corporation in 1966.

Since its inception, Mead Products has developed and marketed numerous items that stand as all-time best-sellers in the retail school supply and stationery markets. Perhaps it is most famous for its line of Spiral brand wire-bound school supplies that uses a unique method of wire-binding large quantities of tablet paper, and revolutionized the design and production of notebooks, theme books, and memo pads.

The Organizer, a tri-fold pockets and pad binder introduced in 1972, was the industry's best-selling school supply item for three consecutive years. Other exclusive Mead Products' introductions include The System (in 1973), The Spiral Organizer (in 1974), the Data Center (in 1975), and The Pinchless One (in 1976). These also have been best-sellers.

Other well-known Mead Products include The Big Chief writing tablet, a best-seller for over seven generations; The Valet tablet and envelope stationery line, which started a revolution in the 59 cents-per-item market; Academie brand artists pads, books, water colors, and crayons; and Montag, famous name in quality boxed stationery.

The company traditionally has been a trendsetter in the industry. In 1966, for example, Mead Products was the first to replace the drab, blue canvas coverings on loose-leaf binders with various fabrics in fashionable colors and designs. More recently, through innovative manufacturing techniques, "photo-graphics" have been applied to the covers of numerous school supply items.

Another industry first was Mead Products' decision 12 years ago to advertise on national network television. During the season the commercials are running (late August, early September), Mead Products becomes one of the largest TV advertisers in the country—of any product.

Today, Mead Products, with its own sales force, markets over 3,000 separate items. National distribution is obtained through wholesalers, distributors, and jobbers, as well as direct to chain discount, drug, variety, food and convenience stores, and depart-

Exhibit 2: Mead Facilities Locations

Headquarters
Mead Products
Mead World Headquarters
Courthouse Plaza, Northeast
Dayton, Ohio 45463

Plants
Garden Grove, California
Atlanta, Georgia
Kalamazoo, Michigan
St. Joseph, Missouri
Salem, Oregon
Alexandria, Pennsylvania
Garland, Texas

Sales Offices/Showrooms
Garden Grove, California
San Jose, California
Atlanta, Georgia
Des Plaines (Chicago), Illinois
Braintree, Massachusetts
Kalamazoo, Michigan
Shawnee Mission (Kansas City), Kansas
Union City, New Jersey
Salem, Oregon
Dallas, Texas

ment and college stores. The company operates seven plants and 12 sales offices/showrooms in 10 states. See Exhibit 2 for facility locations.

How the Trapper and the Trapper Keeper Originated

The idea for The Trapper and The Trapper Keeper was identified by extensive informal exploration of the school supplies market and its total environment. "Management requires us to do a complete situation analysis," Crutchfield points out. "We have to understand what's happening in the marketplace."

A situation analysis at Mead Products entails extensive study of everything that happens from production of products, through the channels of distribution, to their consumption. It includes analysis of educational trends, consumer trends, sales trends, product usage, competition, the trade, and pertinent external factors.

Consumer Definition

People of all ages involved in the learning process are the consumers of school supplies. The range is from the preschooler just learning how to hold a crayon up to and including the adult taking refresher courses to update professional skills.

Consumer Population

The total student population was projected to continue to increase over the next five years but at a lesser rate than in the past. While the number of grade, junior, and senior high school students was declining slightly, the decline would be more than offset by increases in two other consumer segments: (1) preschool kids who in just a few years will become primary customers and (2) college enrollment and adult basic and occupational education. See Exhibit 3 for consumer population/enrollment trends.

Product Usage

Consumer product usage in the growth market segments (except for preschoolers) was basically the same as that of students in grade and high school: wirebounds, filler, binders, and portfolios. Increasing in popularity were portfolios, wirebound notebooks, and selected binders. These select binders were those having pads and pockets that provide for versatile storage of a variety of materials. The demand for filler paper and ring notebooks was relatively flat. See Exhibit 3 for product usage by consumer group and consumer expenditures by product category.

Exhibit 3: Consumer Population/Enrollment Trends

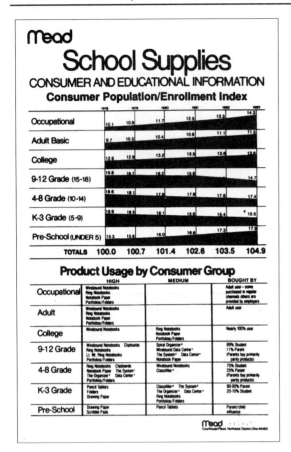

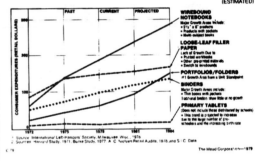

Educational Trends

Important educational trends were identified, along with implications for future demand of various kinds of school supplies. It was learned, for example, that students were taking more courses, more advanced courses, and more individualized instruction. Also uncovered were increased use of timely, specialized portable materials, more use of shared classrooms, and smaller lockers. The impact of the energy shortage and the emergence of a market for left-handed students were also assessed. See Exhibit 3 for detailed analysis of educational trends.

Trade Analysis

As changes in education were affecting the need for and usage of school supplies, so changes in retail shopping patterns were affecting the opportunities for effective distribution of school supply products.

Competition

The school supplies market was very fragmented. Competition was mostly regional owing to the high cost of freight. Only one or two companies other than Mead Products were selling nationally. Mead was the leader nationally, but this varied by product line and by region.

A Need Unfulfilled

The outcome of the situation analysis led Crutchfield to formulate the following thesis: *There is a need for a notebook to hold and organize the portfolios.*

"We saw that students were taking more courses—some of these a variety of 'mini' courses. We saw an increase in the use of pocket portfolios—growth in excess of 20 percent annually. We knew from research that they were using one portfolio per subject or class. With the increased number of classes and portfolios, a student needs some place to keep them organized. What's more," Crutchfield points out, "tra-ditional ports with horizontal pockets have a tendency to spill their contents when mistakenly turned upside down. So, the Trapper Portfolio and the Trapper Keeper notebook would provide the student with both better portfolios and a place to keep them organized." Exhibit 4 shows a picture of the two products.

The best-selling portfolio on the West Coast

Exhibit 4: Trapper Portfolio and Trapper Keeper Notebook

(Pee-Chee) has a vertical pocket—but it had never been popular east of the Rockies. It is interesting to note that part of the rationale for the item occurred to Crutchfield as the result of a conversation at home with his 13-year-old daughter. In retrospect, he describes the experience as one of "creative listening." In asking his daughter about the usage of portfolios in her classes, Crutchfield thought he heard her relate how the teacher required the students to submit their assignments in portfolios as a time-saving device. The teacher wanted to use the ports both for collecting assignments and for redistributing them, along with handouts, so that students could pick up their own portfolios and save class time. When Crutchfield dispatched a Mead researcher to talk with the teacher, he discovered that the teacher never said that. And when the 13-year-old daughter was questioned further, it was found that she never said that either. But the results of the research were positive. The teacher thought the "nonexistent procedure" was a good one.

Testing the Trapper Keeper

"We saw this to be a fantastic concept," Crutchfield recalls. "A portfolio with vertical pockets so that everything is trapped inside when they're closed and a Trapper Keeper to keep Trapper ports organized." Other features added to the inside pockets included a metric ruler, an English ruler, multiplication tables, metric conversion charts, and more. The portfolio (the Trapper) was punched to fit on rings inside a special portfolio notebook (the Trapper Keeper) designed to hold the Trapper ports. The Trapper Keeper was designed, in turn, with nylon pinchless rings, three Trapper ports, a pocket for holding loose materials, and a clip that holds a pad for notes and a place for the pencil. After school or class everything can be snapped together for transporting home—nothing falls out.

Teacher Research

The next step in the development of the Trapper and Trapper Keeper was to determine if the basic product concept had merit. Before making any product, illustrations of the concept were drawn and used to conduct a focus group session with teachers. Was there truly a need for this product? Would teachers recommend it?

Basically, the results were: teachers said that student organization was their biggest problem, and that they would recommend this or any product that helped students improve their organization.

Market Test

To get some measure of student reaction, a test market was set up in Wichita, Kansas. The primary objectives of the test were to determine

1. Product salability.
2. Rate of sale compared to The Organizer, the Data Center, and The System, plus comparable competitive products.

Pricing of the Trapper Keeper was pegged at the same level as the Data Center and The Organizer, ranging from a low of $1.99 (on a weekend sale) to a high of $3.99—the most frequent price being $2.49. The Trapper ranged from four for 98 cents to 29 cents each—the most frequent price being 29 cents.

The total market was monitored from a sell-in and a sell-through standpoint. Fifteen representative stores were audited: seven discount, three variety, three drug, and two food. The product was advertised on TV at 180 gross rating points (GRPs), which is equivalent to everyone seeing the commercial 1.8 times. A photoscript of the commercial is presented as Exhibit 5.

The market test results, in audited stores, were as follows:

1. For every 100 Trapper Keeper notebooks purchased by the consumer, 77 Trapper portfolios, 90 Data Center, 65 The Organizer, and 39 The System notebooks were sold.
2. Trapper portfolios totally sold out in over 90 percent of the stores, so the top potential was not known.
3. There was very little cannibalization of The Organizer, Data Center, or The System notebooks. These items sold at approximately the same level this year as last, in some cases, they were totally sold out.
4. Total unit sales of all items increased 38.5 percent in the monitored stores.

Consumer Post-Test Research

Consumer cards were placed in all the test market products offering a free memo book for filling out and

Exhibit 5: Photoscript of Trapper Commercial

Teacher Research

Teachers exposed to the product concept in a focus group session concluded the idea was good—it helps solve one of their greatest problems — students organization. The teachers said they would recommend students use Trapper Keeper notebooks or any school product that helps them organize their school work.

Market Test

The products were tested for salability and rate of sale compared to The Organizer, Data Center, and comparable competitive products. Trapper Keeper outsold them all in monitored stores. For every 100 Trapper Keepers, 90 Data Centers, 65 Organizers, and 39 The Systems were sold. Best of all, total unit sales (all items) increased 38.5% in the monitored stores. This means plus business for you as new users were created.

Post Use Research

A sample of Trapper Keeper notebook purchasers/users were interviewed via phone after 2½ months of product use.
- 96% rated the Trapper Keeper notebook excellent or good.
- 88% said the Trapper Keeper notebook was better than previous product used.
- 84% intended to repurchase the Trapper Keeper notebook.
- Trapper Keeper notebook users tended to be older.

Introduced to educators in early 1979

Educators will be introduced to Trapper portfolios and Trapper Keeper notebooks through contacts at the Board of Education level and through teachers' magazines.

Presold on Network TV in August

The following commercial will be shown on network TV in August. Approximately 250 GRP's, which is equivalent to everyone seeing the following ad 2.5 times.

TWO HIGH SCHOOL BOYS AT THEIR LOCKERS, TAKING OUT THEIR TEXT BOOKS FOR THE NEXT CLASS. ONE BOY HAS ONLY A TRAPPER PORTFOLIO THE OTHER HAS A THICK NOTEBOOK BRIMMING WITH LOOSE PAPERS. (BELL RINGS)

1ST BOY: That's all you're taking to class?

2ND BOY: Everything I need is in my Trapper Portfolio.

1ST BOY: Trapper?

HE OPENS THE TRAPPER, SLIDES PAPERS IN AND OUT TO DEMONSTRATE

2ND BOY: It traps in all my papers. The pocket is built this way . . . so . . .

HE CLOSES THE TRAPPER . . . THEN SHAKES IT UP AND DOWN DEMONSTRATING HOW THE PAPERS CAN'T FALL OUT

2ND BOY: . . . close the Trapper and the papers are trapped in. One Trapper for each class.

1ST BOY: Where do you keep um?

CUT TO THE TRAPPER KEEPER

2ND BOY: In the Trapper Keeper.

2ND BOY: . . . which also has a note pad and pencil clip.

HE CLOSES THE TRAPPER KEEPER NOTEBOOK AND SNAPS IT SHUT

2ND BOY: After school snap everything in my Trapper Keeper and take it home. What could be neater.

GIRL APPROACHES

1ST BOY: (GESTURING TOWARD THE GIRL) a date with her.

CUT TO PRODUCT SHOT

SUPER: TRAPPER TRAPPER KEEPER MEAD

VO ANNCR: The Trapper and Trapper Keeper only from Mead.

2ND BOY INTRODUCES GIRL TO 1ST BOY. THE COVER OF 1ST BOY'S BINDER FLOPS OPEN SPILLING THE PAPERS

2ND BOY: Hi

MEAD SUPER APPEARS

Exhibit 6: Selected Comments from Consumer Cards

- "Because it's new, slender, and the way it's put together."
- "One reason, it had separate folders, but mainly because of the colors."
- "My mother got it by mistake but I'd seen it on TV, so decided to keep it."
- "Because I like things neat, and things are easy to find. Thanks."
- "Our teacher made us buy one—but I have been very pleased with it."[a]
- "I heard it was good. My girlfriend had one."
- "If you trip all your papers won't go flying all over the place."
- "Because they keep your papers where they belong. They're really great—everybody has got one."
- "I saw ad on TV."
- "Instead of taking the whole thing you can take only one part home."
- "So when the kids in my class throw it, the papers won't fly all over."
- "It was the only one left in the store."

[a]Several cards with comments like this were received and traced back to a ninth grade teacher (Mrs. Willard) in Wellington, Kansas. Mrs. Willard agreed to endorse the Trapper Keeper; and her comments were used in an ad campaign to other teachers. See ad in Exhibit 7.

returning a questionnaire card. Over 1,500 cards were returned. Some of the results were:

- 62 percent of the purchasers were female.
- 35 percent were between the ages of 9 and 12; 44 percent between 13 and 15; 10 percent between 16 and 18.
- 81 percent of the portfolio users preferred the Trapper pocket design over traditional horizontal pockets.
- Only 56 percent of the purchasers had used portfolios prior to finding the Trapper.

Exhibit 6 contains some of the comments of purchasers as to *why* they purchased Trapper Keeper rather than other type binders.

Six weeks after the test market, a number of purchasers were interviewed and asked to evaluate the products. The key results of this research were as follows:

General reaction:

95 percent	—believe Trapper Keeper to be excellent or good
88 percent	—rate Trapper Keeper better than product used previously

Trapper Keeper features most liked:

89 percent	—ports inside, paper won't fall out, and one portfolio for each subject

84 percent	—intended to repurchase the Trapper Keeper

Trapper features most liked:

47 percent	—vertical pocket/papers won't fall out
21 percent	—helpful information (metric conversion, etc.)

National Plans

It was decided to introduce the Trapper Keeper nationally for school opening 1981. The introduction was to be backed by a national, prime-time, network television campaign of 230 to 250 GRPs—approximately 20 spots.

Products were to be presented to teachers and boards of education during the spring for approval and recommendations at school opening in August/September. Teachers' magazines and personal calls were planned to reach the teachers and administrators. Teachers were offered a sample Trapper Keeper at a special price to cover handling and postage. A copy of the "Mrs. Willard Testimonial" advertisement to teachers is reproduced in Exhibit 7.

The Trapper portfolio had a suggested retail price of 29 cents each. Three colors—red, blue, and green—were packaged per assortment. The Trapper Keeper had a suggested retail of $4.85 each. These

Exhibit 7: Sample Print Ad

Why did Mrs. Willard in Wellington, Kansas advise her students to purchase a Mead Trapper Keeper Notebook? For the same reasons you will.

"As a 9th grade teacher, I'm always on the lookout for products that will help my students do a better job in school. Last year, I found the Trapper™ portfolio and Trapper Keeper™ notebook from Mead and recommended them to my class.

Mead developed the products because today's students are taking more courses than ever. They average over seven courses per student. They can't carry seven notebooks, so they are switching to portfolios.

Mead has designed a new portfolio called the Trapper. It

traps in all the student's papers so they won't fall out. Mead has also developed a notebook to carry all these portfolios, called the Trapper Keeper.

Most students keep the Trapper Keeper in their locker. Then, they just change Trappers from class to class, taking only one Trapper to each class. With no large notebooks to carry around, they travel light and easy. After school, they take the Trapper Keeper home with all the Trappers inside.

The Trapper and Trapper Keeper have been tested in actual use. Everyone, teachers and students alike, agree that the Trapper and Trapper Keeper make school easier and better."

Special Teacher Offer. Because the Trapper and Trapper Keeper may help you in organizing your classes, Mead wants you to have a sample of the Trapper Keeper (with 3 Trapper portfolios included) for the cost of postage and handling ($2.00). These products will be available to your students the start of school next fall. So, it's a good chance to try it out ahead of your students. You might find you want to recommend it.

mead

I'd like to try the Trapper and Trapper Keeper. I'm sending along $2.00 to cover postage and handling. Would you please send me a set of the 3 Trappers and a Trapper Keeper.

Send to: Mead Products, P.O. Box 148, 11th & Mitchell Avenue, St. Joseph, Missouri 64502.

Name _____
Address _____
City _____
State _____ Zip _____

Offer expires December 31, 1979.

---

were available in three solid colors and three designs: soccer, dog and cat, and Oregon coast.

The distribution plan covered all major types of outlets: mass merchandisers, food, drug, combo stores, variety stores, and others. The strategy would be to concentrate on major regional and national chains. The sales presentation methods were to include use of a "sell brochure," a slide presentation, a

TV commercial, a TV storyboard, and a chain survey sheet.

A sales forecast, by region, would be needed by December 1980. The national account contacts would be made in December and January, with regional selling taking place in February through May. Key account activity would be monitored weekly.

CASE

7-3 BATES INDUSTRIAL SUPPLY*

Phil Harper had been recently appointed marketing manager for Bates Industrial Supply. Bates was a regional wholesaler of industrial cleaners and related chemicals. Phil directed the field sales force and was in charge of reordering stock for the warehouse. Recently, the company had been having trouble balancing orders against inventory. Customers were complaining about late shipments and items being short on delivery. The company president asked Harper to look into the problem and come up with some recommendations.

Phil realized that establishing direct computer links with manufacturers who supplied them with chemicals could reduce their out-of-stock problem. However, it would take months to buy the necessary equipment and debug the programs. Anticipated costs for direct computer links would be several hundred thousand dollars. A simpler approach would be to study the variations in sales of inventoried items to see if improved demand forecasts would help. Phil decided to call up some sales figures for four popular industrial cleaners on his desktop computer (Exhibit 1). The numbers on the screen represented three years of monthly sales for the four items. Several series seemed to exhibit seasonal patterns, and others were dominated by trends and unknown components. Bates normally prepared forecasts for each inventoried item 12 months into the future so that purchase discounts could be taken and delivery charges minimized. The usual procedure was to use simple projection methods to obtain the forecasts.

Phil decided to look through his computer's Internet service menu to see what forecasting programs were available from outside suppliers. He found several standard programs for moving averages and exponential smoothing that calculated seasonal indexes. However, these programs required the user to specify parameters for the length of the moving av-

erage and the size of the smoothing constants. What Phil needed was a program that found appropriate values for forecasting parameters and compared the accuracy of different techniques across historical data. Forecasting parameters could, of course, be derived using trial-and-error procedures, but that could take forever.

Phil took a sip of coffee from the cup in his hand and winced at the bitter aftertaste. Perhaps the industry should be working on a substitute for the coffee bean; everyone knew the vending machines needed help. As despair at finding a solution to the forecasting problem began to grow, his eyes focused on the title of the program called FORECAST. The description indicated that the program searched old sales data for optimum parameters and then compared techniques by calculating mean absolute percentage forecasting errors (MAPEs). FORECAST tried different lengths of moving averages and different exponential smoothing constants by making a series of one-period-ahead forecasts on past data. Parameters that produced the lowest average errors could then be used to forecast the future. FORECAST was also set up to make seasonal and trend adjustments. Other forecasting methods available in the program included naive, simple regression, moving regression, multiple regression, unit rate of change, percentage rate of change, and Holt's two-variable exponential smoothing techniques.

Phil decided to start with the sales data from SH60 to see if he could find the best forecasting technique for this series. Then the FORECAST program could be used to project sales for periods 37 through 48. One issue Phil was not sure about was whether the technique that worked best for SH60 could be used to forecast sales of the other chemicals. Certainly, it would save him a lot of time if he used the same forecasting procedure for all the products. He also wondered whether trend and seasonal adjustments were worth the bother. Once he had some results for the four chemicals, he would be in a better position to decide whether improved forecasting procedures would solve the out-of-stock problem. Before he

*This case was prepared by Douglas J. Dalrymple of Indiana University.

Exhibit 1: Sales of Four Industrial Cleansers

Time Period	SH60	PN25	SX80	TL75	Time Period	SH60	PN25	SX80	TL75
1	3848	362	5666	885	19	4667	1132	6104	884
2	4024	346	5405	870	20	3555	1360	6812	878
3	3416	382	5001	866	21	3101	1589	8367	874
4	3671	526	4688	859	22	3507	1137	8130	865
5	3762	675	5492	862	23	3131	1739	7525	868
6	4444	440	5231	855	24	3639	1380	6918	855
7	5375	547	4813	857	25	2762	1366	6737	857
8	3752	655	4780	839	26	2929	915	6900	865
9	2884	313	4611	847	27	3137	1651	6112	861
10	3324	555	5201	836	28	2975	1282	6717	853
11	3133	806	5136	876	29	3274	1128	7937	860
12	3048	678	5124	873	30	3422	1397	7647	863
13	3163	568	6149	865	31	4507	1102	6993	882
14	3217	741	6202	860	32	4054	769	8089	876
15	3106	631	5808	846	33	4426	1412	9279	883
16	3196	1006	5572	839	34	4083	1161	9547	875
17	3118	1216	7069	852	35	3924	1210	8064	861
18	3305	862	6839	864	36	4274	1133	8188	864

started, Phil would have to decide whether to base his comparisons of the different techniques on forecasts for periods 25 through 48 or 13 through 48. While a 12-month forecasting horizon seemed appropriate for the future, he was not sure whether to base his evaluations of alternative approaches on one or two years of historical forecasts. Since it was getting late, Phil decided that he'd better begin, and he called up the FORECAST program to the hard drive on his personal computer.

▶ 8 ◀

Organization*

The same old way doesn't work anymore.
ANONYMOUS

*Chapter Consultant: B. J. Polk Customer Business Development Manager Procter & Gamble.

LEARNING OBJECTIVES

After studying this chapter, you should be able to:

▶ Discuss the principles of sales organization.

▶ Explain geographic, customer, product, and functional specialization.

▶ Understand the role and limitations of telemarketing.

▶ Recognize the need for National Accounts Programs.

▶ Tell why and when sales agents are utilized.

▶ Discuss evolving trends in sales force organizations.

▶ HEWLETT-PACKARD REORGANIZES

Before the sales force reorganization, a salesperson for Hewlett-Packard's Computer Systems Organization (CSO) would jump from customer to customer within a defined geography. That meant that one day a salesperson could be working with a clothing manufacturer, the next with a government agency, and the next with a securities firm. After the reorganization, a salesperson might call on only banks, for instance. This helps the salesperson become a specialist in the information problems of a particular industry. The changes seem to have impressed customers, who say that H-P salespeople ask more thoughtful questions about customer needs and implementation of computer systems, something customers say they don't see from H-P's competitors. Success of the reorganization is also reflected in H-P's CSO sales, which exceed $7 billion today compared to only $4.7 billion in 1991.

In part, a technological revolution in computing drove the need for a sales reorganization. H-P anticipated that the reduced instruction set computing (RISC) chip would lead the industry away from proprietary systems to open systems where customers could mix and match components from several vendors. As a result, computer hardware would no longer be the main discussion point; now, whether "you can solve my business problems" would be the center of discussion.

H-P's sales effort is divided into red, blue, and green teams. The red team represents the heart of H-P's sales force, with salespeople specializing in either financial services, federal government and discrete manufacturing, or telecommunications, media, and utilities. The green team represents channel partners, such as VARS (Value-Added ReSellers) and independent agents, whom the company relies on to sell to smaller firms. The blue team includes telemarketing and geographically organized accounts that don't fall neatly into any of the strategically targeted industries on which H-P focuses.[1]

As the Hewlett-Packard example illustrates, changes in the competitive environment may require reorganization of the sales force. When the way your customers purchase evolves, you must follow. Decisions must be made about how many salespeople are needed, how they should work together, and how they should be organized to ensure both efficiency and effectiveness in accessing an identified customer base. In addition, lines of authority and areas of responsibility must be defined so that all sales activities are properly coordinated.

The discussion in this chapter is organized as follows. First, we review a set of principles that should be considered in building any sales organization. Second, the question of sales force specialization and major accounts is addressed. This is followed by a discussion of the advantages and pitfalls of telemarketing and independent agents, alternatives to the traditional field sales force. The chapter closes with a discussion of ways to determine how many salespeople are needed, along with emerging issues such as accessing global markets and TQM.

▶ ORGANIZATIONAL PRINCIPLES

Organizations function best when they support groups of work activities and when these groups respond to existing market opportunities. With the growth of personal

computers, IBM's customers don't need all the selling support traditionally offered by IBM in mainframe sales. Customers are looking for quality, service, and price. As one observer notes, "IBM has got to bring down the cost of sales and marketing. IBM can't support the overhead they used to because the individual sales aren't as large as they used to be."[2]

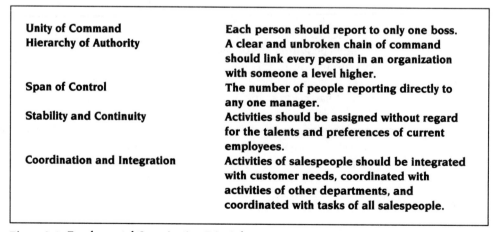

Unity of Command	**Each person should report to only one boss.**
Hierarchy of Authority	**A clear and unbroken chain of command should link every person in an organization with someone a level higher.**
Span of Control	**The number of people reporting directly to any one manager.**
Stability and Continuity	**Activities should be assigned without regard for the talents and preferences of current employees.**
Coordination and Integration	**Activities of salespeople should be integrated with customer needs, coordinated with activities of other departments, and coordinated with tasks of all salespeople.**

Figure 8-1: Fundamental Organization Principles

Too often, as in IBM's case, the structure of the sales force evolves over time; layers of supervision and staff specialists are added to solve particular problems that may arise. After a while, the organizational structure is taken for granted until major sales and profit problems surface. Measuring the effects of organizational structure on performance is difficult, but there are some basic principles that should be considered when building and evaluating a sales organization. These principles are summarized in Figure 8-1.

Three principles are prominent in current sales force organization decisions—span of control, centralization versus decentralization, and integration and coordination.

Span of Control

Span of control refers to the number of subordinates who are supervised by each manager. Ratios of 1 manager for every 10 salespeople are typical for many American firms.[3] Narrow spans of control are more common in small firms and with high-tech products such as aerospace equipment (7:1). Narrow spans of control are appropriate when salespeople are inexperienced. New salespeople benefit greatly from one-on-one coaching in the field from sales management.

Although the narrow span of control used by many U.S. companies allows closer control, it also tends to complicate the communication process, to isolate management from grass-roots operations, and to increase operating costs. These problems occur because a narrow span of control requires more layers of supervision, which add to selling expenses and separate management from the final consumer.

A recent article suggests that today's salespeople are better educated (65% have college degrees), know more about their customers' business, are more comfortable with technology, and can function with wider spans of control. Caradon Everest, a British maker of replacement windows has equipped its reps with laptops loaded with software that allows them to configure customized products on the spot and calculate their prices.[4] These changes allow firms to move to wider spans of control in the range of 10 or 20 salespeople. For example, a Dartnell survey shows insurance firms have average spans of control of 16:1, food products companies 14:1, real estate 14:1, and paper products 13:1.[5] These ratios lead to fewer levels of management and this forces sales managers to become facilitators of change, cheerleaders, and visionaries. Procter & Gamble has recently eliminated three levels of management to make the company a swifter global marketer. A wider span of control also requires organizations to delegate more responsibility and authority to the lowest level.

Wide spans of control and fewer layers of management present important sales management challenges. In recruiting, management may need to look for people with an entrepreneurial outlook who would be more suited to work in this new environment. Experienced, better-trained salespeople who can operate with less supervision may need to be recruited. Training must be changed, additional information funneled to the sales force, and professional development of salespeople emphasized and improved. At Kodak, for instance, sales reps are fed a continual stream of financial data—on units sold, revenues, and even costs and profits. The company has been reorganized into geographic zones, and each zone is "empowered to take umbrella strategies that we develop for the U.S. as a whole and adjust and manipulate them in a way that's appropriate for their specific area."[6]

Fewer levels of management will also lead to fewer promotion opportunities for salespeople within a sales organization. Therefore, sales managers have to learn how to challenge and reward salespeople in order to keep experienced people motivated and productive. This also requires top management to change the traditional corporate culture, in which success is measured by how many times a person is promoted. National Semiconductor (Santa Clara, California) addressed this issue by creating two career paths of equal importance—an individual contributor path and a management path.[7]

Centralization versus Decentralization

A recurring point of discussion in sales management is to what extent control and authority over the sales force should rest in the hands of top management versus field sales managers (e.g., regional or district managers). In a completely *decentralized* organization, field sales managers have the resources and responsibility for performing recruiting, selecting, training, compensating, motivating, and evaluating salespeople. With a highly *centralized* operation, these activities are mostly controlled by central headquarters. In addition to the substantial economies from centralizing certain functions, highly centralized decision making, it is argued, is one way to encourage coordination and integration of salespeople's behaviors and efforts. It also helps to ensure uniformity in an organization's product and service offerings and consistency with the marketing plan.

Despite the possible benefits of centralized decision making, the trend is toward greater decentralization. This is occurring in part to meet the needs of a more diverse customer base served by many organizations and to deal with local competitive conditions. This was part of the motivation by Hewlett-Packard to reorganize.

Advances in technology, especially communications technology, are also making decentralization more feasible while not sacrificing the greater control and internal communications associated with centralized organizations. "Mobile offices" are being created with the use of corporatewide electronic mail systems, wireless access to headquarters' mainframe information, and cellular phones.

Many firms attempt to combine the advantages of centralized and decentralized sales organizations. They may use sales offices to provide service to customers but centralize part of the training and recruiting functions to increase efficiency. Companies like IBM, Alcoa, and Xerox use line managers from local sales offices to recruit from nearby areas and corporate staff recruiters to travel across the country looking for prospects. These firms do some training at sales branches to reduce fixed overhead and encourage on-the-job contact. They also use centralized training facilities where new employees can be brought in for short, intensive training sessions using specialists and equipment not available at the sales branches.

There is no one best way to organize a sales force that meets the needs of all companies. Sales Management in Action 8-1 describes why Hyatt has centralized its sales force despite the many advantages being touted for decentralization. What is

---

Sales Management in Action 8-1
What, Another One?

A customer seeing more than one salesperson from the same company is common, but 62 salespeople from one company trying to sell the same person seems a little extreme. This is how many of Hyatt Hotels' 650 salespeople call on the American Bankers Association (ABA). Hyatt salespeople market rooms in bulk to travel agents, associations, and corporations. Each salesperson pitches the hotel he or she works for, which is how ABA came to know so many Hyatt people. "Looking back on it," comments Hyatt's president, "I think 'How could we have been so bloody dumb?' " So Hyatt pulled in its salespeople located at

individual facilities, such as those in Maui and Waikiki, and relocated them to central selling offices in Chicago and Omaha, where they were assigned specific customers to target. Not surprisingly, the troops rebelled and Hyatt had to back off its plans for a year. Results after the move was finally made have been very encouraging. Bookings in Hawaii were 25 percent higher than during the same period of the previous year.

Source: Patricia Sellers, "How to Remake Your Sales Force," *Fortune* (May 4, 1992), p. 99.

---

the right way to structure a sales job? A good way to start is to take a hard look at the purchasing processes and needs of your customer base and distribution channels.

Integration and Coordination with Other Functions

The traditional flow of communications has been directed outward from the organization to the customer through the sales force. This called for some interaction among other functional areas—R&D, production, logistics, and accounting and finance—but the need for coordination was somewhat limited by the unidirectional flow of communications.

With an increased focus on solving customers' problems, the flow of communications between sales and other departments is becoming more two-way. The sales force now communicates customers' needs and expectations back to the organization. Wal-Mart's and Procter & Gamble's teams have constructed a formal, written Code of Conduct, for instance, in which each has agreed to be the other's advocate within their respective firms. If both teams agree that a particular type of promotion would work best in Wal-Mart, for example, then the P&G sales team is responsible for selling the program inside P&G. To facilitate more honest and candid exchange of information between functional areas, some companies are turning to networked personal computers to facilitate consensus building and brainstorming.[8]

With which functional areas is the sales force most likely to interact? Depending on the organization and situation, sales will need to work smoothly with the following departments on these issues:

- **R&D**—new product and product modification ideas
- *Marketing*—advertising themes and media, cooperative advertising efforts, development of sales aids, channel issues, competitive pricing, and competitive market information
- *Production*—product availability, sales forecasting, production scheduling, technical product information, special product features and characteristics, and delivery schedules
- *Accounting and Finance*—special pricing and credit schedules, customer credit information, establishing budgets and quotas, developing compensation programs, and controlling expenses
- *Customer Service*—equipment installation, customer training, equipment upgrades, addressing ordering problems, warranty servicing, and meeting the customer's emergency needs

Ensuring proper coordination and communications between sales and these functions is not often easy. It can and often does involve adjustments in training programs, communication technology, compensation, and perhaps reorganiztion. Nevertheless, the benefits of a coordinated effort to address customer problems are often worth the effort.

▶ SPECIALIZATION

With the exception of startup businesses or very small organizations, some degree of specialization occurs in most sales forces. Sales forces are usually assigned geographic areas. In addition, sales organizations are increasingly specializing their sales efforts by organizing their sales force into customer, product, or functional specialists.[9] Specialization, however, presents important challenges in terms of coordination, integration, and, most important, higher expenses. A review of the advantages and possible pitfalls of the most common types of sales force specialization follows.

Geographic Specialization

The most common and least complicated way to organize a field sales force is by geographic territories, with a salesperson assigned to sell all products to all customers within a specified geographic area. For example, Figure 8-2 shows the eastern third of the United States divided into 18 sales territories, where each salesperson sells to all customers and prospects located within a designated state. The 18 territories are grouped into three geographic districts, each headed by a District Sales Manager. In this case, all the territories, districts, and regions are based on specific geographic (i.e., state) boundaries.

An important advantage of changing from a completely open sales force structure to *geographic specialization* is that travel time and expenses are reduced. Customer ser-

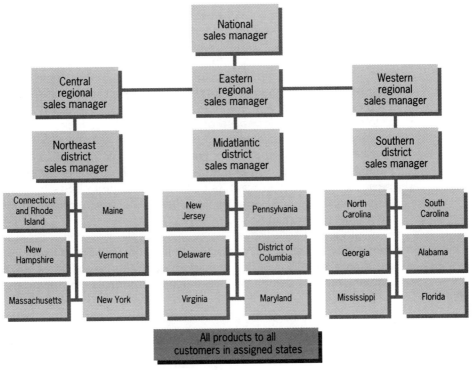

Figure 8-2: Geographical Sales Organization

vice may also improve because the number of customers to be serviced is limited and geographically concentrated. This organization also minimizes conflict over who is responsible for getting the job done in each area. A geographic organization works best when the product line consists of related products or services that appeal to a rather homogeneous group of buyers.[10]

Serious shortcomings may arise because salespeople sell the entire line to all types of customers. Salespeople may find themselves at a competitive disadvantage if there are many diverse products they are asked to sell and if customer problems and needs are diverse and complex as was the case with Hewlett-Packard in the opening vignette of this chapter. When salespeople sell many products, there is a tendency for them to degenerate into order takers, and brands can turn into commodities. There is also the risk that salespeople will spend too much time with customers that are easy to sell to but not necessarily profitable or high-growth opportunities. These problems can be partially solved by providing close supervision, giving incentives to perform strategic activities, and hiring better than average candidates and supporting them with extra training and technical support.

Product Specialization

There are 164 operating companies at Johnson & Johnson producing and selling products such as orthopedic implants, pharmaceuticals, and sutures. How could one person know enough about each product line? The answer is they couldn't, so J&J has organized its sales force around defined product lines. An organization of salespeople by products is shown in Figure 8-3. In this organizational structure, each salesperson specializes by selling only a few of the products in the organization's total product portfolio. Companies may switch to product specialization for one of several reasons. For instance, salespeople may need greater product knowledge to sell technologically complex product lines. If competitors' salespeople are able to offer more help to customers during the purchase process, then our salespeople may find themselves at a competitive disadvantage.

Not wanting to distract their current sales force from pushing existing lines was the reason Harford Steam Boiler Inspection and Insurance Company (HSB) added a specialized sales force to sell its new product, called All Systems Go. Customers for this product were much smaller than those purchasing policies for heavy machinery and atomic power plants.[11]

While *product specialization* allows salespeople to become experts in a particular product line and selling process, this type of organization is likely to be more expensive than a simple geographic organization. This is one reason Colgate-Palmolive Company recently combined its two main sales forces, household products and per-

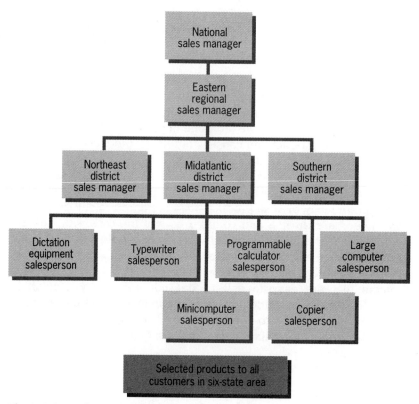

Figure 8-3: Product Specialized Sales Force

sonal care products, into a single sales force. Both product lines are now serviced during a single store visit, and if one buyer is tied up, the Colgate-Palmolive salesperson can speak with the person in charge of the other product line. As usual, other facets of sales management had to be adjusted accordingly. Both the sales force training program and compensation plan were altered to fit the new organization.

High overhead costs were also a driving force behind Procter & Gamble's recent reorganization of its sales force. An internal study discovered that P&G had the highest overhead costs in the business. No wonder: Its sales force had five divisions in three sales layers organized around product groups, selling more than 2,300 stock-keeping units in 34 product categories. The quarterly sales promotion plan for health and beauty products, for instance, ran to more than 500 pages and was sent to every salesperson. P&G has reorganized around 35 specific customers that account for nearly 80 percent of their sales.

Duplication of calls on customers may also become a problem. Separate sales forces frequently do not coordinate their customer contacts and sometimes compete for the same purchasing budget. This was the reason 3M recently reorganized its almost 50 division sales forces into customer-focused teams it refers to as its Integrated Solutions program. An extreme example of duplicate sales calls is described in Sales Management in Action 8-1.

Customer Specialization

In *customer specialization*, which is also referred to as *vertical marketing*, each salesperson or sales team sells the entire product line to select types of buyers. Thus the six salespeople in Figure 8-4 are assigned to banks, retailers, and other types of customers, instead of to geographic regions or product lines, as before.

This organizational structure is said to be more market driven. A customer organizational structure is particularly attractive when buyers are geographically concentrated, as are aerospace firms in Los Angeles and auto assembly plants along I-75 from Detroit to Memphis. The most important advantage of customer specialization is that salespeople gain a better understanding of the customer's special needs and problems and become experts in a particular industry. This strategy is an important selling advantage when emphasizing a marketing relationship strategy with your customers, where trust and cooperation are needed to maintain a long-term, beneficial relationship. It also offers a good opportunity to develop the consultative selling skills discussed earlier in the text.

Salespeople must be well supported to be customer experts; this may even influence hiring practices. To support its focus on the education market, Apple Computer often hires ex-teachers as sales representatives because of their excellent rapport with user customers. As with other forms of sales force specialization, costs and coordination are potential problems. The sharing of information across the different specialized sales forces of a company can also be problematic.

Functional Specialization

A fourth type of specialization in sales organizations, *functional specialization*, focuses on the jobs or functions performed by customer contact people (Figure 8-5). American

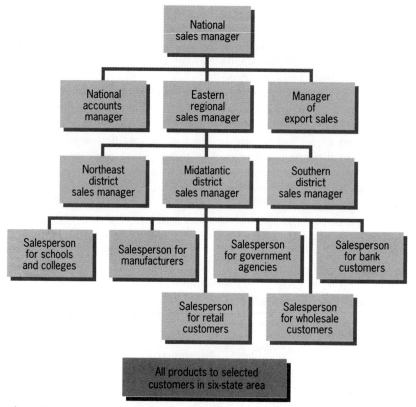

F*igure* **8-4:** Customer Specialized Sales Force

Express profits by having some salespeople generating initial sales and others ser-vicing the account later. Gillette, for instance, has salespeople sell and market prod-ucts, while a separate group of merchandisers perform point-of-sale activities such as shelf management, setting up displays, and other in-store activities.

There is no one best way to organize the sales force, and companies are experi-menting with many different forms in order to compete profitably. A company should start by examining its customers and looking at its organization from the customer's position. There is research suggesting that that when superior selling skills are required, some form of specialization works best; however, there is some danger of role stress and job ambiguity.[12]

▶ MAJOR ACCOUNTS PROGRAM

Regardless of whether the sales force consists of specialists or generalists, many orga-nizations find it necessary to develop a major account program, also known as a national accounts program, in addition to their regular sales force. A *major account program*, as discussed in Chapter 6, is more than a selling strategy. It is a marketing

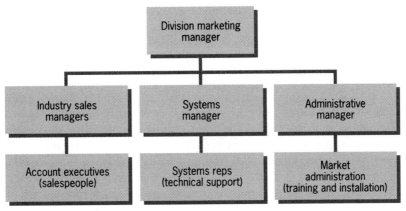

Figure 8-5: Functional Specialization

philosophy directed at a select group of customers that account for a disproportionately large share of the seller's total revenues and have complex needs and problems. These customers put more emphasis on value-added options such as education, electronic data interchange, and management information system compatibility. They typically have multiple divisions with geographically dispersed operations. An example of value-added services is described in Sales Management in Action 8-2.

Sales Management in Action 8-2
"What More Can We Do for You?"

This is an often asked question, but the answer is different if you are a major account. Procter & Gamble planted a crop of executives in Arkansas to work every day with Wal-Mart. The team consists of sales managers, but also of managers from other areas of the company—marketing, finance, distribution, and operations. This team works on such problems as reducing the cost of warehousing Pampers and planning new-product introductions. Black & Decker went so far as to set up Home Depot divisions to cater specifically to those fast-growing accounts. In each account, a vice president oversees a group composed of salespeople, marketers, an information systems expert, and a financial analyst. This gives the team the capability of designing promotion programs specifically for the account, including package redesigns. The payoff for such expensive efforts had better be huge. Wal-Mart is now P&G's largest account, bigger than its total business in every country outside of the United States except Germany. Sales of Black & Decker products sold to Home Depot have climbed almost 40 percent.

Source: Patricia Sellers, "How to Remake Your Sales Force," *Fortune* (May 4, 1992), pp. 100–102.

Despite the successes with major accounts and the current popularity of the major accounts approach, companies often encounter problems when setting them up. Two problems are particularly noteworthy—account selection and organizational structure.

Who Are Major Accounts?

An important issue to be addressed is which customers, if any, should be treated as *major accounts*. There is often a tendency to focus on customer size. If purchasing is negotiated at each of many locations, however, then even a large customer may not be appropriate. Major account programs are usually quite expensive. Many companies initially choose too many accounts to participate in the program, resulting in an overworked major account sales force and underserviced customers.

The emerging view is that customers who qualify for a major account program are those that purchase a significant volume and exhibit one or a combination of the following characteristics:

- Involve multiple people in the buying process.
- Purchase centrally.
- Desire a long-term, cooperative working relationship.
- Expect specialized attention and service.

As with many marketing decisions, deciding who should be a major account depends on finding out your customer's needs. Major accounts are those that are after better service on a national or international basis. The characteristics listed above are indicators that a customer may desire and need special attention.

How to Organize?

Companies have taken a variety of approaches in organizing their national accounts programs. What works for one company and is appropriate for one situation may not work in another. The major organizational alternatives are:

Existing Sales Force   As an initial effort, companies often rely on their existing sales force to service the national account customer. This strategy has the advantage of being less risky and less expensive than setting up a separate sales force. On the other hand, the relationship with these national accounts may not be very different from that with regular accounts, thus raising the question of whether a national accounts program is needed. There is also some evidence that salespeople will focus mostly on closing orders and securing revenue rather than building relationships.[13]

Management   A step up from this initial organization is to assign national account responsibility to management. Computer Task Group, Inc., an Atlanta-based software services firm, assigns a national account to each of the top 25 executives in the company. In addition to being relatively low cost, executives are likely to have the authority and power to meet special customer needs. An additional advantage is that it keeps management close to the customer.

Separate Sales Force   Where the need for a national accounts program is greatest, a separate sales force devoted strictly to national accounts often evolves. The Gold

Bond Building Products division of National Gypsum is organized in this manner. Successful field salespeople are promoted to the national accounts sales force. These people report to a national accounts manager, who in turn reports to the national sales manager. Hewlett-Packard, Xerox, MCI and other companies have similar arrangements.

Sales Teams   Where the selling process is very complex, sales teams may be assigned to national accounts. AT&T has 370 such national account teams. Each team is headed by an account manager with broad product and account knowledge. Providing technical support to the team are two or three product specialists and staff technical specialists. IBM and Pitney Bowes also employ national account teams. The major drawback to this type of organization is its expense. A recent two-day planning meeting for just one national account cost AT&T $5,000.

Regardless of the exact organization of the program, it is critical that the national accounts salespeople have access to and support of top management. A recent survey of national account programs found that in 23 percent of the companies, the vice president of national accounts reported directly to the president. In 67 percent of the companies, national accounts executives reported to the vice president of either sales or marketing.[14]

► TELEMARKETING

Customers are demanding more attention just when many companies—including Apple Computer, IBM, Merck, and Procter & Gamble—are reducing their sales forces. Major account programs pay off for large customers, but no company has the time or money to offer these kinds of services to all customers. An increasingly popular and cost-effective way to serve small and even medium-sized customers is with a telemarketing support system. *Telemarketing* refers to customer contacts utilizing telecommunications technology for personal selling without direct, face-to-face contact. Business-to-business telemarketing is growing at a rate of 30 to 40 percent a year and generates sales in excess of $100 billion yearly.[15] Over 2 million people are employed in consumer and business-to-business telemarketing operations. The effectiveness and opportunity that telemarketing represents are shown by the $1,000 value of the average business-to-business telemarketing sale. Corporations such as IBM, Procter & Gamble, Chase Manhattan Bank, and Union Pacific Railroad have all developed telemarketing systems.[16]

Advantages

One reason for the growing popularity of telemarketing is that it allows companies to make cost-effective sales calls, especially on smaller customers. Telemarketing is 5 to 15 times more efficient and 70 to 95 percent less expensive than field sales because telemarketing representatives cover their territory using the telephone instead of battling traffic.[17] See Table 8-1 for a comparison of field sales and telemarketing costs.

The situation at the Medical and Surgical Products Division of 3M is typical of that found in many firms. The company determined that it cost $200 for each call by field

Table 8-1   Doing the Math on Account Management

	Field Rep	Telemarketing
Sales calls per day	5	25
Sales calls per quarter	325	1624
Sales calls per year	1300	6500
Reps required	6.5	1.2
Cost per sales call	$250	$15
Cost per year	$1,998,750	$117,000

salespeople. Since each sale required 4.3 calls, the selling cost per sale averaged $860. Small hospitals did not generate enough sales to cover this cost, and about half of the hospitals serviced by 3M's salespeople were considered small. To address this imbalance, 3M instituted a telemarketing program. Because telemarketing reps can make many more calls per day than field salespeople, the average cost of a telephone sales call is $25.

A second reason for telemarketing's popularity is that many business customers like it. With increasing demands on their time, purchasing agents often appreciate the speed of telephone purchasing. A study of the wholesale distribution industry conducted by Arthur Andersen and Company predicted that in the near future half of the average wholesaler's sales force would be telemarketers.[18] The demand for field sales reps dropped to eighth place in the study (Table 8-2).

Scope

The use of telemarketing differs from one business to the next. Some of the more common ways in which telemarketing is utilized will now be considered.

Customer Service   Companies provide customers with a number they can call if they have any questions. General Electric built what is referred to as the "Answer Center" in Louisville, Kentucky, to answer questions about products 24 hours a day, 7 days a week. Reps answer up to 15,000 calls per day, using information in a computer database on 120 product lines with 85,000 models and 1,100 operating and repair procedures.[19]

Table 8-2   Ranking of Customers' Wants

	1970	1980	1990
Contact with outside salesperson	1	3	8
Frequency and speed of delivery	2	1	2
Price	3	2	4
Range of available products	4	5	3
Capable inside salesperson	5	4	1

Prospecting and Lead Qualification Instead of simply waiting for prospects to call, some firms are taking a proactive approach to prospecting by having telemarketers call prospects or qualify them for face-to-face selling. AT&T built its National Sales Center to house and train telemarketers in lead generation and qualification. Prior to using telemarketers to qualify prospects, the national closing ratio on sales visits by AT&T salespeople was 1 in 10. After only one year of the telemarketing program, the close ratio was improved to 6.5 in 10. The Center handles over 300,000 contacts a year.

Customer Retention Many companies find it economical to service small customers and sell peripheral or secondary product lines by phone, thereby freeing their salespeople to concentrate on key customers and strategic product lines. IBM uses telemarketing to sell computer supplies, typewriter ribbons, and so on, through their IBM Direct operation. A. B. Dick is a prime example of using telemarketing to maintain contact with over 100,000 small accounts whose average order ($50.00) is too small to cover the cost of a sales call ($66.88).

Advertising and Promotions Today you often see newspaper and magazine ads that feature either a local or an 800 number to get information or to place an order. Merrill Lynch, Chevron, and Blue Cross–Blue Shield are among the many companies that rely heavily on this approach.

Challenges

Despite considerable merit, telemarketing presents several unique management challenges. Among these are gaining acceptance for telemarketing by the field sales force and managing telemarketers.[20]

Acceptance Integrating telemarketing with a traditional sales force can be challenging. Many field salespeople feel threatened by telemarketers. Often salespeople fear that management will eventually cut their commissions on orders placed with the telemarketing reps. Salespeople may withhold critical customer information and refuse to integrate telemarketers fully into the selling process.[21]

Management Hiring the right person for telemarketing can be a potential problem area. What is frequently needed is a person who combines some of the attributes of good customer service people with those of successful salespeople. The best telemarketers are concerned with details and possess the positive outlook and aggressiveness of good salespeople. However, customer service people are often reluctant to make the first call, and salespeople tend to like one-on-one relationships and are apt to spend a lot of time on the phone with one account. Many firms find it necessary to look outside the firm for the right person.

Motivation and retention are also potential problem areas. Telemarketers do not have the freedom of movement of field salespeople and may be required to make 20 to 30 calls per hour. Adding to the problem is lower pay than outside salespeople and the status of second-class citizens relative to salespeople. Average compensation for telemarketing reps is just over $25,000.[22] Companies have tried to provide telemarketers with significant bonuses based on performance, greater training, and increased interaction with salespeople and customers. In general, motivation and retention continue to be problems.[23]

Organizational Structure Summary

Sales management is much more complex and exciting in today's environment. In organizing the sales effort, a large number of specialized sales options are now available, including inside telemarketing specialists, pure product or system specialists, vertical market or customer specialists, and national account specialists. Deciding when and how to specialize is not easy because of the trade-offs that are present. The attractiveness of specialization will depend on a firm's objectives, strategies, capabilities, and external environment. Some points to consider when evaluating specialization options are the following:

- If a company's objective is to reduce costs, then full-line salespeople and telemarketing are the best low-cost options.
- If a company's objective is to increase revenue, then specialization (product, customer, functional, and major accounts) supported by telemarketing should be considered.
- Exceptional training capabilities are frequently critical to the success of specialized salespeople. Specialization by itself is rarely sufficient to produce exceptional results; development of specialized skills must be fostered and enhanced by appropriate training programs.
- When specializing, a firm must have the capability of developing new products and modifying existing products for individual product lines and/or markets. Sales force reorganization cannot solve a product problem.
- If your market is susceptible to demand or margin downturns, then specialists may prove too expensive and are difficult to redeploy.

These factors are likely to vary with the products/markets in which an organization competes. Thus, many large companies combine a variety of specialized sales force structures within their overall selling organization. This also suggests that there is no optimal way for all companies to organize.

▶ INDEPENDENT SALES AGENTS

Up to this point, we have focused on how to organize a company sales force in which all the salespeople and managers are employees of the firm. An important alternative is to hire *independent sales agents* (sometimes referred to as manufacturer's reps) to perform the selling function. Sales agents are not employees, but independent businesses given exclusive contracts to perform the selling function within specified geographic areas. They take neither ownership nor physical possession of the products they sell and are always compensated by commission. Agents are often used to develop new markets through a combination of persuasive selling skills and technical competence. This technical competence exists in part because agents usually handle five to eight noncompeting but related product lines that they know fairly well and sell to similar types of buyers.

When to Use Sales Agents

An estimated 45,000 to 50,000 U.S. manufacturers sell through sales agents.[24] Though agents often handle the products of smaller manufacturers, large manufacturers such as ITT, Corning, Monsanto, Teledyne, and Mobil Oil use sales agents in secondary markets. Xerox, for instance, sells strictly through agents in rural areas and recently switched to selling smaller metropolitan accounts through agents (see Sales Management in Action 8-3).

The decision to pay sales agents to cover a particular product/market is not an easy one to make or to implement. Management should consider three factors: (1) economic consequences, (2) level of control, and (3) competitive market environment.

Economic Consequences   The economic issue centers on the fixed-cost nature of a dedicated sales force versus the largely variable cost associated with sales agents. A simplified representation of cost differences between sales agents and a company sales force with a straight salary compensation plan is shown in Figure 8-6. Although there may be some fixed costs associated with sales agents, sales administration costs are usually a relatively small proportion of total selling costs. Additionally, agents receive neither salary nor reimbursement for travel and entertainment expenses. Since agents are paid strictly on commission, costs rise as sales volume increases. Consequently, there is a break-even sales volume below which sales agents are less

Sales Management in Action 8-3
From Employee to Partner

In the midst of a streamlining process that includes cutting 10,000 employees in 1996, Xerox is attempting to cut the size of its sales force by offering salespeople a plan called the Employee to Partner Program. Xerox is offering qualified sales personnel severance of up to 26 weeks' pay and as much as $15,000 in bonuses to become independent Xerox sales agents to sell copiers to small customers (fewer than 30,000 copies per month) in metropolitan areas. In 1992, Xerox started selling these smaller accounts through sales agents because their research indicated that small businesses were afraid of dealing with large bureaucracies like Xerox. With agents, neighborhood businesses get to do business with other neighborhood businesses. As for workforce reductions, Xerox expects to save more than $1 billion in 1994 and 1995.

Source: Joe Mullich, "Xerox Pits Workers vs. Agents," *Business Marketing* (April 1994), pp. 1, 45.

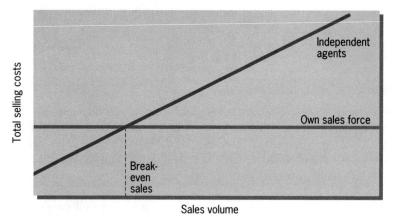

Figure 8-6: Total Costs of Independent Agents vs. Own Sales Force

expensive and above which a company sales force costs less. These economic factors are one reason agents may be used by small companies and in secondary markets.

Suppose that independent sales agents receive a 5 percent commission on sales and administrative overhead costs $50,000. Company sales personnel receive a 3 percent commission plus a salary. Total salary and administrative expenses are estimated at $550,000. At what sales level would the cost of a company sales force equal that of sales agents? This question can be answered by setting the cost equation for both types of sales forces equal to each other and solving for the sales level amount as follows:

$$\text{Cost of company sales force} = \text{Cost of sales agents}$$
$$0.03x + \$550,000 = 0.05x + \$50,000$$

where x is the break-even sales volume.

Solving for x, we see that break-even sales volume equals $25 million. If sales are expected to be below $25 million, then sales agents are less expensive. The cost of a company sales force is less when sales exceed $25 million.

While Figure 8-6 accurately depicts the essential economic relationships when comparing agents with a dedicated sales force, the situation is often more complicated than one might expect. Adding new salespeople to produce greater volume, for instance, results in fixed costs increasing in a stair-step fashion. Thus, there may be multiple break-even points at ever-increasing levels of sales. Agents may also be able to pick up a competing line of goods, thereby reducing actual sales volume below that expected from switching to a dedicated sales force. These and other considerations can make the decision to build a dedicated sales force far less clear-cut than may appear at first glance.

Level of Control Costs are not the only consideration. Managers can control a company sales force through the selection, training, and supervision of salespeople; establishment of operating policies and procedures; and various evaluation and reward programs. With an in-house sales force, salespeople spend 100 percent of their time on the company's products.

When selling through agents, you face competition at two levels: manufacturers selling competing products and firms selling products through the same agents. In other words, the company competes for the agent's selling time. While management should try to establish a personal relationship with their agents and sell the agents on the company's marketing program, the primary control mechanism with agents is the commissions paid on sales.[25] This is a market-driven control method, and agents can be expected to spend their time in a manner that will enable them to meet their income objectives. That is, they will evaluate both the amount of commission and the time it will take to earn the commission when deciding how to spend their time. This is supported by Erin Anderson's study of companies' use of agents. She found that companies tended to use their own sales force when the product lines were complex and hard to learn and when considerable nonselling activities were required.[26]

Additional Issues   When speed and timing are important, such as when you need to enter a new geographic area or product market quickly, sales agents may be the best alternative. Sales agents have an established relationship with customers in a geographic area and offer quick access to targeted buyers. They will still need to learn about the product, but they should already be familiar with the general product line since they are selling related items. Manufacturers competing in high-risk industries with short life cycles or rapidly changing technologies will often rely on sales agents to preserve their flexibility and minimize the downside losses from the expense of an in-house sales force. An in-house salesperson, for instance, may cost $75,000 a year to keep on the road.[27]

Agents' contracts are usually signed annually. Contracts generally call for 30 days' notice, so agents can be dismissed relatively quickly. Despite the tenuous nature of the relationship, sales agents have maintained a strong presence in the distribution of both consumer and industrial products. According to U.S. Department of Commerce statistics, sales agents have accounted for approximately 10 percent of all domestic sales in the United States since 1972.[28] One study found that companies are reluctant to switch from sales agents to an in-house sales force because of the difficulty of setting up a new system. An equally important consideration should be the potential difficulties of dismantling the existing sales agent system.[29]

▶ NUMBER OF SALESPEOPLE

If an in-house sales force is used, management must determine its proper size. The decision is complicated by variations in territories, specialized sales force organizations, and differences in customers and compensation plans. See Management in Action 8-4 for an example of why one company decided to increase its sales force despite higher costs. A rough estimate of the number of people needed, however, can be obtained by looking at three different approaches that consider affordability, workload, and sales volume.

Sales Management in Action 8-4
How Many Salespeople Are Enough?

Loctite North America sells adhesives and sealants to heavy industry. To improve short-term profitability, Loctite allowed its field sales force to decline through attrition. When salespeople left, territories were combined and telemarketing people hired to fill in the gaps. Although profits increased, sales growth stalled. A careful examination of the situation revealed that salespeople were paying attention to and getting many large new orders. However, overall sales were not growing and Loctite was losing business with existing customers. Because of the greater size of the sales territories, Loctite's reps were unable to provide adequate service to existing customers. Industrial adhesives is a special applications business that requires a lot of technical support. This could not be provided over the phone by telemarketers. The solution in this case was to hire 30 additional salespeople during a one-year period. This added expense depressed profitability for six months, but soon afterward, sales began to grow. Loctite has since hired 10 more field reps.

Source: "How Lean Is Too Lean?" *Sales & Marketing Management* (January 1988), p. 53.

Affordability Approach

The size of the sales force is often a compromise between the number of people needed to call on existing and potential customers and what the firm can afford. For example, how many salespeople can a computer company with $20 million in revenues afford to hire, if its sales force is organized by geography, and 6 percent of revenues are allocated for field sales activities? The number of salespeople could be derived as follows:

$20,000,000 Expected sales

$\underline{\times\ .06}$ Field sales expense ratio (wages, commissions, and travel expenses)

$ 1,200,000 Sales budget

$\underline{\times\ .85}$ Percent for sales force (i.e., 15% for supervisor)

$ 1,020,000 Available for salespeople

$$\frac{\text{Dollars available}}{\substack{\text{Wages and expenses} \\ \text{per person}}} = \frac{\$1,020,000}{\$51,000} = 20 \text{ (number that can be hired)}$$

The above example indicates that of the $1,200,000 expected sales budget, $1,020,000 would be available to hire salespeople after supervisory expenses had been deducted. If salespeople cost an average of $51,000 per year for wages and expenses, then the company could afford to hire a total of 20 people. This *affordability approach* has the advantage that costs will be in line with current sales from the outset, and the company need not wait until some future time before expense-to-sales ratios are reduced to acceptable levels through sales growth. The main drawback to this strategy is that it does not consider market potential or customer needs.

Workload Approach

The *workload approach* to determining the size of the sales force is based on decisions regarding the frequency and length of calls needed to sell to existing and potential customers. An estimate of the total number of salespeople required using this approach can be made using the following formula:

$$\text{Number of salespeople} = \frac{\left[\begin{array}{c}\text{Number of}\\\text{existing}\\\text{customers}\end{array} + \begin{array}{c}\text{Number of}\\\text{potential}\\\text{customers}\end{array}\right] \times \begin{array}{c}\text{Ideal}\\\text{frequency} \times\\\text{of calls}\end{array} \begin{array}{c}\text{Length}\\\text{of}\\\text{call}\end{array}}{\text{Selling time available from one salesperson}}$$

For example, if the computer firm had 3,000 existing customers and 2,250 potential clients to be called on five times per year for two hours (including travel time), and if available selling time per salesperson is 1,500 hours per year, the size of the sales force would be:

$$\text{Number of salespeople} = \frac{(3000 + 2250) \times 5 \times 2}{1500} = 35$$

This estimate of 35 salespeople is based on the assumption that the desired frequency and length of calls are the same for all customers. If it is decided that these should vary according to the size and type of customer, then the formula can be modified accordingly.

Perhaps the biggest weakness of the workload strategy is its failure to consider the costs and profits associated with different levels of customer service. Since the ideal call frequencies used in the model are based on judgment, the firm never really knows whether it has set the number of calls to maximize sales and profits. Thus, the workload approach finds the number of salespeople needed to cover the market, but it does not lead to an optimum solution. An alternative approach considers what happens to sales and profits over time as existing territories are divided to make room for more salespeople.

Incremental Approach

Experience has shown that as firms add salespeople within an existing trading area, the increase in new business is usually smaller with each new employee. Sales grow because customers receive better service, but the total number of potential accounts does not change. That is, eventually all prospective customers are adequately covered, and sales do not increase as selling expenses grow. This situation suggests that salespeople should be added until the gross profit on new business is equal to the costs of deploying another person. That is what is referred to as an *incremental approach* to determining sales force size. Since the new business associated with additional sales staffing varies over time and among salespeople, firms must continue to monitor sales activities closely and determine whether they are approaching the point where costs exceed potential benefits.

Each of the methods for determining sales force size focuses on a particular aspect of the problem—cost, revenue, workload. Since the decision involves consideration of each of these factors, the best advice may be to calculate an ideal size using all three methods to determine the boundaries of the problem. With the results of this analysis as decision aids, management judgment is needed to determine the final choice of sales force size.

▶ EVOLVING SALES FORCE ORGANIZATIONS

Three issues related to sales force organization are getting increasing management attention—global sales organizations, sales teams, and TQM.

Global Sales Organization

Firms operating in other countries, referred to as *global sales organizations*, must decide how to organize their selling efforts across national boundaries. While there is added complexity in organizing and managing multinational sales efforts (see Sales Man-

---

Sales Management in Action 8-5
"What? Only a 20 Percent Raise?"

This is what you are likely to hear from a salesperson in Brazil, where national labor laws and rampant inflation make a 20 percent raise equivalent to a pay cut. Cultural differences and economic obstacles make it difficult for U.S. companies to recruit, retain, and motivate a native sales force in foreign countries. Here are a few examples of sales management challenges: In Japan, the use of a commission plan and individual quotas is at odds with Japan's team approach to business and its cultural focus on membership in a larger social group. In India, it is difficult for salespeople to sell outside of their own social and language groups because of the strong social caste system and the multitude of spo-

ken languages. In Saudi Arabia, hiring salespeople is difficult because selling is considered an undesirable occupation and because there is a shortage of labor. In Hong Kong, it is also difficult to hire salespeople because many people of Chinese descent are leaving in anticipation of the return of Chinese control. While there are many challenges in adapting to cultural differences, "shaping" these environments with U.S. sales skills may also be an opportunity. For instance, customers in India may welcome the informality and commitment to promises that are more typical in the United States.

Source: Study by the Personnel Corporation of America, as reported in *Marketing News* (May 8, 1989), p. 7.

agement in Action 8-5), the basic questions to be answered are the same as those faced in domestic markets: Should we use independent agents? Should we have a general sales force or specialists? Should we organize by geography, products, customers, or functions?

A recent study of multinational corporate practices sheds some light on how companies are organizing their sales forces.[30] About 25 percent of the companies used independent agents, about the same as in the United States. Independent agents were most likely to be used in countries where sales are relatively small and geographically dispersed. Agents are more likely to be used in Canada, Brazil, and Mexico, for instance, where company salespeople are uneconomical in outlying areas. This is consistent with the earlier discussion of independent agents in the United States. A consideration not discussed earlier is language. In multilingual markets (as in Sri Lanka, Thailand, and Singapore), companies tend to hire agents with the language and dialect skills necessary to a particular region. Slightly less than half (48.5 percent) of the firms surveyed used some kind of specialized sales force organization. The reasons given for specializing and the type of specializing indicate that multinational firms resolve organizational issues largely the same way they do in the United States.

Sales Teams

Today's customers have increasingly customized and complex needs—needs that frequently cannot be met by individual salespeople. In these situtions, success depends on the ability to marshal resources effectively across a range of buying locations, buying influences, product lines, and internal organizational boundaries. Now, companies such as AT&T, Baxter, Dun and Bradstreet, and Procter & Gamble are discovering that meeting customer procurement requirements and perfecting the overall customer interface requires a customer-focused *sales team* consisting of salespeople, customer service, technical specialists, and other functional areas. The objective of these teams is to bring together greater knowledge and skills at one time to focus on a more creative and complete solution to a customer's needs with the intention of building stronger customer relationships.

Dun and Bradstreet recently formed teams to concentrate on meeting with D-B's top 50 accounts. Previously multiple salespeople representing D-B's different divisions would all call on the same customers. The switch to teams was made to streamline the organization, present a more unified image to customers, and to increase revenue with a focus on building business with existing customers.[31] Xerox has used a team approach for some time, utilizing the slogan "Team Xerox." The account team is made up of an account representative, a high-speed duplicating specialist, an electronic printing specialist, an office systems and networking specialist, an electronic keyboard and workstation specialist, a copier specialist, and an account manager.

Sales teams need not be limited to in-house personnel. To make a presentation to a company about setting up a data application network, MCI's team made the presentation along with representatives of IBM and Rohm. MCI provided the information on data communication, IBM on computer hardware and software, and Rohm on switching equipment.[32]

Sales Management in Action 8-6
Help Wanted Now—A Temporary Sales Force

When in a pinch, companies don't think twice about hiring temporary secretaries, support staffers, and computer programmers. So why not bring on temporary salespeople when the need arises? The idea is apparently catching on with companies under time pressure when launching a new product or extending the reach of an existing one. Prudential HMO needed to saturate a target area quickly and decided that its full-time sales force wasn't sufficient to do the job. Prudential called on temporary staffing firm Sales Staffers International (SSI) to recruit about 75 insurance sales professionals with health care experience to blanket the area. The temporary reps are actually SSI employees, and receive regular sales training. The largest project SSI handled was a two-year stint requiring 1,200 salespeople.

Coordination is critical to the success of sales teams. Three issues are of particular importance in the coordination of sales team efforts: the reward system, the goal-setting process, and staffing and training. Compensation must be flexible, focus on the results of the team rather than the individual, and focus on a longer time frame since the selling cycle is usually longer. The goals of the team and the individuals on the team need to be clarified with respect to each person's responsibilities and the desired team accomplishments. Disseminating information about company strategy helps to clarify team sales goals and the effort top management wants. Teamwork in sales is the sum of individual efforts working cooperatively toward a common goal. This means that recruiting people with the aptitude for teamwork and developing skills such as delegating responsibility and working with and through others are important. This is quite different from the past, where sales was the vocation of a single energetic, persistent individual. Selling skills and product knowledge are still important, but additional skills are also needed for sales teams to function effectively.

Total Quality Management

As you now know, TQM represents a fundamental change in how businesses and business problems are seen. It should not come as a surprise, therefore, that a TQM perspective would include recommendations on how a sales force is organized. Following are some of the principles that should guide sales organization structure:

- The majority of people should be placed in direct customer support functions, with fewer staff positions.
- Fewer levels of management should drive down overhead costs while shortening the decision-making process.

- The organization should be flexible enough to change quickly to support new sales opportunities.
- There should be continuous improvement in the effectiveness of selling processes.[33]

Many of the most respected companies in the United States are adopting these principles. We noted earlier the reduction in sales forces and the use of fewer layers of management. Process speed is also getting more attention. DuPont adopted telemarketing to handle early stages of new account prospecting to reduce the selling cycle time. Xerox, having made a similar change, estimates that it has taken three months off the selling cycle for its most expensive printing systems.[34] Sales management in Action 8-6 shows how one firm used temporary salespeople to raise efficiency.

▶ ETHICAL SITUATIONS

Reorganizations are among the most challenging tasks management can undertake. Not only do they require a lot of planning, but management must anticipate negative reactions by at least some people in the sales force. After all, reorganizations will often affect the pay or income potential of salespeople, and will almost always affect their activities and responsibilities.

Let's reconsider a situation mentioned earlier in the chapter—resistance to telemarketing by the field sales force. If you were a first-level field sales manager, how would you handle this situation? Your company has recently initiated a telemarketing program to call on your smaller customers for their regular reorders on products they currently purchase. In private discussions with the national sales manager, you have been told that if the program works well, the company may be able to reduce the size of its field sales force by 40 percent the next year. You have been asked not to share this information with your sales force because of its potentially adverse effect. What would you say if one of the salespeople told you that he was not cooperating fully in the use of telemarketing because those were his customers, and if he gave them up, then he would not be as valuable to the company? What would you say if he asked you if some salespeople will lose their jobs because of telemarketing?

▶ SUMMARY

The building of an efficient sales organization is guided by several principles. Effective sales organizations usually have a hierarchy of authority and responsibility that extends in a direct line from the chief marketing officer down to the district sales manager and the field salesperson. The span of control should allow economical yet adequate supervision of employees. Sales organizations often make effective use of staff executives to analyze sales data, help with sales training, and recruit new sales personnel. Sales managers must consider when to centralize authority to conserve funds and when to decentralize control to boost sales through better customer service.

Almost all sales organizations use some sort of geographic breakdown to help control the costs and activities of field salespeople. Firms with diverse lines of high-technology products often can improve their sales performance by specializing selling efforts by product. Where buyers have special needs, customer specialization can improve efficiency by eliminating duplication of calls and by more effectively identifying and meeting customers' needs. With complex products, the sales organization may be divided along functional lines into initial contact people and account maintenance people. Recent developments in competition and technology have led to the addition of national accounts and telemarketing programs. Future complexity is likely with the evolution of global competition. Although there is no single best sales organization plan for all firms, careful attention to organizational principles and costs generally can lead to improved operating results.

► **KEY TERMS**

Affordability approach	Major accounts
Centralization	Major account program
Customer specialization	Product specialization
Decentralization	Sales teams
Functional specialization	Span of control
Geographic specialization	Stability and continuity
Global sales organization	Telemarketing
Hierarchy of authority	Unity of command
Incremental approach	Vertical marketing
Independent sales agents	Workload approach

► **REVIEW QUESTIONS**

1. Why is span of control important in planning the design of field sales activities?
2. Explain the conflict between the need to centralize and the need to decentralize sales responsibilities.
3. What are the advantages of geographic sales force specialization?
4. When is product specialization desirable?
5. What are the advantages and disadvantages of functional specialization?
6. How does customer specialization solve some of the problems associated with product specialization?
7. Why has telemarketing become so popular in business-to-business selling?
8. What is a major account program, and why is it being instituted by many organizations?
9. What issues must management consider when using independent sales agents?
10. When would it not be wise to replace salespeople with independent representatives?

11. When operating in other countries, when do U.S. companies choose to hire independent sales agents to represent their products? Is this different from the way agents are used in the United States?

12. Why are companies organizing salespeople into teams and how can the efforts of sales teams be controlled?

13. Which TQM principles are recommended when organizing the sales force effort?

▶ PROBLEMS

1. Ron and Joseph Mauro ran the Tombstone Tap, a Wisconsin bar named for its proximity to a cemetery. They also made pizza in the back room for their customers. Word of the delicious pizza quickly spread, and the Mauros began shipping to local taverns, using a refrigerated truck. In less than three years, production climbed to 3,000 pizzas a day and several delivery routes were established with independent distributors. Shortly thereafter, a large supermarket chain in the Chicago area expressed interest in buying pizzas from Tombstone. At about the same time, however, the Mauros began to have problems. The inexperienced distributors let inventories and unpaid bills pile up. It seemed as if the very growth that had expanded their business might be their undoing. Should they accept the Chicago supermarket's offer? What changes could be made in the sales organization to keep pace with the dynamic environment?

2. Suppose an office supplies dealer has 750 large customers that need to be called on each month, 1,500 medium-size firms that should be called on every six weeks, and 3,000 small organizations that need to be serviced once every quarter. Given that salespeople make 10 calls per week, how many salespeople are needed?

3. Mattel Toys has about 30 major customers (retail chains, for the most part) and thousands of smaller ones, including toy stores not affiliated with chains and drugstores. Sales have not been favorable recently, and the national sales force has gotten its share of the blame. Currently, salespeople call on all potential customers, big and small alike, that fall in their territory. One criticism is that not enough attention is given to the major accounts, which provide a great deal of revenue. Suggest a possible reorganization of the sales force that might alleviate this problem.

4. The world of business-to-business management is changing, radically and permanently. New selling methods, especially national accounts programs and telemarketing, have altered the role of traditional face-to-face selling. The role of the traditional field sales force has shrunk, while telemarketing focuses on small customers and national accounts programs sell to the largest customers. How do you think these developments will affect the role of the traditional sales manager and the skills required for the position? How does the sales manager's role compare with the roles of national accounts managers and telemarketing managers?

5. The 3M Company offers an 800 number to assist its telecommunication equipment customers. The 3M National Service Center, located in St. Paul, Minnesota, is staffed 365 days a year, 24 hours a day, with skilled technicians and coordinators. Through systematic questioning and a variety of facsimile, ASCII communication terminals, the latest monitoring and testing equipment, and a sophisticated on-line computer system, the staff can isolate an equipment problem or operator error. The 3M Center has found that in more than 30 percent of the calls, the equipment failure can be corrected in minutes, without dispatching

a service technician. What are other possible telemarketing applications besides customer service?

6. Corporate restructuring is becoming an everyday occurrence in today's business environment. Such restructuring may happen when one company acquires another or picks up a new product line. It may also occur in the process of divesting a business or product line or when merging several product lines, each with its own sales and distribution forces, into a single division. Restructuring both offers opportunities and poses threats to sales force management. If, for example, a national company has decided to combine its separate housewares and audio business sales forces, what are the issues that must be considered? What kinds of analysis would you do prior to any reorganization? How would you execute a merger between these two sales forces?

▶ IN-CLASS EXERCISES

8-1: Damage Control

Six months after joining Pilot Pen Corporation, the national sales manager is informed by the president that the company has decided to switch to an in-house sales force of 40 salespeople instead of having independent sales agents sell the company's product line of pens, pencils, markers, and accessories.

Pilot Pen's sales are headed for $57 million this year. It has sold through sales agents throughout its 32-year history. Sales have grown rapidly over this time, and 100 sales agents currently represent the product line to Pilot's customers. The agents sell directly to retailers, and to office product distributors, who, in turn, sell office products to retailers such as college book stores, office supply stores, drugstores, and grocery stores. The marketplace is changing as large discounters such as Wal-Mart and K-Mart are growing. The fastest-growing market force is the large office product stores such as Office Max, which sell to businesses as well as to the walk-in retail trade.

In addition to the national sales manager, there are two regional sales managers at Pilot Pen, a subsidiary of Japan's Pilot Corporation. Along with the national sales manager, the regional managers are responsible for recruiting high-quality sales agents and working with them to ensure that Pilot gains full line distribution. The sales manager will need their help to put together an in-house sales force and to undertake damage control when the sales agents are informed of the new organization.

After briefly discussing some current sales issues, the president informs the sales manager that Pilot wants to change from independent agents to an in-house sales force. Among other reasons for the change, the company has decided to open its first U.S. manufacturing facility next year and wants to leverage its production capabilities as soon as possible. The president also mentions that he feels the sales agents have grown "older and wealthier" and are losing the "energy and drive" of earlier years.

The sales manager's reaction is one of surprise, followed by a realization of the magnitude of the undertaking. The president informs the sales manager that he has two months to complete a plan for starting the new sales force. The sales manager says that he had better get started right away, and suggests that he get together with the two regional sales managers this week.

In the initial meeting with the two regional sales managers, the sales manager informs them of the impending change in organization. After expressing their surprise, the regional sales managers focus on their concern with agents' reaction. They say there is no way that this plan can be kept a secret until it is implemented and that the agents are likely to be angry about losing the 20 percent commissions they have become used to receiving over a long period of time. During this discussion, possible retaliatory actions by the agents are discussed. At the meeting conclusion the vice president suggests that they all think about how to "ease out" the 100 agents without suffering undue economic recriminations and calls a meeting for next week to discuss alternative plans.

Questions:

1. As national sales manager, how would you handle the meeting with the two regional sales managers?
2. What issues would you have to address in starting your own sales force?
3. How would you attempt to control the potential economic damage that may occur when switching from sales agents to your own sales force?
4. What would you suggest doing if one of your agents confronted you with the question of whether it was true that Pilot Pen was going to release all its agents and switch to a dedicated sales force?

▶ REFERENCES

1. DANIEL LEVINE, "Justice Served," *Sales & Marketing Management* (May 1995), pp. 53–61.

2. TIM CLARK and JAN JABEN, "IBM's Destiny," *Business Marketing* (May 1993), p. 25.

3. CHRISTIEN HEIDE, *Sales Force Compensation Survey* (Chicago, Ill: The Dartnell Corporation 1996), p. 175.

4. "Technology Raises Bar for Sales Jobs," *Wall Street Journal*, January 21, 1997, p. B-1.

5. HEIDE, p. 175.

6. "Eastman Kodak Brings Training into Sharper Focus," *Sales & Marketing Management* (September 1992), p. 62.

7. MILAN MORAVEC, MARSHALL COLLINS, and CLINTON TRIPODI, "Don't Want to Manage? Here's Another Path," *Sales & Marketing Management* (April 1990), pp. 70–76.

8. PAUL DISHMAN and DREGG AYTES, "Exploring Group Support Systems in Sales Management Applications," *Journal of Personal Selling & Sales Management* (Winter 1996), pp. 65–77.

9. JEROME COLLETTI and GARY TUBRIDY, *Reinventing the Sales Organization* (Scottsdale, Ariz.: The Alexander Group, Inc. 1993), p. 2.

10. ROBERT RUEKERT, ORVILLE WALKER, and KENNETH ROERING, "The Organization of Marketing Activities: A Contingency Theory of Structure and Performance," *Journal of Marketing*, 49 (Winter 1985), pp. 17–21.

11. MARTIN EVERETT, "Send in the Specialists," *Sales & Marketing Management* (April 1991), pp. 46–47.

12. RAVIPEET SOHI, DANIEL SMITH, and NEIL FORD, "How Does Sharing a Sales Force Between Multiple Divisions Affect Salespeople?" *Journal of the Academy of Marketing Science* (Summer 1996), pp. 195–207.

13. THOMAS WOTRUBA and STEPHEN CASTLEBERRY, "National Account Marketers: Who They Are and What They Do," *NAMA Journal*, 27 (Winter 1992), p. 9.

14. JEROME COLLETTI and GARY TABRIDDY, "Effective Major Account Sales Management," *Journal of Personal Selling & Sales Management* (August 1987), p. 4.

15. *Economic Impact: U.S. Direct Marketing Today* (New York: The Direct Marketing Educational Foundation, Inc. 1995).

16. KATHY HALEY, "Telemarketing Boosts Sales Effectiveness," *Business Marketing* (August 1995) , pp. B2–B5.

17. PEGGY MORETTI, "Telemarketers Serve Clients," *Business Marketing* (April 1994), pp. 29, 31.

18. MORETTI, "Telemarketers," p. 31.

19. JOHN TSCHOHL, *Achieving Excellence Through Customer Service* (Englewood Cliffs, NJ: Prentice-Hall, 1991).

20. For an excellent discussion of these issues, see WILLIAM MONCRIEF, SHANNON SHIPP, CHARLES LAMB, and DAVID CRAVENS, "Examining the Roles of Telemarketing in Selling Strategies," *Journal of Personal Selling & Sales Management* (Fall 1989), pp. 1–12.

21. For a good discussion on how to address these problems, see JUDITH MARSHALL and HARRIE VREDENBURG, "An Empirical Study of Factors Influencing Innovation Implementation in Industrial Sales Organizations," *Journal of the Academy of Marketing Science*, 20 (Summer 1992), pp. 205–215.

22. American Telemarketing Association, 1993 *Salary Survey of Members.*

23. DANA MILBANK, "Telephone Sales Reps Do Unrewarding Jobs That Few Can Abide," *Wall Street Journal* (September 9, 1993), p. A1.

24. MARILYN STEPHENS, DONALD WEINRAUCH, and KARL MANN, "Leading Manufacturers Representatives Voice Their Perceptions and Recommendations for the Future: A Challenge to Marketing Educators," *National Conference for Sales Management* (1993), p. 95.

25. For more on nonfinancial means of motivating sales reps, see EDWIN BOBROW, "Reps and Recognition: Understanding What Motivates," *Sales & Marketing Management* (September 1991), pp. 82–85.

26. ERIN ANDERSON, "The Salesperson as Outside Agent or Employee: A Transaction Cost Analysis," *Marketing Science* 4 (Summer 1985), pp. 234–254.

27. STEVE ZUNIER, "Finally, Reps Get Some Respect," *Industrial Distribution*, 80 (June 1991), pp. 27–30.

28. U.S. Department of Commerce, *Census of Wholesale Trade* for 1972, 1977, 1982, 1987, Vol. 1.

29. ALLEN WEISS and ERIN ANDERSON, "Converting from Independent to Employee Salesforces: The Role of Perceived Switching Costs," *Journal of Marketing Research*, 24 (February 1992), pp. 101–115.

30. JOHN HILL and RICHARD STILL, "Organizing the Overseas Sales Force: How Multinationals Do It," *Journal of Personal Selling & Sales Management*, 10 (Spring 1990), pp. 57–66.

31. "Sales Management in the Age of Cross-Functional Organizations," *Sales Manager's Bulletin* (August 30, 1995), p. 10.

32. JOSEPH CONLIN, "Teaming Up," *Sales & Marketing Management* (October 1993), pp. 98–104.

33. JAMES CORTADA, TQM for Sales and Marketing (New York: McGraw-Hill, Inc., 1993).

34. TOM EISENHART, "Telemarketing Takes Quantum Leap," *Business Marketing* (September 1993), p. 75.

▶ **SELECTED READINGS**

DOUGLASS, MERRIL, and DONNA DOUGLASS, *Time Management for Teams* (New York: Amacom, 1992).

CORTADA, JAMES, TQM *for Sales and Marketing Management* (New York: McGraw-Hill, 1993)

HELLRIEGEL, DON, and JOHN W. SLOCUM, JR., *Management*, 6th ed. (Reading, Mass.: Addison-Wesley, 1992).

SONTER, JAMES A., and R. E. FREEMAN, *Management*, 4th ed. (Englewood Cliffs, N.J.: Prentice-Hall, 1990).

CASE

8-1 JEFFERSON-PILOT CORPORATION*

On February 28, 1993, Roger Soles, Jefferson-Pilot's (J-P) President, Chairman of the Board, and Chief Executive Officer for the last 25 years, retired, J-P Corporation had 1992 revenues of $1.2 billion from its four business segments (individual, group, casualty and title insurance; and a communications group) and from investment income.

Soles had used a strong leadership style to guide J-P during his tenure. Decision-making and management had a top-down focus, and Soles exercised a high level of control. Despite J-P's success under Soles' leadership, however, revenues had been basically flat for the last five years (1988–92). Low interest rates, which affected investment earnings, and declining life insurance sales contributed to the sluggish revenues and earnings. The corporate culture also seemed resistant to change and fixed on retaining the status quo—the traditional way of doing things.

J-Ps Board of Directors felt the company needed aggressive new leadership if the company were to be a market leader. In order to provide for a smooth transition following Soles' retirement, the Board selected David A. Stonecipher to become President-elect and brought him on board in September 1992. Stonecipher had been the president and CEO of Life of Georgia, an Atlanta-based insurance company. He also served as President of Southland Life Insurance Company and had recently become President of Georgia US Corporation, the parent company of both Life of Georgia and Southland Life.

Stonecipher had a reputation as an aggressive, outgoing leader who was willing to change and try new things. He realized that increased sales would be the key to J-P's revenue growth and that he needed a strong management team if he were going to make the necessary changes. With that in mind, one of his first acts was to appoint Kenneth Mlekush as Executive Vice President of Individual Insurance. Mlekush, who had previously served as President and CEO of Southland Life, brought over 30 years of experience to the position and specialized in marketing individual life and annuity products. Mlekush later asked Ron Ridlehuber, who had worked with him at Southland, to join J-P as Senior Vice President for Independent Marketing. Ridlehuber had 18 years of experience in marketing and field sales management. Stonecipher also promoted Bill Seawell from his position as an agency manager in J-P's career sales force to serve as Senior Vice President for Ordinary Marketing. Seawell had been with J-P since 1976 and had managed the Greensboro agency since 1981. During that time, the Greensboro agency had consistently been among J-P's leading agencies.

A Strategic Review

After assembling his management team, Stonecipher asked a major consulting firm that specialized in working with life insurance companies to conduct a strategic marketing review of the firm. Now, in early 1993, Stonecipher had assembled the new team in a conference room in the firm's corporate offices in Greensboro, North Carolina, to hear the consultant's report. He knew this report would provide a basis for the strategic decisions the group would have to make if the company were going to meet the Board's and the shareholders' expectations. The managers knew that a key focus of the report and of the decisions facing them would be how J-P should structure and manage its sales force because life and annuity sales would need to grow dramatically in order to increase revenues significantly.

J-P's Sales Force

J-P distributed its individual insurance products through three separate systems: career agents, inde-

*This case was prepared by Dr. Lew G. Brown, Associate Professor, and Michael Cook, MBA, of the University of North Carolina at Greensboro. The authors express their appreciation to Jefferson-Pilot Corporation for its cooperation in development of this case. Copyright © by Lew G. Brown and the North American Case Research Association. Reproduced by permission.

pendent producing general agents, and financial institutions. J-P hired career agents and provided them with extensive training, an office, and full staff support. The company paid the agents a salary subsidy during their training year and then changed them to a commission-only basis. The agents earned a commission on the premiums each policy generated. The agent earned a higher commission rate on the first-year premium and then earned a lower commission rate on renewal premiums thereafter as the policyholder renewed the policy year after year. The career agents were very loyal. In fact, the company was very selective in choosing career agents. Becoming one was difficult, and those who were successful were very proud of their position. But growth based on a career system was slow, and the costs of maintaining the sales force were high.

In early 1993, J-P had approximately 800 career agents. They sold about 90 percent of its life insurance policies. Agents on average during 1992 wrote about 30 policies and earned about $26,000 in first-year commissions (the commissions paid on the policy's first-year premium). The first-year commission rate averaged 50 percent of the first-year's premium. The average career agent earned total income, including commissions on renewal policies, in the high $40,000 range. Bill Seawell was responsible for managing the career sales force.

At the beginning of 1993, there were approximately 1,400 independent personal producing agents (PGAs) distributing J-P's life and annuity products. Twelve salaried regional directors recruited about 15 to 20 PGAs each year, seeking agents who were already established in the insurance business. Although the independent agents did not work directly for J-P, the company provided extensive training and support. The PGAs allowed J-P to extend its marketing operations (in a limited way) beyond its core geographic distribution areas. Although there were more PGAs than career agents, many of them sold few J-P policies each year. They had contracts with J-P as well as with other insurance companies and could sell policies offered by any company they represented. First-year commission rates on policies PGAs sold by were in the 80–85 percent range. These rates were higher than those for career agents because J-P did not pay any of the PGAs' expenses, as it did for career agents. Ron Ridlehuber was responsible for managing the independent sales force.

J-P also used an additional distribution channel consisting of 19 relatively small community banks and savings institutions that contracted to distribute life and annuity products. J-P designed the annuity products for these institutions and controlled pricing. Jefferson-Pilot financial data are presented in Exhibits 1 and 2.

The Consultants' Presentation

David Stonecipher glanced around the conference room to make sure everyone was ready. "Well, gentlemen, let's begin." Aaron Sherman and Larry Richardson, who directed the project for the consulting firm, began the presentation.

"Gentlemen, I have given each of you a detailed report summarizing our findings. We wanted to meet with you today to present an overview of the key points and to answer any questions you have," Aaron Sherman began. "As you are aware, we began this process by holding a workshop with J-P's executives at which we asked them to rate issues the company faces. The number one issue they identified was that your total annualized premium income has declined during the past five years while most of your major competitors' revenues have grown. Although J-P has an excellent core of field and home-office people and is in excellent financial condition, our analysis highlights areas where you need to take action.

Target and Managerial Peer Companies

"In conducting our analysis, we looked at a group of 13 companies, 7 of which we call 'managerial peers' and 6 of which we call 'target companies.' The target companies are those you face on a day-to-day basis in competing for policyholders and new agents. Some of these operate using a 'general agent,' that is an independent agent who is not a company employee. The managerial peer companies are those you compete with when you sell policies or recruit agents, but all of them use a career system like J-P, with agency managers who are responsible for the agents who work out of their offices. J-P has the highest rating in terms of claims-paying ability from both A.M. Best and Standard and Poor's rating services. Only 5 of the 13 peer companies have similar ratings. Some of your

Exhibit 1: Consolidated Statements of Income

(Dollar Amounts in Thousands Except Per Share Information)	Year Ended December 31		
	1990	1991	1992
REVENUE			
Life premiums and other considerations	$238,326	$230,369	$230,034
Accident and health premiums	375,872	382,624	383,552
Casualty and title premiums earned	$47,078	45,270	44,815
Total premiums and other considerations	661,276	658,263	$658,401
Net Investment income	342,053	352,772	360,882
Realized investment gains	28,201	33,963	48,170
Communications operations	127,330	125,045	129,734
Other	3,753	3,433	5,142
Total Revenue	1,162,613	1,173,476	1,202,329
BENEFITS AND EXPENSES			
Death Benefits	111,444	104,131	105,013
Matured endowments	5,223	4,455	4,576
Annuity benefits	13,903	14,912	15,054
Disability benefits	1,224	1,151	1,185
Surrender benefits	59,297	47,174	38,485
Accident and health benefits	322,922	318,876	317,350
Casualty benefits	34,605	36,657	30,025
Interest on policy or contrast funds	89,651	93,995	94,106
Supplementary contracts with life contingencies	4,997	5,346	5,637
(Decrease) in benefit liabilities	(10,050)	(764)	(1,292)
Total benefits	633,216	625,933	610,139
Dividends to policyholders	16,950	16,598	16,997
Insurance commissions	63,396	57,237	54,382
General and administrative	125,101	124,470	128,501
Net (deferral) of policy acquisition costs	(15,745)	(12,214)	(11,536)
Insurance taxes, licenses and fees	22,750	24,351	24,660
Communications operations	95,356	92,334	93,560
Total Benefits and Expenses	941,024	928,709	916,703
Income before income taxes	221,589	244,767	285,626
Income taxes (benefits):			
Current	68,031	77,839	88,889
Deferred	(4,079)	(8,759)	(6,501)
Total Taxes	63,952	69,080	83,388
Net Income	$157,637	$175,687	$203,238
Net Income Per Share of Common Stock	$2.94	$3.42	$3.99

Source: Jefferson-Pilot 1992 Annual Report.

Exhibit 2: Jefferson-Pilot Segment Information

	(Dollars in Thousands)		
	1990	1991	1992
REVENUE			
Life insurance	$946,262	$956,426	$965,862
Other insurance	55,164	53,472	53,907
Communications	127,330	125,045	129,734
Other, net	33,857	38,533	52,826
Consolidated	$1,162,613	$1,173,476	$1,202,329
INCOME BEFORE INCOME TAXES			
Life insurance	$179,725	$202,349	$217,635
Other insurance	6,575	919	7,820
Communications	16,902	18,023	24,262
Other, net	18,387	23,476	35,909
Consolidated	$221,589	$244,767	$285,626
IDENTIFIABLE ASSETS AT DECEMBER 31			
Life insurance	$4,132,811	$4,535,398	$4,817,482
Other insurance	136,449	147,309	158,741
Communications	111,130	102,836	99,938
Other, net	74,518	139,677	159,676
Consolidated	$4,454,908	$4,925,220	$5,235,837
DEPRECIATION AND AMORTIZATION			
Life insurance	$5,031	$5,741	$6,055
Other insurance	155	209	194
Communications	9,980	10,013	8,425
Other, net	324	327	172
Consolidated	$15,490	$16,290	$14,846

Source: Jefferson-Pilot 1992 Annual Report.

agents see the company's financial strength as a competitive weapon, while some others question whether the company has been too conservative.

Performance Analysis

"This overhead (Exhibit 3) presents a summary of your operating performance over the 1987–91 period as compared with the 13 target and managerial peer companies. As you can see, premium income and net gain before dividends have grown more slowly than the target group's average but faster than the managerial peers' average. Over this same period, the number of J-P's career-ordinary life agents has shrunk from 1,186 to 546. As a result, you have seen a decline in the percentage of your total premium income coming from life insurance. This results also from a decline

in the number of policies written and in the face amount per policy. It also appears that the productivity of your agents has lagged behind competitors. You also rely heavily on the business you develop in North and South Carolina and Virginia, as this overhead indicates (Exhibit 4).

Customer Analysis

"Next, we looked at your customers. This overhead (Exhibit 5) first compares J-P and the peer groups on the basis of premium per policy and average size per policy. Then, we break down your customers into male, female, and juvenile groups. As you can see, J-P has a lower premium per policy, average size policy, and premium per $1,000 coverage than do the peer companies. Like the peers, however, your typical cus-

Exhibit 3: Jefferson-Pilot's Summary of Operations 1987–1991 (Dollar Amounts in Millions)

	1987	1988	1989	1990	1991
Premiums & annuity considerations	$648.1	$718.0	$716.3	$727.2	$768.9
Net investment income	250.1	295.3	313.0	326.6	338.7
Other income	32.0	25.8	24.1	28.0	26.8
Total income	930.2	1,039.1	1,053.4	1,081.8	1,134.4
Total expenses	802.3	916.8	890.0	896.9	930.6
Net gain before dividends	127.9	122.3	163.4	184.9	203.8
Dividends to policyholders	18.8	25.3	24.7	23.8	22.5
Net gain after dividends	109.1	96.9	138.7	161.1	181.3

	Change from 1987–1991			Average Annual Percent Change		
	JP	Target Group Average	Managerial Peers Average	JP	Target Group Average	Managerial Peers Average
Premiums & annuity considerations	$120.8	$850.9	$3,182.0	4.4%	7.5%	11.7%
Net investment income	88.6	371.7	723.4	7.9%	9.1%	6.2%
Total income	204.2	796.5	3,590.1	5.1%	4.7%	8.6%
Deductions	(128.3)	(528.9)	(3,337.8)	(3.8)%	(3.5)%	(8.8)%
Net gain before dividends	75.9	267.6	252.3	12.4%	14.4%	6.3%

Source: Jefferson-Pilot.

Exhibit 4: Jefferson-Pilot 1991 Market Share for Selected States

	JP Share of Ordinary Life Insurance			JP's Ordinary Life Premiums (000)
	% Premium	% Issues	% In-Force	
Core Southeastern states:				
North Carolina	3.97%	2.86%	3.57%	$ 63,794
South Carolina	2.08	1.62	1.86	15,884
Virginia	0.94	0.54	0.88	13,017
Other major Southern states:				
Texas	0.58	0.36	0.50	19,368
Florida	0.37	0.19	0.35	10,268
Georgia	0.59	0.39	0.55	8,785
Tennessee	0.57	0.30	0.52	5,865
Louisiana	0.51	0.52	0.55	4,352
Alabama	0.36	0.07	0.28	3,108
Mississippi	0.63	0.29	0.68	2,794
Kentucky	0.33	0.35	0.31	2,181
Outside the South:				
Virgin Islands	3.73	0.60	3.28	433
Puerto Rico	2.58	1.15	1.89	3,853
California	0.07	0.03	0.05	3,738
U.S. total	0.32%	0.20%	0.29%	$175,446

Source: Jefferson-Pilot.

Exhibit 5: Comparison of Premiums and Average Size Per Policy

Premium/Policy Size	Jefferson-Pilot	Target Group	Managerial Peers
Premium per policy	$889	$1,211	$966
Average size policy	$101,470	$126,940	$91,580
Premium per $1,000	$8.76	$9.54	$10.55

PERCENT OF POLICIES
(PREMIUM PER POLICY)

Customer Demographics	Jefferson-Pilot	Target Group	Managerial Peers
Male	51%	57%	53%
	($1,213)	($1,567)	($1,257)
Female	38	33	36
	($639)	($879)	($744)
Juvenile	11	10	11
	($233)	($255)	($303)

By Whom Sold	Full-Time Agents	PGAs
Percent of policies	91%	9%
Premium of policy	$837	$1,439
Average size policy	$100,920	$127,580
Premium per $1,000	$8.29	$11.28

Source: Jefferson-Pilot.

tomer is a male, under 35 years old who is employed in a professional or executive position. Your career agents sell 91 percent of your policies, but the policies they sell are smaller in terms of size and premium than those sold by your PGAs.

"Because adult males account for a little over half of your policies and 70 percent of your premiums, we wanted to look more closely at this group. This overhead (Exhibit 6) shows the occupation, age, and income distribution for your male customers and those of the peer companies. Although we saw earlier that your typical customer is under 35 years old, you will note that the peer companies have larger percentages of their customers in this group and that you have a higher percentage of your customers over 45 years old. This would suggest that you should have higher premiums per policy, yet your premiums per policy are lower in both the younger and older groups and overall. Our analysis indicates that your typical male customer has a median income of $37,500."

"Why do you think our premiums are typically lower than those of the peer companies?" Ken Mlekush asked.

"That's a good question, Ken," Larry Richardson responded. "Our feeling is that the lower premiums are the result of your company's concentration in the Southeast, where incomes are generally lower than in the Northeast. A number of the peer companies have a major presence in the Northeast. Also, some of your agents may not be capitalizing on the opportunities in their markets, but we believe the regional difference is the key factor."

Product Comparison

"If that answers your question, Ken, we'll move on to our discussion of your products," Aaron Sherman resumed. "Our next overhead (Exhibit 7) presents an analysis of J-P's product mix, based on first-year commissions, as compared with the peer companies. As the exhibit shows, J-P has been steadily selling less life insurance, down from 76 percent of first-year commissions to 63 percent, just since 1989. The other companies' life insurance shares have held relatively constant over this time. Your salespeople are selling considerably more disability income and health insurance and annuities than are the other companies."

Exhibit 6: Analysis of Adult Male Consumer by Occupation, Income, and Age

Occupation	PERCENT OF POLICIES (PREMIUM PER POLICY)		
	Jefferson-Pilot	Target Group	Managerial Peers
Executive	37% ($1,756)	36% ($2,003)	28% ($1,728)
Professional	33 ($1,234)	41 ($1,651)	28 ($1,492)
Blue Collar	21 ($710)	18 ($884)	38 ($772)
Clerical	9 ($866)	5 ($1,664)	6 ($734)
Income			
Under $25K	26% ($625)	14% ($582)	24% ($603)
$25K–49.9K	45 ($841)	41 ($811)	51 ($956)
$50K or over	29 ($2,421)	45 ($2,400)	25 ($2,541)
Age			
Under 35	39% ($561)	47% ($671)	47% ($688)
35–44	31 ($1,169)	32 ($1,647)	27 ($1,034)
45 or over	30 ($2,056)	21 ($3,536)	26 ($2,494)

Source: Jefferson-Pilot.

"Why do you think our agents are selling more annuities and disability income policies?" David Stonecipher asked.

"Our experience indicates that agents find it easier to sell disability income and annuities as compared to life insurance," Aaron Sherman answered. "Consumers can understand these policies better and salespeople find them easier to explain. Thus, the salespeople go for the easy sale. What is more important to understand, however, is that it is unusual for a company with a large career sales force to stress universal life. Whole life policies provide more support for the field sales force because consumers tend to keep the policies in force longer and the renewal premiums are higher."

Sales Force Comparison

"How do our salespeople feel about the products we give them to sell?" Bill Seawell asked.

Larry Richardson responded by presenting an overhead (Exhibit 8). "This overhead summarizes our findings on that question. As you can see, relative to the norm for other companies we have surveyed, your agents were less pleased with the variety of products and were significantly less pleased with new product development. They also seemed to feel that the company is not as market driven as it should be."

"Larry, while we are on the subject of how the salespeople feel, how did we stack up relative to recruitment and retention of the sales force?" Ron Ridlehuber wondered.

"That's an important question, Ron. Our study shows that only 35 percent of J-P's new agents made it through the first year, 15 percentage points below the industry average, and only 24 percent made it through the first two years. Moreover, only 7 percent stay more than four years.

"This overhead (Exhibit 9) summarizes your sit-

Exhibit 7: Product Mix Trends (Percent of First-Year Commission)

	1989	1990	1991
JEFFERSON-PILOT			
Life	76%	70%	63%
DI/health	9	12	12
Annuities	11	13	17
Investment Products	4	5	7
Group	0	0	0
Total	100%	100%	100%
TARGET GROUP			
Life	78%	75%	75%
DI/health	7	6	6
Annuities	4	6	7
Investment Products	5	6	8
Group	7	7	5
Total	100%	100%	100%
MANAGERIAL AGENCY PEERS			
Life	76%	78%	77%
DI/health	5	5	5
Annuities	8	9	9
Investment Products	3	3	4
Group	7	6	4
Total	100%	100%	100%

Source: Jefferson-Pilot.

uation pretty well. The first part of the overhead shows that in 1991, recruits represented 48 percent of your base sales force, as compared with 29 percent and 38 percent for the two peer groups. Further, as we've noted, your base sales force has been declining while your peers' sales groups have been stable or increasing. Likewise, your turnover rates have been consistently higher than your peers. Finally, the overhead shows that only 35 percent of your sales force has been with you more than 5 years as compared

Exhibit 8: Sales Force's Ratings of JP's Products (Percent of Agents Agreeing)

Agents' Overall Assessment of Companies' Products	Jefferson-Pilot	Norm
I am pleased with the variety of products our company offers.	66%	78%
I am satisfied with our company's development of new products.	33	65
Our company is market driven, responding to the needs of its target market with appropriate products and services.	25	66

Source: Jefferson-Pilot.

Exhibit 9: Sales Force Recruitment and Retention

RECRUITS AS A PERCENT OF BASE FORCE

	Jefferson-Pilot		Target Group	Managerial Peers
	Rate	**No. of Recruits**		
1991	48%	280	29%	38%
1990	58	378	31	41
1989	34	316	30	40
1988	40	459	30	45
1987	42	501	33	41

PERCENT CHANGE IN BASE FORCE

	Jefferson-Pilot[a]	**Target Group**	**Managerial Peers**
1991	−6%	−1%	−1%
1990	−11	b	2
1989	−31	b	1
1988	−2	b	9
1987	−2	1	6

TURNOVER RATE

1991	36%	24%	28%
1990	44	24	28
1989	48	23	28
1988	30	23	25
1987	31	24	25

DISTRIBUTION OF SALES AGENTS BY YEARS OF SERVICE
Years of Service

1	35%	24%	29%
2	15	14	15
3	10	9	9
4	5	7	7
5+	35	46	40

[a] The field force has declined from 1,161 to 546 full-time agents.

b Less than ½ of 1 percent.

Source: Jefferson-Pilot.

with 40 percent and 46 percent for the two comparison groups. And after five years, we expect agents to be in their most productive period."

"Larry, what did you determine about our agents' productivity versus the peer groups?" David Stonecipher asked.

"We looked closely at the issue of productivity. We found that J-P agents earned on average lower first-year commissions (not including renewal commissions) in each year as compared with the peers. Your base sales force had average first-year commis-

sions of about $22,000 versus $31,000 for the target group and almost $25,000 for the managerial peer group. When we looked at number of policies sold, we also found that your agents sold fewer individual life policies."

"Do you have any ideas as to why our productivity is lower, Larry?"

"Yes, David. Although there are many factors that affect productivity, it seems to the project team that J-P's production standards are low compared to the peers' standards. This may cause more experienced

Exhibit 10: Results of Agent Survey—Production Goals

IN OUR AGENCY, A GOOD JOB IS DONE OF HELPING AGENTS
SET CHALLENGING BUT ATTAINABLE PRODUCTION OBJECTIVES:

	Percent Agreement
Agency Manager	88%
Sales Manager	73
Agent	49
Norm for FT agent	52%

IF VALIDATION REQUIREMENTS WERE A PRODUCTION LEVEL
GOAL TOWARD WHICH I WAS WORKING, I WOULD SEE IT AS:

	Jefferson-Pilot	Target Group	Managerial Peers
Challenging	30%	40%	48%
Modest	51	35	33
Too low	18	23	14
Too high	1	2	5

IN THE PAST MONTH, HOW MANY:

	Jefferson-Pilot	Target Group	Managerial Peers
Prospects have you mailed to	99	231	278
Prospects have you phoned	113	211	147
Cold calls have you made	41	74	63
Appointments have you had	29	49	41
Fact-finders have you completed	22	17	17
Closing interviews have you done	17	18	18

Source: Jefferson-Pilot.

agents to place less business with J-P. They may meet their performance goals with you and then place other business with other firms in order to meet goals there.

"There is also evidence that the agents feel that the production levels are too low. As this overhead (Exhibit 10) shows, your managers believe that they help agents set high but attainable goals, yet slightly less than half of the agents feel that way. In looking at the validation requirements, the performance standards that first-year agents must meet, 69 percent of the agents believed they were modest or too low. Finally, your agents had considerably less activities in direct mail, telephone prospecting, etc., than did agents from the peer companies. Many salespeople don't like to perform these activities, but experience shows that the activities are a key part of building a clientele.

"Your managers and agents also seem to have different perspectives on what is required of new agents. This overhead (Exhibit 11) indicates that over

90 percent of your managers felt they give a realistic picture of an agent's career to an agent they are recruiting, yet only 32 percent of the agents felt that way. Moreover, when we asked the managers which activities they required of a new agent prior to signing a contract with them, we got a very different set of responses than we got when we asked the new agents the same question. Seventy-three percent of your new hires have not been full-time life agents previously, so it is not hard to understand that they might not fully understand what being a career agent requires."

Marketing Costs

"How did we compare as far as marketing costs, Aaron?"

"Ken, our analysis indicates that your marketing costs are generally in line with the managerial peer group. As you know, because of the one-time cost of issuing a policy and the high first-year sales commis-

Exhibit 11: Results of Agent Survey—Precontract

IN OUR AGENCY, NEW AGENTS ARE GIVEN A REALISTIC PICTURE OF THE AGENT'S CAREER:	Percent Agreement
Agency Manager	100%
Sales Manager	93
Agent	32
Norm for FT agent	39%

MANAGERS: WHICH ACTIVITIES DO YOU TYPICALLY REQUIRE OF PRODUCERS PRIOR TO CONTRACT?	Jefferson-Pilot	Target Group	Managerial Peers
Learn a sales talk	100%	63%	83%
Make joint calls	93	57	60
Market opinion surveys	93	74	78
Complete sales	81	57	53
Basic insurance knowledge	70	79	77
Become licensed	59	82	93

AGENTS: WHICH OF THE FOLLOWING ACTIVITIES WERE YOU REQUIRED TO COMPLETE PRIOR TO BEING CONTRACTED?			
Market opinion surveys	64%	24%	39%
Basic insurance knowledge	51	54	51
Become licensed	49	62	66
Complete sales	47	28	27
Learn a sales talk	39	36	40
Make joint calls	30	19	18
None	8	17	12

Source: Jefferson-Pilot.

Exhibit 12: Components of Marketing Costs: 1991 (Per $100 of Weighted New Premiums)

	Jefferson-Pilot	Target Group	Peer Group
Producer Compensation[a]	$61	$55	$62
Management Compensation[b]	26	23	19
Field Expenses Paid by Company[c]	37	36	43
Field Benefits	17	17	24
Sub-Total	141	131	148
Home Office Marketing Expenses	24	14	18
Total	$165	$145	$166

[a]Includes all compensation *other than* renewal commissions; includes first-year commissions on management personal production.

[b]Includes compensation paid to agency managers and second-line supervisors.

[c]Includes all operating expenses paid by Company (e.g., clerical salary, rent, postage, telephone, etc.).

Source: Jefferson-Pilot.

Exhibit 13: 1991 Average Agency Characteristics

	Jefferson-Pilot	Peers
Manager income[a]	$100,913	$150,145
Agency first-year commission revenue	$247,941	$778,431
Managers' years of service	9.9	6.1
Number of agents	11.1	32.9
Number of recruits	5.7	11.2
Number of 2nd-line managers	1.5	2.2
2nd-line manager income[a]	$23,489	$52,075
Number of agencies	35	473

[a]Excludes personal production

Source: Jefferson-Pilot.

sion, it costs J-P about $1.65 for each $1.00 of premium income in the first year. In other words, you lose $.65 for every dollar of premium income in the first year. That's why it is so important to keep policies on the books. It takes into the second or third year before the company makes any money on the policy.

"Your $1.65 figure compares with $1.66 for the managerial group, but it is higher than the target group's average of $1.45. We think that comes from your having more smaller offices. When we controlled for office size, your costs seemed to be in line. This overhead (Exhibit 12) shows the elements of your costs as compared with the peer companies. Your costs are higher for both producer (agent) compen-

sation and management compensation due to your competitive bonus structure and your agent financing plan. Your home office expenses are probably higher simply because you are a smaller company than some of the peers, and there are certain fixed costs you have to bear. You should be able to grow and spread those fixed costs. To help you compare your agencies' costs with the peer group's, I prepared this overhead (Exhibit 13). It shows that your agencies are on average about one-third the size of the average peer agency."

"How do our agents feel about their compensation, Larry?"

"Bill, I prepared this overhead to summarize our

Exhibit 14: Attitudes Toward Compensation

FULL-TIME AGENT RESPONSES (PERCENT AGREEMENT)

	Jefferson-Pilot	Norm
I have a secure income.	39%	46%
I have a good compensation plan.	46	58
My compensation plan is competitive.	38	49
My compensation plan is clear and understandable.	51	53
I have good fringe benefits.	51	64

MANAGERS' RESPONSES

	Jefferson-Pilot	Norm
I have a secure income.	33%	58%
I have a good compensation plan.	67	65
My compensation plan is competitive.	56	55
My compensation plan is clear and understandable.	66	57
I have good fringe benefits.	44	73

Source: Jefferson-Pilot.

findings on that point (Exhibit 14). As you can see, your full-time agents are below the norm in every category for all agents in our survey. On the other hand, your managers are above the norm in each category except for how secure they feel about their income.

"David, I think that about covers the points we wanted to present at this time. We will, of course, be available to answer additional questions you have as you proceed with your planning," Larry concluded.

"Thank you, Larry and Aaron. Your work will be very helpful. We'll let you go now while we continue our discussion."

Options

"Well, I don't know that any of the consultants' findings surprised us, but hearing them all together is certainly sobering," David began. "We've got our work cut out for us if we are going to achieve the growth and profitability goals the Board has set. It wants us to grow earnings per share by 10 percent per year and achieve above average returns on capital. Ken, what do you think our options are?"

"David, even if we choose the option of continuing to have the same kind of company we've had, that is one focused primarily on using the career agent to sell our products, we've got to make a number of changes to address the issues in the report. We seem to be in a cycle of declining performance. Fewer agents lead to less new business. This causes an expense problem. Due to that problem, we don't do the things we need to do to develop competitive products. It's a vicious cycle. Don't you agree, Bill?"

"Yes, Ken. But I think it is important for us to remember that our career-agent system is our key strength. We are known as a company because of that system. We have many long-term, loyal agents. As you know, my father worked here and was in charge of our career agents. We need to improve the quality of our recruits, train them better, and keep them with us. If we can do those things, we will grow faster and be more profitable."

"That's true, Bill," Ron joined in, "but it seems to me that we need to look more closely at complementing the career system by increasing our emphasis on the independent agent. We have many independent agents now, and the report shows that

they are very productive. But they have never been the focus of our system. Under a new system we would contract with existing insurance agents, allowing them to offer our products. This avoids the problem of having to hire and train new recruits, and it would allow us to expand our geographic coverage more quickly. Further, we would not have to pay the office costs and associated salaries. We could pay these independent agents on a comission-only basis. Instead of using our 12 regional directors to recruit, we could license independent marketing organizations to recruit for us, with them earning an override commission on sales their agents made."

"Ron, I know you used this kind of system at Southland, but it would be such a radical change for J-P," Bill responded. "If you increased the size of our sales force substantially by using independent agents, I'm not sure how our career force would react. I'm afraid they'd be terribly threatened. And the folks in the home office are used to working with career agents. The independents would not be loyal to the company. We would have less control over what they sell and over the quality of their work with policyholders. And can you imagine what will happen the first time one of our career agents runs into an independent agent trying to sell the same product to the same customer!"

"David, you asked about options," Ken continued. "I guess this exchange points out that we could continue with a predominantly career-based system, move to a predominantly independent system, or have a combination of the two approaches. We're going to have to make significant changes under any of the options, and I'm sure there will be problems we'll have to address. A final growth option, of course, is to acquire other insurance companies. We certainly have the financial strength to do that, but even then we are going to have to address the issue of how we distribute, how we sell, our products to our policyholders."

"Yes, Ken, distribution is a key issue. I can see that there are many issues we need to think carefully about before we make a decision. Here's what I'd like for you to do. I'd like for each of you independently to consider our situation and develop recommendations as to how we should proceed. I'd like to meet again in two weeks to hear your presentations. I'll call you to set up a specific time once I check my calendar."

CASE

8-2 SHANANDOAH INDUSTRIES (B)*

In November 1986, Shanandoah merged with Lea-Meadows Industries, a manufacturer of upholstered furniture for living and family rooms. The merger was not planned in a conventional sense. Charlton Bates's father-in-law died suddenly in August 1986, leaving his daughter with controlling interest in the firm. The merger proceeded smoothly, since the two firms were located on adjacent properties and the general consensus was that the two firms would maintain as much autonomy as was economically justified. Moreover, the upholstery line filled a gap in the Shanandoah product mix, even though it would retain its own identity and brand names.

The only real issue that continued to plague Bates was merging the selling effort. Shanandoah had its own sales force, but Lea-Meadows Industries relied on sales agents to represent it. The question was straightforward, in his opinion: "Do we give the upholstery line of chairs and sofas to our sales force, or do we continue using the sales agents?" John Bott, Shanandoah's sales vice president, said the line should be given to his sales group; Martin Moorman, national sales manager of Lea-Meadows Industries, said the upholstery line should remain with sales agents.

Lea-Meadows Industries

Lea-Meadows Industries is a small manufacturer of upholstered furniture for use in living and family rooms. The firm is over 75 years old. The company has some of the finest fabrics and frame construction in the industry, according to trade sources. Net sales in 1986 were $3 million. Total industry sales of 1,500 upholstered furniture manufacturers in 1986 were $4.4 billion. Company sales had increased 15 percent annually over the last 5 years, and company executives believed this growth rate would continue for the foreseeable future.

*Prepared by Professor Roger A. Kerin of Southern Methodist University. Reproduced by permission.

Lea-Meadows Industries employed 15 sales agents to represent its products. These sales agents also represented several manufacturers of noncompeting furniture and home furnishings. Often a sales agent found it necessary to deal with several buyers in a store in order to represent all lines carried. On a typical sales call, a sales agent would first visit buyers. New lines, in addition to any promotions being offered by manufacturers, would be discussed. New orders were sought where and when it was appropriate. A sales agent would then visit a retailer's selling floor to check displays, inspect furniture, and inform salespeople on furniture. Lea-Meadows Industries paid an agent commission of 5 percent of net company sales for these services. Moorman thought sales agents spent 10 to 15 percent of their in-store sales time on Lea-Meadows products.

The company did not attempt to influence the type of retailers that agents contacted. Yet it was implicit in the agency agreement that agents would not sell to discount houses. All agents had established relationships with their retail accounts and worked closely with them. Sales records indicated that agents were calling on furniture and department stores. An estimated 1,000 retail accounts were called on in 1986.

Shanandoah Industries

Shanandoah is a manufacturer of medium- to high-priced living and dining room wood furniture. The firm was formed in 1902. Net sales in 1986 were $50 million. Total estimated industry sales of wood furniture in 1986 were $7.1 billion at manufacturers' prices.

The company employed 10 full-time sales representatives who called on 1,000 retail accounts in 1986. These individuals performed the same function as sales agents but were paid a salary plus a small commission. In 1986 the average Shanandoah sales representative received an annual salary of $50,000 (plus expenses) and a commission of 0.5 percent on net company sales. Total sales administration costs were $112,500.

The Shanandoah sales force was highly regarded

in the industry. The salespeople were known particularly for their knowledge of wood furniture and their willingness to work with buyers and retail sales personnel. Despite these points, Bates knew that all retail accounts did not carry the complete Shanandoah furniture line. He had therefore instructed John Bott to "push the group a little harder." At present, sales representatives were making 10 sales calls per week, with the average sales call running three hours. Remaining time was accounted for by administrative activities and travel. Bates recommended that the call frequency be increased to seven calls per account per year, which was consistent with what he thought was the industry norm.

Merging the Sales Effort

In separate meetings with Bott and Moorman, Bates was able to piece together a variety of data and perspectives on the merger question. These meetings also made it clear that Bott and Moorman differed dramatically in their views.

John Bott had no doubts about assigning the line to the Shanandoah sales force. Among the reasons he gave for this approach were the following. First, Shanandoah had developed one of the most well-respected, professional sales groups in the industry. Sales representatives could easily learn the fabric jargon, and they already knew personally many of the buyers who were responsible for upholstered furniture. Second, selling the Lea-Meadows line would require only about 15 percent of present sales call time. Thus he thought the new line would not be a major burden. Third, more control over sales efforts was possible. He noted that Charlton Bates's father-in-law had developed the Shanandoah sales group 25 years earlier because of the company commitment it engendered and because it provided customer service "only our own people are able and willing to give." Moreover, "our people have the Shanandoah 'Look'

Additional background information on the company and industry can be found in case 2-3, Shanandoah Industries (A).

and presentation style that is instilled in every person." Fourth, he said it wouldn't look right if we had our representatives and agents calling on the same stores and buyers. He noted that Shanandoah and Lea-Meadows Industries overlapped on all their accounts. He said, "We'd be paying a commission on sales to these accounts when we would have gotten them anyway. The difference in commission percentages would not be good for morale."

Martin Moorman advocated keeping sales agents for the Lea-Meadows line. His arguments were as follows. First, all sales agents had established contacts and were highly regarded by store buyers, and most had represented the line in a professional manner for many years. He, too, had a good working relationship with all 15 agents. Second, sales agents represented little, if any, cost beyond commissions. Moorman noted, "Agents get paid when we get paid." Third, sales agents were committed to the Lea-Meadows line: "The agents earn a part of their living representing us. They have to service retail accounts to get the repeat business." Fourth, sales agents were calling on buyers not contacted by Shanandoah sales representatives. He noted, "If we let Shanandoah people handle the line, we might lose these accounts, have to hire more sales personnel, or take away 25 percent of the present selling time given to Shanandoah product lines."

As Bates reflected on the meetings, he felt that a broader perspective was necessary beyond the views expressed by Bott and Moorman. One factor was profitability. Existing Shanandoah furniture lines typically had gross margins that were 5 percent higher than those for Lea-Meadows upholstered lines. Another factor was the "us and them" references apparent in the meetings with Bott and Moorman. Would merging the sales efforts overcome this, or would it cause more problems? Finally, the idea of increasing the sales force to incorporate the Lea-Meadows line did not sit well with him. Adding a new salesperson would require restructuring of sales territories, potential loss of commission to existing people, and "a big headache."

Recruiting and
Selecting Personnel*

*The biggest mistake you can make is to think you are
working for someone else.*
ANONYMOUS

*Chapter Consultant: John Schreitmueller Senior Vice-President and
Partner Reedie & Company, L.C.

LEARNING OBJECTIVES

After studying this chapter, you should be able to:

▶ Discuss how to plan for recruiting and selection.

▶ Identify relevant hiring criteria for sales jobs.

▶ Identify the different sources of recruits.

▶ Understand the selection process.

► RECRUITING AT PROCTER & GAMBLE

At Procter & Gamble (P&G), the college *recruiting* effort begins long before the candidates are first interviewed. Prior to the interview day, P&G's recruiters, always line managers, visit the college campus on which they will interview. Instead of relying on the chance that good sales candidates will sign up to interview with them, they ask key people on campus—faculty, administrators, coaches—which students P&G should interview. The selection criteria is based on evidence of success in academics, leadership, and work experience.

Students who pass a screening interview are given an *aptitude test* that P&G has developed to indicate a person's ability to solve problems. This is typically followed by a comprehensive interview with a more senior manager, which is usually held at the regional headquarters. The purpose of these interviews is to select the best candidates from among those qualified. Each candidate on the short list will spend a day in the field with one of P&G's senior salespeople. The purpose of this day is to give the candidate a clear idea of the work of Customer Business Development at P&G.

There is a final interview, often in the Headquarters in Cincinnati, with a panel of three Associate Directors, who must all concur with evidence gathered previously from the candidate. The job offer is almost always made immediately following the panel interview, so that the candidate can return home with a specific offer and location to enroll a spouse or family members in their decision.

Your success as a sales manager will depend largely on how effective you are in attracting, matching, and motivating the right people. Regardless of how well you train, motivate, coach, or counsel your sales staff or develop your sales and marketing strategy, without properly qualified people, you are in the same predicament as a great basketball coach with a team of six-footers who can neither run, jump, shoot, nor rebound.

The costs associated with a poor hiring decision are significant. An often-quoted figure is that out-of-pocket costs associated with recruiting and selection range from 20 to 80 percent of a salesperson's annual salary. Costs go up dramatically, however, when a poor hiring decision is made. Costs associated with a poor hiring include (1) initial training and subsequent training costs needed to overcome deficiencies; (2) costs of absenteeism, poor customer service, and excessive expense account spending associated with gradual withdrawal from the organization; and (3) the opportunity cost associated with lost profits that a qualified person would have generated during the time a poor hire occupies a territory. Experts estimate that the costs of firing a bad employee, and hiring and training a new one, can run as high as 150 percent of the fired employee's salary.[1]

In addition to the costs involved in a poor hiring decision, the impact of such a decision on the organization cannot be exaggerated. Especially in the case of a termination, employee morale, productivity and client relationships all potentially suffer. In the workplace of the 1990s, where downsizings and layoffs have often done more damage to organizations than the organizations anticipated in the forms of negative press, litigation and other issues, the most effective sales managers will be especially aware of the costs, direct and indirect, of poor hiring decisions.

Despite these costs, recruiting tends to be an area of underinvestment by most companies, perhaps because many of the costs are so difficult to quantify. It has been estimated that over half of all people in sales positions are not suited for such a career.[2] Selection of good salespeople obviously represents an important opportunity to gain a competitive advantage. Why is the selection of good salespeople so difficult? One reason is the pressure to fill open territories. One manager summed it up graphically when he said, "Bad breath is better than no breath." According to many sales managers, lack of time is most responsible for their hiring mistakes.[3] Another reason recruiting and selection is difficult is that many companies do not provide effective interviewing training for key line managers who complete the interviewing process.

Our discussion of the recruiting and selection process is based on the following plan. Recruiting and selection does not start with looking for a good salesperson, but with proper planning. First, the number of people to be recruited must be determined, along with an analysis of each sales job. A careful review of the activities to be performed by salespeople helps sales managers prepare a list of specific job qualifications, which can then be used to build a profile to guide the search for successful recruits. Next, management must decide where it will look for recruits. From a pool of recruits, sales managers then must select job candidates. We start our discussion with the planning phase of the recruiting process.

▶ PLANNING CYCLE

The recruiting planning process should include a preliminary analysis of personnel needs, a job analysis, and a review or creation of a job description and job qualifications. Based on the results of these analyses, sources of sales recruits and selection procedures should be planned. Proper planning will help ensure the success of the recruiting process and provide more time for locating the best candidates.

Personnel Needs

The number of new salespeople needed will depend on a number of factors, including sales growth targets, distribution strategies, changes in sales force organization, and sales force turnover. Northwestern Mutual Life Insurance, recognized as one of the top sales organizations, was recently looking to recruit 1,400 full-time agents and 500 college agents in a single year. *Turnover* is the rate at which salespeople leave the sales force because of separations such as resignations, retirement, and promotions. The rate is calculated by dividing the number of separations during a year by the

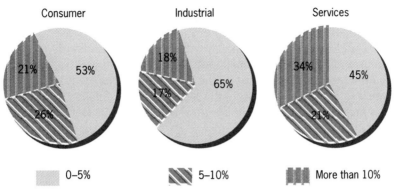

Figure 9-1: Sales Force Turnover Rates

average size of the sales force. Thus, if 15 people leave each year and the size of the sales force is 150, the turnover rate would be

$$\text{Turnover rate} = \frac{\text{Separations per year}}{\text{Average size of sales force}} = \frac{15}{150} = 10\%$$

Because of the recruiting and training expenses incurred, sales managers often try to keep turnover as low as possible. The average sales force turnover rates for service, consumer, and industrial goods companies are illustrated in Figure 9-1. Notice that turnover is highest among service companies. Many, but not all, service sales positions are in industries where it is very difficult for new salespeople to build a list of clients. It is estimated that the first-year retention rate in the insurance industry is just a little over 50 percent. As a result, Northwestern Mutual Life, believed to have one of the best life insurance sales forces, has an objective of recruiting 1,400 agents in 1996.[4] The somewhat higher turnover rate among consumer goods companies may be due to the faster promotion tracks of these companies. In the Personal Products Division of International Playtex, for example, new college recruits are expected to be promoted to sales managers or a staff position within 12 to 20 months. Some turnover, therefore, is not dysfunctional.

Turnover can be too low as well as too high. A well-entrenched sales force may be unable to adjust to a changing environment. While promoting company loyalty, low turnover may also indicate a lack of career growth opportunity by promotion or lateral movement. This suggests that turnover is not something to be minimized or maximized; rather, it is a useful guide for administrative action. The objective is to have enough turnover so that new personnel and enthusiasm can be added to the sales force, yet not so much that sales managers spend all their time recruiting and training new employees.[5]

Company Culture

In addition to the preliminary analysis of personnel needs and other factors, a specific definition of the organization's culture is necessary for the planning cycle's validity.

A well-educated, high-energy, articulate candidate might look like a superb addition to the sales team. However, if he or she does not perceive the company's cultural needs and demands as a match with his or her values, the potential for turnover increases dramatically. For instance some people thrive in a highly competitive environment, while others abhor it. The fact that cultures are likely to vary from one sales branch to another even within the same company, makes the task more difficult but even more necessary. The importance of cultural "fit" between the company and the recruit is tremendous.

Job Analysis

Before managers can effectively recruit new salespeople, they must clearly understand the activities, tasks, and responsibilities of their sales representatives. A *job analysis* is a systematic way to describe how a job is to be performed, as well as the tasks that make up the job. There are a number of different procedures for performing a job analysis. One is the *job analysis interview*, whereby in-depth interviews are conducted with management and salespeople. Management would be queried, for instance, about the sales and marketing plans of the company so as to clarify the role of the sales force. Salespeople would be interviewed to determine how they see their role and how much time they spend on particular activities. In addition to the interviews, the sales force may be sent questionnaires in which they indicate the frequency of performance as well as the importance of each task in their job. Standard questionnaires are available for this task, such as the Position Analysis Questionnaire (PAQ), which lists 194 items describing behavior at work.

While considering management's plans, a job analysis should focus on what salespeople are actually doing today. This can serve as a "reality check" on management's assumptions. For example, a sales manager might describe a job as the merchandising of sales promotions to store managers. However, if salespeople actually spend their time stocking shelves and checking inventory, those salespeople hired to sell to store managers are likely to be unhappy when they find out that the job is really that of a glorified stock clerk. In short, job analyses must incorporate the unpleasant as well as the attractive aspects of the job.

One of the best ways for a company to analyze a selling position is to send an observer into the field. The observer can record the amount of time salespeople spend talking to customers, traveling, record keeping, setting up displays, and attending meetings. Additional information concerning sales jobs can be obtained by interviewing customers, using daily diaries, and reading sales reports to pinpoint critical incidents that spell the difference between success and failure.

Job Description Information from the job analysis should be used to produce a *job description*, which is a written document that spells out the job relationships and requirements that characterize each sales position. The job description explains (1) to whom the salesperson reports, (2) how the salesperson interacts with other staff marketing people, (3) the customers to be called on by the salesperson, (4) the specific tasks to be carried out, (5) the mental and physical demands of the job, and (6) the types of products to be sold.

An example of a job description for a field sales position at Armstrong World Industries is presented in Figure 9-2. Notice that the job description states that the field representative works under the district manager and is responsible for achieving maximum profitable sales within an assigned territory. In this example, the major emphasis is placed on improving the operations of wholesalers. The field representative is expected to work closely with wholesalers to implement promotional programs, train salespeople, and expand coverage of retail accounts. The Armstrong representative is also expected to make regular calls on key retailers, control expenses, handle complaints, and keep the district and Lancaster offices advised on competitive conditions, product needs, prices, and market conditions.

Armstrong	Position Title Marketing Representative (all levels)		Pos. No.	
			Date 8/87	
Incumbent As assigned	Plan/Dept. Floor division	Writer J. A. Gingrich	Approved	
			S.A.D.	MGR.

Job Function

Under general supervision of the District Manager or Assistant District Manager, this position is responsible for developing and achieving maximum profitable sales volume of Division products in an assigned territory.

Dimensions

Sales Volume—ranges from $1–7 million.

Territory—the District is typically divided into geographic areas, with this position responsible for one of those areas; additionally, the position will be given direct responsibility for 1–4 Armstrong wholesalers.

Product Line—consists of a wide range of resilient flooring products including Corlon and Solarian sheet flooring; resilient tile; vinyl sheet flooring; and adhesives and sundries.

Distribution—is achieved by sales to wholesalers, who in turn sell to flooring specialty stores, flooring contractors, furniture stores, department stores, building supply stores and home improvement centers.

Major Emphasis—is directed toward developing and improving the wholesalers in all their functions through such means as training and assisting wholesaler salespeople, helping these people make specific sales, developing new business, and generally contributing to the effectiveness of their operations.

Figure **9-2**: Job Description for a Field Sales Representative

Organization Supervised   None

Principal Activities
1. Develops and achieves maximum sales volume consistent with realistic sales projections within assigned territory. Controls expenditures within approved expense budget.
2. Develops and maintains favorable wholesale distribution of entire Division line within assigned territory. Recommends on the addition or termination of wholesalers. Develops thorough familiarity with wholesaler's business, sales activity, potentials, and requirements.
3. Closely oversees operations of assigned wholesalers. Advises or assists them in such areas as inventory selection and control, service to customers, profit opportunities and rations, etc. Investigates and corrects problem situations such as duplication of orders, receipt of poor quality goods, etc. Draws on Armstrong staff services as special assistance is indicated.
4. Translates promotional goals into concrete plans and assignable responsibilities, determining what is to be done and achieved, and who is to achieve it.
5. Identifies the work which must be done to achieve intended results. Divides this work into parcels that can be performed by single individuals.
6. Maintains proper relationships and interrelationships to assure teamwork and a unified effort between wholesaler and retailer.
7. Promotes Armstrong product line and its features and sales points, and an understanding of Armstrong policies and procedures, among the entire wholesaler organization. Keeps personnel informed on new products, price changes, and related concerns. Adapts Lancaster promotional services to local needs and conducts sales meetings to explain same; follows through on all promotions.
8. Assists wholesalers, sales personnel in concerned territory in their selling efforts, and trains same through promotional meetings, traveling with each person on a regular basis, helping in making specific sales, and developing new business.
9. Plans territory coverage. Regularly calls upon key retail accounts (current and prospective). Takes orders; promotes the marketing and display of Armstrong products; encourages dealer to capitalize on Armstrong's advertising and promotional efforts; introduces new materials; trains counter personnel; provides literature and samples.
10. Investigates and evaluates field complaints; recommends disposition of complaints accordingly.
11. Keeps District Manager's Office and Lancaster advised on matters of specific business interest such as market conditions, competitive situations, product needs, etc. Consults with District Manager's Office concerning matters of policy, unusual situations, pricing, etc.

Figure 9-2: (Continued)

Job Qualifications

While a job description focuses on the activities and responsibilities of the job, *job qualifications* refers to the aptitudes, skills, knowledge, and personality traits necessary to perform the job successfully. A statement of job qualifications would typically include education, previous work experience, technical expertise, aptitudes, and interests. These qualifications, based on the job description, serve as a set of selection criteria that will help sales managers choose the best prospects from among those who apply. Typical of many other companies, the Invacare Corporation, a manufacturer of wheelchairs and other medical products, looks for people with drive, interpersonal skills, common sense, intelligence, and experience selling.[6] It is incumbent on every company to be able to demonstrate to the Equal Employment Opportunity Commission that their job qualifications are required for the job.

In addition to creating a job description, some large firms evaluate the personal histories and skills of current salespeople to build a profile of the successful salesperson with their company. G. D. Searle and Company, a large manufacturer of health care products, recently did this with the help of the SRI/Gallup Organization.[7] Salespeople were divided into two groups based on performance. The two groups were compared on innate intelligence, selling aptitude and basic personality test scores, job application forms, and interview records. Notice that these are personal characteristics that cannot be developed through training or job experience.

Research   Almost everyone has a stereotyped image of the kind of person who will be successful at sales. A review of over 400 studies of the relationship between personal characteristics and salesperson performance found some interesting results and drew the following conclusions:[8]

- Sales aptitude, personal characteristics (e.g., physical traits, experience), selling skills, role perceptions, and motivation are not consistently related to sales performance.

- Personal variables such as family background, personal history, and current marital and family status are some of the best predictors of sales performance among the many personal characteristics examined. However, it is generally illegal to ask these sorts of questions.

- General management skills, such as organization and leadership ability, are critical to success in personal selling.

- Educational level, intelligence, and sociability are not consistently related to sales performance.

In the aggregate, these results suggest that widely held stereotypes of what is needed to be successful in sales are often not accurate. Part of the problem may be that different kinds of personalities may be successful in different kinds of sales positions (see Sales Management in Action 9-1).[9] In addition, this study concluded that developmental characteristics such as specific selling skills, motivation level, and role perceptions, are generally more closely related to performance than are lasting,

---

Sales Management in Action 9-1
"Which Seller Belongs Where?"

Matching the right personality with the right sales position is critical to recruiting and sales success. The Gallup Organization, in Lincoln Nebraska, has interviewed half a million salespeople during the past 22 years to help companies hire and develop sales talent. Here are five typical selling situations and the personality types that Gallup thinks are best suited for each situation:

- **Remote Office.** These salespeople cannot rely on management for constant reinforcement, so they have to rely on themselves to set and accomplish their own goals. Salespeople with strong, personal loyalty to customers may also thrive in a remote office.

- **Team Selling.** This person must have an unselfish desire to contribute; to put the team first. The best people in this situation are service-driven.

- **Growth Market.** This is a dream for a competitive person who gets a real kick from closing orders. It's wide-open, and the opportunities to win seem limitless.

- **Mature Market.** This is one of the most difficult people to find. It takes hypercompetitive people because they must love to take business away from rivals. At the same time, these people must be strong in building lasting, loyal relationships.

- **Telesales.** This takes a person with a strong ego to handle the rejection and isolation that is a huge part of the job. Being very goal driven is also important.

Source: Geoffrey Brewer, "Which Seller Belongs Where?" *Sales & Marketing Management* (May 1994), pp. 33–34.

---

innate characteristics. This suggests that sales managers can and do have an important influence on the performance of a sales force.

On the other hand, it is important to understand that the hiring manager's perceptions play an absolutely critical role in the hiring decision. Ultimately, regardless of education, experience, or any other tangible qualification, it is often the hiring manager's impression of "fit" that stack the deck in favor of a particular candidate. This underscores again the role of "culture" in the process, and places a significant burden on the applicant to understand it.

Buyer's Perspective A survey of 205 purchasing agents concluded that the most valued traits of salespeople were those shown in Table 9-1. The results suggest that sales managers should hire people who are loyal to the customer, willing to fight for them, thoroughness, and follow through on promises. Although product knowledge was fourth on the list, it is usually not a key hiring criterion because deficiencies can be addressed during sales training. Note that the preferred traits in Table 9-1 are not those easily discerned from a resume.[10]

Table 9-1   What Purchasing Agents Like About Salespeople

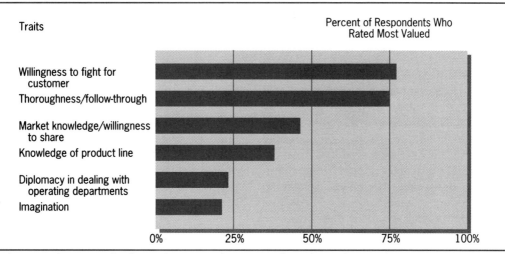

Source: "The Best Sales Reps Will Take on Their Bosses for You," *Purchasing* (November 7, 1996); p. 81.

Today some people are taking a different approach to identifying desirable personality traits in sales candidates. Instead of identifying personality traits associated with overall performance, they are looking for traits related to desirable selling abilities, such as the ability to adjust sales behaviors based on the nature of the selling situation. Sales adaptiveness, for example, has been found to be associated with an internal locus of control (i.e., performance is caused by behavior, not luck), empathy, self-monitoring (i.e., sensitivity to other people's behavior), and androgyny (i.e., both assertive and yielding).[11] This approach is new but holds promise for improving sales force selection. Another example of using personality traits as selection criteria is described in Sales Management in Action 9-2.

Sales versus Technical Skills   One of the perennial dilemmas for sales managers is whether to hire technicians and teach them to sell or to hire experienced salespeople and teach them the technical aspects of the job. Either strategy can succeed; the key factor is the company's approach to selling and the training capability of the firm. Pharmaceutical giants Bristol-Meyers, Eli Lilly, SmithKline, and Parke-Davis prefer candidates to have a science or health care background. Eli Lilly, for example, only hires people with technical degrees, and only 20 percent of their sales force have a business degree.[12] Other leading health care companies such as Pfizer, Merck, and Baxter-Travenol, on the other hand, do not insist on technical backgrounds for their sales applicants. There appears to be no clear consensus as to whether a technical background is needed in sales.

Legality of Job Qualifications

Although lists of qualifications are useful in recruiting for sales positions, they must be employed with caution. The main concern is to avoid employment discrimination caused when qualifications are used to exclude some individuals from certain jobs.

Sales Management in Action 9-2
"Everything Will Be All Right"

It is a part of personal selling's conventional wisdom that optimists perform better than pessimists. Now there is research indicating why this might be true. It appears that people who are optimists (people who expect the best possible outcome) handle stress differently from pessimists. When given a challenging objective, optimists believe it is possible to achieve the goal and focus their attention on devising strategies for achieving it. Pessimists, on the other hand, think there is little chance of achieving the goal, so they believe they can only endure the situation. As a result, they focus their attention inwardly, in an attempt to assuage their own negative feelings, instead of developing plans for meeting their goals. This is another example of how personality traits have been found to be related to desirable behaviors such as coping.

Source: David Strutton and James Lumpkin, "The Relationship Between Optimism and Coping Styles of Salespeople," Journal of Personal Selling & Sales Management, 13 (Spring 1993), pp. 71–82.

The Civil Rights Act of 1964 was the first of several laws designed to prevent illegal employment discrimination. This was followed in 1967 by the Age Discrimination in Employment Act and in 1973 by the Vocational Rehabilitation Act, which was designed to protect the rights of the handicapped. These laws make it illegal to use as job qualifications any attributes that result in discrimination against people of a given race, religion, nationality, sex, or age. The only exception occurs when the employer can show that the characteristic is essential to the successful performance of the job.

Guidelines explaining the discrimination laws have been issued by the Equal Employment Opportunity Commission (EEOC) and the Office of Federal Contract Compliance (OFCC). The regulations issued by the EEOC apply to firms with 25 or more employees. The OFCC rules apply to companies with 100 or more employees that have contracts with the federal government.

Legal guidelines and laws affecting recruiting and selection are constantly evolving and changing. A particularly important new federal civil rights law is the Americans with Disabilities Act (ADA), which became effective in 1992.[13] This law makes it illegal to discriminate in employment against qualified individuals with disabilities. Disabilities covered by the law include visual, speech, and hearing impairment, human immunodeficiency virus infection, cancer, mental retardation, emotional illness, drug addiction, and alcoholism. Although originally protected by the law, illegal drug users are not currently protected.

The law also specifies that employers have an obligation to make reasonable accommodation to the known physical or mental limitations of an individual. Examples of accommodations include making facilities available, restructuring jobs, reassignment, modifying work schedules, modifying equipment, and providing readers or interpreters. The implications of this new law are clearly far-reaching.

► RECRUITING

The goal of recruiting is to find and attract the best-qualified applicants for sales positions. The number of applicants needed to meet personnel requirements will be larger than the number of people to be hired. Not every applicant will have the job qualifications, and not everyone offered a job will accept the offer. The number of applicants needed can be determined by using a simple formula based on the company's experience from past recruiting efforts. The number of recruits (R) is

$$R = \frac{H}{S \times A}$$

where

    H = *required number of hires*
    S = *percentage of recruits selected*
    A = *percentage of those selected who accept*

Thus, if a company needs to hire 10 people and expects to select 10 percent of those applying, and if 50 percent of those offered a position typically accept, then $R = 10/(0.10 \times 0.50)$ or 200. Therefore, the company needs to plan its recruiting process so as to attract 200 applicants.

Notice that the number of recruits (R) can be reduced by either increasing the percentage of people selected (S) or increasing the percentage of those selected who accept an offer (A). You may wish to speculate as to whether increasing A and S in order to reduce R is necessarily beneficial to an organization. What else must be considered besides reducing recruiting time and costs?

Table 9-2 shows the sources typically used by American firms to recruit salespeople. Sources of applicants vary widely, depending on the job to be filled and past

Table 9-2   Recruiting Sources for Salespeople

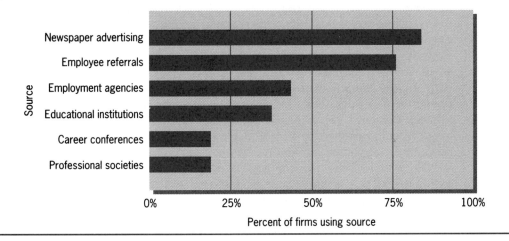

hiring success. For example, educational institutions and employment agencies are the most popular sources for sales trainees. On the other hand, present employees and personal referrals of people working for other firms in the industry are popular sources for sales jobs involving technical product knowledge and industry experience. Companies rarely rely exclusively on one source for sales applicants because each source has advantages and limitations. These sources are discussed in the following sections.

Classified Advertising

Classified advertisements in newspapers and trade journals are often used to attract sales people, as suggested by the 84 percent of firms mentioned in Table 9-2. The *Wall Street Journal* and trade journals such as *Women's Wear Daily* are full of ads for experienced sales reps, sales managers, vice presidents of sales, and general sales managers. Classified ads have the advantage of reaching a wide audience and may attract candidates who are not actively looking for a job. McNeil Consumer Products Company, a pharmaceutical firm, and Boise Cascade Office Products rely on newspaper ads to recruit salespeople.[14]

Advertising's strength in attracting job applicants may also be its greatest drawback. There is a tendency to overburden the selection process with underqualified applicants, resulting in an extensive and costly screening process. This produces a high cost per hire despite a low cost per applicant.

Present Employees

Present employees often make good candidates for sales jobs. They are familiar with the company's products and procedures and do not require as much training as prospects recruited from outside sources. They have established job histories with the firm and can be observed in action when evaluating their potential as sales representatives. People usually consider a transfer to the sales department to be a promotion because of the job's independence and frequently higher earnings potential. One pharmaceutical company found that people employed by the company in non-selling positions yielded better long-run profits than candidates from any other source. While their sales did not increase as rapidly as those of people with previous pharmaceutical sales experience, profits were higher because of lower compensation expenses.[15]

Candidates for major account sales positions are most likely to come from company sources. Sources of candidates for these sales positions are likely to be different from those of regular sales positions because of the differences in the responsibilities in major account sales. A recent study found that 90 percent of companies recruit major account salespeople from among the regular salespeople with the firm, with 44 percent also considering referrals from their major account salespeople.[16]

Hiring from within the company has potential pitfalls. Bad feelings may arise, for example, if managers think that their best people are being pirated by the sales force. In addition, some companies find that employees may harbor hidden prejudices about sales and rely too much on their previous experience. Engineers, for example, may tend to use facts and figures, while customer service people may find it hard to take a tough negotiating stance.

Referrals/Networking

A second major internal source of recruits is recommendations by present employees. As shown in Table 9-2, this is the second most frequently used source of sales recruits. Statistics prove networking and informational interviewing to be among the top conduits for effective recruiting in today's workplace. Well-informed students and graduates in entry-level positions learn each day the values of networking with other sales professionals, executives, senior executives, faculty members and others whose daily routines immerse them in the business community. Because the informational interviewer has probably gained significant grasp of the company's cultural, ethical and business issues ahead of time, it is those individuals who often make superb candidates for sales accountabilities, and at reduced risk for the company.

References from managers and salespeople are particularly valuable because these people tend to have wide social contacts and often meet individuals who make good prospects for the sales team. Company executives understand the needs of the sales program and are in a good position to convince others of the merits of a sales career. Moreover, they are apt to know when people are looking for new jobs and to have some personal knowledge of their qualifications. Some companies even design reward systems for recruiting new salespeople. One lighting company, for instance, awards salespeople bonus points for each recruit they recommend that the company eventually hires. The bonus points can be used to pick merchandise from a catalog.

Employment Agencies

Table 9-2 indicates that *employment agencies* are a frequently used source of salespeople. One-third of the companies responding in one recent survey reported depending on agents to help fill the vacancies in their ranks.[17] Employment agencies are popular because they can save busy sales managers time and money. The agencies advertise, screen resumes, interview prospects, and present qualified applicants to the client. At this point, the sales manager chooses candidates for further interviews. A private agency is paid only when people are actually hired. Employment agencies that charge applicants a fee for placement must be given a detailed set of specifications, since they tend to refer candidates on their current lists. Agencies that charge the employer a fee are more likely to find recruits who match a particular job. Often firms find that the best agencies with which to work are those that specialize in finding sales recruits, such as SALESworld and Sales Consultants. Sales Consultants, for example, advertises that it places more sales management talent than any other organization.

Schools and Colleges

Perhaps the best source of sales trainees is educational institutions. For some firms, such as Dresser Industries, a manufacturer of power transmission equipment, and

Hewlett-Packard, colleges are the focal point of their total hiring process. Armstrong International, for instance, hires 60 percent of its new sales personnel from college graduates.[18] Digital Equipment Corporation (DEC) has switched from relying on transfers from engineering to eager college graduates as their primary source of sales candidates.[19] Recognized for recruiting the best salespeople in the pharmaceutical industry, 50 percent of Merck & Company's new salespeople came from its college recruiting efforts.

College graduates are an attractive source of salespeople for a number of reasons. Graduates tend to be more easily trained and are often more poised and mature than people without college training. Successful college students typically know how to budget their time and, perhaps most importantly, have the perseverance needed to get jobs done.[20]

College students, however, usually lack sales experience and require considerable training and one-on-one coaching before they become productive salespeople. Often they expect to be promoted rapidly to positions in management, becoming impatient if promotion opportunities are not soon made available. Philip Morris Company, for instance, has found that college graduates become bored calling on retail stores to set up displays and sell cigarettes, and has reduced turnover by hiring people with two years of college experience and three to five years of experience selling to retailers.

Customers, Suppliers, and Competitors

Customers and suppliers may also be a source of good recruits. They know the business, are familiar with the company, and may know what is expected of a salesperson. Care should be taken to ensure that the customer or supplier is aware of the recruiting process and is willing to cooperate.

Hiring competitors' salespeople is particularly attractive when a firm's training capabilities are limited, when customers are loyal to the salesperson and will therefore buy from the new company, and when new salespeople must be productive in a short period of time. When it decided to sell to large corporate accounts, Apple Computer targeted experienced salespeople with IBM, DEC, and Data General in its recruiting. Competition is the source for about 80 percent of new salespeople hired by Wang.[21] This practice is also common among insurance firms, stockbrokers, office equipment suppliers, and clothing representatives.

Hiring competitors' salespeople and customers' employees is controversial and gives rise to ethical and legal issues when the suspicion of divulging company secrets is involved. Retaliation and lawsuits are often the reaction of firms in industries where salesperson raiding is not common. Furthermore, because people rarely leave a job they like strictly for reasons of money, the new company may "buy" an unhappy employee. Only 10 percent of firms responding to a recent survey, for example, listed competitors as the best source of sales candidates.[22] A study in the pharmaceutical industry concluded that while salespeople hired from competitors produced the highest initial sales volume, the higher costs associated with attracting these people more than offset their higher productivity, making this source of sales candidates the least profitable.[23]

► SELECTING PROSPECTS

After recruiting a pool of sales candidates, managers must screen out candidates who do not meet the *hiring criteria*. The procedure for *selecting prospects* is a sequential filtering process, as depicted in Figure 9-3. The recruiter begins the selection process by evaluating application blanks and resumes and proceeds to interviews and background checks. In this way, obviously unsuitable prospects can be eliminated with low-cost methods, and the more expensive testing procedures can be saved for a smaller group of promising candidates. Each of the major selection tools is discussed in this section.

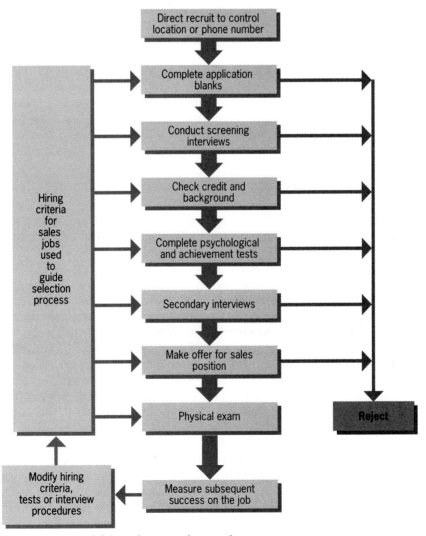

Figure 9-3: A Model for Selecting Salespeople

Application Forms

A popular way to gather personal history data is to have candidates fill out an *application blank*. It is easy to administer and requires very little executive time since the information is in a standardized format, as opposed to a resume. The basic purposes of application forms are to (1) provide information useful in making a selection decision and (2) to obtain information that may be needed during an individual's employment.

Sales managers are primarily interested in several types of information found on application blanks. First, the sales manager wants information about the candidate's educational background. A second category of information is the past employment record. Sales managers are looking for any employment gaps and prefer candidates whose employment records show a natural progression in job responsibilities and wages. One study found that high-performing salespeople with a high propensity to remain with the firm have a job history of extensive selling experience on their resume and view sales as a career position rather than as a stepping stone to another position.[24]

Noticeably absent from the application blank in Figure 9-4 are questions about marital status, gender, religion, race, handicaps, and age exceeding 18 years. These questions have been removed from employment applications for fear that the answers would be used by recruiters to discriminate against certain candidates. Application forms usually do ask for data on military service, so that the firm can comply with affirmative action regulations on the employment of veterans.

Personal Interviews

The *personal interview* is a crucial part of the selection process for all sales positions, since interpersonal skills are so important in sales. Interviews are typically conducted at two levels. The first interview is used primarily to inform the candidate about the job and look for *knockout factors*. These are characteristics that would eliminate a person from further consideration, such as poor speech patterns, unacceptable appearance, or lack of necessary maturity, to mention a few of the more common factors. This initial interview is followed by the main interview, in which candidates are interviewed in order to identify people who best match the job's qualifications. The main interviewing process may include a series of interviews with sales managers, typically including the person to whom the candidate would report. After an initial interview with a divisional manager, Hewlett-Packard holds a series of five or six more interviews at the regional sales office where the job opening exists. SmithKline has changed to a "team interview" process in which the candidate meets with a team of managers including the appropriate sales manager, service manager, sales director, and technical director. They switched to this format because previously candidates had learned the "right" answers by the end of a series of interviews.[25]

One of the benefits of interviews is that managers can follow up on information obtained from application blanks. For example, candidates can be asked to explain gaps in their employment or educational record and defend decisions to leave previous employers. A second advantage of interviews is that they allow sales managers

Form 350- R24

PRE-EMPLOYMENT APPLICATION

An Equal Opportunity Employer
Male and Female

Date _____

OWENS-ILLINOIS

Personal Data

Name	(Last)		(First)		(Middle)	Social Security Number

Permanent Address	(No. & Street)	(City)	(State)	(Zip Code)	Telephone

Present Address	(if different from above)	Until What Date	Telephone

Age (if under 18)	Have you worked for Owens-Illinois before? ☐ Yes ☐ No If Yes, what location	Date available for work

Position for which you are applying

Application received from	Location	Date

Educational Background
Complete all sections applicable

			From	Major or Specialization
High School	Name			
	City		To	Received Diploma ☐ Yes ☐ No
College	Name		From	Major Specialization
	City		To	Type of Degree Received
College	Name		From	Major or Specialization
	City		To	Type of Degree Received
Graduate School	Name		From	Major or Specialization
	City		To	Type of Degree Received
Other	Name		From	Major or Specialization
	City		To	Type of Degree Received

Stenographic And Clerical Applicants

What types of office machines can you operate

Do you take shorthand ☐ Yes ☐ No	Please indicate any other clerical skills or qualifications

U. S. Military Service

Date Entered	Date Discharged	Branch of Service	Highest Rank	Military Job

Affirmative Action Assistance
Vietnam Era Veterans, Disabled Veterans & Qualified Handicapped

As a government contractor, we are required to take affirmative action to employ and advance in employment Veterans of the Vietnam Era, Disabled Veterans, and qualified Handicapped. If you feel that you qualify under this program, please tell us on a voluntary basis if you would like to be considered under the Affirmative Action Program.

Job Category

Name

FOR OFFICE USE ONLY

Figure 9-4: Application Form Used by Owens-Illinois

Employment Record (Begin with most recent)
Include prior employment with Owens-Illinois and part time work if college student

1.

Employer	Job Responsibilities
Address (No. & Street) (City & State)	
Date Began **Date Left** **May we contact** ☐ Yes ☑ No	
Immediate Supervisor's Name **Ending Rate of Pay**	**Reason for Leaving**

2.

Employer	Job Responsibilities
Address (No. & Street) (City & State)	
Date Began **Date Left** **May we contact** ☐ Yes ☐ No	
Immediate Supervisor's Name **Ending Rate of Pay**	**Reason for Leaving**

3.

Employer	Job Responsibilities
Address (No. & Street) (City & State)	
Date Began **Date Left** **May we contact** ☐ Yes ☐ No	
Immediate Supervisor's Name **Ending Rate of Pay**	**Reason for Leaving**

4.

Employer	Job Responsibilities
Address (No. & Street) (City & State)	
Date Began **Date Left** **May we contact** ☐ Yes ☐ No	
Immediate Supervisor's Name **Ending Rate of Pay**	**Reason for Leaving**

Qualifications And Achievements
Please tell us about your personal qualifications for the work for which you have made application. Use additional sheet if necessary.

The applicant herein authorizes the Company to investigate information supplied by him or her and to inquire further in regard to the applicant's background including academic, occupational and health records in its consideration of him or her as a prospective employee. In making this application for employment, it is understood that an investigation may be made whereby information is obtained through personal interviews with your neighbors, friends or others with whom you are acquainted. This inquiry includes information as to your character, general reputation and general characteristics. You have a right to make a written request within a reasonable period of time for a complete and accurate disclosure of the nature and scope of this investigation. It is understood that as part of our Health Program each applicant is required to complete a health examination.

I verify that the above information is true and that I have read and understand the last paragraph of this application.

Form 360- R24 (back)   Signature of Applicant _____

Figure 9-4: (Continued)

Why should we hire you?

Regardless of the company and type of sales position for which you may interview, there are some interview questions that are typically asked. You may not be asked each of these questions in every interview, but you should be prepared to answer them all. After reading each question, think about what the interviewer's purpose may be in asking the question. What is he or she trying to determine? What would your response be to each question?

- What was the most monotonous job you ever had to do?
- In thinking about the people you like, what is it you like most about them?
- Up to this point in your life, what do you consider to be your biggest disappointment?
- How willing are you to relocate? To what extent are you willing to travel?
- How do you feel about the way your previous employer treated you?
- What are your long-term financial objectives, and how do you propose to achieve them?
- What was the most difficult decision you ever had to make as a leader?
- Why should we hire you?
- Sell me this pen.

Figure 9-5: Typical Interview Questions

to assess the applicant's level of interest and desire for the job. Interviews also allow managers to observe a candidate's conversational ability and social skills. Figure 9-5 includes some typical questions asked in sales interviews. The candidates for any professional selling position should be prepared to present their background and career goals in a capsulation of approximately 2 minutes. This is often referred to as a "Two Minute Drill," and responds to the question most typically asked at the beginning of the interview cycle, "Tell me about yourself."

Interviewing is a subjective process, and unfortunately there will be mistakes. Substantial evidence indicates that applicant ratings based on personal interviews vary dramatically among interviewers (Table 9-3). Worse yet, studies have found that personal interview ratings are a very poor predictor of subsequent job success. One laboratory study, for instance, found that experienced interviewers *incorrectly* interpreted smiling, gesturing while talking, and talking more than other applicants as indicators of motivation.[26] Because of the personal nature of selling, the interview has remained the preferred selection tool of most sales managers. One way to minimize selection mistakes is to train sales managers on what questions to ask, how to ask each question, and how to rate applicants. An example of this type of training is discussed in the Behavioral Event Interview described in Sales Management in Action 9-3. Another way to improve the interviewing process is to inform recruiters regularly about the progress of candidates previously hired. Feedback on successes and failures can help refine or improve interviewing techniques.

Table 9-3 Validity of Predictors for Entry-Level Jobs

Predictor	Validity
Ability composite (tests)	.53
Job tryout	.44
Biographical inventory	.37
Reference check	.26
Experence	.18
Interview	.14
Training and experience ratings	.13
Academic achievement	.11
Education	.10
Interest	.10
Age	.01

Source: John Hunte and Ronda Hunte, "Validity and Utility of Alternative Predictors of Job Performance," *Psychological Bulletin*, 96 (July 1984), p. 90.

Patterned Interviews   There are several types of interviewing styles from which to choose. One type of interview is a *patterned interview*, in which the sales manager asks each prospect a set of questions and records the responses on a form. The primary advantage of such structured interviews is that they facilitate comparison of candidates when more than one person is conducting screening interviews. If different questions are asked of each candidate, then a comparison of candidates is often based on impressions rather than on recall of relevant information.

Semistructured Interviews   A completely structured interview may not always be appropriate or best for choosing among candidates. When interviewing veteran salespeople or for a major account sales position, an interviewer may be looking for someone who will take control of the situation, since this is expected of the individual. In such a situation, it may be more appropriate to use a *semistructured interview* that is planned to gather critical pieces of information, but the questions are not repeated word for word and the candidate is expected to take a more active role in the direction an interview takes. An example of a form used to record information from semistructured interviews is shown in Figure 9-6. The key section of the form requires that the interviewer rate each candidate on education and training, work experience, skills and abilities, and career interests, using a scale from 1 to 5. These ratings are based on responses given by the candidate.

Field Observation   A special kind of interview that has proven effective for some organizations is *field observation*, which includes taking candidates out to observe a day of field sales work. The prospect travels with a salesperson, making calls on regular customers. The major benefit of the field interview is that prospects see exactly what the job entails, and those who feel they aren't likely to measure up to the challenge can eliminate themselves before being hired.

Sales Management in Action 9-3
"Why Did You Do That?"

This question is likely to be asked in a Behavioral Event Interview (BEI). A BEI interview relies on asking a series of questions focusing on three or four critical events in the applicant's career in which the individual accomplished something significant, influenced someone, or solved a problem. Interviewers are trained to use open-ended questions, to press for examples, and to probe the applicant's thoughts and feelings during the event. Some sample questions include the following:

"How did you first get involved in selling?"

"What were your initial goals?"

"When you approached customers, how did they respond to you?"

"What exactly would they say?"

According to BEI experts, the thought process a candidate went through is more important than the result. Interviewers are told to suspend judgment and continually ask, "Why did you do that? What were you thinking?" What the interviewer is looking for are patterns of thinking that are appropriate for the position that is open. If prospecting is important, for instance, then they would look for indications of persistence, an ability to handle rejection, and any indication of resistance to meeting new people.

One of the biggest mistakes interviewers make is to lead the candidate by unwittingly prompting the answer they desire. For example, "Are you a high achiever?" will usually elicit only one response.

Source: Jill Neimark, "He Sounds Great, But Can He Sell?" *Success* (March 1988), pp. 51–54.

Follow-up

The interview does not end when the face-to-face discussion has ended. Sales management should track the timely response of candidates for sales positions by their responses in the forms of letters, notes, or other means. This tends to correlate to on-the-job accountabilities, where the most successful selling professionals typically have penchants for following up on their telephone and face-to-face encounters with customers, suppliers, and other key contacts.

Background and Credit Checks

How honest are people about their educational and employment histories? In a review of records from the past 20 years, one executive search firm found that nearly half of all job applicants lie about their salaries and job responsibilities with previous employers. The message is clear: Don't assume that people are telling the truth.

Form 2680-R3

HR SELECTION, RECRUITMENT &
EMPLOYMENT
QUALIFICATION SUMMARY

OWENS-ILLINOIS

Social Security Number	Insert Letter in box at right				
	A = College Recruit **B** = Write-In **C** = Employment Agency **D** = Other				
Surname	First Name	Initial	Interview Date (mo., day, year)	Date Available for Employment	
Street Address	City	State	Zip Code	Telephone	
College / University	Major	Degree B, M or D	If degree M or D, denote undergrad course and college		
Graduation Date (mo., year)	Grade Point Average	Geographic Preference			

Education and Training		
Work Experience		
Skills and Abilities		
Career Interests		
Overall Rating		
Remarks (if any)		

Insert Number in boxes at right   1st ☐   2nd ☐

1 = Corporate Comptroller Training Program	**7** = Industrial Engineering	**13** = Research & Development
2 = Financial (Accounting, Auditing, etc.)	**8** = Plant Engineering	**14** = Manufacturing Supervision
3 = Purchasing	**9** = Manufacturing Engineer	**15** = Adv. Degree Program
4 = Information System / Data Processing	**10** = Product Engineer	**16** = Other (list below)
5 = Sales / Marketing	**11** = Package Engineer	
6 = Personnel / Ind. Relations	**12** = Ceramic / Material Sci. Engineer	

☐ **Refer**   ☐ **Reject**

Division	Location	Date Referred	Division	Location	Date Referred
Division	Location	Date Referred	Division	Location	Date Referred
Was candidate given an O-I application and return envelope ☐ Yes ☐ No	Interviewing Staff or Division	Interviewer		Location	

Source: Owens-Illinois, Inc.

Figure 9-6: Interview Evaluation Form

Failure to check resumes results in hiring overpaid and unqualified salespeople. Scientific Data Systems recently found that 30 percent of their sales force had faked either their educational or work experience.[27] They also found that typically the top performers had told the truth and the bottom performers had lied.

Credit checks are commonly used to assess the financial responsibility of applicants, since financial responsibility goes hand in hand with job responsibility. Though no research has verified this relationship, Equifax, Inc., of Atlanta claims it sold 350,000 of its credit reports to 15,000 employers in 1989. Under the Credit Reporting Act of 1971, applicants must be told that a credit check is being conducted, and they must be given the name and address of the source if the check results in the rejection of a candidate.

Testing

Some form of testing is being used more often today than in the past to help select field salespeople. Tests often provide more objective information than can be obtained from subjective conversation. Interviewers frequently reject prospects on the basis of personal biases and whims. Candidates have been rejected after interviews for such minor matters as speech accents or wearing short-sleeved shirts, short socks, or light-colored suits. These biases can be offset by the use of valid and reliable tests. Referring once again to the results in Table 9-3, notice that testing was found to be the most reliable predictor of entry-level job success, nearly three times as valid as interviews.

Three types of tests are being used in sales force selection: (1) intelligence, (2) personality, and (3) aptitude tests.

Intelligence Tests   *Intelligence tests* measure the ability to learn. These tests are used to determine if people have the minimum capabilities to perform the job. As such, the test is used as a knockout factor; that is, not meeting a minimum level will eliminate a candidate, but scores beyond the minimum will not determine the final candidate selection.

Personality Tests   General *personality tests*, such as the Edwards Personal Preference Schedule, evaluate an individual on numerous personality traits. Some companies use tests designed to measure particular personality traits felt to be important to a particular sales position and company. These are likely to be quite helpful in selecting candidates if properly validated by careful job analysis, as is done at Pfizer.[28]

Aptitude Tests   *Aptitude tests* are designed to determine whether a candidate has an interest in certain tasks and activities. The Strong Vocational Interest Blank, for example, asks respondents to indicate whether they like or dislike a variety of situations and activities. Responses can be compared with those of successful people in a certain type of sales position to determine if the candidate will be successful in the position. Sales Management in Action 9-4 tells how aptitude tests are being used to select sales talent in the Czech Republic.

Sales Management in Action 9-4
From Socialist to Sales Rep

The Czech economy is booming and many American companies with facilities in the country are hiring. The challenge is that the local work force is steeped in the traditions of socialism and nobody has a track record in selling and servicing in a free market economy. Companies such as Warner Lambert, Kmart, and Amway have turned to Caliper Corporation for help.

How does Caliper choose the right person for the job? Much the same way it does in the United States—with a sales aptitude test. Translated almost verbatim from the test used in America, the test looks for qualities such as ego drive, empathy, growth, and leadership. Says a company representative, "We are seeking the same thing that motivates people all over the world—getting to yes."

Source: Weld Royal, "From Socialist to Sales Rep," *Sales & Marketing Management* (August 1994), p. 63.

Recommendations One common error made by recruiters is to adopt some readily available intelligence or psychological test that may be inappropriate for selecting field salespeople. Better results are achieved when tests are tailor-made by testing experts and human resource specialists for the needs of a particular firm or industry. It is also important to base the test on an analysis of the job in question and to validate the relationship between test scores and subsequent job performance. This can be done by comparing scores of the most successful and least successful salespeople currently employed by the firm. Also, use tests as part of the selection process but not as the sole decision criterion.

Physical Examination

Traditionally, the last step in the selection process for salespeople has been a routine physical examination. Field selling is strenuous, often involving extensive travel and the hauling of sample cases into and out of customers' offices. Salespeople typically must endure a lot of stress and frustration. So, the sales manager wants to be certain that the candidate has the stamina needed for the job, as well as to avoid excessive medical costs.

A recent survey of 320 firms revealed that 45 percent of the companies require new hires to complete a physical exam successfully.[29] This same survey showed that 62 percent of the firms conduct *drug testing* of new employees. The popularity of drug testing has increased in recent years with the recognition that drug use can interfere with job performance through more frequent absences, higher medical expenses, and more problems on the job.

With passage of the ADA, preemployment medical examinations have been prohibited.[30] Examinations are permitted once an employment offer is made and prior to commencement of the job. An employer could therefore make a job offer contingent on successful completion of the physical. However, questions about whether the person has a disability, and the nature and severity of the disability, are prohibited.[31]

Additional Selection Tools

Some companies are using additional selection tools to help choose the right sales candidate. One such tool is the *assessment center*, in which candidates participate in exercises related to the job. Assessment centers were first used by the German military to select officers during the 1930s.[32] Merrill Lynch uses a sales simulation process in the selection of account executives. At one brokerage house, candidates are asked to sell a particular stock to a prospect, who is really a psychologist hired by the firm. The prospect greets the telephone caller with a story about how busy he is at the moment. In this simulation, the employer is assessing the candidate's persistence, an important attribute to the job.

More and more companies are using *internship* programs, not only to determine if the person has selling skills, but also to see if he or she fits in with the company culture. With an internship, an individual is hired for a limited period of time, during which he or she is asked to perform certain tasks and gets the chance to observe and work with other people in the company. Northwestern Mutual Life recruits approximately 500 sales interns, called college agents, each year. The internship program is also considered a major part of the recruiting process at Dow Chemical Company. Dow finds that it can attract good people at an early stage of their college careers and that it operates as a good screening device for choosing the best people. The majority of salespeople hired at Dow have previously worked as interns.[33]

Mistakes to Avoid

Sales managers often hire people in their own image, believing they can best relate to people who share their values. Cloning yourself may simplify interpersonal relationships, but it does not ensure sales effectiveness. People who think differently from you may be better for your organization. They may also be harder to supervise, but then the best salespeople often are. Ultimately, what is best depends on what the company wants to do. If pure diversity is what the organization seeks, cloning will most likely fail. If replication is in order, the applicants who genuinely parallel attributes of the sales manager probably represent sound choices.

Beware of applicants who don't really want to sell. These candidates often are looking at several career options, fail to understand the selling environment, and have vague reasons for choosing sales. Interest in travel, a desire to meet people, and making a lot of money are not good enough reasons to hire someone. Look for assertiveness and a clear desire to sell, demonstrated, if possible, by past experience.

Sometimes candidates for sales positions are rejected because the manager feels they cannot grow beyond the immediate opening. This is a serious mistake because many excellent sales prospects are apt to be passed over. Also, candidates selected for their future administrative skills often do poorly as field salespeople. The best approach is to hire for the current opening, not on the basis of what the person may be able to do tomorrow.[34]

Another trap that sales managers fall into is hiring the "best available" candidate. Despite an extensive search and many interviews, the best prospect you can find may not be up to company standards. You are probably better off with an empty territory than one filled with an incompetent. In the short run you can handle an empty territory with temporary help, phone calls from inside salespeople, and major account calls by the sales manager. Don't hire the best of a bad lot; start over with a new search.

An Issue of Integrating Diversity

It should come as little surprise that America is becoming more diverse than in the past. The problem is not the changing composition of the work force itself, but the difficulties companies are having in integrating and utilizing a truly heterogeneous work force at all levels in the organization. Consider the following trends:[35]

- Analysis indicates that 65 percent of new jobs created during the 1990s will be filled by women.
- By 2050, one-half of the U.S. population will be African-American, Hispanic-American, Native American, and Asian-American.
- The median age of the U.S. population is projected to rise from the current 32 years to 36 years by 2000 and to 39 years by 2010.

Companies that attempt to address diversity issues by meeting hiring quotas are not likely to be successful. Changes must be made in the way corporations work. Though the solutions are not clear, some of the problems companies are grappling with include the following:

- Identifying and eliminating discrimination in hiring and management based on age, sex, and ethnicity
- Developing creative ways to encourage productive people to stay in the work force longer by offering part-time, flexible schedules and retraining to upgrade skills
- Recognizing the concerns of men and women with different family structures and family responsibilities by addressing the issue of family care

One reason it is important for corporate America to address these concerns is that employee differences must be taken into account or companies will be unable to attract a sufficient number of qualified people to fill their needs. Another reason is that the markets for products are becoming more diverse, and there is a need to have an in-depth understanding of these markets that may be facilitated by employee diversity. Throughout this text, there are examples of how global companies must recognize and adjust to cultural differences in other countries. It is at least as important that companies make similar adjustments in dealing with employees at home. Some of the international issues are discussed in Sales Management in Action 9-5.

Sales Management in Action 9-5
"Whom Should We Hire in Belgium?"

Hiring successful salespeople becomes much more complicated when American corporations go overseas. The numerous social differences between the U.S. and foreign markets complicates the process. Following are some examples of the social class, religious, and ethnic differences affecting salesperson selection.

- Latin American cultures are largely stratified into high and low, with a very small middle class. Respect is automatically given to superiors. Lighter-skinned groups are generally ascribed higher social status.

- While Europeans on the surface appear to be similar to Americans, there are a number of subtle differences. In Germany,

ethnic biases favor hiring native Germans over those of Turkish or Yugoslav origin. Belgium is ethnically and linguistically split between Flemish and French. About 150 families control much of Belgian commerce.

- Malaysia has U.S.-style affirmative action laws to encourage the participation of native Malays (55 percent of the population) but not for the Chinese (33 percent). Malay society is highly stratified. How a person is treated depends on background, family, and social status.

Source: John Hill and Meg Birdeye, "Salesperson Selection in Multinational Corporations: An Empirical Study," *Journal of Personal Selling & Sales Management*, 9 (Summer 1989), p. 45.

▶ VALIDATING THE HIRING PROCESS

The last step in the hiring process involves validating the relationship between the selection criteria used by the firm and job success. Information collected on the progress of sales personnel is fed back into the system to modify the factors considered in the hiring process. *Validation* requires that managers specify exactly what constitutes success on the job.

A new insurance salesperson, for instance, might have to meet the following criteria by the end of the first year of work: sales premiums of $120,000, renewal of policies at a rate of 60 percent or more, and submitting orders, reports, and paperwork that are legible, accurate, and timely. Those who achieved the standard would be examined carefully to see what common traits they share. The objective of the validation process is to build a profile of the successful performer that can be used to select additional salespeople.

Suppose that an analysis of 50 first-year insurance salespeople reveals that the typical successful salesperson has six months' or more prior experience in sales, a score of 65 or better on the Selling Aptitude Test, and a college diploma or better. These results could then be used to help standardize the hiring criteria to screen applicants. Persons who did not have a college degree or six months' sales experience could be weeded out on the basis of information supplied on their application forms. Those who survive the initial screening hurdles would have to take the Sales Aptitude Test. Candidates who scored below 65 on the test would be dropped before the final interviews.

Validation seeks to build a set of hiring criteria that filters out poor prospects and makes offers to people who will have a high likelihood of succeeding. No system can be 100 percent correct, but a carefully designed program can improve the ratio of successful hires to failures. The stringency of the hiring criteria will depend on the type of sales job for which the person is being recruited. For some routine sales jobs, a set of fairly easy hiring criteria may be adequate. In more specialized industrial selling jobs where a heavy investment in training is required, a more rigorous set of experience and educational criteria may be justified. The goal of validation is to find out what factors are related to success so that they can be used to select new additions to the sales force.

▶ ETHICAL SITUATIONS

The pressure to fill an open sales position frequently leads to situations in ethically gray areas. Earnings potentials may be slightly inflated or optimistic three-year predictions may be made. Relating how one person was promoted in only 18 months, even though this was highly unusual, may leave the candidate with the impression that quick promotion is very probable. What if your company is in a changing industry in which the role of the salesperson is likely to be quite different in the near future and the earnings potential limited? What if you, the interviewer, are thinking of quitting? Should you let the candidate know? Should candidates be informed when it is likely the organization will go through a "downsizing" event sometime in the forseeable future?

▶ SUMMARY

The recruitment and selection of salespeople constitutes one of the primary responsibilities of field sales management. After a thorough analysis of each sales job, the sales manager prepares a list of qualifications to be used in recruiting. Depending on the type of job to be filled and company policy, the sales manager then seeks applicants through various sources—educational institutions, other departments within the firm, employment agencies, classified advertising, and even competing or customer firms. Managers must evaluate the pool of applicants in order to select the most promising candidates. The selection process involves the use of application blanks, interviews, background and credit checks, and examinations in order to identify those persons who meet the job qualifications. Then the sales manager must decide which, if any, of the candidates should be offered selling positions. Hiring criteria should be validated by identifying traits associated with success on the job and including these traits as screening criteria for new candidates.

▶ KEY TERMS

Application blanks	Job description
Aptitude tests	Job qualifications
Assessment centers	Knockout factors
Classified advertisements	Networking
Credit checks	Patterned interview
Drug testing	Personal interview
Employment agencies	Personality tests
Field observation	Recruiting
Hiring criteria	Selecting prospects
Informational Interview	Semistructured interview
Intelligence tests	Turnover
Internship	Validation
Job analysis	
Job analysis interview	

▶ REVIEW QUESTIONS

1. Why is a job description needed for recruiting sales personnel?

2. Is it useful to hire salespeople who are similar in background to the buyers? Why or why not?

3. Explain how personality and appearance contribute to success in sales jobs.

4. What are the most popular sources of sales trainees? of experienced salespeople?

5. Describe the factors that influence where a firm goes to find salespeople.

6. When should classified ads be used to attract salespeople?

7. What is the main advantage of using employment agencies to get salespeople?

8. Why are sales candidates asked to complete an application blank?

9. Explain why interviews are used to screen sales applicants.

10. Can testing be used to screen applicants? What problems are associated with testing?

11. Why do firms attempt to validate hiring criteria for salespeople?

12. Which is the better selection tool, personal interviews or job experience? What are the problems of each tool as a predictor of job performance?

13. Should drug testing be included in physical exams for new sales representatives? Why or why not?

▶ PROBLEMS

1. A district sales manager said, "I have a rule I never break. I only hire salespeople who are in their thirties, married, with three or more kids, and carrying mortgages as big as the Ritz. That way, they'll need me more than I'll need them, and I know they'll be back on the job each and every morning." Comment on this statement. Are there other ways to minimize turnover of the sales force?

2. NCR manufactures point-of-sale terminals and other data processing equipment. Their recruiting effort for sales representatives has a number of interesting features. Along with

the standard interviews by sales managers, they have applicants take two tests. The first is a spatial relations test in which the applicants are required to perceive a three-dimensional relationship on a piece of paper and count the number of edges that touch. In the second test, the applicant is given two minutes to write down as many words as possible that begin with one letter of the alphabet. What can these tests tell the company about the possible success of its applicants that an interview and resume would not show? Is this approach superior to the old-fashioned "seat of the pants" method used by many firms?

3. Representatives in the pharmaceutical sales industry deal with two distinct groups. They call on physicians, attempting to convince them of the product's superior quality, and they call on pharmacists, who must be convinced to stock the product instead of a competitor's products. In recruiting salespeople, some firms hire only pharmacy school graduates, whereas others hire business or liberal arts majors and put them through an intense training program. What are the advantages and disadvantages of each method? What implications might this have for sales management? Will there be a difference in the number or type of persons moving into middle and upper management?

4. Which is the more common reason for salesperson failure: poor planning and organization or inability to get along with buyers? Two hundred sales managers were asked to rank the following factors contributing to the failure of salespeople. How would you rank these factors?

   a. Lacks customer orientation
   b. Lacks proper training
   c. Lacks enthusiasm
   d. Unable to get along with buyers
   e. Lacks personal goals
   f. Lacks initiative
   g. Poor planning and organization
   h. Inadequate product knowledge

   Salespeople were also asked to rank the factors. Do you think their rankings differed from those of sales managers? If so, how?

5. How would you rank the following as important indicators of selling aptitude in an applicant?

__High persuasiveness	__Follows instructions
__Sociability	__Highly recommended
__Enthusiasm	__High verbal skills
__Well organized	__General sales experience
__Obvious ambition	__Specific sales experience

6. About two weeks after starting a new job, doubts creep into your mind. The gap between what you were told and what's actually happening gets wider by the day. When you've been on the job for three weeks, you say to yourself, "I think I made a mistake." One way to avoid making a costly mistake like this is to ask the right questions when interviewing. What questions would you ask when applying for a field sales position to avoid accepting the wrong job?

7. Using the job description in Figure 9-2, develop a set of job qualifications for Armstrong World Industries, along with interview questions to determine if a candidate has these qualifications.

8. Following are some practical questions about how to conduct a job interview if you are the interviewer:

   a. How much of the time should you spend listening to the candidate?

   b. If the applicant seems stressed, should you change the subject or dig further to discover the source of the stress?

   c. How should you wrap up each sales interview?

9. The first few days on the job can be very important in determining how quickly the new salesperson gets started in the territory. How would you answer the following questions about the initial socialization of salespeople into the company? Should new people set their own pace during their first week on the job? Should new salespeople be asked to assess their territory before taking it over?

▶ IN-CLASS EXERCISES

9-1: Which One to Pick

Armstrong World Industries is interviewing candidates for its next training class, which begins in July at its headquarters in Lancaster, Pennsylvania. Armstrong anticipates enough territory openings in the coming year to fill a full class of 35 trainees. The trainees from this class will be placed somewhere in the United States in the Floor Division of Armstrong.

The Floor Division is considered the main division of Armstrong World Industries, accounting for a majority of company sales and profits. A copy of the job description for a sales position in the Floor Division is provided in Figure 9-2. The starting salary is $28,500, with the potential for up to a 10 percent bonus based on annual sales to quota results for the territory and the district. If the qualifications of the candidate warrant it, however, up to $30,000 in base salary can be offered.

The expected career path for salespeople in this division is to manage a territory for between 18 months and 3 years. Promotion is to a staff position to assist a regional sales manager. This assignment is used as field training for the district manager position. This staff assignment may be anywhere in the country and is expected to last from six months to a year. Turnover in the first year of employment averages about 30 percent.

There is one position left in the fall training class, and you must choose from one of the following two people. The first candidate is a senior and will graduate this May. This candidate has answered well all the questions posed, has a good grade point average, and has been involved in a number of extracurricular activities. Overall, the candidate is strong.

The second candidate is a 23-year-old person who currently works for one of the wholesalers carrying Armstrong floor products. The candidate is a salesperson for the wholesaler and has performed well. The owner of the wholesale firm has been listed as a reference that can be contacted. The candidate has graduated from a community college with average grades and currently makes $28,000.

Questions:

1. With your understanding of the job description and possible career path, what questions would you prepare for the interviews of both candidates?

2. What additional questions would you prepare for the first candidate? The second candidate?

3. What are the arguments for and against each candidate and what would be the basis for your choice between the two candidates?

9-2: An Offer I Couldn't Refuse

A competitor is courting one of your best salespeople. T. S. has been with your company for over eight years since being recruited from a nearby college campus. T. S. is well respected by your 26 other salespeople, especially the younger ones, and has never caused you any trouble. You had once talked to T. S., in fact, about the possibility of being promoted to sales manager. T. S. declined, however, indicating no desire to do anything but sell because of the freedom it provided.

The company, a wholesaler of office supplies and furniture, has been in business for 23 years, with sales last year of just over $21 million. Most of your business is in office supplies such as paper pads, computer forms, pencils, pens, and other supplies used regularly by most businesses, both retail and commercial. Salespeople personally call on their customers at least once a week to take orders to replenish supplies. This continuous contact with the customer provides salespeople with the opportunity to sell office furniture when the customer has a need.

One of the competitive advantages you feel your company enjoys is a young and aggressive sales force. Unlike many of your competitors, you hire almost all of your salespeople straight from college campuses in the area. Building a list of customers is not easy, and the aggressiveness, "hunger," and learning skills of college graduates help to build sales during the first years on the job. In order to maintain a high-quality sales force, you pay a 30 percent commission on gross margin dollars, while the industry average is somewhere between 25 and 27 percent.

While they want the lowest competitive price, customers expect high service levels from their office supply salespeople, such as frequent office visits for resupply, quick delivery, especially in an emergency, and information on ways to make their job easier. It is not unusual for salespeople from three or more office supply houses to call on a customer, so the personal relationship between the customer and the salesperson is often a critical factor in determining who gets the sale. If a salesperson switches companies, 35 to 85 percent of the salesperson's customers continue to order from the salesperson.

T. S. has asked to see you privately to tell you about the offer. A competitor has offered him a $15,000 signing bonus on top of a 32 percent commission on all sales. T. S. states, "Frankly it is an offer I can't refuse. You have been very good to me and supported me in every way. That's why I wanted to let you know about this offer and to give you a chance to make a counter offer. I really don't want to leave, but I feel this is a once-in-a-lifetime situation."

You are stunned and point out to T. S. all the advantages of working for your company. Despite your best efforts at dissuading T. S., the meeting concludes with T. S. saying that the competitor wants an answer in the next week. You tell T. S. not to make a move until you get back to her and state that you must talk with the president.

When you tell the president about the situation, the president is surprised at the 32 percent commission rate plus signing bonus and asks, "How can competition do this?"

As sales manager you point out that T. S. produced almost $300 thousand in sales last year and a 30 percent gross margin. Furthermore, T. S. is well liked and respected by others in the sales force, and the sales manager wonders whether others will be tempted to leave if T. S. does.

Questions:

1. Why is T. S. informing you of the competitor's offer?
2. Why is T. S. considering the offer?
3. If you feel that the company can afford it, should you make a counter offer to T. S.?
4. What are the possible negative consequences of a counter offer?
5. If T. S. leaves, what actions would you take to minimize customer defections in T. S.' old territory?

▶ EXPERIENTIAL EXERCISE

This exercise is a practice hiring interview. Assume the role of a district sales manager of Armstrong World Industries who supervises people calling on wholesale and retail stores. You have an opening and are looking for a college graduate to fill the position. Your company offers a competitive compensation program for salespeople based on salary plus bonus, a free company car, and an expense account. Based on the job description in Figure 9-2, develop a profile of the qualifications required for the job. Devise a set of questions that will help screen out unqualified candidates. Since your instructor will pick two students to perform this role play in front of the class, you must be prepared to act the part of the candidate as well. Think of several selling points in your background as a candidate that go beyond the items listed on your resume and be prepared to talk about them. Develop a list of questions that will impress the recruiter and prevent the interview from lagging.

▶ REFERENCES

1. GEOFFREY BREWER, "Shrink Rap," *Performance* (September 1995), p. 30.

2. HERBERT M. GREENBERG and JEANNE GREENBERG, "Job Matching for Better Performance," *Harvard Business Review*, 58 (September–October 1980), p. 128.

3. WILLIAM KEENAN, "Time Is Everything," *Sales & Marketing Management* (August 1993), p. 60.

4. GINGER CONLON, "The Top: Northwestern Mutual Life Insurance," *Sales & Marketing Management* (November 1996), p. 44; for more information on the success of first-year insurance agents, see JACQUELINE LANDAU and JAMES WERBEL, "Sales Productivity of Insurance Agents During the First Six Months of Employment: Differences Between Older and Younger New Hires," *Journal of Personal Selling & Sales Management*, 15 (Fall 1995), pp. 33–43.

5. For more information on the causes of turnover and how to manage turnover, see ELI JONES, DONNA MASSEY KANTAK, CHARLES FUTRELL, and MARK JOHNSTON, "Leader Behavior, Work-Attitudes, and Turnover of Salespeople: An Integrative Study," *Journal of Personal Selling & Sales Management*, 16 (Spring 1996), pp. 13–23; PRADEEP TYAGI and THOMAS WOTRUBA, "An Exploratory Study of Reverse Causality Relationships Among Sales Force Turnover Variables," *Journal of the Academy of Marketing Science*, 21 (Spring 1993), pp. 143–153; and JEFF SAGER, "A Longitudinal Assessment of Change in Sales Force Turnover," *Journal of the Academy of Marketing Science*, 19 (Winter 1991), pp. 25–36.

6. CHARLES BUTLER, "What Does it Take to Sell for Invacare," *Sales & Marketing Management* (July 1995), p. 70.

7. WILLIAM KEENAN, "Taking Aim at Tomorrow's Challenges," *Sales & Marketing Management* (September 1991), p. 70.

8. Review reported in GILBERT CHURCHILL, NEIL FORD, STEVE HARTLEY, and ORVILL WALKER, "The Determinants of Salesperson Performance: A Meta-Analysis," *Journal of Marketing Research* (May 1986), pp. 103–118; and NEIL FORD, GILBERT CHURCHILL, STEVE HARTLEY, and ORVILL WALKER, "Selecting Successful Salespeople: A Meta-Analysis of Biographical and Psychological Selection Criteria," *Review of Marketing*, ed. MICHAEL HOUSTON (Chicago: American Marketing Association, 1988), pp. 90–131.

9. For more on the importance of person-job fit, see JAMES WERBEL, JACQUELINE LANDAU and THOMAS DeCARLO, "The Relation-

ship of Pre-entry Variables to Early Employment Organizational Commitment," *Journal of Personal Selling & Sales Management*, 16 (Spring 1996), pp. 25–36.

10. GEORGE FREEHERY, "The Role of Empathy in Personal Selling," *National Conference of Sales Management* (1992), pp. 130–135.

11. ROSANN SPRIO and BARTON WEITZ, "Adaptive Selling: Conceptualization, Measurement, and Nomological Validity," *Journal of Marketing Research*, 27 (February 1990), pp. 61–69.

12. "Eli Lilly Lauded for Its Bedside Manner," *Sales & Marketing Management* (February 1992), p. 68.

13. SUSAN MEISINGER, "The Americans with Disabilities Act of 1990: A New Challenge for Human Resource Managers," *Legal Report*, Society for Human Resource Management (Winter 1990), pp. 1–16.

14. MARIANNE MATHEWS, "If Your Ads Aren't Pulling Top Sales Talent . . . , " *Sales Marketing Management* (February 1990), pp. 75–79.

15. RENE DARMON, "Where Do the Best Sales Force Profit Producers Come From?" *Journal of Personal Selling & Sales Management*, 13 (Summer 1993), pp. 17–29.

16. THOMAS WOTRUBA and STEPHEN CASTLEBERRY, "Job Analysis and Hiring Practices for National Account Marketing Positions," *Journal of Personal Selling & Sales Management*, 13 (Summer 1993), pp. 49–65.

17. WILLIAM KEENAN (1993), p. 60.

18. Conversation with STEPHANIE N. CRISARA, Manager of Professional Employment, Armstrong Cork Company, Lancaster, Pennsylvania.

19. GARY MCWILLIAMS, "Reveille for DEC's Sleepy Sales Force," *BusinessWeek* (August 30, 1993), p. 74.

20. For more information on how to recruit college students, see DAN WEILBAKER and NANCY MERRITT, "Attracting Graduates to Sales Positions: The Role of

Recruiter Knowledge," *Journal of Personal Selling & Sales Management*, 12 (Fall 1992), pp. 49–58.

21. DICK SCHAAF, "Lessons From the 100 Best," *Training*, 27 (February 1990), p. S19.

22. KEENAN, "Time Is Everything," p. 62.

23. RENE DARMON, "Where Do the Best Sales Force Profit Producers Come From?" *Journal of Personal Selling & Sales Management*, 13 (Summer 1993), p. 27.

24. MYRON GABLE, CHARLES HOLLON, and FRANK DANGELLO, "Increasing the Utility of the Application Blank: Relationship Between Job Application Information and Subsequent Performance and Turnover of Salespeople," *Journal of Personal Selling & Sales Management*, 12 (Summer 1992), pp. 51–58.

25. KEENAN, "Time Is Everything," p. 61.

26. MARTIN EVERETT and BETSY SIESENDANGER, "What Does Body Language Really Say?" *Sales & Marketing Management* (April 1992), p. 40.

27. LIZ MURPHY, "Did Your Salesman Lie to Get His Job?" *Sales & Marketing Management* (November 1987), p. 54.

28. THOMAS WOTRUBA and EDWIN SIMPSON, *Sales Management: Text and Cases* (Boston: PWS-Kent, 1992), p. 380.

29. *Wall Street Journal* (March 6, 1991), p. 131.

30. MEISINGER, "Americans with Disabilities Act," pp. 4–7.

31. CATHY OWENS SWIFT, ROBER WAYLAND, and JANE WAYLAND, "The ADA: Implications for Sales Managers," *National Conference for Sales Management* (1993), pp. 146–148.

32. ROY COOK and JOEL HERCHE, "Assessment Centers: An Untapped Resource for Global Salesforce Management," *Journal of Personal Selling & Sales Management*, 12 (Summer 1992), pp. 31–39.

33. "Internship Program Attracts Quality Recruits," *Sales Manager's Bulletin* (July 15, 1993), p. 5.

34. W. E. PATTON and RONALD KING, "The Use of Human Judgment Models in Sales Force Selection Decisions," *Journal of Personal Selling & Sales Management*, 12 (Spring 1992), pp. 1–14.

35. The discussion in this section is based on JOHN FERNANDEZ, *Managing a Diverse Work Force: Regaining the Competitive Edge* (Lexington, Mass.: Lexington Books, 1991).

▶ SELECTED READINGS

CASCIO, WAYNE, *Managing Human Resources: Productivity, Quality of Life, Profits* (New York: McGraw-Hill, 1989).

FERNANDEZ, JOHN P. *Managing a Diverse Work Force* (Lexington, Mass.: Lexington Books, 1991).

ROSENBLUTH, HAL and DIANE MCFERRIN PETERS, *The Customer Comes Second* (New York: William Morrow, 1992).

TEPPER, RON, *Power Resumes* (New York: 1989).

YATE, MARTIN, *Hiring the Best* (Holbrook, Mass.: Bob Adams, 1990).

YATE, MARTIN, *Keeping the Best* (Hobrook, Mass.: Bob Adams, 1991).

C A S E

9-1 FORTRESS ELECTRICAL TAPE COMPANY*

Ralph Harris, sales manager of the Fortress Electrical Tape Company of Boston, Massachusetts, was attempting to select one candidate among three to fill an opening in his sales force. Fortress executives had for some time retained the services of a psychologist, Dr. Robert Gold, to assist them in selecting new employees. Dr. Gold's reports on these three candidates were available to Harris.

Company Background

Fortress's 1992 sales were in excess of $100 million. The company manufactured and marketed rubber and plastic electrical tapes. These tape products were sold by a sales force of five industry specialists to utilities, transportation firms, industrial plants, and electricians through a network of approximately 3,000

*This case was prepared by Derek A. Newton. Copyright © 1993 by the University of Virginia Darden School Foundation, Charlottesville, VA. All rights reserved. Reproduced by permission.

independent distributors. These latter were serviced by 27 manufacturers' representative organizations ("reps"). Exhibit 1 shows a partial organization chart of the sales operation.

The industry specialist's job was to acquaint end users with the specific technical advantages of Fortress electrical tape. The specialist also had to learn each customer's splicing requirements and other technical problems to be able to develop new applications for Fortress tape. The specialist actually spent only one-fourth of his or her time working directly with present or potential end users, however. Most of the specialist's time was spent working with the reps, arranging and conducting frequent regional sales meetings to pass on new information. The industry specialist also attended similar regional meetings held by the rep groups for their distributors. Typically, the specialist spent one-half of his or her time away from the main plant in Boston.

The industry specialists were typically in their thirties and earned about $60,000 a year. All had previous sales experience. According to company exec-

Exhibit 1: Sales Organization

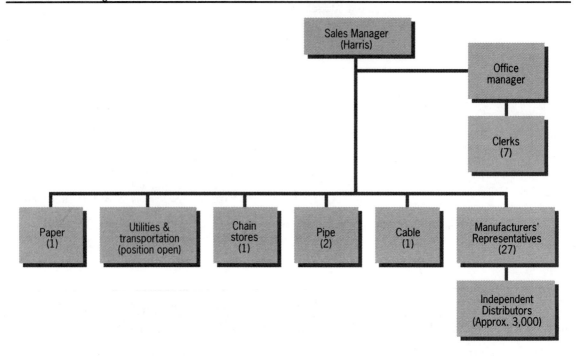

utives, the most desirable background for an industry specialist would include a college degree and selling experience. Fortress executives also looked for candidates familiar with the Fortress product line or with a group of Fortress customers, and who could handle a fast-paced work schedule and a good deal of traveling.

During the past few years, a sharp increase in business—especially in small orders—from the public-utility and transportation industries led Harris to believe that his company could support a full-time specialist serving these markets. This new position would free the paper-industry specialist, who currently served the public utility and transportation markets, to develop the considerable potential in the paper industry.

Harris planned to have the new specialist report directly to him, as did the other industry specialists. The specialist would be based in Boston and would travel at least three-fourths of the time. He or she would initially assist the reps by making missionary and follow-up sales calls on large-volume prospects. After two years, Harris believed, this missionary sell-

ing activity could be reduced. The new industry specialist could then give more effort to maintaining a few key customers and guiding the reps.

This job could lead to the position of assistant sales manager to Harris, or to the position of regional sales manager, a post that Fortress sales executives planned to create within a few years to provide independent representatives and distributors with better supervision and assistance. A candidate's promotability, then, was important to Harris in determining which applicant to select.

The Selection Procedure

Harris and other Fortress executives were dissatisfied with interviews, résumés, and references as means of evaluating candidates. Harris felt that hiring judgments based on interviews were often subjective. While résumés provided concrete data, such information was often difficult to interpret. And Harris had never seen a negative reference. Moreover, most candidates requested that their present employers not be contacted, so Harris felt that the most pertinent information about their job histories was not available to him.

To make better hiring decisions, Fortress executives employed a psychologist, Dr. Robert Gold, to gather and assess more information about prospective employees. Dr. Gold's qualifications included a B.S. and an M.A. in Psychology and Sociology from Tufts University and a Doctor of Education degree in Psychology from Boston University. He had an established practice in Brookline, Massachusetts, was on the faculty of a local college, and had done consulting work for various businesses and public-school systems. Dr. Gold was widely regarded as an expert in dealing with psychological variables in normal and abnormal human functioning. Dr. Gold charged Fortress $1,500 per candidate. In return for this fee, Fortress executives received an interpretation of the applicant's personal history and a discussion of the applicant's qualities for the position.

Among the tests used by Dr. Gold were the following standard individually or self-administered psychological tests: Wechsler Adult Intelligence Test; Reading Comprehension Test; FACT Arithmetic Test; FACT (verbal) Expression Test; FACT Judgment and Comprehension Test; Sales Comprehension Test; Strong Vocational Interest Test; and various projective personality tests. Dr. Gold also used special performance situations and his clinical judgment to assess other personal qualities, such as emotional stability, mental organization, resourcefulness, flexibility, tact, creativity, and motivation.

During the past several months, Harris had interviewed more than a dozen people for the position of industry specialist in the public-utility and transportation industries. He had chosen three candidates to receive psychological testing. His impressions and those of other Fortress personnel are presented below, together with excerpts from the reports submitted by Dr. Gold on each of the three candidates.

Joseph Waring

Joseph Waring had been referred to Harris by the company's largest distributor, who was enthusiastic about Waring's selling and managerial abilities. Although Waring was not actively seeking a job, he was interested enough in the opportunity at Fortress to arrange an interview.

Harris believed that Waring made a good appearance and would probably be an excellent salesman, although he tended to be "a little cocky." Waring knew Fortress's customers very well and had experience calling on these customers, especially the larger distributors. He also responded very well to several questions about the electrical-tape industry.

Harris recalled meeting Waring at a trade show earlier in the year. They had a mutual interest in sailing, and Harris believed that he would enjoy working with Waring. The office secretarial staff was also favorably impressed with Waring.

During a luncheon with Fortress top management, Waring impressed these executives with his selling ability, but they wondered whether he had the capacity to assume a management position at a later date. This doubt was generated largely by Waring's comments about the problems of dealing with excessive paperwork.

Dr. Gold interviewed the candidate and reported the following information about Mr. Waring's background and personal history:

> Waring is the youngest of four children; he has one older brother who is an engineer; his two older sisters are married. His father put himself through engineering college and owned a small company. Waring characterized his childhood as excellent, but says that he has not struggled as hard as his father did. He has been married for eight years. His wife is one year younger than he. They have a good marriage, according to him. They have three children, all boys, and there are no problems. His hobbies include boating, other water sports, hunting, fishing; his wife loves boating. He enjoys an occasional drink. He was in the Army Reserves for a little more than 10 years before resigning.
>
> Waring has a long history of not applying himself, and his academic background and work history underscore this pattern. He was a fair-to-poor student in elementary and high school because, as he states, he did not "get kicked hard enough." He attended a local university for one year in the school of business administration, where he did fair work and, again, did not apply himself. He then moved to another local university "because of the school-work program." However, because the work program required very long hours (7 P.M. to 7 A.M., six days per week), he decided to leave school and work full time at this job (a government project). He remained in this position for four years; his

work was largely technical, but he also did some work for the purchasing director. He felt that he was getting good experience, but the job offered little chance for advancement. He then worked for two years with a builder-realtor.

Waring ran a branch office and supervised construction as well as property sales. He left because he preferred "more technical sales and getting around more." He then sold diesel motors for a large distributor for a year, but "the money wasn't there." His most recent job has been with a small company where he began as a product manager, then became an assistant sales manager, and then assistant to the vice president. He was let go along with many other administrative personnel during a company downsizing. He has been without work since last April. He does not need to make a hasty decision about future employment because he runs a two-boat business with his brother. He stated that he is interested in Fortress but is considering another job as well.

After reviewing the test results, Dr. Gold submitted his assessment of Waring's abilities and potential.

Waring's reaction to the assessment procedures was only fair. He complained about the tests to my assistant and also told her that he does not like to take tests. He has a tendency to talk a lot, but he expresses himself well and has a good sense of humor. He was well groomed. He had previously taken an extensive battery of tests for a position with another company. Only one of the present tests was a repetition, however.

Waring has excellent practical reasoning ability. He approaches problems well and thinks before he acts, and his thinking is organized, flexible, and resourceful. He is above average in judgment and comprehension. His vocational preferences and work history show strength in business and sales. He performed at an average level in reading comprehension, arithmetic ability, and sales comprehension. He shows fairly good tact and fair creativity.

In general, Waring has good basic intelligence. He apparently has not done too much with it, however. He lacks self-discipline and the ability to apply himself consistently to the tasks at hand. This lackadaisical quality prevents him from fully using his talents. He also has difficulty making decisions; he procrastinates and avoids responsibility. He needs outside direction, but he has good interpersonal relationships with authority figures, so he is able to take direction well. He is emotionally immature but basically stable. He shows real warmth in his relationships with other people.

Robert Mann

Mann was referred to Harris by a well-known personnel-placement agency in downtown Boston. The agency was especially enthusiastic about Mann and convinced Harris to come to their offices to interview him. After a very successful interview, Harris invited Mann to Fortress to visit the plant and meet other company executives. Harris enjoyed Mann's sense of humor and believed that the candidate would work out well at Fortress. Harris especially liked Mann's initiative in working his way through college and his general desire to move ahead. Harris also believed that Mann knew as much about Fortress's customers and products as some of the present industry specialists—his answers to questions on technical aspects of electrical tape were flawless. His previous experience seemed to be ideal preparation for the job.

During a luncheon with Fortress top management, Mann made a favorable impression and managed to keep the conversation relaxed with several humorous stories. The only reservations that the executives later expressed stemmed from some dissatisfaction with Mann's appearance and from some perplexity over his lack of progress in his career.

Dr. Gold's interview with Mann produced the following information about his personal history and background:

He grew up in greater Boston and attended public schools. He stated that his marks in high school were below average: He had good marks in English and social sciences, but passed by "the skin of my teeth" in other subjects. He also stated that he did very well in grammar school. After high school he worked for a year as a clerk with a supermarket chain; he felt that he was good with the customers. He then had a short enlistment in the Navy, where he went to electronics school and college preparatory school, and achieved the rank of seaman 2nd class. He hated the Navy saying "they wouldn't let you think." He then spent one year at a junior college where he did very well; following that he spent three years at a local university and finished with a low "B" average. While at college, he worked a full nightshift to pay for his college career; he lost a great deal of weight because of overwork.

Following college he worked for the telephone company for three years as a communications consultant; he left for more money. He then spent seven years with a local company. He trained inside for a year, then moved to outside sales; he left for more money. He then spent seven weeks with a small company and left because it was an "impossible situation and the wrong place"; apparently, the job had been misrepresented to him, for it turned out to require 100% travel. He then worked for a large company in selling for two years; he was asked to resign, and he is not sure why. He is presently selling computer software; he is leaving because "Every order I have sold has been fouled up." "The quality is adequate, but I am used to selling the best." He also says, "There is no place to go." He is currently interested in more responsibility. He feels that he is a proven salesman; he is now looking to make his last move. He feels that Fortress is a dynamic company and says "I have a real solid feeling" toward Fortress.

Mann is the second of four boys; he characterizes his childhood as happy. As a child he had a temper, and he correlates his red hair with his fighting to defend himself. Both of his parents are living; his father has been a jobber and real-estate salesman; his brothers are in sales and marketing. Mann has been married 12 years. His wife graduated from high school and secretarial school. They have three children: The oldest is a girl who is a good student, the next is a boy who is bright but has no motivation for school, and the youngest is a girl who is not yet school age. He states that he has an excellent marriage and that his physical and emotional health are excellent. He mentioned that he had an ulcer at age 30, due to tension. He feels that he has done a good job as a father in that he represents security to his children; that is, he does not vary in his discipline. His hob-

bies are fixing up around the house, reading, coaching a Little League team, and fishing; he and his wife do not go out very much. He is a beer drinker—three or four in the evening, and apparently each evening. He has an occasional highball with customers but says that he does not like to drink at noon.

After reviewing Mann's test results, Dr. Gold submitted the following report:

Mann reacted well to the assessment procedures. He was alert, fresh, and motivated both at the beginning and at the close of the evaluation sessions. He stated that he had taken such tests on two previous occasions. He makes a good impression, speaks well, but he has a tendency to wander from the subject under discussion. He appeared to be tense, and he exhibited a constant small-amplitude hand tremor; the tremor did not vary even under stress. He has a ruddy complexion, and he chain-smokes cigarettes. He tended to try to impress me about the way he handles himself in selling situations.

Mann's vocational preferences suit him for work in sales, personnel, and public administration. Mann's mental performance was very high in nearly all the skill and ability tests: basic intelligence, reading, verbal expression, business judgment, and sales comprehension. Only in mathematical ability is he merely a little above average. He is very good in practical and abstract reasoning. He catches on quickly, thinks clearly, and approaches problems well in that he figures things out before responding. He does not become rattled under pressure. He also performed well in the tests for mental organization, resourcefulness, flexibility, tact, and creativity.

Emotionally, he is expansive, optimistic, motivated, and generally mature. He also has a good sense of humor. However, all of the personality tests showed that he is defensive—he held back in his responses, making them difficult to analyze. His defensiveness suggests that he may be hiding some emotional problem. He is tense, has constant hand tremors, and had an ulcer at age 30. Clinically, I wonder if he may be an alcoholic. An essential feature of his overall performance was his excellent stamina. We can infer that this stamina would carry over to the work situation. On the other hand, if he does in fact have some basic emotional disturbance and/or is an alcoholic, he would not be able to cover up his problems indefinitely.

John Turner

The third candidate, John Turner, was referred to Harris by a small suburban sales-placement agency. Harris went to the agency for a morning of interviews, and Turner was by far the best of the candidates. He was currently working for an ashtray manufacturer, and during the interview he showed his selling process by picking up the table ashtray, selling it to Harris. He cleverly described product differences among various ashtrays and convincingly demonstrated superior features of a particular style of ashtray. His relaxed and positive manner during this sales presentation convinced Harris of his natural sales ability. Turner also mentioned that he had traveled to Europe some years ago, working his way across the Continent. He had also worked his way through college. This initiative also impressed Harris, and he invited Turner to Fortress for a plant tour.

Turner arrived early in a Mercedes-Benz and accidentally met Harris in the parking lot. They walked into the Fortress building together. Turner made a noticeable impression on the Fortress receptionist and displayed a very winning manner to Harris's office staff. As a result, the entire office staff believed that Turner would make a valuable and personable contribution to the sales force.

Although Turner knew very little about Fortress products or customers, he assured Harris that he would have little difficulty in this respect. Turner said that it had taken him less than two months to learn the specifics in his present position.

At a luncheon with top company executives, he impressed the group so favorably that they later decided that he did not have to be assessed psychologically. However, Harris had already scheduled the evaluation procedure and could not cancel it.

Dr. Gold reported the following information about Turner's personal history:

Turner has one younger brother who sells electronic calculators. He described his family as close, saying that "we have a great deal of fun together." He characterized his father as strong

willed but said that he and his brother "survived" and now have a good relationship with him. Turner has been seeing a woman for two and a half years and has plans to marry her. She has a staff position at a university. He has not been engaged previously. His hobbies are skiing, scuba diving, and tennis. He describes himself as having been a "hard drinker" while in the service, but he has cut down a great deal since then; he now rarely drinks during the week.

He lived in many parts of the country while he was growing up because his father was a salesman. He describes himself as an erratic student in the various public schools that he attended. He went to prep school for three years, where his performance was also erratic; at one point he won a prize for raising his average more than any other student in the space of one year. He then went to college for one year with the hopes of studying to be an industrial engineer, but he found engineering courses uninteresting. He left college to join the Marine Corps, where he remained for two years, elevating himself to private 1st class. He then attended a business college here in Massachusetts. He said that the courses made sense to him and he did well the first year, although his grades went down the second year. Following his junior year, he left to tour Europe for six months. He states that he always worked during his schooling, primarily cutting trees on a contract basis. He stresses his need for money and his desire for the "finer things in life," and the fact is that he did make good money. When he returned to school, he achieved average grades.

After graduation he worked for a brokerage firm in New York for 20 months. Because he still wanted to do industrial sales, he left the brokerage firm and went to work for his father as a manufacturer's representative. He left this job after three and a half years because the "rep business folded" (apparently only for him, not for his father). He did not like the work because, as he says, "you had to be less than honest in getting in to see a person" and "you had to wrench the customer's money away from other things he wanted to spend it on." Thus, he says, "I could only go so far and not quite far enough to close the sale." He left the job after six months.

He has been looking for a new position for more than a month now, but says that he is not looking too actively because he wants to make sure that he is going into the right thing. He went to a prominent national personnel-counseling firm for evaluation. He was told that he should aim for management through sales and marketing. He has found that he should stick to selling, and to tangible products. He states that he has had a couple of "interesting offers," but that he is favorably disposed toward Fortress. He feels that he is too "fidgety" to take an office job at this time. He also states that his value is a little higher than most companies are willing to pay for.

After testing Turner, Dr. Gold submitted the following assessment of the candidate's strengths and weaknesses:

Turner's reaction to the assessment procedures was fairly good at the outset. Initially, he seemed quite alert, peppy, interested. He showed a good command of the English language and generally spoke well, except that he tended to ramble and his explanations were not always to the point. He displayed a fairly good sense of humor and was at times quite definitely flip. However, about two-thirds of the way through the tests and interviews he began to wilt. He was visibly tired and was comparatively unkempt in appearance and demeanor. It appeared that he had put up a front at the beginning of the assessment but had lost it by the end. He stated that he had not previously taken so extensive a battery of tests.

In general, the test results showed that Turner has very high intelligence, verbal expression, reading ability, and judgment and comprehension, although his sales comprehension was well below average. His vocational preference is for work requiring verbal expression.

Analysis of his intellectual behavior shows that he has excellent practical and abstract reasoning abilities. He thinks well on his feet and was not visibly bothered by pressure; he did not become rattled when he was obviously having difficulty with a task. He was methodical in his approach to problems, yet his thinking was resourceful, flexible, and creative. However, his performance was sometimes erratic, probably due to periodic lapses of interest. His performance was relatively weaker on tasks calling for immediate effort.

Emotionally, Turner is immature, egotistical, selfish, and spoiled. He seems to have little emotional interaction with others, although he presents himself well in interpersonal encounters. He projects a need for nurturance from father figures. He avoids responsibility and decision making, although he can evaluate situations quite well up to the point of making decisions. He is a talker rather than a doer. His behavior is generally erratic, and there seems to be no stable pattern to his life.

Harris wanted to add the needed sales support as soon as possible, and he did not believe that further searching would glean any better candidates than these. He now had to decide which of the three people would be the best addition to his sales force.

C A S E

9-2 ADAMS BRANDS*

Ken Bannister, Ontario Regional Manager for Adams Brands, was faced with the decision of which of three candidates he should hire as the key account supervisor for the Ontario region. This salesperson would be responsible for working with eight major accounts in the Toronto area. Bannister had narrowed the list to the three applicants and began reviewing their files.

Company

Warner-Lambert, Inc., a large, diversified U.S. multinational, manufactured and marketed a wide range of health care and consumer products. Warner-Lambert Canada Ltd., the largest subsidiary, had annual sales exceeding $200 million. Over one-half of the Canadian sales were generated by Adams Brands, which focused on the confectionery business. The major product lines carried by Adams were:

1. Chewing gum, with brands such as Chiclets, Dentyne, and Trident.

2. Portable breath fresheners including Certs and Clorets.

3. Cough tablets and antacids such as Halls and Rolaids.

4. Several other products, including Blue Diamond Almonds and Sparkies Mini-Fruits.

In these product categories, Adams Brands was usually the market leader or had a substantial market share.

The division was a stable unit for Warner-Lambert Canada, with profits being used for investments throughout the company. Success of the Adams Brands was built on:

1. Quality products.

2. Strong marketing management.

*This case was prepared by Gordon McDougall, Wilfrid Laurier University, and Douglas Snetsinger, University of Toronto.

3. Sales force efforts in distribution, display, and merchandising.

4. Excellent customer service.

Adams was organized on a regional basis. The Ontario region, which also included the Atlantic provinces, had 46 sales representatives whose responsibilities were to service individual stores. Five district managers coordinated the activities of the sales representatives. As well, three key account supervisors worked with the large retail chains (e.g., supermarkets) in Ontario and the Atlantic area. The key account supervisor in the Toronto area had recently resigned his position and joined one of Adams's major competitors.

The Market

The confectionery industry comprised six major competitors that manufactured chocolate bars, chewing gum, mints, cough drops, chewy candy, and other products. The 1993 market shares of these six companies are provided in Exhibit 1.

In the past few years, total industry sales in the confectionary category had been flat to marginally declining in unit volume. This sales decline was attributed to the changing age distribution of the population (i.e., fewer young people). As consumers grew older, their consumption of confectionery products tended to decline. While unit sales were flat or declining, dollar sales were increasing at a rate of 10 percent per annum as a result of price increases.

In the confectionery business, it was critical to obtain extensive distribution in as many stores as possible and, within each store, to obtain as much prominent shelf space as possible. Most confectionary products were purchased on impulse. In one study it was found that up to 85 percent of chewing gum and 70 percent of chocolate bar purchases were unplanned. While chocolate bars could be viewed as an indirect competitor to gum and mints, they were direct competitors for retail space and were usually merchandised on the same display. Retailers earned sim-

Exhibit 1: Major Competitors in the Confectionery Industry

Company	Market Share (%)	Major Product Lines	Major Brands
Adams	23	Gum, portable breath fresheners, cough drops	Trident, Chiclets, Dentyne, Certs, Halls
Nielsen/Cadbury	22	Chocolate bars	Caramilk, Crunchie, Dairy Milk, Crispy Crunch
Nestlé Canada	15	Chocolate bars	Coffee Crisp, Kit-Kat, Smarties, Turtles
Hershey	14	Gum, chocolate bars, chewy candy	Glossette, Oh Henry, Reese's Pieces, Lifesavers
Effem Foods	11	Chocolate bars, chewy candy	Mars, Snickers, M&M's, Skittles
Wrigley's	9	Gum	Hubba Bubba, Extra, Doublemint
Richardson-Vicks	2	Cough drops	Vicks
Others	4		

Source: Company records and industry data.

ilar margins from all confectionary products (25–36 percent of the retail selling price) and often sought the best-selling brands to generate those revenues. Some industry executives felt that catering to the retailers' needs was even more important than understanding the ultimate consumers' needs.

Adams Brands had always provided store display racks for merchandising all confectionery items, including competitive products and chocolate bars. The advantage of supplying the displays was that the manufacturer could influence the number of prelabeled slots that contained brand logos and the proportion of the display devoted to various product groups such as chewing gum versus chocolate bars. The displays were usually customized to the unique requirements of a retailer, such as the height and width of the display.

Recently, a competitor, Effem, had become more competitive in the design and display of merchandising systems. Effem was regarded as an innovator in the industry, in part because of their limited product line and their new approach to the retail trade. The company had only eight fast-turnover products in their line. Effem had developed their own sales force, consisting of over 100 part-time merchandising salespeople and 8 full-time sales personnel, and focused on the head offices of "A" accounts. "A" accounts were

large retail chains such as 7-Eleven, Beckers, Loblaws, A&P, Food City, Shopper's Drug Mart, K-Mart, Towers, and Zellers. Other than Adams, Effem was one of the few companies that conducted considerable research on racking systems and merchandising.

The Retail Trade

Within Adams Brands, over two-thirds of confectionary volume flowed through wholesalers. The remaining balance was split between direct sales and drop shipments to retailers. Wholesalers were necessary because, with over 66,000 outlets in food, drug, and variety stores alone, the sales force could not adequately cover a large proportion of the retailers. The percentage of Adams sales through the various channels is provided in Exhibit 2.

The volume of all consumer packaged goods sold in Canada was increasingly dominated by fewer and larger retail chains. This increased retail concentration resulted in retailers becoming more influential in trade promotion decisions, including dictating the size, timing, and number of allowance, distribution, and coop advertising events. The new power of the retailers had not yet been fully wielded against the confectionary business. Confectionery lines were some of the most profitable lines for the retailer. Fur-

Exhibit 2: Adams Brands Sales by Distribution Channel

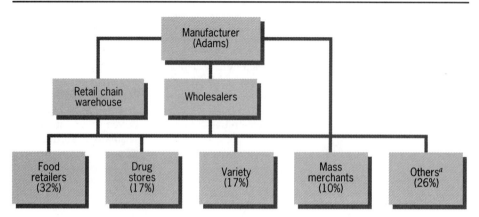

^aConsists of a wide variety of locations, including vending machines, restaurants, cafeterias, bowling alleys, and resorts.

^aConsists of a wide variety of locations including; vending machines, restaurants, cafeterias, bowling alleys, resorts.

ther, the manufacturers were not as reliant on listings from any given retailer as were other food and household product manufacturers.

The increased size of some retail chains also changed the degree of management sophistication at all levels, including that of the retail buyers—those individuals responsible for deciding what products were carried by the retail stores. At one time, the relationship between manufacturers' sales representatives and retail buyers was largely based on long-term, personal associations. Usually the sales representative had strong social skills, and an important task was to get along well with the buyers. Often when the representatives and buyers met to discuss various promotions or listings, part of the conversation dealt with making plans for dinner or going to a hockey game. The sales representative was the host for these social events.

More recently, a new breed of buyer had been emerging in the retail chains. Typically the new retail managers and buyers had been trained in business schools. They often had product management experience, relied on analytical skills, and used state-of-the-art, computer-supported planning systems. In some instances, the buyer was more sophisticated than the sales representative with respect to analytical approaches to display and inventory management. The buyers frequently requested detailed plan-o-grams with strong analytical support for expected sales, profits and inventory turns. The buyer would also at times become the salesperson. After listening to a sales presentation and giving an initial indication of interest, the buyer would attempt to sell space, both on the store floor and in the weekly advertising supplements. For example, the buyer for Shopper's Drug Mart offered a dump bin location in every store in the chain for a week. In some instances, both the buyer and the representative had the authority to conclude such a deal at that meeting. At other times, both had to wait for approval from their respective companies.

The interesting aspect of the key account supervisor's position was that the individual had to feel comfortable dealing with both the old and new schools of retail management. The task for Bannister was to select the right candidate for this position. The salary for the position ranged from $31,000 to $54,200, depending on qualifications and experience. Smith expected that the candidate selected would probably be paid somewhere between $38,000 and $46,000. An expense allowance would also be included in the compensation package.

The Key Accounts Supervisor

The main responsibility of the key accounts supervisor was to establish and maintain a close working relationship with the buyers of eight A accounts whose head offices were located in the Toronto area. An important task was to make presentations (15 to 30 minutes in length) to the retail buyers of these key accounts every three to six weeks. At these meetings, promotions or deals for up to five brands would be presented. The supervisor was responsible for all Adams brands. The buyer might have to take the promotions to the buying committee, where the final decision would be made. In addition, the representative used these meetings to hear about and inform the buyer of any merchandising problems occurring at the store level.

Midyear reviews were undertaken with each account. These reviews, lasting for one hour, focused on reviewing sales trends and tying them into merchandising programs, listings, service, and new payment terms. Another important and time-consuming responsibility of the key account supervisor was to devise and present plan-o-grams and be involved with the installation of the displays. The key account representative also conducted store checks and spent time on competitive intelligence. Working with the field staff was a further requirement of the position.

Bannister reflected on what he felt were the attributes of the ideal candidate. First, the individual should have selling and merchandising experience in the retail business in order to understand the language and dynamics of the situation. On the merchandising side, the individual would be required to initiate and coordinate the design of customized display systems for individual stores, a task that involved a certain amount of creativity. Second, strong interpersonal skills were needed. The individual had to establish rapport and make effective sales presentations to the buyers. Because of the wide range of buyer sophistication, these skills were particularly important. Bannister made a mental note to recommend that whoever was hired would be sent on the Professional Selling Skills course, a one-week program designed to enhance listening, selling, and presentation skills. Finally, the candidate should possess analytic skills because many of the sales and performance reports (from both manufacturers and retailers) were or would be computerized. Thus, the individual should feel comfortable working with computers. Bannister hoped that he could find a candidate who would be willing to spend a minimum of three years on the job in order to establish a personal relationship with the buyers.

Ideally, the candidate selected would have a blend of all three skills because of the mix of buyers he or she would contact. Bannister felt it was most likely that these characteristics would be found in a business school graduate. He had advertised the job internally (through the company's newsletter) and externally (in the *Toronto Star*). A total of 20 applications were received. After an initial screening, three possible candidates for the position were identified. None were from Warner-Lambert (Exhibit 3).

In early August 1994, Bannister and a member of the personnel department interviewed each of the candidates. After completing the interviews, brief fact sheets were prepared. Bannister began reviewing the sheets prior to making the decision.

Exhibit 3: Lydia Cohen

Personal:	Born 1963, 168 cm; 64 kg; Single
Education:	B.B.A. (1985), Wilfrid Laurier University, Active in Marketing Club and intramural sports
Work:	1992–94 Rowntree Macintosh Canada, Inc.—District Manager
	Responsible for sales staff of three in Ottawa and Eastern Ontario region. Establish annual sales plan and ensure that district meets its quota.
	1985–91 Rowntree Macintosh Canada, Inc.—Confectionary Sales Representative
	Responsible for selling a full line of confectionary and grocery products to key accounts in Toronto (1990–91) and Ottawa (1985–89). 1991 Sales Representatives of the Year for highest volume growth.
Interests:	Racquet sports
Candidate's Comments:	I am interested in working in the Toronto area, and I would look forward to concentrating on the sales task. My best years at Rowntree were in sales in the Toronto region.

Lydia Cohen (*continued*)

Interviewer's Comments:	Lydia presents herself very well and has a strong background in confectionary sales. Her record at Rowntree is very good. Rowntree paid for her to take an introductory course in Lotus 1-2-3 in 1991, but she has not had much opportunity to develop her computer skills. She does not seem to be overly ambitious or aggressive. She stated that personal reasons were preeminent in seeking a job in Toronto.

John Fisher

Personal:	Born 1967, 190 cm; 88 kg; Single
Education:	B.A. (Phys. Ed.) (1992), University of British Columbia
	While at UBC, played four years of varsity basketball (team captain in 1990–91). Assistant Coach, Senior Basketball, at University Hill High School, 1988–92. Developed and ran a two-week summer basket-ball camp at UBC for three years. Profits from the camp were donated to the Varsity Basketball Fund.
Work:	1987–93 Jacobs Suchard Canada, Inc. (Nabob Foods)
	Six years' experience (full-time 1992–93, and five years part-time, 1987–92, during school terms and full-time during the summers) in coffee and chocolates distribution and sales; two years on the loading docks, one year driving truck, and three years as a sales representative. Sales tasks included calling on regular customers, order taking, rack jobbing and customer relations development.

John Fisher (*continued*)

	1993–94 Scavolini (Professional Basketball)
	One year after completing studies at UBC, traveled to Western Europe and Northern Africa. Travel was financed by playing professional basketball in the Italian First Division.
Candidate's Comments:	I feel the combination of educational preparation, work experience, and my demonstrated ability as a team player and leader make me well suited for this job. I am particularly interested in a job, such as sales, that rewards personal initiative.
Interviewer's Comments:	A very ambitious and engaging individual with a good record of achievements. Strong management potential is evident, but interest in sales as a career is questionable. Minored in computer science at UBC. Has a standing offer to return to a sales management position at Nabob.

Barry Moore

Personal:	Born 1954, 180 cm; 84 kg; Married with two children
Education:	Business Administration Diploma (1979), Humber College
	While at school, was active participant in a number of clubs and political organizations. President of the Young Liberals (1978–79).
Work:	1991–94 Barrigans Food Markets—Merchandising Analyst
	Developed merchandising plans for a wide variety of product categories. Negotiated merchandising programs and trade deals with manufacturers and brokers. Managed a staff of four.

Barry Moore (*continued*)

1988–91   Dominion Stores Ltd.—Assistant Merchandise Manager

Liaison responsibilities between stores and head office merchandise planning. Responsible for execution of merchandising plans for several food categories.

1987–Robin Hood Multifoods, Inc.—Assistant Product Manager

Responsible for the analysis and development of promotion planning for Robin Hood Flour.

1982–87   Nestlé Enterprises Ltd.—Carnation Division Sales Representative.

Major responsibilities were developing and maintaining sales and distribution to wholesale and retail accounts.

1979–82   McCain Foods Ltd.—Inventory Analyst
Worked with sales staff and head office planning to ensure the quality and timing of shipments to brokers and stores.

Barry Moore (*continued*)

Activities:	Board of Directors, Richview Community Club
	Board of Directors, Volunteer Centre of Etobicoke
	Past President of Etobicoke Big Brothers
	Active in United Way
	Yachting—CC 34 Canadian Champion
Candidate's Comments:	It would be a great challenge and joy to work with a progressive industry leader such as Adams Brands.
Interviewer's Comments:	Very articulate and professionally groomed. Dominated the interview with a variety of anecdotes and humorous stories, some of which were relevant to the job. Likes to read popular books on management, particularly books that champion the bold, gut-feel entrepreneur. He would probably earn more money at Adams if hired.

▶ 10 ◀

Sales Training*

*If you have tried to do something and failed,
you are vastly better off than if you had tried
to do nothing and succeeded.*
ANONYMOUS

*Chapter Consultant: Jerry Willett National Sales Manager Software Spectram.

LEARNING OBJECTIVES

After studying this chapter, you should be able to:

▶ Explain why sales training is needed.

▶ Determine specific training needs for a sales force.

▶ Discuss the topics to include in a training program.

▶ Describe the advantages of centralized and decentralized training.

▶ Understand the use of line, staff, and outside trainers.

▶ Recognize the value of alternative training methods and media.

▶ Describe the different methods for evaluating training results.

▶ Explain the need for follow-up to formal training.

▶ SALES TRAINING AT IBM

As much as any U.S. company, IBM has remade its sales force in an effort to reflect its new market strategy and the emerging needs of the market place. In the past two years, the company has cut its cost of selling by close to $1.5 billion. Its worldwide sales and marketing team, now 70,000 strong, is close to half the size it was in 1990. Most significantly, it is attempting to be a problem solver and consultant to its customers. Consultants obviously need a more sophisticated set of skills than "metal pushers."

The training does not stop after the initial training program. The company has developed a year-long certification program for which the 300 salespeople who head client teams must be nominated to attend. Acceptance into the program depends on demonstrated achievement in such areas as adding value beyond traditional IBM products, strategic partnering with the customer, and solving strategic issues through the IBM team. The classroom component of the program consists of three one-week stints at Harvard, where one week is devoted to general business knowledge, one to consulting, and one to the industry they specialize in serving. Throughout the rest of the year, enrollees work on case studies and write a thesis, which is graded by Harvard professors, on their particular customer.[1]

National surveys of sales and marketing executives consistently indicate that good salespeople are made, not born. Research results also indicate that characteristics that can be developed—such as selling skills, motivation, and role perceptions—are more closely related to sales performance than enduring traits like appearance, aptitude, and personality.[2]

Training requirements and spending are closely related to other management decisions, for instance, recruiting and selection procedures. If a firm believes it needs to hire young, aggressive people with little prior experience in selling, then training of new recruits takes on special significance. Nearly every one of Armstrong World Industries' salespeople has been recruited right out of college. Initial training is conducted at Lancaster, Pennsylvania, near company headquarters. Trainees live in a dormitory-style building called The Manor. While the total cost of recruiting and training is quite high, Armstrong believes the benefits of hiring people without industry-related biases and conflicting opinions are worth the cost.

If a firm hires mostly veteran salespeople from within its industry, then training of new salespeople is less expensive and generally focuses on company procedures. DuPont almost always hires people with technical backgrounds. While their compensation is higher than that of trainees with a nontechnical background, the training period is shorter, only a couple of weeks, and focuses on "people sensitivity." There are also obvious differences in the type and level of compensation plans that are appropriate for each situation. The point is that the various management decisions are related and must be compatible. Spending less in one area must often be compensated for by spending more in another area.

The main sales training issues covered in this chapter are highlighted in the following diagram. Deciding whether a sales training program is needed often involves balancing training costs against alternative methods of obtaining effective field sales coverage. Management frequently finds that not all salespeople need the same kind

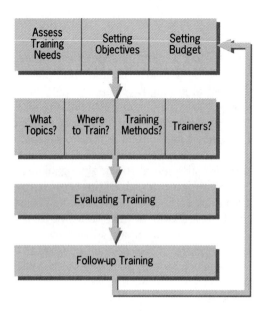

of training. If a training program is recommended, then sales managers must decide what topics will be covered, where the training sessions will take place, who will conduct the sessions, and what methods of instruction will be employed. Although most formal training programs are designed for newly hired personnel, sales managers must also schedule periodic retraining sessions for experienced salespeople because the environment, products, and marketing programs change over time. The manager of sales training activities must then evaluate the contributions of the training program. The primary concerns are to ensure that training objectives are met and to determine whether programs are cost-benefit justified.

► WHY TRAIN SALESPEOPLE?

Sales executives and purchasing agents generally agree that inadequate training of salespeople is one of the most common problems they encounter. When asked what qualities make a top salesperson, purchasing agents frequently mention qualities that can be influenced by training. This is why some of the most respected companies are willing to spend a great deal on sales training. Consider the following examples:

- Xerox spends $100,000 for salary and training during a salesperson's first year on the job.
- IBM budgets more than $1 billion per year for training. Moreover, IBM pulls its best salespeople from the field to help conduct the company's training programs.[3]

These companies treat training costs as an investment in the future success of the firm rather than simply as a current expense.

What are some of the benefits that these and other organizations hope to gain from their sales training programs?

Reduced Turnover

Turnover in a sales force is the ratio of the number of people who leave to the average size of the sales team. Salespeople who go into the field without adequate training typically find it difficult to see buyers, answer questions, or book orders. The resulting confusion and disappointment often lead novices to quit before they have a chance to learn how to sell effectively. A study of the insurance industry found that the likelihood of turnover peaks at 15 months of employment and is highest among low-productivity agents.[4] Management may be able to reduce turnover by helping new agents become more productive through developing better selling skills.

Improved Customer Relations

Industrial buyers, in particular, complain that too much of their time is wasted in dealing with untrained salespeople. Buyers do not like to spend their days counseling salespeople on market conditions and product needs. They prefer to work with trained salespeople with a thorough knowledge of the industry, their firm's business, and their own product lines. Companies are attempting to respond to these concerns. "We train our sales force to understand why customers buy our products," says Pat Dalton, business operations manager for Caterpillar's North American commercial division "we want them to know what their needs are, the importance of follow-up, the need to let a customer vent his anger, and how to help a customer resolve problems without passing the responsibility on to someone else in the company."[5]

Better Morale

Sales training increases product knowledge and improves selling skills; it also builds self-confidence and enthusiasm among the sales force. When salespeople know what they are supposed to do, they are in a better position to withstand the disappointments and meet the challenges of a sales career. Trained salespeople start producing orders faster, and the increased earnings help boost morale. The significance of this objective is reinforced by a recent survey of sales trainees, in which attitude was the most frequently mentioned characteristic of successful salespeople. When brought together for training, people get a sense of belonging to a team in which they can exchange successful selling techniques and ideas.

Increased Productivity

The ultimate objective of any training program is to produce profitable results. The Nabisco Biscuit Company recently estimated that they realized a return of 122-to-1 on a program that teaches salespeople to plan for and make professional sales presentations to retail customers. It cost Nabisco $1,008 to put each salesperson through the program and preliminary results equate to an increase of $122,640 in sales per year per salesperson.[6] While money spent on poorly conceived and executed training programs is largely wasted, the Nabisco example illustrates the potential for significant returns on money spent on training. Sales trainers report that companies are increasingly requiring this type of sales justification from training investments.

▶ PLANNING FOR SALES TRAINING

Planning for sales training involves three related processes: (1) assessing sales training needs; (2) establishing specific objectives for the training program; and (3) setting a budget for the program. Each of these processes is discussed in this section.

Assessing Training Needs

Without oversimplifying the issue, sales force productivity needs generally break down into one of three elements. The sales force either does not know "what to do," or "how to do it," or "why they should do it." A *training needs analysis* is a process for determining where problems and opportunities exist and whether training can best address the issues. A complete training needs analysis includes a review of the firm's strategic objectives, management observation and questioning of salespeople, customer input, and a review of company records.

Management Objectives   An organization's strategic programs frequently imply an emphasis on certain products, customers, and customer relationships. Because Caterpillar embraces a corporate strategy of selling premium products at a premium price, its selling process emphasizes total customer value. As a result, Caterpillar trains its people in consultative selling requiring intimate customer knowledge, including costs, benefits, and profits. Due to changes in DuPont's marketplace, new and veteran salespeople are taking more courses in international areas, in addition to technical and product-oriented courses. These examples illustrate the necessity of identifying training needs as a result of changes in strategy, market environment, and competitive environment. This recommendation is reinforced by surveys of sales management practices which indicate that judgments of upper management and sales management are considered most important in determining sales training needs.[7]

Sales Force Observation and Survey   Observation of salespeople is an excellent way to identify shortcomings, especially when successful and unsuccessful sales calls and salespeople are compared. Observation of sales calls of a company selling auto parts, for example, revealed that the discussion during successful sales calls focused on which products the customer should order. Less successful salespeople spent far more time waiting or talking about nonbusiness subjects. This type of salesperson observation often identifies areas in which to improve. For example, it was also discovered that sales managers needed to be better at coaching salespeople.[8]

Customer Information   Sending customers questionnaires can also be quite revealing. Questions to be asked may include: What do you expect from a salesperson in this industry? How do salespeople disappoint you? Which company in the industry

---

Sales Management in Action 10-1
Getting Customers into the Act

In an effort to include "the voice of the customer," 3M revised its training program for veteran salespeople by asking customers to tell 3M where salespeople needed to improve skills and get additional training. It wasn't that 3M hadn't been surveying its customers before, but the questions had been too general and tended to focus on product quality and technical values rather than on personal selling skills. Corporate training developed a questionnaire to assess skills in six areas—knowledge of products and services, strategic skills critical to leveraging time with the customer, interpersonal selling, sales negotiations, internal influence and teamwork, and customer-focused quality. Salespeople or their managers deliver questionnaires to six customers, chosen by the salesperson, who assess the importance of each skill to the selling relationship, and the

salesperson's application of each skill. With the feedback report in hand, salespeople and their managers determine a training curriculum focusing on the salesperson's three most significant gaps according to the customer survey. Following the voluntary sales training, sales managers are expected to follow up with reinforcement and field coaching, while salespeople return to the customers who were given the survey to review the composite results and to ask for additional direction in closing the gap. Divisions of 3M participate in this program on a voluntary basis, but it has been 3M's experience that veteran salespeople will pay attention to what the customer says more than what other people may have to say.

Source: William Keenan, "Getting Customers into the A.C.T.," *Sales & Marketing Management* (February 1995), pp. 58–63.

---

does the best job? In what ways are its salespeople better? An alternative to surveys is to do a series of focus group sessions with 6 to 10 customers. A focus group is essentially a meeting with a group of customers to elicit specific information, in this case information on training needs. See Sales Management in Action 10-1 to see how 3M incorporates customer input into its training program.

Company Records   Companies with a degree of computer sophistication may have a great deal of useful data for analyzing training needs, especially if call reports are available. Cross-tabulating performance records may also be helpful in identifying which salespeople need what type of training. *Cross-tabulation* involves examining performance by certain sales force characteristics, such as years of experience, geographic area, or area of specialization.

Table 10-1 illustrates how a cross-tabulation may be useful in identifying training needs. Three intermediate measures of performance are crossed with two characteristics of the sales force—years of experience and geographic region. Experience was chosen as a characteristic based on concerns expressed by management that both new and senior salespeople were felt to be having a problem. Regional differences

Table 10-1   Cross-Tabulations from Company Records

	Average Order Size per Salesperson	New Customers per Salesperson	Total Customers per Salesperson
Experience			
Less than 2 years	392	21	86
2–5 years	593	29	145
5–10 years	565	5	152
Over 10 years	470	8	139
Regions			
Northeast	528	6	140
Southeast	520	8	161
Midwest	512	18	107
Southwest	421	26	111
West	544	21	131

were also of interest because managers had considerable latitude in the training of salespeople and complete responsibility after the initial six-week training of new salespeople.

The results in Table 10-1 suggest that there may be a problem with both new and senior salespeople. New salespeople have the lowest average order size and lowest total number of customers. This may suggest that new salespeople need more training in how to increase business with existing customers. At the same time, senior salespeople with over 10 years of experience appear to have a problem with prospecting for new customers. There also seems to be a problem with the Southwest region, since it has the lowest average order size and total customers per salesperson.

What is the next step? Design a training program on prospecting for senior salespeople? Implement a whole set of training programs for the Southwest region? The answer is "no" because we have not yet investigated the sales force's needs in sufficient depth. Cross-tabulating experience with regions may reveal that the Southwest region has mostly new salespeople. There may be competitive reasons for the results. There may be demand and economic differences between the various regions. In short, the needs analysis should return to a dialogue with salespeople and sales managers to identify the causes of the problems. This hypothetical situation points out an important principle when investigating training needs: Use multiple sources of information and cross-validate the information whenever possible.

Setting Objectives

After assessing the training needs of the sales force, specific sales training objectives should be established and put in writing. Like all good objectives, training objectives should be specific enough and measurable so that the extent to which they have been met can be evaluated following the training program. This will also help avoid the problem of training for training's sake. Written objectives are also a good means to gain top management's commitment and willingness to provide budget support for training. As one sales training consultant noted, "I've seen excellent programs fail—and poor programs succeed. The difference has always boiled down to one thing—*management commitment.*"[9]

Setting a Training Budget

New Salespeople Companies spend millions of dollars a year on new salesperson training. Table 10-2 shows the average cost of training new salespeople, including salary during the training period. Table 10-2 also shows the average length of formal training for sales trainees. The more technically oriented industrial and service industries spend more money and take more time to train new salespeople. Intel, for instance, almost exclusively hires engineers for sales positions, and the company puts them through a two-year training program before deploying them to its field offices.

While the overall numbers indicate a relationship between time to train and cost of training, this need not be the case for individual organizations. A study of paper and plastics wholesalers found that top-performing sales forces took more time to train salespeople, but did not spend more money training than their low-producing counterparts.[10]

Retraining Veteran Salespeople Most managers believe that the need to learn is never-ending and that even the most successful sales representatives can benefit from refresher training. Products change, markets shift, territories are reorganized, and salespeople need additional training to help adjust to these new environmental situations. Table 10-3 indicates how much various types of companies are spending on training of experienced salespeople. Burlington Industries' training for experienced salespeople is typical of that offered by many firms. Each division's salespeople meet four times a year for one-day sessions. In these sessions, sales and products are reviewed against the competition, and selling skills are honed. Bell Atlantic has taken a different approach. At Bell, 60 top salespeople from a sales force of 250 representatives were picked for an intense 13-week course that examined emerging technologies in the communications-information services complex.[11] Veteran salespeople at

Table 10-2   Average Cost and Training Period for Sales Trainees

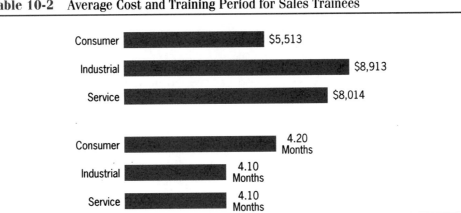

Source: Reprinted with permission from *Salesforce Compensation Survey*, Dartnell Corporation (1992).

Table 10-3   Average Cost and Training Period for Veteran Salespeople

Source: Reprinted with permission from Salesforce Compensation Survey, Dartnell Corporation (1992).

Owens-Corning participate in seminars on topics such as time and territory management, problem solving, and consultative selling.[12]

▶ DEVELOPING THE TRAINING PROGRAM

After determining the needs of the sales force, and setting specific objectives and a budget for training, a number of decisions critical to the success of the individual training program must be addressed. These decisions include (1) what topics to cover, (2) where to conduct the training, (3) who should do the training, and (4) what training methods to use. These four decisions are interrelated so that one decision will impact the others. We will take a close look at each decision in this section to get an understanding of the trade-offs that are made.

Training Topics

The choice of subjects to be covered in a sales training program depends on the products to be sold, purpose of the training, and the background of the people being trained. Firms that sell complex products, of course, have more material to include in their programs than firms selling simpler products or services. Val-Pak, which distributes home-delivered coupons of local retailers, recruits on college campuses and puts new hires through a 17-week training program where they learn about direct mail and selling. Eastman Chemical's training program lasts six to nine months and requires trainees to spend several weeks in technical service labs learning to process chemicals, plastics, and fibers. The purpose of the training may be to provide initial training for new hires, continuing development, or training for a specialized situation. Likewise, initial training may vary depending on the selling experience of the new sales-people. This section discusses topics typically found in training programs.

Product Knowledge A common misconception is that sales training is designed primarily to improve the selling skills of sales representatives. However, more sales training time, usually around 40 percent, is spent presenting product information. This information is frequently related to the introduction of new products. Merck, a $17 billion pharmaceutical company, has a short time to bring a new product to market following FDA approval. In just one week, Merck's 3,000 salespeople will attend an off-site training session where—with the help of physicians—they learn about the new product and get familiar with the disorder it treats. Six weeks after product intro-duction, salespeople are brought together once more to solidify their product knowl-edge. Product understanding is considered essential if sales representatives are to communicate effectively and address customer needs, and has been found to be closely related to product success.[13]

Selling New recruits must be shown how the sales process works before they can be effective and productive field representatives. Even recruits with previous selling experience must often receive this training because selling approaches may differ from one company to the next. Veteran salespeople will also benefit from training in how to sell in specific situations and when presenting new products.

Some experts have suggested that sales training in the future will likely place more emphasis on basic selling as a result of new training methods such as interactive video technology.[14] This technology allows salespeople to react to a specific selling situation. A videotaped customer, for instance, may be programmed to respond based on the salesperson's reaction. The realism and versatility of this technology make it possible to train salespeople in specific selling techniques.

Supporting recent developments in selling skills is research on *cognitive selling scripts*. A script is the knowledge an expert, such as an experienced salesperson, pos-sesses based on remembered similar experiences. Experts are said to possess two types of knowledge. The first type of knowledge, referred to as *declarative knowledge*, permits them to recognize a selling situation requiring a somewhat unique selling process. The other type of knowledge is called *procedural knowledge*. This knowledge consists of the process or sequence of behaviors that should be undertaken to achieve a successful selling conclusion in a particular situation. Research techniques have been recently developed to capture knowledge structures of experts.[15] The implica-tions for sales training are significant. Novices can be taught how to identify selling situations and what approaches are most likely to be successful in each situation based on the knowledge of experts.

Customer and Market Information Training time is also devoted to giving recruits customer information and the general background on the market for the goods and services produced by the firm. This information helps salespeople identify prospects that need products and services offered by the company. Sales recruits are given facts about the size and location of present customers, their buying patterns, needs, and technical processes. Trainees who understand their customers are in a better position to identify customer problems and to talk about how they can solve the buyer's problems. This is why IBM, as discussed in the opening vignette of this chapter, has its account managers study their customer's industry for a week at Harvard.

U.S. Surgical, a manufacturer of surgical and laparoscopic instruments, felt that its salespeople must be conversant with medical terminology and comfortable enough in an operating room to coach skeptical surgeons in its products. To accomplish this, U.S. Surgical's new salespeople must complete a six-week training course with daily exams in anatomy, scrub technique, and the intricacies of company products. Some 20 percent of trainees fail. Each year, salespeople must pass a recertification exam.[16]

Company Orientation   Salespeople who represent a company to the outside world must be well versed in the company's history, organization, and policies, as well as having an understanding of corporate citizenship and building core workplace competencies. Salespeople must have pride and confidence in their company and its offerings. Training sessions include discussions of policies on returns and warranties, credit arrangements, production sources, and sequencing of orders. Trainees must know about exclusive merchandise, price guarantees, discounts, and latitude on pricing. When customers are desperate for an order, salespeople must know how to expedite delivery. Dow Chemical Company's initial sales training program, for example, "aims to produce a fully balanced seller, not just someone trained in product knowledge."[17] During its year-long program, trainees work on three related training projects involving such things as working in Dow's customer service center taking customers' calls and orders, or producing an in-depth marketing study involving customers or new markets.

Other Topics   Due to changes in technology and the marketing environment, new topics are finding their way into sales training programs. Many companies now require their salespeople to use personal computers (PC) to plan sales calls, check on orders, prepare presentations and proposals, aid in presentations, check on inventories, and place orders. Training in how to use computer software is needed to ensure the use of PCs in the field. For this reason, Northwestern Mutual Life trained its agents on how to use its LINK system, a computer network that ties agents directly to the home office in Milwaukee.

Other topics in which some salespeople are receiving training include time and territory management, handling price objections, and resolving legal and ethical issues. Some of the more exotic topics on which salespeople may be trained include reading body language, understanding eye movement, identifying people's decision-making styles, and teamwork. Opinions differ as to the effectiveness of some training. Companies should establish for themselves the costs and benefits of these programs.

Where to Train

Having determined training topics, a company must still decide where and how training will be conducted and who will lead the training sessions. Although the decisions are interrelated, we discuss alternative locations for training salespeople in this section. First, we look at whether training should be centralized or decentralized.

Centralized versus Decentralized Training   One of the recurring controversies in sales management is whether sales training should be centralized or decentralized.

Some managers contend that centralized training leads to greater efficiency, and others insist that training should be done in the field where skills are used.

Centralized training occurs when all the salespeople to be trained are brought to one central location—a plant, the home office, or a training facility. A major advantage of centralized training is the quality and consistency of training. Quality is enhanced through the use of specially trained instructors, custom designed materials, and audiovisual equipment such as closed-circuit television systems. Furthermore, communications and coordination are enhanced when everyone receives the same training. It is also possible to give trainees exposure to top-level managers and other specialists, which can help boost morale and provides valuable insights into sales procedures and customers' needs.

On the negative side, centralized training is very expensive and time consuming. Training facilities and equipment are expensive, and trainees have to be reimbursed for travel to the central site and for lodging. As a result, managers usually attempt to keep the length of these sessions fairly short. In an effort to offset high costs, Xerox now offers its training facilities, once confined to its own sales force, to all kinds of organizations. Hewlett-Packard, Aetna Life & Casualty, and even the U.S. Navy are among those that have taken up the offer to learn Xerox's brand of salesmanship at Xerox Document University in Leesburg, Virginia.

One way some companies are attempting to reduce the cost while preserving the advantages of centralized facilities is by broadcasting training sessions from headquarters facilities. This is fairly new technology, however. A recent survey found that less than 20 percent of respondents utilized videoconferencing or teleconferencing (audio only) to train salespeople.[18]

Decentralized training of salespeople is usually held in field or regional sales offices, which moves the learning process closer to the customers and directly involves field sales management. New recruits get to observe top salespeople selling to customers similar to those they will encounter in their own nearby territories. Location of the training at sales branches also reduces travel and instructional expenses.

Despite these advantages, there are number of potential problems. Perhaps the most common one is that sales managers are so busy supervising the existing sales force that they do not take the time needed to train new recruits. Sales managers whose income is based on a percentage of their salespeople's commissions (called *commission overrides*) are apt to be most concerned about current income and may give training of new employees a low priority. As a result, the content and quality of the training process may vary widely across the branches.

A common resolution of the centralized versus decentralized training issue is to use some combination of the two approaches. Xerox, for example, brings new recruits into the branch offices for a few weeks of familiarization with company procedures and products. With this background orientation, the novice salespeople are then sent to a central facility for a short session of intensive training. This program allows those who are not committed to the company to drop out before the expensive portion of the program begins. After completing the centralized training, Xerox salespeople go back to the field for more practical experience and coaching by their sales managers. At the end of six months of sales experience, the new salespeople return to the central facility for another week of advanced training.

Sales Management in Action 10-2
Getting a Quick Start

It is estimated that about one-third of the nation's major firms have formal mentoring programs, with senior managers providing personal counseling and career guidance for younger employees. The objective is to help young people get a quick start so they can move up to a better job rather than leave in frustration. At Schering-Plough, mentoring ensures that new hires get off the mark the first day. The program lasts for one year, during which each person tackles a specific marketing or sales assignment under the tutelage of one or more mentors. Georgia-Pacific gets around the problem of mentoring people who spend a lot of time on the road by using immediate superiors, usually a sales manager, as mentors for new salespeople. The company has also created some literature that offers advice that is sent directly to the field reps.

Source: Arthur Bragg, "Is a Mentor Program in Your Future?" *Sales & Marketing Management* (September 1989), pp. 54–63.

Field Training   Field or *on-the-job training* (OJT) is the most widely used method of sales training for new recruits. According to a recent survey, 82 percent of responding firms indicated using this method of training. Small companies especially rely on this method of training new salespeople because of the high cost of developing alternative training methods when only a few people are to be trained.

The basic idea of on-the-job-training is that every time salespeople call on customers, they should learn from the experience. To facilitate and encourage learning, new salespeople are often paired with successful veterans. Georgia Pacific and Ortho Pharmaceutical's Biotech Division, for instance, take this approach to OJT. Another alternative is to have the immediate supervisor travel with the new salesperson and observe sales calls. See Sales Management in Action 10-2 for creative ways in which companies are utilizing mentors.[19]

While this experience is important and people should be taught to learn from their experiences, OJT should not be relied on as the sole means of learning. First, experience is costly; while salespeople are gaining experience, sales are lost. Second, the quality of training is likely to be uneven. Some people are simply better at training than others. More important, the new salesperson may pick up the bad habits of the veteran salesperson resulting in a lack of consistency in how salespeople are going to market. It was precisely for this reason that Johnson Controls, Inc. established a new six-month training program for new salespeople. The best means of development is not experience alone, but experience in combination with a planned program.

Training Media

A variety of media are used by companies for sales training. Technology and cost reductions are increasingly making it possible to use alternative media, regardless of

Table 10-4   Instructional Methods Used in Training

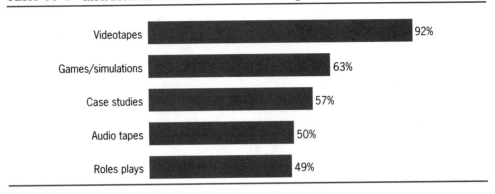

Videotapes	92%
Games/simulations	63%
Case studies	57%
Audio tapes	50%
Roles plays	49%

the training location. Table 10-4 lists the five most frequently used training media according to a recent survey. As the percentages in the table indicate, most companies rely on a variety of media for sales training. While students are usually quite familiar with videotape and case study methods of learning, you may not be as familiar with the use of role plays, games and simulations, and audiotapes as instructional media. Some emerging computer-based training media are also discussed.

Role Playing   *Role playing*, typically of simulated sales presentations, is also quite common in sales training (49 percent). Merck and Company relies heavily on role playing to train new salespeople in how to sell pharmaceuticals.[20] One Cleveland radio station instituted daily role-playing exercises for its sales representatives. This technique is quite effective when used to reinforce information presented in videos and lectures by requiring active participation and practice. Role play helps to determine if the trainee can apply the information. Video cameras are often employed to capture role plays on tape so that they can be reviewed for critique and self-observation.

Despite its wide use, role playing has some pitfalls. The biggest concern is the stress caused by the videotaping. People may not be able to focus on the subject to be learned when under too much stress. One way to reduce the stress is to conduct a critique immediately following the role play, emphasizing positive points and encouraging self-analysis: What did I do right? What will I do differently next time?[21]

Games and Simulations   One of the fastest-growing sales training media are simulations designed to encourage the learning of specific behaviors. *Behavioral simulations* use business games, simulations, case studies, and role playing in which trainees assume a specified role in a selling situation. Companies such as Chase Manhattan Bank, BMW's Motorcycle Division, Caterpillar, and Ford's Heavy Truck Division regularly use games to encourage the learning of product knowledge.

Microsoft has new sales hires participate in games which include props and facilitators who play roles and dress in costumes. In "Gold of the Desert Kings" for instance, teams compete to manage their resources and limited supplies to successfully cross a harsh desert, mine for gold, and return home with the most gold. The

---

Sales Management in Action 10-3
"The Sales Training Book Club"

At Orion Systems Group, Inc. (Ronkonkoma, NY), salespeople can use their corporate credit cards to purchase books and cassettes on any area of sales and business that they wish. All the company requests is that once they have finished the books or tapes, they donate them to the company's professional training library and jot down a few comments and thoughts on the checkout card. The comments are intended as additional guidance to the next borrower. If salespeople want to keep a copy for themselves, they are free to purchase two copies—one to keep and one for the library. Orion feels that the library is an invaluable resource and well worth the expense of between $500 and $800 a year.

---

game is designed to teach the importance of planning, teamwork throughout the organization, and communication. It is felt that this type of learning takes people by surprise and opens the mind to receive the information much more than simply talking to them.

Another popular game is the quiz-show format, in which teams of salespeople compete on stage, complete with emcee and electronic score board. Customized questions deal with realistic selling situations and product knowledge. This quiz-show format in sales training is used by such companies as Coca-Cola, Sherwin-Williams, Minolta, Nabisco, and Shearson Lehman Hutton.[22]

Audiotapes   Audiotapes are an effective way to present and reinforce selling and product information because of the time salespeople spend traveling and waiting. At a recent national meeting for the American Society of Training and Development, there were over 500 exhibitors of audiocassette training material. Tape Rental Library (TRL) offers over 2,000 titles for sales training, which it offers to clients such as Pfizer Labs, Moore Business Forms, Scott Paper, Johnson & Johnson, and Gillette.[23] The biggest limitation to audiotapes as a training medium is their ability to get and hold the listener's attention for a significant period of time. For this reason, audiotapes are frequently used in conjunction with other training media and to reinforce previous training information. Sales Management in Action 10-3 describes how one company encourages its reps to buy sales tapes and books.

Emerging Training Methods   The computer is increasingly being integrated into sales force training. To aid in the redeployment of 11,800 employees in the field as marketing representatives and system engineers, IBM developed a self-study system called InfoWindow. InfoWindow combines a PC with a laser videodisc to provide an *interactive system*. Before attending classes in Atlanta, a sales trainee can practice making sales calls. The onscreen actor is programmed to portray a customer in a particular industry whose response depends on the sales trainee's behavior. Trainees can also film themselves as they interact with the actor.

Sales Management Technology 10-1
"Training Without Travel"

Regular training is crucial for keeping your people abreast of new developments, but it can be a real hassle to gather your entire sales staff together for a training session. New technology for the Internet may move companies into the videoconferencing age. In the past, videoconferencing required special rooms where everyone would gather. Today, for around $150 per location, a sales manager with either IBM PC compatibles or Macintosh machines can buy a small video camera to take a video image. With this technology, a group of up to eight participants can gather,

each in his or her own office, at a convenient time. That means no more travel time or costs, and no expense for renting other people's equipment.

There are limitations in the technology. For instance, the image is in black and white. Further, the pictures and sound are not broadcast-quality—yet. These limitations should be kept in mind when planning for the training. However, the internet appears to offer a cost- and time-effective answer to some of the challenges of training a far-flung sales force.

IBM is not the only company using such interactive systems. Warner-Lambert's training for veteran salespeople is largely conducted in field offices through the use of interactive videos. While the videos may cost $50,000 or more to produce, they have an extended shelf life due to their customization to Warner-Lambert's needs. Hewlett-Packard uses interactive TV/satellite training sessions to help regional sales groups whose customers might benefit from new H-P products.[24] For information on training over the internet, see Sales Management Technology 10-1.

Companies have been slow to adopt high-tech training tools, despite their promise. The Conference Board reported that only 8 percent of firms surveyed had fully implemented computer-based training methods. The reason for slow adoption appears to be the high startup costs and uncertain benefits associated with these training methods. The most widely adopted techniques incorporate a high degree of trainee-computer interaction, while allowing for flexibility and creativity.[25]

Who Should Train

The three most popular types of sales trainers are regular line executives, staff personnel, and outside specialists. Because each has certain advantages, it is not unusual to find organizations using all three types. The selection of trainers for individual firms depends on where the sessions are held, the size of the firm, the characteristics of the product line, and the focus of the training.

Staff Specialists   When centralized sales training is used, companies often have staff specialists prepare the materials and conduct the classes. Staff trainers must not only be good teachers, but also experts in selecting the proper methods and audio-

Sales Management in Action 10-4
"They Really Paid Attention"

Faced with the need to offer his salespeople something new in the way of insight and perspective, Steve Guest of Comdoc Office Systems took a different approach to sales training. "When managers told salespeople something," says Steve, "they paid some attention. But when a customer told them the same things, they really paid attention. Customer information really hits home strongly with the sales force." Once a quarter Steve would invite the president or general manager of a plant to discuss a topic they wanted to address. The customers seemed to enjoy the opportunity to discuss their needs and how Comdoc could help them meet those needs. Occasionally, Steve would invite people to speak who were not customers, but rather prospects or former customers.

Source: Sales Manager's Bulletin, No. 1316 (November 15, 1993), pp. 4–5.

visual equipment needed to meet program objectives. If sales training is conducted on a decentralized basis, staff specialists in the central office usually prepare the program materials, and the instruction is carried out by line managers.

There are some disadvantages to using staff trainers. One complaint is that despite their teaching skills, they often lack experience in realistic field-selling situations, making it difficult for trainees to apply the classroom instruction to real-world customer contacts. In addition, a staff trainer's salary commonly runs up to $45,000 or more, and small firms simply cannot afford this cost.

Outside Specialists   The employment of outside specialists to conduct sales training is a fairly common business practice. Outside consultants may be entirely responsible for the training programs or brought in to conduct specific sessions within a total training program. Outside consultants usually tailor training programs to some degree to meet the special needs of individual firms and industries. Large companies tend to use outside specialists more than small companies and they report being very satisfied with their experience.[26] The main attraction of outside trainers is the variety, inspiration, and excitement they can bring to the training program. Some companies have taken a different approach by inviting customers to be present at their sales training sessions (see Sales Management in Action 10-4).

The potential problems with outside specialists are similar to those of staff specialists. In addition, outside trainers may be unfamiliar with a company's selling situation (lack of familiarity with industry jargon, customers, and competitors). For example, a trainer may discuss price discounting in a presentation when the company is emphasizing value-added selling to avoid price discounting. Salespeople may disregard the training altogether as a result or, worse yet, be misled.

Line Executives   Using line executives, usually sales managers, as sales trainers lends credibility to the program because these people have successful sales backgrounds and salespeople are more likely to recognize their knowledge base.[27] They know how to sell, and they know what skills trainees need in order to perform well in the field. The scheduling of line executives for sales training sessions enables these managers to become better acquainted with the entire sales force. When sales managers who actually supervise the salespeople do the training, new recruits are more likely to put the ideas into practice.

Line executives are not always asked to lead sales training for a variety of reasons. Although line managers know a great deal about selling, they may not be trained in how to communicate the information to a group of people in a classroom setting. Furthermore, line executives are usually preoccupied with current sales problems and may not have the time to do a good job of training. Solutions to these problems include giving managers "release time" so that they can prepare for their training classes and instructing the managers in better communication techniques. Smaller firms, in particular, must deal with these problems, since they often cannot afford staff trainers and are forced to use line executives or outside specialists.

▶ EVALUATING SALES TRAINING

The costs of training are substantial, and sales managers must continually ask whether this investment is paying off. However, it is not easy to establish clear-cut relationships between initial sales training and sales performance. As a result, training managers have often relied on instinct to determine if the training was worthwhile. According to industry experts, this attitude has changed in many companies to one in which management is asking, "What did we get from our training dollars?" This change in attitude came immediately after the recession of the early 1990s, when trainers became the victims of corporate budget cutting. Figure 10-1 describes the four levels on which sales training can be evaluated.

Level One:	Reactions	Are trainees satisfied with the training? This also provides information so that the parts they don't like can be improved.
Level Two:	Learning	Did the training change attitudes, increase knowledge, or improve the skills of the trainees? This usually requires testing before and after training.
Level Three:	Behavior	Are salespeople using their knowledge and skills on the job? This may be measured in a variety of ways: asking salespeople, sales manager observation of salespeople, and questioning customers.
Level Four:	Results	What effect does the training have on the company? The bottom line results of training can include increased sales, higher profits, more new customers, and reduced costs.

Figure 10-1: The Four Levels of Training Evaluation

Table 10-5   Sales Training Evaluation Practices

Measure	Criteria Type	Importance Rank
Trainee feedback	Reaction	1
Supervisory appraisal	Behavior	2
Self-appraisal	Behavior	3
Bottom-line measures	Results	4
Customer appraisal	Behavior	5

Despite the emphasis on showing demonstrable results from training, as shown in Table 10-5, companies still are most likely to use trainee feedback to evaluate training programs. Sales management's appraisal of the trainee's behavior following the training is also frequently used for training assessment, as is a salesperson's evaluation of his or her own behavior.

Bottom-line measures of performance (e.g., sales and profits) were ranked only fourth in frequency of use. One problem with using sales as a performance measure is that sales may change as a result of factors outside of salespeople's control. One way to overcome this problem is to compare the results of people who have gone through a training program with those of people who have not but who are in otherwise similar situations. The Nabisco estimate of a 122-to-1 return on its sales training program, discussed at the beginning of this chapter, was based on the sales results of the 104 salespeople who went through the training compared to 386 other salespeople in the same region who were not trained.

Field experiments to control for outside influences on sales are not easily designed or conducted. People with similar experiences, previous performance, and other characteristics, for instance, should be assigned to both the control group (salespeople not given training) and the group of salespeople given training. Results must usually be measured shortly after training, as well as several months later, to enable comparison between short-term and long-term effects. Likewise, outcomes should be measured before training to determine the extent of the change that can be attributed to training. These are just some of the issues that must be considered.[28]

▶ FOLLOW-UP

Regardless of management's philosophy toward the training issues discussed in this chapter, one of the biggest mistakes management can make is to not follow up on training. One-shot training is a proven formula for failure and a big waste of company money. No one can train salespeople once a year at the annual sales meeting. According to a study at Xerox, 82 percent of skills learned in a training session are lost if not reinforced. Training efforts are most successful when training is scheduled at regular intervals throughout the year. At American Bankers Insurance Group, for instance, twice a year the sales force goes to Miami for a week-long training session. Also, salespeople meet once every two weeks for a full day with their regional managers to go over things taught in the training sessions. Consistent, ongoing training and reinforcement lead to development and improvement as part of an organization's culture. This obviously must start with top management's support and participation. American Bankers demonstrates this commitment when the chairman, vice chairman, or national sales manager holds quarterly meetings with each salesperson.

▶ ADDITIONAL SALES TRAINING ISSUES

Developing Salespeople

Salesperson development involves helping people develop goals, skills, and habits beyond those necessary for the present job. Many experts feel that developing personnel is the most important responsibility of first- and second-line sales managers. This process is sometimes known as *career planning* and often involves retraining salespeople to expand their responsibilities.

Being stuck in a job where there is little or no opportunity for further personal development can be very demotivating. Most people are stimulated by new challenges and the possibility of having an important impact on the performance of the organization. Salespeople who face a future of no new responsibilities beyond their present territory are likely to be less motivated and less committed to the organization than salespeople who have these prospects. Their sales performance may also level off or decline.

What can first- and second-line sales managers do to help salespeople develop their full capabilities and prevent career stagnation? Here are a few suggestions:

1. Help salespeople gain a realistic understanding of the process and of their chances of getting promoted. This should begin with the initial socialization of the new salesperson into the organization and continue with veteran salespeople.

2. Give people opportunities to develop new skills within their present job. For example, a veteran salesperson who has the appropriate skills and desire may be asked to train a new salesperson or to open a new territory.

3. Be creative in letting veteran salespeople know that they are successful and important to the company even if they are not in management. Recognition is particularly effective in this regard. For example, an expensive attaché case could be awarded for achieving a particular sales level.

4. Be constantly on the alert for salespeople with the skills and desire for management or other advanced sales positions. Watching how other salespeople react to the individual in an informal setting is particularly important. Periodic checking of the person's career aspirations is also necessary since these may change, especially as an individual's family situation changes.

5. Design a program for developing salespeople for their next assignments, either in management or in an advanced sales position. Like the sales training program, this program should begin with the tasks to be performed in the next position

that can be practiced and modeled in the current position. For example, a salesperson could be given responsibility for designing and conducting part of the next district sales meeting.

For a career development system to be effective, a company must reward managers for developing their people. In some companies, this is part of the regular evaluation process of sales managers. Without such rewards, managers often have a tendency to hold on to good representatives rather than develop them for their next position.

Ethical Situations

According to recent surveys, almost half of the companies include ethics in their training programs.[29] One reason for this emphasis is the multimillion-dollar judgments against some companies because of their ethically questionable practices. General Dynamics, which was charged with overbilling the government on defense contracts, has a 20-page code of ethics telling salespeople how to behave. The code includes items such as these:

- In countries where common practice might indicate conduct lower than that to which General Dynamics aspires, salespeople will follow the company's standards.
- Under no circumstances may an employee give anything to a customer's representative in an effort to gain influence.
- If it becomes clear that the company must engage in unethical or illegal activity to win a contract, that business will not be further pursued.

The other reason for including ethics in sales training is that salespeople want more direction from management on how to handle certain situations. On the job, salespeople are likely to face a number of ethical and legal dilemmas. Salespeople like to know how the company wants them to act in ethically gray situations. Some such situations have been discussed in the Ethical Situations sections and other chapters in this book.

Improving Teamwork

With its emphasis on customer satisfaction, addressing customers' problems, and building long-term relationships, companies that have adopted a TQM philosophy are finding it necessary to supplement their sales training programs with additional topics and methods. Working in teams requires new competencies from people who formerly worked mostly independently of other employees. Procter and Gamble, for instance, found that people needed to be trained in such skills as how to evaluate other team members, coordinate projects, arrive at mutually agreed-upon objectives, settle disputes within the team, and give honest feedback to team members. Notice that many of these topics were once the concern only of management personnel.

Increased interaction with other functional areas within a company has also meant a change in training methods. Eastman Chemical's 500 salespeople are responsible for $4 billion in sales and often find themselves in the position of coordinating many of Eastman's 18,000 total employees in team efforts focused on improving customer relationships. Eastman realized that they needed to give their salespeople greater working knowledge of the company, its products, and how these products were produced than was previously required. A "working" knowledge is just what Eastman provides. Part of the six-to-nine-month basic training of all Eastman Chemical salespeople is an extended stint in the technical services labs, where salespeople learn to use the same equipment that their customers use to process Eastman chemicals, plastics, and other products. This allows salespeople to talk to the technical people and to communicate customers' problems more effectively inside Eastman.[30]

► SUMMARY

Initial and refresher training sessions are vital to the success of any field sales organization. Sales personnel must understand their products, their customers, and the marketing program of the firm. Company-run training programs generally are the best way to instill the knowledge, and a variety of teaching methods can be used, including lecturers, case studies, videotapes, and programmed instruction.

Salespeople need effective selling skills, which can be acquired through previous jobs or outside seminars. Alternatively, these skills can be taught through role-playing exercises and one-on-one coaching. Filming and videotaping of trial presentations are good ways to increase participation and to polish skills during training sessions.

Training can be conducted by staff specialists, line managers, or outside consultants. Professional trainers are usually involved with centralized training activities and the preparation of classroom materials. First-line sales managers are more likely to conduct one-on-one training. This method allows sales managers to take immediate corrective action to improve the skills of the people working under their supervision.

Sales training requires substantial investment in facilities and materials, and sales managers must continually justify these expenditures. Training programs should be evaluated on a regular basis to measure their impact on sales force turnover, morale, product knowledge, and sales revenues. Knowing the results of training efforts can help managers refine these programs for maximum efficiency and effectiveness. Remember, a firm must follow up on training in the field, where sales happen.

► KEY TERMS

Behavioral simulations	Interactive system
Centralized training	On-the-job training (OJT)
Cognitive selling scripts	Procedural knowledge
Commission overrides	Role playing
Cross-tabulation	Salesperson development
Decentralized training	Training needs analysis
Declarative knowledge	Turnover

► REVIEW QUESTIONS

1. Why do most firms have sales training programs?

2. What prevents some companies from having formal training field programs for salespeople?

3. What are the most important topics in sales training?

4. How can a company determine the training needs of its sales force?

5. Why is so little time spent on learning selling techniques?

6. How much do companies spend, on average, to train new and veteran salespeople?

7. Why do some companies spend more than others on sales training?

8. What decisions must be made when developing a sales training program?

9. Explain why some firms use centralized training, while others decentralize training to the field sales offices.

10. Why do some firms use line executives to train salespeople and others use professional staff?

11. How important is retraining of experienced company salespeople?

12. What methods should be used to evaluate sales training activities?

► PROBLEMS

1. Quaker Oats is a large consumer foods company whose products include Aunt Jemima's pancakes, Quaker Natural cereal, Puss 'n' Boots cat food, and a host of other products. Their sales training program can be summarized as a three-step process:

   a. The recruit attends a one-week classroom training session with a regional trainer whose only job is to work with new recruits. Topics include general company information, product knowledge, and sales techniques.

   b. The recruit then goes into the field and works with a district manager. Before a territory is assigned, the manager and recruit work together on basic selling skills.

   c. After three months in the field, the new salesperson comes back to headquarters for a refresher course on advanced selling techniques and territory management. After this, a similar refresher course is held annually.

   What do you think of this program? Do you see any problems? The trainer in step (a) is often a former sales manager who is two or three years from retirement. Would you like to see anyone else in that position?

2. Roche Labs manufactures and sells pharmaceutical products. Their sales training program is considered the most difficult in the industry. They send their salespeople to participating hospitals to go through a training routine very similar to that given to medical interns. Is this program necessary, or are they overtraining their salespeople? Similarly, should an industrial salesperson work in the manufacturing facility for a period of time?

3. Westvaco uses the computer to augment its sales training program. Sales managers are given data on costs, profit, volume, and other information and asked to make recommendations on business alternatives. The computer responds with estimated results for sales

dollars, profits, and inventories. The simulation is set up as a game, with managers competing against other managers. List the possible benefits of this unique program.

4. As the sales manager for a medium-sized industrial firm, you have just finished reading an article in a business journal that praised the benefits of providing field sales training for experienced salespeople as a refresher. The author claimed that a sales manager observing the calls of veteran salespeople spotted and eliminated bad habits and techniques. When you suggested doing the same thing, your sales force strongly objected. One salesperson was afraid it would look bad to have the manager come along on calls. Another said that after 10 years on the job, he didn't need any further training. You are still convinced that there would be some benefits to this type of training. Would you go ahead with the program, despite the objections? If you do, how do you plan to sell the sales force on the need for such a program?

5. You are the regional sales manager for a wholesaler of automotive parts. You supervise 15 salespeople who are responsible for sales within carefully defined geographic areas. Your salespeople are paid a commission based on gross margin dollars. They are mostly veterans with established customers. A major part of your training program involves having new trainees spend time observing how a successful senior salesperson sells to his or her accounts. You usually assign new people to spend a week with Jack, a veteran salesperson with the highest volume in the region. While this is typical of training programs in small and medium-sized firms, what are the potential pitfalls of this training method? What alternatives does the company have?

6. The use of audiocassettes as a sales training tool has attracted sales trainers for many years because of the amount of time salespeople spend traveling between accounts. (The history of recorded sales materials can be traced back to 1959, when Bob Stone and Don Reaser started The Business Man's Record Club.) Most companies, however, have been unable to sustain a regular schedule of tapes to the field beyond a few months or, in some cases, only three or four basic tapes. The biggest difficulty has been to produce material that salespeople will find worthwhile and to which they will be willing to listen. What would you recommend to someone producing sales training tapes for a field sales force to ensure that the salespeople will listen to and learn from the tapes? Reflect on what would be necessary for you to listen to a tape, enjoy it, and learn from it.

▶ IN-CLASS EXERCISES

The Greatest Product Since Sliced Bread

As the marketing manager, you are very excited about a new product R&D has developed. You know it will sell because you have tons of market research data to back it up. You are also painfully aware that the product and its benefits are complex to the customer, so that it will take significant sales force backing to make it successful. No matter how often you tell the sales department about how great this product is, you know that their instinct for selling won't automatically translate into a passion for selling *this* product.

You decide to ask the sales manager for some time at the next sales meeting to present your product. During your meeting with the sales manager, you explain that this product represents an important opportunity to the company and a chance for the sales force to make more commissions, but sales support is absolutely critical if the product is to succeed. The sales force must put significant time behind it.

The sales manager points out that there may be some skepticism from the sales force after the last new product dud that marketing pushed on them. It will be critical to convince them of the merits of this product. The meeting must get them excited about the product and convince them that it will sell.

The quarterly sales meeting will take place in two weeks. The sales manager will need the morning and part of the afternoon, but you can have two to three hours late in the afternoon. She would like to review your plans for the session next week. She is especially interested in how you will conduct the meeting, what topics will be covered, any media aids you will need, and so on.

Questions:

1. If you were the sales manager, what directions would you give the marketing manager in preparing for the training session?
2. What will salespeople want to know about the new product?
3. What are the alternative training approaches (e.g., lecture) that you could use in this training session?
4. Develop a detailed outline of how you will run this meeting along with a time schedule.

▶ EXPERIENTIAL EXERCISE

Visit a local retailer, wholesaler, or manufacturer and set up an appointment with the person responsible for purchasing. Depending on the size and type of business, this may be the purchasing agent, store manager, owner, or branch manager. You should choose the person on whom salespeople call. Select your company carefully since some firms are too small, so not many salespeople call on them, or the purchasing is done at headquarters. What you want to find out is what the best salespeople do well and what average salespeople do not do well. Have your questions prepared ahead of time; you may need to do some probing. You may recognize this as part of a customer analysis in assessing training needs. You may wish to review that section of the chapter. Ask the person being interviewed to identify the company of the best salesperson who calls on them—and also the worst. There may be more than one company in each category. After you have gathered and analyzed your information, determine if training could overcome the gap between the good and poor salespeople. If training would be effective, outline a program to overcome the deficiencies of the poor salespeople.

▶ REFERENCES

1. Based on discussions with Ygnacius Dominguez, Client Manager, IBM and Jaclyn Fierman, "The Death and Rebirth of the Salesman," *Fortune* (July 25, 1994), p. 86.

2. Neil Ford, Orville Walker, Gilbert Churchill, and Steven Hartley, "Selecting Successful Salespeople: A Meta-Analysis of Biographical and Psychological Selection Criteria," in *Review of*

Marketing, ed. Michael Houston (Chicago: American Marketing Association, 1988), pp. 90–131, and Kay Keck, Thomas Leigh, and James Lollar, "Critical Success Factors in Captive Multi-Line Insurance Agency Sales," *Journal of Personal Selling & Sales Management* 15 (Winter 1995).

3. Dick Schaaf, "Lessons from the 100 Best," *Training*, 27 (February 1990), p. S19.

4. WILLIAM MONCRIEF, RONALD HOVERSTAD, and GEORGE LUCAS, "Survival Analysis: A New Approach to Analyzing Sales Force Retention," *Journal of Personal Selling & Sales Management*, 9 (Summer 1989), p. 26.

5. *Sales & Marketing Management* (September 1993), p. 61.

6. ROBERT KLEIN, "Nabisco Sales Soar After Sales Training," *Marketing News*, January 6, 1997, p. 23.

7. ROBERT ERFFMEYER, RANDALL RUSS, and JOSEPH HAIR, "Needs Assessment and Evaluation in Sales Training Programs," *Journal of Personal Selling & Sales Management*, 11 (Winter 1991), pp. 17–30.

8. SAUL GELLERMAN, "The Tests of a Good Salesperson," *Harvard Business Review*, 90 (May–June 1990), pp. 64–72.

9. JOHN MAROHL, "More on Training," *Sales & Marketing Management* (July 1993), p. 7.

10. ADEL ELN-ANSARY, "Sales Force Effectiveness Research Reveals New Insights and Reward-Penalty Patterns in Sales Force Training," *Journal of Personal Selling & Sales Management*, 13 (Spring 1993), p. 86.

11. WILLIAM KEENAN, "Are You Overspending on Training?" *Sales & Marketing Management* (January 1990), pp. 56–60.

12. KERRY ROTTENBERGER-MUTHA, "Owens-Corning Fiberglas, Corp." *Sales & Marketing Management* (September 1993), p. 56.

13. ERIN ANDERSON and THOMAS ROBERTSON, "Inducing Multiline Salespeople to Adopt House Brands," *Journal of Marketing*, 59 (April 1995), pp. 16–31.

14. MICHAEL MAJOR, "Sales Training Emphasizes Service and Quality," *Marketing News* (March 5, 1990), p. 5.

15. For more information on salespeople's cognitive scripts and knowledge structures, see THOMAS LEIGH and ARNO RETHANS, "Script-Theoretic Analysis of Industrial Purchasing Behavior," *Journal of Marketing*, 48 (Fall 1984), pp. 22–32; THOMAS LEIGH, "Cognitive Selling Scripts and Sales Training," *Journal of Personal Selling & Sales Management*, 7 (August 1987),

pp. 39–48; and THOMAS LEIGH and PATRICK McGRAW, "Mapping the Procedural Knowledge of Industrial Sales Personnel: A Script-Theoretic Investigation," *Journal of Marketing*, 53 (January 1989), pp. 16–34.

16. JENNIFER REESE, "Getting Hot Ideas from Customers," *Fortune* (May 18, 1992), pp. 86–87.

17. "Dow Makes It Big by Thinking Small," *Sales & Marketing Management* (September 1991), p. 44.

18. "Vital Statistics: 1995 Industry Report," *Training* (October 1995), p. 62.

19. For more on mentoring, see ELLEN PULLINS, LESLIE FINE, and WENDY WARREN, "Identifying Peer Mentors in the Sales Force: An Exploratory Investigation of Willingness and Ability," *Journal of the Academy of Marketing Science*, 24 (Spring 1996), pp. 125–136.

20. WILLIAM KEENAN, "Merck Co.," *Sales & Marketing Management* (September 1993), p. 62.

21. For more on role playing in a classroom setting, see JOSEPH CHAPMAN, "Building Block Method for in-Class Role-Playing," *National Conference for Sales Management* (1992), pp. 27–30; LYNN METCALF, "Role Playing in the Classroom: Enriching the Sales Management Course in a Resource-Limited Environment," *National Conference for Sales Management* (1992), pp. 8–12; RICHARD REXELSEN, "Developing Role Play as an Interactive Learning Resource," *National Conference for Sales Management* (1992), pp. 13–18.

22. "To Reinforce and Motivate Your Sales Team, Use TV-Style Quiz Shows," *Personal Selling Power* (July–August 1990), pp. 44–46.

23. JACK FALVEY "The Most Neglected Training Tool," *Sales & Marketing Management* (June 1990), pp. 51–59.

24. WILLIAM KEENAN, "Hewlett-Packard Strives to Connect with Its Customers," *Sales & Marketing Management* (September 1991), p. 48.

25. K. RANDALL RUSS, JOSEPH HAIR, ROBERT EFFMEYER, and DEBBIE EASTERLING, "Usage and Perceived Effectiveness of High-Tech Approaches to Sales Training," *Journal of Personal Selling & Sales Management* (Spring 1989), pp. 46–54.

26. KEENAN, "Are You Overspending on Training?" p. 59.

27. LAWRENCE CHONKO, JOHN TANNER, and WILLIAM WEEKS, "Sales Training: Status and Needs," *Journal of Personal Selling & Sales Management*, 13 (Fall 1993), pp. 81–86.

28. For more on evaluating sales training effectiveness, see RICK MENDOSA, "Training: Is There a Payoff?" *Sales & Marketing Management*, (June 1995), pp. 64–71.

29. "Types of Training Provided by Companies," *Sales & Marketing Management* (June 28, 1993), p. 75.

30. WILLIAM KEENAN, "What's Sales Got to Do with It?" *Sales & Marketing Management* (March 1994), pp. 66–70.

▶ SELECTED READINGS

WARD, NICHOLAS and KATHRYN WOLFSON, *Sales Training Handbook: A Guide to Developing Sales Performance* (Englewood Cliffs, NJ: Prentice-Hall, 1993).

SILBERMAN, MEL, 101 *Ways to Make Training Active* (New York: Pfeiffer, 1995).

CASE

10-1 WESTINGHOUSE ELECTRIC CORPORATION*

Bob Ray, the marketing manager for the Overhead Distribution Transformer Division (OHDT) of Westinghouse Electric Corporation, was concerned about his field sales engineers. It had been four years since OHDT had initiated any sort of formal training program directed at the field sales force. Company information revealed that the sales force had an annual turnover of 10 percent. His concern for newer salespersons' depth of training was paralleled by his conviction that the veteran sales engineers would benefit from more exposure to product knowledge, especially in light of recent innovations. Interpretation of direct and indirect feedback revealed that both groups were reaching for more depth in product knowledge.

*This case was prepared by Norman A. P. Govoni, Babson College; Richard R. Still, Florida International University; and Kent Mitchell, the University of Georgia. Copyright © by Joseph C. Latona. Reproduced by permission.

Westinghouse Electric Corporation

Westinghouse was the world's oldest and second largest manufacturer of electrical apparatus and appliances. Founded by inventor George Westinghouse in 1886, the corporation marketed some 300,000 variations of about 8,000 highly diversified basic products ranging from a simple piece of copper wire to a complex commercial nuclear power plant. The firm employed over 145,000 men and women in laboratories, manufacturing plants, sales offices, and distribution centers from coast to coast and around the world. Over 1,800 of its scientists and engineers were actively engaged in research and development activities. The corporation had more than 160,000 stockholders.

Because of its size and the diversity required to serve a variety of markets, Westinghouse was organized into four companies operating within the corporation. The companies were Power Systems; Industry and Defense; Consumer Products; and Broadcasting, Learning and Leisure Time.

Each company was headed by a president, who had full responsibility for designing, building, and selling the company's products and services throughout the world. Each company had its own staff of specialists in certain fields. It also could draw on corporate resources for additional specialized support in fields such as marketing, manufacturing, engineering, design, research, personnel and public affairs, finance, and law.

The basic organizational unit of the company was the division, each with its own line of products and services. Each division, in turn, was grouped with a number of other divisions with related products and services, such as major appliances, construction products, or power generation equipment.

Combined sales before taxes were $5.1 billion. The Power Systems Company was the leading contributor to income after taxes, with a 43 percent contribution. The Power Systems Company was divided into two main areas: the Power Generation Group and the Transmission and Distribution Division located in Athens, Georgia.

Overhead Distribution Transformer Division (OHDT)

OHDT considered itself first in facilities, developments, and service; and rightfully so, for it had led the nation in overhead distribution transformer sales since 1971, with a fairly consistent market share of about 23 percent. Industry sales were projected to be nearly $900 million by the early 1980s.

Since 1958, all Westinghouse overhead distribution transformers were designed and manufactured in the Athens plant. The previous manufacturing site was in Sharon, Pennsylvania. OHDT was particularly proud of its engineering leadership. In the past few years, Westinghouse had expanded its staff and facility in a time when others were cutting back. Bob Ray was instrumental in making this crucial marketing decision and was later honored with the Corporation's highest award, "The Order of Merit," an award given to three employees each year. In the capacity over demand ratio, the company had been 131 percent, 85 percent, and 88 percent, respectively, for the past three years.

Competition

Westinghouse had been recognized for several decades as the primary innovator in the distribution transformer industry. Four other companies, each of which had active R&D facilities, were considered major innovators: General Electric, RTE, Allis-Chalmers, and McGraw-Edison. Other strong companies among the 29 national competitors were Wagner, Kuhlman, and Colt.

The Westinghouse product was generally ranked tops in its field, representing true value for dollar investment. Some competitors, though, had been successful in promoting a less expensive product.

The Customer and Pricing

The electric utility companies were the consumers for distribution transformers, and they were divided into three major classes: investor-owned utilities, rural electric cooperatives, and municipalities. There were approximately 300 investor-owned utilities, which accounted for about 80 percent of consumption. The coops and municipalities numbered about 920 and 2,000, respectively, and together accounted for the remaining 20 percent. With the increasing migration of families and industries to metropolitan outskirts, the coops were expected to represent a considerably larger share of consumption in the years to come. There were about 33 million overhead distribution transformers across the nation. Sales in this market represented about 60 percent changeouts (i.e., replacements in an area where power consumption had increased) and 40 percent new development units.

In pricing, the major utilities negotiated year-long purchasing commitments during November–December of each year. Fierce price competition was prevalent among the investor-owned utilities, and large discounts off list prices were normally expected. Pricing for the coops and municipalities was more stable, with smaller discounts from list being offered. The method of negotiation was small orders throughout the year for the smaller utilities and the sealed bid method for the publicly owned companies.

Promotion

Westinghouse advertised its electrical transmission, generation, and distribution equipment in leading electrical trade journals. Additionally, it was a member of the National Electrical Manufacturers Association (NEMA), which set standards for the industry. NEMA issued monthly reports to its members which included total market volume and member market share information. Distribution was by a field sales force selling direct to customers.

Marketing Management

The marketing department of OHDT consisted of a marketing manager, a marketing services manager, and four area sales managers who were assisted by a staff of their own. The sales areas were divided geographically. Almost all personnel in the marketing department had an engineering background, which was considered a must in this complex field. The department had ultimate responsibility for the success of its product. They were particularly proud that Westinghouse had been number one in market share of transformer sales each year since 1971.

The marketing department had been located in Athens since 1968, when it moved down from Sharon, Pennsylvania. Exhibit 1 shows where the marketing department fit into the organization of the Athens firm.

The Field Sales Force

Overhead distribution transformers were sold through two of the four Westinghouse companies: the Power

Systems company and the Industry and Defense company. Each company had its own sales network, as shown in Exhibit 2.

There were over 300 Westinghouse corporate field sales engineers, district managers, and zone managers located throughout the country handling OHDT accounts. In addition to being loaded with OHDT products, the salespeople were responsible for other Westinghouse utility products. For example, they represented the Electrical Relay Division, the Circuit Breaker Division, and the Electric Meter Division, each of which was managed through other corporate channels. The field sales engineers, in serving several product divisions, reported to district managers for product loading.

The area sales managers and their staffs (of OHDT) served the field sales engineers by taking and expediting product orders, answering product questions, and collecting feedback. Additionally, they traveled into the field to hold training seminars and to assist salespeople on important sales. Bob Ray often got involved in following through with especially important customers.

Training a Field Sales Engineer

Westinghouse sales engineers were required to have a Bachelor of Science in Engineering. When brought

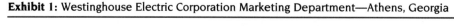

Exhibit 1: Westinghouse Electric Corporation Marketing Department—Athens, Georgia

Exhibit 2: Westinghouse Electric Corporation Sales Organization Chart

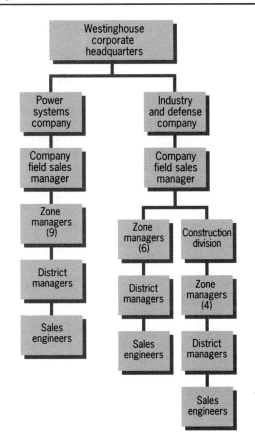

into the corporation, the new recruit was first sent to Pittsburgh for a basic 3-week orientation to the Westinghouse company. The recruit was then assigned to a corporate "graduate studies program" which lasted from 3 to 12 months, depending on his or her skills. Upon completion, he or she was assigned to the field as an assistant sales engineer to serve a training tenure, which lasted anywhere from 6 to 24 months, again depending on individual requirements. During this period, the person would travel for a 2-week period visiting the various manufacturing plants he or she would later serve. Each plant gave the future salesperson a 2-day training and orientation seminar. Ideally, the sales engineers were supposed to return to these parent manufacturing divisions annually for refresher training. Additionally, they would attend dis-

trict or zone training seminars held by representatives of the parent divisions.

A sales engineer, depending on experience and length of service to Westinghouse, drew a base salary averaging about $35,000 a year, not including the bonus. The number of calls and the type of customer were established according to ability, experience, and product loading. It took, on the average, about $500,000 worth of sales to support a sales engineer in the field.

Thoughts of an OHDT Area Sales Manager

Marvin Jones was one of the four area sales managers for the OHDT division. Prior to his present assignment, he was a field sales engineer for over 12 years. Reflecting on his days in the field, he remembered quite well the difficulties involved in attending training seminars held by the various divisions. Salespeople recognized that training was essential, that effective selling required sound training, and that a person's potential (not to mention the quota) really could not be realized without training. However, getting a salesperson to a training seminar was a difficult task, because when there was a sale to be made, there wasn't time for training. The training, as important as it was, would have to wait. At least this was the common thing when attendance at refresher training was more or less left to the individual sales engineer.

The Need to Train

Bob Ray was very concerned about the field sales force's depth of knowledge about overhead distribution transformers, especially in light of fairly recent innovations (a trend which would be expected to continue). He knew Westinghouse had become the leading producer of transformers, but he attributed this more to excellent engineering, excessive demand, and the expertise of his department.

As questions were coming in to the area sales managers at a slightly higher than normal rate, he pinpointed the problem to training. He also knew that the economy might be expected to take a slight decline. With the growing threat that demand might slacken in the months to come, he felt that competition would really start getting rough. In addition, he realized that an unprepared sales force might not fare so well when the time came to give more in-depth and high-quality sales presentations. And it had been a while since Athens had initiated a formal training program. The previous program, which was considered a success, consisted of a campaign to inform the sales force about the overhead distribution transformer, and, as a gimmick, miniature transformer parts were sent to the salespeople.

Unfortunately, a salesperson's time was an extremely valuable commodity, and Bob Ray knew it. Training in any organization was one of the most difficult tasks to pull off effectively, even when the trainees were geographically close to management; but the Westinghouse field sales force, scattered across the nation, was another matter. Making the training task even more burdensome was the fact that these sales engineers had more than just the OHDT account to worry about. It was realized that Athens would have to compete for both time and attention.

From Ideas to Action

With the facts on the table, Bob Ray called on Larry Deal, who headed Marketing Services, and his assistant, Glynn Hodges, who at that time was involved with marketing communications. Hodges was sent to Pittsburgh a few times to work jointly with Earl Swartz, the corporate contact to the ad agency used by Westinghouse. By June, Hodges had the layout completed for the proposed solution to the training problem—a training campaign to be called "The Problem Solvers." Bob Ray liked it. It was estimated that the campaign would ultimately cost about $20,000 representing a large slice of the OHDT marketing budget. Exhibit 3 gives an idea of the estimated costs.

About "The Problem Solvers" Campaign

An overview of "The Problem Solvers" appears in Exhibit 4, which contains the following: background, problem objectives, program implementation, elements of the program (Stages 1 and 2), and a summary of elements and timing.

To catch the salesperson's attention, the proposed campaign would consist of expensive, eye-catching adult games which emphasized puzzle problems. The games would cost $4–$5 each; a good example was a three-dimensional tic-tac-toe game made of three clear plastic decks mounted on top of each other. Each player was represented by either clear blue or yellow marbles about an inch in diameter each. The game could be won horizontally, vertically, or diagonally.

Along with the mailing of each game would be a cover letter and an information bulletin emphasizing a particular feature of the overhead distribution transformer. As the salesperson read each information bulletin, he or she would fill in "clues" to a master crossword puzzle. When the mailings were completed, the salesperson would send in the completed crossword puzzle and picture of himself or herself (along with the rest of the family if desired) to the marketing department in Athens. Athens would have the picture made into a jigsaw puzzle and return it to the participant a few weeks later.

The Marketing Services Division—A Special Project

Larry Deal's Marketing Services Division had been assigned the responsibility of supporting the ad agency by providing the technical information necessary for turning "The Problem Solvers" idea into a manageable campaign. Brian Kennedy, assigned to marketing communications, and assistant Jody Unsler had been asked to design the instruction brochures and crossword puzzle. Also, coordination with Earl Swartz had resulted in the initial selection of a container for the games. The container was a cardboard box with a design of jigsaw puzzle parts; each part had a letter on it, which when put together spelled out "The Problem Solvers." Kennedy put in long hours working on the instruction brochures. In explaining the various components of the transformer, he had decided to set a conversational sales presentation scene between a Westinghouse salesperson and a purchasing agent. The salesperson, who was "Mr. Problem Solver" or "Ms. Problem Solver," was smoothly answering the questions asked by a purchasing agent, who was appropriately labeled "Mr. A. Gent" or "Ms. A. Lady."

Early November

One morning in early November, Bob Ray was relaxing at his desk sipping a cup of coffee. He was thinking about "The Problem Solvers" campaign. Things were

Exhibit 3: Westinghouse Overhead Distribution Transformers: "The Problem Solvers" Promotion

General
This document summarizes various elements of the "Problem Solver" promotion. The costs are based on quotations from suppliers who have seen initially prepared layouts.

Puzzles
Five puzzles will be purchased directly from supplier by Westinghouse.

Shipping Boxes for Puzzles
Five puzzles each of the five different size boxes plus one 6"-by-6" envelope (for crossword puzzles and brochure mailing), each to be printed in two colors using the same "Problem Solver" design. (Suggestion: each box to have a different color on the design.)
Delivery time: six weeks from receipt of order.
Cost: including converting boxes, design preparation, color plates and printing: $2500.

Crossword Puzzle
To be completed by salesperson and submitted with photo to get personalized jigsaw puzzle prize.
Timing: Six weeks from receipt of words and clues from Westinghouse. Puzzles to be printed in simple 4-page format and inserted in envelope along with cover letter and brochure.
Cost: $800.

Jigsaw Puzzle
One 11"-by-14" puzzle will be sent to every salesperson submitting photo along with completed crossword puzzle. Photos will be held and sent in bulk to puzzle manufacturer, who will then send completed puzzle directly to each salesperson along with the original photo.
Timing: four weeks delivery from receipt of photographs.
Cost: $1,300.

Cover Letters
Total of five (one for each puzzle mailing), 400 copies of each.
Cost: including artwork for masthead, copy editing, typesetting, and printing: $600.

Brochures
One brochure will accompany each of the five puzzle mailings. Each brochure will focus on one aspect of the overhead transformers. The cover will have a full color cover of the puzzle being sent; inside pages will be black and white and use existing line art.
Cost: including photos, typesetting, tissue layout and key art, copy editing, and production supervision for five 20-page booklets: $12,000.
Total Cost: up to $20,000.

---

moving along pretty well. At the present rate, he would be able to meet the January 15 target date for the first mailing. He knew $20,000 was a lot of money for OHDT to spend on a training campaign of this type, but he was confident in the overall idea and felt it was the best way to reach such a broad and isolated target. However, a few decisions remained. There was some question about the two-month interval between each of the five mailings. He definitely wanted the sales force ready for November–December when the big utilities would negotiate year-long contracts for the following year. In a way, he wanted the campaign to last a good while, as it represented a big chunk of the budget, but he wondered whether the field sales force's attention would be held over such a period. Another thought entered his mind about the effectiveness of the campaign's feedback mechanism. He remembered Glynn Hodges saying he anticipated a

Exhibit 4: Westinghouse Overhead Distribution Transformers: An Overview of "The Problem Solvers"

Background

The total market for overhead distribution transformers is very good. For Westinghouse, it is excellent. While Athens is producing at full capacity and the current problem is meeting demand, there still remain several conditions with which Athens must cope if it is to achieve its long-range potential:

1. Many Westinghouse and agent salespeople do not understand the advantages of Westinghouse transformers.
2. There are competitors who manufacture and sell transformers at a cheaper price. These transformers are inferior to those at Westinghouse. The Westinghouse story, which must be communicated through sales personnel to customers, is a *value* story.
3. The present sales boom cannot be expected to continue indefinitely, and the sales force must be prepared to conduct tougher, more effective sales presentations.

Program Objectives

The object of this program is to make Westinghouse and agent sales personnel more effective representatives for Athens by showing them why Westinghouse is the value leader and by giving them the information and tools needed to make more effective presentations.

By accomplishing these objectives, the sales representatives will become more confident of their abilities—and the Westinghouse line. This growing confidence will, in turn, create even greater success.

Program Implementation

This is a two-stage program. The Stage 1 phase, the more important, is directed to the Westinghouse sales force and includes an explanation of the program, a summary of the transformer market (and the profit contribution made by Westinghouse transformers), and detailed instructions on transformers (using the theme "The Problem Solvers") along with unique mailings.

The Stage 2 phase is the person-to-person contact between salespeople and customers. Having been effectively indoctrinated into the advantages of Westinghouse transformers, the salespeople are now supplied with effective sales presentation material, which will make contact between sales representatives and customers more productive for the Athens division.

Elements of Program—Stage 1

1. Cover letter No. 1 from Mr. Meierkord (general manager, OHDT) or Mr. Ray spelling out the theme "The Problem Solvers" and the purpose of the program.
2. Instruction brochure No. 1 on Cover and Bushing Assembly along with puzzle.
3. Cover letter No. 2 from Meierkord or Ray.
4. Instruction brochure No. 2 on Tank Assembly along with puzzle.
5. Cover letter No. 3 from Meierkord or Ray.
6. Instruction brochure on Core Assembly along with puzzle.
7. Cover letter No. 4 from Meierkord or Ray. Letter to state that crossword puzzle answers are found in instruction booklet. If salesperson returns completed crossword puzzle along with any photograph of his or her choice, Athens will return a custom-made jigsaw puzzle made out of the photo.
8. Instruction brochure No. 4 on CSP (completely self-protected transformer) features along with crossword puzzle. Crossword puzzle will contain such clues as:
   CSP Transformers (OUTLAST) conventional types by 60 percent.
   CSP arresters (LOWER) discharge voltage on high surge currents.
   After overload trips breaker, breaker can be reset to (TEN) percent more capacity.

Elements of Program—Stage 2

After salespeople have studied the four bulletins, they are better prepared to make more effective presentations to their customers. To help them in their calls, they will be furnished with the following:

1. Cover letter (No. 5) again from Meierkord or Ray, reiterating the profitability of transformers, that they are great "Problem Solvers," and that the salespeople (the ultimate "Problem Solvers") are now well

Exhibit 4: (*continued*)

prepared to communicate to their customers why Westinghouse transformers are truly tops in the field. Cover letter will dwell on the importance of customer presentations, preparation, and follow-through.

2. Flip chart presentation entitled "Westinghouse Distribution Transformers: 'The Problem Solvers.' " The presentation will summarize the most important "Features/Functions/Benefits" from the four technical bulletins. The presentation will be designed in a horizontal format so that the pages are adaptable for photographic slide or strip film production.

3. Customer booklet to be prepared using same text and artwork from the presentation flip chart. Booklet will be left with the customer as a reminder of what was presented and as a source document for later reference.

4. Capabilities brochure, about to be produced, can be an added ingredient to the presentation. While it emphasizes Athens' manufacturing capability—as opposed to the engineering emphasis of the presentation—the booklet is prestigious and will reflect Westinghouse distribution transformers as being a value line.

If not used as part of the presentation, the capabilities brochure would make an impressive mailing to the customer, along with a "thank you" letter for listening to the presentation.

Summary—Elements and Timing

Stage 1	
First Mailing:	Cover Letter No. 1 (Program Summary)
	Bulletin No. 1 Cover and Bushing
	Puzzle No. 1 (Adult Game)
	Master Crossword Puzzle
Second Mailing:	Cover Letter No. 2
	Bulletin No. 2 Tank Assembly
(Two months later)	Puzzle No. 2
Third Mailing:	Cover Letter No. 3
	Bulletin No. 3 Core and Coil Assembly
(Two months later)	Puzzle No. 3
Fourth Mailing:	Cover Letter No. 4
	Bulletin No. 4 CSP Features
(Two months later)	Puzzle No. 4
Stage 2	
Fifth Mailing:	Cover Letter No. 5 (Customer Presentations)
	Flip Chart Presentation
(Two months later)	Presentation Summary for Customer
	Athens Capability Brochure
	Puzzle No. 5

65 percent response. Another point that was undefined in the campaign was what stand OHDT should take on the future newcomers to the field sales force. Since the previous campaign, the new people learned through OJT (on-the-job-training) and sales materials, as well as by picking up what they could from OHDT bulletins. However, this provided only short-range coverage and would break down in the long run or when making sales got tough. This had been one of the factors contributing to the present situation.

With those thoughts in mind, Bob Ray decided to call a division head meeting that afternoon.

CASE

10-2 SANDWELL PAPER COMPANY*

George Murphy, Sandwell Paper Company's Bakersfield branch manager, undertook a careful study of his operation. The study was in keeping with his philosophy of having an alert, informed management, and it dealt with both the managerial and sales aspects of the distribution center.

Company Background

The Sandwell Paper Company, a large paper wholesaler, originated in Omaha, Nebraska, in the 1890s. During its early years, the firm was involved mainly in sales and distribution to final users and bought its paper from other wholesalers. However, as sales grew, the Sandwells soon began a warehouse operation of their own. The product line was quite diversified and included both printing (fine) and industrial (wrapping) grades of paper. Paper merchants carrying both product lines became known as *dual distributors*. To meet the rapid growth of markets on the West Coast, the company established several divisions in that area. Murphy's operation was the Bakersfield branch of the Los Angeles division. There were two other California divisions located at San Diego and San Francisco.

Murphy was quite pleased with the decentralized profit center arrangement of Sandwell and the independence it afforded him. He felt that the challenge of earning a satisfactory rate of return on investment for the branch provided sales incentive for his organization.

George Murphy was in his early fifties and had been in paper sales work for the past 25 years. He had graduated in business administration from the University of Southern California and had gained sales and management experience with two other firms (a paper manufacturer and another paper wholesaler) before joining Sandwell.

*This case is reproduced with the permission of its author, Dr. Stuart V. Rich, Professor of Marketing, and Director, Forest Industries Management Center, College of Business Administration, University of Oregon, Eugene, Oregon.

The Bakersfield sales force under Murphy consisted of three salespeople of fine paper and two of industrial paper. The division had formerly prepared its salespeople in a special sales trainee program that had consisted of daily classroom instruction in products and methods of selling. The instruction involved lectures, cases, and role playing. Regular written homework was required of all trainees. However, because of the company's high turnover of sales personnel, Murphy had terminated this formal method of training. The new method required sales trainees to work at various warehouse jobs, thereby learning firsthand about the products and problems of the business.

According to Murphy, about one-third of his time was spent dealing with problems of warehousing, accounting, and credit extension and about two-thirds with sales meetings, forecasting, quota setting, and actual selling to his own accounts.

Product Line

Sandwell Paper had always been a dual house supplying both printing (fine) and industrial (wrapping) paper goods. In addition to traditional paper goods, the company stocked plastics and other nonpaper items to promote unitized selling.

The objective of unitized or packaged selling was to enable the salesperson to supply all customer needs, thereby simplifying customer ordering and billing and maximizing selling efficiency. Sandwell had been concentrating its unitized sales effort in the meat market and custodial service or janitorial supply areas.

The Sandwell paper product line was divided into two sections—printing and industrial. The fine (printing) paper line (Exhibit 1) represented the more specialized and profitable of the two sections. Printing grades had the best gross trading margin for the Bakersfield branch. Printers did not want to maintain large inventories, yet they wanted quick delivery on the many grades listed in their sample books. They were willing to pay a premium to wholesalers for

Exhibit 1: Printing Grade Categories

Categories	Percent Sales
Bond—Ledger	40
Bond	
Ledger	
Flat writing	
Safety papers	
Mimeograph	
Duplicator	
Index—Bristol	20
Index	
Bristol	
Blotting	
Boards	
Cardboards	
Cut cards	
Tags	
Information	
Book—Cover	20
Book	
Cover	
Envelopes	
Specialty	20
Announcements	
Thin papers	
Gummed	

Exhibit 2: Industrial Grade Categories

Categories	Percentage of Sales
Bags (cellophane, bakery, grocery, department)	20
Industrial (towels, tissue, wrap, lumber wrap)	21
Packing (filter, wadding, corrugated)	3
Waxes, glassine, parchment	6
Boxes, cases, board	7
Food containers, plates, napkins	20
Twine, ribbon, tape	14
Sanitary tissues	9

maintaining inventories of wide ranges of grade sizes, weights, and colors. In the printing paper field, Sandwell Paper was a franchised distributor for Medallion Paper Company, a large, recognized manufacturer of printing paper. In areas serviced by more than one wholesaler, Sandwell had exclusive sales of the Medallion paper line. As a result of handling the complete line, ordering and inventory problems were minimized. Uniform quality could be depended on. Although competitive price inroads were being made on some of Medallion's grades, Murphy and other company managers had elected to continue to carry the line since Medallion's trade name commanded such recognition of excellence.

The Sandwell industrial paper line consisted of those paper goods utilized by manufacturers in making wrapping or in transporting their products. Exhibit 2 lists those items carried by the branch. Industrial grades were characterized by volume selling and price competition, and these grades greatly over-taxed warehouse space. Murphy indicated that industrial sales out of stock were 72 percent and that direct mill shipments (orders taken by the wholesaler) were 28 percent. Also, because of Sandwell's policy of selling its customers unitized service, many other non-paper items were carried in stock. Goods such as cleaning fluid, floor wax and waxing machines, light bulbs, and polyfilm and plastic containers were coupled with paper goods to make up unitized or packaged sales to meat markets, building custodial firms, and other user groups.

George Murphy also commented that the branch's inventory turnover rate was 5 to 6 times per year, while the national average for dual houses was 4.5 times.

Nature of Sales Activities

According to Murphy, Sandwell Paper divided its customer market into three parts—printing, industrial, and resale (retail). The resale market consisted mainly of retail grocery stores and variety stores. The majority of paper wholesalers did not sell directly to this market but let the regular grocery and dry goods wholesaler serve it. Murphy felt that this was a growing market and wanted his salespeople to spend more time developing it.

Company sales to each market segment were as follows: printing, 13 percent; industrial, 62 percent; resale, 25 percent. The same items might be sold to all three customer types. The market segments differentiated the customer, not the type of paper commodity.

Murphy continually had to make decisions on the performance of his salespeople, market trends, price changes, and quotas. He gleaned much of this information from month-old sales invoices, informal talks with salespeople, and quick calls to the divisional sales manager.

In 1995 the Los Angeles division decided to re-evaluate its present sales position and effectiveness. As illustrated by Exhibit 3, the sales volume had continued to expand, while the gross trading margin had declined. Both gross margin and net profit were below the industry average (Exhibit 4). The problems observed by the division, according to Murphy, were present on the branch level and had in part caused the present study to be done. The pricing in the in-dustrial grades had become very competitive, and warehouse space was critical. Murphy felt that expansion of the warehouse was not economically feasible because of the low profit margin in industrial grades.

Despite the apparent downturn in trading margin, the number of accounts in the resale area was increasing. Murphy noted that customers were continually calling in orders and requests for service even though branch salespeople were constantly on the go, many times calling in their orders instead of dropping them off at the warehouse (as they had once done).

Each salesperson had an established monthly draw (salary). The draw was an advance in anticipation of the coming month's sales. The sales quota was set in profit dollars—that is, dollars above item and operating costs. The salesperson had to cover the draw for the month. Because the draw was a minimal amount, once the draw was covered, the salesperson could keep 15 percent of each additional dollar of profit.

George Murphy pointed to the schedules of his salespeople, "They've got as many calls crammed into a day as possible," he said. "They really use their effective selling time [i.e., time with the buyer]." Murphy pointed out that certain aspects of paper selling, especially in selling printing grades, were highly technical in nature. Printers could put an inexperienced salesperson on the spot.

Murphy discussed what he felt was very important in selling—talking to the person who was responsible for the buying. He also pointed out that those who used the paper could help influence the buyer.

As was noted earlier, industrial grades had become quite competitive. Murphy stated that competitors often engaged in price cutting to secure new customers. However, it had been Sandwell's policy to maintain their price against competitive inroads and defend their position by supplying "quality service and good will." This policy was still upheld, with the exception of some large-volume competitive goods like toweling and freezer wrap.

New product items were continually being added to the product line, two or three items quarterly. The division headquarters had tried to encourage sales of new items by organizing sales contests. These attempts had been partially successful. Some salespeople had immediate success with a new item, whereas others were unable to move it. With the next new item the success situation might be reversed.

Exhibit 3: Company Trend in Sales and Gross Margin

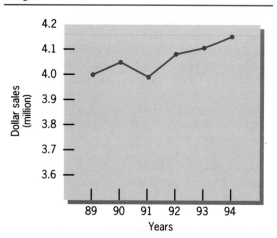

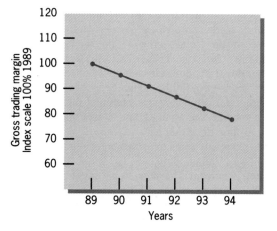

Exhibit 4: Gross Margin and Profit Performance (figures represent percentages)

	Industry Average (NPTA)		Sandwell	
	Warehouse	Direct	Warehouse	Direct
Gross trading margin	22.3	8.5	20.1	8.1
Total expense	19.7	6.5	18.1	7.0
Net profit (before tax) as percent of sales	2.6	2.0	2.0	1.1

Source: National Paper Trade Association, Paper Merchant Performance.

George Murphy decided that the best way to study the selling techniques of his salespeople was to have Phil Edwards, a sales promotion staff member from the Los Angeles division headquarters, accompany the salespeople on calls. Phil had planned on making such a tour for general information and could combine the two projects.

Printer Selling

Mason Printers was a medium-sized printing account specializing in offset and letterpress printing. The business was located on Eleventh Street just off the main business section of Bakersfield. Bud Williams, who had been with Sandwell for three years, was precise in his call schedule and arrived at the shop at 10:30 A.M. each Thursday. While walking to the shop, Bud discussed the account with Phil Edwards.

BUD: Roy Mason is a real artist. When a job is running smooth, he's as agreeable as all get-out. Other times—look out. Sometimes he's out and I waste time just sitting out front waiting for him. He knows I'll be here, so he sometimes leaves an order or note for me. He's the fellow that buys and I sell him Medallion paper on price, quality, and press runability.

EDWARDS: I hear Mason's shop is one of only two in town that has a multisection offset press in operation.

BUD: I know they are making some expensive additions. I try to keep up on the technical stuff, but it's really complicated. Sometimes Roy starts in on what's wrong with an order of paper we sent, and I just can't defend it at all.

The two arrive at the shop and go in. Roy Mason is in the front office (the print shop is in the rear) and makes a gesture of setting his watch at Bud's approach.

BUD: Good morning, Roy.

ROY: Right on time.

BUD: Roy, this is Phil Edwards of our L.A. sales staff. They've sent him over to visit some of our good customers.

EDWARDS: Pleased to meet you, Roy.

BUD: What's up for today, Roy?

ROY: Oh, things are okay. That offset grade you sent over for our regular Smith Company job is going all right. I wish you fellows hadn't run out of that light pink coated cover we always use.

BUD: (*with "Well, so long as it's going through the press okay" relieved look*): Have you got enough of your other stock grades to keep you through the week? Maybe I should check inventory. I know how you like to keep the bare minimum in there.

ROY: We're all set. We have a special job to do for the city. I got out the sample books, and we picked out this grade and color (shows sample). They'd like it with this textured finish. How do you think that will reproduce on the offset press?

BUD: Perfect reproduction! Medallion always runs good.

ROY: I thought it'd be okay, but Ed, my pressman, didn't like the look of it.

BUD: I think it'll be all right. The mill rep is in town, so I'll check with him and let you know.

ROY: Okay, but I'll be in and out all afternoon.

BUD: Say—you know that 25-pound letterpress grade you've been buying from Mentons [another wholesaler]?

ROY: Yes?

BUD: Well, we've got the same color and weight made by Simplin at 5 percent off because the sheet didn't pass the mill quality control specifications. The jobs you use that grade for don't demand quality, so you could use up this off-quality stuff and make yourself a good margin.

ROY: Do you think it will give Ed any trouble on the press? You know he gets pretty angry when a sheet picks, lints or is so porous that the vehicle (ink solvent) carries the pigment into the sheet.

BUD: It shouldn't give you any trouble.

ROY: All right, we'll order it from you this month.

(Glancing quickly at his watch, Bud saw he was going to be late for his call at Fan Fair Supermarket.)

ROY: You know, with this new press we just put in, we're trying to compete for some big accounts. I've got some notes and questions here; maybe we could go over some of them.

BUD: I'll tell you what, Roy, the Simplin rep will be here till next Tuesday. Maybe he and I could get in here Monday morning and talk about your plans.

ROY: Okay, fine by me.

A call from the press room ends the discussion. Roy bids good-bye and Bud and Edwards leave. They walk quickly to the car.

BUD: I'm a little late for Fan Fair. Even though they're a small outfit, their school supplies section really sells the paper. Did you want me to drop you at the office?

EDWARDS: Yes, I've got to meet with Jane Austin (one of two industrial account salespeople) after lunch.

The two drive off.

Industrial Selling

Jane Austin stopped by the office (adjacent to the warehouse) and picked up Edwards. Jane had been selling at the branch for about a year. She started work, as did most prospective Sandwell salespeople, in the warehouse. After four months she had moved to the office order desk, where orders were called in by customers and salespeople. This procedure had been used to prepare Jane for field selling.

Edwards got into the car, and Jane drove out of the parking area.

EDWARDS: Where are we headed?

JANE: Sun Fair Market. I've got to check with the meat department manager. I think he left an item off his order list. And if he runs out of board trays on a weekend, we'll be sure to get the blame for it. This unitized selling puts a lot of pressure on the salespeople.

EDWARDS: I can't think of a quicker way to lose a market customer than to have him come up short of wrapping film or trays on a busy weekend. What calls do you regularly make on Thursday?

JANE: Well, last year, when I started out, Thursday afternoons were for my three big department store accounts. Ted Richards and I—you remember Ted, he's the rep for Thall's Specialty Bag Company—we used to spend a lot of time with store managers laying out the designs for their store merchandise bags. Things have really picked up this year, though. I'll make about eight calls this afternoon, it's a real clockwork schedule. In a way it helps, because people know when you'll be in and they plan on it.

They arrive at the market and walk to the meat department. The man behind the counter waves and points in the direction of the cutting area.

JANE: Jack must be doing some cutting.

They turn the corner and see Jack Wilson.

JACK: What in the world are you doing here today?

JANE: Want to double-check your order for the weekend. You don't have any meat trays down.

JACK: Sure I do! Let's see.

Jack looks at the order sheet developed by Sandwell and Sun Fair executives for ease of ordering.

JACK: Well, I'll be . . . ! Guess I don't. Boy, that would have finished us.

JANE: Jack, this is Phil Edwards, one of our staff salespeople from L.A.

EDWARDS: Pleased to meet you, Jack.

JACK: The same.

JANE: Say, Jack, remember you asked me why we didn't carry the new polyvinyl wrap for chicken? Well, I received a sales bulletin from the division office, and not only do we carry it, but the price is below that of the film you're buying now.

JACK: That's a good one. You guys sell so much, you don't have time to find out everything you're selling. Next time we'll switch over to that new wrap. I hope it "breathes" good and lets the tissue gases escape. We had 50 chickens spoil last month, you know.

JANE: Don't worry! It won't cause any spoilage.

JACK: Well, I better get to work. Thanks for catching my error.

JANE: Okay, Jack. We'll see you.

The two leave, walk to the car, and drive away.

JANE: Now I'm going up to South Eleventh to call on the manager of the New Towers Building. I'm trying to get him to purchase our new custodial service unit. This unit selling works fine sometimes—like at the market—but other times these people don't want to buy everything from you. Are you going to come in?

EDWARDS: No, Jane, I'll sit here and catch up on my study notes.

JANE: Okay.

She parks the car and goes in to see the manager. Twenty minutes later she returns.

JANE: I don't understand it. I've talked with that fellow about using our service on three separate occasions. He's real interested, listens, asks questions, but when I try to get an order all he says is, "I'll check into it." I wish he'd let me know one way or the other.

EDWARDS: Who's next on your call schedule?

JANE: Dairy O, that high-volume hamburger and milkshake outfit. Ed Stenuf is the manager.

EDWARDS: Let's go.

They arrive at the Dairy O, and Austin and Edwards go in. Ed Stenuf is out front waiting on customers.

JANE: Hi, Ed.

ED: Hello, Jane.

JANE: Ed, this is Phil Edwards from our L.A. headquarters.

EDWARDS: Good to meet you, Ed. Jane tells me you've got a good business here.

ED: Oh, we're doing pretty good.

JANE: Well, Ed, can we stock up your bag, napkin, and container-cup inventories?

ED: Well, you know, your competition was in yesterday offering prices below yours. So if you people can't match 'em, we'll have to switch over.

JANE: Well, Ed, Sandwell likes to be as competitive as the next guy. We give our customers quality goods with the best service of any other supplier. We keep track of your supplies, and you never have to worry about being short.

ED: I know, Jane, but these fellows are offering a good hard dollar-and-cents deal. Those shake containers go for $12.70 a three-gross box, and they're offering the same for $12.00.

JANE: I'll have to check at the office tomorrow, and I'll come out and talk price with you.

ED: Okay, Jane. Excuse me, I've got a customer.

JANE: See you tomorrow, Ed.

They walk out to the car.

JANE: There goes some good business. Do you think we can match their price?

EDWARDS: We just can't let everyone who wants a little more business scare us into dropping our prices, after all we've done to stabilize our price level. You better check with George [Murphy] this afternoon and see what develops.

JANE: You bet! Now comes the big push—I call on all my Dairy Queen stores. My big accounts take a lot of time. These little stores don't seem to be worth the time the other fellows give them. Say, it's about 2:30. Did you want to go back to the office?

EDWARDS: Yes, I've got to see George about a warehouse mix-up. Medallion sent out the wrong paper in a carton with proper order labels on it.

Jane drops Edwards off and starts her calls on the Dairy Queen stores.

Resale Selling

Edwards had told salesperson Bob Thomas to pick him up before making calls Friday morning. Bob had been with Sandwell for four years, selling mainly industrial goods to resale dealers or retail merchants. Before joining Sandwell, Bob had been employed as a salesperson for a grocery products company. He was to meet Edwards at the office at 8:30 A.M.

EDWARDS: Who do we see today?

BOB: I'm after my resale picnic supply outlets [independent retail stores and chain supermarkets]. The sales department finally got out the new picnic supplies display rack. I guess there was quite a battle deciding what suppliers would get on it.

EDWARDS: Yes, that's an excellent point-of-sale display.

BOB: Do you think the division is going to make the quota for the salmon-fishing trip?

EDWARDS: The way we're going, it'll be close. You guys have got to dig in.

BOB: What about the new bakery bag order I called Murphy about yesterday? There's good profit in those white multisized baked-goods bags. I don't see all the fuss about whether to put them on an open account so they'll have credit till the end of the month.

EDWARDS: We don't know much about that outfit. You know the policy on doubtful accounts. You guys get big orders with these accounts, but the office has to collect them.

BOB: Well, we need orders to make the quota. It doesn't make much difference to me whether they wait till the end of the month to pay.

EDWARDS: Spoken like a true salesperson. Say, George tells me he's got you fellows keeping a list of all the prospective customers you've called on about the new polyvinyl strapping for unitized lumber.

BOB: Yes, I called on the Medford and the Sellers Lumber Companies Monday. Put on a little demonstration for their salespeople. I'm afraid the introduction fell a little flat, though I told them that the vinyl was stronger than the steel strapping they're now using to hold their unitized lumber packets together during shipment . . . but they started asking some technical questions about strength and shipping and I was having enough trouble getting the band taut and crimped around the lumber unit.

EDWARDS: George said they think this item should be very competitive. The vinyl is 8 to 20 percent cheaper, yet performs as well as steel strapping. It's sure to click.

They arrive at the Careways Market and enter the store. Bob approaches Joe Martin, a buyer for the Careways chain. Introductions are made.

BOB: Say, Joe, it's about time you started stocking up on picnic items.

JOE: How much markup can we expect to get this year?

BOB: Fifteen percent on most.

JOE: How fast did they move last year?

BOB: Stores that got their display racks out near the cash registers, and other good selling points, ordered weekly.

BOB: We've rearranged and substituted some of the items on the rack for maximum sales effect. This year should be the best yet.

JOE: Some of the stuff on the rack we already have in stock from other suppliers. I don't think I'll use the rack. You go ahead and see what we need from the inventory listing, and I'll check back with you in a few minutes to see what you have.

Joe walks off. Bob checks inventory figures and writes up an order for various tissue and toweling items.

BOB: Phil, the pricing on these consumer products is really getting ridiculous. With so many distributors handling them at such low margins, we'll all be out of business. Every day someone is cutting the price, or a manufacturer is handling the account direct or something!

EDWARDS: Yes. Pricing on those high-volume consumer items is a problem.

The two return to Joe Martin.

JOE: Let's see what you came up with. Yes, that's about right. The toweling and napkins stay about the same. Send eight car-

tons of plates, instead of six. Same for the cold cups. Oh, and we won't need any of the plastic knives. They aren't used as much as the forks and spoons.

BOB: All right, Joe. We'll have this order delivered tomorrow.

JOE: Good. So long.

As they leave the store and walk to the car, Bob wonders how he can change Joe's mind on installing some display racks.

BOB: I'll get that rack in there. I'll get back to see him Monday for a little chat. I've got lots of accounts to call on, but I have a flexible schedule, so I can put in a little extra selling effort when I think it's worthwhile.

EDWARDS: A few racks in that Careways chain would really up sales.

BOB: I'll say. I'm going to Smith Company. Did you want to go up there too?

EDWARDS: Well, if you could drop me off at the office on your way up there, it would be convenient for me. I'm supposed to see George at 11:00.

BOB: Okay, fine.

Back at the office, Phil Edwards talked with George Murphy about the weaknesses of the three salespeople and how additional sales training could remedy the problems.

▶ 11 ◀

Territory Design

Remember that time is money.
BENJAMIN FRANKLIN

LEARNING OBJECTIVES

After studying this chapter, you should be able to:

▶ Decide when sales territories should be used.

▶ Explain the advantages of sales territories.

▶ Design territories using the workload and buildup methods.

▶ Understand how computers help build sales territories.

► WHY USE TERRITORIES?

A *territory* is defined as customers located in a geographic area that are assigned to an individual salesperson. The primary benefit of using sales territories is improved market coverage—which usually means better customer relations. Having each field rep assigned to a specific group of customers and prospects enables the salesperson to know each customer's needs, which, in turn, leads to improved service on orders and delivery. Many customers prefer building an enduring relationship with a single field rep rather than having to get acquainted with a new person on each call. Sales Management in Action 11-1 describes how technology is making territory design easier.

Motivation and Cost Savings

The use of territories also benefits salespeople. When salespeople know that all of the customers in an area are their responsibility they are more likely to put forth extra efforts to satisfy customers' demands. This sole responsibility for a territory increases salespeople's involvement and pride in their jobs. They participate in goal setting

---

Sales Management in Action 11-1
Territories by Design

Dividing up sales territories is an infrequent event because of the complexity of the task. However, today even small firms are able to employ computer mapping software to simplify the process. For example, a sporting goods rep organization with seven salespeople used a program offered by GeoQuery of Naperville, Illinois, to create sales territories. When the company plotted the location of its 200 top accounts on the territory maps, they found examples of overlapping coverage and misallocated resources. The maps were so vivid and convincing that the salespeople voluntarily adjusted their account assignments with little or no hassle.

Western Sales Company, a rep firm that sells to 300 plumbing distributors, used mapping software to help fuel a 20 percent sales increase in a 40 percent down market.

Their objective was to divide up the work load of four outside salespeople to create equitable territories and increase sales. Western begins with the selection of an arbitrary geographic area near the salesperson's home. The accounts and contacts from the company database are displayed on Geo-Query maps. The territories are each reviewed to be sure a salesperson can write enough business to justify the territory's existence. If it is too big it is divided or shared with another salesperson. Even before hiring is done, an area can be plotted to see whether there is enough volume for another rep. Now the company can try out territories in a few minutes where before it would have taken 90 days.

Source: Richard Lewis, "Putting Sales on the Map," *Sales & Marketing Management* (August 1993), pp. 78–80.

and have benchmarks by which they can evaluate their own success. Hiring sales-people to match customers' requirements in each territory can greatly improve the effectiveness of the sales force.

Sales territories can be justified economically because they help reduce market-ing costs. When only one person covers each geographic area, *duplication of sales calls* and related travel costs are eliminated. Salespeople in well-designed territories spend less time traveling and more time selling, resulting in lower sales costs as a percentage of sales.

Evaluation and Control

The performance of individual salespeople can be more easily controlled and eval-uated with sales territories. When territories are well balanced in terms of potential, differences across territories can be attributed to the abilities of individual salespeo-ple. Thus when salespeople have their own areas, performance can be more easily compared across time, and against sales potential and sales quotas.

When Are Territories Unnecessary?

Although sales territories have many benefits, companies that sell directly to consum-ers, such as real estate brokers, stockbrokers, insurance salespeople, and some door-to-door salespeople, do not have assigned territories. Territories are not essential when salespeople contact customers infrequently and spend most of their time pros-pecting for new clients. For example, one salesperson sold an amazing $1.3 million of Mary Kay Cosmetics to friends in Minneapolis in a calendar year. This feat would not have been possible if Mary Kay had restricted its consultants to specific areas.

▶ TERRITORY DESIGN PROCEDURES

The effective design of sales territories is basically a six-part decision process (Figure 11-1). A variety of events can trigger adjustments in field sales territories. When two firms merge, there is often a need to combine sales forces to save money and ensure adequate market coverage. Territories are also redesigned when sales in an area grow to the point where the existing salesperson is unable to handle the business. Some-times territories are revised to take into account product line changes or relocation of the company's or customer's plants. Each step in the territory design process can be done manually or with the help of a computer. We will start by discussing each step and then describe how territories can be designed using computer programs.

Select Control Units

The first step in the process is to select appropriate *geographic control units* that can be combined to form sales territories. Control units must be small enough to allow flex-ibility in setting boundaries but not so small as to require massive data manipulation. These units must have less area than a territory and clearly recognized boundaries. Examples of commonly used geographic control units are described in Table 11-1. At first glance, countries would seem to be too large a unit for designing sales territories. However, a firm that is exporting goods to Europe might combine several small coun-tries such as Holland, Belgium, and Luxembourg into one territory. States or provinces

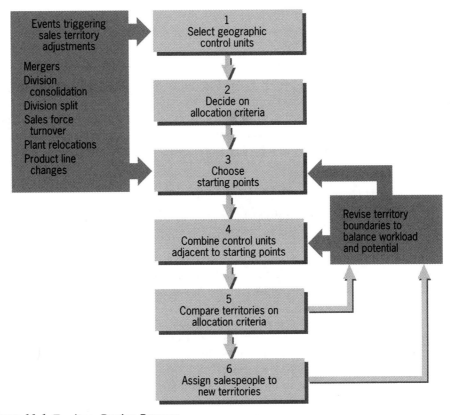

Figure 11-1: Territory Design Process

may also appear to be too big for combination into territories. States are most often used as control units when a firm attempts to cover a whole country with a few sales-people. Small states such as Rhode Island, Connecticut, Massachusetts, and New Hampshire are frequently combined to create single territories.

When a firm does a lot of urban business, cities or metropolitan areas can be desirable control units. Firms that divide up cities into several sales territories often rely on zip codes or census tracts as control units. The ultimate control unit involves building territories by combining groups of customers. This approach is not often followed because the computational burden becomes excessive. Only when a company has a very limited number of large customers can accounts serve as territorial design control units. The most common approach in the United States is to build up

Table 11-1   Geographic Control Units Used in Territory Design

Countries	Cities
States or provinces	Zip codes
Counties	Census tracts
Metropolitan areas	Customers

territories using counties. They are small enough to expedite territory construction, and potentials data are routinely published for these units.

Decide on Allocation Criteria

A variety of criteria such as *equality of opportunity*, number of current customers, and sales potential can be employed to combine control units into viable sales territories. The idea of building sales territories to ensure equality on some dimensions has great appeal to both sales managers and salespeople. Equality among territories should provide a sense of fair play since every salesperson has a chance to earn equal pay.

Quantitative Factors   Three basic *allocation criteria* include:

1. Number of current customers.
2. Potential (number of possible accounts or Buying Power Index).
3. Size (square miles or square kilometers).

The current customer base provides a good estimate of the present workload. It is desirable to include some existing customers in each sales territory you create. Having some regular customers helps boost sales force morale and provides a minimum income for reps paid on commission. Current dollar sales in an area should not be used as the sole allocation criterion, as it ignores future potential. Furthermore, a salesperson who has worked hard to build up a territory will be quite unhappy if his or her territory is split up on the basis of current sales and a new person reaps the benefits of those past labors.

Potential is an important design factor because sales managers are interested in new business growth. Potential can be measured as the number of customers who could use your product or as an index such as the Buying Power Index. When potentials are poorly allocated across territories, salespeople often spend too little time opening accounts. Balancing territories on the basis of geographic size has a direct impact on sales force efficiency. When some territories are much larger than others, salespeople will spend excessive time driving between accounts and not enough time closing sales. Remember that when you make territories compact, you also help reduce travel expenses.

Additional Factors   Other factors that influence the design of sales territories include the location of rivers, lakes, bridges, mountains, and roads. Sales managers often keep relief maps in their offices so that they can see how topographical features will influence sales force travel patterns. The availability of bridges and superhighways often influences how boundaries are drawn for sales territories. Sometimes information on the special needs and requirements of large accounts has an effect on territory design.

Choose Starting Points

The third step in territory design is to select geographic locations to serve as *starting points* for new territories. A common choice is the salesperson's present home, because the cost of relocating salespeople can be avoided and representatives remain near family and friends. Another popular starting point is a large city. Salespeople in urban locations usually have access to a large number of customers, and there is less need for extensive travel. An alternative method is to design the sales territory around the needs of major clients. In this case, the location of the largest customer in an area might be selected as the home base for the salesperson, and other areas might be added to complete the territory. Occasionally a starting point will be a central geographic location, and the preferences of the salesperson or the presence of a city is disregarded. This approach assumes that a place can be found for the salesperson to live after the territory has been created.

The problems of finding starting points for sales territories can be illustrated by looking at a map of the state of Kentucky (Figure 11-2). This map shows the location of counties, major cities, and county population as a measure of potential. If two salespeople are placed in Kentucky, then one would probably be located in Louisville to cover the western half of the state. The second would be placed in Lexington to handle the east. Neither location is very good because they are on the extreme northeastern or northwestern edges of the two territories. In addition, the Lexington-based salesperson would have to travel to the northern tip of the state to cover Covington, which is across the Ohio River from Cincinnati. The heavy concentration of business in the Cincinnati area would probably lead this salesperson to neglect some of the mountainous areas in the southeastern part of the territory. One possible solution would be to give Boone, Kenton, and Campbell counties to the Cincinnati-based salesperson.

If three salespeople are assigned to Kentucky, then the third territory would be placed in the western part of the state. Possible starting points for this territory would be Bowling Green, Owensboro, and Paducah. Owensboro has the disadvantage of being on the northern edge of the territory, and Paducah is too far to the west. A Paducah location would require extensive travel in an east–west pattern. Also, the north–south orientation of Kentucky Lake and Lake Barkley further complicates travel patterns in the area. One answer would be to carve off the seven most westerly counties and give them to a salesperson in another state. This example shows how difficult it is to find starting points for sales territories when you have an irregularly shaped state bounded by rivers and containing noncentral population clusters. You can also see why some firms use independent agents to cover sparsely populated areas.

Combine Adjacent Control Units

Once starting points have been selected, the next step is to begin combining control units. The most popular way to do this is known as the *buildup method*. To be effective, you need to keep running totals on the allocation criteria for each new territory. If number of customers per county is the criterion, you first combine the counties adjacent to each starting point and keep track of the total number of customers in each territory. Then you assign counties between different starting points to territories to balance the number of customers across the new territories. The process of allocating counties to starting points continues until all control units are assigned to individual salespeople.

An example of three sales territories that were built up around the suggested starting points for Kentucky is shown in Figure 11-3. The territories were constructed

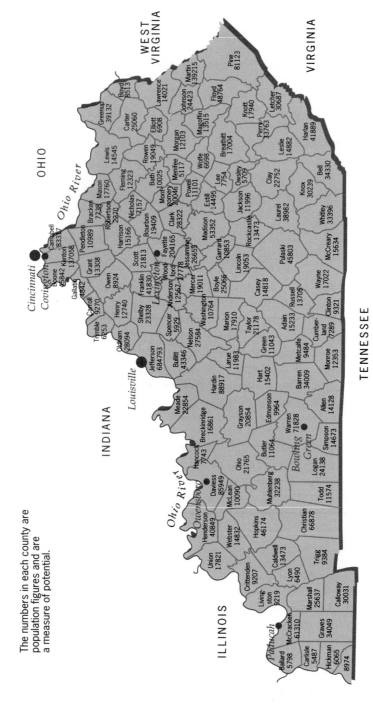

Figure 11-2: Kentucky Counties, Major Cities, and Population Centers

The numbers in each county are
population figures and are
a measure of potential.

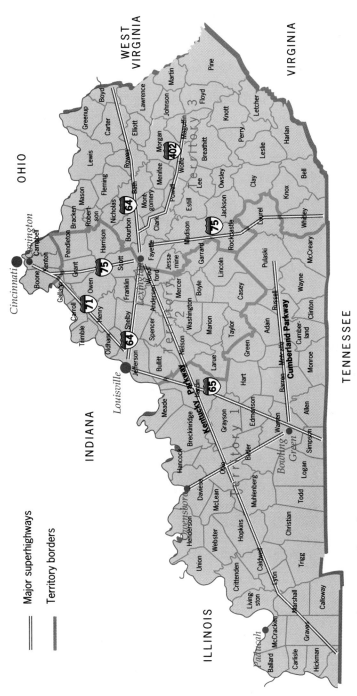

Major superhighways

Territory borders

Figure 11-3: Three Kentucky Sales Territories

using the county population figures shown in Figure 11-2. Note that the solution was simplified by including the three northernmost counties in the Cincinnati territory. Territory 2 turned out to be the smallest because of the heavy population concentration in the Louisville–Frankfort area. Territory 1 is large and ungainly, but it can be covered quite well from Bowling Green using Route 64, Cumberland Parkway, Kentucky Parkway, and the Green River Parkway. Routes 64 and 75 are available to travel the northern and western parts of territory 3. However, the rest of territory 3 is mountainous and will be extremely difficult to cover.

Compare Sales Territories

After you make an initial allocation of control units to starting points, you need to compare territories using other criteria. For example, if a set of territories has the same number of customers, you would then calculate the square miles in each territory to see how the territories compare in size. If there is an imbalance, you look at counties on the borders of the territories to see if some switching could improve the initial allocation. The solution may be to shift a large county with few customers from the biggest to the smallest territory. Unfortunately, large and small territories are not always contiguous, and switches often must be made across several territories. *Balancing territories* on several important criteria, such as customers, potential, and size, is often very difficult.

A comparison of three sales territories created for Kentucky (Figure 11-3) is provided in Table 11-2. The three territories are well matched in terms of potential as measured by population. The largest and smallest territories vary less than 1 percent on this dimension. In terms of size, however, territory 2 is only 60 percent as large as the other territories. This means that territory 2 would be relatively easy to cover, whereas the others present some problems. With the present boundaries, the salesperson in territory 3 has to cross part of territory 1 to get to Whitley County in the south (Figure 11-3). If the salesperson has to cross Laurel County, why not shift Laurel from territory 1 to territory 3? Although this move would help balance the territories in terms of size, it would lead to greater imbalance on potential. The salesperson in territory 1 would have to give up potential represented by 38,982 people. In this particular case, territory 1 might be willing to give up Laurel County because the Cumberland Parkway stops in neighboring Pulaski County. Given the uneven distri-

Table 11-2   Comparing Three Kentucky Sales Territories

Territory[a]	Potential as Measured by Population	Number of Counties
1	1,124,897	47
2	1,129,290	27
3	1,131,137	43

[a]Boundaries of the territories are shown in Figure 11-3.

bution of potential across Kentucky, there is no way that the three territories can be perfectly balanced on both size and potential.

The problem of designing three territories for Kentucky gets more complicated when you introduce a third allocation factor, such as the number of customers. Many salespeople receive commission income, and it is important to balance territories based on existing customers so that wages do not get out of line. However, keeping track of three allocation variables as you move counties back and forth among territories gets rather confusing. One solution that we will discuss later is to use a computer to help you design sales territories.

A Workload Approach

An alternative to the traditional buildup method of creating territories is the *workload approach*. This technique focuses on the development of territories that are equivalent in terms of the work to be performed. The key step is the determination of the optimum call frequency for particular classes of customers. Present and potential customers are located on a map, and the number of firms in each class is multiplied by the theoretical call frequencies to give a total number of planned calls for each area. Adjacent areas are then combined to create territories with a proscribed number of annual sales calls.

An example showing how the workload approach was successfully employed occurred recently at Kodak's professional imaging division.[1] Kodak was experiencing problems with customers because salespeople had to call on a wide variety of clients and sell a vast array of products. Sally Malloy had to sell film and paper to portrait and wedding labs, commercial color labs, and professional resellers. Each type of customer had special needs and Sally had to be familiar with over 60 types of film. To improve customer service, Kodak shifted from straight geographical territories where reps had to sell everything to everyone, to customer-oriented territories that recognized the special skills of each salesperson. The new territories were created with a geographic mapping program. This showed the locations of different types of customers on a computer screen and the home bases of each salesperson. Annual call frequencies were developed for each account and the special selling skills of the 300 salespeople were identified. The sales force was reorganized into three groups for commercial services and six for portrait/wedding and photographer/resellers. Sally Malloy is now assigned to a new territory in Chicago where she calls exclusively to commercial photo labs. Sally's dollar volume is less and her customer base has dropped from 500 to 60. However, Sally is a lot happier, her compensation has remained the same, and her new territory allows her to do a better job of solving customers' problems. A workload approach to territory design was successful for Kodak because salespeople are paid salaries and are not compared on the basis of sales volume.

Dividing a Large Territory

A common problem that you will encounter as sales manager is how to divide a territory that has too many present and/or potential customers for one person to

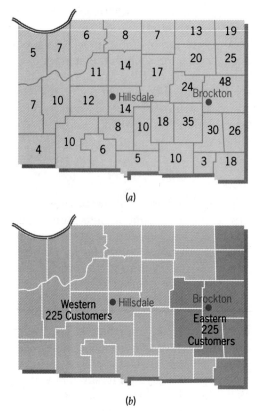

(a)

(b)

Figure 11-4: Dividing a Large Territory

handle. A map of an area to be divided into two sales territories is shown in Figure 11-4a. The map shows the present number of customers per county for one sales-person working the territory from Brockton. A logical home base for the second sales-person is Hillsdale, located in the west–central part of the territory. If these two cities are used as starting points, new territories can be constructed by adding and sub-tracting adjacent counties until all counties are assigned and the number of customers is the same for both territories.

Proposed new territories are shown in Figure 11-4b. Note that the heavy concen-tration of customers in the Brockton area has produced one small territory in the eastern region and one very large territory in the west. Although the two new terri-tories have the same number of customers (225), the western territory requires con-siderable travel since the customers are more scattered. This solution may be acceptable if the current salesperson is located in Brockton and has reached an age where a smaller geographic territory would be appreciated. An alternative solution is to divide the area into northern and southern territories, with Brockton located at the boundary between the two. While the size of the territories, number of customers, and travel time would be equalized, the territories would be wide and narrow. If both salespeople were traveling west from Brockton, travel expenses would be greater than with the solution in Figure 11-4b.

The next step in the buildup process is to consider sales potential figures for each county. The western territory has more undeveloped potential than the eastern region, and the two new territories would be more balanced on size and potential if four or five western counties are shifted to the Brockton territory. Unfortunately, the current workload is then out of balance, since the eastern territory would have about 50 more customers. The example shows that variations in the dispersion of customers and potential across areas make it extremely difficult to construct territories that are equivalent in terms of travel time, number of present customers, and sales potential. Since both the buildup and workload methods create territories by combining geographic areas according to a set of rules, computers can be employed to speed the search for the most efficient territory boundaries.

▶ DESIGNING TERRITORIES BY COMPUTER

Computers are now routinely used to help design sales territories. Sales managers can save a great deal of time by building territories with computer programs. In one firm where it took up to a day to redefine boundaries for a single territory, the whole job can now be done in a few hours on a computer.[2] Territory design programs function by automating some or all of the design processes shown in Figure 11-1. There are basically three types of these programs. The simplest are inexpensive mapping programs. More complicated approaches employ simulation or optimization routines.

Territory Mapping Programs

Mapping programs are used to display territory data on computer screens. First, you feed the computer basic information on potentials, number of present accounts, home locations of salespeople, and geographic boundaries of the control units. Then you draw tentative territory boundaries, using a mouse or numeric key pad. The program displays your planned territories in color on the screen, along with summary data on potentials, current accounts, and geographic size. Through an interactive process of trial and error, you reallocate control units to balance your territories.

STARmanager Advanced Edition, published by TTG, Inc., is an example of a commercial mapping program. This microcomputer program can be purchased for $995 and used to reallocate territories and draw maps for salespeople. The program has the advantage that territory maps are tied in with spreadsheets that show current potentials, sales, and target number of calls. Any changes made in allocations of control units to territories are automatically reflected in the spreadsheet data. You should be aware that STARmanager is an interactive program that helps you create territories, but it does not find an optimum design. A recent survey turned up 12 different mapping programs that were available for an average price of $598.[3] Descriptions of some of these programs are given in Table 11-3. Sales Management in Action 11-2 shows how one company uses an interactive mapping program.

Table 11-3 Sales Territory Mapping Programs

Vendor	Package	Description	Price
GeoQuery Corp.	GeoQuery	Interactive maps for travel planning and territory analysis. Direct links to contact management programs.	$295
TTG, Inc.	STARmanager Advanced Edition	Territory mapping system that integrates sales and marketing data for interactive territory analysis, realignment, and monitoring.	$995
Sammamish Data Systems	GeoSight Professional	Geographic information systems for sales territory creation and management. Includes address matching.	$1,850
Metron, Inc.	TerrAlign	Optimal sales territory alignment and analysis. Exclusive OptAlign technology automatically balances territories and decreases driving time.	$20,000+

Source: Sales & Marketing Management (December 1994), pp. 59–60.

Sales Management in Action 11-2
Interactive Mapping Programs

Dividing up sales territories is a headache for most companies. Stephanie Thompson, manager of marketing programs at Perdue Frederic Pharmaceuticals, recalls: "We used to sit down with our district sales manager for days and do a ton of manual calculations to put together our territories." As the company grew in size, they found they could no longer manage their territories by hand, and they turned to a microcomputer software package. The mapping software allowed Thompson to reconfigure regions in just half a day instead of the several days she previously needed.

The interactive computer program selected uses data on zip code locations of physicians, current call activities, and major highway routes to build territories. As the territories are put together, they are shown as maps on a computer screen and summarized on spreadsheets. This allows managers to balance territories on potentials and other variables. The computer-generated territories are fine-tuned during meetings with regional and district managers. Although "the software is a wonderful thing, nothing takes the place of a district manager's knowledge."

Perdue Frederic believes the computerized system works better than the old approach. Salespeople can see that new assignments are fair because objective criteria are used. The company no longer makes the arbitrary assignments of physicians that were common under the old plan. Also, salespeople now get printed maps and lists of physicians to be called on that were not available with the manual program.

Source: Tom Eisenhart, "Drawing a Map to Better Sales," Business Marketing (January 1990), pp. 59–61.

Simulating New Territories

A more advanced approach to territory design employs computer simulation procedures. With simulation, you set up an objective function and attempt to minimize it, subject to a set of constraints. Some computer programs use an objective function designed to ensure compactness, called the *moment of inertia*. This is simply the sum of the squares of distances from the control units to the trial territory centers weighted by the potential in each area. The smaller the moment of inertia, the greater the compactness of the territories that make up the sales district.

Simulation leads to improved territory designs because the computer examines more combinations than a manager is likely to review using an interactive mapping program. However, simulation does not produce the best possible or optimum territories, and multiple runs are needed to find a good solution.

Optimizing Territory Design

The most sophisticated design programs balance territories optimally, using several factors, and minimize driving time. These optimizing programs are quite complicated and must be run on high-powered computers. TerrAlign, published by Metron, Inc., requires a Windows operating system, and sells for $20,000 and up.[4] This program is described in Table 11-3. Tactics International, Ltd., offers a territory modeling program called Heavy Duty Tactician for $9,995.[5] The high cost of *optimizing programs* suggests that they are most appropriate for firms with large numbers of field salespeople.

Guiding Reps to Clients

Computers can also be used to guide salespeople to the location of customers within the territories you have created. Cars can be equipped with a radio that communicates with a Global Positioning System (GPS) satellite and an onboard computer with detailed maps. The salesperson simply enters the location in the territory that he wants to go to, and the computer provides on-screen directions.[6] The GPS system locates the car within a few feet and can even tell you what lane to be in to make a turn. These systems are available on Avis rental cars in 14 cities and can be purchased as a $1,995 option on new Oldsmobile 88s.

Limitations of the Computer Approach

Computers are being used successfully to build territories and guide reps to customer locations. However, they sometimes make mistakes when they don't know about traffic congestion, the location of rivers, and other natural barriers. One computer-designed sales territory was split down the middle by the Appalachian Trail. This meant that the salesperson would have to spend a great deal of time traveling up and down narrow mountain roads to get from one half of the territory to the other. To avoid these problems, the computer either has to be told about the barriers or managers must make manual adjustments.

► TERRITORY ASSIGNMENTS

The last step in our territory design process is to assign salespeople to individual territories (Figure 11-1). This task is usually completed by district sales managers. The decisions are made by matching the background and needs of salespeople with the opportunities in each geographic area. Factors considered include the present home location, age, and experience of salespeople; the size of the territories; and the customer mix located in each area. For example, some firms try initially to place newly hired young people in territories near the areas where they have grown up or gone to school. This makes it easier for new reps to get started and can reduce first-year turnover. On the other hand, experienced salespeople may be given more remote territories that are full of undeveloped sales potential.

You should realize that territory boundaries do not last forever, and you have to adjust them continually to resolve local issues (Figure 11-1). These include situations where salespeople run into personal problems and are unable to handle all their accounts. Also, you may have a situation where the special needs of a customer require a more experienced rep. Often these problems can be resolved by assigning a few accounts to salespeople in adjacent territories. The idea is to fine-tune territory boundaries without having to go through a complete redesign that would upset everyone.

► ETHICAL ISSUES

Often the success and the income of field reps are directly affected by the size and potential of their assigned territories. However, it is difficult to create territories that are equivalent in terms of potential and travel time. The three Kentucky territories shown in Figure 11-3 are a case in point. Louisville is clearly the best territory, and the sales manager has to decide who gets this plum. Some managers solve this problem by giving the best territories to their friends or relatives. Others may extort favors or cash from reps who get the best areas. Both of these approaches are unethical and not in the long-term interests of the company.

The authors know of one situation where a salesperson was replaced in a sales territory because of a failure to "load up" dealers with inventory. In this case, the manager made territory assignments on the basis of who would best achieve his short-term goals of beating his quota and maximizing his bonus. Sometimes managers are reluctant to reorganize territories because this will force reps to relocate and make them learn to sell in new markets. Managers who become too personally involved with their reps may be unable to make the tough choices that maximize profits to the firm. Ethical territory assignment procedures do not penalize one party at the expense of another.

► SUMMARY

Sales territories are geographic areas assigned to individual salespeople to help improve market coverage and reduce travel time. Territories are often created by combining groups of counties around a home base for a salesperson. The objective of territory design is to build areas that are similar in size, workload, and potential. Sales managers can then identify those salespeople who are performing well and those who are having problems. Territory design involves a six-step process that begins with the selection of geographic control units. Next, you have to decide what allocation criteria to use and pick starting points for the territories.

Then you combine adjacent control units to build up territories and compare them on the basis of allocation criteria. Because of the difficulty of balancing territories using several criteria, computers are becoming popular to solve complex design problems. Computers help keep track of sales and account data and can speed up the creation of new territories. Remember, sales territory boundaries need continual adjustment to respond to changing conditions in the field.

▶ KEY TERMS

Allocation criteria	Mapping programs
Balancing territories	Moment of inertia
Buildup method	Optimizing programs
Duplication of sales calls	Starting points
Equality of opportunity	Territory
Geographic control units	Workload approach

▶ REVIEW QUESTIONS

1. Why do firms go to the trouble of dividing customers' locations into sales territories?
2. What are the most common geographic control units used to construct territories?
3. When sales managers combine control units into different territories, what are their guiding allocation criteria?
4. Describe the most popular starting points used to build sales territories.
5. Why is it so difficult to build territories that are equivalent in terms of number of customers and size?
6. What advantage does the computer offer to territorial design? Disadvantages?
7. What features should you look for in computer programs used to design sales territories?
8. Why is it important to have detailed maps when you are redesigning sales territories?

▶ PROBLEMS

1. Although insurance agents rarely have exclusive territories, insurance companies are finding that mapping programs are quite useful. Sales managers load demographic data, policies in force, and agent locations on computerized area maps. How would a manager use this information?
2. Recently, Merck Pharmaceutical Manufacturing Company bought Medco, a large mail order drug retailer, for $6 billion. Medco also manages pharmaceutical benefit programs for 1,500

health plans. How can Merck use the data available from its new Medco subsidiary to plan its own sales territories?

3. Market Statistics, which produces the *Survey of Buying Power*, is now offering a computer program to help design sales territories. The basic program sells for $5,950 and includes some on-site training. A county data file to use with the program costs $6,950, zip code data sell for $11,950, and both files are priced at $12,950. Major highway data are available for $450. The program displays county and zip code borders on a computer screen and allows you to draw lines to create sales territories. In addition, the program keeps running totals on several control factors. Additional training and support for the program can be purchased for $600 a day plus travel and expenses. How can sales managers justify expenditures of this size to the presidents of their companies? How will you know whether you have an optimum solution with this program? What determines the amount of money you can spend on computer programs to design sales territories?

4. 3M Company in St. Paul, Minnesota, was one of the first corporations to work with computer-augmented territory allocations. The corporate marketing analysis group was given responsibility for reassigning territories in one of 3M's industrial groups. Apparently they were given all the relevant information, including market potential, market share, dollar sales, number of customers, and sales history of each salesperson. Their analysis optimized coverage while minimizing travel costs; the division head was quite pleased. Upon further investigation, though, it turned out that these new territories were useless. For example, one southeastern salesperson was assigned to a territory that was split down the middle by the Appalachian Mountains. It would be almost impossible for him to cover that region. The analysis had left out some important information. What suggestions would you have for the industrial division manager at 3M? For the marketing analysis staff? Is the computer an appropriate tool for territory design?

▶ IN-CLASS EXERCISES

Strike Three

Walker Computer Systems manufactures and sells office computer systems and word processors. It has enjoyed double-digit growth over the past decade due to the growing demand for office automation. Advances in technology have resulted in increased capacity and lower prices in office PCs. As a result, the demand for office automation equipment has exploded as smaller businesses have begun to automate their offices.

One of the consequences of this growth is that Walker has constantly had to increase its sales force, to the point where there are now over 400 salespeople servicing the U.S. market. This has meant constant adjustments to territories, with the result that salespeople are usually given a reduced geographic area to cover. Another adjustment has been in the sales force compensation program because of increased competition and the need to reduce costs. At the same time, the selling cycle time has been decreasing steadily as primary market demand increased and people became more familiar with office automation technology. Just six months ago, Walker introduced a new sales compensation plan designed to place more emphasis on strategic product lines as opposed to total sales volume.

Kim Bryant is the district sales manager for the Texas district. Kim joined Walker six years ago and was promoted to district manager after four years in sales, the last two as the top salesperson in the Southern Region. Kim manages seven people who are located in Dallas, Houston, Austin, Amarillo, and San Antonio. The last person was added just nine months ago in Austin. Due to increased demand, Kim is being asked to add another person to the Dallas–Fort Worth area. Kim's idea is to have the new person cover the Fort Worth area, while Aaron Hughes, the current Walker rep in the area, continues to service the Dallas and mid-cities (cities located between Dallas and Fort Worth) area. This is the second reduction in Aaron's area in the past year, so Aaron will not be happy to hear of the change. This area, however, is believed to have a lot of untapped potential and more demand than one person can cover.

Aaron Hughes currently services the Dallas–Fort Worth area for Walker Computer Systems. For the past three years, Aaron has been the top rep in the Texas district and is one of the top 10 salespeople in the company in terms of total sales volume. Aaron has turned down opportunities for promotion to management on several occasions. One reason for the decision is that Aaron would have to take a cut in pay over the short term. Last year Aaron made just over $160,000 in commissions.

Aaron's Response

"What do you mean 'redesigning' my territory?" bellows Aaron. "Don't you really mean 'reducing' my territory? First, you take Waco away from me. That's strike one. Then you change the compensation plan so that I have to work twice as hard to make as much as I did last year—strike two. Now you want to 'redesign' my territory. That's strike three and I'm out—as in out of this company."

Kim tries to calm Aaron down and tells Aaron that he has no choice in this matter. The order came from headquarters. Aaron is not buying this and replies, "There are a lot of office companies that would like to hire the top Walker rep in the South."

Kim does not want to lose Aaron or have a disgruntled former star salesperson in the district. She is convinced that adding another person to the Dallas–Fort Worth area is the right thing to do for the business. Remember that she is the district sales manager, not the regional or national sales manager. Break into small groups and discuss how Kim should resolve this problem.

Questions:

1. Why do companies redesign territories?
2. What mistakes were made in the Walker territory realignment?
3. What options are available to make territory changes work?
4. Should the company give in to Hughes and not change his territory?

Be prepared to present your group's suggestions when your instructor calls on you.

▶ REFERENCES

1. MELISSA CAMPANELLI, "A New Focus," *Sales & Marketing Management* (September 1995), pp. 56–58.

2. TOM EISENHART, "Drawing a Map to Better Sales," *Business Marketing* (January 1990), pp. 59–61.

3. "Software Directory," *Sales & Marketing Management* (December 1993), pp. 101–102.

4. TERRALIGN, Metron, Inc., 1481 Chain Bridge Road, McLean, VA 22101.

5. "Software Directory," *Sales & Marketing Management* (December 1993), p. 102.

6. Tom Dellecave, "Lost in New York, Onboard Navigation Keeps Reps on the Right Road," *Sales & Marketing Management* (May 1996), pp. 98–103.

CASE

11-1 D. F. HARDWARE COMPANY*

The D. F. Hardware Company was a hardware wholesaler/distributor located in Cleveland, Ohio. The company handled hardware products for a number of manufacturers, selling primarily to retail hardware stores in the greater Cleveland area. Sales were made by a company salesperson, Ted Tyler, who called on the local retailers. D. F. Hardware Co. trucks later delivered the purchased products to these retailers. Tyler reported to Matt Simmons, the company's General Manager, who also acted in the capacity of D. F. Hardware's sales manager. With only one salesperson, this position did not occupy much of Simmons' time.

One of D. F. Hardware's most valued suppliers was the Livingston Tool Corporation, a large manufacturer of hand and power tools. Livingston Tool sold its products in many markets, one of which was retail hardware stores such as were sold by D. F. Hardware. In this particular market, Livingston Tool used selective distributors, since most of the stores were small and widely distributed. D. F. Hardware had functioned as a distributor for Livingston Tool for a number of years in the Cleveland marketplace. The association between the two companies was very amiable; D. F. Hardware valued the Livingston Tool distributorship and its line of high quality products, and Livingston Tool was also pleased with D. F. Hardware's performance in the marketplace.

In April 1978, Cecil Andrews, the national sales manager of Livingston Tool, approached Simmons with an interesting offer. Livingston Tool was revising its policy on its distributor network. Instead of using several distributors to cover a market area, Livingston Tool was consolidating and attempting to cover the same area with an exclusive distributorship. In Ohio,

for example, Livingston Tool had been using distributors in Columbus, Toledo, Cincinnati, and Steubenville in addition to D. F. Hardware in Cleveland. Andrews wanted to replace the five with a single distributor that would be granted the exclusive right to sell Livingston Tool products in the state of Ohio. He offered the exclusive Ohio distributorship to Simmons and D. F. Hardware.

The Dilemma

The Livingston Tool offer was an exciting one for Matt Simmons. As was stated, D. F. Hardware had been pleased with the Cleveland area distributorship, and the thought of having this position for all of Ohio really excited Simmons. The Livingston Tool product line was of high quality, profitable, and fast moving, and Simmons saw it as a major profit maker for D. F. Hardware.

As inviting as the Livingston Tool offer was, Simmons knew its acceptance would involve profound change for his company. The new franchise would necessitate an expansion of D. F. Hardware's sales force, with the establishment of sales territories and sales quotas in the entire Ohio market area. Ted Tyler could continue to sell the Cleveland area, but he could not be expected to cover the entire state of Ohio. In addition, Simmons knew that an acceptance of the Livingston Tool offer would involve changes in his company's physical distribution network, inventory policy, credit policies, and other such related areas.

Simmons found none of these changes formidable enough to warrant the rejection of the Livingston Tool offer. The prospect of having the profitable Livingston Tool franchise for all of Ohio seemed to overshadow any possible obstacles. In addition, he felt that such a move would be the first his company might make in regard to increasing its market penetration and its size. He envisioned that D. F. Hardware would someday be a large regional distributor and that this move was but the forerunner of several similar ones. After weighing all the pros and cons, Simmons accepted Andrews' offer as Livingston Tool's Ohio ex-

*This case was prepared by Robert W. Haas of San Diego State University. From Robert W. Haas, *Industrial Marketing Management*, 3rd ed. (Boston: Kent Publishing Company, 1986), pp. 522–528. © 1986 by Wadsworth, Inc. Reprinted by permission of Kent Publishing Company, a division of Wadsworth, Inc. An adaptation of a publication of the U.S. Government Printing Office.

clusive distributor. Andrews then informed the other four Ohio distributors (in Columbus, Toledo, Cincinnati, and Steubenville) of Livingston Tool's decision and told them that as of June 1, 1978, D. F. Hardware would serve as exclusive distributor in the Ohio market area.

After signing the contract, Simmons felt that his first task was to develop sales territories and quotas and determine how many salespersons the company would need to adequately serve the newly enlarged market area.

Market Characteristics

Not long after the contract was signed, Simmons met with Andrews. This meeting was set up so that Andrews could provide Simmons with market characteristics and other information that would help D. F. Hardware in its new territory. In addition, the meeting was intended to establish the sales volume performance that Livingston Tool expected from D. F. Hardware in Ohio for the coming year. More specifically, Andrews informed Simmons of the following:

1. D. F. Hardware was to sell the Livingston Tool products *only* to retail hardware stores in the Ohio area. Although Livingston Tool products were distributed through other retail outlets such as discount houses, department stores, and farm equipment dealers, the company used other channels to reach these types of customers. Livingston Tool wanted its distributor to cover basically the retail hardware store marketplace.

2. Total U.S. shipments by hand and power tool manufacturers, such as Livingston Tool, had been $2,196.6 million in the previous year, according to data generated by the *Survey of Industrial Purchasing Power*. In that same year, Livingston Tool's shipments amounted to $140.6 million, or 6.4 percent of total shipments. Andrews thought that this 6.4 percent market share estimate was appropriate for the state of Ohio.

3. Andrews estimated that 21.8 percent of hardware store retail sales were accounted for by products similar to those manufactured by Livingston Tool, based on analyses his company had conducted over time. This percentage would give Simmons a good idea of the size of the Ohio retail sales market for the types of products D. F. Hardware would distribute.

4. Andrews expected sales of Livingston Tool products in Ohio to increase by 3.75 percent over the previous year because of increased sales effort due primarily to consolidation of distributors and expected D. F. Hardware's increased sales performance. Livingston Tool would provide D. F. Hardware with sales materials and would participate in cooperative advertising with the distributor to assist in reaching this 3.75 percent objective.

5. Andrews had determined that a typical distributor salesperson could average about 5 sales calls per day, or approximately 1,250 calls in a 250-day work year, based on past experience with other successful distributors across the country. He believed these figures to be appropriate for Ohio but cautioned Simmons to make certain that sales territories were drawn on the basis of both the number of calls to be made and an equal distribution of the total company's sales quota. If these

Exhibit 1: Estimated Total Retail Sales by Hardware Stores SIC 5251 in Ohio by SMSA

SMSA	Estimated Total Retail Sales ($000)	Number of Establishments
Akron	$ 11,797	59
Canton	13,837	49
Cincinnati	31,635	133
Cleveland	39,901	191
Columbus	23,595	93
Dayton	20,139	79
Hamilton–Middletown	4,510	19
Huntington–Ashland	10,037	41
Lima	7,808	36
Lorain–Elyria	6,555	27
Mansfield	2,695	14
Parkersburg–Marietta	2,310	17
Springfield	3,843	16
Steubenville–Weirton	5,300	15
Toledo	16,963	84
Wheeling, W. VA–Ohio	3,531	21
Youngstown–Warren	14,837	40
Total	$219,293	934

Source: U.S. Census of Retail Trade, 1977.

points were not adequately considered, sales-person dissatisfaction would occur and problems would develop. Simmons understood and agreed.

6. Andrews also had determined that a distributor salesperson should call at least once every month on the larger retail accounts (20 or more employees) and at least once every three months on the smaller ones (fewer than 20 employees). He recommended that this would be a good rule of thumb for Simmons to follow, at least initially, in setting up his sales force.

Simmons found the meeting with Andrews to be quite helpful. After their meeting, Simmons began to outline the approach he would use to develop sales territories and quotas and then to determine the optimum number of salespeople for D. F. Hardware to employ. He immediately recognized the need for pertinent data on his Ohio marketplace. The next morning, he visited the library of a large local state

Exhibit 2: Estimated Total Retail Sales by Hardware Stores SIC 5251 in Ohio by Counties Not Included in SMSA Classifications

County	Estimated Total Retail Sales ($000)	Number of Establishments
Ashtabula	$ 3,456	17
Columbiana	5,437	18
Erie	D[a]	5
Hancock	1,383	13
Huron	2,157	12
Licking	D	9
Marion	1,601	11
Muskingum	910	8
Ross	D	5
Sandusky	D	6
Scioto	D	6
Seneca	2,186	4
Tuscarawas	D	10
Wayne	4,839	17
Total	$21,969	141

[a]D indicates counties where retail sales were withheld to avoid disclosing data for individual companies.

Source: U.S. Census of Retail Trade, 1977.

Exhibit 3: Number of Hardware Stores SIC 5251 by Size in Each SMSA and Other Counties in Ohio

SMSA	Outlets with Less Than 20 Employees	Outlets with More Than 20 Employees
Akron	58	1
Canton	45	4
Cincinnati	133	0
Cleveland	186	5
Columbus	88	5
Dayton	75	4
Hamilton–Middletown	18	1
Huntington–Ashland	41	0
Lima	36	0
Lorain–Elyria	26	1
Mansfield	14	0
Parkersburg–Marietta	17	0
Springfield	15	1
Steubenville–Weirton	14	1
Toledo	83	1
Wheeling	21	0
Youngstown–Warren	34	6

Other Counties Outside SMSAs

Ashtabula	16	1
Columbiana	18	0
Erie	5	0
Hancock	13	0
Huron	12	0
Licking	9	0
Marion	11	0
Muskingum	8	0
Ross	5	0
Sandusky	6	0
Scioto	6	0
Seneca	3	1
Tuscarawas	10	0
Wayne	16	1

None of the remaining counties show retail hardware outlets.

Source: Adapted from *Census of Retail Trade*, 1977, and *County Business Patterns*, 1977.

Exhibit 4: Standard Metropolitan Statistical Areas for Ohio

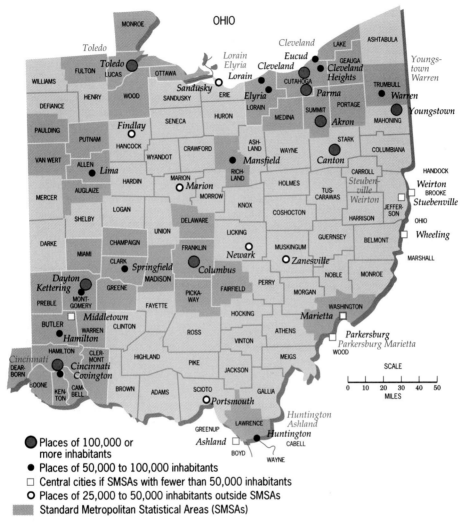

● Places of 100,000 or
  more inhabitants
● Places of 50,000 to 100,000 inhabitants
□ Central cities if SMSAs with fewer than 50,000 inhabitants
○ Places of 25,000 to 50,000 inhabitants outside SMSAs
▨ Standard Metropolitan Statistical Areas (SMSAs)

U.S. Department of Commerce, Bureau of the Census

university to seek out the data he required. Using such sources as the U.S. Department of Commerce's *County Business Patterns* and the *Census of Retail Trade*, he developed Exhibits 1, 2, and 3. He also located a map of Ohio that outlined all standard metropolitan statistical areas (SMSAs) and showed their relationships to all other Ohio counties. This map is shown in Exhibit 4. Since these data were published in the previous year, 1977, Simmons believed they were reliable enough to use in any calculations he might want to make. From these sources, he estimated there were more than 1,000 hardware retail stores in his new market area with total estimated retail sales exceeding $240 million.

With these data, Simmons believed he had sufficient information to determine sales territories and appropriate quotas and decide on the optimum number of salespeople to employ.

CASE

11-2 KENT PLASTICS*

The regional sales manager for Kent Plastics, Jill Hayes, was considering how to reorganize the Indiana district. This area had been divided into two sales territories in the past, with Bill Hicks covering the northern half of the state from Kokomo and Sally Hall covering the southern counties from Columbus (Exhibit 1). However, market growth suggested that four salespeople were now needed. Company policy stated that, when sales in an area exceeded $900,000 per territory, the district had to be divided into smaller segments. Sales in Indiana were currently running $3 million per year.

The Kent Plastics Company began operations as a supplier of plastic parts to manufacturers, but it had expanded into selling plastic bags and meat trays to retailers. Sales personnel were paid a salary plus an annual bonus based on district performance and achievement of territory sales quotas. Travel expenses were paid by Kent, and each salesperson was supplied with a company car.

Jill Hayes wanted to create four compact territories in the state of Indiana that would be similar in terms of sales potential and work load. She felt that equal-opportunity territories would improve morale and make it easier to compare the performance of individual salespersons. Travel expenses would be lower if the territories were designed to minimize the distance from the salespersons' home to different customers' locations. Jill realized, however, that the job of selecting home bases for salespeople was complicated by the heavy concentration of customers located in Marion County in the center of the state.

Counties seemed to be the most logical control units for building new territories, and Jill quickly assembled some statistics for Indiana from secondary sources (Exhibit 2). She obtained the location of each county and major population centers from maps supplied by the Indiana Highway Department (Exhibit 1).

As Jill Hayes looked over the available figures, she wondered what factor or factors would make the

best allocation criteria. Jill had recently obtained a copy of a territory design program published by TTG. Perhaps it was time to call this program up on her computer to help redesign the Indiana district. She knew she had only a few days left to carve out four new territories from the Indiana district before she presented the plan to the sales force at the annual convention. She also had to decide which of the new territories to assign to Bill and Sally.

Exhibit 1: Current Sales Territories and Location of Indiana Counties and Major Cities

*This case was prepared by Douglas J. Dalrymple of Indiana University.

Exhibit 2: Selected Statistics for Indiana Counties

County	Number of Retail Stores	Number of Manufacturing Firms	Value Added by Manufacturing (millions)	Buying Power Index (BPI)	Number of Kent Customers	Kent Sales (thousands)	Square Miles
Adams	273	46	82	.011	3	15	345
Allen	2187	421	832	.150	50	140	671
Bartholomew	542	70	327	.029	10	35	402
Benton	128	5	2	.005	2	3	409
Blackford	174	32	57	.006	2	6	167
Boone	301	38	19	.015	4	8	427
Brown	105	3	1	.004	5	2	319
Carroll	141	19	21	.007	10	16	374
Cass	429	61	88	.019	4	15	415
Clark	642	78	221	.042	32	61	384
Clay	249	13	11	.010	2	6	364
Clinton	307	43	65	.004	10	11	407
Crawford	90	6	3	.005	3	1	312
Daviess	283	38	30	.010	9	18	430
Dearborn	259	30	159	.012	15	24	306
Decatur	213	27	49	.009	8	12	370
DeKalb	324	60	82	.013	22	17	366
Delaware	1153	185	275	.060	21	68	396
Dubois	309	102	101	.012	3	7	433
Elkhart	1229	609	751	.070	15	91	468
Fayette	244	35	99	.012	2	4	215
Floyd	449	73	80	.025	10	21	149
Fountain	257	27	37	.008	3	5	397
Franklin	127	14	9	.006	3	7	394
Fulton	207	40	29	.007	12	13	368
Gibson	313	35	16	.013	15	26	498
Grant	769	120	330	.037	5	45	421
Greene	304	35	15	.011	30	31	549
Hamilton	513	68	55	.029	11	28	401
Hancock	299	39	20	.019	17	27	305
Harrison	175	22	16	.008	8	15	479
Hendricks	381	32	8	.027	23	52	417
Henry	505	55	111	.024	10	17	400
Howard	790	92	535	.047	16	43	293
Huntington	349	71	65	.016	9	32	369
Jackson	331	59	65	.015	7	8	520
Jasper	246	22	95	.010	3	10	562
Jay	239	31	69	.010	12	16	386
Jefferson	279	37	59	.012	4	13	366
Jennings	153	15	14	.008	7	6	377
Johnson	551	55	49	.031	17	49	315
Knox	457	48	49	.018	7	20	516
Kosciusko	564	144	164	.023	24	23	540
LaGrange	203	50	44	.010	5	10	381

Exhibit 2: Selected Statistics for Indiana Counties (*continued*)

County	Number of Retail Stores	Number of Manufacturing Firms	Value Added by Manufacturing (millions)	Buying Power Index (BPI)	Number of Kent Customers	Kent Sales (thousands)	Square Miles
Lake	3746	387	1874	.267	93	310	513
LaPorte	933	169	293	.051	28	63	607
Lawrence	363	60	66	.017	17	18	459
Madison	1281	146	603	.069	8	52	453
Marion	6259	1178	2297	.422	173	527	392
Marshall	428	111	75	.017	3	27	443
Martin	113	12	25	.004	4	6	345
Miami	348	53	46	.015	15	17	377
Monroe	671	60	321	.041	27	54	386
Montgomery	394	41	80	.016	3	11	507
Morgan	352	38	12	.020	19	21	406
Newton	147	13	8	.017	1	6	413
Noble	370	84	76	.013	2	8	412
Ohio	35	2	1	.002	4	2	87
Orange	182	25	23	.006	3	7	405
Owen	121	10	4	.005	1	4	389
Parke	151	8	4	.005	8	9	445
Perry	208	30	51	.007	7	11	384
Pike	149	18	7	.005	3	5	335
Porter	631	69	293	.045	11	63	424
Posey	198	12	8	.008	4	6	412
Pulaski	145	17	12	.003	1	4	433
Putnam	255	25	42	.011	17	21	490
Randolph	321	68	86	.012	15	24	457
Ripley	234	29	77	.010	3	8	442
Rush	196	28	17	.008	7	12	409
St. Joseph	1915	388	486	.109	42	189	466
Scott	153	11	4	.007	2	5	193
Shelby	307	58	68	.012	19	18	409
Spencer	188	7	2	.007	3	11	396
Starke	204	28	12	.009	4	4	310
Steuben	344	45	36	.012	8	14	309
Sullivan	188	29	9	.007	5	6	457
Switzerland	57	8	8	.004	1	2	221
Tippecanoe	871	95	258	.052	51	88	500
Tipton	138	21	16	.006	4	5	261
Union	56	5	1	.003	1	3	168
Vanderburgh	1547	243	523	.077	62	172	241
Vermillion	202	15	81	.007	3	9	263
Vigo	994	143	266	.056	26	99	415
Wabash	363	74	107	.015	19	17	398
Warren	58	7	3	.008	2	5	368
Warrick	233	19	21	.012	14	24	391

Exhibit 2: Selected Statistics for Indiana Counties (*continued*)

County	Number of Retail Stores	Number of Manufacturing Firms	Value Added by Manufacturing (millions)	Buying Power Index (BPI)	Number of Kent Customers	Kent Sales (thousands)	Square Miles
Washington	165	27	25	.007	7	7	516
Wayne	726	125	212	.038	3	58	405
Wells	205	36	66	.010	4	13	368
White	276	31	18	.009	8	7	497
Whitley	236	49	41	.010	4	3	337

▶ 12 ◀

Leadership

Of the best leader, when he is gone, they will say:
we did it ourselves.
CHINESE PROVERB

LEARNING OBJECTIVES

After studying this chapter, you should be able to:

▶ Explain what is meant by leadership.

▶ Determine the appropriate leadership styles for a particular situation.

▶ Know when and how to coach salespeople.

▶ Discuss what is involved in planning and conducting a sales meeting.

▶ Recognize common people problems.

▶ WHERE IS RICHARD WAXLER?

"Where is he now?" Sales managers want to know where their staff is, but there is always one person who marches to the beat of a different drum. In this case his name is Richard Waxler—whereabouts unknown.

He operates as though he hasn't a care in the world. Company policy requires planned itineraries, but you never know when he will roll into the office. He has made the best of a slow territory, so what's the gripe? Richard is popular and well liked by the rest of the sales team, but he is not turning in the documents needed for lost-sales reports. You can't tell where the market is going when you have only half of the information. The usual procedures have been tried, but Richard goes his own way, merrily or otherwise. Now is the time to do something about it, but you don't want to smother his high energy. You must make him realize that he is part of a team.

You are considering several options. Which is the best choice?

1. Set an exact time and place to meet with Richard. At this meeting, tell him that he will not leave the office without first filing an itinerary with you. Also tell him that you expect a written sales report within three days of his return. If he does not abide by these rules, you will hold back bonuses and commissions.

2. Tell other salespeople about the problem and ask them to do what they can to get Richard to fall into line with your policies and procedures.

3. At the next sales meeting, have a major discussion concerning the need for the information that Richard has been omitting. Don't mention any names, but be sure that everyone knows the consequences of not filling out and submitting the proper reports. The guilty should get the hint.

4. Tell Richard that you need to travel with him for a week in order to better critique his methods. Have him prepare the itinerary and include all the details of the upcoming trip.

The most important assets of every company walk out the door each day at 5:00 P.M. Developing and protecting this highly mobile asset is more demanding for sales managers than for other managers. Salespeople may not even come into the office in the morning. They're out in the marketplace every day, and your best salespeople are subject to all sorts of attractive temptations from other companies. Important as money is in ensuring sales force performance, it alone does not inspire loyalty. This is where leadership and supervision are critical.

Which option do you favor to get Richard Waxler to complete his written reports? Some of the options are better than others. Each option is discussed in this chapter.

▶ LEADERSHIP

Leadership is defined as the ability to influence and inspire the actions of people to accomplish worthwhile goals. Leaders inspire trust and loyalty, and they understand how to direct the talents of others toward achieving important objectives. Leadership goes beyond employee supervision to create a vision in which people can believe.

Figure 12-1: Leadership

Research on leadership has revealed that salespeople have more positive views of their jobs, greater commitment, and improved performance when managers clarify sales roles, and demonstrate how salespeople can execute their tasks and how they will be rewarded for their efforts.[1] Great leaders are able to identify sales force needs and show reps the benefits of accomplishing individual and corporate objectives.

Skills

Joe Clayton, Vice President of Sales for Thomson Consumer Electronics describes leadership as "partly ingrained and partly learned. Experience, both successes and failures, provides the intuition needed for successful leadership. To me, leadership is the ability to influence the decision-making process or change the course of events."[2]

Research suggests that there are five skills that the best leaders develop during their careers (Figure 12-1).

1. *Empowerment* refers to a leader's ability to share power with others by involving them in setting objectives and planning. This requires spending time with your salespeople, particularly top people.

2. *Intuition* refers to the ability to anticipate change and take risks. Terry Bradshaw of the Pittsburgh Steelers feels that the distinguishing characteristic of NFL quarterbacks is their intuition. Outstanding quarterbacks have an instinct for when they should run or throw the ball.

3. *Self-understanding* implies a willingness to receive and understand both positive and negative feedback from other people, including subordinates. It also means knowing how it feels to lead and coping with those feelings. One manager said, "You have to recognize that every 'out front' maneuver you make is going to be lonely, but if you feel entirely comfortable, then you're not far enough ahead to do any good."[3]

4. *Vision* is future oriented and includes the idea of change. A successful vision exists when you picture where the sales organization needs to go, communicate and sell that belief throughout the organization, get endorsement from all levels, and then execute plans to get there.

5. *Value congruence* means that everyone in the organization is striving for the same business objectives. Achieving it requires good communication ability, as well as the ability to convince others that certain ideas are good and worth implementing. Value congruence allows a leader to delegate to others the authority to run their own operations.

Power

Power is critical to leadership because it explains why subordinates follow leaders. Five sources of power are legitimate, reward, coercive, referent, and expertise power.

1. *Legitimate power* is based on the manager's position in the organization. Salespeople put extra effort behind products that a sales manager has targeted for special promotion because they think the manager has a right to expect this effort.

    In the case of Richard Waxler the second option, which asks other salespeople to help solve the problem, undermines your legitimate power as district sales manager. To some degree, you are transferring your role as manager to your salespeople. This may make you appear weak.

2. *Reward power* relies on a leader's ability to award subordinates for outcomes that they value. For example, salespeople may put extra effort behind a particular product because the sales manager has offered to pay a bonus for each unit sold over a three-month period. This power depends on the size of the bonus and the importance of extra compensation to the salesperson.

3. *Coercive power* leads to compliance due to fear of punishment. Salespeople who feel that they could be fired will spend extra time prospecting for new customers. However, if the person is already thinking of quitting, then the power of this threat is minimal. This leadership style is rapidly losing favor and the role of the manager today is to support the efforts of the team, not to control and direct.

    The option of setting up a meeting with Richard Waxler and requiring an itinerary is an example of coercive power. This option is loaded with threats. The warning that you will hold back bonuses and commissions that Richard has earned could be illegal.

4. *Referent power* is the leader's influence on others because of friendship with the leader. Salespeople comply because they feel that friends help friends or because they so admire the manager that they want to be like this person.

5. *Expertise power* is based on the perception that a manager has special knowledge, usually based on past success. Thus, new salespeople may put extra effort into targeted accounts because a sales manager has told them that this is the key to future success and because the manager has a long and distinguished district sales record.

Any of the five power bases can lead to desired behavior by subordinates, but salespeople are more satisfied with supervision when they feel a sales manager is particularly knowledgeable (expert power) and makes good decisions and suggestions (expert power), and when they identify closely with the sales manager (referent power). Too much reliance on reward power leads to a mercenary attitude among salespeople rather than a commitment to the overall vision of the organization. Coercive power leads to mere compliance, but employees lack the enthusiasm that accompanies commitment to a course of action. This commitment is usually critical since sales involves more than avoiding mistakes.

► LEADERSHIP STYLES

When you are trying to influence the behavior of others, you need to think about your leadership style. *Leadership style* is the pattern of behaviors that others perceive you to use when trying to influence their behavior. While your perceptions of your own behavior are important, these are not very useful unless they match the perceptions of others.

Every sales manager has a leadership style that he or she uses when dealing with a sales force. Research has shown significant correlations between the type of leadership style employed by first-line field sales managers and their performance ratings.[4] Managers who tie rewards to their sales rep's efforts fairly and do not intervene in their lives unless there are problems tend to get higher evaluations.

Situational Leadership

A *situational leadership* model with four types of leadership styles is shown in Figure 12-2. These leadership styles are based on two characteristics: directive and supportive behavior. D*irective behavior* is the extent to which a leader engages in *one-way* commu-

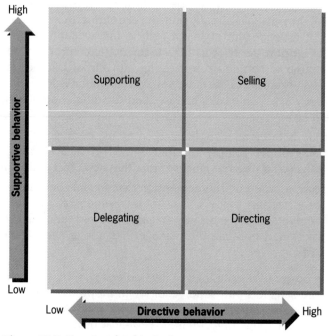

Figure 12-2: Four Leadership Styles

nications, spelling out what, where, when, and how to do it. Performance is closely supervised and controlled by the leader. The canned sales presentation is an example of this behavior. *Supportive behavior* is the extent to which a leader engages in *two-way* communication involving listening and providing support and encouragement. With supportive behavior, a sales manager involves the salesperson in the decision process. Participation in quota setting often involves supportive behavior.

Four Leadership Styles

The four leadership styles shown in Figure 12-2 are referred to as telling, selling, supporting, and delegating. Each style results from a combination of high or low supportive and directive behavior.

1. A *telling style* (low supportive/high directive) is where managers tell a salesperson what, when, how, and where to do various tasks. Identifying the problem and stating how the salesperson will accomplish the goal are initiated by the manager. Communication is largely one way. For example, a sales manager establishes a call frequency pattern for all the customers in a salesperson's territory. No deviations from the pattern are permitted.

2. With a *selling style* (high supportive/high directive), leaders provide a great deal of direction with their own ideas, but salespeople's ideas are solicited. In this case, the sales manager may ask the salesperson for a reaction to the call frequency schedule and will consider exceptions to the general policy that the salesperson feels are justified.

3. A *supportive style* (high supportive/low directive) calls for a shift of day-to-day problem solving from the sales manager to the salesperson. The sales manager's role is to provide recognition, to listen actively, and to facilitate problem solving by the salesperson.

    With a supportive leadership style, management decides that a call schedule is required but would allow the salesperson to devise a call plan. The sales manager may provide past call report information and suggest changes in the schedule that are felt to be necessary.

4. A *delegating style* (low supportive/low directive) has the sales manager discussing problems in the territory with the salesperson. Decision making is then delegated to the salesperson, who decides how a problem is to be handled. The focus of the sales manager–salesperson interaction is to agree on what is causing a problem. The salesperson may decide that a revised call pattern, for example, is the answer to a problem of small orders in the territory.

► TEAM BUILDING

Teamwork in sales organizations has become much more important in recent years as shown by the following quotes.

- "I called our district manager in Phoenix and explained that I was preparing an important proposal for this big account, and would he please help with the part having to do with an account location in his district. He reluctantly agreed, but I haven't seen anything yet, and he hasn't returned my last two phone calls."

- A sales rep selling equipment, while salespeople in another sales force sell related supply items to the same accounts, comments, "Many customers want to coordinate their purchases of equipment and supplies because of the impact they have on their production processes. I meet a lot with my supply brethren because while we share all of our accounts, what's often not shared or clear are our individual goals."[5]

The most common reasons given for a lack of sales team cooperation include such things as rewards and compensation that focus on individual performance rather than team efforts. Also information systems often do not keep team members supplied with pertinent data. Another problem is that organizational structures foster internal competition rather than cooperation. Finally the mindset of some people makes them unwilling to set aside position and power for mutual gains.[6] The job of the sales manager is to help break down these barriers and reduce competition among reps. An example of the type of problems sales managers face is shown in Sales Management in Action 12-1.

Sales Management in Action 12-1
The Case for Effective Team Building

Fred Kennedy is regional sales manager for Mebco Equipment Company. His operation covers a 50-mile radius and includes five salespeople, two secretaries, and two planning and layout specialists. Also sharing the office is the regional service manager.

Fred has been reviewing negotiations with young Tom Plankton. Fred says, "I'm sorry I had to be down state when the Hillman job broke for you. Did you get your bid in as we discussed?"

"I made it," replies Tom. "And by the skin of my teeth. I couldn't get hold of anyone at the factory who could fill in the spec data, for one thing—"

Dan breaks in. "What about Ralph here in the office? He's sold so many of those drives that he knows more about them than the engineers." "I asked him if he would help, but he said he had to work on another job of his own," says Tom.

"I had to estimate the installation figures," Tom continues. "Our illustrious service manager said he was too busy and we would probably lose it anyway. I ended up typing it myself at the last minute. The typists said they had to get their invoices out because it was the end of the accounting period."

After Tom leaves, Fred thinks about what had just been said. "It's a good office, with highly capable people," he muses, "except that they're all a bunch of individualists going in their own directions instead of pulling together to the same drumbeat.

Source: David Stumm, *The New Sales Manager's Survival Guide* (New York: Amacom, 1985), p. 119.

The job of getting individual members of a sales organization to work together to form a functioning and supportive team is made easier when you have a better understanding of how groups operate. One of the most useful ways to describe how groups function is the *Homans system* model, developed by George Homans.[7]

The Homans System

Homans thinks of a group as an interacting system of activities, sentiments, and norms (Figure 12-3).

Activities   Activities include many types of behaviors. In Tom's case (see Sales Management in Action 12-1), it includes developing formal bids. Other tasks may include analyzing problems, evaluating alternatives, making decisions, and writing proposals. These task-related activities will take up most of the salesperson's time and are likely to be of primary interest to the group members, rather than social activities such as coffee breaks, talking, and playing cards.

Interactions   Interactions are communications that take place between two or more people. The amount of interaction may be identified by answering the following questions:

- With whom do the salespeople talk?
- How often do they talk to one another?
- How long do they talk?
- Who starts the conversation?

In Sales Management in Action 12-1, what would you guess is the level of interaction between the sales force and engineers in the factory? between the sales force and customer service personnel?

Sentiments   Sentiments reflect the emotional climate of a group. They may be described in terms of day-to-day feelings, such as anger, happiness, and sadness, as well as deeper feelings, such as trust, openness, and freedom. Deeper sentiments are important because the more these positive sentiments are present, the more likely it is that the group will be effective and productive. Negative sentiments of

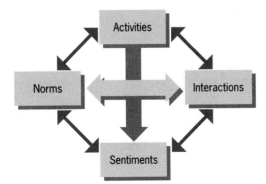

Figure 12-3: Internal Systems of a Group

distrust and lack of interdependence are implicit in the service manager's statement in Sales Management in Action 12-1.

Norms   Informal rules of behavior that are widely shared and enforced by groups are referred to as *norms*. Norms of a work group may define how much work members should do, how they act toward other departments, how they feel about the organization, how they act around the manager, and even what they wear.

Norms develop in one of three ways.[8] (1) Sales managers or salespeople explicitly state what should or shouldn't occur. For example, Fred may have unwittingly established the norm for not helping a fellow salesperson by telling reps during evaluations that salespeople are responsible for their sales results. (2) Events in a sales department's history also lead to the development of norms. These events frequently occur early in the formation of a group or when a new sales manager takes over. In Fred's example, he may have encouraged salespeople to review all bid specifications with him in an effort to get to know each salesperson in the Central Region. (3) A carryover of norms from past experiences may influence the formation of norms in new situations. Perhaps the regional sales manager before Fred discouraged salespeople from helping each other in developing formal bids because one salesperson was being asked to do too much of the work. Obviously, it would help Fred to know how the norms evolved in order to address the team-building issue.

External Conditions   There are a number of outside conditions that can also influence how sales teams operate. These include such things as organizational structure, technology, and management values. For example, in the Mebco case Fred may want to evaluate his sales force compensation program since commission plans often do not reward teamwork or encourage salespeople to help each other. Alternatively, Fred may wish to devise an incentive or recognition program to reward team efforts.

Unlike many other leadership situations, key activities and even the location of the field sales offices are geographically separated from company headquarters. This spatial isolation raises the importance of leadership activities of local sales managers. Two key leadership activities of sales managers are one-on-one coaching and conducting sales meetings.

▶ COACHING

An important function of first-line sales managers is to aid in the development and training of their salespeople. One of the byproducts of corporate downsizing is fewer corporate-level sales trainers and field sales managers are now being asked to pick up more of the coaching burden.[9] *Coaching* consists of on-the-job interactions between a sales manager and field reps to reinforce skills that are needed to reach sales objectives. Coaching sessions may take place in the office, but most sales coaching is done in the field during visits by sales managers. A good way to begin sales coaching is to first talk with customers, reps, and other sales managers to identify skills that need improvement.

What Is Involved

You need to be aware of sales force behaviors that detract from sales effectiveness. Questions that can be used to elicit information are:

1. **Planning.** Includes setting territory and call objectives, routing of sales calls, and use of time. "Before we go in, what is your objective for this call? What do you specifically want to achieve?"

2. **Attitude.** Includes the attitude toward products, specific customers, the company, the salesperson's career, company programs, and company policies. "I have the feeling you didn't care for that assistant buyer. Your attitude is pretty evident."

3. **Knowledge.** Product related, customer business, competition, territory, company, and policies. "The benefits he was asking about were pretty clearly covered in our last sales bulletin. How well do you keep up with these releases?"

4. **Selling skills.** Prospecting, selling steps, handling objectives, buying-center roles, negotiating skills. "Let's talk about the timing when you ask for the order." "Who else in a key buying position are you familiar with at this account?"

The best time for coaching is just prior to and following a sales call. This takes advantage of the important learning principle of recency. Feedback should be given immediately after the behavior. Instead of providing salespeople with negative feedback alone, tell why the behavior was not correct, how a better response could have been made, and why this response would lead to the desired outcome.

During the Sales Call

When a manager accompanies a salesperson, the manager must be sure to let the salesperson control the situation. At times, a manager may be called on to address a particular issue, but should keep his or her remarks focused on that issue while giving the salesperson responsibility for the overall call. Otherwise, the salesperson will turn sales calls over to the manager whenever a tough issue arises. When coaching is your purpose for being together, sales calls should not become a team selling effort. You are there to observe the salesperson's selling skills. Prior to the call, you should establish an understanding that the salesperson is making the call and that you will not jump into the selling process.

Salesperson Maturity

With a mature, veteran salesperson, it is probably most useful to use the post–sales call phase of coaching to identify strengths, build on them, and challenge salespeople to stretch in the areas where they do their best work. Any correcting may be accomplished prior to the next call, using the methods described earlier.

For less mature salespeople, the post–sales call phase of coaching may be best used to establish and reinforce self-evaluation of performance by the salesperson. Questions that may be asked include: "How do you think it went?" "What went well?"

"What could you have done differently?" Positive feedback provides both information and motivation, while negative feedback communicates only information. It is not surprising, therefore, that positive feedback has a greater impact on performance and satisfaction than negative feedback.[10]

By now you may have recognized that the last option in the Richard Waxler case is an example of coaching. Since coaching takes place one-on-one, Richard is not as likely to be defensive as in a more social situation. By instructing Richard in preparing an itinerary and a call report, you are giving him an important and specific demonstration of how to manage his time and territory. This is a positive approach with a high probability that the lessons learned will be retained. Coaching is the option with the highest probability of success.

► SALES MEETINGS

Coaching is best suited to individual training and motivational issues. When a sales team needs help on how to sell a new product, for example, it is often better to address the need in a group setting.

The most common method for motivating and communicating with the sales team is the sales meeting. In some door-to-door sales organizations, sales meetings are held every morning. During these meetings, sales managers give inspirational speeches to help overcome the disappointment that comes from the frequent rejection inherent in door-to-door selling, or review sales objectives and progress toward these objectives. Other types of businesses have sales meetings less often.

Meeting Objectives

Every sales meeting should have a set of meaningful objectives, the most common involving communication, reward, encouragement, and training. Group meetings accomplish these goals effectively and economically. Not only can the sales manager be sure that everyone is exposed to the same message, but effective use can be made of speakers, training films, and special entertainment. Specific objectives for sales meetings include the following:

- Present restyled, redesigned, or new products.
- Explain new marketing and advertising programs.
- Train salespeople in advanced selling methods.
- Motivate salespeople through interaction with senior executives and celebrities, such as television or movie personalities who promote a product.
- Recognize contest winners or superior performers.

The most popular topic covered in sales meetings—sales force feedback—comes as a surprise to many readers. Meetings are usually thought to be a way to give out information, but effective sales managers also see them as a good opportunity to learn about conditions in the field.

Objectives of meetings should be relevant to all salespeople. In the case of Richard Waxler, one of the options was to hold a sales meeting. In this situation, itinerary reports were an issue only with Richard. It is a good idea to review reporting requirements with the sales team, but it may not be wise to state the dire results one can expect for not fulfilling the requirements. People who are already completing the reports are likely to wonder why you are being so negative. Your veiled threats could ultimately lower the productivity of the sales team. On the other hand, sales meetings are nice occasions for providing personal rewards. Senior salespeople could be given single rooms. High performers could come in the night before the meeting for dinner. Never miss the opportunity to recognize your people.

Meeting Budgets

Annual budgets for sales meetings (excluding travel) typically range from $10,000 to $70,000. A two-day meeting for 48 people in New Orleans, for example, is estimated to cost $41,213, or $858 per person.[11] Most businesses do not have a lot of money to spend and hold meetings locally at company sites. Sales managers must control expenses without sacrificing effectiveness. A few firms are trying to reduce costs by using teleconferences. Others are stretching their budgets by having fewer meetings or shorter meetings, by doubling up on room assignments, or by cutting back on hospitality suite time.

Locations and Timing

Pulling salespeople away from their territories for meetings means that some sales opportunities will be lost, but this problem can be minimized by careful scheduling. Sales meetings are usually held during slack times so that they will not interfere with normal customer contacts. Sales meetings can be classified as local, regional, or national.

Local Sales Meetings   *Local sales meetings* are usually run by field managers and are held frequently, perhaps as often as every week, month, or quarter. These meetings are informal and take place in a conference room at the branch sales office or in a nearby motel. With advances in video technology, involvement of home office personnel in local meetings is enhanced.

Regional Sales Meetings   *Regional sales meetings* include salespeople from several states and are usually held quarterly or less often. These meetings are more structured and often feature presentations by sales executives and training specialists from headquarters. With regional meetings, personnel from the head office do most of the traveling, which can save time and reduce expenses for salespeople.

National Sales Meetings   *National sales meetings* bring the entire sales force together at a central location, and usually occur once a year or less. These meetings require higher travel expenditures, and firms tend to stage more elaborate speeches, presentations, and entertainment at these events. The objective of national meetings is to boost the sales force's morale and promote "psychic bonding" among salespeople so that they feel more like a team.[12] At a national sales meeting at the Seth Thomas Company, for example, the baseball theme "Covering All the Bases" was used. The top salesperson was named "Most Valuable Performer," and the meeting culminated with attendance at the opening home game of the Atlanta Braves, with T-shirts and baseball caps for all. When the Travelers insurance company asset management division was in the dumps over low sales, two vice presidents in black suits stepped to the microphone at the annual sales meeting and lip-synched the Blues Brothers song "Soul Man." This was followed by acts from other regional sales offices. The enthusiasm from the entertainment boosted spirits and made the rest of the meeting more successful.[13]

Common Problems

Interest   The most damning outcome of a sales meeting is when participants find it boring and a waste of time. Unproductive meetings are demoralizing and worse than no meeting at all. Surveys have shown that salespeople expect sales meetings to be exciting and fast paced and to make good use of the time available. Problems can be partially avoided by careful scheduling, hiring inspirational speakers, and using films, slides, and other audiovisual equipment. Sales Management in Action 12-2 describes how sales meetings can go wrong.

Sales Management in Action 12-2
It's Always Something

Here are some true stories demonstrating just how off-key sales meetings can become.

- **R2D2.** At the national sales meeting of a medical product manufacturer, a remote-controlled robot was the star attraction. The robot operator was reading a script on the firm's products but kept stumbling over words like "spectrophotometry," which caused everyone to laugh. To make matters worse, the robot was stuck in the "on" position and rolled through the first three rows of people. Meanwhile the person speaking through the robot had no idea what was going on and continued to mispronounce words.

- **Cost-cutting.** At a cosmetics company, cost-cutting hit a new low. "The lunch was designed around a picnic theme," says one sales rep, "which was ludi- crous, given that we were in a window-less conference room on a gorgeous Sunday afternoon in May." Even worse, the luncheon consisted of one hot dog per person.

- **"I like myself."** Emphasizing self-esteem at a meeting held by a bank, the trainer had each person stand up and exclaim "I like myself!" Getting caught up in the spirit, the trainer would yell "Say it louder" as the whole group now screamed "I like myself." The meeting was held at the bank during normal business hours and there were still customers in the building. Suddenly, a customer yelled back, "So do I." Everyone became extremely embarrassed.

Source: Betsy Wiesendanger, "It's Always Something," *Sales & Marketing Management* (November 1993), pp. 113–116.

Participation   Another common complaint about sales meetings is that salespeople spend most of their time listening and do not get a chance to participate and interact with management. This problem can be handled by keeping the meeting groups small so that each speaker leads a discussion rather than presents a formal talk. Also, large groups can be broken into small teams for problem-solving and discussion sessions. Small groups encourage audience participation and enhance learning.

Follow-Up   Problems can also result from a failure to provide follow-up after a sales meeting. Sales managers should give participants materials to take with them so that they can review the information and use it in their day-to-day activities. Moreover, there should be reminder letters and checks by local managers to see that new procedures are being implemented by salespeople.

► SALES FORCE PERSONNEL ISSUES

Sales managers face difficult personnel issues in their development of effective selling teams. Several of these problem areas are reviewed and suggestions are made on ways to manage these situations.

Plateauing

Plateauing occurs when people stop growing as sales professionals. They reach a stage where they are just holding their own or are falling back in performance. Perhaps they have even stopped showing an interest in the job itself. Sales managers report that 15 percent of the typical sales force is plateaued and that the percentage may be as high as 40 to 50 percent in some sales organizations.[14] Plateauing is most likely to occur when salespeople are in their forties, but it may occur even during their thirties.

Causes of Plateauing.   The primary causes of plateauing among salespeople are shown in Table 12-1. Notice that the number one reason for plateauing is the lack of a clear career path for salespeople. This reinforces our discussion of the benefits of

Table 12-1   Sales Managers' Rankings of the Causes of Plateauing

	Overall	Mostly Women	Commission Only
No clear career path	1	2	4
Not managed adequately	2	4	1
Bored	3	3	5
Burned out	4	1	2
Economic needs met	5	7	3
Discouraged with company	6	5	6
Overlooked for promotion	7	6	8
Lack of ability	8	9	7
Avoiding risk of management job	9	10	9
Reluctance to be transferred	10	8	10

Source: William Keenan, "The Nagging Problem of the Plateaued Salesperson," *Sales & Marketing Management* (March 1989), p. 38.

developing a career path for salespeople who do not want to go into management. It also reinforces the suggestion made in Chapter 9 that a realistic picture of the sales position and future opportunities be presented to all recruits.

Sales managers feel there are some differences among sales forces in terms of what causes plateauing. The most important reason for women is burnout (Table 12-1). Burnout is also an important reason for plateauing among salespeople on commission. Other common reasons for commission salespeople to plateau is that their economic needs have been met or that they have not been managed adequately. These results suggest that there are limitations to compensation plans and that people want more from their jobs once their basic compensation needs are satisfied.

Business strategy also influences the incidence of sales force plateauing. Only about 7 percent of salespeople are plateaued in companies that emphasize growth through the development of new products. Within companies defending market share in low-growth markets with commoditylike products, the incidence of plateauing is 34 percent.[15] This suggests that people can be left in a job too long, and a job that is highly structured is more likely to lead to plateauing.

There are signals of the early stages of plateauing that should warn managers that this process is happening. Sales managers say the most important early signal is when salespeople do not prospect hard enough. Other signals are a lack of follow-through in customer servicing and working fewer hours.

Signals of plateauing appear even when interviewing a person for a sales position. For example, people who subsequently plateau are more likely than nonplateaued salespeople to mention circumstances beyond their personal control for leaving their previous job. On the other hand, among people who do not plateau, the two most common reasons cited for changing positions are better compensation and a new opportunity.[16]

Solutions to Plateauing   Managers need to respect the experience that plateaued salespeople have and at the same time find ways to get them to try new approaches to serving customers. Frequently mature salespeople resist change because they do not want to make mistakes and appear foolish. One manager gets his reps together and places a $100 bill on the table. He then says: "I'm going to tell you about a mistake I made last week and what I learned from it. The $100 is for anyone who can top it."[17]

Another way to prevent plateauing and possible turnover is to develop alternative career paths. These positions should provide new challenges to salespeople in order to help them develop professionally. National Semiconductor of Santa Clara, California, recently instituted a dual-career path for salespeople with nonmanagement positions ranging from marketing engineer to senior marketing technician. An important reason for National's organizational change was that the cost of replacing one salesperson ranged from $125,000 to $175,000.[18]

Another suggestion is to confront plateauing as soon as indicators suggest that it may be occurring. Sales managers should look for ways to enrich current sales positions. For example, plateaued salespeople could be trained to help coach new salespeople, to help introduce new products, or to develop key customer accounts. Another alternative is to give these salespeople responsibility for gathering competitive intelligence. Tough-to-crack new accounts could be reassigned, along with the award of valuable and unusual perquisites if the salesperson is successful—such as vacations and bonuses. The number of job-enrichment solutions is limited only by the sales manager's imagination.[19]

Termination of Employment

Termination of salespeople should be considered an option of last resort. At some point in their career managers will find it necessary to terminate a rep. After this decision has been made, termination should be performed in a humane manner, with concern both for human feelings and for staying out of court.

Court dockets today are crowded with wrongful termination suits charging broken promises, invasion of privacy, violation of public policy, and failure of good faith. In California, court awards have run as high as $350,000. Awards are high because a company may have to pay for past and future wages and lost benefits, as well as mental and emotional suffering.[20] In this environment, one misstep by a small company could drive it out of business.

There is no way to eliminate the chance of a lawsuit, but you should follow several steps prior to terminating a salesperson. The first step is to establish a paper trail. The trail should begin with employee manuals that spell out specific company policies and procedures. Performance reviews should occur on a regular basis, documented in writing, and include both positive and negative elements. The written reviews should be accompanied by a candid discussion between you and the salesperson in unambiguous language.

Legal aspects of termination are important, but humanitarian issues are of major concern. One suggestion for softening the blow is to offer an attractive benefit package to terminated employees. This may include an outplacement service to help the person focus on the future and sizable severance pay. Severance pay may range from one to four weeks of pay for each year of employment.

Firing sessions should be brief because neither side gains from a lengthy discussion. Also, the firing session should take place at the beginning of the week and never on a Friday. This allows people to get started immediately on their future rather than spending the weekend reflecting on the past. Never do it over the phone. Always do it in a way that preserves the person's dignity.

Sexual Harassment

Women occupy 28 percent of all sales positions (Table 12-2). In some industries, such as communications, the majority of the salespeople are women. Studies indicate few gender differences in job attitudes and performance, but the issue of *sexual harassment* is becoming more common.[21] Although no information exists on its incidence in sales compared to other occupations, many sales jobs place people in a position where sexual harassment is possible. A client may misinterpret sales enthusiasm as personal attraction. Many positions call for extensive overnight travel, and social interaction is frequently required.

Complaints of sexual harassment filed with the Equal Employment Opportunity Commission (EEOC) doubled in two years, to 7,273 in 1993.[22] Discussions with female salespeople suggest that women will experience some form of sexual harassment—

Table 12-2   Women in Sales: Percentages by Industry

Industry Group	Percent of Women in Sales Force
Business services	33.2
Chemicals	5.9
Communications	50.9
Electronics	35.0
Fabricated metals	7.3
Food products	24.9
Instruments	35.0
Insurance	28.5
Miscellaneous manufacturing	22.7
Office equipment	33.9
Printing/publishing	39.4
Retail	32.2
Rubber/plastics	26.9
Utilities	20.2
Wholesale (consumer)	19.7
Wholesale (industrial)	30.9
Average	**27.9**

Note: Industry groups reflect categories selected and reported by the Dartnell Corporation. The overall average has been calculated by *Sales & Marketing Management* based on data from these 16 industries.

Source: Dartnell Corporation, 25th *Survey of Sales Force Compensation.* © 1989, Dartnell Corporation.

physical, verbal, nonverbal, intentional, unintentional—at some point, and that it is more likely to occur early in their career.

Women who have had such experiences in sales have several suggestions to offer when confronted with this situation:[23]

- **Direct approach.**   The direct approach can be the most effective, especially with established customers. This technique may be as simple as looking the person in the eye and saying, "Don't you ever do that again."

- **Consequence approach.**   Most people agree that humor is often the best tactic. For example, say, "If I kiss you, I expect you to drop your wife."

- **Leave.**   Many women prefer to avoid confrontations, especially if they are alone with someone with whom they are not familiar. Thus, they immediately leave.

- **Aftereffects.**   If it is impossible to avoid the offender in the future, then it is best to get back to the person as soon as possible about some work-related matter. This eases the tension for both people and doesn't jeopardize the business relationship.

Saleswomen surveyed all agreed that the best advice is to avoid getting into potentially embarrassing situations in the first place. They offered several suggestions:

- Conduct yourself professionally.
- Dress appropriately.
- Be cautious in drinking at business functions.
- Don't listen to sob stories.
- Avoid being alone in a one-to-one situation when possible.
- Use independent transportation.

Sexual abuse is most often discussed from a female viewpoint. Men may also experience subtle or explicit instances of sexual abuse. The influx of women into sales, sales management, and buying positions makes this all the more likely today. The possible reactions and preventive suggestions discussed are just as appropriate for men as for women.

Companies can help prevent sexual harassment by having a written policy with examples of illegal behavior and by including the subject in its initial employee training and socialization program.[24] It should be made clear what constitutes sexual harassment, what procedures a victim of sexual harassment should take, and what the consequences are for being an offender.

As a sales manager, what should you do to help salespeople deal with harassment? First, recognize that your salespeople may not tell you about an incident because they are embarrassed and may feel that they are taking a risk by going to the boss. Rather than asking you for advice, they may ask to drop a particular account, request a transfer within the company, or ask for advice in general on how to handle such situations. Most important, do not dismiss the problem. Second, you may offer the alternatives discussed above. If appropriate, you may share some of your own experiences and tips. If the offender is a colleague, the manager should confront the person directly. If the offender is a customer, the manager should offer to join the salesperson on the next call. You must be careful to handle the customer carefully, however, to avoid giving the impression that the salesperson cannot handle the situation alone. You should also be aware of your legal responsibilities to the employee. According to the law, if managers have knowledge of an alleged incident, they must investigate and resolve the matter, or liability can fall on them.

Alcohol and Chemical Abuse

There is no evidence that alcohol and chemical abuse are more prevalent among salespeople than among people in other occupations. However, alcohol and chemical abuse is a national concern, and there is no reason to feel that it is less prevalent among salespeople. Estimates suggest 5 percent of the nation's work force are addicted to alcohol, and another 5 percent are serious alcohol abusers. Salespeople spend a lot of time on the road, which is conducive to escape behaviors, including alcohol and drug abuse.

Most sales managers believe that alcohol abuse is a problem in their sales force, which mirrors findings for the work force as a whole. Sales managers usually detect the alcohol problems through personal observation: the second source of information is fellow salespeople. Very few firms have a company or divisionwide policy for dealing with alcohol abuse. The most common reaction of sales managers is to engage in informal counseling with the abuser. Other common reactions are to refer the salesperson to an alcohol abuse program and to terminate, either after a warning or at once.

In most cases, the responsibility for determining alcohol and chemical abuse rests with the sales manager. Where there is no formal company policy, a sales manager is advised to develop one and ensure that all salespeople understand exactly what the policy is. You should not ignore the signs of abuse or tolerate it among your salespeople. You are also advised to resist the temptation to engage in informal counseling with the problem drinker or chemical abuser. Alcohol and chemical abuse is a complicated psychological and physical problem that requires trained professionals. Finally, sales managers must lead by example. They should ensure that they are sending the right signal by carefully watching their own drinking on and off the job.

▶ ETHICAL SITUATIONS

Most business decisions involve some degree of ethical judgment. Consider the following situation described by an executive with the Aurora-Baxter Corporation, a company that makes construction materials:

> A couple of years ago, following a scandal in the awarding of highway contracts, the state legislature enacted some very stiff laws forbidding state purchasing officers from accepting any gifts—even free lunches. This can be a little awkward in certain respects. When our marketing guys are in the middle of negotiations with them it's natural to go out with the buyers for drinks and a nice meal. Everybody knows that each person there is supposed to pay for his or her own meal. Our guys are told that they have to make that clear. So at some point one of them will say, "OK, everybody, chip in. You know the rule." Maybe there are five of them and three of us and say the bill is $300. When the meal's over they've put in $2 each and we pick up the rest of the tab.[25]

Direction by upper management establishes the ethical climate in which sales managers act. Many corporations have established codes of conduct to guide their employees. Codes are only one of the signals that management provides about ethical behavior. If managers at all levels are seriously interested in creating an environment conducive to ethical behavior, there are certain actions that they should take:

- Underscore the importance of moral conduct by their efforts to perpetuate the "stories" that help to shape the corporate culture.
- Share the process for developing a corporate code of conduct. The process itself will have a constructive influence on behavior.
- How results are achieved should be taken into account when evaluating performance, and not simple reliance on quantitative outcomes.
- Develop a corporate culture that encourages whistleblowing if subordinates are aware of illegal or unethical behavior at higher levels of management.

- Build a sense of job security for those who want to behave ethically. It is often those who feel insecure in their job who are tempted to bend the rules to achieve results.[26]

► SUMMARY

Leadership is defined as the ability to influence the behavior of other people. Sales managers must be aware of the skills necessary to be an effective leader and understand the power bases that are available to influence salespeople under their control. Self-understanding is critical to successful management, but the most successful leaders are also flexible in their style of leadership. We have discussed four leadership styles: directing, coaching, supporting, and delegating.

Field sales managers should also be responsible for the professional development of individual salespeople by providing feedback in the field. The best time for this coaching is before and after actual sales calls. Immediate comments on the salesperson's behavior can be effective in improving the selling and territory management skills of the salespeople. Managers must be careful, however, to always emphasize the things salespeople do well and to praise them for their accomplishments.

High performance depends on cooperation between salespeople and others within the company. One of your jobs as a sales manager is to develop a team effort emphasizing mutual support and respect. In order to develop effective teams, sales managers must understand how groups function. One of the most commonly used methods for influencing the sales team is through sales meetings.

In today's environment, sales managers are likely to be faced with a number of personnel issues that can reduce the effectiveness of selling teams. Chief among these issues are plateaued salespeople, management development problems, termination practices, sexual harassment, and alcohol and chemical abuse. Managers must develop policies to handle them when and if they arise.

► KEY TERMS

Coaching	Plateauing
Coercive power	Power
Delegating style	Referent power
Directive behavior	Regional sales meetings
Empowerment	Reward power
Expertise power	Self-understanding
Homans system	Selling style
Intuition	Sexual harassment
Leadership	Situational leadership
Leadership style	Supportive behavior
Legitimate power	Supportive style
Local sales meetings	Telling style
National sales meetings	Value congruence
Norms	Vision

▶ REVIEW QUESTIONS

1. What is meant by leadership?

2. What skills do the most effective leaders develop during their careers?

3. Why is power necessary for leadership, and what are the sources of power that a leader can draw upon?

4. What is meant by leadership style? Describe the four styles identified in the situational leadership model.

5. What are the objectives of a one-on-one postcall coaching session between a sales manager and a salesperson? How may these objectives be accomplished?

6. Why is team building important for sales effectiveness? What should a manager know about how a group functions?

7. What are the potential topics and objectives of sales meetings? What are the differences among local, regional, and national sales meetings?

8. What is meant by a plateaued salesperson, what are early warning signs of plateauing, and how can the negative consequences be minimized?

9. What are the dangers in promoting your best salesperson to a district sales manager's position? How can companies ensure that a pool of management will be available to fill new vacancies?

10. How can a company minimize the chances of a wrongful termination suit?

11. If a female salesperson informs you that she is having a sexual harassment problem with an important male client, what should you, as her district manager, do?

▶ PROBLEMS

1. Julie has the talent and experience to greatly improve sales in her territory. A veteran salesperson with fifteen years with the company, Julie has been a top performer in the past, but just gets by now. Her husband is a doctor and their children are on their own, so Julie's financial needs are fully met. Julie's sales volume is third in the district of five people, so it's not that she doesn't sell, it's just that her sales volume has not increased much in the past three years and you believe there is opportunity for greater sales out of her territory. Your company has recently downsized and budgets are tight. It's time to do something about Julie. How would you address this situation without losing a strong salesperson?

2. You are the district manager and have all the accountability that comes with the job. You have the feeling that your salespeople are not following many of your instructions. Are you becoming paranoid? John seems to be the informal leader of the salespeople in his district. Deliberately or not, he seems to have become very influential. John is also one of your top salespeople. However, district sales overall are dropping. Is there a connection? You must correct the situation soon, and you do not want to lose John because he is a valuable salesperson. Why did an informal leader emerge? How do you handle John? What can you do to prevent a recurrence?

3. Susan, who sells oil products to industrial and construction clients in the Midwest, left her car in a multilevel car park and joined her customer who had also parked there. Riding up in the empty elevator together, he suddenly turned around and said, "Kiss me." "No," she

replied. "Kiss me," he insisted, getting closer and closer. "I'm married," Susan said, backing away. "So what? I'm married, too," the customer said. If you were in Susan's position, how would you handle this situation at this point? If Susan came to you, her manager, with this information, what would you do?

4. Your company is a wholesaler of disposable medical supplies sold primarily to independent physicians. Among your other responsibilities, you manage a sales force of 27 people who call on physicians throughout the state. These salespeople are paid a commission as a percentage of gross margin, and most have been with your company for more than eight years. Several competitors have been expanding geographically by hiring veteran salespeople away from other wholesalers, with bonuses for changing companies of as much as $10,000 to $20,000. Veteran salespeople are able to take 50 to 80 percent of their customers with them when they change companies. To avoid this problem you feel that you must tie your top salespeople closer to your company. One method of doing this is to increase the status of your senior salespeople within the company and the sales force as a whole. What steps should you take to accomplish this?

5. Sales managers who are new to managing women find them far easier than men to manage in some areas and more complex in others. When traveling out of town on sales calls, one manager commented that he observed that women on his staff tend to overestimate their ability to carry what they've packed and that it takes them much longer to get ready in the morning. Another sales manager mentioned a particular coaching problem. "I've accompanied women on sales calls," he said, "and sensed instantly that the customer was not happy to see me—a third party." How would you handle these situations? More generally, what do you think are the special problems women may have as sales professionals?

▶ IN-CLASS EXERCISES

Why Me, Lord?

Assume the role of a first-level sales manager. You have six people who are at least moderately successful and look to you primarily for support in their selling efforts. On the other hand, there are two people who have been real headaches for you in your first year as sales manager. You keep asking yourself, "Why me, Lord?"

If nothing else, Xavier has a great deal of bravado and confidence. Xavier's sales have been the highest in the district for each of the last five years. A natural leader within the sales force, Xavier has been with the organization for 12 years and is well known throughout the company. The problem is that Xavier hates sales meetings, especially those focusing on training, and despises paperwork. Given the way other people look up to Xavier, you fear that his failure to get to meetings on time and to submit call reports will spread to other people in the district.

The second person with whom you are concerned is Sam. Sam has been with the company and in the same territory for 14 years and is one of your top salespeople. You believe that sales could be even higher in Sam's territory if you obtained greater penetration of the warehouse stores. Sam does a great job with traditional supermarkets, but warehouse stores are gaining more of the business in your product lines. The problem is that Sam prefers to be left alone. He feels he has demonstrated his ability, knows the territory better than anyone else (he is probably correct), and has earned the right to be left alone.

Xavier enters your office after receiving a call from you requesting a meeting and asks, "What's up?"

You tell Xavier that he had another exceptional year in sales and profits, and that this really helped the district. "Best record in the district," replies Xavier.

"My problem is, you were once again late for our district meeting," you continue. "You disrupted the meeting when you finally arrived, and on top of that, you haven't turned in any call reports or competitive activity reports for the past month."

Obviously taken aback, Xavier replies, "I'm a salesman. I sell, and I'm very good at it. I really have no interest in management's problems; I just want to sell."

The next day after a district sales meeting you invited Sam to stop by your office. After exchanging some comments about how the sales meeting went, you get down to business, saying, "Sam, I have received more market information suggesting that the warehouse stores are gaining market share in our product lines. I feel we must get greater penetration of these retail outlets. I'm going to be in your territory next week Monday. I want to spend at least half a day with you, calling on the warehouse stores in your territory." Sam's reaction is immediate and clear. "You know how I feel about this. I've worked alone for 14 years in this territory, and the company pays me to run it. When I need your help, I'll call on you. My territory is different; I just don't think the warehouse stores in my territory are doing very well. They are not very well run."

Break into small groups and discuss what to do with Xavier and Sam. Be prepared to explain your ideas when your instructor calls on your group.

Questions:

1. Did the sales manager take the right approach in discussing the problems with Xavier?
2. What options do you have in handling Xavier?
3. Who owns the territory, Sam or the company?
4. How do you handle veterans who think they know more about selling than you do?
5. How do you get Sam to be a team player?

Next year's district quota is very demanding, and you must get the most out of each rep and territory. How can you get Xavier to turn in his reports and Sam to be a team player?

▶ REFERENCES

1. ALAN J. DUBINSKY, FRANCES J. YAMMARINO, MARVIN A. JOLSON, and WILLIAM D. SPANGLER, "Transformational Leadership: An Initial Investigation in Sales Management," *Journal of Personal Selling & Sales Management*, Vol. 15, No. 2 (Spring 1995), p. 27.

2. Interview with JOE CLAYTON, Executive Vice President of Marketing and Sales—Americas, Thomson Consumer Electronics (1993).

3. JAMES CORTADA, TQM *for Sales and Marketing Management* (New York: McGraw-Hill, 1993), pp. 40–41.

4. FREDERICK A. RUSS, KEVIN M. MCNEILLY, and JAMES M. COMER, "Leadership, Decision Making and Performance of Sales Managers: A Multi-Level Approach," *Journal of Personal Selling & Sales Management*, Vol. 16, No. 3 (Summer 1996), pp. 11–12.

5. FRANK CESPEDES, STEPHEN DOYLE, and ROBERT FREEDMAN, "Teamwork for Today's Selling," *Harvard Business Review* (March–April 1989), p. 44.

6. "Why Teams Don't Work," *Sales & Marketing Management* (April 1993), p. 12.

7. This section is based largely on DON HELLRIEGEL and JOHN SLOCUM, *Management*, 6th ed. (Reading, Mass.: Addison-Wesley, 1991), pp. 544–554.

8. D. C. FELDMAN, "The Development and Enforcement of Group Norms," *Academy of Management Review*, 9 (1989), pp. 47–53.

9. MELISSA CAMPANELLI, "Can Managers Coach?" *Sales & Marketing Management* (July 1994), pp. 59–66.

10. BERNARD JAWORSKI and AJAY KOHLI, "Supervisory Feedback: Alternative Types and Their Impact on Salespeople's Performance and Satisfaction," *Journal of Marketing Research*, 28 (May 1991), pp. 190–201.

11. *Sales & Marketing Management* (June 22, 1992), p. 42.

12. ELAINE EVANS, "How to Create Sales Meeting Magic," *Personal Selling Power* (September 1990), pp. 34–35.

13. "Weary Travelers," *Sales & Marketing Management* (March 1996), p. 68.

14. WILLIAM KEENAN, JR., "The Nagging Problem of the Plateaued Salesperson," *Sales & Marketing Management* (March 1989), pp. 36–40.

15. JOHN SLOCUM, WILLIAM CRON, RICHARD HANSEN, and SALLY RAWLINGS, "Business Strategy and the Management of Plateaued Employees," *Academy of Management Journal*, 28 (1985), pp. 133–154.

16. JOHN SLOCUM, WILLIAM CRON, and LINDA YOWS, "Whose Career Is Likely to Plateau?" *Business Horizons*, 30 (1987), pp. 31–38.

17. MINDA ZETLIN, "Is It Worth Keeping Older Salespeople?" *Sales & Marketing Management* (April 1995), p. 148.

18. MILAN MORAVEE, MARSHALL COLLINS, and CLINTON TROPODI, "Don't Want to Manage? Here's Another Path," *Sales & Marketing Management* (April 1990), p. 70.

19. ROBIN PETERSON, "Beyond the Plateau," *Sales & Marketing Management* (July 1993), pp. 78–80.

20. LIZ MURPHY, "The Art of Firing Smarter," *Sales & Marketing Management* (February 1988), pp. 37–40.

21. PATRICK SCHUL and BRENT WREN, "The Emerging Role of Women in Industrial Selling: A Decade of Change," *Journal of Marketing*, 56 (July 1992), pp. 38–54.

22. JOE MULLICH, "Sales Forces Hit by Harassment," *Business Marketing* (February 1994), p. 42.

23. Based on LINDA LYNTON, "The Dilemma of Sexual Harassment," *Sales & Marketing Management* (October 1989), pp. 67–71.

24. JULIA LAWLOR, "Stepping Over the Line," *Sales & Marketing Management* (October 1995), p. 94.

25. RAYMOND COREY, "Marketing Managers: Caught in the Middle," in *Ethics in Marketing*, ed. Craig Smith and John Quelch (Homewood, Ill.: Richard D. Irwin, 1993), p. 41.

26. Corey, "Marketing Managers," pp. 44–45.

▶ SELECTED READINGS

LARSON, CARL E., and FRANK LaFASTO, *Team Work: What Must Go Right/What Can Go Wrong* (Newbury Park, Calif.: Sage, 1989).

OSBURN, JACK, LINDA MORAN, ED MUSSELWHITE, and JOHN ZENGER, *Self-Directed Work Teams: The New American Challenge* (Homewood Ill.: Business One–Irwin, 1990).

RYAN, KATHLEEN, and DANIEL OESTREICH, *Driving Fear Out of the Workplace: How to Overcome the Invisible Barriers to Quality, Productivity, and Innovation* (San Francisco: Jossey-Bass, 1991).

SLOAN, A. E., JR., *My Years with General Motors* (New York: McFadden, 1965). For a review, see PETER F. DRUCKER, "The Best Book of Management Ever," *Fortune* (April 23, 1990), pp. 145–150.

SMITH, N. CRAIG, and JOHN QUELCH, *Ethics in Marketing* (Homewood, Ill.: Richard D. Irwin, 1993).

STAUNTON, J. DONALD, *Coaching Field Salespeople for Improved Sales Performance* (Sanford, Fla.: National Society of Sales Training Executives, 1990).

CASE

12-1 FIRST NATIONAL BANK*

"I'm concerned about Karen," said Margaret Costanzo to David Reeves. The two bank officers were seated in Costanzo's office at the First National Bank's branch in Federal Square.

Costanzo was a vice president of the bank and manager of the Federal Square branch, the third largest in First National's 92-branch network. She was having an employee appraisal meeting with Reeves, customer service director at the branch. Reeves was responsible for the Customer Service Department, which coordinated the activities of the customer service representatives (CSRs, formerly known as tellers) and the customer assistance representatives (CARs, formerly known as new accounts assistants).

Costanzo and Reeves were discussing Karen Mitchell, a 24-year-old customer service rep, who had applied for the soon-to-be-vacant position of head CSR. Mitchell had been with the bank since graduating from junior college with an associate in arts degree three and a half years earlier. She had applied for the position of what had then been called head teller a year earlier, but the job had gone to a candidate with more seniority. Now that individual was leaving—his wife had been transferred to a new job in another city—and the position was once again open. Two other candidates had applied for the job.

Both Costanzo and Reeves were agreed that, against all criteria used in the past, Karen Mitchell would have been the obvious choice for head teller. She was both fast and accurate in her work, presented a smart and professional appearance, and was well liked by customers and her follow CSRs.

However, the nature of the teller's job had been significantly revised nine months earlier to add a stronger marketing component. (Exhibit 1 shows the previous job description for teller, Exhibit 2 shows the new job description for customer service representative.) CSRs were now expected to offer polite suggestions that customers use automatic teller machines for simple transactions. They were also required to stimulate customer interest in the broadening array of financial services offered by the bank. "The problem with Karen," as Reeves put it, "is that she simply refuses to sell."

The New Focus on Customer Service At the First

Although it was the largest bank in the state, the "First" had historically focused on corporate business, and its share of the retail consumer banking business had declined in the face of aggressive competition from other financial institutions. Three years earlier, the Board of Directors had appointed a new CEO and given him the mandate of developing a stronger consumer orientation at the retail level. The goal was to seize the initiative in marketing the ever-increasing array of financial services now available to retail customers. The new CEO's strategy, after putting in place a new management team, was to begin by ordering an expansion and speed-up of the First's investment in electronic delivery systems. The bank had tripled the number of automatic teller machines in its branches during the past 18 months, and was engaged in an active branch renovation program. One year ago, the First had also joined a regional ATM network, which boasted freestanding 24-hour booths at shopping centers, airports, and other high-traffic locations.

These actions seemed to be bearing fruit. In the most recent six months, the First had seen a significant increase in the number of new accounts opened, as compared to the same period of the previous year. And quarterly data released by the Federal Reserve Bank showed that the First was steadily increasing its share of new deposits in the state.

Customer Service Issues

New financial products had been introduced at a rapid rate. But the bank found that existing platform staff—known as new accounts assistants—were ill-equipped to sell these services because of lack of

*This case was prepared by Christopher H. Lovelock. Copyright © by Christopher H. Lovelock. Reproduced by permission.

Exhibit 1: First National Bank: Position Description for Teller

FUNCTION

Provides customer services by receiving, paying out, and keeping accurate records of all monies involved in paying and receiving transactions. Promotes the Bank's services.

RESPONSIBILITIES

1. Serves customers
    Accepts deposits, verifies cash and endorsements, and gives customers their receipts.
    Cashes checks within the limits assigned or refers customers to supervisor for authorization.
    Accepts savings deposits and withdrawals, verifies signatures, posts interest, and balances as necessary.
    Accepts loan, credit card, utility, and other payments.
    Issues money orders, cashier's checks, traveler's checks, and foreign currency and issues or redeems U.S. savings bonds.
    Reconciles customer statements and confers with bookkeeping personnel regarding the discrepancies in balances or other problems.
    Issues credit card advances.
2. Prepares individual daily settlement of teller cash and proof transactions.
3. Prepares branch daily journal and general ledger.
4. Promotes the Bank's services:
    Cross-sells other bank services appropriate to customers' needs.
    Answers inquiries regarding bank matters.
    Directs customers to other departments for specialized services.
5. Assists with other branch duties:
    Receipts night and mail deposits.
    Reconciles ATM transactions.
    Provides safe deposit services.
    Performs secretarial duties.

product knowledge and inadequate training in selling skills. Recalled Costanzo:

> The problem was that they were so used to waiting for a customer to approach them with a specific request, such as a mortgage or car loan, that it was hard to get them to take a more proactive approach that involved actively probing for customer needs. Their whole job seemed to revolve around filling out forms.

As the automation program proceeded, the mix of activities performed by the tellers started to change. A growing number of customers began to use automatic teller machines for cash withdrawals and deposits, as well as for requesting account balances. The ATMs at the Federal Square branch had the highest utilization of any of the First's branches, reflecting the large number of students and young professionals served at that location. Costanzo noted that custom-

ers who were older or less well educated seemed to prefer being served by "a real person, rather than a machine."

A year earlier, the head office had selected three branches, including Federal Square, as test sites for a new customer service program. The Federal Square branch was in a busy urban location, about one mile from the central business district and three blocks from the campus of the state university. The branch was surrounded by retail stores and close to commercial and professional offices. The other two branches were among the bank's larger suburban offices and were located in a shopping center and next to a big hospital, respectively. As part of the branch renovation program, each of these three branches had previously been remodeled to include no fewer than four ATMs (Federal Square had five), a customer service desk near the entrance, and two electronic information terminals that customers could activate to

Exhibit 2: First National Bank: Position Description for Customer Service Representative

FUNCTION

Provides customers with the highest quality services, with special emphasis on recognizing customer needs and cross-selling appropriate bank services. Plays an active role in developing and maintaining good customer relations.

RESPONSIBILITIES

1. Presents and communicates the best possible customer service.
   Greets all customers with a courteous, friendly attitude.
   Provides fast, accurate, friendly service.
   Uses customer's name whenever possible.
2. Sells bank services and maintains customer relations.
   Cross-sells retail services by identifying and referring valid prospects to the customer assistance representative or customer service director. When time permits (no other customers waiting in line), should actively cross-sell retail services.
   Develops new business by acquainting noncustomers with bank services and existing customers with additional services that they are not currently using.
3. Provides a prompt and efficient operation on a professional level.
   Receives cash and/or checks for checking accounts, saving accounts, taxes withheld, loan payments, Master Card/Visa, mortgage payments, Christmas clubs, money orders, traveler's checks, cashier's checks, premium promotions.
   Verifies amount of cash and/or checks received, being alert for counterfeit or fraudulent items.
   Accepts deposits and withdrawals, verifying signatures where required by policy.
   Cashes checks in accordance with bank policy. Identifies payees; verifies signatures; checks dates and endorsements; compares written dollar and figure amounts; ensures that numbers are included on all counter checks, deposit slips and savings withdrawal and deposit slips; watches for stop payments and holds funds per bank policy.
   Where applicable, pays credit card cash advances and savings withdrawals. Accepts credit merchant deposits. Receives payment for collection items, safe deposit rentals, and other miscellaneous items.
   Confers with head CSR or customer service director on nonroutine situations.
   Sells traveler's checks, money orders, and cashier's checks and may redeem coupons and sell or redeem foreign currency.
   Handles sale and redemption of U.S. savings bonds.
   Sells monthly transit passes.
   Ensures timely batching and preparation of work for transmittal to proof department.
   Prepares coin and currency orders as necessary.
   Services, maintains, and settles automatic teller machines as required.
   Ensures that only minimum cash exposure necessary for efficient operation is kept in cash drawer; removes excess cash immediately to secured location. Ensures maximum control over cash drawers and other valuables on hand throughout daily operation.
   Prepares accurate and timely daily settlement of work.
   Performs bookkeeping and operational functions as assigned by customer service director.

obtain information on a variety of bank services. The teller stations were redesigned to provide two levels of service: an express station for simple deposits and for cashing of approved checks, and regular stations for the full array of services provided by tellers. The number of stations open at a given time was varied to reflect the volume of anticipated business. Finally, the platform area in each branch was reconstructed to create what the architect described as "a friendly, yet professional, appearance."

Human Resources

With the new environment came new training programs for the staff of these three branches and new job descriptions and job titles: customer assistance representatives (for the platform staff), customer service representatives (for the tellers), and customer service director (instead of assistant branch manager). The head teller position was renamed head CSR. Position descriptions for all these jobs are reproduced in Exhibits 2, 3, 4, and 5. The training programs for each group included sessions designed to develop improved knowledge of both new and existing retail products. (CARs received more extensive training in this area than did CSRs.) The CARs also attended a 15-hour course, offered in three separate sessions, on basic selling skills. This program covered key steps in the sales process, including building a relationship, exploring customer needs, determining a solution, and overcoming objections. The sales training program for CSRs, by contrast, consisted of just two 2-hour sessions designed to develop skills in recognizing and probing customer needs, presenting product features and benefits, overcoming objections, and referring customers to CARs.

All staff members in customer service positions participated in sessions designed to improve their communication skills and professional image: clothing and personal grooming and interactions with customers were all discussed. Said the trainer, "Remember, people's money is too important to entrust to someone who doesn't look and act the part!" CARs were instructed to rise from their seats and shake hands with customers. Both CARs and CSRs were given exercises designed to improve their listening skills and their powers of observation. All employees working where they could be seen by customers were ordered to refrain from smoking, drinking soda, and chewing gum on the job.

Although First National management anticipated that most of the increased emphasis on selling would fall to the CARs, they also foresaw a limited selling role for the customer service reps, who would be expected to mention various products and facilities offered by the bank as they served customers at the teller window.

For instance, if a customer happened to mention a vacation, the CSR was supposed to mention traveler's checks; if the customer complained about bounced checks, the CSR should suggest speaking to a CAR about opening a personal line of credit that would provide automatic overdraft protection; or if

---

Exhibit 3: First National Bank: Position Description for Head Customer Service Representative

---

FUNCTION

Supervises the customer service representatives in the designated branch office, ensuring efficient operations and the highest quality service to customers. Plays an active role in developing and maintaining good customer relations. Assists other branch personnel on request.

RESPONSIBILITIES

1. Supervises the CSRs in the branch.
    Allocates work, coordinates work flow, reviews and revises work procedures.
    Ensures that teller area is adequately and efficiently staffed with well-trained, qualified personnel.
    Assists CSRs with more complex transactions.
    Resolves routine personnel problems, referring more complex situations to the customer service director.
    Participates in decisions concerning performance appraisal, promotions, wage changes, transfers, and terminations of subordinate CSR staff.
2. Assumes responsibility for CSRs' money.
    Buys and sells money in the vault, ensuring adequacy of branch currency and coin supply.
    Ensures that CSRs and cash sheets are in balance.
    Maintains necessary records, including daily branch journal and general ledger.
3. Accepts deposits and withdrawals by business customers at commercial window.
4. Operates teller window to provide customer services (see Responsibilities for Customer Service Representative).

Exhibit 4: First National Bank: Position Description for Customer Assistance Representative

---

FUNCTION

Provides services and guidance to customers/prospects seeking banking relationships or related information. Promotes and sells needed products and responds to special requests by existing customers.

RESPONSIBILITIES

1. Provides prompt, efficient, and friendly service to all customers and prospective customers.
   Describes and sells bank services to customers/prospects who approach them directly or via referral from customer service reps or other bank personnel.
   Answers customers' questions regarding bank services, hours, etc.

2. Identifies and responds to customers' needs.
   Promotes and sells retail services and identifies any existing cross-sell opportunities.
   Opens new accounts for individuals, businesses, and private organizations.
   Prepares temporary checks and deposit slips for new checking/NOW accounts.
   Sells checks and deposit slips.
   Interviews and takes applications for and pays out on installment/charge card accounts and other credit-related products.
   Certifies checks.
   Handles stop payment requests.
   Responds to telephone mail inquiries from customers or bank personnel.
   Receives notification of name or address changes and takes necessary action.
   Takes action on notification of lost passbooks, credit cards, ATM cards, collateral, and all other lost or stolen valuables.
   Demonstrates automatic teller machines to customers and assists with problems.
   Coordinates closing of accounts and ascertains reasons.

3. Sells and services all retail products.
   Advises customers and processes their applications for all products covered in CAR training programs and updates.
   Initiates referrals to the appropriate department when a trust or corporate business need is identified.

---

the customer mentioned investments, the CSR should refer him or her to a CAR who could provide information on money market accounts, certificates of deposit, or the First's discount brokerage service. All CSRs were supplied with their own business cards. When making a referral, they were expected to write the customer's name and the product of interest on the back of a card, give it to the customer, and send that individual to the customer assistance desks.

In an effort to motivate CSRs at the three test branches to sell specific financial products, the bank experimented with various incentive programs. The first involved cash bonuses for referrals to CARs that resulted in the sale of specific products. During a one-month period, CSRs were offered a $50 bonus for each referral leading to a customer's opening a personal line of credit account: the CARs received a $20 bonus for each account they opened, regardless of whether or not it came as a referral or simply a walk-in. Eight such bonuses were paid to CSRs at Federal Square, with three each going to just two of the seven full-time CSRs, Jean Warshawksi and Bruce Greenfield. Karen Mitchell was not among the recipients. However, this program was not renewed, since it was felt that there were other, more cost-effective means of marketing this product. In addition, Reeves, the customer service director, had reason to believe that Bruce Greenfield had colluded with one of the CARs, his girlfriend, to claim referrals which he had not, in fact, made. Another test branch reported similar suspicions of two of its CSRs.

A second promotion followed and was based upon allocating credits to the CSRs for successful referrals. The value of the credit varied according to the nature of the product—for instance, a cash machine card was worth 500 credits—and accumulated credits

Exhibit 5: First National Bank: Position Description for Customer Service Director

FUNCTION

Supervises customer service representatives, customer assistance representatives, and other staff as assigned to provide the most effective and profitable retail banking delivery system in the local marketplace. Supervises sales efforts and provides feedback to management concerning response to products and services by current and prospective banking customers. Communicates goals and results to those supervised and ensures operational standards are met in order to achieve outstanding customer service.

RESPONSIBILITIES

1. Supervises effective delivery of retail products.
    Selects, trains, and manages the customer service representatives and customer assistance representatives.
    Assigns duties and work schedules.
    Completes performance reviews.

2. Personally, and through those supervised, renders the highest level of professional and efficient customer service available in the local marketplace.
    Provides high level of service while implementing most efficient and customer-sensitive staffing schedules.
    Supervises all on-the-job programs within office.
    Ensures that outstanding customer service standards are achieved.
    Directs remedial programs for CSRs and CARs as necessary.

3. Develops retail sales effectiveness to the degree necessary to achieve market share objectives.
    Ensures that all CSRs and CARs possess comprehensive product knowledge.
    Directs coordinated cross-sell program within office at all times.
    Reports staff training needs to branch manager and/or regional training director.

4. Maintains operational adherence to standards.
    Oversees preparation of daily and monthly operational and sales reports.
    Estimates, approves, and coordinates branch cash needs in advance.
    Oversees ATM processing function.
    Handles or consults with CSRs/CARs on more complex transactions.
    Ensures clean and businesslike appearance of the branch facility.

5. Informs branch manager of customer response to products.
    Reports customer complaints and types of sales resistance encountered.
    Describes and summarizes reasons for account closings.

6. Communicates effectively the goals and results of the Bank to those under supervision.
    Reduces office goals into format which translates to goals for each CSR or CAR.
    Reports sales and cross-sell results to all CSRs and CARs.
    Conducts sales- and service-oriented staff meetings with CSRs/CARs on a regular basis.
    Attends all scheduled customer service management meetings organized by regional office.

could be exchanged for merchandise gifts. This program was deemed ineffective and discontinued after three months. The basic problem seemed to be that the value of the gifts was too low in relation to the amount of effort required.

Other problems with these promotional schemes included lack of product knowledge on the part of the CSRs and time pressures when many customers were waiting in line to be served.

The bank had next turned to an approach which, in David Reeves' words, "used the stick rather than the carrot." All CSRs had traditionally been evaluated half-yearly on a variety of criteria, including accuracy, speed, quality of interactions with customers, punctuality of arrival for work, job attitudes, cooperation with other employees, and professional image. The evaluation process assigned a number of points to each criterion, with accuracy and speed being the most heavily weighted. In addition to appraisals by the customer service director and the branch manager, with input from the head CSR, the First had recently instituted a program of anonymous visits by what was popularly known as the "mystery client." Each CSR was visited at least once a quarter by a professional evaluator posing as a customer. This individual's appraisal of the CSR's appearance, performance, and attitude was included in the overall evaluation. The number of points scored by each CSR had a direct impact on merit pay raises and on selection for promotion to the head CSR position or to platform jobs.

To encourage improved product knowledge and "consultative selling" by CSRs, the evaluation process was revised to include points assigned for each individual's success in sales referrals. Under the new evaluation scheme, the maximum number of points assignable for effectiveness in making sales—directly or through referrals to CARs—amounted to 30 percent of the potential total score. Although CSR-initiated sales had risen significantly in the most recent half-year, Reeves sensed that morale had dropped among this group, in contrast to the CARs, whose enthusiasm and commitment had risen significantly. He had also noticed an increase in CSR errors. One CSR had quit, complaining about too much pressure.

Karen Mitchell

Under the old scoring system, Karen Mitchell had been the highest-scoring teller/CSR for four consecutive half-years. But after two half-years under the new system, her ranking had dropped to fourth out of the seven full-time tellers. The top-ranking CSR, Mary Bell, had been with the First for 16 years but had declined repeated invitations to apply for a head teller position, saying that she was happy where she was, earning at the top of the CSR scale, and did not want "the extra worry and responsibility." Mitchell ranked first on all but one of the operationally related criteria (interactions with customers, where she ranked second) but sixth on selling effectiveness (Exhibit 6).

Costanzo and Reeves had spoken to Mitchell about her performance and expressed disappointment. Mitchell had told them, respectfully but firmly, that she saw the most important aspect of her job

as giving customers fast, accurate, and courteous service.

I did try this selling thing [she told the two bank officers], but it seemed to annoy people. Some said they were in a hurry and couldn't talk now; others looked at me as if I were slightly crazy to bring up the subject of a different bank service than the one they were currently transacting. And then, when you got the odd person who seemed interested, you could hear the other customers in the line grumbling about the slow service.

Really, the last straw was when I noticed on the computer that this woman had several thousand in her savings account, so I suggested to her, just as the trainer had told us, that she could earn more interest if she opened a money market account. Well, she told me it was none of my business what she did with her money, and stomped off. Don't get me wrong, I love being able to help customers, and if they ask for my advice, I'll gladly tell them about what the bank has to offer.

Selecting a New Head CSR

Two weeks after this meeting, it was announced that the head CSR was leaving. The job entailed some supervision of the other CSRs (including allocation of work assignments and scheduling of part-time CSRs at busy periods or during employee vacations), consultation on—and, where possible, resolution of—any problems occurring at the teller stations, and handling of large cash deposits and withdrawals by local retailers (see position description in Exhibit 3). When not engaged in such tasks, the head CSR was expected to operate a regular teller window.

The pay scale for a head CSR ranged from $7.00 to $12.00 per hour, depending on qualifications, seniority, and branch size, as compared to a range of $5.40 to $9.00 per hour for CSRs. The pay scale for CARs ranged from $6.20 to $10.50. Full-time employees (who were not unionized) worked a 40-hour week, including some evenings until 6:00 P.M. and certain Saturday mornings. Costanzo indicated that the pay scales were typical for banks in the Midwest, although the average CSR at the First was better qualified than those at smaller banks and therefore higher on the scale. Karen Mitchell was currently earning $7.80 per hour, reflecting her associate's degree, 3½ years' experience, and significant past merit increases. If pro-

Exhibit 6: First National Bank: Summary of Performance Evaluation Scores for Customer Service Representatives at Federal Square Branch for Two Half-Year Periods

CSR Name[a]	Length of Full-Time Bank Service	Operational Criteria[b] (max: 70 points)		Selling Effectiveness[c] (max: 30 points)		Total Score	
		1st Half	2nd Half	1st Half	2nd Half	1st Half	2nd Half
Mary Bell	16 years, 10 mos.	65	64	16	20	81	84
Richard Dubois	2 years, 3 mos.	63	61	15	19	78	80
Bruce Greenfield	1 year, 0 mos.	48	42	20	26	68	68
Karen Mitchell	3 years, 7 mos.	67	67	13	12	80	79
Sharon Ronsky	1 year, 4 mos.	53	55	8	9	61	64
Naomi Rubin	7 mos.	—	50	—	22	—	72
Jean Warshawski	2 years, 1 mo.	57	55	21	28	79	83

[a]Full-time CSRs only (part-time CSRs were evaluated separately).

[b]Totals based on sum of ratings against various criteria, including accuracy, work production, attendance and punctuality, personal appearance, organization of work, initiative, cooperation with others, problem-solving ability, and quality of interaction with customers.

[c]Points awarded for both direct sales by CSR (e.g., traveler's checks) and referral selling by CSR to CAR (e.g., ATM card, certificates of deposit, personal line of credit).

moted to head CSR, she would qualify for an initial rate of $9.50 an hour.

When applications for the positions closed, Mitchell was one of three candidates. The other two candidates were Jean Warshawski, 42, another CSR at the Federal Square branch, and Curtis Richter, 24, the head CSR of one of the First National Bank's smaller suburban branches, who was seeking more responsibility.

Warshawski was married and had two sons in high school. She had started working as a part-time teller at Federal Square three years previously, switching to full-time work a year later in order, as she said, to put away some money for her boys' college education. Warshawski was a cheerful woman with a jolly laugh. She had a wonderful memory for people's names, and Reeves had often seen her greeting customers on the street or in a restaurant during the lunch hour. Reviewing her evaluations over the past three years, Reeves noted that she had initially performed poorly on accuracy and at one point, while still a part-timer, had been put on probation because of frequent inaccuracies in the balance in her cash drawer at the end of the day. Although Reeves considered her much improved on this score, he still saw room for improvement. The customer service director had also had occasion to reprimand her for tardiness during the past

year. Warshawski attributed this to health problems with her elder son who, she said, was now responding to treatment.

Both Reeves and Costanzo had observed Washawski at work and agreed that her interactions with customers were exceptionally good, although she tended to be overly chatty and was not as fast as Karen Mitchell. She seemed to have a natural ability to size up customers and to decide which ones were good prospects for a quick sales pitch on a specific financial product. Although slightly untidy in her personal appearance, she was very well organized in her work and was quick to help her fellow CSRs, especially new hires. She was currently earning $7.20 per hour as a CSR and would qualify for a rate of $9.10 as head CSR. In the most recent six months, Warshawski had ranked ahead of Mitchell as a result of being very successful in consultative selling (Exhibit 6).

Richter, the third candidate, was not working in one of the three test branches, and so had not been exposed to the consultative selling program and its corresponding evaluation scheme. However, he had received excellent evaluations for his work in the First's small Longmeadow branch, where he had been employed for three years. A move to Federal Square would increase his earnings from $8.20 to $9.10 per hour. Reeves and Costanzo had interviewed Richter and considered him intelligent and personable. He had joined the bank after dropping out of college midway through his junior year, but had recently started taking evening courses in order to complete his degree. The Longmeadow branch was located in an older part of town, where commercial and retail activity was rather stagnant. The branch had not yet been renovated and had no ATMs, although there was an ATM accessible to First National customers one block away. Richter supervised three CSRs and reported directly to the branch manager, who spoke very highly of him. Since there were no CARs in this branch, Richter and another experienced CSR took turns handling new accounts and loan or mortgage applications.

Costanzo and Reeves were troubled by the decision that faced them. Prior to the bank's shift in focus, Mitchell would have been the natural choice for the head CSR job, which, in turn, could be a stepping stone to further promotions, including customer assistance representative, customer service director, and, eventually, manager of a small branch or a management position in the head office. Mitchell had told her superiors that she was interested in making a career in banking and that she was eager to take on further responsibilities.

Compounding the problem was the fact that the three branches testing the new customer service program had just completed a full year of the test. Costanzo knew that sales and profits were up significantly at all three branches relative to the bank's performance as a whole. She anticipated that top management would want to extend the program systemwide after making any modifications that seemed desirable.

CASE

12-2 ROMANO PITESTI*

Events had come to a head in Tickton-Jones Ltd. and the Marketing Director, Jack Simpson, had called in his Consumer Products Sales Manager, David Courtney, to sort out the problem.

"To come straight to the point, David," said Jack, "I'm about up to here with this sales rep of yours. Romano Pitesti. . . . Am I sick of hearing the guy's name! Everywhere I go, someone bends my ear about him. Last week it was the receptionist complaining about his making personal telephone calls during company time. Yesterday it was the security people about his untidy parking habits. And this morning, the accounts department is abuzz with outrage over his expense returns. Quite frankly, David, these are not isolated instances—he's out of control and I want to know what you intend to do about him, before the whole company is in uproar."

*This case was prepared by A. F. Millman of the Coventry Polytechnic, England. Copyright © by A. F. Millman. Reproduced by permission.

Background

Tickton-Jones Ltd. was formed two years previously, when Tickton Flexible Products Ltd. acquired Samuel Jones Ltd., a local family-owned company. At the time, Tickton's annual sales were approaching $12 million and they employed 230 people; compared with Jones' $4.5 million and 110 people, respectively. Tickton was well established as a compounder of polyurethane and rubber materials and had its own molding facility for a wide range of industrial components. Jones, after years of steady business as a manufacturer of shoes, ladies' handbags, and travel goods, had recently moved successfully into sports shoes and for the first time had made an impact in the export field.

Ben Jones was the Chairman and majority owner of Samuel Jones Ltd. He was the grandson of the founder and the last of the Jones family line with an active participation in the business. At age 63, he wanted to sell out and retire to the Channel Islands with his wife, who had a health problem. The remaining two senior Directors were willing to accept early retirement on generous terms.

Ben Jones had been very happy to accept Tickton's offer and was satisfied that the new company would not involve too much upheaval for his employees. He was a paternal Chairman with a strong Protestant work ethic, but in recent years this had softened, and the organization had become somewhat looser in all aspects of its operations.

Not everyone on the Tickton Board had been in favor of the acquisition, largely because it represented a major diversification into consumer products. But the Managing Director had swayed the decision on grounds of too much current dependence on declining customer industries (e.g., motor vehicles, railways, general mechanical engineering). Jones was considered to have good products in growth markets. In the words of Tickton's Managing Director: "An opportunity like this might never pass our way again. Ben Jones assures me that he has a sound labor force and, like our own, they're not strongly unionized. The sports and leisure shoe business looks particularly attractive. Put our expertise in molding technology alongside their distribution network, and it could be one of our main product lines in five years. It's now or never—it would be virtually impossible to find equivalent facilities within a five-mile radius." Within four weeks, the acquisition was agreed upon.

Due to the departure of Jones's senior Directors, integration of managerial staff provided few problems. Jones's production manager, Bill Thompson, was retained and placed in charge of the Jones site, which was effectively reduced to a manufacturing operation. All nonproduction staff, including the sales manager, David Courtney, were moved to the Tickton site.

However, the absorption of middle/lower-level administrative staff had not been easy, and there were still cliques of former Jones employees who felt aggrieved. For example, certain secretaries had found themselves reporting to managers of lower status; friction in the sales administration office and accounts office caused internal divisions; and there was growing rivalry among the industrial sales engineers and the consumer sales representatives.

The organization of Tickton-Jones's marketing department is shown in Exhibit 1. From the marketing point of view, Jack Simpson had merely added another arm to his departmental organization—the Consumer Products Group under David Courtney.

Exhibit 1: Organization of the Tickton-Jones Marketing Department

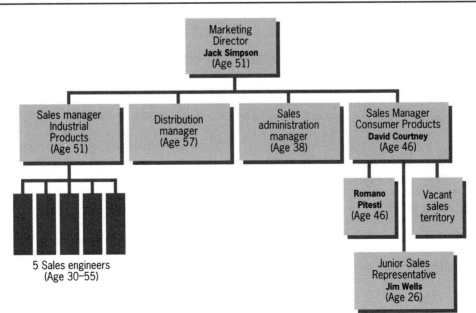

Prior to the acquisition, David Courtney had been very much a field sales manager. He was responsible for the usual sales management tasks of forecasting and budgeting, and spent most of his time dealing with major existing accounts or on the road developing new accounts. David Courtney, Romano Pitesti, and Jim Wells were all paid a salary plus commission. The commission element accounted for 20–25 percent of their annual pay. On joining Tickton-Jones's salary structure they received salary only, though in money terms this did not constitute a loss of total pay.

On the question of company car policy and day-to-day business expenses, there were major differences. Indeed, since at Samuel Jones Ltd. they applied to so few people, there were no formal procedures and Ben Jones signed off on everything, almost without question. In contrast, Tickton had a written document clearly setting out the type of car applicable to particular grades; spending limits for travel and entertainment, and so on. There was also a handbook covering Tickton's general conditions of service, which automatically became the Tickton-Jones handbook.

Romano Pitesti

To say that Romano Cesare Pitesti was *different* from the industrial sales engineers would be an understatement. While they "toed the line" and had quite similar training and attitudes, Romano "sailed close to the wind."

Romano liked to feel that he was an *individualist* and repeatedly proved disruptive in formal group situations. Though basically conscientious and hardworking, he operated in bursts of enthusiasm that usually came to nothing but sometimes, through sheer tenacity on his part, brought the company an important order.

He was the master of the *instant opinion* and often entered into conversation on a range of issues of which he had only cursory knowledge and experience. This led him into a number of embarrassing situations, reflecting his gullibility and boyish naiveté.

There were occasions when he could be charming, understanding, and a good listener, especially in female company. And even more so in the presence of Sheila Jones, his previous Chairman's wife! It was

well known that she had a soft spot for Romano and had once saved him from serious trouble following an incident involving a secretary after the office Christmas party.

Romano was flamboyant in all things, yet beneath this facade lay a caring and deeply sensitive person. His colleague, Jim Wells, summed him up as "part hero, part villain, and part clown."

From the day he transferred to Tickton-Jones, Romano was regarded as a curiosity and a "figure of fun." The reasons were not hard to find. He dressed impeccably and in the height of fashion. Some would say that he overdid it for a 42-year-old, and he was soon dubbed "The Great Gatsby," "Peter Pan," and "The Aging Lothario."

In his first year with Tickton-Jones, Romano married Wendy Churchill, a 28-year-old set designer with a regional television company. This brought him in contact with numerous television personalities and turned him into a prolific name dropper. The stories he told provided unlimited ammunition for the industrial sales engineers, who cruelly taunted him at every opportunity. But Romano, unperturbed, shrugged off their remarks, usually with some witty return.

Despite all these oddities and eccentricities, Roman's sales performance was exemplary.

The Meeting with David Courtney

With Jack Simpson's words ringing in his ears, David Courtney summoned Romano to a meeting. Romano insisted that it would upset his call schedule, but after some cajoling agreed to attend the following morning.

David opened the meeting with firm words: "Romano, something has to be done about the way you operate in this company. It has been put to me that you are out of control. I'm taking the kicks at the moment and I don't like it! I've got a list of incidents to review with you—and you had better have good answers."

1. **David:** Your time-keeping leaves a lot to be desired, and you've been accused of wasting your own time and other people's. The normal starting time is 8:30 A.M. and not some time after 9:00 A.M. when you can make it!

Romano: That's all very well, but I'm entitled to a little freedom on time. Only yesterday I left home at 6:00 A.M. to visit a customer and didn't return home until late in the evening. How many of those complaining about my time-keeping would be prepared to join me at such times of the day and night without overtime payments?

David: And what about time wasting? You seem to spend a fair amount of time with secretaries and typists.

Romano: No more than anyone else. It's just that other people spread their time over the week and mine's more concentrated. You know how much importance you attach to letter and report writing. Well, they all have to be typed.

2. **David:** That brings me to the time you claim to spend report writing. Taking Fridays off is a favorite for sniping by the industrial sales engineers.

Romano: If you want me to write reports, you have got to allow me time to write them—it's as simple as that.

David: The industrial sales engineers write their reports over their lunch break or between sales calls. Why can't you? There's a rumor circulating the company that you played golf last Friday.

Romano: Yes, that's right. I played golf with Arthur Dixon—you know, Singleton's Purchasing Manager. I'm pretty close to a regular order from them. I'm playing with Arthur again on the 29th—should I cancel it?

David: No, no—I only wish you to make yourself a little more *visible* on Fridays. Not every Friday, just now and then.

3. **David:** Are you aware that you have higher claims for replacement of damaged clothing than anyone in the company? Why?

Romano: I can't help it if I wear trendy Italian suits and shoes. That damaged briefcase I claimed last month really was two-tone crocodile skin and cost me $180. I can't visit my customers dressed like those scruffy *Herberts* in the Industrial Group. They wouldn't let me on the premises.

David: OK, OK, just try to moderate your claims in future. I'm the poor guy who has to sign them off.

4. **David:** The biggest problem, as always, surrounds your company car. It's like a big orange blotch on the company landscape!

Romano: I can't see what you have against my car, David. It's only a Ford Escort 1.3 and bought within the company rules. We have very little flexibility on choice of model. After all, it's my mobile office—I live in it for 15 hours per week.

David: Yes, but do you have to choose bright orange and add all those accessories? The industrial sales engineers all have more sober colors such as bottle green and navy blue. Do you really need two large spot lamps with checkered covers, a rear spoiler, and whiplash radio aerial?

Romano: I paid for the accessories myself. You could do the same if you wish. Incidentally, there's a nice vivid green in the Ford Sierra right now!

David: I can almost bear the color with my sunglasses on—but not when you park your car on the double yellow lines near the reception area.

Romano: I knew it! That receptionist has got it in for me. It would be her who complained and not the security people. I only popped in to the switchboard to collect my telephone messages from the overnight answering machine.

David: I can accept that as an isolated incident. But your car is so obvious—everywhere you go, it's instantly recognizable. Which leads me to a very serious issue—did you or did you not use your company car to ferry voters to the local Council elections?

Romano: Yes, I did. I had my doubts about it and was on the verge of opting out. Then I realized Bill Thompson, the Production Manager, was using his company car for the Labour Party, so I thought, what's good enough for Labour is good enough for the Liberals.

David: Perhaps I had better have a word with Bill about the matter. We'll pick this one up later.

5. **Romano:** You've mentioned all these minor irritations, David. Have you ever had cause to question my sales performance? I'm the best salesperson in this company, and you know it! When did I last fail to meet my targets? And have

you received any complaints from customers? I was the same at Samuel Jones. Don't forget, we're a rep short at the moment. A few more salespeople like me and we would be a market leader in no time. Who was it who secured the Milan export order?

But at that particular moment there was an interruption. Romano's telephone paging beeper was signaling an incoming call, and he picked up David's telephone. It was Joe Pinkerton. Romano's number two customer, with an urgent query.

Romano sat back in his chair, put his feet on David's wastepaper basket, and entered into a drawn-out conversation. Twenty minutes later he was still engrossed in conversation. David shook his head and decided to abandon the meeting. Romano gave him a wry grin as he left the office.

▶ 13 ◀

Motivating Salespeople*

*Success is often nothing more than moving from one
failure to the next with undiminished enthusiasm.*
WINSTON CHURCHILL

*Chapter Consultant: Michael Mahan Team Leader IBM Global Services.

LEARNING OBJECTIVES

After studying this chapter, you should be able to:

▶ Define motivation and explain sales managers' concerns with
motivation.

▶ Tell how and why individual needs may differ.

▶ Describe a basic model of the motivation process.

▶ Discuss the different types of quotas and the administrative
issues involved in using quotas.

▶ Describe how to design incentive and recognition programs
and their limitations.

▶ THE PRESIDENT'S CLUB

Leo Kelly is a Philadelphia-based senior sales executive for the Business Systems Group of Xerox Corporation. Last year he finished at 247 percent of quota. In his 20 years with Xerox, Kelly has been a member of the President's Club 17 times. (This is the company's top incentive award, a four-day, first-class trip for a salesperson and spouse to a designated resort.) Says Kelly, "The President's Club is what we all strive for because it's how our success is measured within Xerox. I use it as a yardstick for minimum accomplishment. Other people might use 100 percent of plan; I would consider 100 percent of plan abject failure."

How does Leo Kelly feel about a turndown? "A no is like a buying signal to me," says Kelly. "I make money on no's. If a person is still talking to me, I'm still selling. I say, 'I'd appreciate it if you'd tell me where I have a problem—is the problem me, is the problem my product, or is the problem the way it was presented?' Then I shut up, sit back, and start taking notes—and I'm back in the sales call again."

What does Leo Kelly feel it takes to be a high performer? "The performers—the people who succeed—have tremendous discipline. There's always a reason not to call on someone. There's always a reason to go home early. There's always a reason not to come to work. Sales is a matter of being in the right place at the right time, and the only way you're going to be in the right place at the right time is if you're in a lot of places a lot of times. If you do that, you're going to be successful."[1]

A key management principle states that salespeople's performance is based on opportunity and on their level of ability and motivation. This principle is often expressed by the following formula:

$$\text{Performance} = f(\text{opportunity} \times \text{ability} \times \text{motivation})$$

Although the combination of these factors limits overall performance, deficiencies in one factor may be offset by the others. With Xerox, Kelly enjoyed the opportunity to succeed with a great company, but just as important, he had the ability to sell and the motivation to be very successful.

This chapter is concerned with motivation and will follow the topical outline shown in the following diagram. First, we define motivation and discuss why sales managers are concerned with sales force motivation. Next, we discuss individual needs and how people's needs differ. This is followed by a model of motivation that identifies the variety of factors that promote needs satisfaction. Finally, we explain how to develop effective quota, incentive, and recognition programs. Although these programs are widely used to motivate salespeople, their limitations are also discussed.

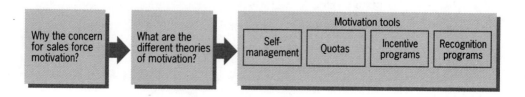

► WHAT IS MOTIVATION?

Sales force motivation is a hot topic with sales managers. If the product or service is right and sales force selection, organization, and training are right, then motivation becomes the critical determinant of success. Another reason sales managers are concerned about motivation is the demanding environment in which salespeople operate. Field salespeople are continually going from the exhilaration of making a sale to the disappointment associated with being turned down. Salespeople frequently must talk with strangers who are not always ready or willing to buy what the salesperson has to sell. Some salespeople, furthermore, must routinely spend long hours on the road away from their families and friends. Faced with these conditions, it is understandable that salespeople may need extra support to do an effective job.

A second reason why motivation is critical is that most salespeople are not under direct supervision in the physical presence of their manager. Veteran salespeople often meet with their immediate sales managers less than six times a year. In the absence of direct supervision, self-motivation is critical.

Third, motivation not only affects what activities salespeople perform, but also their enthusiasm and the quality of their work. A salesperson's conviction that a product or service is best for the customer will have a profound influence on a customer's purchasing decision. Customers are unlikely to purchase if they get the feeling that the salesperson is not truly interested in being there and helping them.

What do sales managers mean when they talk about motivating a salesperson? We define *motivation* as an individual's willingness to exert effort to achieve the organization's goals while satisfying individual needs. Inherent in this definition are three components: effort, needs, and organizational goals. We have discussed typical sales force–related organizational goals—sales volume, market share, profits, customer retention, and so on—and will return to these goals when describing quotas later in this chapter. Let's focus for a moment on effort.

Effort

Over 25 years ago in a classic article on motivation, Herzberg noted that a KITP, which he coyly explained stood for "kick in the pants," may produce compliance, it never produces motivation.[2] When describing someone as being motivated, sales managers are talking about three characteristics of effort:

1. *The drive to initiate action on a task.* A common concern among sales managers is to get salespeople to call on targeted prospects.

2. *The quality of effort on a task.* It's not enough to get people to call on prospects; they must also be motivated to put forth the effort to prepare to prospect properly and call on a potential customer.

3. *The persistence to expend effort over a period of time sufficient to meet or exceed objectives.* It is not enough to put forth the effort some of the time; high performers show up to win every time. Leo Kelly's discussion of what it takes to be a high performer ("There's always a reason not to come to work") is an excellent example of this drive.

Notice that all three of these dimensions of effort originate within the person. No one can motivate a salesperson to do anything, but a sales manager can help salespeople to motivate themselves.

Behavior is not random; it is caused. What causes people to exhibit certain behaviors in defined circumstances? In addressing this question, we look at individual needs, what they are, and how they are related.

▶ INDIVIDUAL NEEDS

In sales, the future of the business—and maybe even the sales manager's job—depends on managers' ability to understand the psychology of their salespeople. A good sales manager knows what his or her salespeople want—what drives them. If a sales manager feels that the need for status, control, respect, and routine are most important, a number of actions can be taken to motivate a sales force, as shown in Figure 13-1.

A number of formal theories have been developed to understand differences in individual needs. Some of the classic theories include Moslow's needs hierarchy, Alderfer's ERG theory, Herzberg's motivation-hygiene theory, and McClelland's theory of learned needs. Since you have undoubtedly reviewed these theories in earlier courses, we assume you're familiar with them. Nonetheless, we've summarized them briefly in Figure 13-2. Sales Management in Action 13-1 describes how Maslow's hierarchy of demand would apply in China.

These classic motivation theories are concerned with unique individual needs. While each individual is unique, motivational and personality profiles of salespeople's wants and patterns of behavior have been identified. After 22 years and interviews with over a half a million salespeople, the Gallup Management Consulting Group's research has revealed that high-performers tend to exhibit one of four per-

Sales Force Needs	Company Actions to Fill Needs
Status	Change title from "salesperson" to "area manager."
	Buy salespeople more luxurious cars to drive.
Control	Allow salespeople to help plan sales quotas and sequences of calls.
Respect	Invite salespeople to gatherings of top executives.
	Put pictures of top salespeople in company ads and newsletters.
Routine	Assign each salesperson a core of loyal customers that are called on regularly.
Accomplishment	Set reasonable goals for the number of calls and sales.
Stimulation	Run short-term sales contests.
	Schedule sales meetings in exotic locations.
Honesty	Deliver promptly all rewards and benefits promised.

Figure 13-1: Sales Force Needs and Ways to Fill Them

Theory	Author	Description
Hierarchy of needs	Abraham Maslow	Physiological, safety, belonging, esteem, and self-actualization needs are ranked in a hierarchy from lowest to highest. An individual moves up the hierarchy as a need is substantially realized.
ERG theory	Clayton P. Alderfer	Hierarchically classifies needs as existence, relatedness, and growth needs. Like Maslow, suggests that people will focus on higher needs as lower needs are satisfied but, unlike Maslow, suggests that people will focus on lower needs if their higher needs are not satisfied.
Motivation-hygiene	Frederick Herzberg	Argues that intrinsic job factors (e.g., challenging work, achievement) motivate, whereas extrinsic factors (e.g., pay) only placate employees.
Theory of learned needs	David McClelland	Proposes that there are three major professional needs: achievement, affiliation, and power. A high need for achievement and affiliation has been related to higher sales force performance. A high need for power has been related to higher sales manager performance.
Equity theory	J. Stacy Adams	Proposes that people will evaluate their treatment in comparison to that of "relevant others" and that motivation will suffer if treatment is perceived to be inequitable.

Figure 13-2: Summary of Classic Motivation Theories

sonality types, each with different drives: the competitor, the ego-driven, the achiever, and the service-oriented.[3] Each of these is described in Figure 13-3. While no one is purely one type of person, you might think about how you would motivate each type of person and what are the potential pitfalls associated with each type of person.

Career Stages

Experienced sales managers have long understood that motivation varies according to the age and experience of the salesperson. Career stages provide a framework to understand how individual salespeople differ and how their approach to work is likely to change over time.

Sales Management in Action 13-1
The Chinese Needs Hierarchy

Maslow's *hierarchy of needs* is a peculiarly North American–based theory of needs. With the globalization of business, you should be aware of assumptions and perspectives that may not be valid in other nations and cultures.

Consider the Chinese culture and history. The importance of the group, rather than the individual, is a common thread running through Chinese culture and management concepts. It is consistent with the values of national loyalty, equity, communal property, reluctance to recognize personal accomplishment, and emphasis on motivating through group forces. A basic assumption in the Chinese culture is that a good member of society always places group objectives before individual needs. If, for example, you compliment a Chinese citizen on his or her accomplishment, the usual reply is, "I am only doing my job" or "It is my duty." Based on these cultural assumptions, the Chinese hierarchy of needs may look like the accompanying figure. Notice that self-actualization is in service to society rather than individual development. The Chinese stress loyalty and unity; Americans stress the integrity of the individual and individual achievement. Also, notice that affiliation is expected within the culture and consequently is considered a basic need. On the other hand, things that many people take for granted, such as food, clothing, and shelter, must be strived for in China.

Source: Adapted from E. Nevis, "Using an American Perspective in Understanding Another Culture. Toward a Hierarchy of Needs for the People's Republic of China." *Journal of Applied Behavior Science,* 19 (1983), pp. 249–264.

The Competitor	This person not only wants to win, but derives satisfaction from beating specific rivals—another company or even colleagues. They tend to verbalize what they are going to do, and then do it.
The Ego-driven	They are not interested in beating specific opponents, they just want to win. They like to be considered experts, but are prone to feeling slighted, change jobs frequently, and often take things too personally.
The Achiever	This type of person is almost completely self-motivated. They usually set high goals and as soon as they hit one goal, they move the bar higher. They like accomplishment, regardless of who receives the credit.
The Service-oriented	Their strengths lie in building and cultivating relationships. Winning is not everything to this person, but they do respond to feelings of gratitude and friendship from other people.

Source: What Makes Great Salespeople," *Sales & Marketing Management* (May 1994), pp. 82–92.

Figure 13-3: Profiles of Top Salespeople

	Exploration	Establishment	Maintenance	Disengagement
Career Concerns	Finding an appropriate occupational field	Successfully establishing a career in a certain occupation	Holding on to what has been achieved; reassessing career, with possible redirection	Completing one's career
Motivational Needs Job Related	Learning the skills required to do the job well. Becoming a contributing member of an organization	Using skills to produce results. Adjusting to working with greater autonomy.	Developing broader view of work and organization. Maintaining a high performance level	Establishing a stronger self-identity outside of work. Maintaining an acceptable performance level
Personal Challenges	Establishing a good initial professional self-concept	Producing superior results on the job in order to be promoted.	Maintaining motivation, though possible rewards have changed. Facing concerns about aging	Acceptance of career accomplishments
Psychosocial Needs	Support Peer Acceptance Challenging position	Achievement Esteem Autonomy Competition	Security Helping younger colleagues	Detachment from the organization and organizational life

Figure 13-4: Career Stage Characteristics

Jolson was the first to note that salespeople's performance resembled the four stages of the classic S-shaped curve of the product life cycle.[4] Later research suggested that, over their career, salespeople go through four stages during which they focus on certain career concerns, developmental tasks, personal challenges, and psychosocial needs.[5] These are summarized in Figure 13-4 for the four career stages.

Exploration Stage

Early in one's career, during the *exploration stage*, the overall concern is finding the right occupation—"What do I want to do for the rest of my life?" The stress associated with resolving this tough issue sometimes results in lower performance, especially among those unable to resolve this concern at an early age. The challenge facing management is to help people successfully address this concern. One thing managers should do is to give realistic job and career opportunity descriptions during job interviews. Managers should also spend time with new people providing feedback, reinforcing their accomplishments, and pointing out the long-run benefits associated with working for the organization.

Establishment Stage

Most people eventually change their focus from searching for the "best" occupation to committing themselves to getting ahead in their current jobs. People at the *establishment stage* of their careers are usually willing to put in long hours to improve their performance. For most people, settling down will occur sometime during the late twenties to early thirties.

One management concern is that the highest performers during this stage are most likely to change jobs. This is especially likely if the rewards for high performance are not provided by their current organizations. In sales, the most obvious sign of getting ahead is promotion to sales management. Unfortunately, the downsizing of many organizations and the elimination of management layers to lower costs and get closer to the customer have reduced opportunities for advancement. Management's challenge in this case is to broaden salespeople's definition of success as something other than promotion to sales management.

The response to this situation by some companies has been to develop a "sales career path" for salespeople who do not want to pursue the management ranks. A typical sales career path might progress from sales rep to senior sales rep to executive rep to major accounts rep. This has retained senior people with higher base pay, healthier commissions, and a solid growth oriented career path. This has motivated and will continue to motivate salespeople for their entire career.

Maintenance Stage

At some point, usually in their late thirties or early forties, people begin to reflect on their past accomplishments and reassess career choices that they have made. For many people, this coincides with the broader reassessment associated with the mid-life crisis. Being turned down for promotion and realizing that future promotion opportunities are unlikely may trigger this reflective reaction in others. How people react to this reassessment of their careers is referred to as the *maintenance stage*.

People often have very different reactions when reflecting on their careers. Some people decide to switch occupations or organizations, while others choose to stay in the present one. Similar to the stay-or-leave decision in the establishment stage, some people decide that sales is the best occupation for them, while others choose to stay in sales out of fear of change or because of other obligations, especially to their families. Still others choose to take a new direction, often pursuing a dream that had been set aside earlier in life.

Promotion to management is no longer as desired or valued by maintenance-stage people as it was during establishment. These people are most likely to be the backbone of the sales force and tend to have the highest sales volume. For most people this stage will last for a long time, typically 15 to 20 years. The challenge for management is to maintain the high motivation and performance levels by challenging people to use their knowledge in new ways. This also means introducing significant rewards for meeting new challenges and mastering them.

Disengagement Stage

Everyone inevitably withdraws from their job and career. The *disengagement stage* involves giving greater priority to issues other than work and career. For people facing imminent retirement, this transition period helps them to cope with the feeling of loss of focus and to come to terms with the idea they will no longer be making a contribution, something that has been a part of success in their careers.

For others, disengagement may occur as a gradual process, early in life, long before retirement. Some of these people are in their forties and early fifties and will remain on the job for some time to come. On-the-job reactions of these salespeople are quite dramatic. They tend not to be as involved in and challenged by their work. In addition, they are less satisfied with many aspects of the job. The sales performance of these people suffers and is usually significantly lower than that of people in the maintenance stage.

Attempts to motivate these people to achieve greater performance are often frustrating. Increased pay usually does not lead to sustained effort, and these people place less importance on management recognition than people in other career stages. While they feel that it is important to meet sales quotas, they are not usually interested in opening new accounts. In short, their approach is one of achieving the minimum necessary to keep management off their backs.

Perhaps the most useful approach that management can take is to help dissuade people from adopting this approach to their careers when retirement is not an imminent event. The methods mentioned in this chapter for motivating salespeople can be useful. If results are not forthcoming, more drastic measures may be necessary, including termination.

▶ A MODEL OF MOTIVATION

Even when organizations offer rewards valued by individuals, motivation may suffer. Sustained, productive effort requires more than offering the best rewards. Studies have shown that the amount of effort an individual will put into an activity depends on the interplay among three factors shown in Figure 13-5: (1) the relationship between effort and performance, (2) the relationship between performance and rewards, and (3) the importance of receiving more of a certain reward. This process model of motivation is referred to as *expectancy theory*.[6]

Effort-Performance Relationship

Expectancy refers to the salesperson's belief that greater effort will lead to greater performance. The more certain an individual is of this effort-performance relationship, the more effort will likely be expended.

Three aspects of this belief are significant to sales management. First, the strength of this belief (i.e., the degree to which an individual is certain of the effort-performance relationship) will influence one's willingness to "work hard." Leo Kelly at Xerox, for example, sounded very confident in his approach to handling customer rejection.

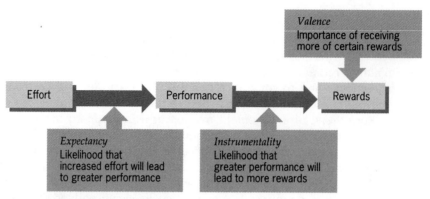

Figure 13-5: Model of Motivation

Second, management should be concerned with the accuracy of salespeople's role perception. Greater effort on the wrong activities will not lead to better performance, but it may lead to the conclusion that performance is not related to effort. Some refer to this as "working smarter." If a salesperson consistently uses an inappropriate selling strategy, for instance, sales call objectives are not likely to be met. The individual may become frustrated, incorrectly believing that no amount of effort will lead to better performance. This shows the interrelationship that exists among effective sales training, coaching, and motivation. No amount of incentive or cajoling will produce the desired level of performance in the absence of a certain level of skill and confidence in that skill.[7]

Finally, people want to know why something happens or doesn't happen and will make attributions about why a certain outcome occurs. An individual may attribute failure to the sales strategy that was used, in which case a search for another sales approach may be undertaken in an effort to make the sale. Alternatively, people may attribute failure to other factors, such as the company, the offering, or the competition. Salespeople who attribute failure to meet the sales quota to themselves are likely to make adjustments and increase their efforts to make the quota in the future. Salespeople who attribute failure to meet quota to circumstances other than their efforts are not likely to make these adjustments and will probably decrease their efforts to meet quota in the future.[8] This points out the need for managers to determine why salespeople believe they performed as they did. This requires having management where it should be—in the field with the sales force.

Performance-Reward Relationship

The second element of the motivation process is the belief that a higher level of performance will lead to greater personal rewards. This element is referred to as *instrumentality*. Motivation will be higher the more certain people are that greater business performance will be rewarded in ways that meet their personal needs. This is one of the reasons commission compensation plans work. Salespeople know how much they will be paid for each sale and understand that their incomes will increase as a result of more sales. This may also explain why limiting the number of winners in a sales contest may not motivate the average salesperson, whose expected level of performance is not likely to be high enough to win.

For the past several years, "pay-for-performance" sales compensation concept has been migrating to other parts of the organization. Marketing, accounting, human resources, virtually all departments, can enjoy additional compensation. Motivating this change in compensation practice, in addition to generating greater performance, is an effort by organizations to foster more of a customer and sales orientation among all functional areas.

Importance of Rewards

How much salespeople desire a particular reward will also influence their motivation to perform and is referred to as *reward valence*. Here we can see the connection between the previous need-based theories of motivation and expectancy theory. Both Maslow's and Herzberg's models suggest that there are limits to how much of any reward people will desire. While many experts believe that salespeople place a high value on pay, this may not reflect a salesperson's day-to-day priorities. If a salesperson's income is already high enough, the benefits of spending an afternoon with the family may outweigh that of higher income. Understanding salespeople's desires for rewards becomes even more complex in an international setting.[9]

People don't simply look at their own rewards; they also make comparisons with other people's rewards. According to *equity theory*, people make inputs (e.g., effort, experience, territories) versus outcomes comparisons with relevant others to determine relative equity. One reaction to an inequitable situation (e.g., Bob puts in less effort but makes more money) is to reduce inputs. Their motivation is decreased. New sales managers are especially vulnerable to equity problems. In an effort to help one person, they may make exceptions or provide extra help. This may be seen by other salespeople as unfair, unless they are also provided extra help in making the sale. This may eventually result in the sales manager doing the job of the salesperson and lead to lower overall performance.[10]

As a final point on rewards, it is important to remember that selling and effort are rewarding in and of themselves. People derive considerable rewards in the form of feeling good about themselves and their work. Organizations and sales management should do everything possible to reinforce these internal rewards and recognize their importance when communicating one-on-one with salespeople.[11]

Our model of motivation provides a framework for managers to understand the internal process by which people are motivated to put forth extra effort. Obviously, helping to motivate salespeople involves more than knowing what they want and need. A breakdown in any of the three dimensions of the motivation process will decrease overall motivation. Therefore, all three aspects of the process must be considered when trying to motivate someone to perform at the desired level.

How can sales managers put these theories to work? The remainder of this chapter looks at several tools available to sales managers to help salespeople put forth greater effort. Quotas, incentives, and recognition programs have been used successfully in a wide variety of organizations to motivate salespeople. A more recent approach, self-management, is gaining more popularity as companies embrace wider spans of control in which people are freed from traditional levels of supervisory control and monitoring. We will discuss this approach first.

▶ SELF-MANAGEMENT

Salespeople typically work independently of direct supervision from their sales managers. In the wake of reengineering and reorganizing, which have eliminated layers of middle management, salespeople in many industries have learned to manage themselves. Companies that are increasingly encouraging self-management, with the sales manager playing a supporting role, are therefore particularly attractive. One approach to self-management is *Behavioral self-management* (BSM), which consists of a series of steps involving monitoring, goal setting, rehearsal, rewards, and self-contracting. A summary of the techniques used in BSM is presented in Figure 13-6.

To better understand how BSM can be used in sales management, consider a situation in which you are attempting to increase the number of calls made each week on new accounts. Self-monitoring in this situation may mean recording the number of calls made on new customers over a four-week period. Having established the current level of effort, a goal is set for the number of new account calls that should be made each week. Stimulus cues may include such things as a small note placed on the dashboard of the car that says "Have You Met Someone New Today?" Alternatively, it may be a special notebook for recording the number of new-customer calls made each week. Consequence management may include stopping at a nicer place than usual for lunch when the weekly objective is met or skipping lunch if the objective is not met by a certain day of the week. Opening presentations with new accounts may be rehearsed in the car while driving to an account and scheduled for the same time each day. Finally, a contract specifying the criteria for rewarding success and punishing failure should be written and witnessed.

Technique	Method	Tools
Self-monitoring	Observe and record behavior.	Can use diaries, counters, tally sheets, charts.
Goal setting	Establish behavior change objectives.	Should be specific and with a short time horizon.
Stimulus control	Modify antecedents to behavior.	May involve introducing or removing cues.
Consequence management	Modify antecedents to behavior.	May involve reinforcement, punishment, or extinction.
Rehearsal	Systematic practice of desired behavior.	May be overt or visualized.
Self-contracting	Specify the relationship between behaviors and their consequences.	May involve public commitment.

Figure 13-6: Self-Management Techniques

The sales manager plays an important role when salespeople use BSM. The manager may help salespeople set goals that are challenging and achievable, while at the same time being consistent with overall organizational goals. The manager can also be helpful in rehearsing desired behaviors through one-on-one coaching and can help reinforce rewards through recognition of successes and encouragement. Again, we can see the importance of having sales managers in the field and knowing what is going on in the territory so that they can encourage and facilitate the use of BSM.

An important step in BSM is self-set goals. Traditionally, goals are set by management for salespeople in the form of quotas. The next section discusses why quotas are used, different types of quotas, and administration issues.

▶ QUOTAS

Quotas are one of the most widely used tools in sales management. *Quotas* are quantitative goals assigned to individual salespeople for a specified period of time. Sales of $150,000 in October is an example of a quantifiable goal for a specific period of time. This is the standard against which performance in October will be compared. While quotas are often based on sales, they should not be confused with sales forecasts or sales potential. A sales forecast is an estimate of what a firm expects to sell during a time period using a particular marketing plan (see Chapter 7). Sales quotas may be set equal to, above, or below the sales forecast. Sales potential, on the other hand, is the maximum demand that a firm can possibly obtain. Potentials are useful for strategic planning and long-range forecasting. Sales quotas are related to sales forecasts and potential but are used for entirely different purposes.

There are three reasons for establishing quotas for salespeople:

1. **To *help management motivate salespeople*.** Achievement-oriented people want specific and challenging goals, with regular feedback on their performance.

2. **To *direct salespeople where to put their efforts*.** When companies assign quotas for each product in their total line of products, they are trying to communicate to their sales force which products should be given priority. V. L. Service Lighting, for example, awards bonus points for each product line that salespeople can receive by exceeding biweekly and annual volume goals.

3. **To *provide standards for performance evaluation*.** Quotas lend themselves to *management by exception*, that is, focusing management's attention on the performance of people who are exceptionally above or below quota. Time can be spent with people whose performance is poor in order to determine if the results are due to the salesperson's efforts or to factors in the environment outside of the salesperson's control. At the same time, management may wish to spend time with high performers to identify key points that could be used to improve other salespeople's performance.

Types of Quotas

There are three widely used types of quotas: sales volume, profits, and activity. Figure 13-7 shows the popularity of each type of quota among large and small firms. Sales

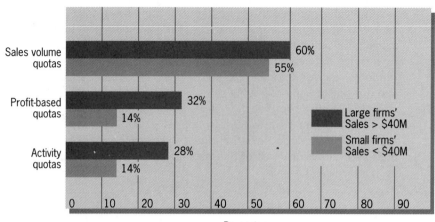

Figure 13-7: Use of the Various Types of Quotas
Source: Alan J. Dubrosky and Thomas E. Barry, "A Survey of Sales Management Practice," *Industrial Marketing Management*, (April 1982), pp. 133–141.

volume quotas are the most widely used and are popular among both large and small companies. Profit-based quotas are far more common among larger firms, as are activity quotas. Each type of quota is discussed below.

Sales Volume Quotas   *Sales volume quotas* are specific volume targets established for each territory, and possibly for each product line, for a specific period of time (usually a month, quarter, or year). The sales volume quota may be stated in a variety of ways, including dollar volume, unit volume, or a point system. A *dollar volume quota* is preferred when there is a large number of similarly priced items to sell (e.g., drugs to wholesalers), when prices reflect management's selling priorities (e.g., higher-priced products are more important than less expensive items), and prices are relatively stable. With *unit volume quotas*, sales objectives are stated in terms of the number of units of each product to be sold. Unit quotas are more popular in businesses that sell a limited number of high-value items (e.g., automobiles) and when price changes frequently. By stating quota in units, the effects of inflation are eliminated from the system. With a *point quota system*, the quota is stated as a certain number of points to be earned for selling each product. The point system provides greater management flexibility since points are assigned to the sale of each type of product. If management wishes to emphasize a new product, for example, they may simply increase the number of points awarded to the sale of the product.

Profit-Based Quotas   *Profit-based quotas* are similar to sales quotas, but focus on profits generated instead of just sales volume. Profit quotas are usually not based on bottom-line profits, but on gross margin (net sales minus cost of goods sold) or contribution margin (gross margin minus direct selling expenses). As such, they attempt to focus the salesperson's attention on profits as opposed to volume. As one sales manager put it, "There's shipping boxes, and there's shipping boxes at the right time to the right customer at the right cost, which is a far bigger idea."

Though more difficult to administer than sales volume plans, setting profit goals has become a growing trend in consumer goods organizations.[12] Profit-based quotas are most likely to be used when salespeople make decisions that dramatically affect the profits of the company. For example, salespeople may choose which of many products to push, or they may have some flexibility in setting prices. Profit contributions often vary considerably among different products. Unless salespeople are aware of these profit differences and know that they will be held accountable for profits, there is no incentive to sell the more profitable products. IBM has developed a special software so that their salespeople have access to cost data, so they can determine the profitability of every transaction.

Activity Quotas   Too much emphasis on volume or profit quotas may lead to neglect of important nonselling activities and to lower long-run performance. This problem may be resolved by introducing *activity quotas*. Activity quotas set targets on specific activities that will help in meeting a firm's sales and profit objectives.

Activity quotas recognize the investment nature of selling; that is, salespeople must often perform activities today that have the potential to produce significant sales volume sometime in the future. Some typical activity quotas include the following:

- Number of calls per day.
- Display racks installed.
- Calls on new accounts
- Dealer sales meetings held.

- Proposals submitted.
- Equipment test sites.
- Product demonstrations.
- Point-of-purchase displays.

One important advantage of activity quotas is that they are based on behaviors that are largely under the control of the salesperson. As a result, a salesperson can be held more accountable for the results and will be more motivated to achieve these quotas.[13]

A serious disadvantage of activity quotas is that the information necessary to track activities is obtained from a salesperson's call reports. Not only does this require the salespeople to do more paperwork, usually on their own time, but there is also an opportunity for misrepresentation. As a result, activity reports may become an exercise in creative writing. Another drawback of activity quotas is that an overemphasis on quotas, such as number of calls per day, may result in salespeople giving management what it wants in calls per day, but sales performance may suffer. Large potential accounts on the fringe of a territory, for instance, may not be called on because of the travel time required.

When Are Quotas Effective?

A good place to start in answering this question is with goal theory. *Goal theory* examines the relationship between goal setting and subsequent performance.[14] This theory proposes that difficult goals, *if accepted*, will lead to higher performance than moderate or easy goals or no goals, such as "Do your best." This means that management must know what a difficult goal is for a particular salesperson versus one that is easy or impossible. Underscoring the motivational influence of difficult goals is the experience of an electronic equipment manufacturer that had set very challenging quotas on its data printer line. Although it took twice as long to sell a data printer compared to the other product lines, the data printer line was considered important to the future of the company. Some salespeople objected to the high quotas, however, so the company relaxed the quotas in six districts to see what the impact would be. A comparison of these six districts with comparable districts with high quotas revealed that the districts with high quotas outsold those with lower quotas. This led the company to conclude that many salespeople are "quota achievers" and that their motivation falls off if they are given quotas that are too easy to reach.[15]

If goal setting is to be effective, management has a much greater role to play than simply setting specific goals. For salespeople to accept the goals as their own, management must also be concerned with the following:

- *Providing feedback.*   Feedback, or knowledge of results, is necessary for goals to improve performance. Sales manager feedback is a very powerful force in shaping salespeople's performance. This suggests that management should give salespeople frequent feedback on their level of sales relative to the quota.[16]

- *Gaining goal commitment.*   Salespeople must consider the goal to be their own. This is what is meant by *goal commitment*; that is, a person's determination to attain a goal. Recall how Leo Kelly described the President's Club: "It is how our success is measured. . . . I use it as a yardstick." Leo has obviously committed himself to meet this objective. There are a number of ways to gain this commitment. One way is salesperson participation in goal setting. This explains why over half of all firms using quotas ask their salespeople for estimates. It has also been found that salesperson estimates are just as likely to be high as they are to be low and that errors in either direction are 10 percent or less.[17] Another approach is to build team spirit and relate individual goals to the greater good of the team. What approach is effective will depend on the leadership style of the manager, the culture of the organization, and the individual salesperson's tendencies.

- *Building self-confidence.*   How people feel about their ability to perform certain behaviors successfully is very important to high performance. Salespeople who are confident in their ability to prospect are likely to perform better than those who are unsure whether they are good at prospecting. This example also points out the considerable benefits of positive feedback. Self-confidence can be encouraged by training and coaching that results in prospecting successes.

This discussion suggests that it takes more than setting quotas to achieve maximum motivation and performance. Motivation is dependent on the total management system. Several issues about quotas remain. The next section examines how to set equitable and fair quotas, how to evaluate performance when multiple quotas are considered, and the relationship between quotas and compensation.

Administering Quotas

Quotas are usually based on one or more of the following: past sales, forecasted sales, sales potential, and individual and salesperson territory adjustments. A "rough" method of determining a sales quota is simply to take sales in a territory for the past year (or an average of several years) and add a percentage based on the company's sales forecast. For example, if sales in territory B are currently $600,000 and the firm wants an 8 percent increase in company sales next year, the new quota would be $648,000. On the surface, this method appears to be equitable and fair. The problem is that past mistakes are likely to be perpetuated. If, in the past, for example, a salesperson has done a poor job covering territory B, then a quota based strictly on past performance will not reflect the true potential that exists in the area. The other problem is that historical sales figures may predate a recent industry slump, or they might fail to account for the product's being at a more mature stage in its life cycle, where the opportunities are different. To be realistic, quotas must also take into account local conditions.

A better approach is to compute sales potential in each territory and to consider this figure when setting quotas. (Procedures for estimating sales potentials are described in Chapter 7.) Suppose the Buying Power Index[18] shows that territory B has 5 percent of the total U.S. potential. If the firm plans to sell $17 million in total volume in the next year, then the quota for territory B would be 0.05 × $17 million, or $850,000. Note that the potential-based quota requires the salesperson to come up with a sales increase of $250,000 for the year.

Basing quotas strictly on sales potential may not always be workable because it ignores past sales and assumes that all territories are the same with respect to the other factors that will determine the actual sales volume achieved. These include environmental factors (e.g., competition, size of customers), organizational factors (e.g., advertising support, proximity to warehouse and manufacturing facilities), and salesperson factors (e.g., experience, ability). Ignoring these may render the quota useless as a performance evaluation tool and for motivating salespeople. Thus, a quota of $850,000 may discourage rather than stimulate a salesperson when current sales in the territory are only $600,000. The best method, therefore, for setting quotas is to consider all three factors: past and forecasted sales, sales potential, and individual territory and salesperson characteristics. Setting quotas requires considerable judgment on management's part. It is easy to see why quotas are a potential bone of contention and why salesperson input can be beneficial.

Another administrative concern of sales managers is how to evaluate performance when salespeople have several quotas to meet. For example, Table 13-1 shows sales volume and activity quotas along with actual results for the salesperson in territory B. Note that although the overall sales goal was achieved, the salesperson was below quota on three of the five factors. Further, only about two-thirds of the allotted displays were achieved. The average quota achievement of 97 percent, however, appears to be good. It would be especially good if all other salespeople in the company reached only 70 to 90 percent of their quotas. What should be this person's overall performance rating?

Although average quota achievement is a convenient summary figure, one potential problem is that "average performance" places equal weight on each element used to arrive at the average. In the example in Table 13-1, for instance, as much value is placed on point-of-purchase displays as on total sales dollar results. Some managers assign different weights to the various quota factors to handle this problem. Quota achievement is weighted by the importance of each quota factor, and the weighted

Table 13-1 Evaluating Quota Performance in Territory B

Quota Factor	Three-Month Quota	Actual	Percentage of Quota Attained
Total sales volume	$83,000	$84,660	102%
Unit sales of Model 75	6	5	82
Point-of-purchase displays	25	17	68
Average calls per day	5	7	140
Percent store distribution	0.75	0.70	93
		Average:	97.2%

ratings are added together to form an overall performance index. You should be careful, however, not to create an overly complicated system.

Another important question is how high management should set the bar. Aiming high is laudable, but setting unattainable goals is a sure way to puncture a sales force's morale. Should a quota be set so that all people will likely exceed it, the top half, or only the few best salespeople? There is no clear-cut answer to this question. Practices vary from one company to the next. If bonuses for exceeding the quota are treated as a normal part of the salespeople's income, then quotas should be set so that most people will achieve them. On the other hand, some companies try to challenge their people to greater performance by setting quotas at higher than expected levels and attach substantial and exceptional financial rewards to beating the quota. In this case, financial rewards for quota achievement may be treated as a way to retain top performers. The level at which a quota is set will depend on the role of quota achievement within the overall financial and nonfinancial rewards system of the organization.

When Not to Use Quotas

In certain circumstances, it is probably not advisable to use quotas. When a significant portion of sales depends on cooperation between salespeople in different territories, then individual quotas may either be unfeasible or discourage cooperation. This is likely to occur when third-party referrals involve prospects in other territories. The referral may not be passed along, especially if quota achievement is evaluated on a relative basis, that is, if bonus quota achievement is evaluated relative to how each salesperson performed.

Another situation not conducive to using quotas is when sales are infrequent with a long selling cycle but the dollar value is very high. In such a situation, no sales may be recorded in a period, followed by extremely high sales volume in a subsequent period. Quota performance is not very meaningful in such a situation.

▶ INCENTIVE PROGRAMS

Incentive programs are short-term promotional events intended to inspire salespeople to a greater than usual performance level and provide them with rewards. Incentives are a proven motivational device with widespread acceptance.[19] It is estimated that two-thirds of all consumer goods companies and over half of all industrial goods companies have sponsored incentive programs. Incentive budgets are estimated to have ranged in size from under $5,000 to over $1 million, with the average firm spending $97,800. In total, over $6 billion is spent annually on sales incentive programs.[20] The large budgets and widespread acceptance of sales incentive programs may be explained by referring back to our model of motivation. Greater rewards will usually lead to greater motivation if the rewards are valued by the salesperson. Our model also explains why incentive programs are usually tied to special customer promotion efforts, a special low price or premium offer, because these should help salespeople see that their extra efforts will lead to higher performance. Recall that these estimates of success are critical to one's decision to put forth greater effort.

Goals and Timing

Incentives are not a giveaway. A generally accepted performance standard is to produce $4 dollars for each $1 put into them. The objectives of a sales incentive program may include more than just producing overall increases in sales volume. Programs have goals such as finding new customers or boosting the sales of special items, counteracting seasonal slumps in sales, and introducing new items to customers. Less frequently used are objectives like obtaining a better balance across product lines or encouraging dealers to build more displays in their stores.

In addition to specific quantitative goals, incentive programs may be used to enhance qualitative goals such as team building. Basing rewards on department or team results is especially helpful in this regard. About 30 percent of all companies with incentive programs, in fact, base rewards on team or department performance.[21]

A sales manager should ask the following questions when deciding on the goal of the incentive program: Is it consistent with our overall marketing strategy? Can the program detract from long-run developmental concerns? Can the salesperson have an impact on the goal? Can the salesperson understand the goal? Can the company measure achievement of the goal? Unless a company can reliably track the money spent servicing each account, for example, profitability is not an appropriate objective.

To maintain enthusiasm, incentive programs should be run for limited periods of time. Salespeople may lose interest in programs that last too long. Alternatively, the program may detract from salespeople's other responsibilities if the program runs too long. A typical program lasts for one to three months, a period that allows salespeople to cover their territories completely and encourages maximum sell-through of the products. Better performance against objectives is generally achieved when the length of the incentive program is two months or less.[22] Salespeople are better able to maintain their focus and interest over this period of time.

An additional timing issue is when during the year to hold a contest. No one answer is appropriate for all situations. Some programs are held during slow times to avoid a dramatic drop in sales. Others are held in peak sales periods because the potential for sales is greater if the sales force gives more effort. The right timing depends on the company and the situation. You should not hold a contest at the same time each year. Salespeople may come to treat the reward as normal income and may play games by withholding orders just prior to the contest.

Prizes

The success or failure of an incentive program often depends on the attractiveness of the awards offered to the participants. There are no firm rules for selecting prizes, except that different prizes should be chosen for each contest and participants should find the prizes attractive. As indicated in Table 13-2, the most frequent awards are cash, followed by merchandise and trips. Cash is a popular award in sales contests because it can be spent on whatever the salesperson wants. However, cash prizes can be more difficult to promote to participants. A common solution to this problem is to offer cash as a substitute for merchandise or travel prizes. In this way, merchandise can be shown and promoted to the sales force, yet winners have the option of accepting cash if they do not want the merchandise. For example, one firm offered an antique car as a contest prize and the winner refused to accept it. The antique car would have been taxed as income to the salesperson at its fair market value; thus the contest winner was better off taking a smaller amount of cash and paying less income tax.

The advantages of merchandise awards are that tangible items can be displayed to the sales force and featured in promotional material. Furthermore, merchandise can be purchased at wholesale prices, giving the awards a higher value than they actually cost the company to buy. However, merchandise prizes can lose their impact if they duplicate things salespeople already own. One solution is to have the salespeople accumulate points by choosing items from a catalog. Another drawback is that winners must pay income taxes on the merchandise that is won.

Travel awards add glamour and excitement to sales contests, and such awards are usually more appealing to older participants. Salespeople making $50,000 a year are less likely to be interested in merchandise prizes, but a week's vacation in Hawaii can be very enticing. As a result, companies in the United States spend over $3 billion annually on travel awards. However, travel awards are the least frequently used type of prize because their substantial cost limits the number that can be offered. In response to this situation, many companies are cutting back on the cost per trip by awarding less exotic trips to places in the United States, such as San Diego, Chicago, and St. Louis. Moreover, the award winner can avoid paying income taxes on the prize by combining the trip with a sales meeting.

Table 13-2 Types of Incentive Awards Used by 168 Firms

Type of Award	Percentage of Firms Using
Cash	59
Selected Merchandise	46
Merchandise Catalog	25
Travel	22

Source: Sales and Marketing Management (February 1990), p. 82.

Administration Issues

While incentive programs have the potential to be very powerful motivators, they must be properly planned and executed. Some of the problems that may arise are described in Sales Management in Action 13-2. One of the keys to successful sales incentive programs is choosing a good theme for the contest. The theme is a unifying statement that ties together the business objective of the contest, the prizes, and the individual. Ideally, the theme will be simple, easy to execute, and something about which the participants can get excited. Common sales contest themes include sports (Super Bowl, World Series), travel locations, treasure hunts, gambling, and detective and mystery themes. These themes are used as reminders during the contest and may also be used to display current standings among the contestants.

A successful program should encourage the average salesperson to expend extra effort, since superior salespeople produce irrespective of the contest and people at

---

Sales Management in Action 13-2
Why Incentive Plans Cannot Work

Some people argue that incentive plans do not work. They argue that incentives produce temporary compliance at best and that once the rewards run out, people revert to their old behaviors. They do not create an enduring commitment to any value or action. By contrast, training and goal-setting programs are believed to have a far greater impact on long-term productivity than any pay-for-performance plans.

Why do most executives continue to rely on incentive programs? Perhaps it is because the temporary benefits are much more noticeable than the long-run problems they cause. Moreover, we have been exposed to manipulation by rewards all our lives, so that incentives are now part of the fabric of American life.

In a recent *Harvard Business Review* article, Alfie Kohn offers the following reasons why incentives do not work:

- *Pay is not a motivator*. When people are asked what matters most to them, pay is usually ranked only fifth or sixth.

- *Rewards punish*. Not receiving a reward one had expected or thinks one deserves to receive is indistinguishable from being punished.

- *Rewards ignore reasons*. Managers often use incentive systems as a substitute for giving people what they need to do a good job: useful feedback, social support, and room for self-determination.

- *Rewards discourage risk taking*. When incentives are used to motivate, predictability and simplicity are desirable job features, since the objective is to get through the task expediently in order to get the reward. Exploration is therefore discouraged.

Source: Alfie Kohn, "Why Incentive Plans Cannot Work," *Harvard Business Review* (September–October 1993), pp. 54–63.

the bottom are less likely to respond to any stimulus. Thus, success depends on setting the qualifications and rewards so that approximately the middle 60 percent of the sales force participates.[23] With this objective in mind, it is often a better approach to have many prizes, instead of having one or two grand prizes that are sure to be won by the superstars. A sales contest can be set up, for instance, with several levels of achievement so that most people win something. One possible approach is to have salespeople who increase volume 10 percent during the program win a $100 camera, while salespeople who achieve a 20 percent gain receive a portable color television set. A third level of achievement might reward the top overall producers with a trip to Las Vegas. A good rule of thumb is that half of the salespeople eligible for sales contests should win some sort of prize.

The incentive program should be highly promoted. Promotion informs salespeople of the incentive program and reminds them of the prizes to be won. A good way to build initial interest is to begin with a kickoff sales meeting in which the sales force can see the prizes and learn the details of the contest. This meeting should be followed by mailings, stories in the company newspaper, and trade advertising to maintain the attention and interest of the field reps. Because sales contests are short-lived, it is essential to issue frequent progress reports to let participants know where they stand and what they must do to qualify for an award.

▶ RECOGNITION PROGRAMS

Without a doubt, recognition and prizes push people closer to their potential than envelopes stuffed with money. This is why almost all sales managers have some sort of recognition program. A *recognition program* is similar to incentives in that an individual or group of salespeople receive an award for exceptional performance. Recognition programs differ from incentive programs in several important ways. While there may be some monetary award involved, the primary award is recognition by management for exceptional performance. There are also timing differences. Where incentive programs are usually short in duration, a recognition program is usually based on performance over a year or longer. In addition, recognition programs usually focus on overall performance rather than the sale of targeted products.

Hewlett-Packard has a reputation for having one of the most professional and successful sales forces in the world. One key to its success is the company's many recognition programs. These programs are based on two principles: (1) Generate enthusiasm and motivation for as many salespeople as possible, and (2) get useful feedback from the sales force to improve performance opportunities even more. Four of H-P's programs illustrate these principles:

- **The 100% Club.** Each sales region sponsors a team-building and recognition program for all salespeople achieving 100 percent of the quota or better for the year.
- **Achiever's Club.** This club consists of the top 10 to 20 percent of salespeople in each region. They win a weekend vacation for two, which includes motivational and recognition activities.

- **President's Club.**   This consists of the top 100 performers in the sales organization—85 salespeople and 15 district sales managers. Nominations are based on eight criteria: sales performance, customer satisfaction, resource management, sales planning, teamwork, leadership, enthusiasm, and being a role model. In other words, being a member takes more than simply producing the highest numbers.[24]

To be successful, recognition programs must become part of the company's culture; that is, they should be longstanding, anticipated, and have lasting value. As you can see, recognition programs focus on the third effort characteristics—the drive to persistently put forth exceptional effort. Successful recognition programs appeal to the highest of Maslow's needs, self-actualization, which, you may recall, is never fully satisfied.

Why does recognition work to motivate salespeople? Part of the reason is that most people strive for recognition by management and peers, and people usually cannot get enough recognition. For high performance to lead to positive job attitudes and subsequent high performance, individuals must have a positive emotional reaction to their performance.[25] A well-administered recognition program can help foster a strong, positive reaction to high performance.

Quality: Changes in Recognition Programs

TQM is having an important impact on what recognition programs reward and how the programs are conducted. One of the most important lessons management should keep in mind is to ensure that the recognition system rewards what the organization values most. If a salesperson is given a large cash award for selling a product, for instance, but the person responsible for installing and fixing the product is given only a lapel pin, this quickly communicates how little the firm values customer service. The change in focus from selling to obtaining a customer for life based on satisfaction is forcing many companies to reevaluate their recognition programs to be sure that they communicate the right set of values.

As organizations embracing TQM expand employee empowerment, they are finding that it is practical to delegate recognition activities to them as well. What a change this is, given that historically all recognition program decisions were the preserve of management! Delegating recognition increases the odds that the right people are recognized since employees always know who really did the work. Instead of giving one salesperson a $10,000 award, for instance, a salesperson is given $10,000 or $15,000 to distribute among the team that made his or her achievement possible, with the salesperson sharing in the financial recognition.

Recognition programs also reflect TQM's emphasis on teams. Instead of recognizing the accomplishments of one salesperson, the entire sales unit is recognized for its overall accomplishments or for working together to close an important sale. Milliken and Xerox recognize teams by having them present the results of their work at Sharing Rallies in which they "pitch" their story to peers. One IBM organization awards a large silver medallion to team members, but only if they are nominated for the award by another team.

In summary, TQM has caused organizations to recognize more than volume and profit, to focus on teams as well as individuals, and to empower employees to recognize the accomplishments of other employees. Still, it is important that management never lose its focus on the individual as a team member. As one sales manager put it: "There still needs to be plenty of room for individual success and achievement. Otherwise, teamwork becomes an amorphous concept that can lead a group to underachieve in harmony."[26]

► ETHICAL SITUATIONS

Despite their widespread use, ethical problems with quota systems, contests, and rewards to motivate people on the job may arise. Some people have questioned whether managers should administer rewards in ways that promote desirable behaviors from the organization's point of view and not worry too much about the individual's freedom to choose which behaviors to engage in to satisfy his or her own desires. When does a manager have too much power to manipulate people into doing what they would not do otherwise? There is also the issue of whether promising rewards detracts from the job. Does promising a reward for doing a job they already enjoy doing lead salespeople to see the reward as the motivation for performing the task, thus undermining their enjoyment of the job? For more on this subject, see Sales Management in Action 13-2.

Poorly run or poorly conceived quotas and contests have high potential for fostering unethical behaviors by salespeople. When salespeople know that a contest is coming up, for example, they may withhold orders prior to the contest in order to have greater volume during the contest. During a contest, "soft" orders, which will be totally or partially returned by the customer, may be submitted. If quotas are set on activities, such as calls per day, salespeople may be tempted to falsify call reports to avoid problems with an overzealous manager or to meet end-of-year objectives for which they are rewarded. If salespeople are rewarded for beating the quota, they may hold back additional orders during the reporting period in order to make their job easier during the next period. Some people have been known to start their own companies during the time they have available after meeting the quota. If a quota or contest is not designed or administered properly, people may easily justify unethical behavior. A good question to consider is how you would design a program so as to prevent or discourage each of these behaviors.

► SUMMARY

Role perceptions, skill levels, aptitude, and motivation all affect a salesperson's performance on the job. Salespeople need basic selling skills, but they also must be motivated to put forth the effort needed to achieve their objectives. Sales managers should understand that people have different needs and that these needs change over time. The motivational process can usefully be explained by a model of motivation based on expectancy theory. Salespeople estimate the chances that their actions will lead to specific goals and that goal achievement will lead to rewards, and they assess the desirability of the rewards offered for achieving those goals. If the objectives seem reasonable and the rewards sufficiently attractive, then salespeople will be motivated. Quotas, set in terms of dollar sales or specific activities, are widely used motivational devices that not only provide goals but also set standards for evaluation of individual performance. Management plays an important role in both setting quotas and ensuring that salespeople accept the goals. Contests are short-run promotional programs that can stimulate salespeople to reach their quotas through the offer of prizes such as merchandise, cash, or trips. Recognition awards, such as "Salesperson of the Month" titles, trophies, and certificates are also effective motivational devices.

▶ KEY TERMS

Activity quota	Incentive program
Attribution theory	Instrumentality
Behavioral self-management (BSM)	Maintenance stage
Disengagement stage	Management by exception
Dollar volume quota	Motivation
Equity theory	Point quota system
Establishment stage	Profit-based quota
Expectancy	Quota
Expectancy theory	Recognition program
Exploration stage	Reward valence
Goal commitment	Sales force segmentation
Goal theory	Sales volume quota
Hierarchy of needs	Self-efficacy
Hygiene-motivation factors	Unit volume quota

▶ REVIEW QUESTIONS

1. Explain the basic factors considered in expectancy theory.
2. What are the propositions of goal theory?
3. What personal factors may influence the motivating ability of specific, challenging goals?
4. Why are quotas used in the management of salespeople?
5. What is an activity quota, and why is it important?
6. Should salespeople participate in the determination of their sales quotas?
7. Why are sales contests used by so many firms?
8. How many prizes should be awarded in a sales contest?
9. Why do many salespeople prefer cash to the merchandise and trips offered in many sales contests?
10. What are recognition awards, and why do they work?

▶ PROBLEMS

1. Bill Tatum, a regional sales manager for a large manufacturer, works long hours, but his department's productivity is low. Everybody else is to blame. For comfort and escape, he occasionally sneaks an extra lunch hour for a tryst with a divorced woman, a trainee in the department. Bill dropped out of college at the age of 20 because of financial problems. When he started work as a salesperson, he worked harder to get ahead than his college-educated peers. He was spotted as bright and aggressive. He kept getting promotions until he became regional sales manager. Although he earns a salary that permits him to pay for a suburban home, membership in a country club, and college for his two children, he's blocked in his job and he knows it. The national sales manager, whom Bill once had a good chance of succeeding, won't retire. Bill's peers, the other regional managers, some younger and more aggressive, are getting the pick of the new salespeople. Bill looks on his own staff as the culls. He has high blood pressure, and his home life has deteriorated. Tatum suffers from job burnout. What should the national sales manager do to help Bill Tatum? What should Bill Tatum do to help himself?

2. Quotas at DSC Technologies are based on the average of sales over the past two years plus a 20 percent increase. The reason for the high increase in sales quota is that DSC manufactures and sells telephone switches in the communications industry, where new technologies are frequently introduced and industry growth over the past decade has averaged just over 20 percent a year. Bonuses are paid on the following schedule:

Bonus Percent	Percent of Quota
5	100–105
7	106–110
10	111–120

   No additional bonus is given for windfall sales over 20 percent of the quota. What are the advantages and disadvantages of this approach? What is likely to happen? How would you change the method?

3. A recent issue of *Sales & Marketing Management* contained more than 20 advertisements for products used in salesperson incentive programs, including trips, cameras, and clothing. As sales manager, you have to select an item to go along with a new-product introduction. What factors will you consider?

4. Hoosier Goods manufactures a complete line of industrial resins and compounds for the construction industry. Of the 40 items in their line, 2 products account for over 50 percent of sales and profits. To improve this situation, management has offered attractive incentives to the sales force to increase sales of the slower products. Recently, however, management has been deluged with complaints by construction firms asserting that the sales force is pushing unwanted products at them. As sales manager, what will you do?

5. You are a sales manager for an industrial manufacturer. The performance of one of your salespeople, James Weber, has slipped and he has achieved only 75 percent of his quota for the past six months. The average sales quota achievement in your district was 90 percent. Weber has worked for your firm for six years and has a bachelor's degree in business administration. Jim's territory is above average in potential but does require considerable travel. At the recent company picnic, Weber seemed depressed and spent his time drinking

rather than interacting with the other salespeople. Weber is divorced, and his ex-wife lives in another city with their three children. You have decided that it is time to call in Weber for a conference. Develop a script for a meeting with Weber that will motivate him to work up to his potential. Be prepared to play the role of the sales manager or Weber in a meeting to be acted out in front of the class.

6. According to Joe Walsh, national sales manager at Thomas Electronics, salespeople should not be involved directly in setting sales quotas for their territories. Says Walsh, "Typical salespeople are either elated over their sales results last month, in which case they will overestimate future sales, or they will underestimate future sales because of poor recent sales. You also have the problem of salespeople playing games with their forecasts in order to make their job easier or to increase their income when bonuses and commissions are tied to quota performance." How do you feel about this? What would be your response to Mr. Walsh?

▶ IN-CLASS EXERCISES

This Is Going to Cost Me My Job

The Ball Corporation is a large packaging manufacturer located in Muncie, Indiana. Most of Ball's sales are in glass, metal cans, and barrier plastic packaging, with glass accounting for over half of all sales. Ball's customers are food packers. Sales calls are built around the ideas of glass's strength (in its pristine state, glass has a tensile strength three to five times that of steel), reducing container weight, solving inefficiencies in packing, and reducing costs through automation. Although some prospecting is involved, most volume growth comes from building sales with existing customers.

Salespeople are compensated by salary plus a bonus based on achieving the quota. To earn any bonus, salespeople must sell at least 90 percent of their quota. The amount of bonus increases up to the point where a salesperson meets the quota, where the bonus is 20 percent of the salary. Salary increases are based on the district manager's performance rating, with one-third of the rating based on quota achievement.

Although district managers provide input into the quota setting process, quotas are set at headquarters and handed down to each district. It is up to the district managers to assign quotas for each salesperson in their district so that they are both fair and distributed in a manner so that the district can hit its quota number.

Two weeks after you have been given your district's sales quota, you have just held a meeting with your district salespeople and have handed them their sales quotas for the coming year. Following the meeting, Sandy McGuire stops by your office and is obviously very unhappy. "My quota is wrong," says Sandy. "I exceeded last year's quota by 5 percent and now this year's quota is 20 percent over what I sold last year. How can you do this to me? I need an adjustment."

Just as Sandy leaves your office, Kim enters. Kim is a lot less outspoken than Sandy, but then again, Kim is on shaky ground with the company and did not make any bonus last year. Kim asks, "How can I make this number? My quota has been increased by 10 percent over last year's and I only made 80 percent of last year's quota. This is going to cost me my job." Kim alludes to problems with increased competition in the territory, lack of support, stress, and personal problems.

Questions:

1. When might a 20 percent sales quota for one district be justified when another district is given only a 12 percent quota increase?

2. What is the role of first-line field sales managers in setting and administering sales quotas?
3. What factors should the district manager consider in setting individual salesperson quotas?
4. What are your alternatives in dealing with Sandy and Kim? Which do you recommend?

► REFERENCES

1. LESLIE BRENNAN, "Sales Secrets of the Incentive Stars," *Sales & Marketing Management* (April 1990), pp. 88–100.

2. FREDERICK HERZBERG, "One More Time: How Do You Motivate Employees?" *Harvard Business Review*, 46 (January–February 1968), pp. 53–62.

3. GEOFFREY BREWER, "What Makes Great Salespeople?" *Sales & Marketing Management* (May 1994), pp. 82–92.

4. MARVIN JOLSON, "The Salesman's Career Cycle," *Journal of Marketing*, 38 (July 1974), pp. 39–46.

5. The discussion in this section is based on the following articles: WILLIAM L. CRON, "Industrial Salesperson Development: A Career Stages Perspective," *Journal of Marketing* (Fall 1984), pp. 41–52; WILLIAM L. CRON and JOHN W. SLOCUM, "The Influence of Career Stages on Salespeople's Job Attitudes, Work Perceptions and Performance," *Journal of Marketing Research* (May 1986), pp. 119–129; and DOUGLAS HALL, "Managing Yourself: Building a Career," in A.R. Cohen, ed., *The Portable MBA in Management* (New York: Wiley, 1993), pp. 190–206.

6. For further discussion of expectancy theory, see WESLEY J. JOHNSTON, and KEYSUK KIM, "Performance Attribution and Expectancy Linkages in Personal Selling," *Journal of Marketing*, 58 (October 1994), 68–81.

7. For a detailed discussion of role perceptions, see JEFFREY SAGER, "A Structural Model Depicting Salespeople's Job Stress," *Journal of the Academy of Marketing Science*, 22 (January 1994), pp. 74–84.

8. GORDON BADOVICK, "Emotional Reactions and Salesperson Motivation: An Attri-

butional Approach Following Inadequate Sales Performance," *Journal of the Academy of Marketing Science*, 18 (Spring 1990), pp. 123–130.

9. ALAN DUBINSKY, MASAAKI KOTABE, CHAE UN LIM, and RONALD MICHAELS, "Differences in Motivational Perceptions among U.S., Japanese, and Korean Sales Personnel," *Journal of Business Research*, 30 (1994), pp. 175–185.

10. LINDA HILL, *Becoming a Manager* (Boston: Harvard Business School Press, 1992).

11. For more on this subject, see STEVEN BROWN and ROBERT PETERSON, "The Effect of Effort on Sales Performance and Job Satisfaction," *Journal of Marketing*, 58 (April 1994), pp. 70–80.

12. NANCY ARNOTT, "Step Right Up!" *Sales & Marketing Management* (October 1994), p. 117.

13. RICHARD OLIVER and ERIN ANDERSON, "An Empirical Test of the Consequences of Behavior- and Outcome-Based Sales Control Systems," *Journal of Marketing*, 58 (October 1994), pp. 53–67.

14. THOMAS WOTRUBA, "The Effect of Goal-Setting on the Performance of Independent Sales Agents in Direct Selling," *Journal of Personal Selling & Sales Management*, 9 (Fall 1989), pp. 22–29.

15. See WILLIAM ROSS, "Performance Against Quota and the Call Selection Decision," *Journal of Marketing Research*, 28 (August 1991), pp. 296–306, for more information on how quota difficulty may influence salespeople's strategies for achieving the quota.

16. For more information on the importance and use of feedback, see BERNARD JAWORSKI and AJAY KOHLI, "Supervisory Feed-

back: Alternative types and their Impact on Salespeople's Performance and Satisfaction," *Journal of Marketing Research*, 28 (May 1991), pp. 190–201; and AJAY KOHLI and BERNARD JAWORSKI, "The Influence of Coworker Feedback on Salespeople," *Journal of Marketing*, 58 (October 1994), pp. 82–94.

17. THOMAS R. WOTRUBA and MICHAEL L. THURLOW, "Sales Force Participation in Quota Setting and Sales Forecasting," *Journal of Marketing*, 40 (April 1976), p. 16.

18. The Buying Power Index is reported by cities, counties, and states each July by *Sales & Marketing Management* magazine.

19. TIM HARRIS, "Incentives," *Sales & Marketing Management* (April 1990), p. 112.

20. REGINA EISMAN, "Justifying Your Incentive Program," *Sales & Marketing Management* (April 1993), p. 43.

21. *Sales & Marketing Management* (February 26, 1990), p. 82.

22. "What Employees Want," *Sales & Marketing Management* (June 1995), p. 41.

23. WILLIAM MURPHY and RAVIPREET SOHI, "Sales Persons' Perceptions About Sales Contests," *European Journal of Marketing*, 29 (1996) pp. 42–66.

24. "Multiple Recognition," *Sales Manager's Bulletin*, 1295 (December 30, 1992), p. 8.

25. STEVEN BROWN, WILLIAM CRON, and THOMAS LEIGH, "Do Feelings of Success Mediate Sales Performance–Work Attitude Relationships?" *Journal of the Academy of Marketing Science*, 21 (Spring 1993), pp. 91–100.

26. FRANK CESPEDES, STEPHEN DOYLE, and ROBERT FREEDMAN, "Teamwork for Today's Selling," *Harvard Business Review* (March–April 1989), p. 8.

▶ SELECTED READINGS

FILSON, BRENT, *Defining Moment: Motivating People to Take Action* (Williamstown, Mass.: Williamstown Publishing, 1993).

HELLRIEGEL, DON, JOHN SLOCUM, and RICHARD WOODMAN, *Organizational Behavior*, 6th ed. (St. Paul, Minn.: West, 1992).

MASLOW, ABRAHAM, *Motivation and Personality* (New York: Harper & Row, 1970).

ROSENBLUTH, HAL and DIANE MCFERRIN PETERS, *The Customer Comes Second* (New York: William Morrow, 1992).

SCHOLTES, PETER R., "An Elaboration on Deming's Teachings on Performance Appraisal," in *Performance Appraisal: Perspectives on a Quality Management Approach*, Gary N. McLean et al., eds. (Alexandria, Va.: University of Minnesota Training and Development Research Center and American Society for Training and Development, 1990).

SCOTT, GINI G., *The Empowered Mind* (Englewood Cliffs, N.J.: Prentice Hall, 1994).

VROOM, VICTOR, *Work and Motivation* (New York: Wiley, 1964).

CASE

13-1 HONGKONG BANK OF CANADA*

"We believe that it will be a very stimulating and productive meeting," said David Bond, Vice-President, Marketing and Public Affairs for the Hongkong Bank of Canada. It was mid-August 1991, and he was talking about a branch managers' meeting that would run early the following month. "Senior management decided in May that we would have a two-day branch managers' meeting and that it would be held at Whistler. They asked Steve Tait, our Vice-President, Human Resources, Jim Francis, our Assistant Vice-President, Training & Development, and myself to put together the meeting program. The 100-plus people that will be there include about 35 managers of the former Lloyds branches, the bank that we purchased and took over operations last year. The program that we have put together for them is very different from previous branch managers' meetings in that we're going to use it as the kickoff of a year-long contest."

The Hongkong Bank of Canada

In 1981, the Canadian federal government passed legislation which permitted banks with foreign ownership to operate in Canada. Several dozen banks started up operations in Canada. One of them was the Hongkong and Shanghai Banking Corporation (HSBC), headquartered in Hong Kong, which established a wholly owned subsidiary called the Hongkong Bank of Canada. The head office was established in Vancouver and operations started with one branch in that city in July 1981. The Hongkong Bank was one of the few new foreign-owned banks to open as a full-service bank, i.e., a bank that generated deposits and made loans to individuals as well as to organizations. This was in contrast to the vast majority of the foreign banks, who

borrowed their loan funds from other financial organizations and confined their loan activities to commercial organizations. Management of the Hongkong Bank considered their full-service orientation as a natural extension of the operational philosophy of their HSBC parent.

Over the years the bank grew through a combination of additional business in existing branches, the opening of new branches, and an aggressive acquisition strategy. In 1985, they bought the Winnipeg and Halifax sites of the foundering Canadian Commercial Bank. The following year they bought the financially troubled Bank of British Columbia, which had extensive retail operations in 38 branches in British Columbia and two in Alberta.[1] In 1988, the bank bought the Midland Bank of Canada which had operated primarily in the corporate lending market. This was followed in 1990 by the purchase of Lloyds Bank Canada with its 52 branches, most of which were in eastern Canada. Lloyds Bank Canada was the outcome of the Lloyds Bank of England purchase of the Continental Bank of Canada in 1986. There was speculation in the industry at the time of purchase that Lloyds had overpaid to get into the Canadian market. There was later talk that the English parent had never really "bought in" to the Canadian operation after its early discovery that it could make a far better return by investing incremental capital in England than it could in investing comparable funds in its Canadian subsidiary.

The Lloyds Bank Canada that Hongkong purchased was focused on the corporate market. The very limited amount of attention to the retail market was devoted exclusively to high net worth individuals. Small net worth customers were actively discouraged. Low Lloyds earnings in recent years had led to drastic reductions in the bank's renovations budget. As a re-

---

*This case was prepared by John R. Kennedy of the John Ivey School of Business at The University of Western Ontario, Canada. Copyright 1993 © The University of Western Ontario. Reproduced by permission.

[1]In 1991, most of the British Columbia branches were still operating with signage that read "Bank of British Columbia" in large letters, followed underneath in smaller letters by the words "A Division of the Hongkong Bank of Canada."

sult, many of the branch physical facilities that the Hongkong Bank acquired were worn and run down. Further, the physical layout in most branches was not appropriate for the Hongkong Bank's emphasis on retail banking. Finally, Lloyds Bank, by Hongkong Bank standards, was overstaffed. This resulted in the departure, in the months following the takeover, of close to 20% of the 1,500 former Lloyds employees.

The acquisition triggered a change in the operating structure of the Hongkong Bank. Four regions were created, Quebec and Atlantic Provinces, Ontario, Western, and B.C., with a senior vice president appointed to head each. One of the major tasks associated with bringing the Lloyds operations into the Hongkong Bank was the integration of computer systems. While substantial work had been accomplished since the merger, it was not expected that the system would be complete until October 1991.

The 1990 Branch Managers' Meeting

The 1990 branch managers' meeting was held in August, just a few months after the acquisition of Lloyds Bank Canada. Thus, it was really the first large meeting of personnel of the two organizations. The day and a half meeting was held in facilities on the University of British Columbia campus, and started with a Thursday evening reception. "The Lloyds folks were understandably a bit wary to begin with," said a Hongkong Bank manager who had been an employee of the Bank of British Columbia at the time it was acquired by the Hongkong Bank. "But the fact that there was even a reception gave a message that most outsiders wouldn't think about. If you are part of a bank organization that is not doing too well financially, one of the first things to go is expenditure on what you might call employee social activities. I can remember back to the dark days of the Bank of BC, where you considered asking employees to pay for their own coffee during a meeting break."

The remainder of the meeting was virtually all one-way communication.

- Here are the Bank's products.
- Here is the way in which they are to be sold.
- Here is the operating system in which you are or will be operating.

"I think it was pretty apparent to everyone at the meeting," recalled another manager originally with the Bank of British Columbia, "that there was going to have to be a lot of work done on systems and organizational integration before we could really get down to the job of focused implementation across the organization."

Planning for the 1991 Branch Managers' Meeting

"When the three of us first got together," said David Bond, "we got talking about our personal experiences with managers' meetings, both here and in other organizations we had worked in. We concluded that they had been, for the most part, one-way communications by head office people designed to provide information and/or motivate the participants, together with some time for leisure and social activities. But when the meeting was over, that was it until the next one. No specific goals. No followup. No nothing! We decided that we wanted to break out of that pattern.

"From there, we spent some time thinking about the objectives we should set for the meeting. After a fair amount of discussion, we concluded that there should be three of them:

- "Stimulate growth of core deposits.
- "Try to build some system to put together the good retailers in our organization with people that don't have those retail skills and abilities.
- "Integrate the Lloyds people into our value system, which is to treat every customer who walks in the door as if they are the most important person on earth.

"It was out of those three objectives that the idea of a contest evolved."

The contest concept and meeting program were fleshed out in a series of meetings which followed.

The Contest

The decision was made that the contest would focus on the growth of core deposits for the one-year period starting September 1, 1991. Core deposits were defined as personal GICs, RRSPs, demand deposits, and time deposits. Extensive discussion went into the development of the contest rules, which are given in

Exhibit 1: Core Deposit Campaign—Contest Rules—

(1)   The Bank's overall deposit target as defined by the 1992 business plan must be met in order for an overall award to be triggered.

(2)   There must be a positive gain in core deposits by a branch on the winning team to be eligible to accompany the winning team to Hawaii.

(3)   A Branch Manager on the winning team must be an employee in good standing at the time of the award allocation to be eligible.

(4)   In the event a Manager is transferred from one branch to another and that branch is not within the same group but the original branch is among the winning teams, then if the Manager had been at the branch for the majority of the year and had accounted for a majority of the deposit growth, he or she will go on the trip. Otherwise, the new Manager will go.

(5)   With the exception of St. Laurent, new branches which open during the campaign will not be included in the contest. Appropriate adjustments will be made to the deposit balances of existing branches which lose core deposits through transfer to a new branch during the first three months of operation.

(6)   Points will be awarded as follows:

    (A)   Team standing following "initiatives" at Branch Managers' Conference:
        1st—2.5 Pts
        2nd—2.0 Pts
        3rd—1.5 Pts
        4th—1.0 Pt
        5th—0.5 Pt

    (B)   Greatest absolute dollar increase in core deposits:
        1st—10 Pts
        2nd—8 Pts
        3rd—6 Pts
        4th—4 Pts
        5th—2 Pts

    (C)   Greatest percentage increase in core deposits:
        1st—5 Pts
        2nd—4 Pts
        3rd—3 Pts
        4th—2 Pts
        5th—1 Pt

    (D)   Best all-around (i.e., most balanced) results (i.e., smallest percentage difference between largest percentage increase and smallest percentage increase on a team):
        1st—10 Pts
        2nd—8 Pts
        3rd—6 Pts
        4th—4 Pts
        5th—2 Pts

    (E)   Largest percentage increase in number of new retail deposit accounts:
        1st—5 Pts
        2nd—4 Pts
        3rd—3 Pts
        4th—2 Pts
        5th—1 Pt

Exhibit 1: Core Deposit Campaign—Contest Rules—continued

(F) Highest absolute increase in net new retail deposit accounts (i.e., new accounts less closed accounts):

    1st—5 Pts
    2nd—4 Pts
    3rd—3 Pts
    4th—2 Pts
    5th—1 Pt

$$\text{Winning} = \text{Highest Points of Sum of}$$
$$A + B + C + D + E + F$$

(7) In cases of dispute, or extenuating circumstances, the judgment of the COO will govern.

Exhibit 1. A rule was developed to break a tie should one occur.

The Teams

After some discussion, the decision was reached to have five teams. Steve Tait, together with the bank's marketing department, assumed responsibility for putting the teams together, within the criteria that teams should be the same size, represent all regions, contain a mix of pretakover Hongkong branches and Lloyds branches, and be balanced in terms of size of existing personal core deposits, percentage growth over the previous year, and potential for growth over the next year. Steve went through a series of iterations in which he put teams together, shopped them around senior management asking for input as to team equivalence, and then made adjustments. The result of this process was the five teams outlined in Exhibit 2.

The Prize

Each branch manager of the winning team, together with a guest, would receive free round trip passage, five nights' accommodation, and a celebratory dinner in Hawaii in October 1992. Two business meetings would be held during the five-day period. Rules were developed to define manager eligibility.

The Meeting Program

"Putting the program together was a lot of fun," said Jim Francis. "We worked hard to get a sequence and mix of activities that would be most effective in development of the team spirit that is necessary not only for the contest but for the kind of organization we want to be. We concluded as well that the presentation of the meeting agenda should be a reflection of our operating style. Finally, we decided that we wanted to put a name on the event that described what we were trying to accomplish. We combined the ideas of the Whistler mountain resort where the conference was going to be, Diamond Head in Hawaii where the contest winners will stay, together with the meeting and contest objectives, to get the meeting title and theme, 'Peak Performance.' "

Arrangements had already been completed to provide each branch manager at the end of the meeting with a framed custom print of Whistler created by a well-known B.C. artist. The meeting schedule appears as Exhibit 3. This schedule had already been distributed to the meeting participants. The titles of the individuals named in the meeting agenda are given in Exhibit 4. While they were not explicitly identified on the schedule, two activities should be highlighted. The first of these would occur early on the morning of September 6. People were to meet in the hotel lobby as teams for the first time, and take a cable car up the mountain to a restaurant for breakfast. There, if the weather cooperated, everyone would be able to see the sun rise over Whistler mountain. Second, part of the Friday afternoon team activities would be devoted to competition on Whistler streets in a number of races, including a Chuckwagon Race in which the wagon would be a child's wagon.

Exhibit 2: Groups for Core Deposit Campaign

Group 1			Group 2			Group 3		
City/Branch	Prov	Origin	City/Branch	Prov	Origin	City/Branch	Prov	Origin
Brampton	Ont	LBC	Abbotsford	BC	BBC	Vancouver		
Calgary			Calgary			Broadway &		
South	Alta	LBC	5th Ave.	Alta	LBC	Ash	BC	BBC
Cranbrock	BC	BBC	Vancouver			Campbell River	BC	BBC
Edmonton			Cambie & 42nd	BC	HKBC	Chicoutimi	Que	LBC
101st Street	Alta	LBC	Vancouver			Edmonton		
Vancouver			Denman Street	BC	BBC	Pacific Rim		
Georgia &			Vancouver			Mall	Alta	HKBC
Thurlow	BC	LBC	Dundas Street	BC	HKBC	Halifax	NS	CCB
Hamilton	Ont	LBC	Edmonton			Vancouver		
Vancover			Jasper Ave.	Alta	BBC	Kingsway &		
Hastings &			Fredericton	NB	LBC	Senlac	BC	BBC
Burrard	BC	BBC	Granby	QUE	LBC	Markham	Ont	LBC
Lasalle	Que	LBC	Vancouver			Mississauga		
Vancouver			Granville & 12th	BC	BBC	Golden Plaza	Ont	HKBC
Lougheed &			Vancouver			Mississauga	Ont	LBC
North Road	BC	BBC	Hastings &			Montreal		
Vancouver			Penticton	BC	BBC	Place Air		
Main & Pender	BC	HKBC	Kelowna			Canada	Que	LBC
Montreal			Richter Street	BC	LBC	Oakville	Ont	LBC
Place Victoria	Que	HKBC	Vancouver			Saint John	NB	LBC
Montreal			Kingsway &			Saskatoon	Sask	HKBC
Rene Levesque	Que	HKBC	Royal Oak	BC	BBC	Sault Ste. Marie	Ont	LBC
Nanaimo	BC	BBC	Laval	Que	LBC	Scarborough		
Ottawa	Ont	LBC	Red Deer	Alta	LBC	Dragon Centre	Ont	HKBC
Regina	Sask	LBC	Richmond			Vancouver		
Richmond			Parker Place	BC	LBC	Sixth & Fifth	BC	BBC
No. 3 & Park	BC	BBC	St. Catherines	Ont	LBC	Vancouver		
Spadina	Ont	HKBC	Vernon	BC	BBC	Main	BC	BBC
St. John's	Nfld	LBC	Victoria			Victoria		
Surrey	BC	BBC	Fort Street	BC	BBC	731 Fort Street	BC	HKBC
Vancouver			West Vancouver	BC	BBC	Victoria		
Tenth & Sasamat	BC	BBC	Windsor	Ont	LBC	Douglas &		
Trois-Rivieres	Que	LBC				Hillside	BC	BBC
						Whitby	Ont	LBC
						White Rock	BC	BBC

Legend:
HKBC = HongKong Bank of Canada
LBC = Lloyds Bank of Canada
CCB = Canadian Commercial Bank
BBC = Bank of British Columbia

Exhibit 2—Cont'd

Group 4			Group 5		
City/Branch	**Prov**	**Origin**	**City/Branch**	**Prov**	**Origin**
Barrie	Ont	LBC	Calgary		
Chilliwack	BC	BBC	8th Ave.	Alta	BBC
Edmonton			Calgary		
South	Alta	LBC	Good Fortune Plaza	Alta	HKBC
Vancouver			Vancouver		
Fraser & 48th	BC	BBC	Columbia St.	BC	BBC
Haney	BC	BBC	Delta	BC	BBC
Vancouver			Kelowna		
Hastings & Gilmore	BC	BBC	Bernard Ave.	BC	BBC
Kamloops	BC	BBC	Kingston	Ont	LBC
Vancouver			Kitchener	Ont	LBC
Kerrisdale	BC	BBC	Lethbridge	Alta	LBC
Langley	BC	BBC	Vancouver		
London	Ont	LBC	Main & Keefer	BC	BBC
Longueuil	Que	LBC	Mississauga		
Medicine Hat	Alta	LBC	Chinese Cultural		
Prince George	BC	BBC	Centre	Ont	HKBC
Richmond			Mississauga		
Johnson Centre	BC	HKBC	North	Ont	LBC
Scarborough			North Vancouver	BC	BBC
Eglinton Ave.	Ont	LBC	Penticton	BC	BBC
Scarborough			Port Coquitlam	BC	BBC
Milliken Square	Ont	HKBC	Saint Leonard	Que	LBC
Ste-Foy	Que	LBC	Sherbrooke	Que	LBC
Thunder Bay	Ont	LBC	St. Laurent	Que	HKBC
Timmins	Ont	LBC	Toronto		
Toronto			Skyway Park	Ont	LBC
70 York Street	Ont	HKBC	Victoria		
			Douglas & Johnson	BC	BBC
			Willowdale	Ont	HKBC
			Winnipeg	Man	CCB

Legend:
HKBC = HongKong Bank of Canada
LBC = Lloyds Bank of Canada
CCB = Canadian Commercial Bank
BBC = Bank of British Columbia

Exhibit 3:

Hongkong Bank of Canada 1991 managers conference

Hongkong Bank of Canada
1991 Managers' Conference

September 5th

3:00 PM SHARP	Bus To Whistler Departs Vancouver	Head Office
6:00 - 7:00 PM	Reception	Ballroom
7:00 - 9:00 PM	Dinner	Ballroom
9:00 - 10:00 PM	Regional Meetings	TBA

September 6th

7:00 AM SHARP	1st Group Initiative	Lobby
7:30 - 8:30 AM	Breakfast	TBA
8:30 - 8:45 AM	Official Opening - Chris Crook	"
8:45 - 9:30 AM	The Opportunity - Clyde Ostler	"
9:30 - 9:40 AM	"A Moment With Mould"	"
9:40 - 10:00 AM	The Challenge - Chris Crook	"
10:00 - 11:00 AM	Team Activity - Name That Team	"
11:00 - 11:45 AM	Service Is The Key - Bill Dalton	"
11:45 - 12:15 PM	2nd Group Initiative	"
12:15 - 1:45 PM	Lunch - Hosted by Bob Hemond	Cheakmus
1:45 - 2:00 PM	"Another Moment With Mould"	Ballroom
2:00 - 2:45 PM	Team Activity - Brainstorming	"
2:45 - 3:15 PM	Merchandising Our Way - Chris Crook	"
3:15 - 5:00 PM	Team Activity - Strategy	Breakouts
5:00 - 5:30 PM	Free Time	Optional
5:30 - 6:00 PM	Reception	Ballroom
6:00 - 8:30 PM	BBQ - Hosted by John Ranaldi	"
8:30 - 9:00 PM	Team Activity - Presentations	"

Exhibit 3: (continued)

Conference Cont'd

September 7th

Time	Red	Blue	Yellow	Green	Pink	
7:15 - 8:20 AM 8:20 - 8:30 AM	Breakfast - Hosted by Dewar Harper "John Goes On!"					Cheakmus "
	Red	Blue	Yellow	Green	Pink	
	Diamond Head	Black Tusk	Board Room	Sutcliffe A	Sutcliffe B	Meeting Rooms
8:30 - 9:05 AM	CEO & COO	Back At The Branch	H.O. Panel	Local Marketing	Credit Connection	"
9:05 - 9:40 AM	Back At The Branch	H.O. Panel	Local Marketing	Credit Connection	CEO & COO	"
9:40 - 10:15 AM	H.O. Panel	Local Marketing	Credit Connection	CEO & COO	Back At The Branch	"
10:15 - 10:50 AM	Corporate Shuffle					TBA
10:50 - 11:25 AM	Local Marketing	Credit Connection	CEO & COO	Back At The Branch	H.O. Panel	Meeting Rooms
11:25 - 12:00 PM	Credit Connection	CEO & COO	Back At The Branch	H.O. Panel	Local Marketing	"
12:00 - 1:30 PM	Lunch - Hosted by Martin Glynn & Bruna Giacomazzi					Cheakmus
1:30 - 1:40 PM	"The Last Mouldy Moments"					Ballroom
1:40 - 2:30 PM	The Strategic Plan - Jim Cleave					"
2:30 - 3:15 PM	Team Activity - Strategic Plan					"
3:15 - 4:00 PM	Questions to Senior Executive					"
4:00 - 4:30 PM	Wrap-up and Farewell					"

Exhibit 4: TITLES OF INDIVIDUALS NAMED IN THE MEETING SCHEDULE

Name	Title
Chris Crook	Executive Vice President, Banking
Clyde Osler	A senior officer with the Wells Fargo Bank
John Mould	Sr. Vice President & Controller
Bill Dalton	Chief Operating Officer
Bob Hemond	Sr. Vice President, Quebec & Atlantic Provinces Region
John Ranaldi	Sr. Vice President, Western Region
Dewar Harper	Sr. Vice President, Ontario Region
Martin Glynn	Sr. Vice President, BC Region
Bruna Giacomazzi	Sr. Vice President, Special Credit
Jim Cleave	Chief Executive Officer

MEMBERS OF THE SATURDAY MORNING PANELS

Panel Name	Panel Member	Title
CEO & COO	Jim Cleave and Bill Dalton	
H.O. Panel	Steve Tait	VP Human Resources
	Jim Mayhew	AVP Human Resources
	Brian Salvador	AVP Compensation & Benefits
Local Marketing	Al Cummings	AVP Marketing
Credit Connection	Steve Wilson	VP Consumer Credit
	Bert McPhee	Sr. Vice President, Credit
Back at the Branch	Phil Scott	President, Scott Consulting Inc.

Exhibit 5: Instructions to the Branch Manager Participants

INSTRUCTIONS FOR FRIDAY AFTERNOON

You have a number of tasks to accomplish in a relatively limited time period.

You will be expected to present at dinner tonight a logo for your team and to have selected a theme song with appropriate words. The logos and the songs will be judged by the Fabulous Four* as to their appropriateness, suitability to the name chosen, ingenuity, originality, and presentation. The results of the judging will count toward the trip to Hawaii.

You will need to prepare yourselves to gain maximum benefit from tomorrow morning's activities. To do that you may wish to spend some time understanding the scope of the challenge that you face. What are the characteristics of the group? Just how daunting is the task ahead? What should be your major objectives and how do you plan to accomplish them? What are the strengths within the group and how can you capitalize upon them?

How will you communicate with each other and provide support to each other? The Bank will not pay for conference calls or travel, so what alternatives are available and how do they get organized and done?

Tomorrow morning between 8:30 and 12 noon you will have the opportunity to meet with five different groups or individuals. Each session is designed to provide you with some "tools" which you individually and as a team can use to help you get to Diamond Head. Each session has provided an outline of what they plan to discuss with you. You need to make sure that you gain the maximum benefit from these sessions with your group. What are the most important things for you to know with respect to each area? How will you organize to make sure that you accomplish your objectives for each of these consultative sessions?

*The "Fabulous Four" were the four senior officers of the bank:
James H. Cleave; President and Chief Executive Officer
William R. P. Dalton; Executive Director and Chief Operating Officer
Maurice R. Mourton; Executive Vice-President, Administration
Chris J. Cook; Executive Vice-President, Banking

Exhibit 6: Instructions to the Session Participants on Saturday Morning

The five teams will be meeting with five different groups for 30 minutes at a time. The purpose of these meetings is to give the individual teams information regarding the "tools" that they will be provided with during the year as they strive to win the trip to Diamond Head.

What you are asked to do is to provide, on one page maximum, an outline of the most salient information that you would be willing to provide to the group during your session. For example, the Marketing/Public Affairs group will be providing information on the detailed marketing campaigns planned for the year, and the type of support that will be provided for each branch.

Each group should be given the opportunity to ask you questions, and provide you feedback on what is of concern to them. Thus, any presentation should not be more than 15 minutes. If you wish, *at the conclusion of the session*, you can provide each manager with take-away material.

Thus, the challenge for the individual teams is to make sure that they have organized themselves to gain the maximum benefit from the opportunity of meeting with you. Your challenge is to present material in an interesting, informative, and inviting manner. Since the time is limited, you will be forced to concentrate on only the most essential matters. The draft of your material should be sent to Elaine Ranger no later than the 15th of August so that it can be reproduced and included in the Managers' packages.

Final Details

"To get the most out of the meeting, the branch managers will have to understand that they have to get actively involved in it," said David Bond. "At the same time, the head office participants in the Saturday morning sessions must understand that they have a specific role to play in those sessions. Therefore, we've put together two sets of instructions. The one for the participants[2] will be given out when the contest is introduced on the Friday[3] morning. The one for the head office people[4] has already gone out."

[2] See Exhibit 5.
[3] Friday, September 6.
[4] See Exhibit 6.

CASE

13-2 GENERAL ELECTRIC APPLIANCES*

Larry Barr had recently been promoted to the position of District Sales Manager (B.C.) for G.E. Appliances, a division of Canadian Appliance Manufacturing Co. Ltd. (CAMCO). One of his more important duties in that position was the allocation of his district's sales quota among his five salespeople. Barr received his

*This case was prepared by Richard W. Pollay, John D. Claxton, and Rick Jenkner. Copyright © by Richard W. Pollay, John D. Claxton, and Rick Jenkner. Reproduced by permission.

quota for next year in October of the previous year. His immediate task was to determine an equitable allocation of that quota. This was important because the company's incentive pay plan was based on the salespeople's attainment of quota. A portion of Barr's remuneration was also based on the degree to which his sales force met their quotas.

Barr graduated from the University of British Columbia with the degree of Bachelor of Commerce. He was immediately hired as a product manager for a mining equipment manufacturing firm because of his summer job experience with that firm. Three years later he joined Canadian General Electric (C.G.E.) in Montreal as a product manager for refrigerators. There he was responsible for creating and merchandising a product line, as well as developing product and marketing plans. Two years later he was transferred to Coburg, Ontario, as a sales manager for industrial plastics. The next year he became Administrative Manager (Western Region) and when the position of District Sales Manager became available, Barr was promoted to it. There his duties included development of sales strategies, supervision of salespeople, and budgeting.

Background

Canadian Appliance Manufacturing Co. Ltd. (CAMCO) was created under the joint ownership of Canadian General Electric Ltd. and General Steel Wares Ltd. (G.S.W.). CAMCO then purchased the production facilities of Westinghouse Canada Ltd. Under the purchase agreement the Westinghouse brand name was transferred to White Consolidated Industries Ltd., where it became White-Westinghouse. Appliances manufactured by CAMCO in the former Westinghouse plant were branded Hotpoint.

The G.E., G.S.W., and Hotpoint major appliance plants became divisions of CAMCO. These divisions operated independently and had their own separate management staff, although they were all ultimately accountable to CAMCO management. The divisions competed for sales, although not directly, because they each produced product lines for different price segments (Exhibit 1).

Competition

Competition in the appliance industry was vigorous. CAMCO was the largest firm in the industry, with approximately 45 percent market share, split between G.E., G.S.W. (Moffatt & McClary brands), and Hotpoint. The following three firms each had 10–15 percent market shares: Inglis (washers and dryers only), W.C.I. (makers of White-Westinghouse, Kelvinator, and Gibson), and Admiral. These firms also produced appliances under department store brand names such as Viking, Baycrest, and Kenmore, which accounted for an additional 15 percent of the market. The remainder of the market was divided among brands such as Maytag, Roper Dishwasher, Gurney, Tappan, and Danby.

Exhibit 1: Organization Chart

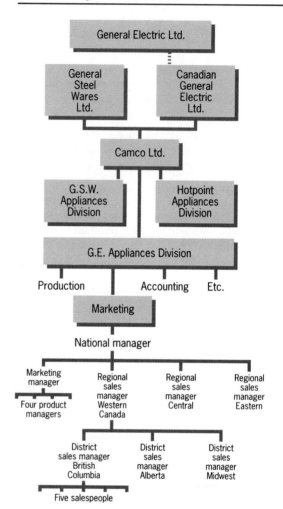

G.E. marketed a full major appliance product line, including refrigerators, ranges, washers, dryers, dishwashers, and television sets. G.E. appliances generally had many features and were priced at the upper end of the price range. Their major competition came from Maytag and Westinghouse.

The Budgeting Process

G.E. Appliances was one of the most advanced firms in the consumer goods industry in terms of sales budgeting. Budgeting received careful analysis at all levels of management.

The budgetary process began in June of each year. The management of G.E. Appliances division assessed the economic outlook, growth trends in the industry, competitive activity, population growth, and so forth in order to determine a reasonable sales target for the next year. The president of CAMCO received this estimate, checked and revised it as necessary, and submitted it to the president of G.E. Canada. Final authorization rested with G.E. Ltd., which had a definite minimum growth target for the G.E. branch of CAMCO. G.E. Appliances was considered an "invest and grow" division, which meant that it was expected to produce a healthy sales growth each year, regardless of the state of the economy. As Barr observed, "This is difficult, but meeting challenges is the job of management."

The approved budget was expressed as a desired percentage increase in sales. Once the figure had been decided, it was not subject to change. The quota was communicated back through G.E. Canada Ltd., CAMCO, and G.E. Appliances, where it was available to the District Sales Managers in October. Each district was then required to meet an overall growth figure (quota) but each sales territory was not automatically expected to achieve that same growth. Barr was required to assess the situation in each territory, determine where growth potential was highest, and allocate his quota accordingly.

The Sales Incentive Plan

The sales incentive plan was a critical part of General Electric's sales force plan and an important consideration in the quota allocation of Barr. Each salesperson had a portion of earnings dependent upon performance with respect to quota. Also, Barr was awarded a bonus based on the sales performance of his district, making it advantageous to Barr and good for staff morale for all his salespeople to attain their quotas.

The sales force incentive plan was relatively simple. A bonus system is fairly typical for salespeople in any field. With G.E., each salesperson agreed to a basic salary figure called "planned earnings." The planned salary varied according to experience, education, past performance, and competitive salaries. A salesperson was paid 75 percent of planned earnings on a guaranteed regular basis. The remaining 25 percent of salary was at risk, dependent upon the person's sales record. There was also the possibility of

Exhibit 2: Sales Incentive Earnings Schedule: Major Appliances and Home Entertainment Products

Sales Quota Realization Percent	Incentive Percent of Base Salary Total	Sales Quota Realization Percent	Incentive Percent of Base Salary Total
70	0	105	35.00
71	0.75	106	37.00
72	1.50	107	39.00
73	2.25	108	41.00
74	3.00	109	43.00
75	3.75	110	45.00
76	4.50	111	46.00
77	5.25	112	47.00
78	6.00	113	48.00
79	6.75	114	49.00
80	7.50	115	50.00
81	8.25	116	51.00
82	9.00	117	52.00
83	9.75	118	53.00
84	10.50	119	54.00
85	11.25	120	55.00
86	12.00	121	56.00
87	12.75	122	57.00
88	13.50	123	58.00
89	14.25	124	59.00
90	15.00	125	60.00
91	16.00	126	61.00
92	17.00	127	62.00
93	18.00	128	63.00
94	19.00	129	64.00
95	20.00	130	65.00
96	21.00	131	66.00
97	22.00	132	67.00
98	23.00	133	68.00
99	24.00	134	69.00
100	25.00	135	70.00
101	27.00	136	71.00
102	29.00	137	72.00
103	31.00	138	73.00
104	33.00	139	74.00
		140	75.00

earning substantially more money by selling more than quota (Exhibit 2).

The bonus was awarded such that total salary (base plus bonus) equaled planned earnings when the quota was just met. The greatest increase in bonus came between 101 and 110 percent of quota. The bonus was paid quarterly on the cumulative total quota. A holdback system ensured that a salesperson was never required to pay back a previously earned bonus by reason of a poor quarter. Because of this system, it was critical that each salesperson's quota be fair in relation to those of the other salespeople. Nothing was worse for morale than one person earning large bonuses while the others struggled.

Quota attainment was not the sole basis for evaluating the salespeople. They were required to fulfill a wide range of duties including service, franchising of new dealers, maintaining good relations with dealers, and maintaining a balance of sales among the different product lines. Because the bonus system was based on sales only, Barr had to ensure that the salespeople did not neglect their other duties.

A formal salary review was held each year for each salesperson. However, Barr preferred to give his salespeople continuous feedback on their performances. Through human relations skills he hoped to avoid problems which could lead to dismissal of a salesperson and loss of sales for the company.

Barr's incentive bonus plan was more complex than the salespeople's. He was awarded a maximum of 75 annual bonus points broken down as follows: market share, 15; total sales performance, 30; sales representative balance, 30. Each point had a specific money value. The system ensured that Barr allocated his quota carefully. For instance, if one quota was so difficult that the salesperson sold only 80 percent of it, while the other salespeople exceeded quota, Barr's bonus would be reduced, even if the overall area sales exceeded the quota (Exhibit 3).

Quota Allocation

The total sales budget for G.E. Appliances division for next year was about $100 million, a 14 percent sales increase over the current year. Barr's share of the $33 million Western region quota was $13.3 million, also a 14 percent increase over the previous year. Barr had two weeks to allocate the quota among his five territories. He needed to consider factors such as historical allocation, economic outlook, dealer changes, personnel changes, untapped potential, new franchises or store openings, and buying group activity (volume purchases by associations of independent dealers).

Sales Force

There were five sales territories within British Columbia (Exhibit 4). Territories were determined on the basis of number of customers, sales volume of customers, geographic size, and experience of the salesperson. Territories were altered periodically in order to deal with changed circumstances.

One territory was comprised entirely of contract customers. Contract sales were sales in bulk lots to builders and developers who used the appliances in housing units. Because the appliances were not resold at retail, G.E. took a lower profit margin on such sales.

G.E. Appliances recruited M.B.A. graduates for their sales force. They sought bright, educated people who were willing to relocate anywhere in Canada. The company intended that these people would ultimately be promoted to managerial positions. The company also hired experienced career salespeople in order to get a blend of experience in the sales force. However, the typical salesperson was under age 30, aggressive, and upwardly mobile. G.E.'s sales training program covered only product knowledge. It was not felt necessary to train recruits in sales techniques.

Allocation Procedure

At the time Barr assumed the job of D.S.M., he had a meeting with the former sales manager, Ken Philips. Philips described to Barr the method he had used in the past to allocate the quota. As Barr understood it, the procedure was as follows:

The quota was received in October in the form of a desired percentage sales increase. The first step was to project current sales to the end of the year. This gave a base to which the increase was added for an estimation of the next year's quota. From this quota, the value of contract sales was allocated. Contract sales were allocated first because the market was considered the easiest to forecast. The amount of contract sales in the sales mix was constrained by the lower profit margin on such sales.

The next step was to make a preliminary allocation by simply adding the budgeted percentage increase to the year-end estimates for each territory. Although this allocation seemed fair on the surface, it did not take into account the differing situations in the territories or the difficulty of attaining such an increase.

Exhibit 3: Development of a Sales Commission Plan

A series of steps are required to establish the foundation upon which a sales commission plan can be built. These steps are as follows:

Determine Specific Sales Objectives of Positions To Be Included in Plan

For a sales commission plan to succeed, it must be designed to encourage the attainment of the business objectives of the component division. Before deciding on the dimensions of a commission plan, you have to decide on which of the following objectives are important.

1. Increase sales volume
2. Do an effective, balanced selling job in a variety of product lines
3. Improve market share
4. Reduce selling expense to sales ratios
5. Develop new accounts or territories
6. Introduce new products

Although it is probably neither desirable nor necessary to include all such objectives as specific measures of performance in the plan, they should be kept in mind, at least to the extent that the performance measures chosen for the plan are compatible with and do not work against the overall accomplishment of the component's business objectives.

Also, the *relative* current importance or ranking of these objectives will provide guidance in selecting the number and type of performance measures to be included in the plan.

Determine Quantitative Performance Measures to Be Used

Although it may be possible to include a number of measures in a particular plan, there is a drawback to using so many as to overly complicate it and fragment the impact of any one measure on the participants. A plan that is difficult to understand will lose a great deal of its motivating force, as well as being costly to administer properly.

For components that currently have a variable sales compensation plan(s) for their sales, a good starting point would be to consider the measures used in those plans. Although the measurements used for sales managers need not be identical, they should at least be compatible with those used to determine commissions.

However, keep in mind that a performance measure that may not be appropriate for individual salespeople may be a good one to apply to their manager. Measurements involving attainment of a share of a defined market, balanced selling for a variety of products, and control of district or region expenses might well fall into this category.

The accompanying table lists a variety of measurements that might be used to emphasize specific sales objectives. For most components, all or most of these objectives will be desirable to some extent. The point is to select those of greatest importance where it will be possible to establish measures of standard or normal performance for individuals, or at least small groups of individuals working as a team.

If more than one performance measurement is to be used, the relative weighting of each measurement must be determined. If a measure is to be effective, it must carry enough weight to have at least some noticeable effect on the commission earnings of an individual.

As a general guide, it would be unusual for a plan to include more than two or three quantitative measures with a minimum weighting of 15–20 percent of planned commissions for any one measurement.

Establish Commission Payment Schedule for Each Performance Measure

Determine Appropriate Range of Performance for Each Measurement. The performance range for a measurement defines the percent of standard performance (R%) at which commission earnings start to the point where they reach maximum.

The minimum point of the performance range for a given measurement should be set so that a majority of the participants can earn at least some incentive pay, and the maximum set at a point that is possible for some participants to obtain. These points will vary with the type of measure used and with the degree of predictability of individual budgets or other forms of measurement. In a period where overall performance is close to standard, 90 to 95 percent of the participants should fall within the performance range.

For the commission plan to be effective, most

Exhibit 3: Development of a Sales Commission Plan (continued)

of the participants should be operating within the performance range most of the time. If a participant is either far below the minimum of this range or has reached the maximum, further improvement will not affect his commission earnings, and the plan will be largely inoperative as far as he is concerned.

Actual past experience of R%'s attained by participants is obviously the best indicator of what this range should be for each measure used. Lacking this, it is better to err on the side of having a wider range than one which proves to be too narrow. If some form of group measure is used, the variation from standard performance is likely to be less for the group in total than for individuals within it. For example, the performance range for total District performance would probably be narrower than the range established for individual sales within a District.

Determine Appropriate Reward: Risk Ratio for Commission Earnings. This refers to the relationship of commission earned at standard performance, to maximum commission earnings available under the plan. A plan that pays 10 percent of base salary for normal or standard performance and pays 30 percent as a maximum commission would have a 2:1 ratio. In other words, participants can earn twice as much (20 percent) for above-standard performance as they stand to lose for below-standard performance (10 percent).

Reward under a sales commission plan should be related to the effort involved to produce a given result. To adequately encourage above-standard results, the *reward:risk ratio* should generally be at least 2:1. The proper control of incentive plan payments lies in the proper setting of performance standards, not in the setting of a low maximum payment for outstanding results that provides a minimum variation in individual earnings. Generally, a higher percentage of base salary should be paid for each 1%R above 100 percent that has been paid for each 1%R up to 100%R to reflect the relative difficulty involved in producing above-standard results.

Once the performance range and reward:risk ratios have been determined, the schedule of payments for each performance measure can then be calculated. This will show the percentage of the participant's base salary earned for various performance results (R%) from the point at which commissions start to maximum performance.

Example: For measurement paying 20 percent of salary for standard performance:

Percent of Base Salary Earned	
1% of base salary for each +1%R	0%
	20%
1.33% of base salary for each +1%R	60%

Percent of Sales Quota
80% or below
100% (standard performance)
130% or above

Prepare Draft of Sales Commission Plan
After completing the above steps, a draft of a sales commission plan should be prepared using the accompanying outline as a guide.

Keys to Effective Commission Plans
1. *Get the understanding and acceptance of the commission plan by the managers who will be involved in carrying it out.* They must be convinced of its effectiveness in order to properly explain and "sell" the plan to the salespeople.

2. *In turn, be sure the plan is presented clearly to the salespeople* so that they have a good understanding of how the plan will work. We find that good acceptance of a sales commission plan on the part of salespeople correlates closely with how well they understood the plan and its effect on their compensation. The salespeople must be convinced that the measurements used are factors which they can control by their selling efforts.

3. *Be sure the measurements used in the commission plan encourage the salespeople to achieve the marketing goals of your operation.* For example, if sales volume is the only performance measure, the salespeople will concentrate on producing as much dollar volume as possible by spending most of their time on products with high volume potential. It will be difficult to get them to spend much time on introducing new products with relatively low volume, handling customer complaints, etc. Even though a good portion of their compensation may

Exhibit 3: Development of a Sales Commission Plan (continued)

still be in salary, you can be sure they will wind up doing the things they feel will maximize their commission earnings.

4. One solution to maintaining good sales direction is to put at least a portion of the commission earnings in an "incentive pool" to be distributed by the sales manager according to his judgment. This "pool" can vary in size according to some qualitative measure of the sales group's performance, but the manager can set individual measurements for each salesperson and reward people according to how well they fulfill their goals.

5. If at all possible, you should test the plan for a period of time, perhaps in one or two sales areas or districts. To make it a real test, you should actually pay commission earnings to the participants, but the potential risk and rewards can be limited. No matter how well a plan has been conceived, not all the potential pitfalls will be apparent until you've actually operated the plan for a period of time. The test period is a relatively painless way to get some experience.

6. Finally, after the plan is in operation, take time to analyze the results. Is the plan accomplishing what you want it to do, both in terms of business results produced and in realistically compensating salespeople for their efforts?

Tailoring Commission Plan Measurements to Fit Component Objectives

Objectives	Possible Plan Measurements
1. Increase sales/order volume	Net sales billed or orders received against quota
2. Increase sales of particular lines	Sales against product line quotas with weighted sales credits on individual lines
3. Increase market share	Percent realization (%R) of shares bogey
4. Do balanced selling job	%R of product line quotas, with commissions increasing in proportion to number of lines up to quota
5. Increase profitability	Margin realized from sales
	Vary sales credits to emphasize profitable product lines
	Vary sales credit in relation to amount of price discount
6. Increase dealer sales	Pay distributor salespeople or sales manager in relation to realization of sales quotas of assigned dealers
7. Increase sales calls	%R of targeted calls per district or region
8. Introduce new product	Additional sales credits on new line for limited period
9. Control expense	%R of expense to sales or margin ratio
	Adjust sales credit in proportion to variance from expense budget
10. Sales teamwork	Share of incentive based upon group results

The next step was examination of the sales data compiled by G.E. Weekly sales reports from all regions were fed into a central computer, which compiled them and printed out sales totals by product line for each customer, as well as other information. This information enabled the sales manager to check the reasonableness of his initial allocation through a careful analysis of the growth potential for each customer.

The analysis began with the largest accounts such as Firestone, Hudson's Bay, and Eatons, which each bought over $1 million in appliances annually. Accounts that size were expected to achieve at least the budgeted growth. The main reason for this was that a shortfall of a few percentage points on such a large account would be difficult to make up elsewhere.

Next, the growth potential for medium-sized accounts was estimated. These accounts included McDonald Supply, K-Mart, Federated Cooperative, and buying groups such as Volume Independent Pur-

Exhibit 4: G.E. Appliances—Sales Territories

Territory Designation	Description
9961 Greater Vancouver (Garth Rizzuto)	Hudson's Bay, Firestone, K-Mart, McDonald Supply, plus seven independent dealers
9962 Interior (Dan Seguin)	All customers from Quesnel to Nelson, including contract sales (50 customers)
9963 Coastal (Ken Block)	Eatons, Woodwards, plus Vancouver Island north of Duncan and upper Fraser Valley (east of Clearbrook) (20 customers)
9964 Independent and Northern (Fred Speck)	All independents in lower mainland and South Vancouver Island, plus northern B.C. and Yukon (30 customers)
9967 Contract (Jim Wiste)	Contract sales Vancouver, Victoria. All contract sales outside 9962 (50–60 customers)

chasers (V.I.P.). Management expected the majority of sales growth to come from such accounts, which had annual sales of between $150 thousand and $1 million.

At that point, about 70 percent of the accounts had been analyzed. The small accounts were estimated last. These had generally lower growth potential but were an important part of the company's distribution system.

Once all the accounts had been analyzed, the growth estimates were summed and the total compared to the budget. Usually, the growth estimates were well below the budget.

The next step was to gather more information. The salespeople were usually consulted to ensure that no potential trouble areas or good opportunities had been overlooked. The manager continued to revise and adjust the figures until the total estimate matched the budget. These projections were then summed by territory and compared to the preliminary territorial allocation.

Frequently, there were substantial differences between the two allocations. Historical allocations were then examined, and the manager used his judgment in adjusting the figures until he was satisfied that the allocation was both equitable and attainable. Some factors which were considered at this stage included experience of the salesperson, competitive activities, potential store closures or openings, potential labor disputes in areas, and so forth.

The completed allocation was passed on to the Regional Sales Manager for his approval. The process had usually taken one week or longer by this stage.

Once the allocations had been approved, the District Sales Manager then divided them into sales quotas by product line. Often, the resulting average price did not match the expected mix between higher- and lower-priced units. Therefore, some additional adjusting of figures was necessary. The house account (used for sales to employees of the company) was used as the adjustment factor.

Once this breakdown had been completed, the numbers were printed on a budget sheet, and given to the Regional Sales Manager (R.S.M.). He forwarded all the sheets for his region to the central computer, which printed out sales numbers for each product line by salesperson by month. These figures were used as the salesperson's quotas for the next year.

Current Situation

Barr recognized that he faced a difficult task. He felt that he was too new to the job and the area to confidently undertake an account by account growth analysis. However, due to his previous experience with sales budgets, he did have some sound general ideas. He also had the records of past allocation and quota attainment (Exhibit 5), as well as the assistance of the R.S.M., Anthony Foyt.

Barr's first step was to project the current sales figures to end-of-year totals. This task was facilitated because the former manager, Philips, had been making successive projections monthly since June. Barr then made a preliminary quota allocation by adding the budgeted sales increase of 14 percent to each territory's total (Exhibit 6).

Barr then began to assess circumstances which could cause him to alter that allocation. One major problem was the resignation, effective at the end of the year, of one of the company's top salesmen, Ken Block. His territory had traditionally been one of the most difficult, and Barr felt that it would be unwise to replace Block with a novice salesperson.

Barr considered shifting one of the more experienced salespeople into that area. However, that would have involved a disruption of service in an additional territory, which was undesirable because it took several months for a salesperson to build up a good rapport with customers. Barr's decision would affect his quota allocation because a salesperson new to a territory could not be expected to sell immediately as well as the incumbent, and a novice salesperson would require an even longer period of adaptation.

Barr was also concerned about territory 9961. The territory comprised two large national accounts and seven major independent dealers. The buying decisions for the national accounts were made at their head offices, where G.E.'s regional sales had no control over the decisions. Recently, Barr had heard rumors that one of the national accounts was reviewing its purchase of G.E. appliances. If they were to delist even some product lines, it would be a major blow to the salesman, Rizzuto, whose potential sales would be greatly reduced. Barr was unsure how to deal with that situation.

Another concern for Barr was the wide variance in buying of some accounts. Woodwards, Eatons, and McDonald Supply had large fluctuations from year to year. Also, Eatons, Hudson's Bay, and Woodwards had plans to open new stores in the Vancouver area sometime during the year. The sales increase to be generated by these events was hard to estimate.

The general economic outlook was poor. The Canadian dollar had fallen to 92 cents U.S., and unemployment was about 8 percent. The government's anti-inflation program, which was scheduled to end next year, had managed to keep inflation to the 8 percent level, but economists expected higher inflation and increased labor unrest during the postcontrol period.

The economic outlook was not the same in all areas. For instance, the Okanagan (9962) was a very

Exhibit 5: Sales Results

Territory	Previous Budget (× 1,000)	Percent of Total Budget	Previous Actual (× 1,000)	Variance from Quota (V%)
9967 (Contract)	$2,440	26.5	$2,267	(7)
9961 (Greater Vancouver)	1,790	19.4	1,824	2
9962 (Interior)	1,624	17.7	1,433	(11)
9963 (Coastal)	2,111	23.0	2,364	12
9965 (Independent dealers)	1,131	12.3	1,176	4
House	84	1.1	235	—
Total	$9,180	100.0	$9,299	1

Territory	Following Year Budget (× 1,000)	Percent of Total Budget	Following Year Actual (× 1,000)	Variance from Quota (V%)
9967 (Contract)	$2,587	26.2	$2,845	10
9961 (Greater Vancouver)	2,005	20.3	2,165	8
9962 (Interior)	1,465	14.8	1,450	(1)
9963 (Coastal)	2,405	24.4	2,358	(2)
9965 (Independent dealers)	1,334	13.5	1,494	12
House	52	.8	86	—
Total	$9,848	100.0	$10,398	5

Exhibit 6: Sales Projections and Quotas

	Projected Sales Results, Current Year				
Territory	Current Year October Year to Date (× 1000)	Current Projected Total (× 1000)	Current Budget (× 1000)	% of Total Budget	Projected Variance from Quota (V%)
9967	$2,447	$ 3,002	$ 2,859	25.0	5
9961	2,057	2,545	2,401	21.0	6
9962	1,318	1,623	1,727	15.1	(6)
9963	2,124	2,625	2,734	23.9	(4)
9965	1,394	1,720	1,578	13.8	9
House	132	162	139	1.2	—
Total	$9,474	$11,677	$11,438	100.0	2

	Preliminary Allocation, Next Year		
Territory	Current Projection (× 1000)	Next Year Budget[a] (× 1000)	% of Total Budget
9967	$ 3,002	$ 3,422	25.7
9961	2,545	2,901	21.8
9962	1,623	1,854	13.9
9963	2,625	2,992	22.5
9965	1,720	1,961	14.7
House	162	185	1.4
Total	$11,677	$13,315	100.0

[a]Next budget = current territory projections + 14% = $13,315.

depressed area. Tourism was down, and fruit farmers were doing poorly despite good weather and record prices. Vancouver Island was still recovering from a 200 percent increase in ferry fares, while the lower mainland appeared to be in a relatively better position.

In the contract segment, construction had shown an increase recently. However, labor unrest was common. There had been a crippling eight-week strike recently and there was a strong possibility of another strike next year.

With all of this in mind, Barr was very concerned that he allocate the quota properly because of the bonus system implications. How should he proceed? To help him in his decision, he reviewed a note on development of a sales commission plan which he had obtained while attending a seminar on sales management the previous year (Exhibit 3).

▶ 14 ◀

Compensating
Salespeople*

I've always been worried about people who are willing to work for nothing. Sometimes that's all you get from them, nothing.

SAM ERVIN

*Chapter Consultant: Robert C. Conti, vice president, The Alexander Group, Inc.

LEARNING OBJECTIVES

After studying this chapter, you should be able to:

▶ Balance the need for wages against company resources.

▶ Select appropriate compensation methods.

▶ Set pay levels.

▶ Determine benefit packages.

▶ Assemble a compensation plan.

► COMPENSATION OBJECTIVES

Compensation is one of the most important tools for motivating and retaining field salespeople. However, compensation is a cost and selling expenses have now increased to the point where they represent 12.2 percent of sales revenue.[1] Thus to maintain profitability you must design compensation plans that encourage salespeople to work efficiently. This is not easy to do and 59 percent of the managers in a survey complain that their pay plans fail to motivate their staffs to make an extra effort and 48 percent gripe that they overpay poor performers.[2] Part of the problem is that young firms often use the same commission rate for all products. Under these conditions, salespeople push low-margin products to maximize their income rather than higher-priced, high-margin, new items. If you want to sell new products, you have to reward salespeople for moving them.[3] A solution is to vary commission rates by item profitability so that salespeople are encouraged to sell a mix of products that maximizes overall company profits.

This example shows that compensation plans must be custom designed to meet the goals of individual firms. It also shows that the natural desire of salespeople to make money for themselves if left unabated can conflict with the firm's need to control expenses. This means that you have the difficult task of designing compensation programs that motivate salespeople to reach company goals and satisfy customers without bankrupting the firm. Since 30 to 40 percent of all sales reps are unhappy with their compensation plans at any one time, you may be continuously challenged to come up with a better program.

A useful tool to begin translating company objectives and the desired sales job into an appropriate compensation plan is to consider the Customer-Product Matrix introduced in Chapter 2. As shown in Figure 14-1, the Customer-Product Matrix divides sales opportunities into combinations of new and old customers and products. In general, sales positions which focus primarily on New Business Development (upper right-hand quadrant) require a greater proportion of incentive (e.g., commissions and bonus) in the compensation plan than those sales jobs in the lower left-hand quadrant (Account Management). Sales jobs consisting primarily of Account Management involve a greater account servicing component and are therefore better suited to a primarily salary form of compensation.

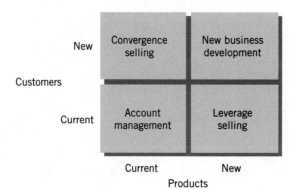

Figure 14-1: The Customer-Product Matrix

▶ COMPENSATION METHODS

There are few theories to guide you in designing sales compensation plans that fit the needs of a specific firm. Building a program is a combination of art and science, and sales managers often feel the need to review or alter compensation plans regularly to increase their efficiency. By far the most common compensation plan combines a base salary with some type of incentives. Table 14-1 shows that 83 percent of firms use combination plans for field salespeople. The most traditional compensation method is straight salary.

Straight Salary

While a familiar form of compensation for most nonselling personnel, straight salary involves paying a fixed amount each pay period. *Straight salary* programs were used by only 7 percent of the 211 firms reported in Table 14-1. The major benefits of salary are more control over wage levels and the ability to easily direct the sales force on nonselling/revenue generating activities. Such activities would include, for instance, taking orders for inventory replenishment, equipment installation and maintenance, and shelf-management programs. A Dartnell Compensation Survey showed that the average salary plan paid middle-level salespeople $36,000 per year compared with $50,700 for salespeople on salary plus incentive programs.[4] This does not necessarily mean that salary plans are inherently lower paying compensation plans, but that the sales activities associated with most straight salary plans are such that they are lower paying. Also, with a salary plan, wages are a fixed cost to the firm, and the proportion of wage expense tends to decrease as sales increase. Another advantage of salary is that it allows maximum control over salespeople's activities. Salaried employees can be directed to sell particular products, call on certain customers, and perform a variety of nonselling jobs for customers. Because a salesperson's income is not tied to the volume of business done with specific customers, it is easier for the sales manager to divide territories and reassign salespeople to new areas. Further, salaried salespeople tend to exhibit higher loyalty to the firm than employees under other plans.

Table 14-1 Use of Compensation Plans

Method	Percentage of Companies Using
Straight Salary	7
Straight Commission	10
Salary Plus Bonus	34
Salary Plus Commission	21
Salary Plus Bonus Plus Commission	24
Commission Plus Bonus	4
Total	100%

Source: Donald W. Jackson, John L. Schlacter, and William G. Wolfe, "Examining the Bases Utilized for Evaluating Salespeoples' Performance," *Journal of Personal Selling & Sales Management*, Vol. 15, No. 4 (Fall 1995), p. 59.

Because salary plans are fairly straightforward, they are easy to explain to new employees but may be more difficult to administer from year to year.

Salary plans provide salespeople with security and a steady, predictable monthly income. Trainees, in particular, tend to favor this payment plan since they run the risk of having low incomes if they start out on a commission plan. The U.S. Chamber of Commerce pays new salespeople a salary for 90 days before moving them to a straight commission plan. Merrill Lynch, for example, has considered paying salaries to new brokers to reduce their temptation to boost commissions in ways that might conflict with client's interest.[5] Salary programs are also often preferred by customers, since they know salespeople are there to help rather than to load the customer with inventory.

Limitations   The most frequently heard criticism is that salaries do not provide strong incentives for extra effort. Even though salary adjustments are made to reward performance, these adjustments are usually annual and lack the more immediate reinforcement of alternative plans. As a result, some salespeople may not put in the extra effort to meet the needs of the company. A second problem is that salaried salespeople usually require much closer supervision by sales managers than salespeople who work under commission plans. Also salary plans often overpay the least-productive members of a sales team, and cause problems when new trainees earn almost as much as experienced salespeople.

Applications   Research has shown that salary is used more often in competitive labor environments, in situations where it is difficult to assess sales force activities and performance, and in companies where salespeople spend a lot of time on service and paperwork.[6] This suggests that salary is most appropriate when it is difficult to relate the efforts of individual salespeople to the size or timing of a sale. For example, the "detail people" for pharmaceutical companies are primarily engaged in missionary activities with doctors and do not sell directly to most of their customers. For years it was impossible to track drug orders prescribed by particular physicians. Now that the information is available, the compensation plans of pharmaceutical sales forces are more incentive oriented and salary is a lower percent of total compensation.

Salary is also used when team selling is important, as in the sales of complex aerospace products to airlines and the government. Salary is widely employed in nonferrous metals such as aluminum. Salespeople in this industry are technical advisors, and it may take years to convert a customer from one material to another. Salary is also appropriate in situations where the products are presold through advertising and the salesperson primarily takes orders. Liquor, for example, is largely presold through magazines and newspaper ads, and salespeople are mainly responsible for in-store merchandising and displays.

Straight Commission

Salespeople on commission are paid a percentage of the sales or gross profits that they generate. The *straight commission* plan rewards people for their accomplishments rather than their time or efforts. On average, salespeople who are paid commissions make more money than with other wage programs. A survey revealed that the average compensation of senior sales reps on straight commission is $84,100 per year compared to $68,300 for reps on salary plus incentive and $54,500 for those on straight salary.[7] Higher wages tend to attract better-qualified applicants and provide a strong incentive to work hard. However, Table 14-1 indicates that straight commission plans are used by a relatively small number of firms. In this study about 10 percent reported using straight commissions.

Advantages   Straight commission plans foster independence of action and provide the maximum possible incentive. They are easy to understand, and it is fairly simple to calculate wages. Since the selling costs are entirely variable, the firm does not pay as much money when sales decline or fail to meet growth objectives. When commissions are paid at the time revenues are received, there are definite cash flow benefits. In addition, the firm can vary the size of sales commissions by product line. This allows the company to pay higher commission rates on high-margin items.

The advantages of a 10 percent commission plan are shown graphically in Figure 14-2. Notice that when sales per person are low, the costs of the commission plan are low. However, a *fixed cost* salary plan ($30,000) gives higher costs. Companies that want to minimize their financial risk can choose *variable cost* commission plans. Firms that want to minimize compensation costs as sales grow use fixed cost salary programs. Thus, in Figure 14-2, when sales are less than $300,000 per year, the salary plan is the high-cost method. But when sales exceed $300,000 per year, the straight salary plan results in lower total costs for the company in the example. Thus, small firms often use commission plans to get started and then shift to salary when they get big. However, financial risk should not be the sole or even primary basis for choosing between a salary or commission compensation plan. The sales job to be performed should be the most important criterion. Note, for instance, that sales jobs with most new small companies will fall in the New Business Development quadrant of the Customer-Product Matrix and compensation should therefore include a significant incentive component.

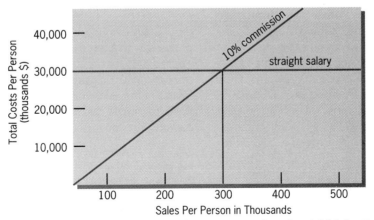

Figure 14-2: Comparing Salary and Commission Plans for Field Sales Representatives

Problems   Despite some advantages, straight commission has a number of drawbacks. The major problems are that sales managers have little control over commission salespeople and nonselling activities are apt to be neglected. Commission salespeople are tempted to sell themselves rather than the company, as well as to service only the best accounts in their territories. Because salespeople's wages are directly related to sales to particular accounts, salespeople are often quite reluctant to have their territories changed in any way. Turnover can become excessive among commission salespeople when business conditions are bad, since they often have little company loyalty. Techniques used by brokerage firms to reduce turnover among their commissioned salespeople are described in Sales Management in Action 14-1. Wide variations in pay under commission plans may also lead to poor morale among lower-paid personnel, and highly paid salespeople may be reluctant to move into supervisory or managerial positions.

Sales Management in Action 14-1
Designing Compensation Plans to Cut Turnover

Turnover among stockbrokers averages 17 percent per year. Brokers earn no salary but are paid a commission (20 to 45%) on the gross profits they generate. Salespeople on straight commission often move from firm to firm, causing disruptions for customers and fights among the remaining brokers for the departing broker's accounts. To provide better service to customers and retain their most productive people, brokerage firms are building in more golden handcuffs. The new plans are designed to counter the fat upfront bonuses rivals are using to steal top producers. To build loyalty Prudential pays brokers who stay 10 to 14 years a bonus of 3.5 percent of their total commissions. This would amount to $140,000 for a $400,000 per year commission producer. They also receive awards for accumulating assets and for selling Prudential's proprietary mutual funds. At the same time, Prudential is cutting the payout of low producing brokers. The new commission

plans offered by Prudential and the other major stockbrokers are designed to boost loyalty and improve customer relations.

Discount brokers follow a different strategy to keep customers happy. Charles Schwab paid its brokers a salary of $26,000 in 1991 plus an average bonus of $5,000 based on surveys showing how satisfied its customers were with their service. Schwab's brokers earn less than one-third the $98,400 made by regular full-service brokers. The company is pleased with their plan because it aligns the interests of its brokers with those of its customers. Also Schwab brokers do not make investments recommendations nor do they have to hustle to make trades to produce commission income.

Source: Michael Siconolfi, "Big Wall Street Houses Devise Pay Plans to Keep Brokers From Going to Rivals," *Wall Street Journal* (November 10, 1992), p. C1; Michael Siconolfi, "Schwab Brokers In '91 Averaged $31,000 in Pay," *Wall Street Journal* (September 29, 1992). p. C9.

Examples   Straight commission works best when maximum incentive is needed and when a minimum of after-sale service and missionary work is required. This situation exists for most door-to-door organizations and many car dealerships, though this is changing somewhat as a result of Saturn's success with "no-haggle" pricing. Other types of businesses that use straight commission plans include life insurance, real estate, stock brokerage, printing, and wholesalers in many industries. Commission rates often run from 5 to 14 percent of sales.

Salary Plus Bonus

Combining a base salary with a *bonus* has several advantages. The base salary provides reps with income security, and the bonus gives added incentives to meet company objectives. Bonuses are discretionary payments for reaching specified goals. They are usually paid annually.

Salary plus bonus programs were the most preferred plan in Table 14-1 with 34 percent of firms using them. The main advantage of salary plus bonus plans is that they balance the need to control selling expenses and provide extra rewards for added results. When products are largely presold by advertising, like many consumer items, it does not make sense to pay a salary plus a commission to get salespeople to push for added volume. Under these conditions, a salary plus a modest bonus is enough to get the job done.

Another possible advantage of salary plus bonus plans is they may lead to lower turnover among salespeople. This is particularly important when buying cycles are long and reps must understand how customers do business. Business Wire, for example, has been able to quadruple revenues over four years using competitive salaries plus performance and year-end bonuses.[8] The security of a salary allows their reps time to both court prospects over the long haul and service existing customers. Business Wire also encourages longevity by gradually raising the share of bonuses and benefits to 60 percent of wages after six years. As a result, Business Wire's sales are up and only two salespeople have left in the past four years.

Probably the most widely used basis for determining bonus pay is sales to quota. Another popular basis is average gross margin achieved by the rep. Other bonus factors are the number of new accounts, unit sales, and overall company performance. In some firms the size of the bonus may be arbitrary. Managers review sales results, customer relations, and after-sale service and decide how much each person should receive. When managers fail to communicate how bonuses are determined they can lose some of their effectiveness as motivational devices. Salary plus bonus plans are commonly used by large food manufacturers, such as Quaker Oats and Procter & Gamble, which sell through supermarkets.

Salary Plus Commission

Industrial sales reps are frequently paid *salary plus commission* to give them the push needed to sell complex products or services. For example, Digital Equipment Corporation has converted its 10,000 computer salespeople from a straight salary plan to a salary plus commission program.[9] These plans pay a base salary plus a small commission of 1 to 6 percent of sales. Twenty-one percent of the firms in Table 14-1 employ salary plus commission programs.

Although most firms start paying commissions on the first dollar of sales, 39 percent establish *commission thresholds* that must be reached before the commissions apply. Often the commission rates vary, depending on sales volume. As an illustration, a salesperson might earn 4 percent on the first $20,000 of sales each month, 5 percent on the next $15,000, and 6 percent on anything over $35,000. *Progressive commission rates* are used when sales increases require extra efforts. Although progressive commission rates reflect the increase in selling effort, they may also increase sales expenses.

Commission rates can also be adjusted to promote the sale of individual products or to intensify efforts among specific market segments. Many firms vary commission rates according to the profitability of products. To prevent windfall earnings due to circumstances unrelated to salespeople's efforts, 42 percent of firms have *wage caps* on the incentive portion of their compensation plans.[10]

Commissions are usually paid monthly, providing fairly immediate reinforcement for the salesperson's efforts. Some firms spread commissions over several months or years to smooth out the pattern of payments and to ensure that salespeople continue to service their accounts after the initial sale. Spreading commissions over a period of time also discourages a salesperson from leaving the firm once a big sale has been made.

The major drawbacks to salary plus commission plans are that they are more expensive and costly to administer. Research has shown that the average maximum wages paid with a salary and commission program are higher compared with salespeople on salary plus bonus plans. Salary plus commission plans are widely used in industrial firms selling building materials, machinery, electrical supplies, and paper products.

Salary Plus Commission Plus Bonus

The most comprehensive payment plans combine the stability of a salary, the incentives of a commission, and the special rewards of a bonus. Table 14-1 indicates that 24 percent of firms surveyed used this plan. The primary benefit of these plans is they allow you to reward virtually every activity performed by salespeople. Field representatives love these plans because there are so many different ways for them to make money. However, their complexity makes them difficult to administer.

IBM recently revised its *salary plus commission plus bonus* plan to make it more workable for its 14,000 reps around the world.[11] Under the old plan reps made most of their commission income in the fourth quarter of the year when business computers are usually delivered. Also the commission system paid lower rates for sales through distributors and salespeople tended to ignore this important channel of distribution. A heavy reliance on contests under the old plan focused efforts on making the quick sale rather than finding solutions that fit customer needs. One of the most serious problems was that many IBM clients need cooperation among sales reps from different states and countries to assure that equipment is installed correctly and the reps were not financially rewarded for these activities. The old plan used 25 different performance factors to determine compensation, far too many for reps to keep track of. IBM's new plan is simpler using 10 performance factors to determine compensation. Also the commission structure was revised so reps make more money selling to distributors. Now contest income is limited to 20 percent of incentive wages and 20 percent is awarded for work team performance across geographic boundaries. These incentives are paid monthly. Sixty percent of incentive income is now tied to personal performance on factors such as growth, customer solutions, channel partners, and profit contributions. This income is paid quarterly. The bonus portion of the plan is based on company profits and customer satisfaction and is paid annually. IBM also gives recognition awards in the form of trips and prizes that provide additional income for sales reps. This example shows that although salary plus commission plus bonus plans provide many ways to reward salespeople, they need to be modified periodically to make sure they are in tune with corporate objectives.

Commission Plus Bonus

Another combination plan used by 4 percent of the firms in Table 14-1 was the *commission plus bonus* program. This approach combines the incentives of a commission plus special rewards for meeting objectives. These plans are particularly well suited to a company that uses brokers or independent sales reps. They are also widely employed for stockbrokers and bond traders. For example, Merrill Lynch pays its brokers commissions plus cash bonuses and memberships in recognition circles. These clubs reward recipients with trips and deferred compensation worth tens of thousands of dollars each year. To maintain their club membership, brokers must sell 10 computerized financial plans a year. Tying the receipt of such perks to quotas on particular products doesn't appeal to every salesperson.[12]

Customer Satisfaction and Sales Force Compensation

Total quality management (TQM) focuses on delivering high-quality products to clients and making sure customers are satisfied. However, only 10 percent of 450 companies surveyed link some portion of sales force compensation with customer service.[13] Part of the problem is that firms have trouble measuring customer satisfaction and they are afraid salespeople will manipulate the data to gain an advantage. Despite these problems there is a growing trend toward tying compensation to customer contentment.

The most common objective in tying compensation to buyer satisfaction is to reduce the attrition of current customers. Companies who use surveys to measure satisfaction ask questions on sales force responsiveness, problem solving, after-sale service, and communication skills. This information is then used to modify some other sales force compensation factor or to calculate a percentage of base salary to award as a bonus. A typical firm assigns about 20 percent of total pay for achievements with customer satisfaction.

An example of a typical plan that ties customer satisfaction to sales force compensation is shown by Appleton Papers, Inc. The year-end bonus at Appleton is a significant portion of overall compensation and is based on volume, profit, and individual objectives. Forty percent of the bonus is awarded for objectives and customer satisfaction is the leading goal. This means that at least 20 percent of the bonus is tied to customer satisfaction.

Team Selling Plans

Team selling is becoming more common in American business, and you must design your compensation programs to accommodate this trend. In its simplest form, *team selling* involves two salespeople in separate territories who need to coordinate their activities to complete the sale. The recommended solution is to establish a system for sharing commissions so that both reps will work for the order. A more complicated team selling scenario has outside salespeople, technical specialists, service reps, and telemarketers all working together to make a sale. Many firms are emphasizing organizational teamwork to improved sales and profits. This means that compensation programs must be designed to reward other members of the selling team besides the outside salesperson. Since technical reps and service people are paid salaries, the usual approach is to share incentive payments with all members of the selling team.[14] Thus technical reps and service people on sales teams may be rewarded with small commissions, but more likely group bonuses. For example, Mine Safety Appliances pays its 28 sales teams with a base salary, plus revenue-based and nonrevenue-based bonuses. Team members fill out questionnaires to help determine salary levels and discuss how to allocate bonuses for outstanding individual achievements.[15]

Profit-based Commissions

The main objective with compensation programs is to provide direction to the sales force to achieve the business' objectives. Unfortunately, this is not an easy task. For example, it has been shown that when incentive payments are based on a percentage of the sales of each product as they are in 47 percent of firms surveyed, it is unlikely that salespeople will sell the mix of items that will lead to the most profits.[16] Since salespeople rarely have data on costs and economies of scale, they will usually look only at the incentive rates and emphasize those items that are easy to sell and carry the highest commissions.

An alternative approach is to pay commissions on the gross margin dollars on each product. With a *gross margin commission* plan, the company and the salesperson share the same pool of money (realized gross margin), so that both are interested in maximizing this amount. Theoretically when this occurs, the company makes more gross profit so they can share the increased profitability with the sales force and the sales reps make more money. Medical supply and retail automobile salespeople are paid a percentage of the gross margin on each sale so that they will negotiate with customers to obtain the highest possible profit for their employer and themselves. An example showing how a switch from sales commissions to gross margin commissions increased profits for Dell Computer is described in Sales Management in Action 14-2.

Sales Management in Action 14-2
Dell's Drive for Profits

In 10 years Dell Computer has grown from sales of nothing to nearly $3 billion in annual revenue. This was accomplished by selling desktop personal computers at low prices directly to customers using telephone salespeople. At the present time 75 percent of sales are over the phone and only 10 percent go through retailers. Dell's success is partially due to a system of paying sales commissions to its phone representatives. Although this approach has allowed Dell to grow rapidly, the company has neglected some other areas of the business. Dell spends less on R&D than any of its major competitors. As a result, Dell's notebook PCs performed so poorly that Dell had to withdraw them from the market and take a $20 million charge in 1993. They were also late getting into the PC server market and their control systems have been so weak they had to take a $71 million inventory writedown in 1993. Also competitors started to narrow the price gap in 1993 and Dell was expected to report an annual loss for the first time. Dell realizes they must now focus on generating greater profits rather than just greater volume. To help make this possible, Dell calculated the profit margins on each of its products and switched its salespeople to a gross margin commission plan. Salespeople are now rewarded for selling the most profitable items instead of the low-margin PCs that salespeople pushed when they were paid commission on sales.

Source: Peter Burrows, "Beyond Rock Bottom," *Business Week* (March 14, 1994), pp. 80–82.

Gross margin plans have not been as successful in all situations. Certain-Teed Corporation, for example, tried paying its building materials salespeople a commission on gross margin but was forced to shift to a salary plus incentive program because the salespeople were bringing in too many low-margin orders. The problem arose because the salespeople viewed making 10 percent on a $1 million order as equivalent to making 20 percent on a $500,000 order (Table 14-2). On both orders, the company makes $100,000 in gross margin and the salesperson collects $15,000 in commission. But if the selling time is similar, the salesperson is likely to work for the

Table 14-2 Comparing Gross Margin Commissions on Two Orders

Order Number	Percentage Gross Margin on Each Order	Size of Order	Gross Margin to Company	Percentage Commission on Gross Margin	Commission Paid to Salesperson
1	10	$1,000,000	$100,000	15	$15,000
2	20	$500,000	$100,000	15	$15,000

prestige of the $1 million order. However, the company is better off with the $500,000 sale, since the smaller order means lower inventory carrying costs and a reduced drain on raw materials and plant capacity. Perhaps a more appropriate plan would have been to pay commissions on a combination of gross margin and order size. The plan could have been designed to pay a lower commission rate when gross margin and the order size were smaller.

▶ SETTING PAY LEVELS

Once a sales manager has selected a compensation method, the next job is to establish the best *wage level* for salespeople. At first glance, this task does not seem too difficult, since there are only three options: The firm can pay the average prevailing wage, pay a premium, or offer less than the going rate. A premium wage level is appealing because it may attract better salespeople and motivate them to sell high volumes. Paying higher than average wages makes it easier to recruit college-trained people who can be promoted into managerial positions later.

Sales managers can obtain guidelines about current pay levels by reviewing surveys published by the Dartnell Corporation, the Conference Board, and trade and industry associations. For example, Table 14-3 shows typical pay levels for combination plans in sales organizations in 1996. Note that the highest pay goes to top sales executives followed by regional sales managers. First-level field sales managers ($83,700) earn more than the key account reps ($71,200). However, sales managers may earn less than the top rep in their district. Also other studies suggest that the relatively low pay of telesales reps ($33,900) can lead to morale problems and high turnover. On the other hand, having positions such as key account rep in the middle of the compensation range provides incentives for trainees and telesales reps to move up the promotion ladder. Although sales trainees start with a base salary of

Table 14-3   Compensation Levels for Firms Using Salary Plus Incentives, 1996

Position	Salary ($000)	Incentive ($000)	Total Compensation ($000)
Top Sales Executive	$91.2	$31.5	$122.7
Regional Sales Manager	69.0	23.3	92.3
National Account Manager	66.9	18.7	85.6
District Sales Manager	61.8	22.0	83.7
Key Account Rep	54.6	16.6	71.2
Senior Sales Rep	45.1	23.2	68.3
Intermediate Rep	34.6	16.1	50.7
Entry Level Rep	28.8	10.9	39.8

Source: *Sales Force Compensation Survey* (Chicago: Dartnell Corporation, 1996), p. 28

only $28,800, they are often provided with a car, an expense account, and an opportunity to earn commissions or a bonus.

▶ EXPENSE ACCOUNTS AND BENEFITS

No discussion of sales force compensation would be complete without mention of expense accounts and other *benefits*. Almost all firms that pay straight salaries or some combination of salary, commission, and/or bonus cover expenses for salespeople. Typical expenses paid by firms include those for automobiles and other travel, tips, lodging, food, samples, telephone, postage, and tickets for sporting and theater events. A typical expense allocation reported in a recent survey averaged $16,151 per year.[17] These expenses run about $17,653 for industrial salespeople, and $11,200 for those selling consumer services.

Expense Reimbursement Programs

Three types of expense plans can be used: (1) unlimited, (2) per diem, and (3) limited repayment.

Unlimited Plans   One type of expense reimbursement plan is to have salespeople submit itemized forms showing their expenditures, and the firm simply pays all reported expenses. This approach allows salespeople wide discretion on where they travel and how they entertain customers. In addition, an unlimited expense plan is cheap to administer since no one regularly spends time checking expense accounts to see if they are overstated.

Unlimited expense plans are often favored by small firms that don't want to bother auditing expense accounts. They are also used by companies that sell expensive products such as airplanes and defense systems, where extensive entertainment of clients is routine. The main problem with these plans is some salespeople get too greedy and try to make money off their expense accounts. This forces management to occasionally fire reps who get out of line.

Per Diem Plans   A per diem expense plan pays the salesperson a fixed dollar amount for each day or week spent in the field. The amount is designed to cover food, gasoline, lodging, telephone calls, and other expenses. A major benefit of a per diem plan is that it is simple and inexpensive to supervise. However, salespeople may try to make money off the plan by spending less than the allowance. This is usually done by cutting back on travel. Instead of driving to distant customers, salespeople could save money by concentrating on nearby prospects. Also, there is less incentive to entertain customers with a per diem plan than with an unlimited plan. These actions may keep salespeople under their expense allowance, but they may also cost the company sales revenues. Another problem is that per diem allocations have to be revised periodically to reflect inflation. Per diem plans are typically used by firms for routine reorder selling of standard items.

Limited Repayment Plans   With this approach the firm sets dollar limits on each category of sales expenses. For example, a firm might allow 30 cents a mile for travel, $8 for breakfast, $12 for lunch, $25 for dinner, and $70 for a room. These limits must reflect actual field experience, and they need to be adjusted frequently to reflect inflation. The objective of this plan is to make salespeople aware of what the company will pay and encourage them to control their expenses. The limited expense approach makes it easier to budget for sales costs and should reduce expense account padding.

One problem with limited reimbursement plans is that new reps may be uncertain as to whether the firm will cover various miscellaneous expenses. Although 87 percent of companies pay for lodging, only 77 percent pay for entertainment, 57 percent pay a mileage allowance, 53 percent pay for car phones, 41 percent pay for home copiers, 40 percent pay for a leased auto, and 56 percent pay for home fax machines.[18] The net result of setting limits is that salespeople may spend their valuable time juggling expenses from one category to another or from one time period to another to make sure they cover their costs. This time could be better spent solving customers' problems.

Another issue with limited repayment plans is that they may be expensive to monitor. One large wholesaler kept 11 full-time clerks to check sales expense accounts. To help reduce expenses, the company stopped having reps fill out expense accounts and relied on a few experienced salespeople to keep track of their actual expenses for one week twice a year. These observed expenses were then used to set repayment rates for all reps. The new plan required only one clerk for administration and gave salespeople more time to sell, so that nine sales positions could be eliminated.[19] Another alternative would be to "spot-check" expense reports by randomly selecting expense reports to be verified.

Selecting Benefits

Benefits can be used to attract and reward salespeople. One study found that salespeople prefer benefits to recognition and incentive awards.[20] Benefit packages range in cost from $3,500 for lumber and wood products salespeople to $16,938 for primary metal products reps, with a typical program costing $7,548.[21] These programs include a variety of hospitalization, insurance, and pension plans, as shown in Table 14-4. The explosion in medical care costs in recent years has made it difficult for many firms to keep the expenses of benefit packages under control. One approach has been to raise the medical deductible levels so that employees pay more of the costs. Another popular solution is to allocate a certain number of benefit dollars to each salesperson and let them choose from a cafeteria line of possible benefits. This allows reps to select a benefit package that fits their individual needs.

You have to decide how much the salesperson should be required to contribute to the benefit program. If the salesperson is asked to pay a portion of the costs, the firm may give the person extra compensation to cover the contribution. However, this extra money is taxable and sometimes will even move the person into a higher income tax bracket. If the firm pays for these benefits directly, so that salespeople receive the tax advantage, they may receive lower total wages than those offered by other firms, but they are better off in the long run.

Table 14-4   Benefits Offered by Companies

Benefit	Percentage of Firms Offering
Hospital costs	96%
Life insurance	79%
Dental plan	69%
Long-term disability	62%
Pension plan	57%
Short-term disability	51%
Profit sharing	45%
Thrift savings	24%
Employees stock purchase plan	24%

Source: Sales Force Compensation Survey (Chicago: Dartnell Corporation, 1996), p. 121.

Expense accounts and benefit packages amount to a substantial portion of the costs of keeping a salesperson in the field. To some degree, cash wages, expense accounts, and benefits may be substitutes for one another, since they all provide rewards and incentives to salespeople. On the other hand, Maslow's Hierarchy of Need theory would suggest that they address different needs.

▶ ASSEMBLING THE PLAN

Sales managers have the responsibility of combining the various wage elements into an appropriate compensation plan and then predicting its effectiveness. This is not an easy task, and software firms have come up with some new computer programs to provide help. VI Comp of Lexington, Massachusetts, has a program that can be used to design and administer complex incentive programs.[22] The program sells for $13,000 to $40,000, depending on the number of salespeople covered by the system.

How Much to Pay?

In determining an appropriate level of wages to pay salespeople, a good starting point is the average wage paid by other firms of the same size in the industry. Other considerations might be the labor market where people are coming from and going to. Assume that comparable firms are paying their midlevel salespeople an average annual total compensation of $50,000. The sales manager now must split this total into salary, commissions, and a bonus. Based on an analysis of the sales job to be performed, the breakdown might be $36,000 for salary, $10,000 for commissions, and $4,000 for a bonus. The monthly salary of $3,000 provides stability of income and amounts to 72 percent of the wage package. For this company the commission rates could be set to vary from 1 to 4 percent of sales, depending on the profitability of the various products in the line and the source of the business. The following break-down shows how the commission portion of the wage would be calculated:

Commission Rate	Type and Source of Business	Sales Achieved	Commission Amount
0.01	Reorders of supplies	$100,000	$1,000
0.02	New equipment	250,000	5,000
0.04	Sales to new accounts	100,000	4,000
Totals		$450,000	$10,000

Note that the compensation plan pays a fairly low commission rate of 1 percent on reorders of supplies that carry low profit margins. However, a 2 percent commission is paid on sales of the more profitable new equipment. Also, a 4 percent commission is paid on all sales to new accounts to encourage sales force prospecting.

The bonus portion of the plan is set up to pay 8.7 percent of salary and commissions to salespeople who exceed their annual quota for the number of new accounts. Assuming the salesperson met this quota, the bonus payment would be 8.7 percent of $46,000 ($36,000 in salary + $10,000 in commissions), or $4,000. The actual payment of the $4,000 bonus would be delayed until the end of the year. The total compensation for the salesperson in this case amounts to $50,000, which is about the average sales representative in Table 14-4 ($50,700).

The following shows the addition of a car, other expenses, and benefits to the compensation program:

$36,000	Salary
10,000	Commission (1 to 4 percent of sales)
4,000	Bonus (8.7 percent of salary and commissions for exceeding new account quota)
7,500	Benefits
7,200	Car expense (24,000 miles at 30 cents per mile)
10,000	Lodging, food, and entertainment
$74,700	Total costs per salesperson

Although car expenses and payments for lodging, food, and entertainment are not part of real wages for salespeople, these expenditures do represent a growing proportion of the cost of keeping a salesperson in the field. Thus, as the price of lodging and entertainment increases, sales managers may have less money available for cash wages. While a current car expense of $7,200 seems like a lot of money, this figure represents only 120 miles a day for a person who is on the road 200 days a year. Also, $10,000 a year for food and lodging seems adequate, but it amounts to only $50 a day for salespeople who are on the road four days a week. Unless sales managers find ways to control escalating entertainment and travel expenses or increase sales volume or profits, they will have trouble keeping cash wages competitive.

Evaluating the Plan

After you have selected an appropriate compensation method and wage level, the plan must be evaluated to see how it will affect salespeople's wages and total costs. This evaluation usually involves taking sales figures from the previous year and calculating expected wages for a group of salespeople under the new program. These calculations are greatly simplified if you have an automated computer program like that described in reference 22. Your objective is to see how above- and below-average salespeople would fare under the new system. You want to avoid having salespeople reap windfall gains or suffer from unfairly low earnings. You should be cautious when introducing new compensation programs that pay lower wages than the current plan. This often produces resistance among salespeople and can lead to higher turnover. In some situations, however, turnover may be welcome. Why?

▶ ETHICAL ISSUES

Compensation is a key motivational factor for field salespeople, and sales managers must be careful that it is employed in an ethical manner. A common problem is that high base wage rates and raises go to people the manager likes or those who complain the most rather than to reps with the best sales records. Fairness in setting wage rates and bonuses can improve sales force morale and help achieve long-run company goals.

Another source of abuse is commission plans that encourage salespeople to overstock their customers with inventory or drive unethical behaviors. As an example, some truck dealers encourage unethical behavior when they pay their parts salespeople straight gross margin commissions. Although gross margin commissions usually increase the profits for the dealer and the salesperson, these plans may burden customers with parts that are costly or inappropriate. There are many suppliers of vehicle parts, and some of the items are rebuilt. Thus gross margin commission plans are apt to encourage parts salespeople to push items that carry the fattest margins, regardless of their safety, durability, or cost. Customers are unlikely to be ecstatic about compensation plans that make salespeople rich at their expense. These examples suggest that managers need to establish controls on compensation programs so that customer relations are not compromised.

▶ SUMMARY

Compensation is one of the key factors in motivating salespeople to achieve the sales and profit objectives of the firm. Compensation plans should allow salespeople to reach their own income goals without overstocking customers or ignoring nonselling duties. Sales managers must learn to combine salary, commissions, bonuses, and benefits so that salespeople and the firm both benefit. Beyond the issue of what plan to use is the question of how much to pay. Field sales reps are sometimes overpaid, and it is the job of the sales manager to constantly balance the costs against the benefits received for sales force expenditures.

► KEY TERMS

Bonus	Salary plus commission
Commission plus bonus	Salary plus commission plus bonus
Commission threshold	Straight commission
Fixed cost	Straight salary
Benefits	Team selling
Gross margin commissions	Variable cost
Progressive commission rates	Wage caps
Salary plus bonus	Wage level

► REVIEW QUESTIONS

1. Why do compensation plans often have so many objectives?
2. What are the advantages and disadvantages of straight salary compensation plans?
3. What compensation plan is most popular among industrial firms? consumer firms?
4. When should a firm use straight commission?
5. Explain the advantages of a salary plus commission plan.
6. Why do so many firms use salary plus bonus plans?
7. Explain why gross margin commission plans can lead to higher wages for salespeople and improved profits for the firm.
8. Can companies pay salespeople too much? too little? Why?
9. Why are fringe benefits so important to salespeople?
10. How should a sales manager evaluate a new compensation program?
11. Why do sales managers place caps on incentive wages?

► PROBLEMS

1. Field salespeople are usually exempt from the Fair Labor Standards Act, which says that employers have to pay time and a half to workers who put in over 40 hours per week. However, inside salespeople and telemarketers who are paid on commission sometimes work more than 40 hours per week. Do you have to pay time and a half to these people?

2. A car salesperson spent three hours selling a new Nissan Maxima for $800 over cost. The dealer kept the first $600 of the gross profit and split the remaining $200 with the salesperson on a 75 percent/25 percent basis. This left the salesperson with only $50 for three hours' work, which he had to divide with another salesperson who talked with the customer over the phone. Is this system good for the dealer? For the salesperson? What changes would you recommend?

3. Sears has cut the base hourly pay of its salespeople who sell big-ticket items and increased their commission rates. Why has Sears made this change, and how well do you think the new plan has been received by the salespeople?

4. Merrill Lynch has recently expanded its broker training period from 20 weeks to two years. Instead of being paid commissions, the new trainees will be paid a salary and a bonus. The trainees are also required to complete successfully courses on money management,

product knowledge, and client service. Why has Merrill Lynch changed its broker training program, and what do you think of the new compensation plan?

5. In 1994, Met Life was accused of using unethical sales practices to sell nurses whole life insurance policies. Sales literature and discussions with customers emphasized a "retirement savings plan" even though the actual policy was insurance. Met Life ended up paying $20 million in fines in 40 states and agreed to refund premiums to 92,000 policy holders. Salespeople liked to sell whole life policies because they earned 55% commissions on first year premiums compared to only 2 percent on savings plans such as annuities. Should Met Life revise its compensation plan for field reps and, if so, how?

6. Designing compensation plans for team selling when the sales cycle is long and complicated is a difficult task. One consultant suggests dividing the selling job into parts, such as identifying the lead, qualifying the prospect, performing technical assistance, writing the proposal, and closing the sale. Then if a 20 percent commission was being paid, 4 percent would be allocated to team members who performed each of these tasks. If some tasks are more important than others, the 4 percent allocations could be changed to reflect these differences. What are the advantages and disadvantages of this system?

7. Car salespeople tend to be a nomadic breed, switching from one dealership to another, depending on what brand is hot. To combat this problem, Volkswagen pays salespeople their commission in three installments, with the final payment coming two years after the car is sold. Audi pays cash bonuses to top salespeople at the end of the year. Both plans require salespeople to stay to collect the money. Why are dealers using compensation programs in an attempt to cut turnover? Which of the two plans is better and why?

8. When discussing the profit-based commission plans in this chapter, it was suggested that one way Certain-Teed could overcome its order size problem was to base its commission rate on both gross margin dollars and order size. Assuming that orders varied in size from $250,000 to $2,000,000 and that gross margins varied from 10 percent to 30 percent, set up an appropriate commission rate plan. Assume that Certain-Teed wanted to pay a commission of 5 percent of gross margin on the average order.

9. As regional sales manager, you have to make salary recommendations for six district sales managers whom you supervise. They have just completed their annual appraisal period and are now to be considered for their annual raise. Your company has set aside 10 percent of salary costs for merit increases. Your total current annual salary cost is $297,300, which means that you have $29,730 for salary increases. There are no formal company restrictions on how you may distribute the 10 percent merit increase. Indicate the size of the raise that you would like to give each sales manager. All managers have the same job classification, and the salary recommendations are secret.

EMPLOYEE PROFILE SHEET

- **John Smith** Age 30, three children, current annual salary $59,000, MBA, Harvard. John is married to the daughter of the chairman of the board and has been with the company five years, the last two as sales manager. He has one of the easiest groups to supervise, doesn't impress you as being very bright, but is a hard worker. You rated him as "slightly above average" (68 percent) on his last performance rating. You checked your view with others you respect; they, too, felt that he was less effective than other managers who work for you, but they reminded you of his potential influence.

- **Larry Foster** Age 27, single, current annual salary $38,300, BA, University of Maine. Larry has been with the company for four years, the last two as sales manager. He has a difficult group to supervise, is bright, often works overtime, and has "turned around" the group he supervises. You rated him as "an excellent manager with a good future" (89 percent) on his last performance rating.

- **Tim Hall** Age 44, four children, two in college, current annual salary $60,000 (three years of college, no degree). Tim has been with the company for the past 18 years and has been in his current position for the past 8 years. He is unhappy that you were named regional sales manager because he was hoping to get the job. He is well liked by all the other managers and by his employees. He rarely works on weekends, and he seems to be easygoing with his salespeople. However, his group had the second highest performance of the groups you manage. You rated him as outstanding (85 percent) on his last performance appraisal.

- **Ellen Panza** Age 30, married, two children, current annual salary $45,000, BA, City University of New York. Ellen has been with the company for two years and worked as sales analyst for the first year before being promoted to manager. You feel that she was given the job because she is a woman, and frankly, you resent it. In addition, you feel that her salary is too high compared to the salaries of others in the company. However, you must admit that she has performed in an outstanding manner, since her group went from last to first place in performance this year. Her score on the rating sheet was 90 percent.

- **Otto Lechman** Age 36, married (wife works for the company as assistant personnel director), no children, current salary $55,000, MBA, University of Michigan. Otto has been with the company for nine years, the past six as manager. He is aggressive and hot-tempered, and though at one time you thought he was your best employee, during the past two years you have found him to be a disappointment. You rated him as "slightly below average" (59 percent) on his last performance rating. You believe that one of the reasons Otto's performance has fallen off is that he has found out about John Smith's and Ellen Panza's salaries.

- **David L. Green III** Age 29, single, current annual salary $40,000, BA, Wayne State University. David has been with the company for six years and became the first black manager in your company five years ago. He has been very instrumental in recruiting other blacks into the company and is often called on by the president to represent the company at civic and social events. You have found David's work to be marginal, and though you assigned him to manage the best group five years ago, the group is now the lowest performing. You rated David as "below average" (60%) and would like to get rid of him, but you don't know how you would replace him.

Your company has a secret pay policy. What information do you plan to share with your employees? What was your decision rule for administering the pay increases?

▶ IN-CLASS EXERCISES

Digital Joins the Rest of the World

For years the sales force of Digital Equipment Corporation (Digital) was the only one in the computer industry not working on commission; salespeople were paid a straight salary. The founder of Digital, Ken Olsen, believed that the engineers, scientists, and educators to whom Digital sold did not need a highly motivated salesperson calling on them. Well, times have changed for Digital's direct sales force of about 10,000. Digital's new compensation program puts all of its salespeople on salary plus commission. In the past, salespeople at Digital were paid a bonus based on how they compared with other Digital salespeople. Under the new plan, commissions are paid on how well a salesperson performs against a plan rather than in comparison to other people.

This exercise involves E. D. Lucente, vice president of worldwide sales and marketing, and one of her regional vice presidents.

Lucente and the regional vice president have been discussing the new sales force's compensation plan. Lucente points out that the company has been in the red for eight straight quarters. More important, Digital's customer base has changed. No longer does it consist of just engineers and scientists who know what they want in a computer.

The vice president agrees that something has to be done, but feels that the new plan will lead to a lot of problems that must be anticipated. After all, things that could be managed easily in a 100 percent salary environment will be looked at very differently when they can impact people's earnings directly. When pressed for specifics by Lucente, the vice president said, "Take, for example, territory design. A reduction in territory will be seen as a limitation on earnings potential rather than less travel."

Lucente indicates that she understands what the vice president means and asks if he sees any other problems. The vice president mentions another issue: "A rep selling PCs, requiring a high volume of low-value transactions, needs a different plan than an account manager on a single account, where you're looking for behavior that looks at the long-term interest of the account. How do we adjust the plan for each of these situations?"

Questions:

1. What is the purpose of adding an incentive to sales compensation?
2. Exactly how should a commission be added to Digital's compensation plan?
3. How should the plan be adjusted for the two types of selling situations mentioned?
4. What other sales management functions will change as a result of the compensation change?

► REFERENCES

1. *Sales Force Compensation Survey* (Chicago: Dartnell Corporation, 1996), p. 117.

2. *Wall Street Journal* (March 6, 1990), p. B1.

3. ROBERT G. HEAD, "Restoring Balance to Sales Compensation," *Sales & Marketing Management* (August 1992), p. 52.

4. *Sales Force Compensation Survey* (Chicago: Dartnell Corporation, 1996), p. 50.

5. BRIDGET O'BRIAN, "Merrill Lynch Considers Paying Salaries to New Brokers to Cut Interest Conflicts," *Wall Street Journal* (November 20, 1995), p. A2.

6. GEORGE JOHN and BARTON WEITZ, "Salesforce Compensation: An Empirical Investigation of Factors Related to Use of Salary Versus Incentive Compensation," *Journal of Marketing Research*, 26 (February 1989), p. 9.

7. *Sales Force Compensation Survey* (Chicago: Dartnell Corporation, 1996), p. 49.

8. GINGER TRUMFIO, "Keeping the Lid on Turnover," *Sales & Marketing Management* (November 1995), pp. 41–42.

9. TIM CLARK, "Digital Displays Signs of Recovery," *Business Marketing* (August 1993), p. 13.

10. *Sales & Marketing Management* (February 1995), p. 32.

11. MICHELE MARCHETTI, "Global Gamble," *Sales & Marketing Management* (July 1996), pp. 64–69.

12. BRIDGET O'BRIAN, "Merrill Lynch Planners Say They Face Too Much Sales Pressure," *Wall Street Journal* (May 3, 1996), p. B1.

13. ANDY COHEN, "Right on Target," *Sales & Marketing Management* (December 1994), pp. 59–63.

14. *Sales Compensation in the 1990s* (Bureau of Business Practice, SMB Special Report, 1991), p. 13.

15. "Rewarding Team Players," *Sales & Marketing Management* (April 1996), pp. 35–36.

16. *Sales Force Compensation Survey* (Chicago: Dartnell Corporation, 1996), p. 163.

17. *Sales Force Compensation Survey* (Chicago: Dartnell Corporation, 1996), p. 119.

18. *Sales Force Compensation Survey* (Chicago: Dartnell Corporation, 1996), pp. 121.

19. PETER DRUCKER, "Permanent Cost Cutting," *Wall Street Journal* (January 11, 1991), p. A15.

20. LAWRENCE B. CHONKO, JOHN F. TANNER, and WILLIAM A. WEEKS, "Selling and Sales Management in Action: Reward Preferences of Salespeople," *Journal of Personal Selling & Sales Management* (Summer 1992), p. 69.

21. *Sales Force Compensation Survey* (Chicago: Dartnell Corporation, 1996), p. 119.

22. MELISSA CAMPANELLI, "Compensation Automation," *Sales & Marketing Management* (March 1993), p. 104.

▶ SELECTED READINGS

CESPEDES, FRANK V., "A Preface to Payment: Designing a Sales Compensation Plan," *Sloan Management Review* (Fall 1990), p. 60.

JOHN, GEORGE, and BARTON WEITZ, "Sales Force Compensation: An Empirical Investigation of Factors Related to Use of Salary versus Incentive Compensation," *Journal of Marketing Research* (February 1989), pp. 1–14.

HEIDE, CHRISTEN, *Dartnell Sales Force Compensation Survey* (Chicago; Dartnell, Inc., 1996), 254 pages.

MATHIS, ROBERT L., and JOHN H. JACKSON, *Personnel/Human Resource Management* (St. Paul, Minn.: West, 1991).

RAO, RAM C., "Compensating Heterogeneous Salesforces: Some Explicit Solutions," *Marketing Science* (Fall 1990), pp. 319–341.

SHANK, MATHEW, and CYNTHIA LUNNEMAN, "Proper Pay and Rewards Help Retain Sales Force," *Marketing News* (March 5, 1990), p. 67.

CASE

14-1 MADISON FIBER CORPORATION*

Early in February 1993, executives of the Madison Fiber Corporation of Baltimore, Maryland, were discussing some proposals to modify the company's sales-force compensation plan. The discussion had been prompted by the recent broadening of the product line and by widespread disenchantment with the current compensation plan, a straight salary system with an annual bonus set by means of subjective evaluations. Furthermore, Madison executives had recently reorganized the sales force. They believed that, if changes in compensation were to be made, now was the most appropriate time to make them.

Company and Industry Background

Madison produced synthetic fibers, yarns, and fabrics. The company was founded in 1955 to serve a rapidly changing carpet-manufacturing industry. Subsequent to its founding, the firm made several major breakthroughs in synthetic fiber technology and production. These advances enabled Madison to become a significant supplier of synthetic carpet fiber as well as to make competitive entries into related fields.

Madison's three major product lines were synthetic carpet fiber, yarns, and industrial fabrics. Madison's synthetic carpet fiber—a monofilament—was used by leading carpet mills that produced tufted and needle-punch carpets for commercial and residential carpeting. The company manufactured synthetic yarns by twisting monofilament synthetic fibers into multi-filament and ribbon styles for a variety of applications, including webbing in aluminum lawn furniture, grilles on high-fidelity speakers, and automobile seat covers. By weaving the yarns the company manufactured industrial fabrics used as bagging for such products as seeds, beans, fertilizer and minerals, and as sheeting for such applications as tents, swimming-pool covers, industrial wraps, and tarpaulins. Because monofilament fiber was the base material for carpet fiber, yarn, and fabric, companies competing in any one of the above markets tended to compete in the others as well. Madison executives expected competitive pressure from industry overcapacity to become intense by the end of 1993. They ranked Madison fifth among its competitors in manufacturing capacity and estimated that the largest firm in the industry was four times Madison's size. Selected market estimates, forecasts, and sales data for carpet fiber and other Madison products are shown in Exhibit 1.

The Carpet Fiber Market

For many years the dominant materials used in carpet manufacturing were of natural origin such as wool. During the 1960s, synthetic fibers began to take a larger share of the market. Madison and its competitors moved quickly to increase their capacities for manufacturing synthetic fiber. By 1988 the synthetic-

fiber industry was operating at capacity. During the period 1989–1991, however, the carpet-manufacturing industry experienced a period of stagnant sales growth. An upturn in 1992 signaled to Madison executives that the period 1993–1998 might promise a 4% annual increase in industry sales. Accordingly, using 1988 capacity as the base of 100, Madison executives were in the process of adding capacity to increase this figure to 115 by the end of 1993 and to 155 by the end of 1995. Most carpet customers (with a few notable exceptions) were located in the South; the majority were in or around Dalton, Georgia.

The Yarn Market

Because of the many potential applications for synthetic yarn and fragmented industry data, company executives could not estimate potential sales volume or Madison's share of the synthetic-yarn market. Company executives believed that Madison's sales were limited only by its ability to create customers and by available machine time. Currently, the company's backlog of firm orders extended into the middle of 1993. The available data indicated to company executives that Madison had a small and spotty share of some of the applicable markets for synthetic yarns in 1992. For instance, they estimated they had 8% of the grille cloth market, 15% of the static automobile seat cover market, and 8% of the declining market for lawn-furniture webbing. Most of Madison's yarn customers were located near Chicago or other large industrial cities. Many potential yarn markets and customers were not being covered at all.

The Industrial Fabric Market

Because executives had waited to develop truly superior products, the firm was late in entering the industrial-fabric market. Madison fabric products were

Exhibit 1: Sales Volume and Forecasts ($ million)

	Actual		Forecast		
	1991	**1992**	**1993**	**1994**	**1995**
Carpet-fiber industry (est.)	$829.7	$846.3	$880.1	$915.4	$952.0
Madison carpet-fiber sales	$87.1	$89.7	$96.8	$106.1	$116.1
Madison market share (est.)	10.5%	10.6%	11.0%	11.6%	12.2%
Madison yarn sales	$35.6	$38.3	$47.2	$57.9	$71.7
Madison fabric sales	_____	$2.6	$12.9	$14.2	$15.6
Madison total sales	$122.7	$130.6	$150.6	$178.2	$203.4

introduced during the last quarter of 1991. Demand for this material was so great in 1992 that the company was able to sell all of its limited production. There was no discernible geographic pattern among potential fabric customers.

Madison's Marketing Activities

Madison was organized into four departments: marketing, finance and administration, operations, and research and development. Each department was headed by a vice president, who reported to the company president. Three of the departments employed fewer than 60 people; operations employed more than 400. Reporting to the vice president for marketing were a customer-service manager, a sales manager, and three product-development managers (one for carpet fibers, one for yarns, and one for industrial fabric).

The customer-service manager handled telephone contacts with customers, solving customers' billing, delivery, and technical problems. She also served as an "inside" sales representative, referring sales leads and requests for product information to the appropriate sales rep. These inside sales activities, however, were always credited to the sales rep assigned to the account.

The product development managers helped sales reps and customers solve technical problems; analyzed the current and potential market for their products; suggested product-development or line-extension opportunities; developed specifications for new and proposed products; and forecasted demand for new, existing, and proposed products by making appropriate economic and profit analyses. The product-development managers were expected to be technically expert with regard to customers' manufacturing techniques, as well as familiar with the marketplace and likely prospects for new and existing product offerings. Unlike a typical "brand manager," the product-development managers had no responsibility for sales volume or profits.

The *sales manager* developed sales plans by product, territory, and account and also directed the sales force. The current sales manager had been promoted to his present position in January 1992, after ten years as a Madison sales rep. He was 42, a college graduate, and earned about $75,000 a year in salary and management bonus.

Because the equipment used to manufacture synthetic fibers, yarns, or fabric represented a substantial capital investment, the company's basic business strategy was to attempt to operate at full capacity (normally two shifts) at all times. Fluctuations in consumers' demand for carpeting and competitive or technological developments, however, often created undersold or oversold conditions.

Capacity-forecasting and profit problems led Madison executives to take steps to reduce the firm's heavy reliance on the carpet-manufacturing industry. Accordingly, they decided in 1990 to broaden research and development in yarn and fabric for other industries. In 1991 Madison diversified into industrial fabric and began a marketing strategy to increase the proportion of sales of products other than carpet fiber.

In the carpet market, Madison's new strategy was to increase its share of business with high volume accounts where it could become the primary supplier. Historically, Madison had been the secondary or tertiary supplier in such acounts, a condition that exacerbated the cyclicality of the business. A second objective was to reduce dependence on small accounts whose positions in the marketplace were marginal from the standpoints of credit and potential growth.

In the yarn market the strategy was to find new applications that would appeal to manufacturers with high poundage or high square-foot requirements. New customers had to be found beyond manufacturers of furniture, automobile seat covers, and grille cloth. Applications that would not generate significant volume were considered unattractive because of their low margins.

In the industrial-fabric market, the strategy was to provide improved material and new applications in volume for customers who were using or were likely to switch to superior synthetic fabrics in some of their present or new end products. Examples of such products were specialty bagging (sacks, bales, bags), swimming-pool covers, tenting, tarpaulins, and industrial product wraps. Management estimated that much of the domestic market was concentrated in 100 large potential accounts. Major marketing efforts were to be undertaken at first, however, with only the largest potential customers with high-volume applications. This strategy required a very high investment in weaving and coating equipment. Madison was obliged to take heavy debt to enter this capital-intensive business.

Sales and Sales Management Activities

The job of the Madison sales reps was multifaceted. First, they were expected to service Madison accounts and obtain orders for all Madison product lines. By virtue of personal acceptability and technical competence, they were expected to assist customers in determining apropriate inventory levels, to monitor and correct possible problems as regards the quality of delivered products, to monitor and correct Madison's delivery service, to handle complaints, and to serve generally as on-the-spot trouble-shooters.

Second, the sales reps were expected to increase the proportion of business that Madison was obtaining from each account. Because most larger companies, particularly those purchasing carpet fiber, preferred to purchase from several sources, it was important that the sales reps penetrate past the customer's purchasing office and become influential with all important decision makers within the customer's operation.

Third, the sales reps were expected to work closely with the product-development managers to seek new applications for existing products and extensions of the product line, and to introduce new products to present and potential customers. In effect, between working with accounts and developing a close liaison with the product-development managers, a good part of the sale reps' job was to manage relations between the Madison plant and its customers.

Fourth—and increasingly important—given the company's efforts to reduce its dependence on carpet-manufacturing customers—the sales reps were expected to prospect for new accounts for yarns and fabrics. They were responsible for generating leads by observing, listening, reviewing such sources as the *Thomas Register*, and following up inquiries forwarded from the customer-service manager.

Thus, sales reps were required to call upon many different kinds of customers, ranging from large carpet manufacturers to small grille-cloth weavers to industrial packaging firms. They could experience considerable difficulty in determining who and where the likely prospects were for a number of quite different product applications. Finally, the company's marketing strategy was still in the process of evolving, forcing sales reps to tailor their activities by industry and by geographic area.

Late in 1991, the sales organization had been reduced from two regional managers supervising 14 Madison sales reps and four commission agents, to a single sales manager supervising 12 sales reps. This action had been taken after a detailed study of the sales reps' activities had revealed that the sales force was underutilized. As a consequence, each territory had been studied to determine the optimum number of calls per day from a well-planned itinerary. Each current account was analyzed to determine how many calls per year were required to offer the desired amount of service and selling time. A similar procedure was undertaken with respect to current and potential prospects. This analysis produced the current teritory assignments and a concomitant increase in the number of required and actual sales calls per week. As Exhibit 2 shows, the dollar sales for 1992 were similar among the sales territories, except for the Atlanta teritory with its large concentration of carpet manufacturers.

The current sales reps had been with Madison from four to twenty years. They had been hired as experienced sales reps and their ages ranged from 33 to 52. The company had no formal training program beyond a two-week tour in the plant to gather technical knowledge and a two-week tour in the field with an experienced sales rep to "learn the ropes."

In 1992, in recognition of the sales manager's increased span of control, three control forms were instituted to monitor the field activities of the sales force. The first was a weekly itinerary submitted by the sales rep to the sales manager. It listed the sales rep's planned calls by account and by day. It was faxed in to the sales manager on Friday to cover the following week. The second form was a trip report, which the sales rep filled out after each call. The sales rep listed the account's name, persons contacted, purpose of the call, results of the call, whatever marketing intelligence he or she had gathered, and whatever follow-up action should be taken by the sales rep or by the Madison plant. For a serious complaint, the sales rep was required to fill out a complaint report in seven copies, which were routed to various departments within Madison, depending upon the nature of the complaint. This form was also used to request price adjustments and to advise other Madison departments of problems with service, billing, pricing, delivery, and quality control.

The sales manager tried to maintain personal contact with each of the 12 sales reps by telephone

Exhibit 2: Individual Territory Results and Earnings–1992

Territory	Number of Actual and Potential Accounts[1]	Carpet Backing ($mm)	Yarn ($mm)	Fabric ($mm)	Total ($mm)	Salary	Bonus
Atlanta	42	$25.2	$1.9	$0	$27.1	$58,000	$5,200
Baltimore	40	8.3	1.8	0	10.1	49,000	4,000
Boston	38	1.9	6.6	0.2	8.7	51,000	4,200
Chicago	48	5.7	3.2	0.6	9.5	52,000	6,000
Cleveland	41	3.5	5.3	0.3	9.1	47,000	5,500
Detroit	50	2.8	6.6	0.4	9.8	48,000	5,000
Houston	44	8.8	0.7	0.2	9.7	44,000	5,700
Los Angeles	45	4.7	3.7	0.5	8.9	54,000	5,500
New York	44	9.5	0.3	0.1	9.9	57,000	4,700
Philadelphia	36	9.0	0.3	0	9.3	47,000	4,200
Pittsburgh	42	3.7	5.0	0.2	8.9	45,000	4,200
San Francisco	42	2.9	2.9	0.1	9.6	48,000	5,800
TOTAL	512	$89.7	$38.3	$2.6	$130.6	$600,000	$60,000

[1]Potential accounts referred to identified prospects whom the sales reps intended to call upon or had been called upon.

at least once a week. His objective was to spend two and one-half to three days a week in the field working with the sales reps and calling on customers with them. This schedule permitted him to work in the field with each sales rep for two or three days in each quarter. An annual sales meeting, usually held in February, brought all the marketing and sales personnel together in Baltimore. This meeting, a combination of social and business activities, was the company's major opportunity to inform the sales force of technical developments in the Madison product line and to review marketing plans.

The sales manager conducted a formal performance review with each sales rep at the end of the year. The review took place either in the field or during a sales rep's visit to the Madison plant. The vehicle for performance appraisal was a two-page sheet that provided space for the sales manager to write a subjective appraisal and developmental action plan in each of six areas: technical knowledge, quality of work, quanity of work, initiative, relations with Madison personnel, and office procedures. These criteria were used throughout the company, and the form was standard for all departments and for all nonmanagerial employees.

The current compensation plan for the sales force paid a straight salary that, in 1992, averaged $50,000,

plus a year-end bonus ranging from $4,000 to $6,000 per person. The size of the bonus depended on the collective subjective judgments of the sales manager, the marketing vice president, and the president. Seldom, according to the sales manager, was the size of the bonus related directly to sales dollars produced. In addition to earnings, the sales rep received all normal fringe benefits, plus a company car. He or she was reimbursed for all normal business expenses after submitting a monthly expense report.

The Compensation Issues

The first problem that senior executives had to deal with was the appropriate amount of compensation. Madison executives estimated that the average sales rep's earnings in the industry were approximately $60,000 a year (including company car), although sales reps for two of Madison's larger competitors probably averaged about $75,000 a year. Earnings for the top sales reps in the industry appeared to be in the neighborhood of $80,000 to $100,000 a year.

The sales manager recognized that Madison sales reps' earnings were close to the industry average. But he argued that, because Madison was a small company relative to its major competitors, Madison should pay more than average compensation in order to attract and keep the best possible sales reps. The controller argued that, because turnover was almost nonexistent, there was no need to pay Madison sales reps more than they were already getting.

The second issue was the method of compensation. Firms in the industry exhibited considerable variety in methods of compensating their sales reps. Two of the large firms paid straight salary only. Some smaller companies used commissioned agents who paid their own expenses from a commission rate of one and one-half percent of their sales. Most of Madison's competitors, however, used a salary system with some form of bonus payment. Each of these methods had its adherents within Madison.

The president indicated that the decision of how the sales reps were to be compensated would be left up to the sales manager, the marketing vice president, and the company controller. He placed two constraints on their decision, however: (1) No sales rep doing a good job should suffer financially from a change in the pay plan and (2) if a bonus system was instituted, no sales rep could earn more than 50% of his or her salary in bonus, because the Madison managerial bonus plan had the same limit.

Accordingly, the marketing vice president, the sales manager, and the controller met to discuss the options they had studied over the past six months. These options are described below.

Straight Salary

The controller advocated paying sales reps a straight salary and basing future salary adjustments on past performance. He argued that a straight salary would give managers tight control over the sales reps' order taking and account servicing. Because much of the sales reps' success depended upon their ability to bring the internal resources of the company to bear on the solution of customer problems, the "credit" for the sale belonged to everyone in the Madison organization. Furthermore, much of their business was "handed to them on a silver platter" and was not a direct consequence of their individual initiative.

The sales manager disagreed. He maintained that straight salary gave sales reps no incentive to develop new business or to increase business with current customers, and that these objectives were the real focus of their efforts. He added that both these activities were critical to the success of the company's strategic shift in product and customer emphasis. Furthermore, he maintained that salary adjustments would be determined by the same subjective evaluations that made Madison executives uncomfortable in determining bonuses under the current system.

Continuation of Current Plan

The major argument for continuing the present plan was based upon the marketing vice president's idea that "the devil you know is better than the devil you don't." He maintained that the current system had the advantages of familiarity and control over unexpected events. He recognized, however, that the current plan was favored neither by the sales reps, who had been complaining about the subjectivity of the bonus determination, nor by the sales manager, who was particularly uncomfortable when explaining to the sales reps the basis for these subjective judgments.

Straight Commission

Straight commission was the plan favored by the sales reps. The commission rate under discussion was 0.6% of sales, paid monthly. The sales reps argued that they would be inclined to work harder if they were treated "as if they were in business for themselves," and that their efforts to maximize their own incomes would maximize the achievement of company objectives. The controller pointed out to the sales manager and the marketing vice president that straight commission meant that, as the firm grew and increased its efficiency, it could never improve its ratio of sales to cost of selling. The marketing vice president expressed the opinion that he did not want the sales reps "in business for themselves," he wanted them "working for Madison." The sales manager sympathized with both of these reservations, but he thought that straight commission might make his managing job easier because he would have to do less "booting them in the tail."

Salary Plus Annual Bonus
Based on Product-Line Sales

The sales manager proposed an annual bonus based on product-line sales "over quota." He favored establishing quotas for each sales rep for each major product line-carpet fiber, yarn, and industrial fabric. At 100% of quota for each product, sales reps would receive no bonuses; for each 3% in excess of quota for each product line, a sales rep would receive a bonus of 1% of salary. Thus, if a sales rep exeeded his or her personal quota for each of the three product lines by 9%, the annual bonus would be 3% + 3% + 3% or 9%

of salary. The maximum bonus would be 50% of salary. The annual bonus would be supplemented by a one-time award given for each new account, to equal one-tenth of one percent of the new account's first-year sales, with a maximum-payment of $500 per account. This payment would be made as soon as possible after the anniversary date of the new account's first order.

The controller was less than enthusiastic about his plan, maintaining that the quotas might be set too low, resulting in overpayment to the sales reps. He also wondered about the effects of windfall sales. The marketing vice president wanted to know how the sales managers planned to make the quotas fair, because sales in the past had sometimes been limited by plant capacity.

Salary Plus Quarterly Bonus Based on "Capitalized Sales Expense"

One of the product managers had passed along to the marketing vice president an article describing the "capitalized sales expense" approach to compensation. This method required that managers first determine the sales expenses that they were willing to incur. This expense was expressed as a percentage of sales. The salary and controllable expenses incurred by a sales rep were then divided by this percentage. The resulting amount, called a "bogey," was to be used as a dollar sales quota. The sales rep would receive a bonus for sales in excess of the "bogey." The bonus would be set at a fixed percentage of these excess dollar sales, at a rate below the figure for the desired sales expenses, expressed as a percentage of sales. No bonus could exceed 50% of a sales rep's salary.

The marketing vice president was intrigued enough by this idea to calculate some percentages illustrating it. He set desired sales expenses at 1% of sales and set the bonus at 0.5% of sales in excess of bogey. He then figured the quarterly bonus for a sales rep who earned a salary of $15,000 for the three-month period, made $2,300,000 in sales, and incurred $5,000 in expenses during the same period.

$$\frac{3 \text{ months' salary} + 3 \text{ months' controllable territory expenses}}{0.01} = \text{bogey}$$

$$(3 \text{ months' sales} - \text{Bogey}) \times 0.005 = \text{bonus}$$

$$\frac{\$15,000 + \$5,000}{0.01} = \$2,000,000 = \text{bogey}$$

$$\$2,300,000 - \$2,000,000 = \$300,000$$
(sales in excess of bogey)

$$\$300,000 \times 0.005 = \$1,500$$
(bonus for the quarter)

The marketing vice president felt that this system would appear too complicated to the sales force, although he recognized that the bogey derived from capitalizing sales expense seemed less arbitrary than a quota "plucked out of the air." The controller felt that the system would be too complicated to administer, although he realized that the cost of sales would decline as the sales reps exceed their bogey. The sales manager noted that this plan neither emphasized sales by product line, nor motivated sales reps to open new accounts. But he acknowledged that the system would encourage sales reps to keep their expenses down, because spending less than budget would lower their bogey.

C A S E

14-2 POWER & MOTION INDUSTRIAL SUPPLY, INC.*

It was 7:00 on Sunday evening when Hal Maybee returned to his office. He had spent the afternoon golfing with one of his customers, and he now had to decide what he was going to tell the head office on Monday morning with regard to new salaries for the sales staff at his branch.

Hal had just been appointed Atlantic Region District Manager for one of Canada's largest industrial distributors. His appointment was made only two weeks before, following the sudden death of Fergie McDonald, who, at 48 years old, had been in charge of the company's most profitable branch. About 70 percent of the sales in Atlantic Canada, including the four most profitable product lines, were for manufacturers that the company did not represent on a national basis. There were many manufacturers in Ontario and Quebec that served central Canada with their own sales forces, and used distributors for the east and west coasts due to the distances from their head offices and the geographical dispersion of customers in those regions. Although Power Motion had sales agreements with over 400 North American manufacturers, only about 100 manufacturers were involved in 80 percent of the sales.

It was a complete surprise to Hal when he was promoted, and he knew there were people at the branch who thought they deserved it more. Exhibit 1 shows the performance evaluations that Fergie had completed on the six salespeople just before he died. Head office had intended to send only five forms to Hal, but one of the secretaries mistakenly included Fergie's evaluation of Hal as well.

Nearly three weeks previously, Fergie and Hal were making some joint calls on some pump mills in

northern New Brunswick, the territory that Fergie kept for himself, even though head office wanted him to stop selling and spend more time on sales administration. During the trip, Fergie told Hal that he was given 6 percent of the total sales staff salary to be divided among them for the coming year. This was the customary way of giving salary increases at the branches, as it gave the head office the discretion to decide the total increase in the salary expense, but it gave the district managers responsibility for allocating salary increases. Fergie was told that nationally, sales increases would average about 3 percent, but his branch was among the lowest paid in the company and had been the best-performing branch for several years.

Hal did not want to express his opinions, as he knew he and Fergie would disagree. However, he did allow Fergie to express his own thoughts on the staff. There were two salespeople that Fergie had a real problem with. He viewed Jim Stanley as his biggest problem. Jim actually had seniority at the branch. He had been hired, as shipper, order desk salesperson, and secretary when the branch was only large enough to support one person other than Bob Laird, the first salesperson the company had in Atlantic Canada. Bob and Jim operated the branch for almost two years when Bob decided to hire Fergie as a salesperson to help develop the territory. When Bob retired, Jim thought he would get the position as District Manager, as he had seniority, and he had experience with all aspects of the business including managing the office and warehouse, which had grown to include seven people. He was very disappointed when the head office gave the position to Fergie, as he had no experience other than sales.

Within a year, Jim decided he wanted to get into sales. He was finally resigned to the fact that office management was a dead-end job, and the only possibility for advancement was through sales. Now, after five years, Jim was not performing as well as he should. In fact, he hated selling and spent an increasing amount of time drinking while away from home. He hinted that he wanted to get back into the office.

---

*This case was prepared by H. F. MacKenzie of Memorial University of Newfoundland, Canada. The case was prepared as a basis for class discussion and is not intended to illustrate effective or ineffective handling of a management situation. All names in the case have been disguised. Copyright © 1994 by H. F. MacKenzie, Memorial University of Newfoundland, Faculty of Business Administration, St. John's, Newfoundland A1B 3X5. Reproduced by permission.

Exhibit 1: Evaluation of Salespeople

Salesperson	Evaluation Criteria	Far Worse Than Average			About Average		Far Better Than Average	
Dave	Attitude	1	2	3	4	⑤	6	7
Edison	Appearance and manner	1	2	3	4	5	⑥	7
	Selling skills	1	2	3	4	5	⑥	7
	Product knowledge	1	2	3	④	5	6	7
	Time management	1	2	3	④	5	6	7
	Customer goodwill	1	2	3	④	5	6	7
	Expense/budget	1	2	3	④	5	6	7
	New accounts opened	1	2	3	④	5	6	7
	Sales calls/quota	1	2	3	④	5	6	7
	Sales/quota	1	2	3	4	⑤	6	7
	Sales volume	1	2	3	④	5	6	7
	Sales growth	1	2	3	4	⑤	6	7
	Contribution margin	1	2	3	4	5	⑥	7
	Total score: 61							

Comments: Current salary $52,000. Territory is Cape Breton Island and the city of Moncton, N.B. Needs more product knowledge but has learned a lot since hired. A bit aggressive, but he has developed some excellent new accounts through attention to detail and follow-up support.

Salesperson	Evaluation Criteria	Far Worse Than Average			About Average		Far Better Than Average	
Arne	Attitude	1	2	③	4	5	6	7
Olsen	Appearance and manner	1	2	③	4	5	6	7
	Selling skills	1	2	③	4	5	6	7
	Product knowledge	1	2	3	④	5	6	7
	Time management	1	2	③	4	5	6	7
	Customer goodwill	1	2	③	4	5	6	7
	Expense/budget	1	2	3	4	⑤	6	7
	New accounts opened	1	2	③	4	5	6	7
	Sales calls/quota	1	2	3	4	5	⑥	7
	Sales/quota	1	2	③	4	5	6	7
	Sales volume	1	2	3	④	5	6	7
	Sales growth	1	2	③	4	5	6	7
	Contribution margin	1	2	③	4	5	6	7
	Total score: 46							

Comments: Current salary $44,500. Has been calling regularly on his existing accounts in southern New Brunswick (except Moncton). Although he has increased the number of sales calls, as agreed at our last review, sales have not gone up accordingly. Some concern with product knowledge. Arne knows all of our major product lines very well, but has not shown much effort to learn about many of the new lines we have added that may become our best product lines in the future. Further concern with his contribution margin. This is the fourth year in a row that it has dropped, although it is almost the same as last year.

Salesperson	Evaluation Criteria	Far Worse Than Average			About Average		Far Better Than Average	
Hal	Attitude	1	2	3	4	⑤	6	7
Maybee	Appearance and manner	1	2	3	④	5	6	7
	Selling skills	1	2	3	④	5	6	7
	Product knowledge	1	2	3	4	⑤	6	7
	Time management	1	2	3	4	5	⑥	7

Exhibit 1: (*continued*)

Salesperson	Evaluation Criteria	Far Worse Than Average			About Average		Far Better Than Average	
	Customer goodwill	1	2	3	4	5	⑥	7
	Expense/budget	1	2	3	④	5	6	7
	New accounts opened	1	②	3	4	5	6	7
	Sales calls/quota	1	2	3	④	5	6	7
	Sales/quota	1	2	3	4	⑤	6	7
	Sales volume	1	②	3	4	5	6	7
	Sales growth	1	2	③	4	5	6	7
	Contribution margin	1	②	3	4	5	6	7
	Total score: 52							

Comments: Current salary $38,500. Although still the Office Manager, Hal has taken over Newfoundland as a territory and travels there four times a year. Hal also travels to northern New Brunswick with me occasionally due to his expert product knowledge on electric and pneumatic products, which we sell to the mines and pulp mills in the two areas. Hal is very focused and successful with the big sales but needs to develop knowledge of and interest in some of the lower sales volume, less technical products, as they are generally higher-margin items. Hal has a lot of respect in the office and our efficiency has improved greatly, as has the general work atmosphere within the office.

Salesperson	Evaluation Criteria	Far Worse Than Average			About Average		Far Better Than Average	
Tanya	Attitude	1	2	3	④	5	6	7
Burt	Appearance and manner	1	2	3	④	5	6	7
	Selling skills	1	2	3	4	⑤	6	7
	Product knowledge	1	2	③	4	5	6	7
	Time management	1	2	3	4	⑤	6	7
	Customer goodwill	1	2	3	4	⑤	6	7
	Expense/budget	1	2	3	④	5	6	7
	New accounts opened	1	2	3	4	⑤	6	7
	Sales calls/quota	1	2	3	4	⑤	6	7
	Sales/quota	1	2	3	4	⑤	6	7
	Sales volume	1	2	3	④	5	6	7
	Sales growth	1	2	3	4	⑤	6	7
	Contribution margin	1	2	3	4	⑤	6	7
	Total score: 59							

Comments: Current salary $36,000. Very impressed with her performance. Has good knowledge of product pricing and sourcing but needs to learn more about product applications. Tanya sells mainly maintenance and operating supplies, but she has a number of accounts that buy large annual volumes, as her territory is the Halifax–Dartmouth area surrounding our warehouse. Tanya is dedicated and dependable. She has opened many new accounts for us, and I predict good success for her as she continues to develop her knowledge and selling skills.

Salesperson	Evaluation Criteria	Far Worse Than Average			About Average		Far Better Than Average	
Jim	Attitude	1	2	③	4	5	6	7
Stanley	Appearance and manner	1	2	③	4	5	6	7
	Selling skills	1	2	③	4	5	6	7
	Product knowledge	1	2	3	④	5	6	7
	Time management	1	②	3	4	5	6	7
	Customer goodwill	1	2	③	4	5	6	7

Exhibit 1: (*continued*)

Salesperson	Evaluation Criteria	Far Worse Than Average			About Average		Far Better Than Average	
	Expense/budget	1	2	③	4	5	6	7
	New accounts opened	1	②	3	4	5	6	7
	Sales calls/quota	1	2	3	④	5	6	7
	Sales/quota	1	2	3	4	⑤	6	7
	Sales volume	1	2	3	④	5	6	7
	Sales growth	1	2	3	4	⑤	6	7
	Contribution margin	1	2	3	4	⑤	6	7

Total score: 46

Comments: Current salary $42,000. Jim seems to be performing quite well, but there is concern with his behavior. I hope that a salary increase and some direction from me will improve his performance next year. He has been making some suggestions that he might like to move back to office management because everyone thinks I will be promoting Hal to full-time sales and letting him take over my territory as well as Newfoundland. I really do not want Jim back in the office, and I think he should be a good salesperson. His sales and contribution margin are good, but part of his sales increase this year came from a new customer that has a manufacturing plant in his region but actually buys from an office located in Tanya's territory. Tanya and Jim have agreed to split the credit for the sales, as Tanya must do the selling but Jim has to service the account.

Salesperson	Evaluation Criteria	Far Worse Than Average			About Average		Far Better Than Average	
Buck	Attitude	1	2	3	④	5	6	7
Thompson	Appearance and manner	1	2	3	④	5	6	7
	Selling skills	1	2	3	4	⑤	6	7
	Product knowledge	1	2	3	4	5	⑥	7
	Time management	1	2	3	④	5	6	7
	Customer goodwill	1	2	3	④	5	6	7
	Expense/budget	1	2	③	4	5	6	7
	New accounts opened	1	②	3	4	5	6	7
	Sales calls/quota	1	2	③	4	5	6	7
	Sales/quota	1	2	3	④	5	6	7
	Sales volume	1	2	3	④	5	6	7
	Sales growth	1	2	3	④	5	6	7
	Contribution margin	1	2	3	④	5	6	7

Total score: 51

Comments: Current salary $49,000. Sells in Pictou County, N.S., where we have a very established customer base and a variety of industries. Buck knows all of his customers very well, as he has lived in the area all of his life. He has very good selling skills and product knowledge and has been the main reason we have done so well in his territory.

However, when these rumors started to spread, the staff let it be known that they did not want to work under Jim again if there were any alternatives.

Fergie was thinking about giving Jim a good salary increase. First, it might make him appreciate his job more, and maybe he would put more effort into sell-ing. Second, it would make the position more attractive than a possible return to the office, as he would not want to take a tremendous salary cut.

The other problem was Arne Olsen, the other senior salesperson. As the territory developed quickly, the branch hired a secretary just after Fergie was hired. A month later, a warehouseman was hired and Jim was promoted to Office Manager. Jim immediately hired Hal Maybee as an order desk salesperson. Within a year, another salesperson, Arne, was hired, along with a second secretary. The branch growth slowed but was steady from that point on. Arne was always an average salesperson. He never really had much motivation to perform, but he always did whatever he had to do, so that he was never in any serious trouble as far as his job was concerned. Lately, he was starting to slip a bit, and rumor had it that he was having at least one affair. He also recently bought a Mazda Miata that he drove on weekends, as he was not allowed to drive anything but the company car through the work week.

Dave Edison was with the company for just under one year. If he had had a few more years with the company, Hal knew he would have probably been the new District Manager. He came to the company from the life insurance industry, and rumor had it that he was slated for a national sales manager position within the next year, as the company was rumored to be taking on a new line of capital equipment from Europe that would be sold nationally, but would have one person at head office responsible for national sales.

Tanya Burt was also in sales for only a year. She had been hired as a secretary, but it soon became apparent that she had exceptional telephone skills. She was promoted to order desk salesperson within a year, and three years later, she requested and was given an outside sales territory. There was some concern with her product knowledge but no concern with her attitude or sales ability. Tanya was the first and only woman to be promoted to one of the company's 80 outside sales positions.

Buck Thompson had a very solid, established territory. He needed little direction, as he was doing most things very well. Fergie was a bit concerned that he was not making enough sales calls, but he certainly was performing well.

As Hal reviewed the performance evaluations, he agreed that Fergie had been very thorough and accurate in his assessment of each of the individuals. Hal wondered about the amount of salary increase he should give to each person. While he had to make this decision immediately, Hal realized there were other important decisions he would have to make soon. He recognized some of the problems Fergie had trying to decide salary increases, and these were more important for Hal, as he had to get the support of the sales staff before he could hope to overcome some of these problems. He also had to start thinking about hiring another salesperson to cover Newfoundland and northern New Brunswick, as the head office was determined that he give up responsibility for all accounts in the region. He would, however, be allowed and encouraged to call on customers with the sales staff.

▶ 15 ◀

Evaluating
Performance

Nothing succeeds like success.
ALEXANDRE DUMAS

LEARNING OBJECTIVES

After studying this chapter, you should be able to:

▶ Conduct a sales force performance review.

▶ Describe the criteria used to evaluate salespeople.

▶ Distinguish between input and output measures of sales performance.

▶ Discuss the importance of cost controls.

▶ Discuss the value of behavioral control procedures for salespeople.

▶ Explain the advantages and disadvantages of MBO.

► SALES PERFORMANCE REVIEW

Evaluation is essentially a comparison of sales force goals and objectives with actual achievements in the field. A general model of the evaluation process is shown in Figure 15-1. First, management must decide what it wants the sales force to accomplish. The most common objectives are the attainment of specific sales revenues, contribution profits, market shares, and expense levels. Then, a sales plan must be prepared to show how the goals are to be achieved. The next step is to set performance standards for individual products for different levels in the organization. Thus, you must set goals for total sales, as well as sales by regions, by product, by salesperson, and for each separate account. You then look at differences between the performance standards and the results attained. Reasons for above- and below-standard performance are analyzed, and modifications are made in the plans for the future.

Selecting Performance Measures

The task of selecting a set of sales performance measures for a firm is difficult because there are so many unique factors that can be used. Some authors suggest that performance measures should be tailored to the goals and objectives of each organization.[1] This leads to the observation that different sets of evaluation criteria can be successful in separate sales environments.[2] The relative usage of 20 output performance measures as reported by 215 sales executives is shown in Table 15-1.

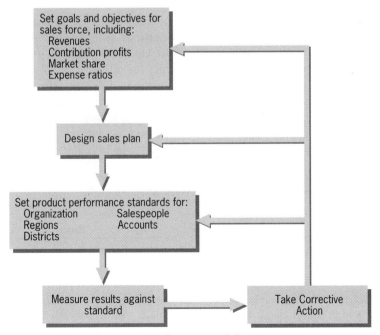

Figure 15-1: A Sales Force Evaluation Model

Table 15-1 Output Measures Used in Sales Force Evaluation

Performance Measure	Percent Using	Performance Measure	Percent Using
Sales		Profit	
Sales volume dollars	79%	Net profit	69%
Sales volume previous year's sales	76	Gross margin percentage	34
Sales to quota	65	Return on investment	33
Sales growth	55	Net profit as a percentage of sales	32
Sales volume by product	48	Margin by product category	28
Sales volume by customer	44	Gross margin dollars	25
New account sales	42		
Sales volume in units	35		
Sales volume to potential	27		
Accounts		Orders	
Number of new accounts	69	Number of orders	47
Number of accounts lost	33	Average size of order	22
Number of accounts buying full line	27		

Source: Donald W. Jackson, John L. Schlacter, and William G. Wolfe, "Examining the Bases Utilized for Evaluating Salespeoples' Performance," *Journal of Personal Selling & Sales Management*, Vol. 15, No. 4 (Fall 1995), p. 61.

A great unresolved controversy in sales management is whether *output measures* (Table 15-1), *input factors* such as those in Table 15-2, or qualitative criteria are best for evaluating sales performance. Output factors look at sales volume, number of new accounts, margins, and the number of orders whereas input criteria measure expenses, number of calls, and days worked. Qualitative measures include things like attitude, communication skills, and product knowledge. Research has shown that qualitative factors are the most widely used, but they are difficult to measure and often lead to biased evaluations.[3] This same study revealed that there has been a decline in the use of input performance measures. Managers are putting less emphasis on such factors as number of sales calls, demonstrations, and letters/phone calls to prospects. Also there is more usage of profit, margin, and expense factors.

Table 15-2 Input or Behavior Bases Used in Sales Force Evaluation

Base	Percent Using	Base	Percent Using
Selling expenses to budget	55%	Number of calls per day	42%
Total expenses	53	Number of reports turned in	38
Selling expenses as a % of sales	49	Number of days worked	33
Number of calls	48	Selling time vs. nonselling time	27

Source: Donald W. Jackson, John L. Schlacter, and William G. Wolfe, "Examining the Bases Utilized for Evaluating Salespeoples' Performance," *Journal of Personal Selling & Sales Management*, Vol. 15, No. 4 (Fall 1995), p. 62.

Table 15-3 Sales Data for Bear Computer Company

Year	1 Company Volume ($ millions)	2 Percentage Change from Previous Year	3 Industry Volume ($ millions)	4 Company Market Share (percent)
1997	26	+8.3	300	8.6
1996	24	+14.0	219	10.9
1995	21	+23.5	165	12.7
1994	17	—	125	13.6

▶ THE BIG PICTURE

A logical first step in a sales analysis is to look at aggregate sales figures for a company or division. Some sample sales figures for the Bear Computer Company are provided in Table 15-3. Bear seems to be doing well. Sales have increased from $17 million to $26 million in only four years, or 18 percent annually. However, the rate of growth is declining. For some reason, Bear has been unable to maintain the sales increases that it achieved in earlier years. One excuse for such a situation is that slow growth simply reflects general economic conditions. However, industry sales have been expanding rapidly at the same time that Bear's sales gains have fallen off. The resulting impact on market share is shown in column 4. Bear's market position has fallen from 13.6 percent in 1984 to only 8.6 percent in 1997. Thus, although Bear's sales have increased 53 percent, its market share has taken a disastrous plunge. A sales increase, like the tip of the iceberg, tells only part of the story. The *iceberg principle* encourages managers to search through their data to find out what is really going on.

There could be many reasons for the 37 percent drop in market share at Bear Computer. Competitors may simply be more aggressive and may have attracted the new business from Bear. Another possibility is that the product itself may be deficient in terms of performance or reliability. Because personal selling is the primary way of selling computers, it is a likely problem area. Bear may not have enough salespeople or sales offices, or the sales force may not be calling on the right prospects.

Dollar versus Unit Sales

Sales can also be broken out in terms of number of units sold (Table 15-4). Unit sales can be useful when inflation and other price changes distort dollar sales figures. For example, dollar sales of Bear computers went from $16.8 million in 1996 to $18.2 million in 1997. However, unit sales actually declined from 560 to 520 over the same period, meaning that the average price of a Bear computer went from $30,000 in 1996 to $35,000 in 1997. Although some of the 17 percent increase in computer prices was due to inflation, some other factor is contributing to this change. The data suggest that the sales force is trading customers up to the most expensive computers in the

Table 15-4   Comparing Dollar and Unit Sales at the Bear Computer Company

	1996 Sales			1997 Sales		
Products	Thousands of Dollars	Units	Avg Price per Unit	Thousands of Dollars	Units	Avg Price per Unit
Computers	$16,800	560	$30,000	$18,200	520	$35,000
Accessories	4,800	4,000	1,200	5,200	4,727	1,100
Software	2,400	1,200	2,000	2,600	1,280	2,031
Total	$24,000	5,760		$26,000	6,527	

line. Another breakdown of sales by individual models of Bear computers would tell you what items are being ignored.

A decline in unit sales is a serious problem in an expanding market, and you should make adjustments in the wage and quota systems to achieve more balanced growth in computer sales. Unit sales growth is desirable because it keeps production lines and employees busy.

A somewhat different situation exists with Bear's line of accessory equipment (Table 15-4). Note that dollar and unit sales both increased between 1996 and 1997. However, unit sales grew much more rapidly than dollar sales, and the average unit price dropped from $1,200 in 1996 to $1,100 in 1997. These results suggest that the sales force may be cutting prices to boost unit volume. This push for market share is to be applauded as long as profit margins are not completely destroyed. Bear's software product line also experienced growth in dollar and unit sales. In this case, the sales force was able to sell more units at higher average prices. These efforts are commendable, but Bear's software sales are still far below the levels suggested by industry and company potential figures.

Sales by Customer Type

Another useful approach is to break down sales by individual customers. These reviews often show that you obtain a high percentage of sales from a small number of customers. When 80 percent of your sales come from only 20 percent of your buyers, you are probably losing money serving small amounts. Some sales managers use the 80–20 *principle* to shift low-volume accounts to mail-order or telephone reorder systems. Other firms give small accounts to independent distributors so that the regular sales force can concentrate their efforts on a reduced number of large accounts. Frequently, a policy of providing extra service to large accounts leads to greater total sales for the firm.

▶ EXPENSE ANALYSIS

Although a sales analysis provides useful data on the operation of a field sales force, it does not tell the whole story. Sales figures show trends, but they do not reveal the effects of price-cutting or the differences in selling expenses, potential, and saturation that exist across products or territories. A more complete picture of sales force efficiency can be obtained by reviewing expense data to show the effects of changes in selling tactics on the profitability of the firm.

What Expenses Are Relevant?

We take the position that controllable expenses such as wages and travel are the figures that are relevant to field sales managers. Thus national advertising and production costs, which are not directly controlled by sales managers, should not be used to judge the efficiency of the sales organization. Of course, cost-of-goods-sold figures are necessary to help measure price-cutting by salespeople. Table 15-2 shows that the most popular expense measures relate selling expenses to budget figures or to sales.

Product Expenses

A logical first step in an expense analysis is to look at the differences associated with each product line. Table 15-5 shows such an analysis for the Bear Computer Company. Note that the cost of goods sold plus commissions is considerably higher for computers (70 percent) than it is for accessories (60 percent) and software (20 percent). These results can be explained in several ways. One possibility is that Bear is paying too much for parts, with the result that its manufacturing costs are simply higher than those of competitors. Another explanation is that competition has driven down selling prices in the market and raised Bear's cost of goods sold as a percentage of sales. A more disturbing possibility is that salespeople are cutting prices on computers to close sales so that they can raise their commission income. If this is the case, then the sales manager may need to place limits on the sales force's authority to negotiate prices. The sales manager could also shift to a gross margin commission system so that there would be less incentive to cut computer prices. A third approach is to revise the commission structure so that salespeople can earn more by pushing the higher-margin accessories and software lines. This discussion shows that a review of the contribution margins produced by different product lines can be very helpful for sales managers.

Table 15-5   Expense Analysis by Product Line, Bear Computer Company, 1997

Product	1997 Sales (000)	CGS and Commission $	CGS as a Percentage of Sales	Contribution Margin	Contribution Margin Percentage
Computers	$18,200	$12,740	70	$5,460	30
Accessories	5,200	3,120	60	2,080	40
Software	2,600	520	20	2,080	80
Total	$26,000	$16,380	63%	9,620	37%

▶ EVALUATING SALESPEOPLE

One of the most difficult tasks you will face as a sales manager is evaluating the performance of salespeople under your control. While appraisals are opportunities to motivate salespeople to higher levels of achievement, at the same time they provide evidence for disciplinary action. Thus performance reviews demand that sales managers play the role of coach and judge. One consultant has said, "I'm not aware of a single company happy with the performance appraisal process.[4]

Why Are Performance Reviews Needed?

Performance reviews are usually conducted on an annual basis.[5] Although these reviews are difficult to administer, they do provide valuable information for staffing decisions. In your role as sales manager, you will be continually asked to decide:

- Who should receive raises, bonuses, and prizes?
- Who should be hired and promoted?
- Who needs retraining?
- What subjects should be emphasized in training classes?
- How should sales territories be adjusted?
- Who should be terminated?

Each of these decisions requires you to look at a slightly different set of evaluative criteria. Moreover, there are a wide variety of procedures to measure how well salespeople are performing on each dimension.

Behavior versus Output Performance Measures

Although behavior control systems are more widely used than output measures, there is considerable debate as to which approach is better. A model highlighting the differences between input- and output-based systems is shown in Figure 15-2. Managers who supervise salespeople who sell cigarettes, pharmaceuticals, and alcoholic beverages are paid salaries and supervisors focus on input measures of performance. For these salespeople, number of calls, demonstrations, and displays erected are key

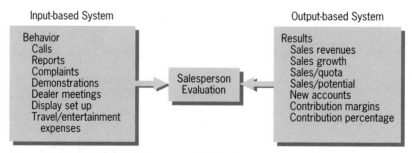

Figure 15-2: A Model of Salesperson Evaluation

success factors. On the other hand, managers who direct stockbrokers, insurance, and real estate agents who are paid on commission tend to emphasize output measures. Despite these preferences, neither group relies exclusively on input or output measures of performance. Sales jobs are multidimensional, and comprehensive evaluation systems must include multiple criteria. Thus your dilemma is how to select and balance a set of input and output factors that will lead to the best results for your organization. Our discussion of this issue begins with a review of input or what we call behavioral measures of performance.

▶ BEHAVIOR-BASED EVALUATION

Behavioral systems are concerned with keeping track of what happens at each stage of the sales operation. This means that management must closely monitor sales force activities and direct and intervene to improve customer relations. For example, Swissôtel reviewed the activities of their ten U.S. salespeople to see how they were allocating their time and how many calls they were making per week.[6] The hotel company found that salespeople were spending too much time in the office preparing proposals and expense accounts instead of talking to customers. Swissôtel set a new goal of six calls per day and they expected their people to spend 80 percent of their time in direct customer contact. To help make salespeople more efficient, they equipped them with cellular phones and laptop computers to give up-to-the-minute inventory of hotel rooms. This provides salespeople with the information needed to close calls on the spot.

Behavior-based systems usually require managers to make some subjective evaluations about individual salespeople. The most common qualitative factors used in these performance evaluations are given in Table 15-6. Note that factors such as communication skills, attitude, initiative, and appearance can only be judged using subjective interpretations and rating scales. This may introduce problems of bias,

Table 15-6   Qualitative Bases Used in Sales Force Evaluation

Base	Percent Using	Performance Measure	Percent Using
Communication skills	88%	Time management	63%
Product knowledge	85	Cooperation	62
Attitude	82	Judgment	62
Selling skills	79	Motivation	61
Initiative and aggressiveness	76	Ethical/Moral behavior	59
Appearance and manner	75	Planning ability	58
Knowledge of competition	71	Pricing knowledge	55
Team player	67	Report preparation and submission	54
Enthusiasm	66	Creativity	54

Source: Donald W. Jackson, John L. Schlacter, and William G. Wolfe, "Examining the Bases Utilized for Evaluating Salespeoples' Performance," *Journal of Personal Selling & Sales Management*, Vol. 15, No. 4 (Fall 1995), p. 63.

halo effects, and credibility into the evaluation process. Despite these limitations, behavioral systems are thought to produce a number of desirable benefits.

Behavior-based evaluation procedures can lead to knowledgeable and expert salespeople who are more committed to the organization. Also, salespeople tend to be self-motivated and react favorably to peer recognition. With behavior systems, salespeople can be expected to spend more time planning their calls and on sales support activities. Finally, behavioral measures encourage salespeople to achieve company goals and better serve the needs of customers.

Support for behavior reviews is shown by a survey of 144 sales executives from a cross section of industries.[7] The managers were asked a variety of questions on behavioral and outcome-based systems. The most interesting finding was a positive relation (+0.17) between the proportion of salary in the compensation system and the achievement of sales objectives. This suggests that a high proportion of wages usually associated with behavior systems produces better results than the high commissions associated with outcome-based plans. These results must be tempered with the knowledge that they reflect the opinions of sales managers rather than the preferences of field salespeople. When 249 salespeople were surveyed, 93 percent said they preferred pay raises over the recognition awards commonly used with behavioral systems.[8]

Another study supporting the value of behavior measures compared activities of top quartile insurance agents with bottom quartile agents.[9] The most successful agents were more likely to be able to leverage their time by having customers deal with other agency personnel, were more willing to spend money beyond the office expense allowance, adopted a numbers approach to setting goals, and were more likely to have employees who could sell back them up when they were out of the office.

Using Behavior-based Systems

Successful implementation of behavioral evaluations requires periodic analysis of data on sales force activities. One popular way to gather this information is through the completion of daily, weekly, or monthly *call reports* by salespeople. These reports detail who was called on, at what stage the prospect is in the sales cycle, and what follow-up activities are needed in the future. Some managers use the 10-3-1 rule that says that for every 10 qualified prospects, 3 will entertain a proposal and 1 will become a customer. By monitoring three key databases, a lead log, a proposal log, and an order log, managers can see how reps are moving leads through the sales cycle.

Firms that do not watch sales force activities can create serious evaluation problems. One company gave its salesperson-of-the-year award to a rep that didn't close any new accounts and lost 40 percent of his old customers. Although this person produced high sales revenues by closing a few existing customers, he was not positioned for the future because he did not have any new prospects to move into the proposal stage. BellSouth managers use ACT!, activity management software developed by Symantec, to help keep track of their salespeople.[10]

A recent innovation is to have salespeople record call data directly on notebook-sized computer screens. Call report forms are presented on the screen, and salespeople make their entries with a pen or keyboard. Pharmaceutical salespeople, for example, have doctors sign their names directly on the screens to request product samples. At the end of the day, reps call in with a modem and information is forwarded to central computers for processing. This speeds the collection of field data and simplifies filling of customer requests for samples, brochures, and merchandise. A side benefit of using notebook computers for call reports is that the machines have built-in clocks. This allows you to monitor field activities to make sure that reps actually make the calls they are reporting.

Management by Objectives   A common behavioral system is *management by objectives* (MBO). With this method, salespeople and sales managers jointly set personal development goals for the subordinate that can be completed within a specific time period. Salespeople then develop an action plan to reach each goal. Written performance appraisals are presented to salespeople during review sessions with sales managers. Reps react favorably to MBO systems because they can see where they stand and know that progress toward their goals will be rewarded.

Although MBO systems work well for some firms, they are not without problems. One issue is that some sales force goals do not lend themselves to expression in quantitative terms. This problem is particularly serious with technical reps when the job often involves problem solving. Also, MBO goals can sometimes become ceilings that salespeople refuse to exceed. Perhaps the biggest weakness of MBO systems is that they require a lot of sales manager time. Implementation of an MBO control system can take a week per subordinate per year. Thus a manager supervising 12 salespeople would spend three months a year on this activity alone.

Behavioral Observation Scales   An improvement on MBO is an approach called *behavioral observation scales* (BOS), which focuses on identifying a list of critical incidents that lead to job success. Salespeople, their superiors, and customers can provide inputs for this task. The key job behaviors that are identified can then be grouped together to form job dimensions. Next, five-point scales are attached to each activity. The behavioral scales that result can be used by regional or district sales managers to measure the frequency with which subordinates engage in critical behaviors.

Scores on scale items are totaled, and categories for adequate, good, excellent, and superior performance are set by management. Use of BOS allows regional managers to measure the personal interaction skills of their district sales managers. Good people skills are often the difference between success and failure among field sales employees. Research has shown that 95 percent of failed managers are weak in this area,[11] and BOS is a good way to identify these problems.

The use of BOS is less time-consuming for sales managers than MBO systems. The main problem with BOS is the expense entailed in preparing the rating scales, and this is not something that is best done by field managers. Also, separate job dimensions and critical incidents must be developed for each level and type of sales job.

Table 15-7   Measuring Sales Force Output for Bear Computer Company

	1	2	3	4	5	6	7	8
Territory	Sales '96 Jan–Sept (000)	Sales '97 Jan–Sept (000)	Dollar Change	Sales Growth	Market Potential Index (percent)	Sales Quota (000)	Percentage of Quota Achieved	Sales Variance (000)
Jones	$ 750	$ 825	+ $75	10.0%	26%	$ 943	87%	−$118
Smith	500	570	+ 70	14.0	15	543	105	+ 27
Brown	1025	1110	+ 85	8.3	32	1160	96	− 50
West	960	1000	+ 40	4.2	27	977	102	+ 23
	$3235	$3505	+$270	8.3%	100%	$3623		

▶ RESULTS-BASED EVALUATIONS

An example of a sales results system employed by Bear Computer Company is shown in Table 15-7. The figures are broken out by territory so that the manager can evaluate the performance of individual salespeople. Columns 1 and 2 show year-to-date sales volumes for 1996 and 1997. Note that Brown and West had the highest sales, with Brown also producing the largest dollar increase. When these changes are converted into percentages, we see that Smith had the best sales growth, followed by Jones (column 4). Up to this point, the figures suggest that Brown ranked number one on revenues, and Smith showed the best sales improvement.

Differences in Potential

One problem with the results-based sales figures given in columns 1 through 4 (Table 15-7) is that they do not adequately measure conditions faced by salespeople in the field. Thus the sales outputs we have observed may simply reflect differences in the size of the territories. This suggests that sales results need to be compared with the potential available in each territory.

Bear's sales potential for the four areas can be estimated from published industry figures, from the *Survey of Industrial Purchasing Power*, or from *Census of Business* data. A detailed discussion of ways to estimate potential was covered in Chapter 7. Once you have reliable measures of potential, the next step is to convert these numbers into sales quotas. For example, Jones has 26 percent of the sales potential in the area (column 5, Table 15-7). Since Bear expected district sales to increase 12 percent to $3,623,000 ($3,235,000 × 1.12 = $3,623,000), the sales quota for Jones would be 0.26 × $3,623,000 or $942,812. Similar calculations can give sales quotas for each territory with actual sales results.

Sales to Quota

Dividing actual territory 1 sales of $825,000 by the quota of $942,812 shows that Jones was only producing 87 percent of company expectations (column 7, Table 15-7). Also, Brown has not achieved his quota even though he has the largest potential of all (32 percent). West, which had the lowest dollar increase, was still able to sell 102 percent of his quota. Thus, two territories with large dollar increases in computer sales actually were the two weakest territories when sales were related to potential. The best performance was achieved by Smith, who had the smallest potential in the division and was third in terms of dollar sales growth. These results suggest that you should consider rewarding Smith with some of the accounts from Brown. This change may increase total sales of the division, since Brown is apparently not covering this large market adequately.

The figures in Table 15-7 also indicate that Jones needs further review. Jones achieved a 10 percent sales increase, which is better than the average for the division. However, computer sales are still $118,000 below potential (column 8). One possible explanation is Jones is new to the territory and has not had time to develop the area properly. Perhaps the area has a history of poor sales because of competitive pressure, or Jones is poorly trained and needs additional coaching from you. These examples suggest that a careful analysis of territorial sales data can help in addressing problems that are beneath the surface of performance results.

Contribution-based Evaluations

Measuring salespeople on the basis of the *profit contribution* that results from their activities is often a useful exercise for sales managers. An example of a contribution profit review for Bear Computer Company is shown in Table 15-8. The analysis begins with net sales for each territory, from which the cost of goods sold and sales commissions are subtracted. This gives a *dollar contribution margin*. Note that Brown had the highest dollar margin. However, when the dollar contributions are divided by sales to give a *contribution margin percentage*, West had a 34 percent margin, compared with only 32 percent for Brown. Brown is apparently pushing a mix of items with low markups or is possibly cutting prices to gain sales volume.

Table 15-8   Measuring Territory Profit Output for Bear Computer Company

	Territory Performance (thousands)[a]			
	Jones	Smith	Brown	West
Net Sales	$825	$570	$1100	$1000
Less CGS and commissions	495	428	754	660
Contribution margin	330	142	356	340
CM as a percentage of sales	40%	25%	32%	34%
Less direct selling costs				
Sales force salaries	55	35	55	65
Travel	15.5	4.1	3.5	5.0
Food and lodging	12.5	4.0	3.2	4.5
Entertainment	11.4	.3	.5	1.0
Home sales office expense	4.5	2.3	2.0	4.5
Profit contribution	$231.1	$ 96.6	$291.8	$260.0
PC as a percentage of sales	28%	17%	26%	26%

[a]Sales figures are from Table 15-7.

Trading Profits for Revenues   The disadvantages of trading profits for volume can be clearly seen by looking at the performances of Jones and Smith. Jones appears to be selling high-profit products at list prices to generate an impressive 40 percent margin. On the other hand, Smith is cutting prices, leaving only a 25 percent contribution margin. These results help explain the sales figures reported in Table 15-7. This earlier analysis showed that Smith achieved a 14 percent sales growth and produced 105 percent of quota. The information in Table 15-8 suggests that the results were related to Smith's selling strategy—offering low prices and pushing low-markup items. On the other hand, the high prices charged by Jones resulted in slower sales growth, and Jones attained only 87 percent of the planned sales quota.

An analysis of the direct selling expenses in the four computer sales territories provides another view of the results of individual efforts (Table 15-8). Even though West had the second-highest contribution margin percentage, he was tied with Brown on net profit contribution as a percentage of sales (26 percent). The reason is that Brown kept direct selling expenses to 6 percent of sales, while these expenses ran 8 percent of sales in West's territory. Part of the problem was that West was paid more than anyone else. In addition, West's expenses for travel, food, and entertainment were relatively high. If these could be reduced to the level achieved by Brown without hurting sales, West's profits would improve substantially.

Buying Customers   Another profitability issue is raised by the activities of Jones. Jones produced a contribution margin that was 6 percent higher than that produced by any other territory (Table 15-8). However, the profit contribution of 28 percent was only 2 percent more than that generated by Brown and West. The explanation for the failure to push this advantage through to the bottom line lies in the various expense categories. Although Jones's salary ($55,000) seems reasonable, the amounts spent on travel, food, lodging, and entertainment appear to be excessive. While salespeople in the other three territories averaged $11,500 for these expenses, Jones spent $43,900. The typical response of a sales manager to expenditures of this size would be to pressure the salesperson to cut back so that the profit contribution would increase. However, the issue of how much control managers should place on sales expenses is a very delicate one. Salespeople need to spend enough to get the sale, but not so much that profits are reduced. Sometimes it pays to entertain customers. For example, a study revealed that the most successful insurance agents were those who exceeded their office expense budgets.[12] Thus Jones's success may be due to his ability to wine and dine clients. On the other hand, it is possible that Jones is using his expense account to offer customers under-the-table discounts on the computers. If these travel, food, and entertainment expenditures are legitimate, the manager might consider asking the other salespeople to spend more on these items.

► USING MODELS FOR EVALUATION

Most sales managers use both behavioral and outcome-based factors. This combination approach allows them to appraise more effectively the multidimensional nature of the field sales job. There are several evaluation models that allow you to review different aspects of selling at the same time.

Four-Factor Model

Perhaps the simplest sales force evaluation model includes just four measures of performance. Individual input is gauged by the number of days worked and the total number of calls made. The output of the salesperson is measured by the number and average size of orders. These factors are combined to give the following equation:

$$\$ \text{ Sales } = \text{Days worked} \times \frac{\text{Calls}}{\text{Days worked}} \times \frac{\text{Orders}}{\text{Calls}} \times \frac{\text{Sales }\$}{\text{Orders}}$$

The *four-factor model* indicates that sales can be increased by working more days, making more *calls per day*, closing more sales with customers, and increasing the *sales per order*. If a salesperson is not generating sufficient volume, then the problem must be a deficiency in one or more of these areas. The model has to be used with caution because of the interactions among the factors. Calls, for example, have a positive correlation with sales but often have a negative relationship with sales per order. This means that even though sales increase as you make more calls, at some point the size of the order begins to decline, as there is less time to spend with each customer. Thus there appears to be an optimum number of sales calls for each salesperson that will maximize profits.

An example of the four-factor model is presented in Table 15-9. The data show that Pete's sales were about average for a salesperson in 1996 and Ann's were a little low.[13] However Ann worked more days, made more calls, had lower expenses, and landed more orders. As a result, Smith made one more call per day and had a 50 percent *batting average* (orders per calls). Although Jones closed the sale on only 40 percent of his calls, he had a high *average order size*. Thus, despite lower values for days worked, calls per day, and batting average, Jones obtained larger orders and a higher total sales volume.

Table 15-9   Evaluating Performance Using Behavior and Outcome Data

Performance Factors	Pete Jones	Ann Smith
Sales (annual)	$1,400,000	$1,100,000
Days worked	210	225
Calls	1,200	1,500
Orders	480	750
Expenses	$19,000	$14,900
Calls per day	5.7	6.7
Batting average (orders per calls)	40%	50%
Sales per order	$2,916	$1,466
Expenses per call	$15.83	$9.93
Expenses per order	$39.58	$19.86
Expenses as % of sales	1.35%	1.35%

In this case, a sales manager might be tempted to encourage Ann Smith to increase the size of her average order. Larger orders should increase total sales, but would result in fewer and longer sales calls and possibly a reduction in her batting average. Fewer calls per day produced larger orders in Jones's territory, but it is not clear that this strategy would work as well for Smith. Also, Pete's expenses are $3,000 above industry averages in 1996 and Ann's are below average.[14] Jones's expenses are also sharply higher than Smith's when expressed on a per-call or order basis. However, *expenses as a percentage of sales* were the same for both representatives. Sales managers must often suggest different selling strategies to account for differences across territories.

Ranking Procedures

A second way to combine sales force evaluations is to use *ranking procedures*. Rankings can be added up to give an overall measure of efficiency. For example, Table 15-10 shows how five salespeople ranked on 10 different input/output factors. The first factor used to evaluate performance is sales per person. Although this variable is a good overall measure, it can be deceiving. Note that Ford, for example, had the highest total sales but was last on sales to potential, suggesting that this high volume was due to a large territory. Gold, on the other hand, had low volume and high *sales to potential*, indicating good coverage of a limited market.

Sales to quota shows a salesperson's ability to increase revenue, and Mann was the best on this factor. Sales per order is important to some firms because they have found that small orders are unprofitable. Ford, for example, achieved a high sales volume by making a large number of calls and selling small amounts to each customer. Gold had the best batting average, ranking first on the ratio of orders to calls. The gross margin percentage achieved by the salespeople shows how well they control prices and sell the right mix of products. The data suggest that Ford's low margins were the result of price-cutting to increase the *number of accounts* and boost sales. Ford was also weak on the behavioral factors measuring the number of reports turned in and expense control.

Table 15-10   Ranking Salespeople on 10 Input/Output Factors

Ranking Factors	Ford	Bell	Shaw	Mann	Gold
Dollar Sales	**1**	2	3	4	5
Sales to Potential	5	3	4	2	**1**
Sales to Quota	5	4	2	**1**	3
Sales per Order	5	**1**	4	3	2
Number of Calls	2	5	**1**	3	4
Orders per Call	4	2	5	3	**1**
Gross Margin Percent	5	**1**	3	4	2
Direct Selling Costs	4	3	5	**1**	2
New Accounts	**1**	4	2	5	3
Number of Reports Turned In	4	3	**1**	5	2
Total of Ranks	36	28	30	31	25

The performance of the five salespeople varied widely across the 10 factors in Table 15-10, and each person ranked first on two criteria and last on at least one factor. When the rankings are added to give an overall measure of performance, Bell, Shaw, and Mann had total scores close to 30, the expected value. However, Ford's score of 36 and Gold's score of 25 suggest that these two representatives require special attention. Although Ford had the best sales volume, he had the poorest scores on four other factors and the weakest overall record. Gold, on the other hand, was doing a good job despite low total sales. The most obvious change suggested is to shift some of Ford's territory to Gold, giving Gold more to do and providing better coverage for some of Ford's customers. Also, Ford should be encouraged to work for larger orders and told to stop cutting prices.

Summing the ranks of the factors in Table 15-10 provides a rough indication of the performance levels of salespeople, but it has some disadvantages. Perhaps the biggest weakness is that it assumes that all 10 criteria are equally important. This is rarely the case, however, since firms may be looking for sales growth at one point in the business cycle and profits at another.

Performance Matrix

Deficiencies of the four-factor model and ranking procedures have led to the development of a new *performance matrix* [15] shown in Figure 15-3. The diagram was constructed

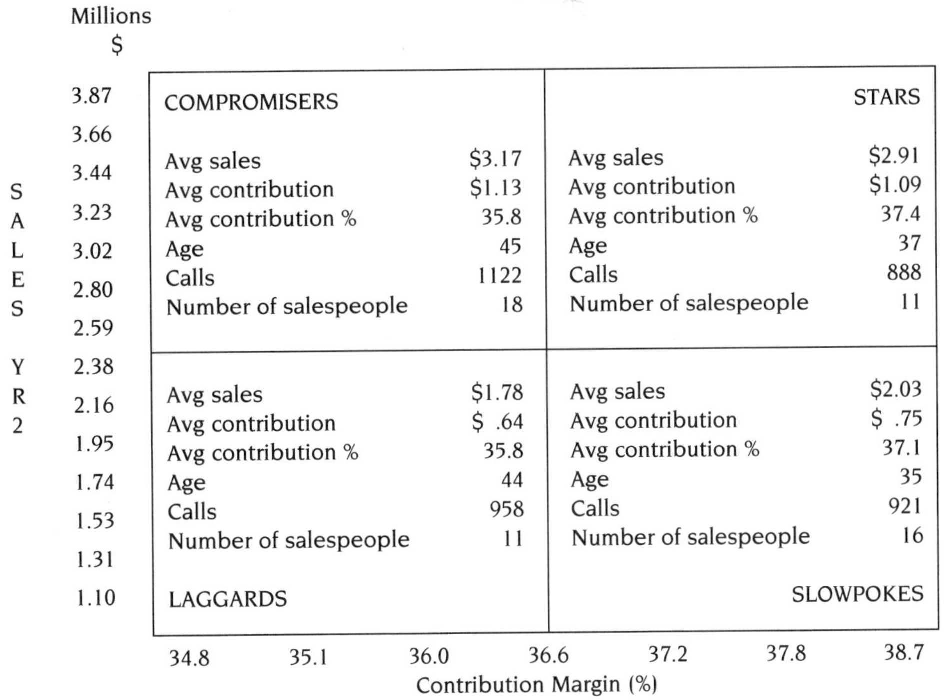

Millions
$

		COMPROMISERS			STARS
S	3.87				
A	3.66	Avg sales	$3.17	Avg sales	$2.91
L	3.44	Avg contribution	$1.13	Avg contribution	$1.09
E	3.23	Avg contribution %	35.8	Avg contribution %	37.4
S	3.02	Age	45	Age	37
	2.80	Calls	1122	Calls	888
Y	2.59	Number of salespeople	18	Number of salespeople	11
R	2.38				
2	2.16	Avg sales	$1.78	Avg sales	$2.03
	1.95	Avg contribution	$ .64	Avg contribution	$ .75
	1.74	Avg contribution %	35.8	Avg contribution %	37.1
	1.53	Age	44	Age	35
	1.31	Calls	958	Calls	921
	1.10	Number of salespeople	11	Number of salespeople	16
		LAGGARDS			SLOWPOKES

| 34.8 | 35.1 | 36.0 | 36.6 | 37.2 | 37.8 | 38.7 |

Contribution Margin (%)

Figure 15-3: Performance Matrix for 56 Building Products Salespeople

by dividing sales force sales and contribution margin percentages into high and low categories. Then averages were calculated for age, calls, and contribution dollars for salespeople falling into each cell. The four cells of the matrix have been given descriptive names to highlight comparisons among different groups. The stars in the upper-right quadrant produced the highest sales and highest gross margin percentages. Slowpokes in the lower-right cell produced good percentage margins but lower sales. Salespeople who fell into the lower-left quadrant were low on both sales and percentage margins. The compromisers in the upper-left cell had high sales and lower contribution margin percentages.

A performance matrix allows you to review and compare the accomplishments of your sales force along several input/output dimensions at the same time. Note that Figure 15-3 includes data on two input measures (calls and age as a proxy for experience) and three output measures (sales, contribution dollars, and contribution margin percentage). In this case, the matrix shows that the youngest building products salespeople are either slowpokes or stars and that the oldest are laggards or compromisers. These data suggest that many reps start their careers by selling a high-margin mix of products and end it by sacrificing margins for revenue.

Data from the performance matrix shown in Figure 15-3 can be used to make a number of managerial recommendations. The 11 laggards represent a plateau problem and therefore are ripe for retraining, redeployment, or dismissal. Also, if these salespeople made more contractor calls, they might be able to move up to the compromiser category. A crucial issue for the building products sales manager is deciding whether to encourage reps to become stars or compromisers. This is a tough choice because although the stars had the highest contribution percentage, the compromisers produced more sales and more contribution dollars. Thus managers looking for dollars would reward the compromisers, and those seeking a higher net profit percentage would reward the stars. After reviewing the data in Figure 15-3, management of the firm changed their compensation plan from straight commission to a salary plus commission plus bonus program to tie sales efforts more closely to the profitability of the different product lines.

This example shows that a performance matrix can provide a useful way to review behavior and the results achieved by salespeople. The matrix is easy to construct, and it neatly summarizes a variety of sales activities in a readable format. With this procedure, the key task for the manager is to select appropriate performance measures for the review process. A copy of the *Sales Manager* computer program that helps you study the relationships among your control factors and prepare a performance matrix is available from your instructor.

Relative Performance Efficiency

Another procedure called the *relative performance efficiency index* uses both inputs and outputs to compare performance to a peer group. This approach employs data envelopment analysis and simulation techniques to prepare a single index of efficiency.[16] Table 15-11 shows a relative performance index of 85 percent calculated for a salesperson selling advertising space to businesses. In this case rep 22 is compared with three other salespeople who had scores of 100 percent operating in similar conditions.

Table 15-11 Relative Performance Efficiency for Sales Rep 22

Variable Type	Variable Name	Value Measured	Value if 100% Efficient	Slack
Output	Percent Quota Attained (%)	100	120	20
Output	Supervisor Evaluation	5	5	0
Output	Sales Volume ($)	45,000	50,500	5,500
Input	Sales Training	5	5	0
Input	Salary ($)	20,000	18,000	2,000
Input	Management Ratio	3	2	1
Input	Territory Potential ($)	60,500	50,000	10,500

Reference Set		Efficiency = 0.85
	Influence	Iterations = 10
Salesperson 7	0.49	
Salesperson 20	0.43	
Salesperson 45	0.08	

Source: James S. Boles, Naveen Donthu, and Ritu Lohtia, "Salesperson Evaluation Using Relative Performance Efficiency: The Application of Data Envelopment Analysis," *Journal of Personal Selling & Sales Management*, Vol. 15, No. 3 (Summer 1995), p. 44.

The analysis is based on a comparison of output measured by three variables relative to the size of four input variables. If salesperson 22 had been as efficient as his peers, he would have exceeded his quota by 20 percent, sold $5,500 more advertising, received $2,000 less salary, had 1 less management support person, and had operated in a smaller territory. The results of the analysis can be used by sales managers to allocate resources and make decisions on retraining. Organizations that pay their salespeople straight commissions to maximize output are rarely concerned with input factors, and relative performance indexes would not be an appropriate evaluation technique.

▶ TQM AND SALES FORCE EFFICIENCY

TQM uses a strong customer orientation, a team-oriented culture, and statistical methods to analyze and improve business processes including sales management. A typical TQM approach groups salespeople into teams to analyze current problems and suggest ways to improve sales procedures. This method includes salespeople in the quality improvement perspective and helps to develop a team orientation. For example, a sales team in Kodak's Chemical Division identified 17 behavioral activities in quality sales calls that were important determinants of territory sales.[17] Sales managers now concentrate sales force evaluation and control activities on the implementation of these behavioral elements. The idea is that continuous improvements in call quality should lead to improved territory sales. Although the use of TQM can improve sales procedures and customer satisfaction, the procedure is not easy to implement in the typical sales organization. The main problem is that TQM focuses on teamwork, whereas most sales force compensation plans reward individual salespeople with commissions based on achieving sales and volume quotas. W. Edwards Deming, one of the founders of the TQM movement, attacks quotas and commissions because they do not focus attention on improving quality or customer satisfaction. One way to solve this problem is to offer salespeople bonuses based on the achievement of quality-related activities. Recommended activities include the following:

- Team participation
- Sales process improvements
- Suggestions implemented
- Customer satisfaction improvements
- Sales opportunities identified[18]

Points could be assigned for achievements in each category, and bonus dollars would then be paid to reward individual or group performance.

► ETHICAL ISSUES

When you focus management's attention on the activities of individual salespeople, you open a Pandora's Box of possible ethical violations. Salespeople are under a great deal of pressure to meet their quotas, and some are not above offering bribes, kickbacks, and lavish entertainment to get what they want. They may even resort to telling lies about competitive products and sabotaging in-store promotional materials. As a field sales manager, you are expected to know when salespeople engage in these activities and how to control them.

Another area for abuse is the awarding of bonuses and salary adjustments to individual salespeople for outstanding performance. Since these awards are often based on subjective evaluation of qualitative factors, it is common for sales managers to give their friends rewards in excess of what they deserve. Firms that base these financial adjustments on objective criteria are more likely to avoid these abuses.

A perennial problem area with field reps is expense account cheating. This issue is so pervasive that it has almost become an acceptable part of the sales culture. The fact that some firms allow a certain amount of expense account cheating makes it difficult or impossible to set standards that are enforceable.

► SUMMARY

Sales force evaluation is a process that compares goals with accomplishments. The most common approach breaks out sales by territories, products, units sold, and customers. However, sales figures do not tell the whole story; you must also evaluate selling expenses and margins. An effective expense analysis will show whether salespeople are wasting company travel funds or cutting prices to boost their commission income. Our discussion has shown that the evaluation of salespeople is an essential but tricky task. You want to be able to motivate reps to higher levels of achievement while at the same time judging them on their accomplishments. Some firms evaluate salespeople on behavioral activities that lead to sales, while others focus on factors that measure results. Most sales managers use both input and output criteria to assess the multidimensional character of sales jobs. Ranking procedures, performance indexes, and performance matrices can be used to combine control factors to show overall effects and interactions more clearly.

▶ KEY TERMS

Average order size	Input factors
Batting average	Management by objectives (MBO)
Behavioral systems	New accounts
Behavioral observation scales (BOS)	Number of accounts
Call reports	Output measures
Calls per day	Performance matrix
Contribution margin percentage	Profit contribution
Dollar contribution margin	Ranking procedures
80–20 principle	Relative performance efficiency index
Evaluation	Sales growth
Expenses as a percentage of sales	Sales per order
Four-factor model	Sales to potential
Iceberg principle	Sales to quota

▶ REVIEW QUESTIONS

1. Explain the 80–20 and iceberg principles used in sales performance analysis.
2. How can a company's sales go up while its market share is declining?
3. Why are market potential figures important in the evaluation of salespeople?
4. Of what value is a breakdown of sales by products, units, territories?
5. What expenses are relevant in an analysis of field sales performance?
6. What criteria do sales managers use to evaluate sales performance?
7. How can you judge performance and motivate salespeople to work harder at the same time?
8. What is the difference between input and output measures of performance?
9. Why are behavioral systems important? When are they used?
10. What is the chief disadvantage of MBO?
11. What are the advantages and disadvantages of BOS?
12. What is the difference between sales to potential and sales to quota? Why do some firms use both?

▶ PROBLEMS

1. The CEO of Vanstar Corporation found that one of his top sales reps came to the office early every morning and called customers' voice mail and left messages with her opening ideas for them for the day. When she called later, the customers always took her calls

personally to respond to the ideas she had left on their machines. Should the CEO incorporate this activity in the company's sales performance evaluation system? How would you measure performance on this activity?

2. To help improve sales performance, some sales managers are asking their reps to become certified. This involves taking some courses prepared by Sales & Marketing Executives International and passing a written test. Do you think these activities are worthwhile?

3. Research shows that a sales call can cost $220 and is rising at a rate of 10 percent per year. Some firms have responded by having salespeople focus on the profit economics of the buyer at major accounts. What does this mean, and how should a firm maintain its contacts with smaller accounts?

4. Merck & Company, one of the largest pharmaceutical companies in the United States, uses a forced distribution of a bell curve to reward its employees. This means that the high-performing reps are paid considerably more than average or below-average reps. The strong emphasis on individual quantitative performance measures has met some resistance from those who believe in promoting group cooperation. Merck has responded to these concerns by offering a 100-share stock option grant to all employees. Staff turnover is running at a low 5 percent per year. How should Merck measure the performance of reps who call on doctors but rarely take orders? Should Merck's plan be used by other firms? Why or why not?

5. Purchasing agents often complain that salespeople are just order takers. In today's increasingly competitive market, purchasing agents prefer salespeople who can talk about technical applications and make suggestions to reduce costs. They also like salespeople who prepare proposals that help the buyer make better decisions. However, most sales managers measure performance by looking at output factors such as number of orders signed. What procedures do you recommend to evaluate more effectively the subjective dimensions of personal selling?

6. A survey of 250 major corporations showed that 77 percent of purchasing agent decisions are based on intangibles such as "I like the people," "They know my business," and "They follow up." How would you measure these factors and build them into your sales force evaluation system?

7. Seminars and demonstrations have proven to be an extremely effective way to sell financial services and computer interconnect systems. However, these systems are expensive, and it often takes 6 to 18 months to close a sale. What criteria would you use to measure the success of seminars? How would you collect and use this information to evaluate your sales force?

▶ EXPERIENTIAL EXERCISES

*Quarterly Sales Review**

Richard Smith is the vice president of sales and marketing for Triton Manufacturers, Inc., which manufactures electric motors. The company has built a large organization in the United States and Canada over the past 100 years. For the past seven years, they have been doing business in Europe. The first three months of the company's fiscal year have ended, and Richard is preparing for the European quarterly sales review meeting.

*Prepared by Professor Camille P. Schuster of Xavier University and Barry Sargeant of Concom Systems.

The *Geschäftsführer* (business leader/managing director), Helmut Schmidt, has an office in Munich and is in charge of two sales managers in Germany, a country manager in Austria, and a country manager in Switzerland. Schmidt is in his mid-forties, was hired for this position three years ago, and is German. For five years before joining Triton Manufacturers, Schmidt worked for another company in the same industry in Canada. Upon returning to Germany, he was hired to replace the person who had been hired for this position when it was created but had not been successful in meeting the company's sales goals.

The country manager in Austria is Michael Wagner, who is based in Vienna. Wagner was originally hired at the same time as the previous *Geschäftsführer* and has been with the company for seven years. He is Austrian born and is in his late fifties. Sales in Austria have consistently been at or about 100 percent of projected sales.

The country manager in Switzerland is Dieder Auffenschweitz, who is German-Swiss and in his late thirties. Auffenschweitz has been with Triton Manufacturers for about two years and has produced a dramatic turnaround in sales. Sales in Switzerland had been poor and are currently above the projected target.

The sales manager for the northern half of Germany is Otto Dietrich, who is based in Hamburg, has been with the company for five years, and is in his mid-forties. He was hired by Schmidt's predecessor in an attempt to boost sales in Germany. The sales manager for the southern half of Germany is Richard Griffiths, who is English and married to a German woman. He is in his late thirties, based in Stuttgart, and has been with the company for two and a half years. Sales in Germany were low before Schmidt took the position as *Geschäftsführer*. Since that time sales have improved marginally, but not at the rate of the industry or at the rate of the competitors. Therefore, Triton Manufacturers is losing market share in Germany.

Helmut Schmidt's assessment of the situation is that he just needs more time and that the Americans don't know how to do business in Germany. His attitude is imperious. He feels in control and believes that he knows best what to do.

The European quarterly sales review meeting will be held on Monday in Frankfurt.

Questions:

1. How should Richard Smith prepare for the quarterly sales review? Who should attend the meeting? What information should he take? What information should he request from the other participants? How long should the meeting last?

2. How do you approach the review process? How do you both congratulate success and stimulate improvement during this process? How should you leave the situation at the end of the meeting?

▶ IN-CLASS EXERCISES

I Know These Sales Figures Stink

At Sara Lee, the large foods company, each district sales manager is required to annually evaluate the performance of each of their salespeople and to hold a face-to-face session with each salesperson to discuss the evaluations. Prior to the meeting, performance results and overall performance ratings are mailed to each salesperson. Both outcome and behavioral measures are taken into consideration in arriving at an overall performance evaluation. Salespeople are paid a salary plus a bonus of up to 10 percent of their salary based on their sales performance vis-à-vis the quota. Salary increases are based on the manager's performance ratings.

This exercise deals with a new sales manager who is conducting an evaluation session with

Jack, a salesperson whose performance she has rated "unsatisfactory." Jack is in his second year in sales with Sara Lee. His first year was rated "satisfactory" by his first sales manager, but no better. Included below are some of the numbers considered in his performance evaluation this year.

Criteria	Jack's Results	Average for the District
Sales to quota	92%	101%
Sales growth	3%	8%
Number of new accounts	5	12
Sales calls per day	13	11
Display setups per day	3	5

When asked how he felt about his evaluation, Jack states, "This is a bunch of bull. I know the sales figures stink, and I'm not happy with them either. I'm saying the sales numbers are not comparable to those of other people because one of my largest customers went out of business last year. It is unfair to compare my sales with a quota set a year ago or with the performance of other reps in this company."

At some point in the discussion, you bring up Jack's poor performance on the other evaluation measures. "Those numbers are meaningless," Jack responds. "Sales volume is the bottom line. If I get the sales figure, the rest of these numbers don't count."

Finally, Jack hits you with the comment, "I want some personal consideration here. An evaluation like this would be the kiss of death for me. What kind of future would I have then?"

Your instructor may break the class into groups to discuss Jack's performance evaluation.

Questions:

1. How should the sales manager respond to Jack's hostile reactions?
2. What consideration should be given to a large customer going out of business?
3. How should the sales manager balance the importance of input versus output measures during the evaluation?
4. Did the sales manager do a good job of supervising Jack and preparing for the performance evaluation?

Be prepared with some answers to these questions and some replies for the manager to give to Jack.

▶ REFERENCES

1. DONALD W. JACKSON, JOHN L. SCHLACTER, and WILLIAM G. WOLFE, "Examining the Bases Utilized for Evaluating Salespeoples' Performance," *Journal of Personal Selling & Sales Management*, Vol. 15, No. 4 (Fall 1995), p. 65.

2. VLASIS STATHAKOPOULOS, "Sales Force Control: A Synthesis of Three Theories," *Journal of Personal Selling & Sales Management*, Vol. 16, No. 2 (Spring 1996), p. 1.

3. DONALD W. JACKSON, JOHN L. SCHLACTER, and WILLIAM G. WOLFE, "Examining the Bases Utilized for Evaluating Salespeoples' Performance," *Journal of Personal Selling & Sales Management*, Vol. 15, No. 4 (Fall 1995), p. 64.

4. *Wall Street Journal* (October 16, 1990), p. 1.

5. MICHAEL H. MORRIS, DUANE L. DAVIS, JEFFREY W. ALLEN, RAMON A. AVILA, and JOSEPH CHAPMAN, "Assessing the Rela-

tionships Among Performance Measures, Managerial Practices, and Satisfaction When Evaluating the Salesforce," *Journal of Personal Selling & Sales Management* (Summer 1991), p. 32.

6. ANDY COHEN, "Movin' Out," *Sales & Marketing Management* (January 1996), pp. 24–25.

7. DAVID W. CRAVENS, THOMAS N. INGRAM, RAYMOND W. LAFORGE, and CLIFFORD E. YOUNG, "Behavior-Based and Outcome-Based Salesforce Control Systems," *Journal of Marketing* (October 1993), p. 54.

8. LAWRENCE B. CHONKO, JOHN F. TANNER, and WILLIAM WEEKS, "Selling and Sales Management in Action: Reward Preferences of Salespeople," *Journal of Personal Selling & Sales Management* (Summer 1992), p. 69.

9. KAY L. KECK, THOMAS W. LEIGH, and JAMES G. LOLLAR, "Critical Success Factors in Captive, Multi-Line Insurance Agency Sales," *Journal of Personal Selling & Sales Management*, Vol. 14, No. 1 (Winter 1995), pp. 17–33.

10. MICHELE MARCHETTI, "Board Games," *Sales & Marketing Management* (January 1996), p. 44.

11. ROBERT TROUTWINE, "Prepare Now and Succeed Later," *College Edition of the National Business Employment Weekly, Wall Street Journal* (Fall 1990), p. 10.

12. KAY L. KECK, THOMAS W. LEIGH, and JAMES G. LOLLAR, "Critical Success Factors in Captive, Multi-Line Insurance Agency Sales," *Journal of Personal Selling & Sales Management*, Vol. 14, No. 1 (Winter 1995), pp. 17–33.

13. *Salesforce Compensation Survey* (Chicago: Dartnell, 1996), p. 20.

14. *Salesforce Compensation Survey* (Chicago: Dartnell, 1996), p. 119.

15. DOUGLAS J. DALRYMPLE and WILLIAM M. STRAHLE, "Career Path Charting: Frameworks for Sales Force Evaluation," *Journal of Personal Selling & Sales Management*, Vol. 10, No. 203 (Summer 1990), pp. 59–68.

16. JAMES S. BOLES, NAVEEN DONTHU, and RITU LOHTIA, "Salesperson Evaluation Using Relative Performance Efficiency: The Application of Data Envelopment Analysis," *Journal of Personal Selling & Sales Management*, Vol. 15, No. 3 (Summer 1995), pp. 31–49.

17. DAVID W. CRAVENS, RAYMOND W. LAFORGE, GREGORY M. PICKETT, and CLIFFORD E. YOUNG, "Incorporating a Quality Improvement Perspective into Measures of Salesperson Performance," *Journal of Personal Selling & Sales Management* (Winter 1993), p. 11.

18. JAMES W. CORTADA, TQM *for Sales and Marketing Management* (New York: McGraw-Hill, 1993), p. 83.

▶ SELECTED READINGS

CRON, WILLIAM, ELLEN JACKOFSKY, and JOHN SLOCUM, "Job Performance and Attitudes of Disengagement Stage Salespeople Who Are About to Retire," *Journal of Personal Selling & Sales Management*, 13 (Spring 1993), pp. 1–14.

GANESAN, SHANKAR, BARTON WEITZ, and GEORGE JOHN, "Hiring and Promotion Policies in Sales Force Management: Some Antecedents and Consequences," *Journal of Personal Selling & Sales Management*, 13 (Spring 1993), pp. 15–26.

MARSHALL, GREG and JOHN MOWEN, "An Experimental Investigation of the Outcome Bias in Salesperson Performance Evaluations," *Journal of Personal Selling & Sales Management*, 13 (Summer 1993), pp. 31–47.

MORRIS, MICHAEL H., RAYMOND LAFORGE, and JEFFREY ALLEN, "Salesperson Failure: Definition, Determinants, and Outcomes," *Journal of Personal Selling & Sales Management*, 14 (Winter 1994), pp. 1–16.

C A S E

15-1 PRACTICAL PARTIES*

George Thomson is employed by the Howard Hills Holding Company, a conglomerate with its headquarters in the UK, but operating worldwide. He has a reputation as a trouble shooter, and has been given a number of assignments in the group where Thompson has successfully carried out turn-round operations on subsidiary companies. Some of these have been acquisitions purchased very cheaply as the companies have been in a state of near insolvency.

Arnold Newby, the group's managing director has invited you to his office to discuss a new assignment. "You are aware of our takeover of Practical Parties about two years ago. We are very unhappy with its performance and would like you to sort it out." This strikes Thompson as surprising, as he knew that the subsidiary concerned is profitable, but Newby goes on to explain further. "We paid a good price for Practical Parties on the basis of its prospects for growth, but to be frank, the growth has not happened. To make matters worse, the executive we put in charge

*This case was prepared by Mark Adams, Mike Easey, and Harry Robinson of the University of Northumbria at Newcastle, England. Copyright © 1991 by the University of Northumbria at Newcastle. Reproduced by permission.

has left suddenly after a major disagreement with us. We thought we had made a major coup in being able to recruit him from another party plan company. All he seems to have done is upset some of our consultants by changing procedures to those of his previous company, and now he says that the growth we looked for is not possible. I would like you to take over from him, produce a plan for growth, and get it started before moving on to a new challenge. It will not be easy, but I know you won't let us down."

Newby explains that if a case can be made for it the group can make investment funds available. He does not expect you to agree to the assignment immediately, but would like your thoughts on how or whether sales and profits growth could be established in the next three years. This is expected in the form of an interim report to be delivered and discussed in only a week's time. To help, Thompson is given a folder prepared by Jane Fraser, a recent Business School Graduate who has worked for Practical Parties for the last year. The folder contains comments and material written by Jane, in addition to photocopies of material she thinks might be useful. On the basis of this material, which follows, Thompson is expected to complete his report.

Exhibit 1: Comments from Jane Fraser

1. Background
   Practical Parties is a successful and profitable company. Its founder worked for another party plan company bringing with him some of the best staff. Unfortunately, sales have been nearly static for the last three years. In fact, after allowing for inflation, sales have declined somewhat.

   Party Plan is a method of selling where a hostess (almost all party plan activities are female oriented) invites friends to her house, light refreshments are provided, and there is the opportunity to buy goods. In the case of Practical Parties, orders are taken and the goods delivered and billed later. This avoids problems of hostesses getting involved with the collection of money and storing goods. The hostess is rewarded with a relatively modest cash payment and a gift from the Practical Parties product range, which can broadly be described as giftware, but has a strong bias to glass and china goods. The hostesses are recruited by Practical Parties consultants, who are paid on commission, and classed as self employed.

   Hostesses are seen as key factors in the success of the company's operations. If a hostess has a wide network of friends and acquaintances then a suitable mix of guests can be found which enables the party to be an enjoyable social and buying occasion. Prior to the arrival of the previous executive of Practical Parties, hostesses received incentives not only on sales made, but also on the number of guests

Exhibit 1: Comments from Jane Fraser (continued)

attending and the number of further parties arranged. A dynamic and expanding network of hostesses, with parties held at regular and appropriate intervals, is the cornerstone of a consultant's success.

In all there are 2500 consultants, of whom about one in twenty are supervisors responsible for a group of consultants under them. These supervisors receive commission on the sales of the consultants under them. They are expected to recruit consultants, and they conduct usually fewer parties themselves than the average for the people under them.

The consultants' role is to demonstrate the product, actively sell gift items, collect orders, and make deliveries. A minimum requirement is that at least one guest at the party agrees to host another party. The consultant is also responsible for recruiting all the hostesses and briefing them on such matters as invitations, refreshments, and the creation of a friendly atmosphere.

The quality of consultants varies considerably. Some consultants produce their own special invitation cards and follow-up brochures to encourage repeat orders independent of the parties. A number of consultants are also agents for other party plan companies and it is suspected that products for these other companies may be sold at functions organized in the name of Practical Parties. Training of consultants is the responsibility of the senior consultants who have themselves often been selected primarily for their sales performance. Training is not standardized, aside from the sales conferences.

Turnover of consultants has recently increased. Some of those with the most successful records have moved to recently started party plan companies undergoing rapid growth. Methods of recruiting more consultants are being considered. With more consultants, there will be more hostesses having more parties, thus giving more sales. Direct payments to consultants to recruit more consultants has been rejected for the time being, as that might be construed as pyramid selling (a form of selling that involves payment for recruiting people who would have to pay fees to join or for stock). This was considered illegal and unethical. Practical Parties was a member of the Direct Selling Association, and adhered to a code of practice which would make sure that it remained a respectable company which did not become involved in dubious practices.

In addition to commission, the company tried to motivate consultants through lavish sales conferences, competitions, and merit awards.

A full-time buyer scours the world for interesting giftware. If we are in the giftware business, perhaps we could consider opening a chain of gift shops using our economies of scale and sourcing knowledge as a distinctive competence. This could perhaps be turned into a franchising operation. On the orders of the recently departed managing director, slightly poorer quality products were being sold in order to at least increase margins if volume could not be increased. This had partly backfired, as it had led to experienced consultants moving on. In the past they had always been able to claim that the company sold reasonable products.

Administration is efficient, with deliveries being accurate and on time. This is made possible with a highly advanced computer operation. The computer manager boasted that the company had records of all the parties indicating who purchases what product, when the product was purchased, and where the purchaser lived. Not much use has been made of this data, but preliminary analysis reveals disappointment with performance in the South-East of England, where it was considered the most purchasing power lay.

Very little advertising is used, as it is deemed inappropriate for this type of operation.

2. The Market

It is very difficult to define the market for Practical Parties. If the market means any product that might be given as a gift, then it means almost any product. However, most of the products are in the china and glass category, and a fair amount of secondary data exist for that.

During the early 1990's retail sales of tableware and kitchenware were valued at approximately £400m, and glassware at around £220m, giving a total of £620m. Both sectors have grown in real terms with tableware growing faster than glassware.

Growth has been attributed to increasing interest in the house, and home entertaining, as well as increases in income. The market was affected by cheap imports in the mid 1980s, but made a recovery.

Since 1990 there have been signs of a downturn due to lower rates of new house formation because of demographic factors, and a reduction in disposable income resulting from higher interest rates for mortgages. As a company we are not sure what the effects will be of the increasing trend to single person and single parent households.

China and porcelain are losing market share to stoneware and earthenware which are cheaper. The glassware market is divided into two categories, hand gathered glass and machine gathered glass.

Hand gathered glass can be either hand made crystal, with a high lead oxide content, or less elaborately cut glass with a lower lead content. Much of the better quality glassware is bought by tourists, especially Americans, and is therefore affected by fluctuations in the number of visitors caused by such things as the variations in exchange rates. Machine made glass is produced for the mass market and everyday use. It is hit at the cheaper end from time to time by petrol retailers using free glassware as promotions. Practical parties tends to sell either lower quality hand made products, or glassware at the higher end of the machine made market.

3. The Competition

If the competition is thought to be organizations selling similar goods, then department stores and gift shops would be considered the main competition. If the "product" is more of the party as a social occasion, then the competition would be other party plan operations, or perhaps other organizations engaged in direct selling.

Direct selling could include such things as direct mail selling and selling insurance door to door. For this reason, statistics from different sources never seem to tally on the total market for goods sold direct.

Overall the direct selling sector is characterized by being very fragmented, with several hundred individual enterprises. The majority of these are very small, and the sector is dominated by a relatively small number of larger organizations. Most of the organizations which sell consumer goods direct, involving personal contact, use party plans. One notable exception is Avon Cosmetics, possibly the largest in personal selling terms, which uses individual to individual contact rather than the groups involved in parties.

The UK market for direct selling of consumer goods involving face to face contact was worth approximately £600m in 1990. The 1980s were characterized by slow growth rates, much of which came from new, smaller companies. Indeed, it appears that all the companies eventually become victims of the product life cycles of the goods they sell, with the company growth slowing as the product category growth slows. An alternative hypothesis is that as well as the advantage of the social occasion, parties need novelty to interest those attending, and once the novelty of a new organization wears off, then the attractiveness of the party also declines.

Brief profiles of some of the chief competitors in various forms of direct selling follow:

Exhibit 2: Profiles of the Major Competitors

Avon

Avon cosmetics is still the largest direct selling company in the UK. The company is a subsidiary of Avon Products Inc, the US conglomerate of New York. It is primarily involved in selling cosmetics and toiletries, and holds significant market share in many product sectors. Avon mainly sell by means of a small catalogue which is regularly changed and updated, although the customer can still sample the products if they wish. The catalogues also features other products such as jewelry items and personal goods.

Rosgill

The Rosgill Group comprises a number of wholly owned subsidiaries which are listed below. It is the largest party plan company in the UK, with a current turnover somewhere in the region of £45m. The company has been quoted as holding 42,000 parties each year, by some 6000 demonstrators. Significantly they appear to be the only party plan company to encourage children to attend their parties, which may well be used as an added pressure to buy.

Rosgill Holdings (Pippa Dee Parties, Dee Minor Limied	Merchandises clothing by direct sales
Pippa Dee International	Jewelry by direct sales
Wanderkurst	Clothing manufacture
Melrose marketing	Consumer goods by direct sales
Matchmaker Parties Ltd.	Housewares by direct sales

Tupperware

Tupperware effectively established the party plan selling method in the UK, however recent years have shown a loss of presence and turnover has fallen slightly. This probably is because plastic housewares are now much more widely available through retail outlets and have lost some of the individual appeal they once had. In response to this, the company has widened its product range to merchandise plastic toys and general household goods.

The company started in the UK in 1960, although it originated in the USA in the 1950s. Internationally in 1996 Tupperware claimed a sales force of 800,000, worldwide net sales of US $1.4 billion, and 97 million attendances at parties worldwide.

The mode of operation remains predominantly Party Plan although it is now far less rigid and "kitchen consultants" are being used for house demonstrations. This is mainly a response to more women working and, as such, attempts have been made to sell the products at places of work. The Tupperware image which launched their initial success is now possibly proving more of a hindrance than a help, for although the company has a huge range of products, it is still strongly identifies with its base products.

Amway

The company is a wholly owned subsidiary of the Amway Corporation and is most strongly identified with the sponsorship and multi-level approach to party plan. The Amway Corporation had worldwide sales of US $6.3 billion in 1995, which marked 11 years of consecutive growth for the organization.

They offer a wide range of merchandise, including household cleaning products, cosmetics, skincare, dietary aids, and jewelry.

Exhibit 3: Practical Parties Consultants

Average number of parties per week per consultant						
0–1	1	2	3	4	5	6+
45%	26%	16%	9%	2%	1%	1%

Interpretation: The table should be read as percentage of consultants arranging a given number of parties, e.g. 45% of consultants arrange on average less than one party a week.

Performance of consultants by length of service		
Length of Service	**% of Consultants**	**% of Sales**
0–12 weeks	4	1
13–18 weeks	8	6
19–24 weeks	12	7
25–30 weeks	12	10
31–52 weeks	15	16
1–2 years	18	25
2–3 years	16	20
3+ years	13	15
Twenty-five percent of consultants leave each year.		

Exhibit 4: Results of Survey of 948 Respondents on Party Plan Attendance

Consumer reaction to Party Plans is difficult to express with any degree of accuracy, given the wide variability in quality of product offerings. Some secondary research, although dated, did indicate that roughly 80% of consumers thought the products were expensive at Party Plan schemes, but over 60% thought they were good value for money. Approximately 90% did feel under some pressure to buy something. The extent to which these finding apply to Practical Parties is unknown.

Percentage Yes response from the survey question "Have you ever been to a party or consultant where goods are sold?"

Base: 948 responses   % Yes response overall = 75%

Age Groups	%	Social Class %		%UK Adults
15–24	69	AB	64	22.3
25–34	75	C1	75	27.1
35–44	92	C2	82	22.5
45–54	81	DE	67	28.1
55–64	74			
65+	58			

Social Class Definitions

A Upper Middle Class: Higher Managerial, administrative or professional.

B Middle Class: Intermediate managerial, administrative or professional.

C1 Lower Middle Class: Supervisory or clerical, and professional, junior managerial or administrative.

C2 Skilled Working Class: Skilled Manual Workers

D Working Class: Semi and Unskilled Manual Worker

E Those at the lowest level of subsistence: State pensioners or widows unemployed, casual or lowest grade workers.

Television Regions

The main Commercial Television Contracts in the UK are awarded on a regional basis

TV Area	Contractor	% Attending Party Plan
London	Carlton/LWT	60
South & South East	Meridian	64
Wales & West	HTV	75
South West	West Country TV	73
Midlands	Central TV	78
East	Anglia	71
North West	Granada TV	75
North East	Channel 3	74
Yorkshire	Channel 3	78
Border	Border TV	72

Exhibit 5: Organization Chart

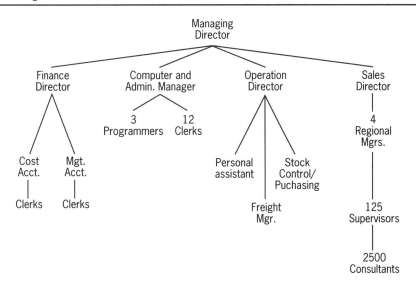

Exhibit 6: Summary Accounts for Practical Parties Ltd (Thousands of Pounds)

	1996	**1995**	**1994**	**1993**
Sales	19379	19808	17629	15395
Commission	6775	6716	6522	6003
Net Sales	12604	13092	11107	9392
Interest paid	50	50	46	38
Sales Expenses	660	587	426	309
Manufacturing and Dist. Exp.	73	81	68	52
Other Expenses	197	183	126	102
Depreciation	420	381	261	222
Advertising	7	11	3	3
Variable Cost	8879	9133	7659	6545
Bad Debt	0	0	0	0
Admin. remuneration	1193	1040	999	943
Total Expenses	11479	11466	9588	8214
Non-trading income	58	50	48	35
Net profit before tax	1183	1676	1567	1213
Exports	0	0	0	0
Fixed assets	1974	2138	1836	1756
Stocks	1892	2004	2403	2399
Trade debtors	0	0	0	0
Other current assets	182	263	192	176
Total current assets	2074	2267	2595	2575
Total assets	4048	4405	4431	4331

Exhibit 6: Summary Accounts for Practical Parties Ltd (Thousands of Pounds) (continued)

	1996	1995	1994	1993
Creditors	1653	1923	1836	1820
Short term loans	96	83	81	69
Other current liabilities	5	0	1	1
Total current liabilities	1754	2006	1918	1890
Net assets	2294	2399	2513	2441
Shareholders funds	1823	2017	2131	2109
Long term loans	471	382	382	378
Capital employed	2294	2399	2513	2487
Ratio Analysis				
Return on Net Assets	51.57	69.86	62.36	48.77
Return on Total Assets	29.22	38.05	35.36	28.01
Operating Margin	6.10	8.46	8.89	7.88
Asset turnover	4.79	4.50	3.98	3.55
Current ratio	1.18	1.13	1.35	1.36
Quick ratio	0.10	0.13	0.10	0.09
Interest cover	23.66	33.52	34.07	31.92
Debt/Equity	0.26	0.15	0.19	0.18
Stock turnover	10.24	9.88	7.44	6.42

CASE

15-2 YORK ELECTRONICS*

York is a medium-sized electronics company that specializes in the manufacture of circuit boards, customized computer chips, and test equipment. The electronic components are sold by company salespeople directly to original equipment manufacturers (OEMs), and test equipment is handled by a second group of independent reps. Bill Hicks was recently appointed national sales manager at York to supervise the company's salespeople and the independent reps.

*This case was prepared by Douglas J. Dalrymple of Indiana University.

Company sales for the Electronic and Test Equipment divisions amounted to $135 million in 1996. Test equipment sold for relatively high prices and made up the major portion of sales revenue. Independent reps were paid straight 6 percent commissions on all York equipment sales in their territories. The volume of test equipment shipments had increased 15 percent the previous year, and Bill was satisfied with the performance of the reps. Also, the reps' compensation plan made it difficult for York managers to direct their day-to-day activities. About all Bill could do with the independent reps was to replace them if they failed to push York's equipment. York's testing products were only one of several lines of equipment carried by these reps.

Exhibit 1: Descriptions of Sales Territories

Territory Number	Salesperson Assigned	Area Included
1	Mary Holmes	Vermont, New Hampshire, Rhode Island, Massachusetts, Maine
2	James Potter	Connecticut, upstate New York (Rochester and east; includes Westchester County)
3	Harvey Stewart	Long Island (Nassau and Suffolk counties), western Pennsylvania (Altoona and west)
4	Jane Thomas	New York City (New York, Kings, Queens, Richmond, and Bronx counties), northern New Jersey, western New York from Buffalo to Rochester
5	Chad Hunter	Eastern Pennsylvania to Altoona, southern New Jersey, Maryland, Delaware
6	Harvey Phillips	Ohio, West Virginia, Kentucky
7	Greg Lewis	Indiana, Michigan
8	Anne Forbes	Missouri, Nebraska, Kansas, Iowa
9	Bill Fredericks	Illinois, Wisconsin, Minnesota, North and South Dakota
10	Sally Smith	California north of Santa Barbara, Oregon, Washington, Idaho
11	Fred Reilly	Los Angeles north to Santa Barbara (includes Santa Barbara, and Ventura counties, and the western part of Los Angeles County)
12	Marilyn Reed	California south of Los Angeles (includes Orange, Riverside, San Diego, and Imperial counties)
13	George Pardo	Los Angeles (most of Los Angeles County and part of San Bernadino County)
14	Henry Dodds	Colorado, Arizona, New Mexico, Utah, Wyoming, Montana
15	Todd Young	Texas, Oklahoma, Arkansas, Louisiana
16	David Wood	Mississippi, Alabama, Tennessee
17	Tammy Cook	Virginia, North Carolina, South Carolina
18	Brad Wolf	Georgia, Florida

Bill Hicks was convinced, on the other hand, that a review of the Electronics Division's sales force would be quite useful. York currently covered the U.S. electronics market with 18 company salespeople. The assignments of individuals and descriptions of their territories are given in Exhibit 1. Electronics salespeople acted as consultants to OEMs and helped them solve product design problems using York boards and customized chips. They were paid a base salary plus a commission and an annual discretionary bonus. Since electronics salespeople did a great deal of developmental work, their base wage amounted to about 60 percent of their total compensation. Commission rates varied from 0.3 to 1.0 percent of sales, depending on the products sold. The highest commissions were paid on items with the largest gross margins. In the past, bonuses had been based on

sales increases, with some attention to profitability. Each salesperson was also given a company car and an expense account to cover travel and entertainment costs.

York's sales of electronic components increased in 1996, but profits were relatively flat. Price competition was intense, and Hicks had been brought in to improve sales force productivity and profits. Bill began his analysis by collecting some performance data on his electronics sales force (Exhibit 2). After reviewing these numbers, he thought it might be useful to calculate some additional control factors such as sales per call, expenses to sales, sales growth, dollars of gross margin, and sales to potential. York measured potential by the number of manufacturers who used electronic components in each sales territory and the value of their finished product shipments. These

Exhibit 2: Sales Force Performance Data

Territory Number	Sales 1995 (millions)	Sales 1996 (millions)	Gross Margin (%)	Calls (1996)	Years of Service	Age	Potential Territory Size in Miles^2 (000)	Total Number of Firms	Total Value of Shipments (millions)	Salary (1996)	Commissions (1996)	Expenses (1996)	District
1	$1.839	$2.214	40%	770	2	32	58.4	1965	$9959	$34,100	$16,500	$4269	1
2	2.398	2.411	38	660	6	40	44.2	1461	10,190	40,150	17,710	7096	1
3	2.497	2.640	33	1250	25	50	16.7	1023	4719	35,860	21,450	9510	1
4	1.509	1.739	36	900	7	34	8.7	2601	10,360	37,950	11,440	15,628	1
5	2.167	2.686	31	678	20	49	46.7	2264	16,287	33,330	22,330	13,027	1
6	1.183	1.190	44	610	3	40	104.8	2286	21,195	33,000	10,450	9785	2
7	2.232	2.431	37	870	12	38	92.9	2465	23,010	33,000	16,610	11,797	2
8	1.561	1.632	45	580	16	46	283.3	1601	14,240	33,000	11,660	22,425	2
9	2.147	2.032	42	630	14	48	334.9	3306	25,600	31,900	18,370	12,014	2
10	2.012	2.621	40	492	3	32	356.3	3329	17,980	39,600	17,380	12,523	3
11	.831	.885	52	600	2	26	4.6	136	540	27,500	8470	4741	3
12	1.658	2.251	28	1030	6	39	16.4	994	4047	33,000	12,100	4938	3
13	1.377	1.146	39	540	5	38	4.0	2127	10,590	46,200	6600	3477	3
14	1.058	1.081	49	480	2	26	662.9	1407	6407	33,000	10,560	14,165	3
15	1.898	3.083	37	460	2	29	427.3	3130	26,280	33,000	12,100	19,431	4
16	1.856	2.578	25	820	5	36	139.1	1603	12,303	33,000	14,520	18,747	4
17	2.090	2.317	23	820	20	50	118.7	2167	18,840	38,500	16,280	9602	4
18	1.224	1.565	39	830	5	28	112.2	2479	13,232	28,050	10,340	25,394	4

numbers were derived from U.S. Census of Business data using SIC codes and territory boundaries. Bill decided to calculate penetration by dividing territory sales by the total value of electronics shipments in each area.

To help with his analysis, Hicks called up the new Sales Manager program that he had recently installed on his computer. By typing SM and hitting *enter*, Bill got a title screen and then a spreadsheet. Down the left side of the screen were a series of numbers to identify 1 to 200 salespeople. The spreadsheet was set up for 22 columns of data across the screen. Twenty of the columns already had headings. Bill entered his 1995 sales figures under the column heading "Sales Yr 1" and the 1996 numbers in column "Sales Yr 2." He noticed that the program automatically calculated a sales growth number for each second-year sales entry. When he typed in gross margin percentages, the program calculated dollar gross margin numbers. Bill then entered the rest of his data in the appropriate columns on the spreadsheet.

The next step in Hicks' sales force analysis was to calculate simple correlation coefficients among his control factors. This was accomplished by touching the F10 key, moving the cursor to "Correlation," and hitting *enter*. The correlations that came up on the screen varied from 0.0 to ±1.0, and they showed the direction and intensity of associations among the performance variables. For example, a strong positive correlation observed between sales and dollars of gross margin (+0.806) was expected because gross margin dollars is simply sales minus the cost of goods sold (Exhibit 3).

Bill was intrigued by the correlations he found among the control factors, and he decided that further analysis was needed. He called up the top menu with the F10 key and moved the cursor to *Plot*. This produced two choices: normal graphs and a performance matrix. He remembered that his business school professors advocated using matrices to evaluate salespeople. When he moved the cursor to "Performance Matrix" and touched *enter*, the program asked him to specify the *y*-axis on the diagram. The program cursor was positioned on Year 2 sales data, and Bill touched the *enter* key. Then the cursor skipped over to the contribution margin percentage, and he hit *enter* again. This gave him a four-quadrant matrix where each salesperson appeared as a yellow diamond. A white arrow on the screen could be moved with the arrow

keys or mouse to highlight data on individual salespeople. By moving the arrow to a yellow diamond and hitting *enter*, Bill got data on each person and summary data on the salespeople in the quadrant.

Once his sales analysis was complete, Hicks had a number of decisions to make. The annual sales meeting was scheduled in two weeks, and he needed to identify the best salespeople in each district and nationwide so that "Salesperson of the Year" awards could be made. He wondered whether these choices should be made on the basis of sales alone or whether he should use some combination of performance variables. The Sales Manager program had a *District* option in the top menu that might help him with this problem. He also had to identify salespeople for retraining and for possible termination. If the data showed evidence of plateauing among his middle-aged salespeople, then changes would be needed to correct this problem. Hicks would have to specify the topics needed to be covered for those picked for retraining. In addition, Bill had $55,000 in annual bonus money that he had to allocate among the electronics salespeople. He was also concerned about whether changes were needed in basic wage levels and commission rates. Another strategic question was whether York had enough electronics salespeople. If extra salespeople were hired, Bill had to decide how old they should be when hired and how much experience was necessary. In addition, he had to decide if the present sales territories needed to be redesigned. A reallocation of the territories would have to consider where to place any new salespeople. The more Bill thought about these problems, the more he was convinced that he needed one of those new computerized territory design programs he had seen advertised. Without a computer program, he would have to draw some maps to analyze the existing territories and plan for possible added salespeople.

Beyond these decisions, Hicks had to make decisions concerning the factors he wanted to emphasize to motivate his electronics salespeople to reach corporate objectives. Bill knew that his goals were unlikely to be reached if he asked his salespeople to improve on 10 different control factors all at the same time. Besides, improving some of the factors conflicted with the achievement of others. What he needed was a short list of prioritized factors to highlight at the upcoming sales meeting.

Exhibit 3: Correlations Among Sales Force Control Factors

	1996 Sales	1996 Calls	Sales/ Calls	Expenses	Exp/ Sales	Exp/ Calls	Years of Service	Age	GM (%)	GM ($)	Terr. Size	No. of Firms	Value Ship.	Penetration	Sales Growth	Commissions
Sales	1.000	.285[a]	.718	.140	-.435	.115	.346	.332	-.666	.806	.000	.353	.389	.279	.637	.738
Calls	.285	1.000	-.430	-.112	-.221	-.492	.499	.371	-.562	-.047	-.583	-.318	-.343	.725	.071	.358
Sales/call	.718	-.430	1.000	.254	-.204	.517	-.079	-.035	-.174	.810	.447	.576	.587	-.203	.611	.355
Expenses	.140	-.112	.254	1.000	.807	.875	.061	-.124	-.021	.174	.428	.369	.359	-.337	.436	-.060
Exp/sales	-.435	-.221	-.204	.807	1.000	.714	-.121	-.302	.379	-.282	.445	.082	.048	-.386	.026	-.412
Exp/call	.115	-.492	.517	.875	.714	1.000	-.120	-.241	.207	.301	.450	.425	.450	-.452	.440	-.147
Years of service	.346	.499	-.079	.061	-.121	-.120	1.000	.874	-.429	.120	.718	-.030	.117	.249	.440	.640
Age	.332	.371	-.035	-.124	-.302	-.241	.874	1.000	-.478	.098	-.216	.057	.244	.180	-.211	.599
GM (%)	-.666	-.562	-.174	-.021	.379	.207	-.429	-.478	1.000	-.117	-.284	-.111	-.125	-.354	-.297	-.430
GM ($)	.806	-.047	.810	.174	-.282	.301	.120	.098	-.117	1.000	.356	.486	.472	.064	.478	.631
Territory size	.000	-.583	.447	.428	.445	.450	.718	-.216	-.284	.356	1.000	.333	.331	-.326	.174	-.075
No. of mfg.	.353	-.318	.576	.369	.082	.425	-.030	.057	-.111	.486	.333	1.000	.846	-.570	.238	.192
Value ship.	.389	-.343	.587	.359	.048	.450	.117	.244	-.125	.472	.331	.846	1.000	-.630	.203	.236
Penetration	.279	.725	-.203	-.337	-.386	-.452	.249	.180	-.354	.064	-.326	-.570	-.630	1.000	.116	.271
Sales growth	.637	.071	.611	.436	.026	.440	.440	-.211	-.297	.478	.174	.238	.203	.116	1.000	.131
Commissions	.738	.358	.355	-.060	-.412	-.147	.640	.599	-.430	.631	-.075	.192	.236	.271	.131	1.000

[a] Correlations of .320 and larger are significant, with a probability of error of <.10.

CASE

15-3 ABBOTT, INC.*

One snowy Saturday in January 1997, Mary Reid was reviewing the performance of her field sales force. Mary was the national sales manager for Abbott, Inc. Abbott produced vinyl siding and plastic plumbing supplies for the construction industry. Their products were sold to 120 distributors in the United States, who made them available to lumberyards, hardware stores, and contractors. The company employed 56 salespeople who worked with the distributors and made calls on contractors, retailers, and architects. Abbott had organized its sales force into five geographic districts headed by sales managers. The five sales managers reported directly to Mary Reid (Exhibit 1). Siding and plumbing fixtures were shipped by truck from company warehouses to distributors and directly to large buyers.

Salespeople were assigned fixed territories and were responsible for increasing sales in their areas. They were given quotas based on potential and past company sales in their areas. Territory performance

*This case was prepared by Douglas J. Dalrymple of Indiana University.

was also measured by the penetration ratio. This ratio compared company sales with published industry data showing the volume of building contracts awarded in each territory. Salespeople who exceeded their quotas were eligible for recognition awards, larger territories, and promotions.

Field reps were paid a straight commission that ranged from 1 to 3 percent of sales. The size of the commission varied according to the experience of the salesperson. In addition, salespeople received an expense allowance that averaged $8500 per year. The five district sales managers were paid a salary and a bonus based on the volume produced in their districts.

Consolidated sales of Abbott, including the overseas division, totaled $355,670,000 in 1996. Although sales were up in 1996, net profits had declined. These results were partially due to increased competition and price cutting. Reid wanted to learn more about her sales force because she was under considerable pressure to improve profits in the new year.

Reid decided to start her analysis by calling up some basic sales force performance data on her desktop computer. These figures are shown in Exhibit 2.

Exhibit 1: Abbott Sales Organization

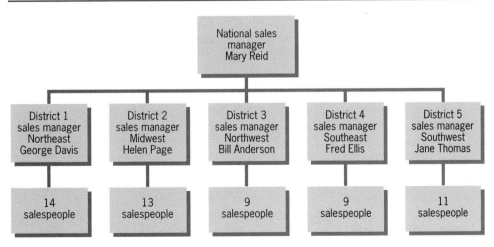

Exhibit 2: Sales Force Performance Data for Abbott, Inc.

Name	Age	Sales 1996 (000)	Sales 1995 (000)	Quota 1996 (000)	Penetration 1996	Calls 1996	Commission per Month 1996	Contribution Margin 1996 (000)	Sales District	Months of Work 1996
Field	54	$3.710	$2.943	$3.548	702	917	$6928	$1318.0	1	12
White	29	2.971	2.070	2.300	419	467	4990	1149.7	2	8
Evans	35	2.927	2.364	2.749	1948	1219	4075	1041.8	1	12
Long	37	2.428	1.773	2.107	315	880	4125	903.8	2	12
Hunt	30	2.298	1.753	1.899	710	1213	4905	854.9	3	12
Reed	32	2.741	2.421	2.879	2820	935	4967	977.0	1	12
Knight	33	2.577	1.948	2.228	527	1096	4198	920.4	5	12
Quinn	36	2.565	2.432	2.847	297	807	4752	961.9	2	12
Reilly	34	2.278	1.684	1.899	957	939	4305	833.8	3	12
Adams	33	1.872	1.308	3.016	338	889	3851	699.4	2	12
Zimmer	37	2.982	2.399	2.649	644	1165	5618	1105.4	3	12
Smith	27	1.669	1.751	2.098	225	780	3250	635.9	4	12
Miller	37	3.589	3.272	3.698	368	1091	6030	1329.2	2	12
Hall	51	3.755	3.322	3.739	306	1181	7107	1366.6	4	12
Vance	29	1.928	2.054	2.391	580	866	3684	698.3	3	12
Martin	27	1.292	.914	1.777	343	1178	3659	465.1	5	10
Sharp	48	3.884	3.301	3.798	1490	1354	6726	1375.9	1	12
Jones	43	3.500	2.836	3.150	1960	1180	6565	1219.1	3	12
Baker	26	2.944	2.256	2.738	571	402	4251	1120.9	2	12
Queen	37	1.945	1.886	2.248	506	492	3402	704.6	2	8
Kelly	35	2.068	1.932	2.141	342	825	4883	759.0	2	12
Lewis	60	1.501	1.295	1.339	448	1199	4466	535.1	5	12
Young	57	2.693	2.067	2.421	1123	806	6070	979.0	1	12
Isom	27	1.551	1.612	1.878	246	832	3137	584.7	2	12
Urban	38	1.099	.716	.962	231	353	3706	387.4	2	12
Green	40	1.262	1.071	1.309	453	1313	3876	468.4	5	12
Scott	67	2.243	2.042	2.767	550	968	5535	793.6	2	12
Norris	33	2.448	2.225	2.558	453	1060	4129	905.5	4	12
Ward	34	2.713	1.567	1.998	267	958	4960	996.7	4	12
Wood	45	2.541	2.670	2.811	873	1260	4918	899.3	1	12
Upchurch	49	2.759	2.583	3.086	365	969	6056	1008.8	4	12
York	65	2.606	2.400	2.697	497	1147	5352	986.7	4	12
Grant	33	2.786	2.400	2.197	441	1461	4279	1009.6	5	4
Taylor	38	2.965	2.174	2.448	1151	1373	5473	1075.8	5	12
Carter	63	3.716	2.704	3.128	1332	1047	6920	1347.0	1	12
Wolf	64	2.384	1.990	2.281	3000	614	6202	835.8	1	12
Olsen	43	2.126	2.050	2.200	455	1173	4240	785.2	5	12
Edwards	47	2.203	1.930	2.600	141	882	5870	818.8	5	8
Summers	32	4.078	2.762	3.183	602	767	6725	1472.1	1	12
Black	53	2.742	2.434	2.682	931	945	5976	998.6	3	12
Allen	38	2.617	2.475	2.898	300	938	3353	968.1	4	8
Owens	32	3.595	3.323	3.848	1861	1135	5339	1346.2	1	12
Day	63	3.358	2.801	3.282	1133	1604	8265	1205.7	1	12

Exhibit 2: Sales Force Performance Data for Abbott, Inc. (continued)

Name	Age	Sales 1996 (000)	Sales 1995 (000)	Quota 1996 (000)	Pene-tration 1996	Calls 1996	Commis-sion per Month 1996	Contri-bution Margin 1996 (000)	Sales District	Months of Work 1996
Parsons	38	1.790	1.842	2.105	203	941	4029	655.9	4	12
Dunn	49	2.596	2.372	2.796	310	1162	5089	927.9	5	12
Thomas	39	1.678	1.571	1.812	907	1281	3136	608.5	3	12
Voss	30	2.192	1.875	2.469	166	673	5824	829.3	4	7
Stone	48	1.879	1.711	2.032	990	1182	5124	679.4	5	12
Zorn	30	2.011	1.739	2.281	243	568	3657	742.2	2	11
Jackson	33	1.903	1.894	2.161	450	840	3790	701.3	3	4
Nichols	36	1.609	1.690	1.898	381	1307	2527	583.3	5	12
Irwin	30	2.631	2.170	2.560	199	697	3803	987.9	2	10
Page	47	3.047	2.939	3.298	806	1200	5846	1099.6	1	12
Cook	37	2.328	2.054	2.398	664	933	4665	859.6	1	12
Walker	39	2.055	2.043	2.399	519	1099	3594	735.9	3	12
Fox	28	3.411	2.689	3.248	3322	706	5335	1187.5	1	12

The territory sales quota, penetration, and contribution margin are given for 12 months, even though a few salespeople worked for less than a year. As a result, Reid adjusted calls and commissions to make it easier to compare salespeople with one another.

Next, Reid transferred her data files to the new Sales Manager program that she had acquired.[1] This program allowed her to create new variables and perform a variety of evaluations on her field salespeople. Reid decided to calculate some simple correlation coefficients among her control variables (Exhibit 3). Age appeared to be related to sales, and there were some interesting correlations with other variables. Reid decided to focus on the most significant associations to see what effects they might have on sales force supervision. Based on a review of the numbers in Exhibit 3, she decided to plot some of the variables using the performance matrix routine in the Sales Manager program.

Abbott's marketing manager had been asking for some recommendations on sales managers and salespeople who could be honored at the national sales

meeting scheduled for February. Reid planned to use the Sales Manager program to rank the salespeople on a national basis. The District subroutine would allow her to rate the performance of the salespeople in each sales district. Although it would be very easy to rank them on sales achievements, Reid wondered if she should prepare some sort of composite index that would evaluate the sales force on a variety of factors.

Reid had recently come across an article in a marketing journal suggesting that salespeople follow a career path that resembles the product life cycle. According to the article, salespeople start off exploring the sales field, go into a development phase, mature, and then experience declining performance measures as they approach retirement. The suggested relationship is shown in Exhibit 4. Note that sales are lowest in the exploration phase, grow rapidly in the development stage, level off in the mature phase, and drop off in the decline stage. Mary wondered whether the career life cycle concept described in Exhibit 4 applied to Abbott salespeople. Abbott employed a variety of sales reps ranging in age from 26 to 67; the median age was 37. Reid thought it would be useful to calculate an age distribution of the sales force to see if there was anything meaningful to be learned.

To help find out whether the career life cycle ap-

[1] Ask your instructor for a copy of the Sales Manager program to help complete your analysis. Some tips on how to use this program are given in Case 15-1.

Exhibit 3: Correlations Among Sales Force Performance Factors, 1996

	Age	Sales	Sales Growth 1993/1992	Sales to Quota	Penetration	Calls	Commission per Month	Contribution Margin Percent	Sales per Call	Contribution per Call
Age	1.00	.21	−.09	.04	.16	.30	.59	−.39	−.15	−.17
Sales	.21	1.00	.22	.45	.39	.17	.76	−.15	.52	.51
Sales growth	−.09	.22	1.00	.64	.08	−.19	.22	−.05	.35	.35
Sales quota	.04	.45	.64	1.00	.19	.03	.34	−.09	.36	.35
Penetration	.16	.39	.08	.19	1.00	.08	.34	−.53	.19	.17
Calls	.30	.17	−.19	.03	.08	1.00	.22	−.28	−.68	−.67
Commission/ month	.59	.76	.22	.34	.34	.22	1.00	−.27	.29	.25
Contribution percent	−.39	−.15	−.05	−.09	−.53	−.28	−.27	1.00	.18	.23
Sales/call	−.15	.52	.35	.36	.19	−.68	.29	.18	1.00	.99
Contribution/ call	−.17	.51	.35	.35	.17	−.67	.25	.23	.99	1.00

Exhibit 4: Sales Force Career Path Life Cycle

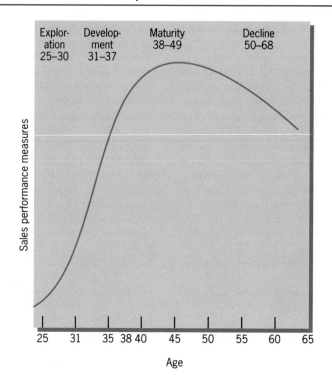

plied to Abbott, Mary decided it might be instructive to calculate the means of various performance factors for groups of salespeople divided according to the career categories described in Exhibit 4. Mary was sure that there was something to be learned about the sales force from the performance data if she just kept her computer humming. The data in Exhibit 2 also gave an indication of the turnover rate in the sales force in 1993, and Reid wondered if some adjustments were needed in the compensation program. Reid was concerned that the results of her performance matrix and career life cycle analyses would require some changes in terms of hiring, firing, training, and motivation.

A In-Class Exercises

► INTRODUCTION

Eleven in-class exercises have been developed for this text. Each in-class exercise presents a realistic sales management dilemma that you are asked to solve. The exercises have been written as an opportunity to address real-life complexities. There is no one right answer, but some solutions are better than others.

Each of these in-class exercises could also serve as the basis for students to develop role plays dramatizing the problem, evaluating alternative solutions, and proposing a preferred solution. Role playing is used extensively in sales and sale management training to give people a realistic preview of what they can expect on the job and to develop skills in handling critical issues. Should you enter sales as a career, you are almost sure to encounter the use of role plays. Experience in developing and participating in role plays should help you in conducting role plays in the future.

The purposes of the exercises are to give you a better overall understanding of sales management, to give you a chance to develop your own ideas regarding sales management issues, and to serve as a basis for class discussion. As with all practical exercises, it is important that all students be familiar with the exercises and develop their own approaches to resolving the main issues of the role play. The purpose of this appendix is to provide help in approaching the in-class exercises in this text.

► PREPARATION

The first step in preparing your solution is to read the in-class exercise and identify the main issue or issues in the situation. Some issues are of immediate concern, while others are more long-term in nature, especially the possibility of establishing a precedent for undesirable behaviors or attitudes. The chapter preceding the role play will often provide additional insight into the general issue under consideration.

The next step is to identify alternative ways of realistically addressing the situation. Several situations will likely occur to you, some fairly quickly. Be careful to evaluate fully the consequences of each solution in terms of potential negative short- and long-term consequences and consider whether the alternative fully addresses the problem in the role play. Be prepared to defend your chosen solution, especially in regard to its realism and the extent to which it fully addresses the core issues of the role play.

If you are asked to videotape a role play of the situation, then it would be helpful to keep the following points in mind:

- Prepare a carefully worded script to guide you through the role play, but do not read from the script during the videotaping of the role play.
- Keep in mind your surroundings for the role play and attempt to integrate appropriate props, such as products and office machines.
- Be sure to check the quality of the sound on the tape before proceeding very far into the role play itself.
- Inject your personality and humor into the exercise.

B   Getting a Job in Sales

Personal selling is often the first job for business students on the pathway to an executive position. All manufacturers and service organizations need qualified sales talent, and they are constantly looking for replacements. You will find sales openings listed daily in almost every newspaper in every region of the country. Although an abundant number of sales jobs are available, your task is to get an offer from a firm that meets your expectations in terms of location, compensation, travel, and opportunities for personal growth.

The easiest way to contact firms that are looking for salespeople is to sign up for interviews with companies through your campus placement office. This allows you to talk with a variety of firms about their sales opportunities in a convenient and inexpensive manner. However, you should realize that for every 30 students interviewed on campus, only three or four will be invited to headquarters for a final round of testing and secondary interviews. Also, the chances are that only one out of four final candidates will be offered a job. Thus, although campus interviews are easy to arrange, competition for jobs is often fierce.

► NETWORKING

Statistics prove networking and informational interviewing to be among the top conduits for effectively locating a job in today's workplace. Off-campus networking has become increasingly important as new job opportunities have moved more to small and medium-size companies that may not interview on campus. Well-informed students and graduates are learning each day the values of networking with other sales professionals, executives, senior executives, faculty members, and others whose daily routines immerse them in the business community.

One thing to keep in mind when networking is that studies indicate that one is most likely to find a job at the third level of networking. The first level of networking consists mostly of people you know right now, while the second level are people that have been referred by the first-level people, and the third level are people to whom you have been referred by the second-level network people. This suggests that you should build a network of contacts by asking people with whom you speak for the names of additional people. It also suggests that you put some time and effort into building your network and not expect to find a job on the first round of interviews.

► DIRECT MAIL CAMPAIGN

To increase the odds of getting the job you want, you may also wish to supplement the on-campus interviews and off-campus networking with a direct mail campaign. The first step in this campaign is to develop a mailing list of firms that you want to approach. Your campus placement office is a good place to look for prospects, as the office will probably have directories, as well as lists of firms that are looking for sale candidates. Also, you may want to target desirable companies whose representatives visited the campus but did not have any openings on their interview schedules. Other names of organizations can be obtained from family and friends who know people in particular firms or work with an organization. Numerous references to specific companies are made in this text and are summarized in the company index at the back of the book. If you have geographical preferences, you should pick firms that are located in the area where you want to live. Once you have a mailing list, you need to prepare your advertising message.

► COVER LETTER DESIGN

Cover letters introduce you to potential employers. Good letters motivate employers to read your resume and subsequently invite you to an interview. Your cover letter expands on your resume and adds a personal touch to your approach. Effective letters present you as a warm, pleasant person who wants to be a salesperson.

Your cover letter should be directed to a decision maker rather than to the nebulous "Dear Sir" or "Dear Madam." There is no reason for a firm to respond to a letter addressed to "Sir" or "Madam." Note that the sample cover letters in Exhibits 1 and 2 are directed to Jane R. Briggs, director of college relations, and C. B. Johnson in the personnel department. When individuals receive letters, there is more of an obligation to respond.

Remember that your cover letters must be customized for each potential employer, individually typed, and personally signed by you. Mass-produced form letters usually get filed in the wastebasket. Cover letters also should be concise, yet have enough bullet points to catch the interest of the reader. The four-paragraph cover letters shown in Exhibits 1 and 2 are close to the maximum acceptable length.

The objective of the opening paragraph in a cover letter is to capture the reader's attention. One sentence describes the position for which you wish to be considered and how you learned of the opportunity. Another states your job interests and career aspirations. When appropriate, you can mention the mutual acquaintance who suggested that you write to the potential employer.

Exhibit 1: Sample Cover Letter for Financial Sales

125 S. High Street
Columbus, OH 43210
333-337-3337
April 1, 1997

Ms. Jane R. Briggs
Director of College Relations
Hewlett-Packard
Palo Alto, CA 94444

Key Points

- Graduating
- Commercial sales
- Financial orientation
- Industry knowledge
- Leadership
- Transcript skills
- Relevant hobby
- Local contact

Dear Ms. Briggs:

In May I will be graduating from Ohio State with a degree in marketing supported by a strong set of courses in finance and computer applications. I am seeking a position in commercial sales which draws equally from my marketing and finance strengths. Your opportunity in calling on corporate financial managers for the purpose of selling financial software and hardware solutions excites me.

Hewlett Packard and other hardware vendors in the computer industry offer a unique opportunity to use many of my skills. My elected leadership activities and involvement in intramural team sports give you some clues to my personality and spirit. My unofficial transcript illustrates the depth and breadth of my skills and interests in your opportunity.

I read several popular computer magazines regularly and have stayed attuned to recent developments in microcomputers and related equipment throughout college. I work part-time at a local computer retailer dealing with everyone from hackers to local business owners.

The enclosed résumé provides detail about my credentials and interests, but I need an opportunity to personally talk to you to best express how I can contribute to Hewlett Packard. If you could put me in contact with a local representative as a shadow for a day, my talents would be clearer. I will call you on Wednesday to see when we might be able to get together.

Sincerely,

Edward R. Bell

Enclosures: Résumé
              Unofficial Transcript

Source: Reproduced with permission from C. Randall Powell, *Career Planning Today,* 2nd ed. (Dubuque, Iowa: Kendall/Hunt).

Exhibit 2: Sample Cover Letter for Pharmaceutical Sales

Apartment 22
Stone Hill Estates
Arcola, FL 2611
407-222-2222
February 27, 1997

Mr. C. B. Johnson
Personnel Department
Professional Pharmaceuticals
Atlanta, GA 30332

Dear Mr. Johnson:

Do you have an opening for a sales representative? With a B.S. degree in marketing and 10 hours of chemistry courses at the University of Florida, I think that my academic qualifications and personality are well suited for a career in pharmaceutical marketing.

Two summers and many part-time jobs in sales-related positions have convinced me that sales is the best entry-level position for me to begin my career as a future marketing executive. I value the freedom and independence that you offer an individual after your training program which I read about in the College Placement Office. Each of my previous employers will tell you that I work hard and thrive under pressure and challenge. Although I have not been active in campus life as a leader because I have had to work to get through school, every work supervisor has expressed pleasure at my enthusiasm to serve customers.
In my last experience at Super Drugs, I worked for a pharmacist and talked with several salespeople who called on us. They all commented on the individual rewards of working in the booming health-related industry. The attached résumé only brushes the surface of my qualifications, so I hope I have the opportunity to elaborate on my credentials in person.

I am willing to work hard, study, learn, and take responsibility. May I have the privilege of an interview? Since we are several hundred miles apart, would it be possible for me to schedule an initial interview with any of your salespeople in this region? I plan to call you within the week to see if something might possibly be arranged. I need a chance to start as a sales representative because I know I can advance on my own merits with Professional Pharmaceuticals. Please call me if you need more information.

Very truly yours,

Mary T. Stuart

Enclosure

Key Points

- Question opening
- Targeted field
- Personal qualities
- Industry interest
- Maturity
- Regional interview
- Will call

Source: Reproduced with permission from C. Randall Powell, *Career Planning Today,* 2nd ed. (Dubuque, Iowa: Kendall/Hunt).

The middle paragraphs of a cover letter sell your credentials to the employer. The idea is to show how your background matches the needs of the job. For example, in Exhibit 1, Edward Bell points to his leadership activities, his readership of computer magazines, and his work in a computer store as reasons he should be hired by Hewlett-Packard to sell financial software.

All sales presentations need a strong and effective close. The last paragraph of your cover letter should ask for the interview. You need to make a positive response easy by presenting alternative interview dates and telling how you plan to follow up. Notice how Ed Bell (Exhibit 1) asks to be put in contact with a local sales rep and says when he will call.

▶ PREPARING YOUR RÉSUMÉ

Employers often receive hundreds of résumés each day, and they spend only a few minutes reviewing each one. This means that your résumé has to be carefully designed if you expect to penetrate the clutter of competitive applicants. Job-focused résumés are more likely to get through the initial 60-second glance than more broadly based résumés. An outstanding example of a position-focused sales brochure résumé is presented in Exhibit 3. This creative résumé features the position description on the cover and shows a picture of Sandra Marinconz making a sales presentation to a doctor.

On page 2 of her résumé, Sandra describes her career goals, education, and activities (Exhibit 3). Observe that Sandra has placed her grades in her major ahead of her overall grade point average. The third page of Sandra's résumé highlights her work experience and her philosophy of success. Notice how well the work data are organized to emphasize Sandra's ties to sales and the pharmaceutical industry.

You should realize that there is no one standard format for résumés. Indeed, most students prepare short résumés for on-campus interviews and develop more creative résumés (Exhibit 3) for off-campus direct mail campaigns. Effective résumés employ large type and plenty of white space to make them easy to read. Heavy-textured buff paper is preferable to white copy machine paper. Often your printer will have some suggestions on what color and weight of paper are appropriate for a power résumé.

▶ RÉSUMÉS THAT SELL

We included Sandra Marinconz's résumé in this section because it was very well received by business recruiters. Sandra actually sent this résumé out and was deluged with requests for interviews. One sales vice president called her immediately after he received the résumé and invited her to St. Louis for a visit to headquarters. Sandra's creative résumé generated a total of six job offers.

What features made Sandra's résumé so effective? First, it was job focused, well organized, and creative (pictures), and it emphasized the match between Sandra's background and pharmaceutical sales. A close reading of Sandra's résumé reveals that her overall grade point average was only 3.1 out of a possible 4.0. Sandra was

Résumé
of
Sandra A. Marinconz

PRESENT ADDRESS
501 D Terry Lane
Bloomington, Indiana 47401
(812) 333-5741

PERMANENT ADDRESS
8802 Branton Avenue
Highland, Indiana 46322
(219) 923-6378

Position Description
PHARMACEUTICAL SALES REPRESENTATIVE

Desire to begin my career in the Health Care Industry marketing a pharmaceutical product line to physicians, pharmacies, and hospitals. Prefer a highly structured training program which combines classroom and field training to fully prepare me to begin a successful career. Would like to eventually participate in the development and achievement of corporate plans and goals. Ambition is to complete advanced sales training programs and advance into a specialty position.

Exhibit 3: (*continued*)

Career Goals

SHORT-TERM GOALS (1–12 months):

- To continue learning and developing
  professional behaviors
- To successfully enter my sales career
  with a desirable and challenging position

INTERMEDIATE GOALS (1–5 years):

- To generate the maximum amount of sales
  and new business within my territory
- To advance either within my sales career
  or move into a sales management position

LONG-TERM GOALS (5 years on):

- To continue learning, developing, and
  sharpening my sales skills to keep up with
  the changing field
- To become an expert at solving problems

Education

College: INDIANA UNIVERSITY SCHOOL OF BUSINESS, Bloomington,
Indiana.
Degree: BACHELOR'S DEGREE in Marketing, May 1994.
Grade Index: 3.6/4.0 in major
3.1/4.0 overall

Coursework includes the completion of 26 hours of Marketing Electives

Activities

ACTIVE MEMBER:

- Indiana University Marketing Club (Promotions Committee)
- Indiana University Student Athletic Board (Revenues Committee)

DEAN'S HONOR LIST CANDIDATE:

- Fall Semester 1992–93

PROFESSIONAL PRACTICE LECTURES:

- Presented the benefits of an internship to Orientation students

VICE PRECINCT COMMITTEE PERSON:

- Registered precinct members to vote
- Helped coordinate community activities
- Attended county conventions

Work Experience

DATES	COMPANY	POSITION/ACCOMPLISHMENTS	SKILLS ACQUIRED
May-August 1993	HALLMARK MARKETING CORPORATION Indianapolis, IN	SALES INTERNSHIP: Detailing, selling and servicing all assigned retail outlets. Assisted with seasonal orders, sales objectives, and current sales programs and promotions.	• Communications • Selling • Analytical • Flexibility • Commitment
May-August 1992	ECKERD DRUGS Dallas, TX	SALES CLERK/CASHIER: Provided quality customer service. Trained new sales clerks. Supervised employees in store manager's absence. Increased the sales of Eckerd brand products.	• Learning Quickly • Managerial Skills • Team Work • Problem Solving
June-August 1990	PEPSI-COLA COMPANY Munster, IN	PRODUCT SAMPLE DISTRIBUTOR: Promoted Pepsi-Cola products in grocery outlets. Distributed samples and communicated sale information to the consumers. Also managed unsupervised working hours.	• Verbal Skills • Creativity • Persistence • Honesty • Self-Discipline

Philosophy of Success

SUCCESS IS . . .

- Never giving up/persistence
- Learning from mistakes and successes
- Assuming responsibility for your own behavior (NO EXCUSES!!!)
- Performing acts without the expectation of immediate rewards
- Putting forth your best effort at *all times*
- Never putting things off

References Listed on Back*

*Sandra listed 4 references on the last page of her résumé. She included: names, titles, addresses, and telephone numbers.

not hired because of her grades, but because she had the skills and interests to get the job done. Does this mean that you should copy Sandra's design when you prepare your own résumé? The answer is clearly no, but you should realize that creativity in résumé design can reap big rewards. We believe that each résumé should be unique so that it highlights the personality, background, and career interests of its creator. Remember that the best résumés are positive, emphasize skills, use action words, stress accomplishments, incorporate buzz words from your field, and use examples to illustrate personality traits. Best of luck with your job search.

KEY TERM AND SUBJECT INDEX

Ability to pay, 178
Account analysis, 183
Account opportunity, 185
Account relationship strategy, 42
Account service/Coordination, 12
Accounts, 124
Acquisition costs, 129
Activity quotas, 495
Administration, 11
Advertising, 5
Advocate, 85, 133
Affordability approach, 302
Age Discrimination in Employment
  Act, 338
Allocation criteria, 422
Alternative choice close, 91
Americans with Disabilities Act
  (ADA), 338
Analyzers, 36
Application blanks, 344
Aptitude tests, 329, 351
Artificial intelligence (AI), 98
Assessment centers, 353
Attitude, 453
Audiotapes, 390
Automobile Information Disclosure
  Act, 234
Awareness, 135

Background check, 349
Balancing territories, 426
Bargaining, 141
Behavioral Event Interview, 347, 349
Behavioral observation scales (BOS),
  571
Behavioral self-management (BSM),
  492
Behavioral systems, 569
Benefiting, 74
Benefits, 86, 541
Best few opportunities, 239
"Bingo" card, 177
Break-even sales volume, 181
Bribes, 230
Build strategy, 36
Buildup method, 423
Business ethics, 219
Business mission, 33
Business portfolio analysis, 36
Buying authority, 178
Buying center, 130
Buying committee, 128
Buying Power Index, 253
Buying signals, 91

Call reports, 570
CALLPLAN, 186
Canned presentation, 74
Career planning, 395
Career Stages, 485
Centralization, 286
Centralized training, 387
Checking questions, 84
Civil Rights Act of 1964, 338
Classified advertisements, 340
Close-ended questions, 84
Closing, 90
Coaching, 452
Coercive power, 447
Cognitive selling scripts, 385
Cold canvassing, 177
Commission, 298
Commission overrides, 387
Commission plus bonus, 537
Commission threshold, 536
Commitment, 137
Commonality, 80
Company culture, 331
Competence, 80
Coordination and Integration, 284,
  287
Competitive position, 185
Complex sales, 87
Contractual relationship, 44
Contribution margin percentage, 573
Conventional morality, 224
Cost per call, 180
Credit checks, 349, 351
Cross-tabulation, 381
Customer based triangle, 40
Customer concerns, 88
Customer satisfaction, 537
Customer-product matrix, 530
Customer specialization, 291
Cycle time, 52

Dealing with dissatisfaction, 48, 49,
  93
Decentralization, 286
Decentralized training, 387
Decision models, 185
Declarative knowledge, 385
Defenders, 36
Delegating style, 449
Demonstrations, 86
Derived demand, 125
Detailors, 54
Differentiation strategy, 35
Direct Inquiry, 176
Direct inquiry directions, 177

Direct personal contact, 79
Direct selling expenses, 229
Directive behavior, 448
Directories, 177
Disengagement stage, 489
Dissolution, 138
Diversity, 354
Divest strategy, 36
Dollar contribution margin, 573
Dollar volume quota, 494
Drug testing, 352

Economic buyer, 131
Effort, 483
80–20 principle, 566
Electronic spreadsheet, 51, 712
Employment agencies, 341
Empowerment, 446
Enhancing the relationship, 93
Entertainment, 231
Equal Employment Opportunity
  Commission (EEOC), 338, 459
Equal opportunity, 422
Equity theory, 485, 491
ERG theory, 485
Establishment stage, 488
Ethics policy statement, 235
Evaluation, 563
Evidence, 86
Expansion, 136
Expectancy, 489
Expectancy theory, 489
Expectations, 140
Expense accounts, 229
Expense analysis, 566
Expense classifications, 50
Exploration stage, 136, 487
Exponential smoothing, 261
Expertise power, 447

Fact-finding questions, 84
Features, 85
Feedback, 496
Feeling-finding questions, 84
Field observation, 348
Follow-up, 92
Foreign Corrupt Practices Act, 280
Four-factor model, 575
Functional specialization, 291

Games, 389
Generic business strategy, 35
Geographic control units, 420
Geographic specialization, 288
Gifts for buyers, 229

Global Positioning System (GPS), 431
Global sales organization, 304
Goal commitment, 496
Goal theory, 495
Golden Rule, 222
Government regulation, 233
Gross margin commissions, 538

Harvest strategy, 36
Hierarchy of authority, 285
Hierarchy of needs, 485
Hiring criteria, 343
Hold strategy, 36
Homans system, 451
House accounts, 229

Incentive program, 498
Incremental approach, 303
Independent sales agents, 298
Individual, 224
Input factors, 564
Instrumentality, 490
Intelligence tests, 351
Intent, 82
Interactive system, 390
Interaction, 73
Interaction phase, 79
Internship, 353
Intuition, 446

Job analysis, 332
Job description, 222, 332
Job qualifications, 335
Job Skills, 10
Jury of executive opinion, 256

Knockout factors, 344
Knowledge, 453

Leadership, 7, 553
Leadership style, 448
Leading indicator, 256
Learned needs, 485
Legitimate power, 447
Low-cost strategy, 35

Machiavellianism, 223
Maintenance stage, 488
Major account program, 292
Major account relationships, 44
Management by objectives, 571
Managing the implementation, 93
Market potential, 252
Marketing mix, 39
Marketing segmentation, 38
Mean absolute percentage error
    (MAPE), 259
Minimum account size, 179
Moment of inertia, 431
Motivation, 483
Motivation-Hygiene, 485

Moving average, 260
Multimedia, 99
Multiple regression, 262

Naive forecast, 258
National sales meetings, 455
Needs discovery, 82
Need recognition, 125
Need—satisfaction presentation, 75
Needs, 178
Networking, 341
New Salespeople, 383
Niche strategy, 35
Nonselling time, 171
Norms, 452
Notebook computers, 98

On-the-job training (OJT), 388
Open systems, 97
Open-ended questions, 84
Organizational goals, 34
Organizational purchasing process,
    125

Partnering selling approach, 43
Patterned interview, 348
Pen computers, 98
Per Diem, 541
Percentage of sales method, 49
Performance evaluation, 129
Performance matrix, 577
Percentage rate of change forecast,
    259
Permission questions, 84
Personal interview, 344
Personal Letters, 79
Personal motives, 83
Personal selling, 5
Personality tests, 351
Phoning ahead, 79
Physical Examination, 352
Planned selling approach, 136
Planning, 453
Plateauing, 457
Point quota system, 494
Possession costs, 129
Postinteraction phase, 73, 92
Power, 447
Precall planning, 76
Preinteraction, 73
Problem—solution presentation, 75
Procedural knowledge, 385
Product Knowledge, 385
Product specialization, 289
Productivity improvement, 74
Profit contribution, 573
Profit-based quota, 494
Programmatic purchasing, 42
Progressive commission rates, 536
Proposals, 127
Propriety, 82

Prospect list, 175
Prospect profile, 174
Prospecting, 173
Prospectors, 36
Pseudoconcerns, 89
Public relation, 95
Purchasing concerns, 173

Qualifying prospects, 173, 178
Quota, 493

Ranking procedures, 576
Reactive selling approach, 42
Real concerns, 88
Recognition program, 502
Recommendations, 352
Recruiting, 329, 339
Reengineering, 52
Referent power, 447
Referrals, 177, 341
Regional sales meetings, 455
Relating skills, 80
Relationship anxiety, 80
Relationship binders, 139
Relationship evolution, 135
Relative performance efficiency
    index, 578
Repeat purchases, 129
Repeat transactions, 43, 44
Results-Based evaluations, 572
Reward power, 447
Reward valence, 491
Robinson-Patman Act, 223
Role morality, 233
Role playing, 389

Salary plus bonus, 535
Salary plus commission, 535
Salary plus commission plus bonus,
    536
Sales budget, 47
Sales force automation, 95
Sales force composite, 255
Sales force segmentation, 616
Sales force strategy, 31
Sales forecasting, 255
Sales funnel, 186
Sales management, 4
Sales managers, 4
Sales Meetings, 454
Sales organization, 6
Sales per order, 775
Sales potential, 252
Sales promotion, 5
Sales promotion "pull", 8
Sales proposal, 87
Sales teams, 305
Sales volume quota, 494
Salesperson development, 395
Satisfaction guaranteed, 74
Search for suppliers, 126

Seasonal forecast adjustments, 257
Selecting prospects, 343
Self-understanding, 446
Selling Aptitude Test, 355
Selling Skills, 453
Semistructured interviews, 348
Sentiments, 451
Sexual harassment, 227, 459
Simple linear regression, 261
Simulations, 389
Single-factor model, 188
Situation analysis, 37, 38
Situation ethics, 224
Situational leadership, 448
Smoothing constant, 261
Social Darwinism, 223
Society, 224
Span of control, 6, 285, 284
Specialization, 288
Specifications, 126
Stability and continuity, 284
Standard Industrial Classification
    (SIC) codes, 254
STARmanager, 429
Stimulus—response presentation, 74
Straight commission, 532
Straight rebuys, 130
Straight salary, 531
Strategic business unit (SBU), 36
Strategic Management Planning, 31, 32
Strategic marketing planning, 31, 37

Strategic partnering, 138
Strategic partners, 45
Strategic partnerships, 45
Strategy, 35
Summary close, 91
Supplier selection, 128
Supporting, 93
Supportive behavior, 449
Supportive style, 449

Target marketing, 38
Task motives, 83
Tasks and Processes, 51
Team selling, 85, 538
Teamwork, 396
Technical Buying Influence, 132
Telemarketing, 295
Telling style, 449
Termination, 459
Territory, 419
Territory Design, 420
Territory Mapping Programs, 429
Thomas Register of American, 177
Time management, 191
Total Quality Management (TQM), 7,
    51, 99, 306, 503, 579
Trade secrets, 228
Trade shows, 177
Training Budget, 383
Training Program, 384
Training needs analysis, 380

Transactional purchasing, 42
Travel, 12
Travelling salesperson problem, 190
Trend projections, 259
Trial close, 90
Trial relationship, 136
Trust, 142
Truth in lending laws, 234
Turning points, 263
Turnover, 330, 379

Unit rate of change, 259
Ungolden Rule, 222
Unit volume quotas, 494
Unity of command, 284
U.S. Census of Manufacturers, 254
User buyer, 131
User friendly, 74

Value, 140
Value analysis, 129
Value congruence, 447
Vendor analysis, 129
Vision, 446
Vocational Rehabilitation Act, 388

Wage caps, 536
Wage level, 540
Whistleblowing, 232
Wireless technology, 98
Workload approach, 303, 427

AUTHOR INDEX

Acito, Frank, 57
Adams, J. Stacy, 485
Adams, Mark, 586
Alderfer, Clayton P., 485
Allen, Jeffrey W., 584, 585
Anders, George, 56, 71, 710, 732
Anderson, Rolph, 17, 103
Anderson, Erin M., 56, 58, 312, 401,
    508
Anderson, James, 148
Anglin, Kenneth, 148
Armstrong, Robert, 18, 26
Armstrong, J. Scott, 268
Anthony, Ray, 103
Arnott, Nancy, 198, 508

Badovick, Gordon, 508
Barrett, Paul M., 240
Bellizzi, Joseph, 149
Beauchamp, Tom L., 241
Berkowitz, Eric, 56, 71

Berner, Robert, 240
Bertrand, Kate, 134, 147, 179
Blalock, Dawn, 240
Blattberg, Robert, 148
Bobrow, Edwin, 312
Boedecker, Karl, 86
Boles, James, 579, 585
Bowie, Norman E., 241
Bradley, Gregory, 60, 71
Bragg, Arthur, 96, 98, 388
Brennan, Leslie, 508
Brewer, Geoffrey, 4, 17, 18, 240, 336,
    361, 508, 510
Brooks, William, 199
Brooksbank, Richard, 57, 102
Brown, Steven, 508
Brown, Dr. Lew G., 313
Brown, Steven, 536, 644
Bunn, Michelle, 147
Burrows, Peter, 539
Burton, Thomas M., 232, 240

Buskirk, Richard, 18
Butler, Charles, 18
Byrne, John, 57, 67, 71

Campanelli, Melissa, 435, 467, 550
Cannito, Michael, 102
Carusone, Peter S., 271
Cascio, Wayne, 363
Caslione, John, 132
Castleberry, Steven, 311, 362, 589
Cespedes, Frank, 550
Chapman, Joseph, 401
Cheneler, John, 149
Chonko, Lawrence B., 402, 550,
    585
Churchill, Gilbert A., 18, 199, 361,
    400
Clancy, Kevin, 149
Clark, Tim, 57, 311, 549
Claston, John, 519
Clayton, Joe, 466

Clifton, Reichard, 177, 189
Close, Wendy, 103
Cohen, Andy, 17, 87, 549, 585
Colletti, Jerome, 18, 311
Collins, Marshall, 311, 467
Comer, James M., 466
Conlan, Ginger, 361
Conlin, Joseph, 312
Cook, Michael, 313
Cook, Roy, 362
Corey, Raymond, 467
Cortada, James, 312
Cortada, James, 17, 57, 466, 585
Covey, Stephen, 199
Coward, Derek, 199
Cox, Craig, 221
Cravens, David, 38, 184, 199, 312, 585,
Crisara, Stephanie N., 362
Cron, William, 35, 37, 149, 467, 508, 535
Crosby, John, 149

Dahlstrom, Robert, 240
Dalrymple, Douglas I., 69, 269, 280, 440, 585, 592, 597
Dangello, Frank, 362
Darmon, Rene, 362
Davis, Duane L., 584
Day, Ralph, 69
DeCarlo, Thomas, 361
Deeter-Schmelz, Dawn, 149
Deighton, John, 148
Dellecave, Tom, 41
Diaz, Manuel, 56, 147
Dishman, Paul, 311
Doherty, Edward, 57, 71
Dominguez, Ygnacius, 400
Donaldson, Thomas, 241
Donthu, Naveen, 579, 585
Douglas, Donna, 199, 312
Douglass, Merrill, 199, 312
Doyle, Stephen, 148, 562, 589, 635, 643
Drucker, Peter, 467, 550
Dubinsky, Alan, 103, 240, 466, 508
Dunn, Dan, 57, 71
Dyer, Jeffrey, 46, 57

Easey, Mike, 586
Easterling, Debbie, 402
Edmondson, Gail, 102
Eisenhart, Tom, 312, 430, 435
Eisman, Regina, 509
Eln-Ansary, Adel, 401
Emshwiller, Joan, 127
Engemann, Kurt, 148
Effmeyer, Robert, 401, 402
Eppon, GD, 199

Evans, Elaine, 467
Everett, Martin, 80, 311, 362

Falvey, Jack, 401
Fento, John, 103
Fernandez, John, 363
Fierman, Jaclyn, 400
Fildes, R., 268
Filson, Brent, 509
Fine, Leslie, 401
Flanagan, Patrick, 172
Ford, Neil, 18, 311, 361, 400
Fox, Dale R., 204
Freehery, George, 362
Freeman, R.E., 312
Friedman, Lawrence, 57, 58, 128, 148
Futrell, Charles, 361

Gable, Myron, 362
Ganesan, Shankar, 148, 585
Gassenheimer, Jule R., 240
Gellerman, Saul, 102, 401
Geyelin, Milo, 240
Goalter, Barbara, 103
Gould, FJ, 199
Govoni, Norman A.P., 402
Greenberg, Herbert M., 361
Greenberg, Jeanne, 361
Groethe, Wylie, 149
Gross, Charles W., 325
Grothe, Peter & Mardy, 149
Guest, Donald, 18, 26

Haas, Robert W., 436
Hair, Joseph Jr., 401, 402
Haley, Kathy, 311
Hall, Douglas, 508
Hammer, Michael, 57, 71
Hanan, Mack, 103
Hardigree, Donald W., 239
Hardwick, Mark, 103, 135
Harris, Tim, 509
Hartley, Stephen, 56, 361, 400
Hawes, Jon, 148
Head, Robert G., 549
Heese, Rick, 199
Heide, Christen, 550
Heide, Jan, 147, 148, 311
Heiman, Stephen, 149, 199
Hellriegel, Don, 312, 509
Hennessey, Hubert, 104
Henthorne, Tony, 102, 135
Herche, Joel, 362
Herzberg, Frederick, 485, 508
Hill, Linda, 508
Hill, John S., 17, 312
Hirsch, James, 9
Hoffman, Douglas K., 239
Hollon, Charles, 362

Hoverstad, Ronald, 401
Hovovich, B. G., 148
Howe, Vince, 239
Hucks, Michael, 103
Hudson, Richard, 57, 71
Hunan, Mack, 199
Hunt, Shelby, 149

Ingram, Thomas N., 18, 585

Jaben, Jan, 311
Jackofsky, Ellen, 585
Jackson, Donald W., 531, 564, 584, 569
Jackson, John H., 550
Johnston, Wesley J., 508
Jaworski, Bernard, 199, 467, 508, 509
Jenker, Rick, 519
John, George, 147, 148, 549, 550, 585
Johnston, Mark W., 17, 198, 361
Jolson, Marvin, 103, 240, 466, 508
Jones, Daniel, 57, 72
Jones, Eli, 361

Kahle, Lynn, 147
Kale, Sudhir, 141
Kalunian, Barbara, 104
Kantak, Donna Massey, 361
Kantin, Robert, 103, 135
Karp, Peter, 199
Kashani, Kamran, 26, 117, 161
Kearns, David, 58
Keck, Kay L., 400, 585
Keenan, William, Jr., 10, 18, 33, 56, 198, 268, 361, 362, 381, 401, 402, 457, 467
Kelley, Bill, 193
Kemp, David S., 174, 198
Kennedy, John R., 509
Kerin, Roger A., 56, 58, 63, 326
Keysuk, Kim, 508
Kimball, James, 57
King, Ronald, 363
Kishel, Gregory, 103
Kishel, Patricia, 103
Klein, Ronald, 401
Klopp, Charlotte, 57, 72
Kohli, Ajay, 467, 508
Kohli, Allie, 501
Kotabe, Masaaki, 103, 240, 508, 509
Krapfel, Robert Jr., 148
Krishnan, Shanker, 199
Kushner, Malcom, 103

LaFasto, Frank, 467
LaForge, Raymond, 18, 184, 199, 585
Lagace, Rosemary R., 240
Lamb, Charles, 311, 376, 393
Lambert, Douglas, 148

Landau, Jacqueline, 361
Larson, Carl E., 467
LaTour, Michael, 102, 135
Lawlor, Julia, 467
Lehner, Urban, 57, 71
Leigh, Thomas, 400, 401, 585
LeBoent, Michael, 199
Leslie, George, 94
Leventhal, Richard, 21
Levine, Daniel, 311
Levy, Michael, 35, 37
Lewandowski, R., 268
Lewis, Richard, 419
Lim, Chae Un, 103, 240
Lohtia, Ritu, 579, 585
Lollar, James G., 400, 585
Lovelock, Christopher H., 468
Lublin, Joann S., 240
Lucas, Allison, 147
Lucas, George, 401
Lumpkin, James, 103, 338
Lunneman, Cynthia, 550
Lynton, Linda, 467

Machiavelli, Niccolo, 240
Macintosh, Gerrard, 148
MacKenzie, H.F., 247, 557
Maggs, John, 57, 71
Magrath, Allan, 56, 373, 393
Mahaijan, Vijay, 58
Major, Michael, 401
Makridakis, Spyros, 264, 268
Mann, Karl, 312, 380, 393, 764, 785
Marchetti, Michele, 549, 585
Marmorstein, Howard, 148
Marohl, John, 401
Marshall, Greg, 585
Marshall, Judith, 312, 379, 393
Maslow, Abraham, 485, 509
Mast, Kenneth, 148
Mathews, Jack, 103
Mathews, Marianne, 362
Mathis, Robert L., 550
McClelland, David, 485
McDougall, Gordon, 370
McGee, Victor E., 268
McGraw, Patrick, 401
McKenna, Regis, 58
NcNeilly, Kevin M., 466
McWilliams, Gary, 362
Meilstrup, Spenser S., 362
Mendosa, Rick, 402
Mercer, David, 103, 198
Meric, Havva J., 18, 26
Merritt, Nancy, 362
Metcalf, Lynn, 401
Michaels, Ron, 103, 240, 508
Milbank, Dana, 312, 379, 393
Mile and Snow, 36, 37
Miller, James, 240

Miller, Robert, 149, 199
Millman, A.F., 476
Mills, Brad, 18, 26
Minninger, Joan, 103
Moncrief, William, 311, 401
Moran, Linda, 467
Moran, Ursula, 57, 72
Moravee, Milan, 311, 467
Moretti, Peggy, 312, 376, 377, 381, 393
Moriarty, Rowland, 57, 71, 233, 253
Morgan, Fred, 86
Morgan, Robert, 148
Morris, Michael H., 584, 585
Moskowitz, Robert, 199
Mowen, John, 585
Mullich, Joe, 299
Murphy, Liz, 362, 467
Murray, Alan, 57, 72
Musselwhite, Ed, 467

Nadler, David, 58
Nanus, Burt, 58
Narus, James, 148
Neimark, Jill, 349
Nevin, John, 147
Nevis, E., 486
Newton, Derek A., 363, 550
Newton, J., 268
Noorewier, Thomas, 147
Norwell, D. Wayne, 149

O'Brian, Bridget, 549
O'Connell, William, 10, 198
Oliver, Richard, 508
Osburn, Jack, 467
Owen, Charles, 147
Owen, Duane B., 268
Owens, Jan, 147

Parzen, E., 268
Patterson, Gregory, 221
Patterson, James M., 241
Patton, W.E., 363
Pecotich, Anthony, 18, 26
Peoples, David, 103
Pepper, Don, 148
Peters, Diane McFerrin, 363, 509
Peterson, Robert, 102, 508
Peterson, Robin, 467
Pickett, Gregory M., 585
Pillai, Uajnadini, 102
Pillai, Rajnandini, 147
Pollay, Richard W., 519
Porter, Michael, 35, 56, 71
Powell, C. Randall, A-4
Prokesch, Steven, 176
Pryce, Adrian, 137
Pullins, Ellen, 401

Quelch, John, 467

Rackham, Neil, 57, 58, 103, 128, 148
Ramsey, Rosemary, 149
Rao, Ram, 550
Reese, Jennifer, 401
Rethans, Arno, 401
Rexelsen, Richard, 401
Rink, David, 148
Robertson, Thomas, 401
Robinson, Harry, 586
Rochford, Linda, 56
Roering, Kenneth, 311
Rogers, Martha, 148
Roos, Daniel, 57, 72
Rosenbluth, Hal, 363, 509
Ross, William, 508
Rottenberger-Murtha, Kerry, 81, 103, 401
Royal, Weld, 352
Rudelius, Bill, 56, 71
Ruekert, Robert, 311
Ruff, Richard, 28, 58, 148, 157
Russ, Frederick, 466
Russ, K. Randall, 400, 401, 402

Sager, Jeff, 361, 508
Schaaf, Dick, 362, 400
Schlacter, John L., 531, 564, 569, 584
Schmidt, CP, 199
Schmitt, Richard B., 240
Schnarrs, Steven P., 258
Scholtes, Peter R., 509
Schonberger, Richard, 58
Schul, Patrick, 467
Scott, Gini G., 509
Sellers, Patricia, 287, 293
Shank, Mathew, 550
Sharma, Arun, 147, 148
Sherlock, Paul, 149
Shipp, Shannon, 312
Shulman, Robert, 149
Siconolfi, Michael, 240, 534
Siesendanger, Betsy, 362
Silberman, Mel, 402
Simon, Stephanie, 240
Simpson, Edwin, 362
Singhapakdi, Anusorn, 240
Sloan, A.E., 467
Slocum, John W., 312, 467, 508, 509, 585
Smith, Daniel, 147, 311
Smith, Craig N., 467
Snetsinger, Douglas, 370
Sohi, Ravipeet, 311
Sonter, James A., 312
Spangler, William, 466
Spiro, Rosann, 57, 362, 618
Stafford, Thomas, 102
Stanton, William J., 18

Stathakopoulos, Vlasis, 199, 584
Staunton, Donald J., 467
Stephens, Marilyn, 312, 380, 393
Stern, Gabriella, 240
Stertz, Bradley, 57, 71
Sterlicchi, John, 57, 71
Stickney, Thomas, 198
Still, Richard R., 17, 312
Stoltman, Jeffrey, 86
Strahle, William, 57, 204, 585
Strutton, David, 103, 338
Stumm, David, 450
Sudir, Kale, 180
Sujan, Harish, 69, 485, 495, 621, 643
Swan, John, 148
Swift, Cathy Owens, 362
Szymanski, David, 148, 199

Tanner, John, 402, 550, 585
Taylor, Thayer, 103, 195
Tepper, Ron, 363
Thomas, Claude, 57, 72
Thurlow, Michael, 509
Trawick, I. Frederick, 148
Tripodi, Clinton, 311, 467
Troutwine, Robert, 585
Trumfio, Ginger, 549
Tubridy, Gary, 311
Tuleja, Tad, 149

Tully, Shawn, 148
Tyagi, Pradeep, 361

Unlim, Chae, 508

Vaccaro, Joseph, 199
Van Doran, Doris, 198
Varadurajan, Rajan, 58
Vavra, Terry, 149
Velasquez, Manuel G., 241
Vitell, Scott J., 240
Vrendenburg, Harrie, 312
Vroom, Victor, 509

Walker, Orville, 18, 311, 361, 400
Ward, Nicholas, 402
Warren, Wendy, 401
Wayland, Jane, 362
Wayland, Rober, 362
Webster, Frederick, 57, 42, 71
Weeks, William, 147, 402, 550, 585
Weilbaker, Dan, 362
Weinrauch, Donald, 312, 380, 393
Weisendanger, Betsy, 456
Weiss, Allen, 147, 312
Weitz, Barton, 362, 549, 550, 585
Werbel, James, 361
Werhane, Patricia H., 241

Wheelwright, Steven C., 264, 268
Whittler, Tommy, 103
Wilke, John R., 56, 240
Williams, Alvin, 102, 135
Wilson Learning Corporation, 89
Wilson, David T., 148
Winkler, R., 268
Winston, Wayne, 199
Witt, Robert E., 200
Wolfe, William G., 531, 564, 584, 569
Wolfson, Kathryn, 402
Woodman, Richard, 509
Woods, Bob, 129, 135, 435, 452
Womak, James, 57, 71
Wortruba, Thomas, 311
Wortuba, Thomas, R., 56, 198, 220, 240, 361, 362, 508, 509
Wren, Brent, 467

Yammarino, Francis J., 466
Yate, Martin, 363
Young, Clifford, 184, 199, 585
Yows, Linda, 467

Zeflin, Minda, 467
Zeiger, Rob, 240
Zenger, John, 467
Zunier, Steve, 312

COMPANY INDEX

Abbott Laboratory, 232
A.B. Dick, 297
Aetna Life & Casualty, 172, 387
Air Products & Chemicals Inc., 41
Alcoa, 286
Allied Signal Aerospace, 127, 138
Allnet Communications Services, 174
American Airlines, 45
American Bankers Insurance Group, 394
American Express, 291–292
American Home Products, 255
AMSCO International, 87
Amway, 352
Apple, 291, 295
Apple Computers, 99, 172, 373, 376
Applied Decision Systems, 265
Armstrong World Industries, 172, 333, 377
Arthur Andersen & Co., 172, 268, 296
Atlantic Software Corporation, 179

AT&T Global Information Systems, 36, 41, 44, 52, 53, 131, 172, 174, 295, 297, 305
Aurora-Baxter Corporation, 462
Avis, 431
Allen Bradley, 7
Avon Products, 74, 177

Ball Corporation, 135
Baxter Healthcare Corporation, 184, 305
Baxter-Travenol, 337
BBN Software Products, 143
Black and Decker, 293
Blue Cross-Blue Shield, 297
BMW, 389
Boise Cascade Office Products, 340
Bose, 46
Boston Consulting Group, 36
Bottomley and Associates, Inc., 127
Briskheat, 2

Bristol-Meyers, 232, 337
Burlington Industries, 303

Caliper Corporation, 352
CAP Gemini Sogeti, 73
Caradon Everest, 285
Caterpillar, Inc., 31, 379, 389
Certain-Teed Corporation, 539
Chase Manhattan Bank, 389
Chevron, 297
Chrysler Corporation, 41, 45, 126
Coca-Cola, 139, 390
Colgate-Palmolive Company, 291
Comcast Cable, 3
Comdoc Office Systems, 392
Compaq, 36
Compaq, 2
Corning Glass Works, 103, 298, 299, 380
Cutco, 74

Dartnell Corporation, 10, 12, 285, 460, 540
Data General, 221, 342
Datacom, 194
Dell Computers, 538, 539
Delphus Inc., 265
Digital Equipment Corporation, 342
Dow Chemical Company, 44, 353, 386
Dow Corning, 178
Dresser Industries, 341
Dun and Bradstreet, 172, 305
DuPont, 45, 172, 236, 307, 377

Eastman Chemical, 52, 384, 396
EDS, 75, 98, 582
Eli Lilly, 337
Encyclopedia Britannica Corporation, 38
Equifax, Inc., 351
Ernst & Young, 172
Exxon Chemicals, 73

Federal Express, 41, 44, 99
Ford, 7, 45, 127, 138, 389

Gallup Organization, 336, 484
Gates Rubber Company, 40
G.D. Searle & Company, 143, 335
General Dynamics, 396
General Electric, 45, 52, 233, 257, 296
General Mills, 41
General Motors, 45, 127, 129, 236
GeoQuery, 419
Georgia-Pacific, 388
Gerber, 232
Gillette, 182, 292, 390
Glaxo Holdings PLC, 37
Gregory Group, The, 90
GTE, 125

Hallmark, 13, 21, 22
Hamilton Company, 80
Harford Steam Boiler Inspection and Insurance Company (HSB), 290
Harley-Davidson, 7
Hewlett-Packard and Company, 39, 129, 139, 182, 187, 238, 286, 342, 344, 387, 502
High Test Safety Shoes Company, 132
Holiday Inn, 41
Home Depot, 293
Honeywell, 45, 298, 574
Holston, 43
Hyatt, 286, 287
Hyundai Motor Company, 41

IBM, 2, 4, 36, 40, 41, 44, 45, 51, 60, 61, 98, 140, 170, 172, 284, 286, 295, 297, 342, 377, 378, 390, 536

Intel, 187, 195
International Playtex, 331
Invacare Corporation, 335
ISL Marketing, 13
ITT, 299

Johnson & Johnson, 289, 388, 390
Johnson Controls, 126

Kaiser, 38
Kodak, 285, 427
K-Mart, 352

Loctite Corporation, 189, 305

Marvin Windows, 134
Mary Kay Cosmetics, 74, 518, 673, 726
MCI, 174, 305
McBride Electric, 13
McLoughlin Body Co., 46
McNeil Consumer Product Company, 340
Mebco, 450
Merck and Company, 33, 295, 337, 342, 385, 389
Merrill Lynch, 297, 353, 532, 537
Metron, Inc., 431
Microsoft, 97, 389
Mid-American Waste System, 230
Milliken, 45, 503
Minolta, 390
Mitsubishi Electric, 233
Mobil Oil, 299
Monsanto Corporation, 45, 96, 299
Moore Business Forms, 390
Motorola, Inc., 98, 127, 140
Multimedia Marketing, 81

Nabisco, 379, 390, 394
National Semiconductor, 458
NCR, 36
NCR Corporation, 36, 373
Nestle SA, 41, 232
Northwestern Mutual Life, 330, 353, 386
Novell Netware, 97

Ortho Pharmaceutical, 388
Owens-Corning, 172
Owens-Brockway, 124, 136, 168, 170, 178
Owens-Illinois, Inc., 124, 345

Pacific Bell, 172
Parke-Davis, 337
Perdue Fredric Pharmaceuticals, 430
Pfizer Labs, 337, 390
Philip Morris Company, 342

Pitney Bowes, 44, 295
Procter & Gamble, 34, 45, 44, 53, 78, 140, 285, 287, 291, 293, 295, 305, 329, 396
Prudential, 534

Rainbird, 127
Rank, 176
Rank Xerox, 176
RELTEC, 126, 143
Rohm, 305

Saga, 139
Sales Consultants, 341
Sales World, 341
Saturn, 535
Schering-Plough, 388
Schwabs, 534
Scientific Data Systems, 438
Scott Aviation, 138
Scott Paper Company, 35, 390
Sears, 221
Seth Thomas Company, 455
Shearson Lehman Hutton, 390
Sherwin-Williams, 390
SmartSoftware Inc., 265
SmithKline Beecham, 337, 344
Southwest Networks, 174
Sprint, 174
SRI/Gallup Organization, 335
Stahl Company, 194
Symbol Technologies, Inc., 37

Tactics International, Ltd., 431
Teledyne, 299
Texas Instruments, 45, 127
3M, 131, 187, 295, 381
Thomson Consumer Electronics, 446
Timeplex, 99
TTG, Inc., 429

United Parcel Service, 137
U.S. Navy, 387
U.S. Surgical, 386

Val-Pak, 384

Wal-Mart, 78, 287, 293
Wang Laboratories, 342
Warner-Lambert, 352, 390
Western Sales Company, 419
Wilson Learning Corporations, 93
Westinghouse, 51
Wright Line, 40
Wyeth-Ayerst International, 3

Xerox, 7, 9, 13, 82, 88, 127, 176, 286, 299, 305, 307, 378, 387, 483, 503

Ziegler Tools, 193

CASE INDEX

Abbott, Inc., 597–601
Adams Brands, 370–375
Arapahoe Pharmaceutical Company, 21–26

Bates Industrial Supply, 280–281
BSI, 58–62

The Case Method, 18–21
The Centrust Corporation, 149–159

Dave MacDonald's Ethical Dilemmas, 242–250
D.F. Hardware Company, 436–439

First National Bank, 468–476
Fortess Electrical Tape Company, 363–369

General Electric Appliances, 519–528

Hanover-Bates Chemical Corporation, 200–204
Honkong Bank of Canada, 510–519

Jefferson-Pilot Corporation, 313–325

Kent Plastics, 440–443

Madison Fiber Corporation, 550–556
Mead Products, 271–279
Mediquip S.A., 117–122

National Saxony Carpet Company, 166–168

Parker Computer, 269–271
Pepe Jeans, 159–166
Power & Motion Industrial Supply, Inc., 557–561
Practical Parties, 586–592

Romano Pitesti, 476–480
Royal Corporation, 104–116

Salco Chemicals S.A., 26–29
Sales Management Simulation, 69–71
Sandwell Paper Company, 410–417
Shanandoah Industries (A), 63–68
Shanandoah Industries (B), 326–327

Texxon Oil Company, 241–246

Westinghouse Electric Corporation, 402–409

York Electronics, 592–596

Zygar Pharmaceuticals, 204–217